PSYCHOPATHOLOGY AND PSYCHOTHERAPY

FROM DIAGNOSIS TO TREATMENT

Len Sperry, M.D., Ph.D.

and

Jon Carlson, Psy.D., Ed.D.

Accelerated Development Inc.
3808 West Kilgore Avenue
Muncie, IN 47304-4896

Psychopathology and Psychotherapy
From Diagnosis to Treatment

Copyright 1993 by Accelerated Development Inc.

10 9 8 7 6 5 4 3 2 1

Printed in the United States of America

Technical Development: Tanya Benn
                           Virginia Cooper
                           Delores Kellogg
                           Cynthia Long
                           Marguerite Mader
                           Shaeney Pigman
                           Sheila Sheward

Library of Congress Cataloging-in-Publication Data

Sperry, Len.
    Psychopathology and psychotherapy : from diagnosis to treatment / Len Sperry and Jon Carlson.
    p.   cm.
        Includes bibliographical references and index.
        ISBN 1-55959-032-7
        1. Psychology, Pathological.   2. Psychotherapy.   3. Psychiatry-
-Differential therapeutics.   4. Adler, Alfred, 1870-1937.
5. Diagnostic and statistical manual of mental disordres.
I. Carlson, Jon.   II. Title.
        [DNLM: 1. Mental Disorders--diagnosis.   2. Mental Disorders-
-therapy.   3. Psychopathology.   4. Psychotherapy--methods. WM   100
S751p]
RC454.S68   1992
616.89--dc20
DNLM/DLC
for Library of Congress   92-17705
                                                             CIP

LCN:92-17705
ISBN:1-55959-032-7

Order additional copies from:

ACCELERATED DEVELOPMENT INC.
PUBLISHERS
3808 West Kilgore Avenue
Muncie, Indiana 47304-4896
Toll Free Order Number 1-800-222-1166

FOREWORD

Arthur Freeman, Ed.D.

As a beginning graduate student at New York University, I took my first course in personality theory. The text for the course was the first edition of the now classic *Theories of Personality* by Calvin Hall and Gardner Lindsey. In the text, after lengthy chapter-long discussions of the works of Freud and Jung, four "social psychologists," Adler, Horney, Sullivan, and Fromm were combined into a single chapter. The outline for the course said that we were going to discuss all of these theories during one class lecture period. The works of these social theorists particularly interested me by their reasonable and social focus. When I inquired of the instructor if we were going to be able to finish all of the discussion of these four theorists in one lecture, he said that since these were all only "minor" theories, they could be "disposed of" easily in a single class.

By purest coincidence, the mental health center in New York in which I did my clinical internship three years later was on the street floor of the apartment building next to the building housing the Alfred Adler Mental Hygiene Clinic. One day I went in to find out more about the Clinic and discovered that there was a training program, and I ended up taking courses over the next three years. I learned about the basis for Individual Psychology from such Adlerian notables as Danica Deutch, Helene Papenek, Kurt Adler, and Alexandra Adler. As a practicing clinician for almost three decades, I have come to see how wrong my graduate professor was about many things, especially about the work of Adler.

In 1990, I was honored by being asked to deliver the Rudolf Dreikurs lecture at the Alfred Adler Institute in Chicago.

A colleague wondered why they had asked me, a non-Adlerian, to deliver the address. After all, I was not identified as Adlerian in my theoretical orientation or clinical practice. In fact I have written about and practiced Cognitive Therapy for the last 15 years, based on my study and work with Aaron T. Beck and my earlier work with Albert Ellis. Of interest to me was that after my lecture entitled, "Cognitive Therapy and the Individual Psychology of Alfred Adler," many members of the audience came to me and told me how they thought that my presentations and subsequent comments were clearly Adlerian. Dr. Eva Dreikurs Ferguson offered one of the greatest compliments when she commented that her father would have agreed with what I had said. Kurt Adler has told me that he believed that Beck's work in Cognitive Therapy was a logical extension of his father's work.

The seminal and groundbreaking work of Alfred Adler, Rudolf Dreikurs, and other Individual Psychologists has too often been given short shrift and only passing notice in the professional psychological and psychiatric communities. In many undergraduate and graduate courses in history and systems of psychology, or in clinical and counseling psychology programs, Adler is not taught at all. Or, if Adler's work is taught, it is as a "minor" theory. This is incredible, given the Adlerian contributions to the development of psycho-therapeutic theory, clinical practice, and delivery of psychological services. For example, Adler's work has been the basis for the development of guidance services in elementary and high schools, has led to the development of the specialty profession of school psychology, and has led to the development of community mental health centers. The theoretical orientation developed by Adlerians has been the basis for Frankl's Logotherapy and the contemporary Ego-analytic approaches of the psychoanalysts, and has been one of the major influences for the development of present day Cognitive Behavior Therapy.

The reasons for the lack of direct Adlerian emphasis in general university and graduate courses, and for the lack of recognition of the Adlerian contribution to general clinical practice have, in my view, been several. (1) Adlerian theory and clinical practice have often had a limited distribution in that they have often been written by Adlerians and for

Adlerians. (2) Often Adler's original works have been used not simply for their historical or theoretical importance, but for their direct clinical applications. Given that the material was written over 50 years ago, the material may not be relevant to modern clinical practice. (3) Adlerians have not been organized as a strong and visible political force. (4) Adlerians have, by and large, kept to themselves and not brought their message to the broader forums of mental health professionals. (5) Based on Adler's early work in schools and in training teachers, many applications of Individual Psychology have been educationally, not clinically, oriented. (6) Discussions of Adlerian theory, principles, and clinical applications have too often been separated, until now.

In this exceptional clinician's volume, two of the most noted American Adlerians, Len Sperry and Jon Carlson, have, in addition to their own superb clinical contributions, drawn together a number of talented clinicians and have asked them to discuss and describe Individual Psychological approaches to the broad range of clinical problems. Included in this group are such distinguished names as Heinz Ansbacher and Bernard Shulman. The stated goal of this volume is to help the clinician-counselor to connect the theoretical view of psychopathological problems and the diagnostic concepts of psychopathology as defined in DSM-III-R with the treatments of those particular disorders from an Adlerian perspective. In this regard it succeeds admirably.

Another strength of the text is the overviews provided at the beginning of each section. These serve to focus the reader on the diagnostic categories to be discussed and to integrate the material. Of course, as I read the material, I view it with my "Cognitive Therapy" eye. I am pleased that so much of what you will read in this volume offers the structured, strategic, systemic, and dynamic focus that was developed by Adler, and has become so much a part of Cognitive Therapy.

The highest order skill of the therapist is the ability to develop a case formulation using the diagnostic data, clinical observations of behavior, and the spontaneous responses on the part of the patient. This conceptual framework is then turned into the therapeutic strategies and the specific intervention that will help realize the strategies as the therapist works towards the treatment goals. By taking the reader through the case formulation process and then illustrating the approach with a representative case, the contributors have helped to clarify the treatment process.

The clear message of the text is that Adlerian therapy is a powerful and viable model for the treatment of the broad range of clinical problems. It is an important tool in the therapeutic armamentarium of clinical psychologists, psychiatrists, social workers, guidance counselors, pastoral counselors, nurses, and any other mental health professional.

Arthur Freeman, Ed.D.
Philadelphia

PREFACE

Most mental health clinicians and trainees complain that abnormal psychology and psychopathology texts are typically lifeless and boring. These books tend to be packed with too many facts, criteria, and lists of symptoms with too few case examples. More importantly, they have limited value and utility for day-to-day clinical practice. This is particularly true of texts that are based primarily on the American Psychiatric Association's *Diagnostic and Statistical Manual* (DSM-III-R) with its seemingly endless and arbitrary lists of categories, labels, and criteria. Clinicians wonder, besides providing diagnostic labels and codes for insurance forms and agency and government records, what value do standardized diagnostic criteria have for treatment? Many systems of psychotherapy have eschewed standardized diagnostic systems claiming that they were irrelevant for treatment. Beutler's research bears out the observations of practicing clinicians and psychotherapy theorists. He reported that, except for specific diagnostic entities such as phobic disorders and sexual dysfunctions like premature ejaculation and primary orgasmic dysfunction, it is not possible to predict effective outcomes for therapeutic interventions based solely on diagnosis (Beutler & Crago, 1987).

Clinicians have suggested that DSM-III-R could be more useful in planning treatment if it provided dynamic or systems formulations for each disorder. Is it unreasonable to expect that a psychopathology text provide both diagnostic criteria and dynamic or systemic formulations?

One of the main purposes of *Psychopathology and Psychotherapy* is to combine DSM-III-R diagnostic criteria with dynamic/systemic formulations. Specifically, this book integrates the diagnostic feature of DSM-III-R with the dynamic and systems-based theory of Individual Psychology. DSM-III-R and Individual Psychology—the theory of personality and treatment developed by Alfred Adler—are surprisingly complementary. This text emphasizes this mutual complementarity and provides the reader a straightforward and easily comprehensible understanding of why a particular client or patient develops one disorder rather than another. Factors such as early childhood experiences, family dynamics, temperament and other biological considerations, as well as dysfunctional cognitions and beliefs are correlated with DSM-III-R descriptions and diagnostic criteria.

A second purpose of *Psychopathology and Psychotherapy* is reflected in the subtitle: "From Diagnosis to Treatment." Based on our clinical practice, teaching, and supervision, we find that understanding why and how an individual develops a particular disorder is extremely valuable and useful in developing treatment intervention and guiding the psychotherapeutic process. Accordingly, a discussion of treatment goals, strategies, and methods supplements follows the description and clinical formulation of each DSM-III-R disorder discussed in this text.

This book is arranged in five sections, beginning with an overview of psychopathology and the diagnostic and treatment process. The more common clinical presentations of children and adults are described in the next four sections. Diagnostic, clinical, and treatment formulation for these disorders are provided along with a representative case example. The last chapter explains the basics of Individual Psychology for readers who would like additional information on this approach.

We believe that the Individual Psychology perspective is particularly valuable and timely as the trend toward integration of the various psychotherapeutic systems gains momentum. The contemporary view of Individual Psychology presented in this text integrates much information from psychodynamic, cognitive-behavioral, and systems schools as well as the neurosciences. Essentially, Individual Psychology is an integrative theory approach.

This book will be useful as both a text for undergraduate and graduate psychopathology courses in all mental health disciplines, as well as for interns and residents in clinical and counseling psychology and psychiatry programs. It also should have clinical value and utility for experienced practitioners in the various mental health professions.

REFERENCE

Beutler, L., & Crago, M. (1987). Strategies and techniques of prescriptive psychotherapeutic intervention. In R. Hales & A. Frances (Eds.), *Psychiatry Update: Annual Reveiw Vol. 6.* Washington, DC: American Psychiatric Press.

ACKNOWLEDGEMENTS

We would like to acknowledge the outstanding work of the many contributors to this text, particularly Michael Maniacci, Harold Mosak, Bernard Shulman, Walter "Buzz" O'Connell, Donald Lombardi, Dorothy Peven, Jim Croake, Kathy Myers, Ronald Pancner, Mark Mays, and Judy Lewis. Dr. Heinz Ansbacher, the dean of Individual Psychology, provided invaluable comments and critiques of parts of the manuscript, as well as inestimable encouragement in the darker moments of this project's life course.

We also would like to acknowledge the gentle direction and support from publisher and colleague Dr. Joe Hollis. Finally, we acknowledge the word processing assistance of Candace Ward Howell, Dawn Stalbaum, and Kim James-Jones.

TABLE OF CONTENTS

LIST OF FIGURES

LIST OF TABLES

PART I

INTRODUCTION

OVERVIEW

In Chapter 1 an overview is provided of Alfred Adler's Individual Psychology and its relation to psychopathology. The three formulations—diagnostic, clinical, and treatment—are discussed to show the relationship.

Differences and similarities between the *Diagnostic and Statistical Manual of Mental Disorders, Third Edition, Revised*, and Individual Psychology are identified and discussed. The DSM-III-R system is based on a pathological model and a psychology of possession, while the Adlerian approach is based on a growth model and a psychology of use. The Alderian approach emphases are (1) psychological reasons in explaining behavior and symptoms (psychodynamic focus); (2) attitudes and beliefs about self and the world (cognitive focus); and (3) family constellation, social interactions, and psychological movement (systems focus).

This first chapter concludes with a case example to illustrate the progression from diagnosis through treatment.

CHAPTER 1

PSYCHOPATHOLOGY AND THE DIAGNOSTIC AND TREATMENT PROCESS

Len Sperry, M.D., Ph.D.

Today, more is known about the process of normal development and psychopathology than ever before. Similarly, the hope is greater that treatment interventions can effectively reduce and even reverse psychopathological processes than in past decades. This chapter has three purposes: First, it describes Alfred Adler's basic view of normality and psychopathology along with some observations which extend and clarify it. Second, it compares the Individual Psychology or Adlerian view with the nosological or classification system of the *Diagnostic and Statistical Manual, Third Edition, Revised* (DSM-III-R) (American Psychiatric Association, 1987). Third, it suggests how diagnostic considerations can be linked to treatment interventions. A case example will highlight these considerations by suggesting how a famous historical case might be formulated by a contemporary clinician.

ALFRED ADLER'S VIEW

Alfred Adler (1956) was the founder of the psychological theory and system called Individual Psychology. Adler chose the term "Individual"—as its Latin derivation meant "indivisible"—referring to the essential unity of the person. Adler believed that the hallmark of the healthy, nonpathological person was the capacity to move through life meeting the various life tasks with courage and common sense. Adler called this hallmark "social interest." In no way did Adler infer that such an individual was perfect or fully self-actualized. Actually, healthy persons can use private logic, experience some discouragement and a sense of inferiority, and compensate in ways that are outside the reaches of social interest. The common perception is that imperfections and failures are part of the human condition. On the other hand, pathological persons believe that they must be perfect and then justify their thinking and actions as the only way to achieve perfection. For Adler, all personality dysfunction was the outcome of erroneous conceptions of how to achieve personal superiority. For the most part, he believed that these faulty conceptions were formed early in one's life (Adler, 1956).

A neurotic disposition, Adler's term for the predisposing conditions which can result in psychopathology, stems from childhood experiences which are characterized either by overprotection or neglect, or by a confusing admixture of both. From these experiences, the young child develops a set of psychological convictions—about self, the world and life goal, which becomes the life-style—of his/her inability to develop mastery or cope with the tasks of life. This conviction is confounded and reinforced by the child's perception of a hostile, punishing or depriving environment at home or school, or one that is subtly demanding or frustrating. Rather than providing encouragement to engage in other efforts involving mastery and achievement, these experiences leave the youngster feeling discouraged and fearful. Rather than experiencing trusting and loving relationships, the young child grows to become distrustful and manipulative. To compensate for these exaggerated feelings of insecurity and anxiety, the child becomes self-centered and uncooperative.

So what is a pathological or dysfunctional life-style? The dysfunctional life-style is an inflexible life-style. Problem solving is based upon a self-protective "private sense" rather than a more task-oriented and socially useful "common sense." Once this set of faulty psychological convictions has coalesced and self-protective patterns of coping are established, the individual has difficulty in seeing or responding to life in any other way. The end result is that the dysfunctional individual cannot cope productively with the tasks of life nor really enjoy the rewards of his/her labors, much less relationships with others. In contrast, a set of psychological convictions and coping patterns that are shaped positively by the child's healthy experiences of mastery, creativity, and loving and pleasurable relationships will result in a flexible life-style.

Adler presented a unitary theory of psychopathology wherein the individual "arranges" symptoms uniquely to serve as excuses for not meeting the tasks of life or to safeguard self-esteem either by aggression or distancing from others. Adler discriminated dysfunctional behavior along the dimensions of social interest and degree of activity. For instance, neurotics respond to the life tasks with "Yes—but." With the "yes" the individual acknowledges social responsibilities, and with the "but" symptoms are presented which excuse responsibility. Mosak (1984) described two types of "yes—but" responses: "yes—but I'm sick" which is the classic response of the psychoneurotic; and, "yes—but I defy it," the acting-out response of the character neurosis or personality disorder. On the other hand, psychotics respond to life tasks with "No" and cut themselves off from the common world. As to activity level, Adler noted a low degree is found in neurotic conditions such as depression and obsessive-compulsion, with a higher degree in anxiety neurosis, schizophrenia, and alcoholism. The highest levels were in manics and sociopaths (Adler, 1964a).

DEVELOPMENTS IN THE ADLERIAN VIEW

Adler believed that three main components were common to all psychopathology: *discouragement, faulty conceptions,* and *life-style beliefs.* Furthermore, he posited that undeveloped social interest and personality dysfunction were basically the outcome of an erroneous way of living. This represents Adler's views of normality versus abnormality at the time of his death. It should be noted that at the outset of his career, Adler felt that psychopathology stemmed from various organ inferiorities. This was a rather biological and reductionistic position. Later, his view changed to a more intrapsychic view in which dysfunctional behavior was seen as a conflict between inferiority and superiority feelings. He described the "neurotic disposition" as the predisposing factor in the development of neurosis. The term "pampered life-style" eventually replaced this term. Still later Adler developed a more sociopsychological view in which psychopathology represented movement toward self-importance at the expense of the common good. In many respects, the last version of Adler's theory represented one of the first attempts at developing a holistic view of psychopathology (Adler, 1964b). Although it encompassed features from the biological (organ inferiority and organ dialect) and the social realms, it was primarily a theory of emotional development and dysfunction which integrated all processes through the prism of the life-style:

> This is notably the case with the lungs, the heart, the stomach, the organs of excretion and the sexual organs. The disturbance of these functions expresses the direction which an individual is taking to attain his goal. I have called these disturbances the organ dialect, or organ jargon, since the organs are revealing in their own most expressive language the intention of the individual totality. (Adler, 1964b, p. 156)

Neufield (1954) differentiated the early psychosomatic approaches from the biopsychosocial and integrative approaches like Individual Psychology. Most psychosomatic theories failed to fully appreciate the multi-faceted dynamics and interdependence of *all* of the biological, the psychological, and the social dimensions of human existence. Failure to appreciate all of these multi-faceted dimensions leads to the same narrow reductionism Neufield criticized in many early psychosomatic theories.

A tendency among those espousing an integrative theory has been to downplay some of these multi-faceted dynamics, particularly the biochemical and neuropharmacological ones.

This is particularly true in the treatment of depressive disorders. A growing awareness is that depression is not a single entity but rather a spectrum disorder. As such, depression is currently viewed by many as a group of discrete illnesses which span a biopsychosocial continuum in which symptom patterns appear to be influenced more by biochemical factors at one end of the continuum and more by psychological factors at the other end. To illustrate the biopsychosocial perspective, a helpful procedure is to speculate about how a depressive disorder develops. Based on recent research findings we can speculate that people who experience a major depressive episode are in some ways genetically susceptible to depression, such that brain pathways and circuits dealing with emotions like pleasure are fragile and poorly buffered from external influences. Add to this some early life traumas such as the loss of or separation from a significant other—such as a parent—that undermines self-confidence and esteem and to which individuals respond with safeguarding patterns. Subjecting individuals to a severe psychological stressor at a later point in life is interpreted by them as a threat which in some way echoes their early experience of loss or separation. When existing social support systems and personal coping strategies or safeguarding methods are not sufficient to neutralize this stressor, the already compromised brain biochemistry is overtaxed, resulting in the familiar biological symptoms of depression such as sleep and appetite disturbance, psychomotor retardation, reduced energy, inability to experience pleasure, and somatic symptoms such as constipation and headache. This reduced physiological functioning serves to further reinforce the individuals' life-style beliefs about self, the world and the future. Pancner (1985a) suggested a similar hypothesis.

On the other hand, a dysthymic disorder, previously called neurotic depression, probably has more psychosocial loading than genetic and biological loading. The dysthymic disorder most often presents with fewer biological symptoms and more dysfunctional life-style beliefs and coping skills. Thus, it is not surprising that dysthymic disorders respond well primarily to psychosocial therapies, while major depressive disorders are more likely to respond to biochemical therapies such as antidepressant medications, often in conjunction with psychotherapy. Psychotherapy will be a necessary adjunctive treatment assuming that a pampered life-style or neurotic disposition interferes with functioning in life tasks. But, when little or no life task dysfunction exists, as is sometimes the situation, then psychotherapy is probably not warranted. Pancner (1985b) proposed a similar view.

FORMULATION: DIAGNOSTIC, CLINICAL, AND TREATMENT FORMULATIONS

A case formulation is a way of summarizing diverse information about a patient in a brief, coherent manner for the purpose of better understanding and treating of the individual. Basically, case formulations consist of three aspects: diagnostic formulations, clinical formulations, and treatment formulations. A *diagnostic formulation* is a descriptive statement about the nature and severity of the individual's psychiatric presentation. The diagnostic formulation aids the clinician in reaching three sets of diagnostic conclusions: whether the patient's presentation is primarily psychotic, characterological, or neurotic; whether the patient's presentation is primarily organic or psychogenic in etiology; and, whether the patient's presentation is so acute and severe that it requires immediate intervention. In short, diagnostic formulations are descriptive, phenomenological, and cross-sectional in nature. They answer the "What happened?" question. For all practical purposes the diagnostic formulation lends itself to being specified with DSM-III-R criteria and nosology. A *clinical formulation,* on the other hand, is more explanatory and longitudinal in nature, and attempts to offer a rationale for the development and maintenance of symptoms and dysfunctional life patterns. Just as various theories of human behavior exist, so do various types of clinical formulations exist: psychoanalytic, Adlerian, cognitive, behavioral, biological, family systems, and bio-psychosocial. Clinical formulations answer the "Why did it happen?" question. A *treatment formulation* follows from a diagnostic and clinical formulation and serves as an explicit blueprint governing treatment interventions. Rather than answering the "What happened?" or "Why did it happen?" question, the treatment formulation addresses the "What can be done about it, and how?" question. The most useful and comprehensive formulations are *integrative formulations* which encompass all three dimensions: diagnostic, clinical, and treatment. The format of the following chapters of this book will highlight integrative formulations. Diagnostic formulation material will emphasize DSM-III-R criteria and codes. Clinical formulation material will review Adlerian interpretations and dynamics, while the treatment formulation material will briefly suggest treatment goals and methods. Because DSM-III-R is so prominent in diagnostic formulation, the DSM-III-R theory will be related to Adlerian psychology throughout this book.

INDIVIDUAL PSYCHOLOGY AND DSM-III-R

Quite unlike other psychological systems which are based on a pathology or disease-model, Adlerian theory is based on a growth-model. It emphasizes the element of discouragement in the dysfunctional individual rather than focusing primarily on psychopathological symptoms (Mosak, 1984). Similarly, because it is a psychology of use rather than of possession, Adlerian theory does not emphasize the diagnostic classification of symptoms. Instead, Adlerians emphasize the meaning, purpose, and use of dysfunctional thinking, behavior, and symptoms. Since the Adlerian approach emphasizes the psychological reasons or mechanisms which are considered to be important in explaining behavior and symptoms, it has a *psychodynamic focus.* And since it also emphasizes attitudes and beliefs about self and the world, it has a *cognitive focus.* Finally, because it emphasizes family constellation, social interactions, and psychological movement it has a *systems focus.* In short, a clinical formulation for an Adlerian integrates psychodynamic, cognitive, and systems features. With this emphasis on the clinical formulation, we do not mean to imply that Adlerian clinicians do not specify a diagnostic formulation. Adlerians will assign a formal diagnosis if requested by an insurance carrier or by clinic policy. But because observations about the individual's movement and descriptions about the uniqueness of the individual are considered more useful than diagnostic categories, nosologies and personality typologies have limited utility in clinical practice among Adlerians. However, for didactic purposes, Adler did characterize four *personality types:* the ruling, getting, avoiding, and the healthy, socially useful person. The first three types describe individuals who are discouraged and low in social interest and so would be considered dysfunctional. Mosak (1959, 1971, 1973, 1985) has briefly described several other personality types and has provided in-depth analyses of the getting and controlling types. Adler considered the obsessive-compulsive neurosis to be the prototype of all neuroses, while the hysterical neurosis was the prototype for Freud. Indecisiveness and doubt, depreciation of others, god-like strivings, and focus on minutiae were the safeguarding methods that Adler routinely noted were used by his compulsive neurotic patients in seeking their goal of personal superiority. He noted that various neurotic and psychotic individuals might use different safeguarding methods, but their movement was nevertheless the same: avoidance or rejection of the life tasks. The standard diagnostic classification adopted by many clinicians and insurance carriers in the United States is the third edition revised of the *Diagnostic and Statistical Manual of Mental Disorders* (1987), usually referred to as DSM-III-R. Unlike the Adlerian approach with its unitary theory of psychopathology, DSM-III-R describes 18 distinct major classifications and diagnostic criteria for more than 200 mental disorders. Each disorder has a unique set of descriptive—rather than dynamic—diagnostic criteria. A DSM-III-R diagnosis can be made when a match exists between the facts from a particular individual's history and clinical presentation and the diagnostic criteria for a particular mental disorder. In short, **the DSM-III-R system is based on a pathological model and a psychology of possession, while the Adlerian approach is based on a growth model and a psychology of use.** Consequently, the Adlerian therapist might not be as concerned about making a DSM-III-R type of descriptive diagnosis as he/she would be in understanding the individual's dynamics, that is, movement and life-style themes. But just as differences exist between the two approaches, some important similarities also exist.

Similar to the Adlerian emphasis on life-task functioning, DSM-III-R views pathology as clinically significant behavioral or psychological syndromes or patterns associated with maladaptive functioning in one or more of three areas: social relations, occupation, and leisure. As the Adlerian approach strives toward an integrative-biopsychosocial understanding of the individual, DSM-III-R allows for a multiaxial classification so that interrelated biopsychosocial or systems facets of a person's life may be considered. Five axes are used:

Axis I: Clinical Syndrome(s) (e.g., Adjustment Disorder with Anxious Mood)

Axis II: Personality Disorder or Specific Developmental Disorders (e.g., Dependent Personality Disorder)

Axis III: Physical Disorders or Conditions (e.g., Hypertension)

Axis IV: Severity of Psychosocial Stressors (e.g., Severity 6—death of spouse, and change of job)

Axis V: Current level of adaptive functioning and highest level of functioning in the past year (e.g., current GAF 55; Highest GAF past year 70)

Many integrative-oriented therapists, including Adlerians, would argue for the inclusion of a sixth axis: a biopsychosocial formulation. The mere listing of biopsychosocial information in the various axes, however, does not in and of itself constitute an integrative formulation.

Practically speaking, can DSM-III-R categories be interrelated with Adlerian theory? Mosak (1968), in what many consider to be a classic in the psychopathology literature, has helped a generation of clinicians to interrelate central themes or basic life-style convictions with DSM-III-R diagnostic categories. These central themes are determined from clinical observation, psychological testing, and particularly through early recollections. Mosak listed the eight most common themes: getter; controller; driver; to be good, perfect, right; martyrs; victims; "aginners"; feeling avoiders; and excitement seekers. He also interrelated combinations of these themes with 19 diagnostic categories. For example, the life-style of a person who would be traditionally diagnosed as a depressive neurosis would likely be a composite, in varying degrees, of the getter, the controller, and the person needing to be right (Mosak, 1979). For the antisocial personality, the themes would likely be those of the getter, "aginner," and excitement seeker.

FROM DIAGNOSIS TO TREATMENT

How does a clinician know whether a client is receiving the most appropriate clinical care? The current consensus favors treatment that is matched or tailored to the client's needs and expectations. Tailored treatment is a logical extension of cooperation between clinician and client in Adlerian Theory. Tailored treatment is based on a comprehensive evaluation and integrative case formulation, as well as on a negotiated, mutual agreement about treatment expectations and methods.

Briefly, a comprehensive clinical evaluation usually includes the presenting complaints and their history, mental status, social and developmental history, health status, previous treatment, and the client's explanation of the condition and expectations for treatment. These last two items represent the client's formulation. In addition, the Adlerian clinician would observe and elicit information on the life tasks and of life-style themes and convictions. The integrative case formulation suggests the origins and meaning of the client's concerns. Because it is an integrative statement it accounts for biological and familial predispositions; the client's coping skills; faulty life-style convictions; as well as interpersonal, occupational, and social system factors. A five axes DSM-III-R diagnosis, problem list, statement of the client's motivation and capacity for treatment, and prognosis round out the formulation.

The **negotiation process** begins with the clinician acknowledging the client's formulation and the similarities and differences from the clinician's formulation. The ensuing discussion allows the clinician to educate the client about his/her illness and clarify misconceptions about it and the treatment process. Discussion of the client's expectations for the treatment process and outcomes facilitates negotiating a mutually agreeable direction for treatment and a therapeutic relationship based on cooperation. Then, the specifics of treatment selection can be discussed.

CASE EXAMPLE:
THE CASE OF MRS. A REVISITED

Perhaps the most famous of Adler's cases was that of Mrs. A. The following is a summary of the Case of Mrs. A as it might be reported by a clinician today along with diagnostic, clinical, and treatment formulations. The reader is reminded that Adler did not treat Mrs. A. She was an ongoing patient of Dr. Hilda Weber, a non-Adlerian at the time Adler was asked to comment on parts of Dr. Weber's written case study. Although Adler did not personally interview Mrs. A, he was able to deduce Mrs. A's life-style themes from a few pages of Dr. Weber's case report. These life-style themes are noted in the clinical formulation section.

Summary

This is a 31-year-old married housewife with two children who presents with a dysphoric mood, a cleaning compulsion, knife phobia, and a fear of seriously harming her younger son.

History of Present Illness

The patient dates these progressively worsening symptoms of 18 months to a terrifying dream in which angels surrounded a coffin. But it appears the symptoms span the eight years of her marriage probably beginning with her immense disappointment that her first child was a boy rather than a girl. In time she became jealous of her husband's popularity and friends, had difficulty relating to her neighbors, and as their marital discord increased, threatened to kill herself and her son if things did not change. Her vanity was severely wounded when a second son was born about three years later. Soon thereafter, a drunken neighbor threatened to kill her with a knife. She soon moved out of their home and took her two children and moved in with her parents. During her absence, her husband had a "nervous breakdown" and begged her to return to care for him. After she returned, her obsessive thoughts and compulsions incapacitated her to the point that she sought psychotherapy.

Past Psychiatric Treatment

Following her suicidal threats, her husband took her for an evaluation at which time she was diagnosed with a "nervous stomach," a functional or psychosomatic condition. Psychotherapy was neither recommended nor requested. This was approximately four years ago.

Family History

The patient denies any family history of psychiatric illness, but notes alcoholism on her father's side of the family. Father was described as a construction worker who was impulsive, physically abusive, and a binge drinker. Mother was described as hardworking but non-assertive. Marital conflict was precipitated by her father's drinking and loud threats to "cut everyone's throat." The patient was the third of eight children, four girls followed by four boys. She described herself as a child as being cheerful, fun loving and well-liked by everyone, except her oldest brother whom she described as selfish and inconsiderate. She described her older sister as selfish because she was silent and reserved, and who was severely disciplined for small matters.

Social/Developmental History

She reports being in excellent health as a child, doing well in school and having many friends. She left high school before graduation—which was not uncommon among her female friends—and had a number of unskilled jobs before marrying. While she lived at home and worked, she did well. But when jobs necessitated, she lived away from home, and developed numerous somatic symptoms including a severe skin condition and an enlarged thyroid gland. After her physician insisted that she return to live at home, her symptoms subsided. Thereafter she was able to return to work choosing male-oriented jobs. She explained she didn't want to work around things like fine glassware or china since she dreaded breaking such items. One day her father threatened to kill her with a shovel because her return home had become a financial drain on the family. She ran from the house and hid at a nearby church, vowing she would never return to live at home again. At the age of 21 she broke off an engagement of three years to a rather passive and clinging male. Soon thereafter, she met her husband while he was recuperating from wounds sustained in the military. He was all she had dreamed of in a mate: tall, handsome, and a non-drinker. Like their marriage, their courtship was conflicted. He left her, and she pursued him when she learned that she was pregnant with their child. A "shotgun wedding" followed.

Diagnostic Formulation

A list of acute problems or symptoms exhibited by Mrs. A include a cleaning compulsion and obsession involving aggressive behavior and fear of knives, indicative of an Obsessive Compulsive Disorder; dysphoric mood of sufficient duration to warrant the diagnosis of Dysthymia; and concerns about the safety of her children given her impulsive style leading to the V-code diagnosis of the Parent-Child Problems. Longer term problems or issues include chronic marital problems (V code), and characterological issues of impulsivity, affective instability, and other symptoms characterized by the Axis II diagnoses.

Axis I: Obsessive Compulsive Disorder (300.30)
Dysthymia (300.40)
Marital Problem (V61.10)
Parent-Child Problems (V61.20)

Axis II: Borderline Personality Disorder (301.83) with Histrionic, Narcissistic, Compulsive, and Dependent Traits

Axis III: Somatic Complaints
Thyroid Goiter by history

Axis IV: Stressors—Moderate Severe (4) Chronic Marital-family issues; Homicidal ideation

Axis V: GAF Now: 46; Highest in past 12 months: 58

Clinical Formulation

Based on Adler's analysis and Shulman's (1969) accompanying commentary on the case, the following life-style themes and convictions are noted. Mrs. A viewed life as hostile, unfair, and overcontrolling. She saw herself as a victim who expected to be humiliated, but also believed she was entitled to be treated differently. Therefore, she demanded that others take care of her, and she utilized obsessions, compulsions, and threats of harming herself and her child to insure that her husband and family continued in their caretaking roles. Mrs. A also utilized interpersonal relationships as a means of gaining dominance and resisting submission, and so she would likely construe cooperation as conquest. Therefore, a clinician might anticipate that the development of a cooperative therapeutic relationship would take some time and that the negotiation phase of therapy would be very important and could not be downplayed. Also, because Mrs. A showed relatively little insight and psychological mindedness, and was rather ambivalent, the initial phase of treatment should not focus primarily on insight and interpretation. In short, a clinician would endeavor to gain Mrs. A's cooperation from the very onset by attending to her expectations of treatment and by encouraging her involvement, while being aware of her ambivalent, controlling, and entitled life-style.

Treatment Formulation

The initial focus of treatment would be to elicit Mrs. A's expectations for treatment, for the therapist's role and for her role in treatment. A mutually agreed upon treatment plan would then be negotiated. Presumably, the treatment plan would involve symptom reduction at first, followed by sta- bilization of marriage and family relations, and in the later stages focus more on characterological or Axis II issues. A short course of treatment with a trial of an antidepressant, anti-obsessive-compulsive medication (i.e., Prozac or Anafranil), and/or focused behavior therapy aimed at symptom reduction is indicated. In addition, whatever measures might be needed to insure that Mrs. A did not harm her children or herself such as consultation with a child protective services agency would be advised. Then, because of the chronic severity of her condition, psychosocial stressors, as well as her histrionic, narcissistic, and borderline personality features, a course of individual supportive therapy, with adjunctive sessions involving her husband and/or children, as well as a consideration of group therapy would be indicated. One half-hour sessions would probably be scheduled twice weekly until sufficient symptom reduction was achieved and a stable therapeutic relationship had developed.

In the second phase of treatment, sessions might be weekly and focus on longer term problem issues such as parent-child and marital relations, characterological features and faulty life-style convictions about entitlement and overcontrol, as well as her need to somatize, and threats of acting out, masculine protest, and so on. Because of these characterological features, Mrs. A might likely prove to be a difficult patient. However, she would merit a fair to good prognosis, assuming she would continue in her commitment to treatment.

REFERENCES

Adler, A. (1956). *The Individual Psychology of Alfred Adler.* In H.H. Ansbacher & R.R. Ansbacher (Eds.). New York: Harper and Row.

Adler, A. (1964a). *Superiority and social interest.* In H.H. Ansbacher & R.R. Ansbacher (Eds.). Evanston, IL: Northwestern University Press.

Adler, A. (1964b). *Problems of neurosis. A book of case histories.* New York: Harper and Row.

Adler, A. (1969). *The case of Mrs. A: The diagnosis of a life style* (2nd ed., with commentary by B. Shulman, M.D.). Chicago: Alfred Adler Institute Publishers.

American Psychiatric Association. (1987). *Diagnostic and statistical manual of mental disorders,* (3rd ed., revised). Washington, DC: Author.

Mosak, H. (1959). The getting type, a parsimonious social interpretation of the oral character. *Journal of Individual Psychology, 15* (2), 193-198.

Mosak, H. (1968). The interrelatedness of the neuroses through central themes. *Journal of Individual Psychology, 24* (1), 67-70.

Mosak, H. (1971). Lifestyle. In A. Nikelly (Ed.), *Techniques for behavior changes: Applications of Adlerian theory.* Springfield, IL: Charles C. Thomas.

Mosak, H. (1973). The controller: A social interpretation of the anal character. In H.H. Mosak (Ed.), *Alfred Adler: His influence on psychology today.* Park Ridge, NJ: Noyes Press.

Mosak, H. (1979). Mosak's typology: An update. *Journal of Individual Psychology, 35* (2), 92-95.

Mosak, H. (1984). Adlerian psychology. In R. Corsini & B. Ozaki (Eds.), *Encyclopedia of Psychology.* New York: Wiley-Interscience.

Mosak, H. (1985, May). Mosak's typology: Behaviors, psychopathology, and psychotherapy. Paper presented at *North American Society of Adlerian Psychology,* Atlanta, GA.

Neufield, I. (1954). Holistic medicine versus psychosomatic medicine. *American Journal of Individual Psychology, 10* (3,4), 140-168.

Pancner, R. (1985a). Biochemical theory and Adlerian psychotherapy. Audiotape. Montreal: *International Association of Individual Psychology.*

Pancner, R. (1985b). Impact of current depression research on Adlerian theory and practice. *Individual Psychology: The Adlerian Journal of Individual Psychology, 41* (3), 289-301.

Shulman, B. (1969). Forward to second edition. In F. G. Crookshank (Ed.), *The case of Mrs. A.* Chicago: Alfred Adler Institute.

PART II

PSYCHOSES
AND
MOOD DISORDERS

OVERVIEW

Adler (1956) stated that "The loftiest goals are to be found in the most pathological cases, that is, in the psychoses" (p. 314). While Freud developed a theory about psychotic disorders, he felt that, by and large, they were not amenable to psychoanalytic treatment. Adler disagreed, unequivocally stating that psychosis

> represents a greater distance from fellow man than any other expression except, perhaps, suicide. But . . . [it] is not incurable if the interest in others can be aroused. It is an art to cure such cases, and a very difficult art. We must win the patient back to cooperation; and we can do it only by patience and the kindliest and friendliest manner. (Adler, 1956, p. 316)

In the next four chapters, the authors examine four of the most difficult and theoretically controversial disorders in DSM-III-R. Ever since the French philosopher Descartes made the distinction between mind and body, theoreticians have struggled with the problem of how to conceptualize "mental illness." For Adlerians, the distinction between mind and body is irrelevant; given the holistic hypothesis and teleological perspective of Individual Psychology, the issue is not what causes what, but for what purpose is this being used. Adlerians are generally receptive to the recent advances and discoveries in the biological sciences, believing that seeking a single, unitary cause to any condition is reductionistic (of note is Freud's opinion in this respect; he felt that symptoms were "overdetermined" and to search for any single cause was fruitless).

Dreikurs (1967) made a distinction which has proved quite useful. He noted the difference between psychosis, neurosis, and character disorders as being one of the relationship of common sense to private logic. In the psychotic disorders (including the organic conditions), common sense is discarded. Private logic prevails, and individuals act as if their private logic were "fact" rather than "fiction." Regardless of the etiology, psychotic individuals operate upon premises which are not grounded in common sense. Whether a condition is primarily psychological or biological is not as relevant for Adlerians as is the individuals' stance about their condition. People must learn to adapt to survive, and as Adler frequently noted, survival is greatly facilitated when it is done cooperatively, with the support and mutual assistance of others.

Sperry and Shulman present Chapter 2 entitled "Schizophrenia and Delusional Disorders." They review the DSM-III-R diagnostic criteria and the classic Adlerian perspectives of each condition. Updating research into the new decade, they present an insightful discussion of the work of Gazzaniga (1988), whose recent work on split-brain patients has offered some fascinating conceptualizations which appear to support a basic Adlerian construct: the life-style as organizer and interpreter of experience.

In Chapter 3, Maniacci discusses the "Organic Mental Disorders." After presenting an overview of the DSM-III-R criteria, he discusses the differences between inferiorities, inferiority feelings, and inferiority complexes, and presents a discussion of the three levels of compensation individuals make when adjusting to illness. He highlights the necessity of understanding patients' conditions not only from a biomedical perspective, but from an individual, family systems, and rehabilitation perspective.

Peven in Chapter 4 discusses "Individual Psychology and Bipolar Mood Disorder." She presents an extensive review of the history and various theoretical perspectives taken toward the condition throughout the years, and discusses the Adlerian perspective cogently and insightfully. Peven offers eight cardinal features found in patients with Bipolar Mood Disorders and the subsequent implications for treatment.

The final chapter of this section, Chapter 5, is written by Pancner and is entitled "Depressive Disorders." After an extensive review of the DSM-III-R, biological, familial, and psychological factors of these varied conditions, he presents an integrated, comprehensive perspective of the conditions which is grounded upon the concept of depression being a spectrum disorder which exists along a continuum.

REFERENCES

Adler, A. (1956). *The Individual Psychology of Alfred Adler.* In H. L. Ansbacher & R. R. Ansbacher (Eds.). New York: Harper and Row.

Dreikurs, R. (1967). *Psychodynamics, psychotherapy, and counseling.* Chicago: Alfred Adler Institute.

Gazzaniga, M.S. (1988). *Mind matters.* Boston: Houghton Mifflin.

CHAPTER 2

SCHIZOPHRENIA AND DELUSIONAL DISORDERS

Len Sperry, M.D., Ph.D.
Bernard H. Shulman, M.D.

Approximately one-fourth of all hospital beds and roughly one-half of the psychiatric beds in the United States are occupied by individuals who have been diagnosed with a schizophrenic disorder. Estimates are that the lifetime risk of developing this disorder is approximately one percent. Basically, schizophrenia is a syndrome consisting of a highly altered sense of inner and outer reality to which the individual responds in ways that impair his/her life. This altered sense of reality, which is the psychotic core of this disorder, shows itself in disturbances of speech, perception, thinking, emotion, and physical activity. The term literally means "splitting of the mind" which in popular parlance connotes a "split personality" or multiple personality disorder. Rather, schizophrenia refers to the incongruity between different mental functions, that is, between thought, content, and feeling, or between feeling and overt activity. For example, the schizophrenic may talk of sad or terrifying events while laughing or showing no affect whatsoever.

Schizophrenia is a syndrome that involves multiple disorders with varying causes, courses, and treatment outcomes. As a diagnostic label, schizophrenia includes a wide variety of clinical presentations. Symptoms can vary so greatly from one individual to another that to present a classic textbook picture of the disorder is difficult. For example, the diagnostic presentation could be that of a hypervigilant accountant who suspects that others are plotting against him/her, the housewife who believes she is controlled by her dead mother's voice, or the withdrawn and apathetic college student who broods incessantly about the reality of existence. Symptoms also can vary within the same individual over time so that the schizophrenic may be floridly psychotic and totally unable to function one week, and then be capable of adequate reality testing and reasonable performance in the workplace the next week.

DSM-III-R Diagnostic Features

The major features of **schizophrenia** can be specified in terms of a series of diagnostic criteria which include an age of onset, disorganization of prior level of functioning, and a tendency toward chronicity, as well as characteristic symptoms such as bizarre delusions, prominent hallucinations, incoherence or marked loosening of associations, catatonic behavior, flat or grossly inappropriate affect, and marked dysfunctioning in the tasks of life. Furthermore, certain other psychiatric conditions which may mimic the disorder must be ruled out. These include schizoaffective disorder, mood disorder with psychotic features, psychoactive substance abuse disorder, organic mental disorder, delusional disorder, or other psychiatric disorders such as brief reactive psychoses and induced psychotic disorder. The reader is referred to the *Diagnostic and Statistical Manual of Mental Disorders, Third Edition, Revised* (American Psychiatric Association, 1987), for a listing of specific criteria.

The onset of schizophrenia is most likely to be noted in late adolescence or early adulthood. Except in rare instances, the diagnosis is not made unless the illness begins before age 45. Clinical experience has indicated that the diagnosis should be reserved for illnesses of at least six months duration. The diagnosis of **Schizophreniform Disorder** is reserved for individuals with symptoms of less than six months duration who otherwise meet the diagnostic criteria for schizophrenia. If the symptoms persist for more than six months the diagnosis is then corrected to that of Schizophrenic Disorder.

Phases and Course of Schizophrenic Disorder

Generally speaking, this disorder first presents with prodromal symptoms, yet manifestations of the active phase sometimes occur without these. Usually, the prodromal phase begins with a noticeable deterioration of functioning prior to the active phase and involves the presence of specific symptoms. These symptoms include social isolation or withdrawal; marked impairment of role functioning; peculiar behavior; poor hygiene; blunted, flat, or inappropriate affect; unusual perception experiences; odd or bizarre ideation or "magical thinking"; and vague, circumstantial, or metaphorical speech. The diagnosis is not made unless two of these symptoms are present.

The active phase is recognized by the presence of certain characteristic symptoms combined with gross impairment in the tasks of life: work, love, and friendship. Symptoms characteristic of this phase include delusions, hallucinations, and marked disorganization of thought and verbal behavior. Typically, delusions are bizarre and include content of either religious, somatic, grandiose, nihilistic, or prosecutory nature. Typically, auditory hallucinations involve two conversing voices, or one voice providing a running commentary on the patient's behavior or is repetitive but unrelated to a depressed or elated mood. Typically, thought disturbance is evidenced by inco- herence, illogicality, loose associations, or poverty of content. However, thought disturbance is not a dependable criterion unless accompanied by a flat, blunted, or inappropriate affect; grossly disorganized behavior; or some type of delusions and/ or hallucinations. Other symptoms may include a disturbance in a sense of self, autistic preoccupation, difficulty in making and carrying out decisions, confusion, obsessions or ritualistic behavior, ideas of reference, or dysphoric moods.

The residual phase gradually follows from the active phase. It is manifested by the same symptoms already described for the prodromal phase. Persistence of at least two of the prodromal symptoms are required by DSM-III-R diagnostic criteria.

According to DSM-III-R, the diagnostician is to classify the course of schizophrenic disturbance in terms of six categories: subchronic, chronic, subchronic with acute exacerbation, chronic with acute exacerbation, in remission, or unspecified. A patient who has a documented diagnosis of schizophrenic disorder but recovers fully is usually considered to be *in remission.* If no recurrences intervene over a period of five years without medication, the diagnosis is then changed to that of "no mental disorder." Patients in remission frequently experience an acute exacerbation of their symptoms, possibly re-hospitalization. Clinicians talk about the *rule of thirds* which predicts that approximately one-third of all patients who meet the diagnosis for schizophrenia will recover fully after a single episode, and another one-third will experience periodic exacerbations of symptoms and periods of remission, while the remaining one-third will experience the ongoing chronic form of this disorder.

The Subtypes of Schizophrenia

In DSM-III-R are recognized five subtypes of schizophrenic disorder. In actual practice, clinicians have found these subtypes of limited value since schizophrenic presentations do not neatly fit into a single diagnostic category. The five types are discussed briefly in the paragraphs that follow.

The *catatonic subtype* is characterized by marked involvement of the motor system with either hypoactivity or hyperactivity. Catatonic rigidity, which is the maintenance of a rigid posture against efforts to be moved, and catatonic posturing, the voluntary assumption of inappropriate or bizarre postures, are particularly characteristic of this disorder. At times a relatively rapid alternation occurs between excitement and stupor. The prognosis for this subtype is relatively good, but is often succeeded by other subtypes.

The **disorganized subtype** is basically the same as the historical designation of "hebephrenia." Clinical features of this subtype are severe incoherence, grossly disorganized behavior, and the presence of flat or grossly inappropriate affect. If present, delusions and hallucinations tend to be fragmentary and poorly organized. These individuals often have a history of poor premorbid functioning and follow a chronic course without significant remission.

The **paranoid subtype** is dominated by relatively persistent and systematized delusions which are usually persecutory, grandiose, or involving jealousy. Or, it may involve auditory hallucinations of similar content. Grossly disorganized behavior, catatonic features, and incoherence or inappropriate affect are not present in this type. The onset of this subtype tends to be later in life than the other subtypes, and the tendency toward deterioration is less.

The **undifferentiated subtype** is characterized by prominent psychotic features that cannot be classified in any of the previous subtypes or includes the features of more than one. This and the disorganized subtype tend to have the worse prognosis.

The **residual subtype** is used to characterize those individuals who have had an episode of schizophrenia, but whose current clinical picture no longer includes prominent psychotic features. Typical residual symptoms of emotional blunting, social withdrawal, eccentric behavior, odd beliefs or magical thinking, or marked lack of initiative, interest, or energy characterize this subtype. Often this subtype is used synonymously with the concept of partial remission.

DELUSIONAL DISORDERS

The essential feature of the delusional disorder is the presence of a persistent, non-bizarre delusion that is not due to any other mental disorder. Delusionally disordered patients do not display the pervasive disturbances of mood and thought found in other psychotic disorders. Absent are flat or inappropriate affect, prominent hallucinations, or markedly bizarre delusions. However, they do have one or more systematic and circumscribed delusions often of a persecutory nature but also involving infidelity by spouses or lovers, grandiosity, somatic changes, or erotomania of at least one month's duration. The differential diagnosis for delusional disorders includes schizophrenia, major depression or manic syndrome, and the organic mental disorders.

The delusional disorder is relatively uncommon and the lifetime risk of this disorder is between 0.05 percent and 0.1 percent. For the most part, this is a mid-life disorder and usually not recognized until the individual's delusional system is noted by friends or family. One reason why this disorder may appear to be relatively rare is that these individuals tend to be distrustful of others, particularly psychiatrists, and typically do not voluntarily seek treatment. Delusionally disordered individuals tend to be hypersensitive, argumentative, and litigious and may be referred for psychiatric evaluation because of ill-founded legal actions that they have initiated. Although these individuals may perform well occupationally and in areas outside the parameter of their delusions, they tend to be social isolates and have difficulty maintaining marriages and friendships.

The delusional disorder appears midway on a continuum between the paranoid personality disorder and schizophrenia, paranoid type. Delusions are common among the elderly and among the stimulant-drug abusers. Similarly, delusional or paranoid reactions are common in medical or surgical patients who experience delirium, in patients who are bedridden, in hearing or sight impaired individuals, as well as among refugees and minority groups. Delusionally disordered individuals have family relationships that are characterized by turbulence, callousness, and coldness. The etiology for this disorder is unknown, and though genetic and biological factors have been postulated none have actually been identified.

Types of Delusional Disorders

In DSM-III-R is recognized six types of delusional disorders based on the predominant delusion being noted. A brief description of each is given in the paragraphs that follow.

Erotomanic Type. The central theme of an erotic delusion involves the belief of unrequited love by another, usually an idealized romantic love and spiritual union, rather than sexual attraction. The person about whom this conviction is held is usually of higher status such as a superior at work, a complete stranger, or a famous person such as a sports figure, movie star, or politician. Much newspaper publicity about erotomanic delusions of individuals who have hounded, attacked, or even killed celebrities has been noted in the last few years. John Hinckley, Jr.'s much publicized effort to contact and "track" actress Jodie Foster is one such example.

Grandiose Type. Grandiose delusions usually take the form of the individual's being convinced that he/she possesses some great but unrecognized talent or insight, or has made some important discoveries. The predominant theme is one of inflated worth, power, knowledge, identity, or special relationship to a deity or famous person.

Jealous Type. When delusions of jealousy are present, the individual is convinced, without evidence or cause, that his/her spouse or lover is unfaithful. Small bits of "evidence" such as ambiguous notes, disarrayed clothing, or spots on the sheet are collected and used to justify the delusion. Inevitably, delusionally-disordered individuals confront their spouse or lover and take extraordinary steps to intervene in the imagined infidelity.

Personality Type. Persecutory delusions are the most common of the six types. The predominant theme is that the individual or someone close to the individual is being malevolently treated. The delusions may be simple or elaborate and usually involve a single theme or series of connected themes involving being spied upon, followed, poisoned or drugged, harassed, conspired against, or obstructed in the pursuit of long-term goals.

Somatic Type. The predominant theme in this type of delusion is that the person has some physical defect, disorder, or disease. Common delusions involve worms under the skin, rotting brain, and various kinds of cancer which have been medically ruled out.

Unspecified Type. This is a delusional disorder that does not fit in any previous category. It is also used to classify delusions of reference without malevolent content.

The differential diagnosis for this disorder includes organic mental disorders such as dementia and organic delusional syndromes such as those due to amphetamines or a brain tumor. Other disorders that must be ruled out are schizophrenia, paranoid type, schizophreniform disorder, mood disorders with psychotic features, body dysmorphic disorder, and the paranoid personality disorder. According to DSM-III-R, when an individual meets the criteria for a delusional disorder and has a preexisting paranoid personality disorder, the personality disorder should be listed on Axis II followed by the modifier "premorbid."

THE ADLERIAN PERSPECTIVE ON PSYCHOSIS

The theory of functional psychosis presented in this section reflects the Adlerian perspective particularly as it has been articulated by Bernard Shulman (1968, 1984), and supplemented with the research-based theory of Michael Gazzaniga (1988), the noted mind-body researcher.

Shulman's model of the psychotic process can be summarized as follows:

*Vulnerability + Life-Style Convictions + Decision + Self-Training and Discouragement →
Psychotic Process and Symptoms*

Briefly, vulnerability (i.e., positive family history for a major psychiatric disorder, some biological predisposition to psychosis, and/or faulty training), when combined with psychotic-like life-style convictions, personal decision, self-training, and discouragement, can result in a psychotic process. One becomes schizophrenic over a period of time in response to cumulative life stresses and a feeling of failure. The "choice" is neither conscious nor planned ahead of time. It is a series of small steps—a self-training in which one step makes taking the next step easier, so that in the end one somehow arrives at one's own illness without recalling the past by which one came.

Like other Adlerians, Shulman espouses a cognitive theory of personality development and psychopathology. Cognitive theory offers a description, an explanation of the internal cognitive structures of the individual. This explanation includes the individual's consistent style of perceiving. For example, schizophrenics extract and process information differently from other persons. They are "over-inclusive," that is, they include too many categories in their thoughts. They do not filter out extraneous information well. Furthermore, they do not abstract with precision and thus make errors in logic. They do not pay proper attention to differences in the semantic context of language, and thus they do not understand precisely what others are saying to them. Therefore, they invest what they hear with meaning prompted by the inner fantasies. In addition, cognitive theory describes the internal schemata apperception—the self-concepts of individuals, their world designs, and their plans for coping with the world. Kelly (1955) devised the term **personal constructs** for the idiosyncratic way people construe events. The word "construe" is apt, since it implies that events are actually **constructs** devised by individuals themselves. It is a personal conclusion about life and themselves that produces a seemingly appropriate action. These personal constructs are contained in the memory organization of individuals and influence how subsequent events are stored in their memory.

The personal constructs contain the world design and the plan of action in the schizophrenic, the **extravagant ideals** that Binswanger (1960) mentioned. Self-concept, world design, and plan of action are all part of what Adler called the life-style (1926). Extravagant ideals grow from normal human motives which have gone awry. Finally, a cognitive theory describes the coping program devised by individuals.

If we know the life-style of individuals, we will know their cognitive blueprint for behavior. Then, we shall be able to see how those who become psychotic have followed a step-by-step progression in their journey toward psychosis. We shall understand how they integrate the events of their lives into this journey in accord with their unconscious blueprint. Thus, knowing their master plan for perceiving stimuli, we shall be able to understand their subjective experiences— the phenomenology of their life. From knowing their phenomenology, we also may reason backwards and plot out their cognitive blueprint.

Arieti (1974, 1980) and Binswanger (1960) have offered useful insights for understanding the psychotic process from a cognitive perspective. Arieti (1980) begins his inquiry by noting the importance of a child's subjective perceptions:

> Certainly it is very important to study what kind of interpersonal world the patient met early in life. That is the first term on our list of inquiries, but only the first. It is also of crucial importance to determine how the child experienced this world, how he internalized and how such internalization affected the subsequent events of his life, which in turn acted as feedback mechanisms. (p. 242)

A more thorough cognitive-phenomenological theory of psychosis and schizophrenia is offered by Binswanger (1960). Starting from the premise that individuals construct their own **world design,** Binswanger asked, "Who is this man and how does this man interpret himself?" He went on to say that schizophrenics construct a world design in which they set up a set of rigid alternatives, a hard and fast either/ or:

> These alternatives are totally inadequate to escape from an unescapable situation . . . he shuts himself off from the world of others and himself, and most especially . . . he shuts himself off from . . . a loving relatedness with others. (p. 160)

Binswanger was saying that those who will become psychotic have created an impossible situation for themselves. As part of their world design, they have constructed a distorted and misguided goal which is impossible to achieve. They do not give themselves permission to cease pursuit of this goal, and they believe they will be a total failure if they do not achieve it. This notion that schizophrenics have inordinate and inappropriate goals is similar to that of Adler (1926)—a concretized, rigid and dogmatic aspiration to be in some way superhuman and a greater interest in this personal goal than in fellowship or enjoyment of life.

The few studies on level of aspiration that have been done on schizophrenics and preschizophrenics confirm that, unlike controls, schizophrenics and preschizophrenics either maintain high levels of aspiration after repeated failure or raise those levels (Lu, 1962).

Vulnerability to Psychosis

Even in high risk situations, most individuals do not experience the psychotic process. Specifically, why does one child in the family become psychotic while others do not? Vulnerability is an important consideration. The basic assumption here is that a person who has a vulnerability to a psychiatric illness has the propensity to develop or express symptoms of the disorder under certain stressful conditions. This, of course, is the basis of what is called the **stress-diathesis model.** Neuchterlein and Dawson (1984) and Liberman (1987) have described vulnerability-stress models of schizophrenia in which the course and outcome of the disorder are in dynamic flux, influenced by biological, psychological, and social-environmental variables. This vulnerability is manifested by genetic predisposition, neurotransmitter abnormalities, and other unknown neurological factors resulting in cognitive, autonomic, and attentional dysfunctions, as well as a host of premorbid psychosocial factors such as faulty early childhood training, high flown goals, and life-style convictions.

Neuchterlein and Dawson (1984) emphasize the information-process deficits that along with autonomic reactivity anomalies, social competence, and coping limitations (called enduring vulnerability characteristics) interact with environmental stimuli (social stressors and nonsupportive social networks) and transient intermediate states (processing capacity overload, autonomic hyperarousal, and deficient processing of social stimuli) to yield the psychotic symptoms of schizophrenia.

Some schizophrenics seem to start life with what Alfred Adler called an **organ inferiority,** a central nervous system organization which is unstable or somehow defective. Gazzaniga (1988) has developed a cognitive theory of psychopathology which addresses this issue of central nervous system dysfunction and incorporates research findings from both the neurosciences and cognitive theory. Gazzaniga proposed that individuals generate a series of internally consistent schemas or beliefs about themselves and life would allow daily living to be both predictable and meaningful. He labeled these cognitive schemas the **brain's interpreter,** which appear similar to what Adlerians call life-style convictions. Gazzaniga's "brain interpreter" is reminiscent of Kurt Goldstein's (1939) compensatory tendency and Adler's theory of compensation. The interpreter does not always have correct data but must interpret this information any way the brain can. Gazzaniga further postulated an urge to create order in the information being processed, which is an effort to compensate for central nervous system dysfunctioning, or "organ inferiority" as it was called by Adler. Gazzaniga believed that schizophrenia is a disease in which the brain's interpreter, typically the verbal, left hemisphere, attempts to create order out of what is most likely endogenous, or inner-generated, brain chaos. By brain chaos, he referred to spurious neural actions precipitated by faulty biochemical brain states, such as sharp rises or decreases in neuro-transmitters which adversely affect the typically symbolic, image-generating right hemisphere. The interpreter makes decisions about what meaning to assign to chaotic events.

The psychotic process in general and schizophrenia in particular reveals how powerful the interpreter may be and how much it wants to succeed in generating reasonable ideas about unreasonable experiences and thoughts that arise out of dysfunctional brain states. As the right hemisphere continues to generate odd, unexplainable images and impressions, the left hemisphere desperately attempts to "interpret" and integrate these aberrations according to some consistent, logical, rule-governing system, which Adlerians would term the life-style.

Endogenous brain changes, particularly changes in the levels of neurotransmitters such as dopamine, create new circumstances to which the brain's interpreter must continually react. That reaction in turn produces perceptions that can become powerful guides for the mental outlook of the patient. An endogenous state that is quickly induced by a change of brain chemistry—such as with a mind-altering drug like LSD—can be dismissed fairly easily as an apparition after the brain's biochemistry returns to a more normal state. However, if the brain change lasts longer, then the interpretations generated by the altered state of mind become more embellished, and the memories associated with them take on their own life and can become powerful influences on the personal history of the individual. Gazzaniga noted that "crazy thoughts" are manageable for the normal person because they occur as part of some unusual context, and thus are easily rejected. On the other hand, continually crazy thoughts, evoked by chronic brain dysfunction, become harder to reject. This occurs because of the accumulative effect of one "crazy memory" welcoming other "crazy ideas."

Gazzaniga speculated that schizophrenia is the fate of the human mind exposed to long-term distortions of reality. The brain's interpreter tries to bring order to the chaos brought about by biochemical or structural brain abnormalities. As a result of processing erroneous data about self, social relationships, and life circumstances over long periods of time, the brain's interpreter constructs strange and psychotic theories about reality which become the bizarre images generated by the right hemisphere.

Gazzaniga was not saying that chronic brain dysfunction such as schizophrenia is the result merely of the overproduction of the neurotransmitter dopamine. Rather, he believed that the dopamine abnormality impacts nerve circuits such that they misfire. In turn, the brain's interpreter creates a specific delusion or set of hallucinations that allow the patient to "make sense" of this phenomenon.

Gazzaniga offered a useful phenomenological description of the overwhelming feelings of vulnerability of individuals entering a psychotic state. The non-psychotic person's sense of worth is usually sustained by the positive feedback from social contacts, interactions, and personal relationships. While individuals may have doubts about the future in known and unknown situations, they can cope with such feelings because life in the past with other people has worked out. But what happens if these individuals start to loose their perception of these automatic rewards? Assuming that accurate perceptions reflect brain circuitry that is functional, good feelings are automatically triggered when individuals have contact with a good friend, but what if seeing that friend did not trigger that response? Gazzaniga believed that this new, negative experience evolves into a state much like schizophrenia. With their personal reference system at loose ends because they had trouble producing those automatic rewards, they feel suddenly uncertain and vulnerable. In this disorienting state, they begin to see the world through a haze of paranoia. Such a change in neurotransmitter activity in the limbic system, also called the reward-generating system, alters brain circuits so that pleasant associations and rewards are no longer produced. Thus, it is easy to imagine how bizarre thoughts fill this void. Without input of thoughts from the normal reward system, schizophrenics are in a chronic information vacuum. They search for information from their current environment, but because of their increasing social isolation, little is to be found. As consensual validation decreases, their interpreter creates an alternative reality which accounts for hallucinations and delusions.

Intrusive thoughts may begin to flood this chronic informational vacuum. As schizophrenics cope with these unwanted intrusions into thought, thought itself becomes very disordered and interrupted. The first response can be wild embarrassment, and schizophrenics then withdraw from social contact as much as possible. However, rather than helping, social isolation further compounds the problem. At first, the brain's interpreter had to deal with imagined sounds and voices, but it now has to comprehend them without the steadying influence provided by contact with friends and family. The same can be said about delusions. At times, all persons experience some paranoid thinking. Episodes of overwhelming vulnerability that arise in the absence of a threatening stimulus are usually due to some transitory biochemical balance in neurocircuitry which the brain's interpreter easily dismisses as unsubstantiated. But when the condition moves beyond the episodic to a chronic condition, the brain's interpreter can create prominent delusions in its attempt to "explain" its neurochemical dysfunction.

Besides brain dysfunction, other vulnerabilities to schizophrenia include a positive family history for a major psychiatric disorder predisposing an individual biologically and psychosocially for an expression of psychotic process, and a difficult childhood in which the individual has become systematically and persistently discouraged by the demands of life. *The childhood of schizophrenics is characterized by unsatisfactory human relationships,* not only with parents but also with siblings and peers. Such unsatisfactory childhood situations, containing deviant personal methods of relating, distorted and confusing methods of communication, marital problems, suppressive parental behavior, and other peculiar and unsatisfying interactions have been described by many theorists and researchers. Adlerians believe that these unsatisfactory situations are not what result in psychosis but rather the child's personal reaction to these childhood problems.

Shulman (1984) noted that the child must conspire with environment pressures to bring about situations which lead to schizophrenia. He noted four common syndromes that predispose or increase the individual's vulnerability to schizophrenia. The four syndromes are the special child syndrome, the bossy child syndrome, the inadequate childhood syndrome, and the child who has to be something to satisfy others syndrome.

Schizophrenia seems to be a final common pathway to which different people can come. Perhaps these concepts do not yet explain who becomes schizophrenic. By looking at the internal schemata of the individual we inevitably find evidence of the kind of world design described by Binswanger (1960), and the kind of life-style described by Kurt Adler (1958).

Shulman proposed that both a vulnerability to psychosis and an extreme stressor are necessary but insufficient conditions for the expression of psychosis. He argued that the sufficient condition is a decision. Therefore, he proposed that the child with a predisposition toward psychosis can choose to be or not to be schizophrenic. The question is basically one of choosing a course of life which is likely to lead to schizophrenia. In their study of families of schizophrenics, Hoover and Franz (1972) found that both normal and schizophrenic siblings selected their responses to parental demands and life situation stimuli by either letting themselves become involved in intense embroilment with the parent or refusing to do so. In each case, some kind of decision or choice is made. Thus, in addition to hereditary and environmental determinants, a *creative self* also is at work. Shulman (1984) stated that this creative self becomes a crucial factor in the etiology of schizophrenia because it leads us to the notion that schizophrenia is a personal choice, unconscious perhaps, but a choice nevertheless. Like Gazzaniga, Shulman is convinced that schizophrenia is more likely to be the result of a plan rather than simply the result of a defect in brain functioning only.

Shulman's theory of schizophrenia and other psychotic disorders will be presented in the remaining sections of this chapter. This material has been adapted from Shulman (1968, 1984).

Life-style Convictions, Decisions, and Self-training for Psychosis

Psychotic individuals create their own meaning for their existence according to their underlying *convictions.* These same convictions are schizophrenogenic; that is, they predispose individuals to schizophrenia. Shulman assumes that a teleological factor must be present, namely, a set of *personal values* which are largely self-determined and which "call forth" the psychosis.

Such personal values are developed during childhood in the context of the family. They include *convictions* about self and life drawn from childhood relationships, the raw material from which they must select data and fashion beliefs.

These psychotogenic values or convictions grow out of faulty training in responding to life's demands and result in the syndromes of behavior described above. The convictions are described in the following hypotheses:

Hypothesis 1. *Individuals who will become schizophrenic are the recipients of faulty training which leads to the following faulty beliefs.*

a. The conviction that they have no place in the world because of their deficiencies and/or the hostilities of the environment.

b. The conviction that they must achieve some special state or position which frees them from all defects in order to have a satisfactory life. This special state or position is always an exaggerated goal, e.g., to be perfect, to be godlike, to be impregnable, to hurt and humiliate, to be utterly masculine, to have "perfect" interpersonal relationships, and so on. Only this longed for state can give them a place in the world. Their goals are therefore relatively inflexible, have an all-or-none quality, and demand absolute fulfillment. They see few or no alternatives.

c. The conviction that any defeat or anticipated defeat, no matter how minor, in the pursuit of this goal is a major threat to their desperate attempt to overcome their defects and will "spoil" their life. From this grows the idea that the schizophrenics are abnormally sensitive to slights or defeats, whereas normal individuals are able to withstand certain disappointments. Schizophrenics are thus seen as having "low frustration tolerance" and "weak egos." For Shulman, persons who are so "sensitive" to failure exaggerate the importance of succeeding in all endeavors. Life must not bring any defeat because that would topple the whole structure. In this sense, schizophrenics have all their eggs in one basket. Thus they make unreasonable demands on life.

d. The conviction that common sense, social participation, and acceptance of the rules of life according to which society operates interfere with their movement toward their chosen goal. Therefore, in order to better pursue the goals and/or avoid defeat in their pursuits, they make all other considerations of lesser value. Thus, good human relations, the customs of society, sex, health, even life itself have less value than the continuation of their pursuits. In short, schizophrenics train themselves to be different because being like others will not work for them.

Hypothesis 2. The crisis occurs when they perceive their life situation does not allow achievement of the goal in accord with "common sense" in a socially acceptable and useful way. Therefore, "common sense" and consensuality are discarded because they interfere with the pursuit of the goal. They decide to stop living in the consensual world. This is the *decision* which constitutes the "psychotic break." At this point is when they discard the obligation to function like other human beings.

Hypothesis 3. Having discarded common sense, they are free to develop their own private logic which permits them to create the fiction that they have reached or will reach their goal of superiority. For example, a divinity student, convinced of his own sinfulness and failing in his schoolwork, spent three days and nights in prayer and fasting eventually resulting in a state of confusion in which he felt himself drawn to Jesus. When found by the school authorities, he claimed that he *was* Jesus, and he was subsequently hospitalized. Schizophrenics-in-process systematically and autistically build a fantasy life to suit themselves. They become independent of the rules which others feel obliged to obey. They can even publicly defecate or masturbate without shame.

Hypothesis 4. Because the world and other people, by their very existence, tend to intrude on their privacy, they must take steps to protect their private world. To this end they isolate themselves and take steps to nullify the efforts of others who attempt to communicate with them. They remove themselves by stupor or drive others away by threats and bizarre behavior. They decide that what others do is wrong, harmful, silly or crazy, and otherwise blunt, impede, or hide from the efforts of others to reach them. They make themselves immune to logic and sentiment: two consensual ways of communicating by which one person can possibly influence another. All this is made easier by having discarded "common sense." If one wants to stop being part of this world and live in the world of one's own making, the efficient procedure is not to accept "common sense."

Once the schizophrenogenic convictions have been reached and the crisis situation has occurred, the decision to discontinue social participation leads to forms of behavior that prevent continued social integration. Such behavior may be universal or limited to certain specific life areas, because sometimes schizophrenics can accomplish their goals by discarding only some aspects of consensuality. They need not discard all of them, nor all of them all of the time.

By continued isolation from social participation, what begins as a device for avoiding personal defeat or catastrophe becomes itself a catastrophe. Schizophrenics may start by playing a game of pretense but often find themselves caught in their own devices. Scher (1962) said that schizophrenics begin to believe their own fanciful constructs; they discarded the social system and now have only their schizophrenic system as a *modus vivendi.* Their only choice is to continue their attempts to strengthen their *fort sans foundation* to work harder at reifying their private sense until they succeed at reaching a state hospital or halfway house. There they are relatively free from the demands of life or until their transcension into schizophrenia permits them to escape the defeats they fear, after which the "acute psychosis" may remit and they resume limited social participation. Otherwise, only strong intercurrent events affect their system. Psychotropic drugs, electroshock therapy, or a skillful therapist may sidetrack them from the pursuit of this fiction; or if they are soldiers and the military situation does not permit them to withdraw from social participation, they may be forced to make some kind of peace with the demands of life.

The "decision" to disregard consensuality is thus the *sine qua non* of the psychotic break. Boisen (1947) compared this to creative thinking, saying that observation of a person experiencing this psychotic process shows evidence of an "unsolved personal problem"; attempts at solution are made which proceed by stages similar to the development of insight and creative thinking. Boisen considered the psychosis as a chosen "solution" to the problem.

Shulman (1984) also noted that schizophrenics must be convinced that common sense is an obstacle, rather than an aid to their purpose. Since common sense is not only sufficient but also necessary for the achievement of those personal goals which are chosen by the majority of persons, it becomes logical to assume that psychotics aspire to achievements which are impossible, or at least highly unlikely, when they remain within the bounds of consensuality. Research has shown that the schizophrenics have a higher level of aspiration than non-schizophrenics, and they tend to raise these levels after repeated failures rather than lowering them as normal persons do (Lu, 1962). Their goal may not only be very high and perfectionistic, it also may be extremely inappropriate, such as wanting to be the Messiah, God, supersexed, nonhuman, wanting relationships only on their own terms, wanting to have no human relationships at all, or wanting to live in a completely different kind of world.

Schizophrenics also must decide that their private personal goals are imperatives which outweigh all other considerations and values. Nothing else has an appeal for them equal to this rigid goal. In their ambitions, all else is considered chaff for the wind. Only in dreams, in toxic states, in narcotic fantasies, in artificial psychoses, in experiments on sensory deprivation, or in times of severe exhaustion can those living by consensual rules arrange to discard common sense and operate according to a private sense which is completely personal and extrasocial. At other times, the *Weltanschauung* we accept constrains us to heed the commonly accepted forms of behavior and communication even though we may resent their limitations.

Since "private sense" cannot stand too much daylight without crumbling, schizophrenics must protect it from close scrutiny. To this end, they severely limit interpersonal communications, either by not speaking at all or deliberately misleading those attempting to speak with them. They may be willing to transact business with others when such transactions do not threaten their private logic, either because the area of transaction is innocuous or because a therapist or other person is willing to accept their rules of the game. This last situation is called "participating in the patient's psychosis."

Basically, schizophrenics remain well integrated in their *own way.* An outside observer may be impressed with the inappropriate quality of the psychotic solution and thinks he sees a person whose "defenses have disintegrated." Actually psychotic individuals have discarded their previous consensual defenses because they were related to consensual modes of functioning and therefore no longer useful to them. This is why they do not use the usual "defense mechanisms," which require that they accept the rules of common sense. The decision to discard common sense still leaves psychotics with the continuing problem of reifying their private sense. In Gazzaniga's language, the brain's interpreter now has to make sense out of chaos. They must support, justify, and defend their point of view until it becomes an article of faith, as when paranoid individuals provoke others to abuse them so they can feel justified in being "victims." At this point, some of their behavior will be exploratory in nature; that is, they will empirically determine which varieties of behavior best serve their purpose of keeping distance. This is why *a far greater variety of behavior is seen in earlier stages of psychosis than in later stages.* Eventually, effective ways of creating distance are evolved, tested, sharpened and refined, and the behavior becomes no longer exploratory and relatively open, but rigid, stereotyped, and concrete.

What others have called "poor ego functioning," "poor drive control," and "emergence of primary processes" are the schizophrenics' careful inattention to those stimuli and perceptions that they want to filter out. Consequently comes the availability of illogic, unreason, illusion, fantasy, and so on, both as modes of perception and as modes of communication. This allows them to be and act "crazy" since the consensual rejection of "crazy" behavior is absent. For example, psychotics first fantasize that the world is astride; then they are justified in rejecting as unreal and false any evidence that the world exists. Now they are free from obligation to observe rules; they emancipate themselves from all powers other than their own and save their self-respect by blaming the outside world or refusing to acknowledge its existence.

The "decision" often seems to occur at times of physical exhaustion or illness. The crisis situation with its attendant fear, indecision, restlessness, exhaustion, sleeplessness, and sleep deprivation provides an easier transition into a psychotic state. When physical resistance is lowered, the integrating functions of the central nervous system diminished as the brain's interpreter "tires," and nonconsensual experiences are more likely to occur. Perhaps if they set out to become reactively psychotic, an easy procedure is to work themselves into a state of frenzy, unclarity, exhaustion, and extreme subjectivity, just as warriors engage in a war dance to work themselves into frenzied readiness before a battle.

Differential Diagnosis of Schizophrenia

Some patients, however, meet the criteria for other psychoses but in some way do not completely fit these hypotheses for schizophrenia. While having had some childhood difficulties, they were neither schizotypal nor paranoid personality types. They can relate interpersonally with families and peers, but from time to time become psychotic under stress. Once the acute psychotic state clears, their underlying personality disorder, usually histrionic, passive-aggressive, or borderline, becomes evident.

The main difference between these cases and schizophrenia is that the psychosis in these cases is temporarily evident in the individual's life and not a way of existence. These individuals are not caught up in what Adler (1926) called the **high-flown goal,** and what Binswanger (1960) termed the **extravagant ideals.** Of the four sets of convictions mentioned earlier in this chapter, seemingly they suffer only from the fourth. This distinction fits the criteria in DSM-III-R for **brief reaction psychosis** as distinguished from schizophrenia.

The psychosis in these cases may be more easily understood if we compared it to a partial retreat from reality in the face of a most unpleasant demand of life. It provides a temporary way out and starts to recede as soon as the life demand is no longer present. It can be compared to the behavior of a child losing a game; one child will lose graciously, another will hide its hurt, the third will depreciate the game, a fourth will accuse the others of cheating, a fifth will cheat to influence the outcome, the sixth will rationalize, and a seventh will grit its teeth and determine to win next time. The eighth child, however, will deny, distort, disturb, and even destroy the game, refusing to let it come to its natural end. This is the mode of reaction of a patient who fits the criteria for "brief reactive psychosis."

Shulman (1984) differentiated the **paranoid** features of the schizophrenic from those seen in the **delusional disorder** and the **bipolar disorder.** In the delusional and bipolar disorder, Shulman noted that they develop some private logic while retaining some consensuality. Patients can become very upset, but do not appear to have undergone an acute disoriented episode. They may have their own private explanation of "causes" and "evil forces at work" and have no intent to expose these explanations to rules of consensual logic. The bipolar disorder, on the other hand, so often can look as bizarre as the schizophrenic that the differentiations become difficult. The acute disoriented state in the manic phase of the bipolar is similar to that of a schizophrenic. Both states can show perceptual distortions and autistic thinking. **Manic states** may contain considerable paranoid features. However, manics do not wish to keep a distance between themselves and others. Although they change the rules of the "reality game" they continue to want social relationships. Their behavior is that of people who constantly seek close relationships. Even in the distrust phase of the bipolar disorder, their behavior is designed to keep others involved with them. This is the essential difference between the bipolar disorder and the schizophrenic. Between attacks, individuals with the bipolar disorder usually accept the human role as the rest of us do, whereas schizophrenics do not.

Psychotic Process and Symptoms

The symptoms of schizophrenia themselves also can be understood as a form of surrealistic creation and its consequences. Schizophrenics have manifold symptoms, not all of them limited to psychotic processes. They can worry, be fearful, become despondent, be self-conscious, suffer feelings of inadequacy, be cynical, be lonely, lose sleep and appetite, have obsessive thoughts, overindulge in alcohol, and be able to concentrate as does the so-called neurotic. On the other hand, some of their symptoms are specific manifestations of schizophrenia, particularly those involving their refusal to use consensuality.

With this in mind, Shulman (1984) has classified the symptoms of schizophrenia as specific markers along the continuum moving away from or toward consensuality. Symptoms are arranged in a developmental sequence rather than in the chronological order. As in any developmental sequence, stages may merge and overlap and should not be considered as sharply delimited from another. In addition, stages may be repeated since schizophrenics sometimes proceed through the same process over and over again. What is more, many schizophrenics will not pass through all these stages but will skip some of them in the course of their illness. Thus, one must not think that every patient follows this exact course of events. Note needs to be made that many psychotic disorders such as acute organic brain syndromes and delusional disorders will not fit into this scheme.

The sequence is described in terms of the symptoms evident to an observer and related to the schizophrenic's subjective experience at the time. Not all of the schizophrenic's symptoms are psychotic symptoms *per se*. Some can more rightly be called neurotic. The sequence of psychotic symptoms is as follows:

1. Symptoms with a purpose of permitting and facilitating the withdrawal from social integration. These include seclusiveness, secretiveness, apathy, shallow affect, lack of interest in normal events, deep concentration, practicing autistic thinking, and even suicide.

2. Symptoms with a purpose of defeating the appeal of social living and the insistence of social demands. These include inappropriate affect, loose associations, private language, mutism, negativism, self-neglect, violence, disgusting behavior, and assaultiveness.

3. Symptoms with a purpose of reinforcing schizophrenic private logic in insuring the correctness of their position. These include hallucinations, delusions, provocation of others, impulsiveness, the need to prove self as no good, and playing the game of being "crazy."

4. Symptoms with a purpose of admitting the reestablishment of conditional social relationships which are sometimes so bizarre that we are constrained to consider them as indications of psychoses. These include some bizarre methods of behavior. However, obsessive-compulsive and hypochondriacal symptoms may be used for the same purpose. Perhaps these symptoms, bizarre as they may be, should be included among those we consider restitutive, because they are not intended to further separate the individual from society.

A composite model of psychotic disorders can now be presented which incorporates the stress-vulnerability research, Gazzaniga's neuroscience theory, and Shulman's view:

$$Stress + Brain\text{-}Mind\ Vulnerability$$
$$+ Coping/Self\text{-}Training + Decision \rightarrow$$
$$Psychotic\ Process$$

Essentially, stressors such as losses, conflicts, and lack of social support can precipitate a psychotic process and symptoms when brain-mind vulnerability—positive family psychiatric history or other biological predisposing factors as well as psychosis-prone life-style convictions/cognitive schema—interacts with deficits in coping skills, self-training, and decisions based on discouragement.

TREATMENT OF SCHIZOPHRENIC DISORDER

Since the middle 1950s antipsychotic medications have been the treatment of choice for schizophrenics, particularly in the active phase. The introduction of antipsychotic medications has had a powerful influence on the management of schizophrenia. Some pharmacologists believe that the antipsychotic medication is the only proven mode of treatment and that psychotherapeutic interventions are of little use. On the other hand, advocates of psychotherapy for schizophrenia argue that medication alone is not sufficient and that the effectiveness of medication depends on the psychosocial context in which it is given. They also contend that medication only reduces psychotic symptoms but does not affect the patient's social or personality functioning. For all practical purposes, talking about a single "correct" treatment is not useful since schizophrenia is a syndrome consisting of a number of disorders. The range of treatments and combinations of treatments used reflects the variability inherent in this disorder. What is useful to some schizophrenic individuals may not be useful or even may be harmful to others. Most effective treatment regimens combine psychopharmacology and psychosocial therapies (Beitman and Klerman, 1986).

Shulman (1984) has described an Adlerian perspective on treatment. He noted that the decision to reverse the psychotic process requires that the individual be willing to consider alternatives to current behavior, to experiment with these alternatives, and to train oneself in new directions. The task is not a simple decision to "buck up and stop thinking that way," but a willingness to reorder one's perceptions in order to permit the growth of a new frame of reference in regard to life. Shulman noted that change must precede through a kindling of hope, a reestablishment of consensual ways of behaving, and an experiencing of satisfaction in consensual living. The keynote of the therapist's behavior is, thus, encouragement. Patient, persistent encouragement is a necessity. "The approach is continued," stated Kurt Adler (1958), "until the patient becomes convinced that fruitful cooperation is possible, becomes more hopeful as to the achievement of some of his goals, learns to feel less of an isolate and more likely the human being."

What must patients learn in order to change? That they have mistaken high-flown goals; that they have misunderstood what it means to be human; that they can become successfully human with human practice; that life will be more satisfying when they join the human community; that they have been training themselves away from the common sense way of looking at life and practicing the use of an isolating private logic; and that their psychotic symptoms are purposeful maneuvers more under their control than they have recognized.

Shulman (1984) noted that the great majority of schizophrenic individuals will not have any systematic individual psychotherapy, nor a relationship between therapist and patient extended over a long enough term to be effective. However, even brief encounters can have far-reaching effects. While therapists will carry out a systematic long-term psychotherapy with relatively few schizophrenic individuals, they will briefly and perhaps casually come in contact with many more patients. Any of these encounters, while making ward rounds, while doing intakes in the clinic, while examining patients or emergency admissions, provide therapists opportunities to intervene therapeutically albeit briefly. Shulman noted that treatment such as group therapy, milieu therapy, family and recreational therapy, music therapy, psychodrama, social clubs, and even medication groups can be very useful treatment interventions. They are social processes and tools of communication with a purpose of encouraging and clarifying self-awareness and self-understanding, overcoming isolation, promoting the use of social skills, and correcting faulty perceptions.

TREATMENT OF THE DELUSIONAL DISORDERS

Generally speaking, treatment of the delusional disorders is extraordinarily difficult. The longer the symptoms have been present, the more refractory they are to simple treatments such as psychoeducation, psychotherapy, or medication. However, some culturally-induced syndromes may respond to relocation—i.e., returning to the patient's country of origin— even if they have taken months to come to clinical attention (Reid, 1989).

When the delusionally disordered individual agrees to psychotherapy, it may be the treatment of choice, but it should be initiated in such a way that the patient is likely to see some benefit from it and some support from the therapist. Emphasis should be on developing a trusting relationship with a neutral and accepting therapist. Ritzler (1981) indicated that systematic desensitization has been effective in reducing delusional behavior. Antipsychotic medication has been noted to be effective in some cases. However, most patients are reluctant to take neuroleptics either because of their suspiciousness of the treatment or because of their exquisite sensitivity to the side effects of medication. It has been shown that antipsychotic medication takes the "edge" off delusions, making psychosocial treatment much more possible. Recent use of antidepressants also has been noted to be effective (Reid, 1989).

Bullard's (1960) short paper on Adlerian psychotherapy with paranoid patients is a classic. Bullard described an approach to engaging the suspicious and distrustful delusional or paranoid patients. Shulman (1984) noted that insofar as possible he tries to save the pride of the paranoid. He stated,

> Our explanations and interpretations are egosyntonic; we treat him with courtesy and respect, while we do not let his delusions pay off; we try to discuss with him his feelings about life, and those areas where he feels threatened by defeat, and try to help him to feel that he is a worthwhile person. It will take longer to convince that he is not surrounded by a hostile world, and that he does not always need to win to be superior or to be right. (p. 156)

CASE EXAMPLE

A 41-year-old single white male had been hospitalized for psychotic reactions five times in the previous 15 years. He presented as a dependent personality disordered individual who lived with an older married sister and was supported by a Veterans Administration pension. Although unmarried, he had had girlfriends in the past and still maintained a sexual liaison with one of them. He had male friends and enjoyed drinking, playing cards, and going to ballgames with them. His downfall always came at work. He was able to get a job whenever he felt well and always showed himself to be a good worker. Soon he would be given more responsibilities. He feared and resisted, but he was not able to speak up effectively to his bosses. He would react by becoming slipshod in his work and taking days off. Shortly thereafter, he would begin to feel agitated, and worried about his job and his health. He would lose his appetite and become unable to sleep. For several sleepless nights, he would begin "having thoughts" which were obsessive ideas that he was getting sick or that he would lose his mind. Eventually he became exhausted and disoriented, would hear voices, imagine that he was dying, fear he was being poisoned, and so on. He would be brought to the hospital by his sister or sometimes would present himself for admission. His stays in the hospital tended to last from six months to two years. After a few months he would begin to calm down, recover his composure, and would slowly regain his confidence to leave the hospital and try working again. He had never been discharged from a job, but voluntarily left when he felt too sick to work. His greatest fear was that he would again have a psychotic episode.

During the psychotic episodes, this male fulfilled all the criteria for the diagnosis of schizophrenic, undifferentiated type. During his periods of remission he was a dependent personality with reasonably superficial adjustment to others. True, he never felt able to undertake many responsibilities such as marriage or advancement at work. He had dropped out of school in the 11th grade because he felt it was too much for him. He was the baby of his family and had been overprotected by his mother until her death. His older sister now filled his mother's role. The pattern of his life is a common one, but why did he become psychotic in times of stress rather than developing an anxiety disorder which might have served his purpose just as well? The psychotic episodes function as ordinary anxiety disorders, as a device for avoiding a difficult situation, or for saving face in it. When faced with the responsibility that is perceived as overwhelming, this patient could defeat the demands of the life situation by "flipping his lid," by "throwing everything up for grabs." However, he does retain a bridge by the non-psychotic states in two ways: First he always remains able to find a job; and second, he willingly returns to the dependent hospital situation where he is relieved of responsibility and stress. The psychotic episodes are situational reactions for this dependent personality.

REFERENCES

Adler, A. (1926). *Über den Nervosen Charakter.* Wiesbaden: J. F. Bergman.

Adler, K. (1958). Life style in schizophrenia. *Journal of Individual Psychology, 14,* 68-72.

American Psychiatric Association. (1987). *Diagnostic and statistical manual of mental disorders* (3rd ed., revised). Washington, DC: Author.

Arieti, S. (1974). An overview of schizophrenia from a predominantly psychological approach. *American Journal of Psychiatry, 131,* 241-9.

Arieti, S. (1980). Psychotherapy of schizophrenia: New or revised procedures. *American Journal of Psychotherapy, 34,* 464-476.

Beitman, B., & Klerman, G. (Eds.). (1986). *Combining psychotherapy and drug therapy in clinical practice.* New York: S.P. Medical & Scientific Book.

Binswanger, L. (1960). Existential analysis, psychiatry, schizophrenia. *Journal of Existential Psychiatry, 1,* 157-165.

Boisen, A. (1947). Onset in acute schizophrenia. *Psychiatry, 10,* 159.

Bullard, D. (1960). Psychotherapy of paranoid patients. *Archives of General Psychiatry, 2,* 137-141.

Gazzaniga, M. (1988). *Mind matters: How mind and body interact to create our conscious lives.* Boston: Houghton-Mifflin.

Goldstein, K. (1939). *The organism: A holistic approach to biology derived from pathological data in man.* New York: American Book Co.

Hoover, G., & Franz, J. (1972). Siblings in the families of schizophrenia. *Archives of General Psychiatry, 26*, 334-342.

Kelly, G. (1955). *The psychology of personal constructs.* New York: Norton.

Liberman, R. (1987). *Psychiatric rehabilitation of chronic mental patients.* Washington, D.C.: American Psychiatric Press.

Lu, Y. (1962). Contradictory parental expectations in schizophrenia. *Archives of General Psychiatry, 6,* 219-234.

Neuchterlein, K., & Dawson, M. (1984). A neuristic vulnerability/stress model of schizophrenic episodes. *Schizophrenia Bulletin,* 10(2):300-312.

Reid, W. (1989). *The treatment of psychiatric disorders: Revised for the DSM-III-R.* New York: Brunner/Mazel.

Ritzler, B. (1981). Paranoia—prognosis and treatment: A review. *Schizophrenia Bulletin, 7,* 710-728.

Scher, J. (1962). Mind as participation. In *Theories of the mind.* New York: Free Press of Glencoe.

Shulman, B. (1968). *Essays in schizophrenia.* Baltimore: Williams and Wilkins.

Shulman, B. (1984). *Essays in schizophrenia* (2nd ed.). Chicago: Alfred Adler Institute.

CHAPTER 3

ORGANIC
MENTAL DISORDERS

Michael P. Maniacci, Psy.D.

Alfred Adler developed a theory and technique of counseling and psychotherapy which has, in time, gained in recognition and acceptance. Individual Psychology, the name he gave his system, postulates a theory of human nature and behavior which emphasizes the holistic, phenomenological, teleological, and interpersonal aspects of people. Adler, perhaps above all else, was a pragmatist. His theory grew out of his work as a clinician, a practicing physician and psychotherapist who placed treatment and prevention highest on his list of priorities. Sigmund Freud, Adler's senior colleague and the founder of Psychoanalysis, was a scientist and had a much more theoretical, research-oriented perspective in mind when he developed his system. For Freud, Psychoanalysis was the focus of his work; he was interested in developing and elaborating upon his theory and technique. Hence, his clinical work was limited by (and directed to) the type of patient who would fit his theoretical system. Traditionally, this applied to psychoneurotics and certian conversion (psychosomatic) disorders. Severe personality disorders, psychotics, and children and families, because they did not fit his system of treatment, were excluded. Adler, by contrast, was much more patient/clinical-oriented. He worked not only in individual outpatient psychotherapy, but also in clinics and schools. In addition, Adler worked in hospitals and sanatoriums with varieties of patients. His emphasis was upon what worked, regardless of the setting, mode, duration, or patient selection. Therefore, if a family needed to be seen, he would develop a strategy for working with them. He did the same for his work with children, criminals (in which he recommended group psychotherapy), and psychotics (Adler, 1956).

The variety of patients with whom Individual Psychologists work is rather broad. Adler's system provides not only the theoretical conceptualizations necessary for such work, but in many instances, the clinical guidelines and strategies. Individuals with organic mental disorders are challenging to work with, yet Adler and his followers have provided clinicians the requisite guidelines and theoretical framework upon which to base treatment. Not only is Adlerian theory applicable to understanding such conditions, but Adlerian therapy is well-suited for working with such individuals. Medical supervision and interventions are required in the treatment of all these conditions and syndromes, yet the psychosocial aspects are gaining in recognition and importance, even in the medical field (Reid, 1983; Rule, 1984; Strub & Black, 1985). As Gallatin (1982) pointed out

> Perhaps the most significant point that emerged [from her research] had to do with the role of social factors . . . whether or not a patient feels "isolated." A person's attitude . . . can help to determine how well he or she recovers from a brain injury. Indeed, it is possible that these social and emotional factors may enter the picture from the start—that some people may be more susceptible to organic disorders because of their isolation and lack of support . . . (p. 201)

Against this ever increasing theoretical awareness, Adler's conceptualizations will be presented in this chapter.

AN OVERVIEW OF THE ADLERIAN PERSPECTIVE

In 1907, Adler first presented his theory of organ inferiority. At that time, he was still a member of the Freudian "inner circle," and his conceptualizations were quite mechanistic and deterministic. In effect, he was writing as a Freudian, not an Adlerian. His position evolved and changed radically since that early monograph, and such a discussion of the process is beyond the scope of this work; interested individuals are referred to Ansbacher and Ansbacher's commentaries in their seminal volume (Adler, 1956). For present purposes, Adler's views will be discussed in their final form.

Dreikurs (1948) pointed out that Adler's final formulation of organ inferiority involved three aspects: (1) a **somatic level,** (2) a **sympathetic level,** and (3) a **psychic level.** An inferior organ, that is, an organ which is deficient in structure or function (for reasons detailed below), will typically require compensatory efforts in at least one or more of the three areas. A person with a dysfunctional limb may compensate somatically by unconsciously developing the unaffected limb to an even greater degree than normal; on the sympathetic side, that same person may assume a certain way of moving which compensates for the deficiency; and on the psychical side, the person may become conscious of it and attempt to deal with it as best as he/she can, or place others into his/her service. In keeping with Adler's conceptualizations of striving from a perceived minus situation to a perceived plus situation, individuals will compensate according to the degree of social interest and level of activity they have (Adler, 1956).

For example, John has epilepsy. He has a low degree of social interest (a sense of community feeling, an interest in the interest of others) and a high degree of activity. His compensatory efforts will most likely develop on the useless side of life using very assertive, aggressive means. He may use his epilepsy to bully others into his service and forcibly "blackmail" those in his social field into yielding to his demands by not taking his medication, overstimulating himself at times he knows he should not, and by being hypersensitive to environmental cues which arouse his sympathetic nervous system too easily (Swonger & Constantine, 1983). How useful or useless John's compensation is for his organic inferiority is contingent upon how much social interest he has and how active he is. Adler conceptualized a four-fold personality description which utilized these two constructs (Adler, 1935).

Erickson and Doppelt (1987), Mosak and Maniacci (1989), and Sperry (1988) have all recently detailed and discussed the biopsychosocial aspects of Individual Psychology. Being a holistic theory, the biological, psychological, and social dimensions of individuals need to be examined in order to better grasp the situation. In working with the organic mental disorders, of crucial importance is to examine and deal with all three aspects in order to better treat the individual—the goal Adler placed foremost in his work. Stopping interventions either at the somatic or psychosocial level is not enough in most cases; it is providing less than optimum care to the patient and is in itself reductionistic. Somatic and psychological problems can coexist and often do in the same individual. In fact, research is beginning to postulate an interrconnectedness that Adler stressed as early as 1907 (Gallatin, 1982; Ornstein & Sobel, 1987). Whether or not the etiological significance of psychosocial factors in biological conditions is ever clarified, one thing is clear: A biopsychosocial perspective entails working with the entire person, not just parts or symptoms.

DSM-III-R: ORGANIC MENTAL DISORDERS

In the third edition (revised) of the *Diagnostic and Statistical Manual of Mental Disorders (DSM-III-R)* (American Psychiatric Association, 1987) are distinguished two broad categories of organic disorders: Organic mental **disorders** and organic mental **syndromes. Disorders** are those conditions which have a known (or presumed known) etiology such as a delirium brought on by alcohol withdrawal. **Syndromes** refer to a constellation of signs or symptoms without reference to etiology, such as in some organic anxiety syndromes. In the syndromes, what is happening is clear; why it is occuring is not. In DSM-III-R are described the following syndromes:

Delirium
Dementia
Amnestic Syndrome
Organic Delusional Syndrome
Organic Hallucinosis
Organic Mood Syndrome

Organic Anxiety Syndrome
Organic Personality Syndrome
Intoxication
Withdrawal
Organic Syndromes Not
    Otherwise Specified

The following disorders are listed in DSM-III-R:

Dementias Arising in the Senium and Presenium
Psychoactive Substance-Induced Organic
    Mental Disorders
Organic Mental Disorders Associated with Axis III
    Physical Disorders or Conditions, or
    Whose Etiology is Unknown

The Psychoactive Substance-Induced Organic Mental Disorders and the Intoxication and Withdrawal Syndromes will be discussed only briefly due to space limitations and the fact that the addictions will be discussed in greater detail in subsequent chapters.

Organic Mental Syndromes

Delirium. Delirium is characterized by a rapid onset. It is typically resolved quickly as well and is seen most often in cases of high fevers and acute trauma to a localized area of the brain. Delirium tends to occur at either end of the age spectrum most frequently (i.e., the very young and those over sixty) but can occur at any age. Primarily, it is a disorder of attention. Damage to the right parietal lobe and inferomedial surface of the occipital lobe, as well as encephalopathy, renal disease, and certain metabolic disorders (e.g., hypoglycemia, ionic imbalances) can precipitate it. The slower the onset (usually no more than hours or at the most, days), the more likely the underlying pathology is systemic or metabolic as opposed to traumatic. The clinical picture tends to fluctuate over the course of a day, with the patient being worse during sleepless nights or in the dark. The person may appear incoherent or rambling and display increased or decreased motor activity. During acute periods especially there may be gross impairment to orientation (person, place, time, situation) and memory.

Dementia. The essential feature of dementia is memory impairment and a more insidious onset. Prognosis may be static, progressive, or remitting, depending upon the particular case presentation. Memory impairment typically follows this course: short-term memory is lost first, followed by immediate, and finally, long-term memory is lost (usually only in the most advanced of cases). Subsequently identity confusion, gross errors in judgment, lack of impulse control, and even personality changes take place. It is found primarily in the elderly. Dementia is diagnosed only when there is loss of intellectual functioning sufficient enough to severely interfere with social or occupational life tasks.

Amnestic Syndrome. Impairment in both short- and long-term memory is the characteristic feature of this condition. Long-term memory with regards to events from the very remote past can sometimes be remembered better than more recent events. Immediate memory, such as the ability to recall digits presented in sequence, is not impaired. In order to "fill in" the memory loss, confabulation is often present (that is, imaginary events are substituted for the forgotten information). The most common form of this syndrome is usually associated with thiamine deficiency, but head trauma or certain forms of encephalitis can precipitate it as well.

Organic Delusional Syndrome, Hallucinosis, and Mood Syndrome. These clusters of syndromes each involve specific symptoms which can be caused by numbers of different factors. In the *Delusional Syndrome,* a false or confabulated belief is postulated in the face of reality that is so extreme so as to defy credibility, and the delusion(s) can be traced to an organic process (e.g., persecutory delusions and paranoia from excessive amphetamine use). In *Organic Hallucinosis,* the perceptual, and not necessarily the cognitive, processes are impaired. Whether the hallucinations are auditory, gustatory, visual, haptic, or olfactory depends upon the nature and type of substance used or stimulation deprived (such as hallucinogens commonly producing visual hallucinations or auditory deprivation producing auditory hallucinations). In the *Organic Mood Syndrome,* individuals have either manic or depressed moods, or in some instances, both. The clinical picture is similar to that seen in the Mood Disorders; however, an organic factor is in this case etiologically linked to the disturbance (such as endocrine dysfunction, pancreatic cancer, or hemispheric strokes). .

Organic Anxiety Syndrome. Clinically, this syndrome is similar in presentation to *Panic Disorder* or *Generalized Anxiety Disorder,* but the etiological factors are determined to be organic, such as hyper- or hypothyroidism, caffeinism, or certain brain tumors. This syndrome is not diagnosed if it occurs only during the course of *Delirium.*

Organic Personality Syndrome. For this condition, a persistent personality disturbance must be present which has affective instability, recurrent outbursts of rage, impaired social judgment, apathy, or paranoia. Causes which are frequently associated with such a condition include frontal lobe damage, head trauma, temporal lobe epilepsy, and in some cases, multiple sclerosis and Huntington's chorea.

Intoxication And Withdrawal. In either of these conditions, the ingestion of certain substances has produced certain physiological changes which lead to maladaptive behavior (e.g., fighting, impaired judgment). Simply drinking socially and becoming euphoric or having slurred speech is not considered clinically intoxicated; if the maladaptive behavior appears, then the diagnosis is warranted. Someone may have *Amphetamine Intoxication* without having the full blown clinical diagnosis of an *Amphetamine Delusional Syndrome.* Similarly, *Alcohol Withdrawal* is (clinically speaking) a noticeably milder presentation than *Alcohol Withdrawal Delirium,* which is not only more extreme but more life threatening. The particular clinical presentation of intoxication or withdrawal is dependent upon the substance ingested.

Organic Mental Disorders

The Organic Mental Disorders, as mentioned previously, are grouped into three categories. The first category involves Dementias.

Primary Degenerative Dementia Of The Alzheimer Type. This diagnosis is given when the primary presentation is a dementia. If present before age 65, it is called *presenile* *onset;* otherwise it is *senile onset.* In either the senile or presenile onset, four types are distinguished:

with delirium   with depression
with delusions   uncomplicated

If no other etiological factor is linked to the onset of the dementia and the onset is insidious with a generally progressive deterioration, then the diagnosis is given.

Multi-infarct Dementia. In this case, dementia is present, but the etiology is linked to cerebrovascular disease. The presentation is "patchy"; that is, some intellectual functions are relatively intact while others are sharply deteriorated. Rather than a slow, insidious onset, the onset is abrupt and the course is fluctuating.

Psychoactive Substance-Induced Organic Mental Disorders. Within this one heading, the DSM-III-R contains a list of 46 specific types, ranging from alcohol, amphetamine, caffeine, and cocaine to opioid, sedative, or anxiolytic disorders. Symptom presentations vary according to what is ingested, how much is ingested, and for how long. Organic conditions, for example, can be created by ingesting too much alcohol, caffeine, or cocaine. What particular behavior or signs are seen depends upon what "goes in," so to speak. Interested individuals are referred to DSM-III-R for specifics.

Organic Mental Disorders Associated With Axis III Physical Disorders Or Conditions, Or Whose Etiology Is Unknown. With this category, someone can have a pneumonia which produces the Delirium. The Delirium would be listed on Axis I and the pneumonia on Axis III. Similarly, an Axis I diagnosis of Amnestic Disorder might have severe head trauma on Axis III.

DYNAMICS: AN ADLERIAN PERSPECTIVE

This is a difficult section to write due to the diverse nature of the above mentioned disorders. What particular disorder appears is primarily biologically determined, as is the course of the disorder. However, as Adler pointed out, how the patient reacts to the disability is dependent upon whether or not the compensatory efforts are useful or useless. On the first level, the somatic level, and the second level, the sympathetic level, biological processes and medical interventions predominate; the third level, the psychic level, is contingent upon the degree of social interest and the level of activity (which is primarily biological in nature). As Shulman and Klapman (1968) pointed out, the agitation or confusion seen in delirium or the affective instability seen in the organic mood or personality syndrome secondary to temporal lobe epilepsy is beyond the individual's control; however, how he/she reacts to having it and how compliant he/she is to managing it usefully is a matter of psychic compensation, and that is a matter of subjective perception and choice.

Nature Of The Inferiority

Dreikurs (1948) made the useful distinction between inferiority, inferiority feelings, and inferiority complex. Briefly, an **inferiority** is objective; that is, it can be measured according to situationally determined standards and criteria. **Inferiority feelings** are subjective; that is, they may have nothing to do with actual inferiorities. **Inferiority complexes** are open declarations of bankruptcy; that is, behaviorally observable presentations of subjectively felt inferiorities. For instance, Sally may have cerebral palsy. That may be an actual inferiority. She may feel inferior because of it and declare bankruptcy; she may refuse to participate in life and force others into her service. However, Kate, with the same organic inferiority, may not feel inferior. She may choose to overcompensate on the useful side of life and become exceptionally helpful, courageous, and productive. The nature of the inferiority imposes certain limits upon what is possible, but not the attitude adopted.

Inferiorities can be genetic/inherited (Cystic Fibrosis, Huntington's chorea), chromosomal (Down's Syndrome, Turner's Syndrome), situational/accidental (head trauma, metabolic or endocrine dysfunction, infarcts), or self-induced (substance abuse, damage from anoxia secondary to some suicide attempts, etc.). The location of the damage may have certain effects upon behavior depending upon a number of complex interrelated factors (such as central nervous system, left or right hemisphere, temporal or occipital lobes, cerebrovascular, etc.). The idiographic nature of Individual Psychology is perhaps nowhere more relevant than here. The numerous factors which make up the particular disorder must be taken into account.

Childhood Training

Adler (1932) classified three situations which he considered to be intensified minus situations; that is, situations which severely tax the social interest and cooperative spirit of individuals. The first of these situations was discussed previously—***organ inferiority.*** Having an inferior organ or organ systems can lead to useless compensation on the part of the individual who may become discouraged in efforts to fit in society in a prosocial way.

The second situation Adler (1932) said predisposed certain individuals to useless compensations was **pampering.** Pampering can be operationally defined as doing anything for children that they can do for themselves (Dreikurs & Soltz, 1964). For Adler, pampering established an expectant attitude in individuals of continued service throughout the life span. These people begin to become dependent upon others for solutions to the challenges of life. As Adler (1932) cautioned, pampering is not only the result of the actions of parents and caregivers, but it is "the creation of the child himself" (p. 89). It is "the exacting attitude of the child which induces pampering" (p. 89).

The third situation which Adler said predisposed individuals to useless compensatory activity was **neglect.** Children who are neglected, hated, or abused can understandably be deficient in developing their social interest. Again, Adler (1932) cautioned: "every pampered child will automatically find himself, later in life, in situations which will make him feel neglected" (p. 89). These forms of training in meeting life's challenges can lead individuals to adopt hesitant, dependent attitudes towards their disabilities.

Family Training

Family training encompasses a more systems-oriented perspective (Sherman & Dinkmeyer, 1987). As Barlow (1984) and Traver (1984) pointed out, families can sometimes encourage the useless compensatory efforts of disabled individuals. The *"systemic lifestyles"* of certain families, according to Barlow, can significantly affect the adjustment, exacerbation, onset and maintenance of many physical conditions and disabilities (p. 63). Family purposes, as well as individual purposes, need to be examined in the training of individuals who use their disabilities for neurotic purposes. Interested individuals are referred to the chapters by Barlow and Traver for detailed family systems descriptions which are in line with the principles of Individual Psychology.

Clinging To The Shock Effects

Adler (1956) spoke of certain patients who tended to cling to the shock effects of some situations. The shock effects could be either biological or psychological. For example, on the psychological side, individuals may experience a disappointment from a "real," exogenous situation, such as the loss of a job. However, they will cling to the effect and use it to further movement towards goals which are self-centered. The disappointment will be used as an excuse to extract special treatment or consideration from others. On the biological side, much the same can be seen with someone who uses a broken leg to dominate those in his/her social field. Individuals with an organic anxiety syndrome secondary to hyperthyroidism may become quite adept at manipulating their families—the mother and older sister(s) especially—into assuming all their major chores and tasks. This builds resentment in their siblings and fathers, who subsequently become angry and resentful at their wives, increasing the already existing distance between certain family members. They cling to their anxiety symptoms long after therapeutic blood levels have been attained on their medication.

Private Logic

Adler (1928) discussed the difference between common sense and private sense, logic, or intelligence. **Common sense** is that which is shared by the general population: it is a sign of empathy, identification with others, and social interest. **Private intelligence,** or **logic,** is that which is not in line with the common sense. The closer the private logic is to the common sense, the more socially adaptive the individual is (Dreikurs, 1945). In the organic psychoses, the private logic of the individual is exposed; that is, as in all psychoses (functional, ideopathic or organic), "as the perception of our common world vanishes or disintegrates, the inner world of the patient becomes dominant" (Dreikurs, 1945, p. 135). This dynamic plays a crucial role in understanding the life-style of the disabled individual (Rule, 1984). In DSM-III-R, with its multiaxial classification system, is utilized a similar concept with its inclusion of Axis II personality disorders. Someone with an obsessive compulsive personality disorder may react to a disability in a radically different way than someone with a premorbid histrionic personality disorder. The particular presentation will depend upon the various factors discussed previously.

Cummings (1988) provided a useful set of guidelines for distinguishing between organic and ideopathic (functional) psychoses. He listed eight characteristics which may be indicative of a clear-cut **organic pathology:**

Late onset—typically after the age of 45

Atypical features—that is, features which do not ordinarily occur in schizophrenia or manic psychoses

A coexistent deficit syndrome—such as delirium, dementia, or aphasia, for example

A normal premorbid personality

An absent history of psychiatric illness

An absent history of psychiatric mental illness in the family

A coexisting neuromedical illness

In addition, two additional signs of which clinicians should be aware when screening for organic psychosis are visual hallucinations and a tendency to make the unfamiliar familiar. In the first case, visual hallucinations are usually (but not exclusively) indicative of toxic processes in clients. In the second, individuals who claim to know strangers or treat people they have never met as if they were relatives ("that nurse, that's my sister Patty!") are compensating for severe perceptual or memory impairment. Both are telltale signs of organic pathology in a number of cases.

GENERAL TREATMENT STRATEGIES

As mentioned previously, medical interventions are always required in the organic conditions. In addition, treatment strategies are directed in four other areas: education, structure and support, counseling, and family interventions. Each will be examined briefly.

Medical

In general, medical intervention is typically directed along two fronts: surgical and chemical. Surgery to relieve intercranial pressure from a tumor which has produced an Amnestic Syndrome can be extremely beneficial. Medicating with antipsychotic medication, such as *haloperidol,* can be very helpful in controlling some cases of *Organic Delusional Syndrome.* The role of anticonvulsants in managing a number of organic conditions is being acknowledged also (Martin, 1986).

Typically, medical assessments are structural assessments that involve examining the brain and its surrounding structures. CAT scans, PET scans, MRI scans, and the like, primarily provide glimpses into the brain itself. Functional assessment, the role of determining what patients can and cannot do, will be discussed later in this chapter.

Education

This is very crucial. Individual Psychology emphasizes the educational component of counseling and therapy. Patients and families can be given information and facts about the type of illness, its course, relapse rate, prognosis, and associated features. Increasing their awareness and ability to make informed choices can prove especially beneficial in virtually all cases.

Structure and Support

In most of the acute conditions, hospitalization is required. Someone in a full blown delirium should be medically monitored and treated. The structure of the hospital and support of the professional staff is necessary. Similarly, rehabilitation centers and support groups can ease the burden and greatly facilitate recuperation.

Counseling

Rule (1984) has provided an excellent volume on this topic for use by Adlerians. In general, counseling interventions involve two dimensions: counseling for rehabilitation and for adjustment.

Rehabilitation involves the distinction between impairment and disability. Two individuals with the same impairment will not necessarily be equally disabled. For example, the loss of a finger to a construction worker is less disabling than to a concert pianist. Again, the idiographic components of the particular case, life-style and family structure in particular, need to be examined.

Adjustment involves adaptation to the impairment. Lifestyle factors are crucial for an understanding of this phase (Rule, 1984). The ability of someone to adjust to the organic condition will influence the efficacy of the rehabilitative efforts.

Functional assessment involves an understanding of what given patients can and cannot do, depending upon the type and severity of the organic condition. Briefly, some of the main assessment instruments are the following.

The Mental Status Examination. Strub and Black (1985) provide an excellent discussion of the procedure. When used by an experienced clinician, it can be done in under an hour and serve quite successfully as a screening device for organic pathology. Two other rapid screening devices used by clinicians are the *Hutt Adaptation to the Bender-Gestalt Test* (1985) and the *Quick Neurological Screening Test—Revised.*

Luria-Nebraska Neuropsychological Battery. This instrument provides a comprehensive overview of patients' functioning, and it can be useful in localizing the site of many injuries to the brain and central nervous system. Along with the *Halsted-Reitan,* it is one of the most frequently used neuropsychological assessment instruments.

In addition to the neuropsychological assessment instruments mentioned, clinicians may be interested in gaining an understanding of the personality variables of their clients. As Rule (1984) aptly pointed out, a **Life-Style Assessment** can prove invaluable. The *Rorschach,* particularly using Exner's (1986) system, can be extremely helpful. Whereas the **Life-Style Assessment** can provide a longitudinal view of personality functioning, the *Rorschach* can provide a rich cross-sectional view of cognitive-perceptual, emotional, and interpersonal functioning in a relatively short period of time.

In general, as Gallatin (1982) and Ornstein and Sobel (1987) pointed out, the individual's adaptation to society can prove crucial in the recovery from serious organic pathology. Clients need to feel connected, useful, and a part of their network. Feelings of inferiority only serve to disrupt rehabilitation efforts and recovery.

Family Interventions

Barlow (1984) and Traver (1984) discussed the role of family dynamics in rehabilitation. Clinicians need to be sensitive and willing to work with concerned family members as partners in the process. In many cases, simply imparting knowledge to the family about the nature, course, and prognosis of the condition can do much to relieve fears and tensions. Explaining the limits of the patients' future functioning and possible, potential difficulties can prove beneficial as well. Many of the organic conditions listed in DSM-III-R are of short duration and recovery is rapid and without complication; however, some such as dementia or the organic hallucinosis or organic personality syndrome can have long-lasting and very disruptive effects upon the lives of patients and families alike. Counseling strategies need to be directed in these cases towards adjustment and compensatory efforts, and the family's role in the process can be crucial.

CLINICAL EXAMPLES

Two brief examples will highlight many of the aforementioned issues. The first involved a relatively acute condition which needed immediate medical attention; the second case was of a more chronic, debilitating nature.

Case of Eddie

Eddie was a young, rebellious man who had been in therapy at a local community clinic for several months. He had an antisocial personality disorder with narcissistic features on Axis II with a long history of "polydrug" abuse on Axis I. He was in treatment under pressure from his family, who threatened to send him back to a halfway house should some improvement not be noticed in his overall behavior. He appeared at the treatment center agitated, somewhat confused, and extremely paranoid. The night before, he had been taken home by a friend who dropped him off at his front door and turned to leave. Eddie came running after him in a panic claiming there was a dead body in his front room. The police were called only to find that there was no body in the room. His friend had calmed Eddie down and told the police he would bring Eddie to the treatment center first thing in the morning. When Eddie was examined, he was oriented times four (he knew who he was, where he was, what time it was, and why he was here) and had a relatively normal presentation except for the agitation and paranoia. He was claiming that others were after him and that the treatment staff (the psychiatric nurse who was his primary therapist and the author who was called in to evaluate his current condition) were going to destroy his life and take away his family. After questioning Eddie and his friend, the possibility of an organic versus functional delusional disorder was raised. The rapid onset of the delusions, the agitation, and overall physical condition of Eddie (extremely rapid pulse, pupil dilation, sweating) lent credence to the possible organic nature of the condition and laboratory tests were ordered. Eddie had ingested a large quantity of amphetamines. His diagnosis was as follows:

Axis I   292.11 Amphetamine Delusional Disorder

Axis II   301.70 Antisocial Personality Disorder with narcissistic features

Axis III None

Axis IV   Psychosocial stressors: parents' divorce
          Severity: 3—Moderate (acute event)

Axis V   Current GAF: 50
          Highest GAF past year: 60

A *Life-Style Assessment* was conducted when Eddie was released back to the treatment center for outpatient psychotherapy. In short, he is a "getter" (Adler, 1956; Mosak, 1959). His early recollection summary stated that

> I am entitled to special treatment, enjoy creating excitement and being rebellious. There are two types of women—those who give to me and those who are unstable, hysterical, and no fun (they are the ones who expect me to be accountable for my actions). There are some things in this world that have to be accepted but I don't like it.

Eddie and his therapist began work on these issues. His substance abuse was related to his style of life. Also of issue was his relationship to his female therapist, who, as predicted from his *Life-Style Assessment,* he viewed as "no fun" and out to hold him "accountable" for his actions. The content of his delusions—his private logic—reflected these themes as well: His life was in threat of being "destroyed" from his perspective and his family might be taken away if he did not "clean up" his life.

Case of Valerie

The second case was very different in nature from Eddie's. Valerie was a woman in her thirties who had been living in a group residential treatment program for most of her life. In the past several months, she had begun acting out, becoming intermittently violent and explosive over apparently inconsequential situations. She would quickly "settle down," however, and claim ignorance for her explosive behavior. Despite numerous behavior modification programs, no improvement had occurred in her bizarre behavior. Psychological assessment was requested, including neuropsychological screening.

Intelligence testing found her to have a borderline normal level of functioning with her performance score, but her verbal and full scale scores were in the mildly mentally retarded range. The 21 point difference between her verbal and performance scores was statistically significant. She appeared to be functioning at a skill level significantly above her ability to comprehend what she was doing. This was reflected in her *Vineland Social Maturity* score and human figure drawings as well; she was functioning well, with her drawing receiving a developmental score in the average to high average range. No evidence for gross neurological impairment was obtained on her *Bender-Gestalt* drawings, yet her *Rorschach* showed strong evidence for cognitive-mediational dysfunction and a tendency for impulsive behavior. In short, her protocol showed the potential for left hemisphere, temporal lobe impairment. Medical and neurological evaluation were requested. Valerie showed an abnormal EEG (electro-encephalograph). Her diagnosis: temporal lobe epilepsy. Her DSM-III-R diagnostic formulation was as follows:

Axis I   310.10 Organic Personality Disorder, explosive type

Axis II   317.00 Mild Mental Retardation

Axis III Temporal Lobe Epilepsy

Axis IV   Psychosocial stressors: none

Axis V   Current GAF: 65
          Highest GAF past year: 80

After a trial of anticonvulsant medication and relaxation training, Valerie's behavior improved remarkably, as did her strained relationship with staff and fellow residents. While she remained somewhat irritable and could still have periods of sexual acting out, her explosiveness and violent outbursts came under control.

Discussion of Cases

In the first case, Eddie's style of life strongly influenced his eventual organic presentation. His getting style and excitement-seeking tendencies led him to an Amphetamine Delusional Disorder. Further complications and management issues could be expected unless some change occurred in his style of life. Even during his organic condition, his delusions reflected his private logic.

In the second case, Valerie's organic condition affected a portion of her brain that influenced her ability to regulate and control her behavior and impulses, and her ability to comprehend and communicate her dysfunction. No overt life-sytle issues were involved; a generally accepted concept is that anyone with damage to the frontal and temporal lobes might experience similar dysfunction.

Eddie's case was more an issue of psychotherapy and reorientation after the acute condition was successfully managed. For Valerie, the issue became one of rehabilitation and adjustment to her disorder. It was not a psychotherapeutic issue; it was more of a counseling situation (i.e., adaptation to the situation without changing the underlying style of life). In her case, family and staff members needed to be counseled as to the extent and prognosis of her disorder, as well as to the importance of Valerie being consistent on her medication.

CONCLUSION

Adler developed a system of psychotherapy and a model of personality that emphasized the biopsychosocial aspects of individuals. For Adler, the patient was the focus of treatment and the crucial component of his theory. Adler developed techniques for dealing with numerous and varied disorders, ranging a wide spectrum of clinical presentations. Within his theory, Adler offered guidelines for work to be directed to a whole array of conditions, including the organic mental conditions.

In general, individuals with organic mental disorders can be taught to compensate for their conditions in socially useful ways. Through the help of family members and professional staff (medical and non-medical alike), patients with organic conditions can be helped. The important aspects of the case to be taken into consideration are the nature of the patients' organic inferiorities/dysfunctions, the direction of the compensatory efforts in either useful or useless ways, the type of support provided by the social network, and the clients' life-styles.

FOOTNOTE

Many Adlerians make a distinction between organ inferiority and handicap. An **organ inferiority** is traditionally referred to when an inherited inferiority is passed down from generation to generation. A **handicap** would be any inferiority that occurs which is not inherited. For present purposes, such a distinction is not necessarily articulated. Compensatory efforts being useful or useless is still the relevant issue.

SUGGESTED READINGS

Martin, R. (1986). *Matters gray and white.* New York: Fawcett Crest.

This is an excellent overview of many of the common neurological disorders clinicians encounter. Martin follows a neurologist for one year and learns about the various clinical disorders and the brain and central nervous system's functioning.

Ornstein, R., & Sobel, D. (1987). *The healing brain.* New York: Simon & Schuster.

This book clearly and convincingly discusses the interrelationship between our biological functioning and our psychosocial relationships. In addition, the authors discuss the role of beliefs and expectations in managing health and illness.

Reid, W. H. (1983). *Treatment of the DSM-III psychiatric disorders.* New York: Brunner/Mazel.

This book, though originally written for DSM-III, is still very relevant for an understanding of DSM-III-R, particularly with the organic mental disorders (which have not changed significantly). The sections offer various descriptions and current treatment recommendations for each specific disorder.

Rule, W. R. (Ed.). (1984). *Lifestyle counseling for adjustment to disability.* Rockville, MD: Aspen Publications.

This is an excellent book for those interested in applying Adlerian psychology to various issues of rehabilitation and counseling the handicapped. Rule has assembled many experienced clinicians (many of whom he trained) and asked them to write chapters on topics they know thoroughly.

Strub, R. L., & Black, F. W. (1985). *The mental status examination in neurology* (2nd ed.). Philadelphia: F. A. Davis.

One of the best books available on administering and interpreting the mental status examination. The authors, in a surprisingly brief and concise fashion, discuss what various responses and findings mean in relation to brain and central nervous system functioning. A book of which every clinician should be aware.

REFERENCES

Adler, A. (1907). *Study of organ inferiority and its psychical compensation.* New York: Nervous and Mental Diseases.

Adler, A. (1928). Brief comments on reason, intelligence and feeble-mindedness. In H. L. Ansbacher & R. R. Ansbacher (Eds.), *Superiority and social interest* (pp. 39-49). New York: W. W. Norton.

Adler, A. (1932). The structure of neurosis. In H. L. Ansbacher & R. R. Ansbacher (Eds.), *Superiority and social interest* (pp. 83-95). New York: W. W. Norton.

Adler, A. (1935). Typology of meeting life problems. In H. L. Ansbacher & R. R. Ansbacher (Eds.), *Superiority and social interest* (pp. 66-70). New York: W. W. Norton.

Adler, A. (1956). *The Individual Psychology of Alfred Adler*. H. L. Ansbacher & R. R. Ansbacher (Eds.). New York: Basic Books.

American Psychiatric Association. (1987). *Diagnostic and statistical manual of mental disorders* (3rd ed., revised). Washington, DC: Author.

Barlow, M. S. (1984). Lifestyle and the family of the disabled. In W. R. Rule (Ed.), *Lifestyle counseling for adjustment to disability* (pp. 61-80). Rockville, MD: Aspen Publications.

Cummings, J. L. (1988). Organic psychosis. *Psychosomatics, 29*, 16-26.

Dreikurs, R. (1945). Psychological differentiation of psychopathological disorders. In *Psychodynamics, psychotherapy and counseling*. Chicago: Alfred Adler Institute.

Dreikurs, R. (1948). The socio-psychological dynamics of physical disability. In *Psychodynamics, psychotherapy and counseling*. Chicago: Alfred Adler Institute.

Dreikurs, R., & Soltz, V. (1964). *Children: The challenge*. New York: Duell, Sloan & Pearce.

Erickson, R. C., & Doppelt, L. H. (1987). Rehabilitation of the chronic psychiatric patient. *Individual Psychology, 43*, 296-307.

Exner, J. E. (1986). *The Rorschach: A comprehensive system. Volume 1: Basic foundations* (2nd ed.). New York: John Wiley & Sons.

Gallatin, J. (1982). *Abnormal psychology*. New York: Macmillan.

Hutt, M. L. (1985). *The Hutt adaptation of the Bender-Gestalt test* (4th ed.). New York: Grune & Stratton.

Martin, R. (1986). *Matters gray and white*. New York: Fawcett Crest.

Mosak, H. H. (1959). The getting type, a parsimonious social interpretation of the oral character. *Journal of Individual Psychology, 15*, 193-198.

Mosak, H. H., & Maniacci, M. P. (1989). An approach to the understanding of "schizophrenese." *Individual Psychology, 45*, 465-472.

Ornstein, R., & Sobel, D. (1987). *The healing brain*. New York: Simon & Schuster.

Reid, W. H. (1983). *Treatment of the DSM-III psychiatric disorders*. New York: Brunner/Mazel.

Rule, W. R. (Ed.). (1984). *Lifestyle counseling for adjustment to disability*. Rockville, MD: Aspen Publications.

Sherman, R., & Dinkmeyer, D. (1987). *Systems of family therapy: An Adlerian integration.* New York: Brunner/Mazel.

Shulman, B. H., & Klapman, H. J. (1968). Organ inferiority and psychiatric disorders in childhood. In E. Harms (Ed.), *Pathogenesis of nervous and mental diseases in children* (pp. 49-62). New York: Libra.

Sperry, L. (1988). Biopsychosocial therapy: An integrative approach for tailoring treatment. *Individual Psychology, 44,* 225-235.

Strub, R. L., & Black, F. W. (1985). *The mental status examination in neurology* (2nd ed.). Philadelphia: F. A. Davis.

Swonger, A. K., & Constantine, L. L. (1983). *Drugs and therapy: A handbook of psychotropic drugs* (2nd ed.). Boston: Little, Brown and Company.

Traver, M. D. (1984). Using selected lifestyle information in understanding multigenerational patterns. In W. R. Rule (Ed.), *Lifestyle counseling for adjustment to disability* (pp. 81-103). Rockville, MD: Aspen Publications.

CHAPTER 4

INDIVIDUAL PSYCHOLOGY AND BIPOLAR MOOD DISORDER

Dorothy E. Peven, M.S.W.

Individual Psychological understanding of mood disorders grows out of a 1914 paper on "Melancholia and Paranoia" by Alfred Adler (Adler, 1968) just as psychoanalytic understanding comes from Abraham (1957) and Freud's 1917 "Mourning and Melancholia" (Freud, 1960). Later elaborations by psychoanalysts and Individual Psychologists have expanded the theories, but the past three decades have seen a remarkable amount of laboratory research which remains to be integrated into psychodynamic formulations.

Recent literature on Bipolar Affective Disorder describes relatively few empirical studies that offer a psychodynamic explanation of bipolar disorders. Personality theorists, on the other hand, have discussed the psychodynamics of Bipolar Affective Disorder but have published few, if any, empirical studies. Neither Adler nor the psychoanalysts addressed themselves at any length to the psychodynamics of bipolar illness nor did any theorist yet distinguish between unipolar depression and the depression of the bipolar.

My purpose is to review some theoretical formulations and current research findings and attempt a synthesis toward an understanding of bipolar illness from the viewpoint of Individual Psychology. The discussion of the psychodynamics of bipolar disorder follows a previous paper by Peven and Shulman (1983).

DIAGNOSIS OF BIPOLAR DISORDER

The phenomenon of dysphoric and euphoric episodes following one another was identified as a syndrome by poets and physicians as early as Homer and Plutarch and was described by Aretaeus of Cappadocia in the first century A.D. Current understanding and classification of bipolar disorder derive from the work of Emil Kraepelin who had been influenced by J. Falret, Sr. and J. Baillarger who termed the illness *folie a double forme.* Kraepelin in 1896 proposed the name "manic depressive insanity" for this group of disorders and wrote vivid and complete descriptions of the syndrome (1902). He added his own observation that a large proportion of manic-depressive patients came from "tainted" families; i.e., his patients had close relatives who had experienced some form of affective (mood) disorder.

Bipolar disorders are distinguished from other affective disorders because of the circularity of the moods: depression follows mania which follows depression in a fashion that colors the whole psychic life even though there are euthymic periods when functioning is not disturbed. In DSM-III-R (American Psychiatric Association, 1987) are listed three bipolar disorders, **mixed, manic,** and **depressed,** and is stated that a diagnosis of a major mood disorder can be made only after finding typical criteria defining episodes of the illness and only if the episode is clearly distinguishable from usual functioning. If the disturbance of mood is depressed, the depression must be sustained for at least two weeks; the diagnosis of manic episode requires a disturbance of mood lasting at least one week.

BIPOLAR DISORDER, MIXED (or CIRCULAR)

The diagnostic criteria for bipolar disorder is evidence of severe mood swings. Along with the disorder of mood there are marked disturbances of thought and behavior. During the manic episode bipolars display elation or irritability, pressure of speech, flight of ideas, and increased motor activity. These people exhibit poor judgment and ignore the logical consequences of their behaviors. Often, they display an inflated self-esteem.

> Frequently, expansiveness, unwarranted optimism, grandiosity, and lack of judgment lead to activities such as buying sprees, reckless driving, foolish business investments, and sexual behavior unusual for the individual. Often, the activities have a disorganized, flamboyant, or bizarre quality. (American Psychiatric Association, 1980, p. 206)

An example would be as follows:

> A, a young woman in a manic state, would sit on a park bench during pleasant weather and trip the male joggers going by in order to start a conversation which would invariably lead to her bringing the chosen man back to her apartment for a sexual interlude.

Or

> M, a manic young man, stood in the middle of one of Chicago's busiest streets (the Outer Drive) and with his coat held as a cape played toreador with the oncoming cars.

Occasionally during the manic state delusions or hallucinations may occur. The uncritical self-esteem and marked grandiosity are often of a delusional nature. "God's voice may be heard explaining that the individual has a special mission. Persecutory delusions may be based on the idea that the individual is being persecuted . . . " (American Psychiatric Association, 1980, p. 207).

A very frightened young man, S, in a manic state marked by extreme fear and depression comingled told me (after he was discharged from the hospital) that he thought that the staff were cannibals and whenever they came in to take care of him they were going to take pieces of his flesh and eat them.

Another male bipolar, B, would drink to excess when he felt "high" and one day threw twenty-dollar bills out of the second-floor window of his office to all his "admirers" on the street.

Manics always have a decreased need for sleep and awaken full of energy. Sometimes they go for days without sleep. Usually a flight of ideas and a nearly continuous flow of accelerated speech with abrupt changes from topic to topic occurs. Sometimes the speech is disorganized and incoherent and a loosening of associations also occurs.

The most common associated feature is lability of mood with rapid shifts from laughter to anger or depression. The depression may last moments, hours, or days and not uncommonly the depressive and manic symptoms intermingle and occur at the same time or alternate rapidly.

Some mania occurs secondary to other conditions like epilepsy, drugs, infections, neoplasms, and metabolic disturbances. A good procedure is to inquire about medications and, especially with younger patients, drugs.

In order to diagnose a manic episode at least four of the following seven symptoms should be present; if the mood is irritable, five symptoms are necessary:

1. increased activity socially, sexually, and at work;

2. increased talkativeness;

3. flight of ideas by objective examination or subjective report of racing thoughts;

4. grandiosity, at times to a delusional degree (For example: Once, there were three young men hospitalized on

the psychiatric unit at the same time, all three of whom claimed to be Jesus Christ. The staff resolved any dissension by allowing each one to have a turn at being Jesus . . . John could be Christ on Monday, Michael on Tuesday, and Peter on Wednesday. Within a week they had all changed their identifications.);

5. decreased need for sleep;

6. distractibility; and

7. poorly thought-out involvement in projects or activities.

The depressive episode is characterized by a change of mood from a usual normal mood to a predominantly dysphoric mood, or by a loss of interest or pleasure in all, or almost all, of the patient's usual activities. At least four of the following eight symptoms should be present:

1. striking change of weight;

2. sleep difficulty, either measurable insomnia or measurable hypersomnia;

3. decreased energy (For example: L, a 23-year-old woman who was recovering from a manic episode and hospitalization, felt herself beginning to get depressed and anergic. She needed a job and found it very difficult to arouse herself for interviews. She sat heavily in her chair, facing me, and said plaintively: "Dorothy, why not let me go off the lithium for three days and I'll bet you I'll get five job offers.");

4. psychomotor retardation or agitation, objectively observable;

5. decreased interest in usual activities or in sexuality;

6. excessive self-reproach or guilt;

7. decreased ability to think or concentrate; and

8. suicidal action or recurrent thoughts of suicide. (For example: A, the woman mentioned above, had been through several manic and depressive cycles, usually hospitalized. During a depressed swing she jumped in front of a train and nearly lost her left leg. She was quite subdued and cooperative during the long recovery and responded better than usual to my efforts to raise her spirits. Long afterwards she did not want to discuss the episode but vowed never to try to suicide again, and she hasn't.)

PHYSIOLOGICAL THEORY AND RESEARCH

Recent researchers have tried to prove Kraepelin's observations about "tainted" families, and many research findings seem to demonstrate a familial proclivity to bipolar disorders (Blehar, Weissman, Gershon, & Hirschfeld, 1988; Winokur, 1975). Bipolars tend to have close relatives suffering from affective disorders and it is difficult not to believe that an inherited factor is at work. Winokur wrote that two ingredients "seem to be necessary" for Bipolar Affective Disorder to occur: (1) a propensity for significant mood change, and (2) a tendency for the mood change to vary in a bipolar fashion.

Kretschmer thought that a disproportionately large number of pyknic body-type individuals develop bipolar disorder (1936), while Sheldon suggested that a constitution of high mesomorphy coincided with a higher than average representation of cyclothymic disorders (Cohen, 1975).

In addition to hereditary factors, constitutional factors, and premorbid personality factors, other etiological theories have been advanced, for example, dysfunctions of (1) the endocrine system, (2) the diencephalic centers involved in affective expressions, and, (3) the processes that in lower animals are involved in hibernation (consideration of the seasonal factor). Genetic and family studies, neurophysiological studies, and neurochemical studies have produced results which suggest that most likely a relationship exists among the various functional, anatomical, and neurochemical systems in the brain and that brain disturbances can lead to affective disorders.

Some researchers have formulated a concept called the **Biogenic Amine theory** of mood disorders which postulates that most depressions may be associated with a relative deficiency of norepinephrine at functionally important adrenergic receptor sites in the brain. Hypomania and mania are supposedly associated with an excess of such amines. "Those drugs which cause depletion . . . of norepinephrine centrally produce sedation or depression, while drugs which increase or potentiate brain norepinephrines are associated with . . . an antidepressant effect" (Schildkraut & Kety, 1967). Kaplan and Sadock disagree and suggest that more current research demonstrates " . . . that mania results from the relative predominance of dopamine function, either through actual excess or as a result of cholinergic deficiencies" (Kaplan & Sadock, 1981, p. 365).

Sleep neurophysiologic and neuroendocrine abnormalities have been investigated and support the hypothesis that mood disorders are limbic-diencephalic disturbances and "give credence to the notion that midbrain homeostatic mechanisms are disrupted" (Akiskal, 1989, p. 7).

The most recent research has focused on the application of recombinant DNA technology and the chromosomal linkage of markers to bipolar disorders. But an active controversy exists over the reproducibility of the X-chromosome findings with researchers on both sides of the controversy (Blehar, Weissman, Gershon, & Hirschfeld, 1988).

Other current research interests have to do with the relationship of "creativity" to bipolar disorder.

> . . . bouts of black melancholy alternating with paroxysms of creative drive figure prominently in the life histories of many productively creative persons. [We] . . . examined rates of mental illness in 30 creative writers, 30 matched control subjects, and the first-degree relatives of both groups . . . [it showed] the writers had a substantially higher rate of bipolar affective disorder and there was also a higher rate of affective disorder and creativity in the writers' first-degree relatives . . . . (Miller, as cited in Hoppe, 1988, p. 388)

Still other people are attempting to analyze the relationship between psychopathology and neuropsychological abnormalities of the right and left hemispheres of the brain. Kyle reported:

> In studies of affective disorders versus schizophrenia, the schizophrenic patients showed significantly more left temporal and left parietal lobe errors. Both schizophrenic and affective disorder subjects (a majority of whom were manic) had more errors relating to both hemispheres than did controls. In general, depressive patients show impairment of the right hemisphere and right frontal functions compared to schizophrenics and to normals. (Kyle, 1988, p. 370)

Kyle quoted Flor-Henry:

> . . . it is probable that the symptomatology of mania— essentially verbal-motor disinhibition, euphoric irritability, and hypersexuality—reflects an abnormal activation of dominant front temporal systems brought about by a fundamental disorganization of the nondominant hemisphere. The characteristic hypersexuality of mania is the result of the activation of the neural systems subtending the orgasmic response in the right hemisphere of which the opposite pole is the hyposexuality of depression. (Kyle, 1988, p. 370)

Seemingly a relationship exists among the various functional, anatomical, and neurochemical systems, but we are just beginning to understand the relationships between these systems and psychopathology. Genetic and family studies all seem to point to some essential difference between the physiology of "normal" people and those who develop bipolar disorder.

The *National Depressive and Manic Depressive Association* is trying to have bipolar illness legally declared a physical illness. In 1989 they filed a class action suit against two insurance companies contending that there is "widespread support in the medical community that manic depression is a physical illness" (The Pendulum, 1990). The Association seeks to have insurers pay the same level of benefits as they would for any other physical illness, such as cancer. The suit claims that insurance companies' payment practices discriminate against victims of the illness by paying less for a psychiatric diagnosis than for other diagnoses. The verdict may not resolve the issue.

A continuing discussion prevails regarding bipolar versus unipolar depressions. Statements in DSM-III and DSM-III-R do not distinguish between a depressive episode in major depressive disorder and a depressive episode in a bipolar disorder. Diagnostic criteria are the same for both groups. Kaplan and Sadock (1981) believed that depressed patients with a history of manic episodes (bipolars) should be separated out and dealt with differently than those patients who have only recurrent episodes of depression (the unipolar group).

> Considerable evidence of possible genetic, familial, personality, biochemical, physiological, and pharmacological differences between bipolar and unipolar affective disorders has been presented. Patients with bipolar disorder show a far higher frequency of positive family history than do patients with only depression. Psychopharmacological studies also indicate differences in the response of bipolar and depressed patient to psychoactive drugs, especially lithium. Patients with bipolar disorder are more likely to develop hypomanic responses to dopa, or to imipramine and other tricyclics, than are patients with depressions. (Kaplan & Sadock, 1981)

In Table 4.1 are clinical features to aid in distinctions among a manic episode, a depressive episode in a major depression, and a depressive episode in a bipolar disorder.

PSYCHODYNAMIC THEORIES: THE RELATIONSHIP OF PERSONALITY TO BIPOLAR DISORDER

Both the empiricists and the personality theorists suggest that the premorbid personality of the bipolar is cyclothymic; that is, marked alternations occur between lively and depressed moods and activities before a psychotic break. Kraepelin (1902), Kretschmer (1936), and Turns (1978), as well as Winokur (1975) and Adler (Ansbacher & Ansbacher, 1956) believed that a certain type of person who has either a particular kind of temperament or a particular set of personality traits becomes ill with bipolar disorder. For example, Adler said: " . . . alterations in manic-depressive insanity are manifested by individuals who showed slight phases of conduct of this pattern in their earlier life. . ." (Ansbacher & Ansbacher, 1956, p. 323).

(Continued on Page 91)

Table 4.1. Clinical Features of Major Affective Episodes

	Manic Episode	Depressive Episode in Major Depression	Depressive Episode in Bipolar Disorder
Essential features	Predominant mood elevated, expansive, or irritable	Depressive mood or pervasive loss of interest or pleasure	A history of alternating episodes of mania and major depression
Symptoms	Hyperactivity, excessive involvement in activities, poor judgment, pressure of speech, flight of ideas, loosened associations, inflated self-esteem, decreased need for sleep, distractibility, hypersexuality	Loss of interest or pleasure, sleep disturbances, appetite disturbance, change in weight, psychomotor agitation or retardation, cognitive disturbance, decreased energy, feelings of worthlessness or guilt, thoughts of death or suicide	As in depressive episode in major depression
Laboratory Findings (inconstant)	Nocturnal EEG: decreased total sleep time, decreased percentage of dream time, increased REM latency (decreased pressure to dream)	Nocturnal EEG*: decreased total sleep time and increased percentage of dream time, decreased REM latency (increased pressure to dream), first REM period very long	Nocturnal EEG*: depressed phase-normal total sleep time and increased percentage of dream time, decreased REM latency, manic phase as in mania
Associated features	Lability of mood, depression within mania, hallucinations, delusions related with mood.	Depressed facies, tearfulness, anxiety, irritability, fearfulness, brooding, phobic attacks, paranoid symptoms, delusions of poverty	As in mania and major depression in different episodes of illness

*Nocturnal electroencephalogram differentiates unipolar from biopolar depressed patients, according to E. Hartman, *Arch. Gen. Psychiatry*, 19:312, 1968.

(Kaplan & Sadock, 1981, p. 367)

Akiskal, Hirschfeld, and Yerevanian surveyed the literature and came to the conclusion that:

> . . . obsessionalism was in fact the only deviant personality measure associated with mania . . . This finding is consistent with the observation that the extroverted, ambitious, and driven person with an inordinate capacity for work . . . a profile frequently linked to bipolar illness—has considerable affinities to the duty-bound and work-addicted compulsive person. (Akiskal, Hirschfeld, & Yerevanian, 1983, p. 803)

A study of the epidemiology of bipolar disorder shows that the higher socioeconomic classes have the highest incidence of bipolar illness. Willerman and Cohen (1990) suggested that if social class is considered an *effect* rather than a cause, the possibility is that the work-oriented, somewhat compulsive person with temperamental qualities of drive and sociability reaches high achievement levels in the society and culture of the United States. They go so far as to say: ". . . while bipolar disorder is a disadvantage, bipolar traits, or mild bipolar *symptoms* may actually confer a distinct advantage" (Willerman & Cohen, 1990, p. 361).

Freud, like Adler and other personality theorists using naturalistic observations, generated hypotheses linking personality to affective disorders but made no distinction between depression in bipolar disorder and other types of depression. In "Mourning and Melancholia," Freud (1960) interpreted depression by comparing it with the normal mourning reaction that follows death of a loved one.

> The mourning work consists of a slow, gradual dissolution of the emotional ties with the lost object, and the incorporation of its idealized picture into the subject . . . it is as if the patient had unconsciously lost an object for which he had ambivalent feelings of love and hatred. As a consequence of its incorporation, the shadow of the object has fallen upon the ego, hence the melancholic self-hatred and suicidal tendencies. (Ellenberger, 1970, p. 512)

For Abraham (1957), following Freud, depression represented the reaction of a feeling of narcissistic injury and loss, as the ego fears the punitive and disapproving superego. Mania is the ego's insistence that the injury has been repaired and the superego conquered. Since the ego has defeated the superego, no longer does a need to control or inhibit impulses exist and the manic has a triumphant feeling of omnipotence. Yet, an underlying uneasiness is present as superego fears persist in the mania " . . . and the patient's frantic, driven quality in part represents his flight from punishment" (MacKinnon & Michels, 1971, p. 188). Mania is thus understood as an attempt to stave off and deny depression. Later, Freud (1960) changed the sequence and hypothesized that when the depression is finally resolved, the energy that is bound up in the depression is liberated and mania appears. No explanation is given for the fact that mania does not follow every episode of depression.

Rado (1956) explained both mania and melancholia by a double incorporation. He believed the lost loved object has been split into good and bad objects. The bad object, incorporated in the ego, is punished leading to melancholia. The good object remains for reconciliation. Mania is an unstable reconciliation achieved through denial of guilt.

The neo-Freudian Fromm-Reichmann, with Cohen, Baker, and Cohen (1954) studied 12 patients with manic-depressive illness and made the following observations: Bipolar patients seem to come from families that are upward striving, and the parents' values lead to the development of ambitious, driven children who feel an obligation to achieve success in accordance with the high achievement standards of the family. Future patients become outwardly extroverted and set their life goals impossibly high which makes them susceptible to any small setback. This orientation is not intrinsic to the child, but comes from conforming to family values (Cohen et al., 1954).

Sullivan believed the psychic pathogen is anxiety:

> The behavior of cyclothymic people may be looked upon as an obscure expression of movements away from the experience of anxiety . . . depression or an unhappy manic state being more tolerable than anxiety itself. The anxiety is apparently rarely felt as such, and it is extraordinarily difficult to isolate the event which threatens to expose the anxiety and in turn sets up the patterns known as manic depressive . . . . (Sullivan, 1954, p. 201)

Later theorists like Beck view depression through an information processing model. Beck's original cognitive theory suggested that depression is a thinking disorder which includes selective abstraction, overgeneralizations, and negative self-attributions. A 1987 paper by Beck elaborates and expands this original thinking. He posited: " . . . six separable but overlapping models" which "integrate genetic, neurochemical, and cognitive processes [as well as] biological processes as different sides of the same coin" (Beck, 1987, p. 5).

Even though Kohut did most of his writing during the last few decades, his followers suggest he did not adequately address the issue of biological predisposition. Kohut had concluded that all psychopathology was best explained by "developmental arrests which inevitably result from parental shortcomings [of empathic failure]" (Baker & Baker, 1987, p. 2).

Galatzer-Levy, a Kohutian, thus explained bipolar disorder as a "self-disorder." "Self object failures threaten catastrophic experiences . . . [manic depressives] are unable to find adequate self-objects . . . Mania and hypomanic states in these patients appear as a *defense against the dangers of the loss of the self-object* . . . these difficulties come into particular prominence with separations" (Galatzer-Levy, 1988, p. 98) (Emphasis mine).

While later contributions to theory do not always follow the original formulations of Freud and Abraham, only fragmentary discussions are in the literature suggesting psychodynamic hypothesis for manic-depressive illness.

ALFRED ADLER AND INDIVIDUAL PSYCHOLOGY

Adler and Organ Inferiority

Genetic and family studies, neurophysiological studies, and neurochemical studies all seem to point to physiological factors in the etiology of bipolar disorder.

This hypothesis is consistent with Adlerian thinking, especially Adler's early formulations about organ inferiority. Early in his theoretical thinking (about 1907), Adler proposed that some children are born with organs that are "developmentally retarded" and that " . . . an inherited [organ] inferiority corresponds to an inherited disease" (Ansbacher & Ansbacher, 1956, p. 24).

Although Adler had not as yet completed his thinking about the role of the creative self in the development of personality, he suggested that being born with an organ inferiority is not absolutely deterministic—many ways exist for "diseased" people to develop in spite of organ inferiority, such as compensation and overcompensation. Beethoven, who was deaf, wrote music; Renoir, who was blind, painted, and so on.

> The fate of the inferior organs is extremely varied. Development and the external stimuli of life press toward overcoming the expressions of such inferiority. Thus we may find approximately the following outcomes . . . inability to survive, anomaly of form, anomaly of function, compensation within the organ, compensations through a second organ, *compensation through the psychological superstructure,* and organic or *psychological* overcompensation . . . . (Ansbacher & Ansbacher, 1956, p. 24) (Emphasis mine)

Later, Adler gave primacy to the psychological processes:

> . . . organ inferiority becomes one of the important objective factors which provide certain probabilities for . . . development, such factors being ultimately subject to the individual's own interpretation. Second, the inferior organ, as the point of least resistance, becomes the preferred means by which the psyche expresses itself through the body. (Ansbacher & Ansbacher, 1956, p. 222)

In conclusion, the findings of laboratory researchers lead to the suggestion that bipolar disorder is an illness that occurs in those people who are predisposed to it by virtue of a familial inherited organ inferiority; but, the lessons of Individual Psychology suggest that the *appearance* of the illness in its morbid form is a function of each individual personality.

Thus, bipolar disorders can be precipitated by life situation stresses or by personality driven stresses which disrupt the "midbrain homeostatic mechanisms" (Akiskal, 1989). This leads to the evidence for the etiologic role of psychodynamic personality susceptibility factors.

Adler and the Affective Disorders

Mania. By 1920 Adler had developed his unitary theory of the neurosis and, therefore, never did address himself at any length to the psychodynamics of bipolar illness.

Adler believed that all humans are motivated to overcome a subjective experience of inferiority by striving for a "fictional" goal of superiority. Those who direct this striving toward **personal** supremacy over their fellow human beings are, to the extent their goal lacks social interest, more or less neurotic.

> . . . the essential tendency of the neurotic is the striving from the feeling of inferiority toward "above . . . [and] the combination of " . . . these two moods . . . [leads to] a neurotic constant back and forth . . . the conduct of powerless exaltation, where at one time the trait of powerlessness, at another time the trait of exaltation, becomes more prominent. This process is most clearly visible in manic depressive insanity. (Ansbacher & Ansbacher, 1956, p. 273)

Bipolar patients are those who display in the most extreme fashion the "hesitating," "back and forth" movement that Adler saw in all neurotic behavior. For Adler all neurosis is an attempt to evade what is subjectively perceived as a challenge. Those who see challenges as situations to be dealt with will move forward directly into problem-solving behavior. Those who see challenges as threats to a precarious self-esteem will either falter or move away from the perceived "danger."

According to Adler, neurotics are distinguished from psychotics by their ability to retain their grasp on reality; that is, they understand a challenge exists that has to be faced and steps must be taken, but they don't like the idea. They feel frightened and behave in timid ways. Psychotics, on the other hand, try to deceive themselves as well as others by acting *as if* the threatening situation is either not there at all and they deal with other issues like "voices," or they behave *as if* the problem has already been successfully solved.

Given these theoretical foundations, one can understand why Adler saw mania as "a bluff to overrun others" (Ansbacher & Ansbacher, 1956, p. 323). Later, in "Life-Lies and Responsibility," Adler (1968) elaborated further by stating that mania occurs in ambitious people who do not believe in themselves to the extent of imagining that they would be able to gain their goal of superiority by direct methods. Therefore, the mania is an "act" meant to deceive both the manic person and his/her fellow humans into believing the deed has already been done. But bipolars cannot continue their deception indefinitely, so even though they begin "every act enthusiastically . . . [they lose] interest soon after . . . " (Adler, 1968, p. 247) and the mania is "a sudden blaze which consumes its fuel . . . [Excitement] rapidly wanes into depression . . . [and] brilliant beginnings and sudden anticlimaxes are repeated at intervals through [the manic-depressives'] life histories" (Adler, 1964, p. 27).

Peven and Shulman summarized Adler's statements on bipolar disorder: (1) a premorbid cyclothymic personality exists, (2) moods swing back and forth between a feeling of omnipotence and exaltation . . . (they feel able to meet any challenge) to a feeling of powerlessness and feeling overwhelmed by the slightest task, (3) bipolars lack faith in their own competence, and (4) mania can be seen as a maneuver to deceive themselves and others (Peven & Shulman, 1983, p. 5).

Depression. Alfred Adler (1959), in "Melancholia and Paranoia," presented his ideas on the etiology, phenomenology, and interpersonal transactions of the depressed "melancholic" person. And Kurt Adler, in 1961, gave an eloquent review of the Individual Psychological position on depression.

For the Adlers, the depressed adult is one who has from early childhood on put other people into his/her service. Adler senior said, "The discouraged child who finds he can tyrannize best by tears will be a cry-baby; and a direct line of development leads from the cry-baby to the adult depressed patient" (A. Adler, 1959). Depressed persons force others to submit to them by acting "as if" they were weak, helpless babies. Their method of operation (which is called "the exploitation of other's good will") is developed early on and carried throughout life.

The self-image of "pampered" children is that of inadequacy. Pampered children are those who have everything done for them. Consequently, they never develop their problem-solving abilities, feel unable and inadequate, and prefer never to be put to a test. This leads to an exaggeration of the inability to meet life's challenges.

According to Alfred Adler, this low assessment of the self suggests that an opportunity for extraordinary success has somehow been missed. Depressives imply, in a disguised manner, how important and extraordinary they are when they take upon themselves ostentatiously the blame for world calamities.

The purpose of the depression is the achievement of a fictive superiority and irresponsibility. By putting a claim on the services of others, by blaming others to induce guilt, by frustrating all efforts to help them, by depreciating others, " . . . the depressive is led to a concealed increase in the feeling of importance" (K. Adler, 1961).

> This, then, is the relentless effort of the depressed [the goal of the depression]: to prevail with his will over others, to extort from them sacrifices, to frustrate all their efforts to help him, to blame them . . . overtly or secretly . . . for his plight, and to be free of all social obligations and cooperations, by certifying to his sickness. (K. Adler, 1961)

The symptoms of depressives are seen as offensive weapons and have as their purpose to increase the "shock" to the environment.

As an holistic theorist, Adler believed the organs of the body are induced to cooperate with the purpose of the behavior. Thus, appetite, sleep, digestion, etc., adjust their functions in response to the depression. This is not to be considered an argument for causation: Adler was not a determinist. For decades the research has shown that all emotions (affects) are accompanied by chemical changes. Emotions, by definition, always include physiological processes. However, some illnesses (cancer of the pancreas) as well as some drugs, by influencing the chemical processes, can produce symptoms of depression. It is believed these drugs produce **the same chemical changes that are produced by a depression from psychogenic causes.** Thus, the chemical findings in depression remind us that body and mind influence each other as interacting systems and that the source of the trouble can come from either system.

For the two Adlers, depression is an attitude toward life, an accommodation to life as perceived through the eyes of a spoiled child who exploits and depreciates others and will force his body knowingly or unknowingly to accommodate to this pathological way of life by producing distressing symptomatology. Under these circumstances, whether the depression is part of a unipolar or a bipolar illness makes no difference.

Adler said:

> . . . It is neither heredity nor environment which determines our relationship to the (world). Heredity only endows us with certain abilities. Environment only gives us certain impressions . . . the interpretation we make of these experiences . . . are the bricks which we use in our own "creative" way in building up our attitude toward life. It is our individual way of using these bricks . . . which determines our relationship to the outside world. (Ansbacher & Ansbacher, 1956, p. 206)

THE WORK OF PEVEN AND SHULMAN

The material in this section is taken from a 1983 paper by Peven and Shulman. They studied 17 well-established cases of bipolar disorder from their private files in an attempt to establish an Individual Psychological view of bipolar disorder. They also reviewed the literature on bipolar illness and found some personality factors which seemed to be universally accepted and had implications for psychodynamic theory. The outstanding factors discussed in historical literature were: (1) bipolars have strong affiliative tendencies, (2) bipolars have a high achievement motive, (3) bipolars seem to have little faith in themselves and their ability to solve life's problems in a straightforward fashion, and (4) bipolars' attitudes and energies shift from one extreme to another.

The group studied consisted of 11 men and six women (bipolar disorder is as common in men as it is in women), and an analysis of their personalities was obtained from *Life-Style* analysis, *Rorschach tests, 16 PF tests,* and the *Lusher, MMPI* and *WAIS.* Of the 17, five had a definite family history of affective disorder.

All the tests and anamneses were reviewed for common material and were factored. No statistical analysis was done, nor was a control group used. The authors found the following eight common personality factors in their 17 bipolar patients.

1. Affectivity in the Perceptual Style

Bipolar people seem to meet Jung's concept of people who use feeling rather than thinking, sensing, or intuiting, as their superior function (1971): that is, they pay a great deal of attention to their feelings. They will often be found taking their emotional temperature, "I feel great," "I feel sad," and so on. The early recollection of R (a young man) is an example:

> Age 6: I was alone with my mother in our apartment. It was dark and dingy and smelled. I hated the smell, it was like an old toilet. My mother was angry about something and I was very unhappy. I felt terrible in that dark, smelly place with my angry mother.

2. Ambition to Achieve

All of the 17 patients studied showed either a high achievement motive or described themselves as coming from families in which a strong press was present for achievement. This finding concurs with earlier studies mentioned in this chapter.

Adlerians see the achievement motive as competitive movement toward an ambitious goal of superiority. Whenever private goals are inordinate, insatiable, or improbable of attainment, they contribute to psychopathology. Although the goals of the patients in the study were not necessarily the "lofty goals" of psychosis (Adler, 1964), they were "inappropriate to the time, place, and method of pursuit. The patients preferred giant steps to ordinary ones, large bites to small ones" (Peven & Shulman, 1983, p. 8).

> One patient decided to be a coin collector. He threw himself into the activity to the extent that he bought them in huge quantities, attended every exhibition, visited all the dealers, and filled a whole room in his house. Then he lost interest and stopped the activity altogether.

But sometimes the goal is "too high up" as in the young man whose *Rorschach* report reads: "His main goal in life is to become the most amazing person in the world."

3. Covert Rebellion Against the Obligation to Achieve

Although achievement was a dominant goal for the bipolars studied, they seemed to harbor resentment toward it. Overt or covert opposition to the burden of achievement was always present.

> The summary of the Family Constellation of one patient reads: "He accepted the family value that one had to achieve all the time, even when he didn't want to . . . " The psychologist's interpretation of his *Rorschach* states: "He views himself as being called upon to accomplish special feats, but he does not want to be pushed around by life; he wants unlimited freedom."

Even when bipolars are angry about the necessity, they cannot permit themselves to stop achieving.

> Perhaps one reason achievement becomes burdensome is the fact that true achievement is most often a gradual, step-by-step process over time—a time sequence bipolars

can hardly tolerate since they are characterized by the trait of impatience. As mentioned above, when bipolars are manic they act as if the success were imminent. The achievement is considered either complete and the burden is lifted or, as in the depression, the burden has returned heavier than ever and paralyzed the bipolar. (Peven & Shulman, 1983, p. 8)

4. Birth Order

Firstborn and only children were overrepresented in the 17 patients. Thirteen of the 17 were either firstborn or only children. (All six women were firstborn or onlies.) This factor has been found in other studies (Berman, 1933) and begs the question; if some kind of physiological causality does occur, why does it appear to morbidly affect firstborns more than others?

> The achievement orientation of firstborn children has been cited by several investigators (Altus, 1970; Fakouri, 1974) . . . Perhaps the reason firstborn and only children are overrepresented . . . is that these birth-order positions are more often associated with our second factor, achievement. . . . and these children are also more likely to have a high desire for parental approval. Thus, firstborns may feel less free to reject the values and tasks their parents assign to them. They may feel rebellious, but are less able to disregard the parental injunction that achievement is important. (Peven & Shulman, 1983, p. 9)

5. Cognitive Styles

Two common cognitive styles were found in the patient group: sharpening (versus leveling) and a high internal locus of control (versus an external locus of control). Those people who tend to minimize differences between two similarly viewed figures are called **levelers.** Those who accentuate differences are called **sharpeners.** Holzman and Gardner (1960) found that sharpeners are more open to new experiences, are willing to expend great effort to get what they want, and show more emotional intensity (than levelers). Peven and Shulman (1983) believed bipolars are sharpeners because they always demonstrate emotional intensity.

Sharpening fits also with the bipolars' search for excitement and extroversion. One of B's early recollections demonstrates this trait.

> Age 5: I went to Florida with my parents to visit some friends. I was playing around the house and I heard the dog barking at something and I saw it was a rattlesnake. I just stood there terrified. The man came out with a shotgun and yelled "get away!" He shot the snake and picked it up on a pitchfork while it was still moving. He said, "They don't stop moving until sundown." It was a grand experience. I was exhilarated.

According to Rotter (1975), people with an internal locus of control see themselves as the responsible agents for the events of their lives and allocate excessive responsibility to themselves. In mania, bipolars attribute great power to themselves; in depression, they attribute exaggerated failures to themselves. This seems to fit Adler's idea that bipolars alternate between feelings of powerlessness and exaltation, and that they start projects enthusiastically and lose interest quickly.

6. The Value of Excitement

Zuckerman (1979) called the tendency to always seek out high levels of excitement the "sensation-seeking motive." Adlerians see this behavior as movement toward the goal of excitement.

> . . . In clinical studies Zuckerman found this motive associated with hypomania, impulsiveness, and overactivity . . . It follows that people who use feeling in this way will seek out feeling experiences. But bipolars value excitement so much that they intensify these experiences until they provide the amount of emotional arousal with which . . . they feel most comfortable. (Peven & Shulman, 1983, p. 10)

The early recollection about the rattlesnake is an example of the high priority given to excitement. Another example is the early recollection of M, the young man who played toreador in the street:

Age 7: My aunt, uncle, cousin, and all my family piled into the station wagon and went to Riverview (an amusement park). I had never seen Riverview, let alone at night when it was all lit up. It was very exciting to me. I said, "This is heaven!" Everybody laughed, but I was very, very excited and enthralled.

7. Extremism

Adler believed that one of the mistakes neurotic people make is to see the world in terms of concrete opposites. Antithetical thinking does not allow for shades of gray; things are either black or white, good or evil, and these kinds of cognitions lead to maladaptive behavior. Kurt Adler believed this tendency is present in the bipolars' emotions and behavior as well as their cognition:

> . . . [They] appear to take literally the "all" in "all or nothing" proposition . . . The effort usually fails, as does the gambler's when he puts all his money on one horse in a desperate attempt to recoup his losses . . . (K. Adler, 1961, p. 60)

Bipolars are either/or people. They throw themselves into life or just as intensely shrink from it. Kurt Adler pointed out that the seemingly contradictory behavior has a singleness of purpose . . . the pursuit of personal superiority through impressive achievements. But, "they never really believe in themselves, [and] they negate reality at the use of a delusion . . . either by foreseeing that everything will be wonderful and that [they] can do anything . . . [or] that everything will be dismal and that [they] can do nothing . . . " (K. Adler, 1961, p. 60). This extremism is exemplified in the *Family Constellation Summary* of one of the young men previously mentioned: it is an example of early training in extremism.

> An only child who grew up in a family with an authoritarian, distance-keeping father and a sweet, close, giving mother. The atmosphere was one of extremes and stressed the closeness to mother and the distance from father. He was both pampered and felt deprived; and while father required accomplishments, mother accepted him as he was.

Bipolars see themselves as first or last, Caesar or nobody.

> Their behavior is like Don Quixote who managed to live
> in the world as a heroic knight even though the age of
> chivalry was past. He would either attack windmills forcefully
> or lie under a tree unmoving and claim to be enchanted.
> (Peven & Shulman, 1983, p. 12)

Another of the young men previously mentioned described himself in extremes by saying, "I was very skinny until I was eight and then I became very fat." He talked about school in the same manner; "Sometimes I got an A, and sometimes I flunked."

Peven and Shulman (1983) saw the extremism of the bipolar as a response style. It is the way bipolars respond to the responsibilities of life and is another way to understand the cyclical nature of the illness.

8. Inept Feelings and the Desire to Impress

Both Adlers believed that bipolars do not really believe in their own competence. The goal of achievement is set too high and since they are unable to reach their goals they feel inadequate and try to compensate. One way in which they compensate is to try to impress others with their greatness. The *Rorschach* of one man states it very clearly:

> Mr. T uses a snow job to impress people when he
> cannot deliver the goods. He uses a verbal smoke screen
> from unconventional areas of knowledge to impress
> others while disguising his inability to understand and
> deal with what is really going on around him. By
> attracting attention to the esoteric, he can distract
> others from the fact that he produces very little by
> common sense standards and can bamboozle others
> into regarding him as a whiz. He creates for himself
> a substitute world of achievement and power, with
> grandiose future plans, which he may believe himself,
> but which are hardly convincing to someone who looks
> for the evidence . . . by selecting areas difficult to

put to the test, he enjoys the liberty of taking the benefit of the doubt about power and achievement, and believing that he is superior to others.

He may make a good beginning, but fails in the follow through.

The world for Mr. T is both strange and frightening; he feels small and overpowered in it. He is at the bottom, and the only way he feels he can make it up is through power and prestige.

He is a discouraged person who sees others as either above or below him (in power, prestige, and achievement) and he is a long way from the top. He has given up trying to reach the top through conventional channels . . . and is reaching for magic . . . He relieves the discouragement by entertaining grandiose plans and substituting fictitious prestige and achievements. (Testing done by Bede Smith, Ph.D.)

This *Rorschach* interpretation of a 28-year-old man reads like an analysis of bipolar disorder as understood from an Adlerian point of view. In the face of high achievement goals bipolars feel inadequate and they attempt to compensate for feelings of inferiority by impressing others with grandiose plans. The plans serve as substitutes for real achievement, for bipolars are concerned with the impression they make on others. They need people for their purposes and do not isolate or withdraw as schizophrenics do. However, they demonstrate little social interest as their desire for approval is for the recognition of their own importance and not about concern for others. (Yet, they are often warm, compassionate friends.) The early memory of S demonstrates the kind of relationships bipolars like . . . impressing others:

Age 9: We had just moved to a new neighborhood and I was with this guy. I told him I was with a gang in my old neighborhood. I had on this great leather jacket and the wind came along and blew my jacket open. There were four little holes in the lining and I told the guy the holes were from shots from a bee-bee gun. I was hoping he would believe me.

SUMMARY

Peven and Shulman believed that bipolar disorder may very well be an organ inferiority, a constitutional predisposition to mood swings. However, as Adler warned, the existence of an organ inferiority does not determine behavior. The "creative self" is that which intervenes between the stimuli (heredity and environment) acting on people, and the response to those stimuli that "determines" behavior. Thus, no matter the "cause" of the disorder, the behavior has psychological significance.

Birth order is not a personality trait, of course. But firstborns, more often than others, are known to be highly achievement oriented and their overrepresentation in the studied cases is explained in this way. But the desire to achieve prominence, status, and prestige was evident in all cases studied. Bipolars are ambitious people who burden themselves with inappropriate goals of achievement. Their method of operation is an impatient lunge in the general direction of their goal which often results in failure. The failure doesn't end the desire to impress, so when they are in the manic phase they try to overwhelm others with their grandiose plans and fantasies. Since their method of operation does not allow for gradual, straightforward movement, they experience feelings of inferiority at their "failures" and withdraw as if in defeat.

Bipolars do not hold themselves in high regard . . . they suffer from low self-esteem and the belief that they are the responsible parties (common feelings in a firstborn). Therefore, instead of recognizing their goals and methods as inappropriate, they blame themselves for their failures.

One interesting finding was the discovery that bipolars carry within themselves a deep feeling of rebellion against what they consider the "burden" of impressive achievement. Consider the following *Rorschach:*

> S views himself as called upon to accomplish special feats. He is supposed to be big but does not feel that

he is. The test indicates that he does not really test himself to see whether he has what it takes. Instead, S only goes through the motions while fooling himself into believing that he is making sincere efforts to achieve. His desire is not to be pushed around by life and to have unlimited freedom. Since he sees life as a struggle (full of hassles) S's immediate goal is to be independent and free of constraints.

But bipolars are not free to throw off the burden because in their limited-range thinking, impulsive and antithetical, they see the world only in concrete opposites. If no grand overwhelming success exists, then only dismal failure occurs. They are people of extremes in what they think, feel, and do.

The relationship between mania and depression is considered.

> Mania can be seen as a heightened attempt to achieve impressive feats; depression as the exhausted refusal to participate in life when it denies bipolars their achievement but leaves them still faced with the *burden* of achieving . . . we do not believe that the purpose of mania is to stave off depression nor do we believe that it is the resulting freedom of energy following resolution of depression. For us, *mania is an intensified attempt to meet a challenge and depression, in this case, is an intensified protest against the 'burdensome task.'* . . . Mania can be a denial of fear (as Kurt Adler says) as well as a denial of sadness (as Freud says). One may attack a challenge when one feels inept or fears defeat, but one can also attack when one smells success. Given the constitutional predisposition and the characteristic ways of behaving, it is also quite possible that mania can result from being aroused by a success or by pleasant excitement and not knowing when to stop or moderate the arousal. Bipolars, in fact, court the arousal since that is the way they feel most comfortable. (Peven & Shulman, 1983, p. 14) (Emphasis mine)

CASE EXAMPLE

Case of Martha

The following case history demonstrates many of the psychodynamics explained in this chapter.

Martha was 30 years old when she was hospitalized for the first time under the care of our group private practice. She was brought to the hospital by her husband who recognized her behavior as manic and realized she needed psychiatric care.

The couple, who had a son four years old, had recently moved to the Chicago area because the husband, Paul, had just become the vice-president of a medium-sized corporation in Chicago. They lived in a suburb known for its upward mobility and transiency; as the men moved up the corporate and financial ladders, couples moved out of suburb A up to suburb B.

The women in suburb A were "corporate" minded and had formed social clubs and voluntary organizations designed to help their husbands' upward mobility. The year was 1971 and large socioeconomic sections of the U.S. had not taken up the banner of the sixties revolution.

Martha wanted to "belong," to be like the other women whom she saw as successful wives and mothers. She worked part-time as a teacher to help them "up" financially, and joined as many of the women's groups as she could. Within a few months she was not sleeping nights, had no appetite, and felt "shaky and excited all the time." She lost control of her classroom and started calling the women in her groups at all hours trying to "make plans" for all the schemes she had concocted. Soon, the women were bewildered by Martha and began to question her judgment. She was beginning to get periods of crying spells mixed with her hyperactivity and excited state.

In Martha's own words:

"Paul was out of town on business and I got all involved in the overplanning of the women's groups. I called Bob [the corporate President] in the middle of the night and his wife thought I was sleeping with him. (I wasn't, but he had many women.) I realized something was wrong, and I thought I'd better get home to my parents [in Minnesota], so I put Richard [the son] in the car and drove two blocks. I knew right away I couldn't make it, so I went to my girlfriend's house and she saw I wasn't normal and she got me and Richard to sleep by telling me I had to lay down with Richard. I fell asleep immediately . . . I hadn't slept in days. She called the office and the President called Paul who came right home and took me to the hospital.

"I felt terrible. Paul was trying so hard and I fell apart. I was in the hospital for six weeks and all I wanted was to get out of the hospital. I hadn't accepted it [her illness]. I was determined not to be like my mother."

Martha's mother had been diagnosed manic-depressive for many years. Apparently, mother never did get "regulated" on her medications. Although mother had not shown extreme signs of mania or depression in Martha's early years, by the time Martha was a teenager mother was spending more and more time in the hospital until, by the time I met Martha, the family considered it a good year when mother spent only two or three months in the hospital.

Martha has a three years younger sister, Jeanette, whom she describes [as a child] as "Belligerent. She fought a lot with the other children and didn't want to go to school. She wet the bed and we didn't get along." Jeanette grew up to be an unhappy, unpleasant adult. Married three times, she is now divorced, has moved all over the country from job to job and is currently back in their home town living with her parents.

The family history of Martha and Jeanette also includes a maternal grandfather who committed suicide by hanging himself. Such a family history, (grandfather, mother, Jeanette) is characteristic of the primary relatives of those suffering from affective disorders. Although Jeanette may not present with classical bipolar signs, she does suffer the irritability and restlessness that is common to sub-affective mood disorders (Akiskal, 1989).

While Martha was in the hospital in 1971 she was treated with phenothiazines and discharged after six weeks, already started on a downward turn toward depression. Within a few weeks:

> "I got depressed because things weren't all well [perfect] and I took all my pills at once. Paul took me to the [nearby] hospital where they pumped my stomach, and then I was back in your hospital for three weeks."

Martha recovered from that bout of depression and was not seen nor did she need treatment for ten years.

Then, in 1982, Paul noticed a change in Martha's behavior and brought her back into treatment. The records show she was "high" and was given phenothiazines, but it wasn't until 1984 that Martha was again hospitalized as "manic." Since that time she has been seeing me regularly for psychotherapy, gets her medications from a psychiatrist, and has not suffered either a full-blown mania or a major depression. We have developed a comfortable relationship and often look forward to seeing each other.

My major problem during Martha's treatment has been to get her to accept the fact of her illness. She had grown up with two "difficult" women and was considered the "star" of her family, the "good girl" who did everything "right." She had no room in her self-image for being "sick." As a child she worshipped the "Goddess of Good Little Girls." A summary of her Family Constellation reads as follows:

> The older of two girls who stayed in the number one position by being the kind of child the parents wanted: a "good girl scout." Sister was discouraged and found her place by being the angry baby. The children were expected to have a "smile on their face and a song in their hearts" because the family values were to have a nice disposition and conduct yourself properly and constructively. The good opinion of others was also important.

The family atmosphere was warm and affectionate, and the people were concerned about each other. Father guided the family as a benevolent authority because he knew what was "right" and had the final say over the kindly but "sick" mother.

Martha took the family values seriously and tried to do the right thing and to please others. She became "Miss Goody Two-Shoes."

Some of Martha's 1971 early recollections were as follows:

Age 4: I was swinging in a swing from the cottonwood tree. Grandmother was swinging me . . . long, huge, soaring swings so that I could look out over everything. Grandmother was saying she would go to town and buy groceries and every time she pulled me back she would tell me another grocery she'd buy . . . bread . . . butter . . . milk . . . Long, huge, majestic swings to swing out as far as I want to. Warm and all engulfing. A soaring feeling.

Age 6: There was a big bonfire. Father had roasted wieners and marshmallows and all the neighborhood kids were there. We put together all the leaves and piled them high and there was the smell of the bonfire and all the kids jumping on the leaves. Happy and excited and romantic.

Age 8: Father ran the town movie projector. A bunch of us went to father's movie house on Saturday night. The popcorn girl was making popcorn. We all held hands while one person touched the machine because it had a short in it so the shock from the machine went around everybody and through everybody. I was frightened. I was not enjoying the fun. I was frightened, but everybody else thought it was fun.

Age 8: It was gym and everybody chose up teams for the softball team, and I was the very last person chosen. Sports was not my thing, but I was crushed. Nobody wanted me, neither team wanted me. It was important to be popular. I felt humiliated.

The summary of the Early Recollections was written as follows:

> I want life to be beautiful, everybody to be happy and have a good time, and life to go smoothly. (Life should be like a picnic.) When life becomes unpleasant I suffer and I don't know what to do.

Out of the summary of the *Family Constellations* and the summary of the *Early Recollections* were found three Basic Mistakes, or self-defeating apperceptions:

1. She doesn't even think in terms of being a decision-maker. She is interested only in meeting the requirements and following the directions. (She doesn't initiate action.)

2. She exaggerates the importance of being a "good girl." In fact, that's all she's got and it's the only way of acting she has. She doesn't have any other way of solving problems.

3. When being a good girl doesn't work, she feels completely at a loss, and suffers.

In 1971, in the new situation, Martha tried hard to "shine." She wanted so much to do the right thing, to please everybody, to be accepted, to overcome, that she created a "crisis situation" for herself. She stopped resting, stopped sleeping, and went into a manic state. When she believed she had failed completely, she became depressed and attempted suicide.

During the years from 1971 to 1984 when we started doing psychotherapy together, Martha had given up teaching and had learned not to overtax herself. She and Paul made the difficult decision not to have any more children because they were concerned about Martha's mental health. She was working in an office in a nonmanagement position and was happy there: "I don't have to take any work home."

After the 1984 hospitalization, Martha was taking pheno-thiazines for a few months. During the course of a session one day I casually asked after Paul, and Martha told me he had "non-Hodgkins lymphoma," that it was "under control," and she always did her best never to think about it: "It's very background and I don't pay any attention to it," and she didn't have to for over four years.

In March, 1985, my notes read: "She wonders why she cycles. We agree that too much stimuli for her sets her off, and she says, 'Any time I'm in a group situation and I have to find my place in the group, it's a difficult situation for me.'" This is reminiscent of one of her early recollections where she wasn't chosen. By then, she understood this constitutes stress for her. In June of 1985 her son graduated from high school, both families came in and stayed with her, the toilet broke down, her car stopped running and she "got high." Paul called and she was put on phenothiazines again for several weeks.

Paul began to notice "differences" in her and was concerned that she was "going crazy" again. But Martha and I dug deeply and discovered she was literally changing her life-style: She no longer believed she had to please everybody, say "yes" to anything asked of her, and always be a "good" girl. She started to do more of what she pleased, and Paul found it disconcerting although it was not a threat to the marriage. An early recollection from that time shows her admitting "nasty" feelings:

> **Age 7:** My sister had done something and I said to my grandmother, "I hate her," and my grandmother said, "No you don't, you love her, she's your sister." I knew my grandmother was wrong and that I really did hate her.

In September, 1985, Martha came in looking dull and bleary and complained of feeling anergic. She said, "I'm a little down right now, but it's not a problem." Yet my notes read, "I think she's more than a little depressed and (maybe) going to get worse. Shall I ask for a change in meds?" By October she was reporting early morning awakening, loss of appetite, low energy, social withdrawal, and inability to concentrate. At this point we wrestled each other to the ground.

Martha had always resisted taking lithium, the treatment and medicine of choice for bipolar illness. She was still (my notes) "very hung up on the embarrassment and shame of 'mental illness.'" I begged and entreated her to treat herself as if she had any other illness, like diabetes, for example, where she would have to be on insulin. I said she had to finally accept the fact that she cycled *like mother* and had to take medicine *like mother* whether she liked it or wanted it or not.

Martha struggled and evaded; I pleaded, cajoled and threatened. She started to cry and finally agreed to start lithium and an antidepressant. By December, 1985, she was "neither up nor down" and she has continued in this mode since then. Her lithium blood level has stayed between 0.76 and 0.95 (therapeutic level is between 0.75 and 1.50). And she has managed to pull through many "crisis situations" without cycling too high or too low.

Suddenly, in the fall of 1986, Paul's lymphoma took a bad turn. Martha reported it to me but said she "preferred not to think about it." Yet all during 1986 and 1987 Paul kept getting worse and failed to respond for any length of time to more and more drastic treatment. Martha came to see me more often and in an interesting development, she became more open and honest with me. She stopped "denying" her fears about Paul's illness, and told me of her "real" doubts and worries. She confessed she had "never liked" her mother, only her father, and really "hated" being on medicine because it made her think of her mother. She couldn't understand why she was without medicine (or treatment of any kind) for ten years and then began to cycle again. (I had no logical or psychological "reason" either.)

Paul kept getting worse until by February of 1988 Martha and I were discussing what "she would do if Paul dies." Paul did die in October of 1988 and my notes throughout 1988 and 1989 consistently read: "She is doing very well." She managed the death, the funeral arrangements, the burial, and the grieving with extreme grace under pressure, watched herself carefully for any untoward signs of depression or mania, and expressed her "worry" that now there was "nobody to tell me when I'm getting high." I promised to do that for her and to watch and help her in any way I could.

The year is now 1990 and Martha has not cycled up or down since 1985 although she did, of course, experience a normal grief reaction when Paul died. Mother, however, has been hospitalized for several months every year.

We see each other about once a month or every six weeks (at her pleasure); she stays on the lithium and is making a good adjustment to her single, widowed life. In fact, a few months ago she told me how life was "easier" for her being alone because she had no pressure of responsibility to anyone. Paul had left her well-provided for; she has friends and goes out; her son is in graduate school and she's feeling all right with the world. I told her I was going to "immortalize" her in this chapter and she was pleased. We went over her record and she corrected some dates and thoughts. I asked for new early recollections and these are what she gave me (1990):

> **Age 3:** There was a big, huge tree with a long swing attached and my grandmother pushed me and told me she was going to take me to places like Japan, and Ireland, and China and all these places that the swing could take me. I knew she loved me. It was fun and there were no rules; you're on your own.
>
> I can go wherever I want and do whatever I want. There are no rules. I'm getting help from someone who loves me so I can do what I want.
>
> **Age 7:** My Dad had built cupboards in the bathroom and had put in the towels and linens. My sister and I got in there and we hid there and scrambled up and down. We climbed and crawled around the cabinet. I had a great sense of freedom.
>
> **Age 7:** It was the middle of winter and we lived up on a hill. They closed the streets and there was no traffic. Lots of kids, and my father, and we took sled

rides. We went clear to the top and all the way to the bottom even to the railway tracks. Great fun.

Since the recollections were repeating themselves, I stopped.

This woman, who is now almost 50 years old, has "come out." She no longer hides her feelings about wanting to be free of all constraints and burdens. She frankly says she enjoys the freedom from responsibility she is now experiencing and no longer has as much of a desire to please and accommodate herself to others. Whereas in the past she thought only about impressing others with her "goodness" and worried herself into a suicide attempt after her first hospitalization, she no longer considers the opinion of others as more important than her own.

Martha has discovered her strength and developed a belief in herself and her ability to handle the exigencies of life. She no longer feels like a failure if she doesn't make it in a group, but can take the rejection in her stride. (She is pleasant, so is seldom "rejected.")

In her desire *not* to be like her mother, Martha has established ways and means of staving off her illness. She makes sure she gets plenty of rest and promises to call me should she miss one night's sleep; she does not overtax or overburden herself in most areas of her life; her job is not a brain-buster and she "doesn't take it home"; she has friends and goes out with them, but makes sure she does not get overtired; and she takes her medicine and gets lithium levels at infrequent intervals. She now understands her illness and knows what she must do to stay on top of it.

Sometimes Martha will bring in dreams to discuss in psychotherapy because she has become more attuned to the nuances of her psyche. Sometimes we discuss her childhood and the meaning of her early recollections. In revealing herself to me she found she is not, in her words, "a terrible person." In fact, she often feels comfortably good about herself and her ability to get on in life.

Martha's case illustrates the interplay between a physiological disorder and personality factors. A firstborn girl born into a family with first-degree relatives suffering from mood disorders, Martha took as her goal to be the "goodest" girl in the world. This inhibited her problem-solving ability since she was only able to see the world in terms of doing the "right thing" and impressing others with her goodness or, failing that, disaster. At a stressful life-situation change she tried harder, became emotionally aroused (the inherited factor) and believed, in her antithetical thinking mode, that if the women in the voluntary groups did not find her "wonderful," she had let down her husband and ruined his career. The cycling started.

This case also demonstrates the beneficial use of psychotherapy in mood disturbances. During psychotherapy Martha learned to regard her bipolar disorder as an illness, and now she watches herself carefully. She has stopped trying to impress others with her goodness. She no longer sees the world in concrete opposites but is able to qualify and make gradations; as much as she loved Paul (and she did), she did not turn his death into a disaster. Martha has learned to reduce arousing stimuli and she accepts her limits gracefully.

I don't believe Martha has completely conquered her bipolar illness; her early recollection about the swing compels me to see symbolic significance in the glorious, soaring feelings she enjoys as she hovers over the world. Perhaps her desire to be without any rules will some day get her into deep trouble. At the very least, she knows what she wants and what constitutes a good time for her. But I am concerned that if she ever loosens up her control of herself, she might climb into mania again. I shall share my thoughts and feelings with Martha and hope she will listen to me should the time ever again come when she leaps off of the long, soaring swing.

REFERENCES

Abraham, K. (1957). *Selected papers of Karl Abraham.* New York: Basic Books.

Adler, A. (1959). Melancholia and paranoia. In *The practice and theory of Individual Psychology*. Towota, NJ: Littlefield, Adams.

Adler, A. (1964). *Problems of neurosis*. New York: Harper & Row.

Adler, A. (1968). *The practice and theory of Individual Psychology*. Towota, NJ: Littlefield, Adams.

Adler, K. (1961). Depression in the light of Individual Psychology. *Journal of Individual Psychology, 17*, 56-67.

Akiskal, H., Hirschfeld, M., & Yerevanian, B. (1983). The relationship of personality to affective disorders. *Archives of General Psychiatry, 40*, 47-60.

Akiskal, H. (1989). New insights into the nature and heterogeneity of mood disorders. *Journal of Clinical Psychiatry, 50*, 5.

Altus, W. D. (1970). Marriage and order of birth. *Proceedings of the Annual Convention of the American Psychological Association, 5*, 361-362.

American Psychiatric Association. (1980). *Diagnostic and statistical manual of mental disorders* (3rd ed.). Washington, DC: Author

American Psychiatric Association. (1987). *Diagnostic and statistical manual of mental disorders* (3rd ed., revised). Washington, DC: Author

Ansbacher, H., & Ansbacher, R. (1956). *The Individual Psychology of Alfred Adler*. New York: Basic Books.

Baker, H., & Baker, M. (1987). Heinz Kohut's self-psychology: An overview. *The American Journal of Psychiatry, 144*, 1.

Beck, A. (1987). Cognitive models of depression. *Journal of Cognitive Psychotherapy: An International Quarterly, 1*, 1.

Berman, H. (1933). Order of birth in manic-depressive reactions. *Psychiatric Quarterly, 7*, 430-435.

Blehar, M., Weissman, M., Gershon, E., & Hirschfeld, R. (1988). Family and genetic studies of affective disorders. *Archives of General Psychiatry, 45*, 289-292.

Cohen, R. (1975). Manic-depressive illness. In A. Freedman, H. Kaplan, & B. Sadok (Eds.), *Comprehensive textbook of psychiatry* (2nd ed.). Baltimore: Williams & Wilkens.

Cohen, M., Baker, G., Cohen, R., & Fromm-Reichmann, F. (1954). An intensive study of twelve cases of manic-depressive psychoses. *Psychiatry, 17,* 103-137.

Ellenberger, H. (1970). *The discovery of the unconscious.* New York: Basic Books.

Fakouri, M. E. (1974). Relationship of birth order, dogmatism, and achievement motivation. *Journal of Individual Psychology, 30,* 216-220.

Freud, S. (1960). Mourning and melancholia. In *Collected Papers, Vol. 4.* New York: Basic Books. 152-170.

Galatzer-Levy, R. (1988). Manic-depressive illness: Analytic experience and a hypothesis. In A. Goldberg (Ed.), *Frontiers in self psychology.* Newark, NJ: The Analytic Press.

Holzman, P., & Gardner, R. (1960). Leveling and sharpening and memory organization. *Journal of Abnormal and Social Psychology, 61,* 176-180.

Jung, C. (1971). *Psychological types.* Princeton, NJ: Princeton University Press.

Kaplan, H., & Sadock, B. (1981). *Modern synopsis: A comprehensive textbook of psychiatry/III* (3rd ed.). Baltimore: Williams & Wilkins.

Kraepelin, E. (1902). Dementia praecox and manic-depressive disease. In T. Millon (Ed.), *Theories of personality and psychopathology,* (3rd ed.). New York: Holt, Rinehart & Winston.

Kretschmer, E. (1936). *Physique and temperament.* London: Routledge and Kegan Paul.

Kyle, N. (1988). Emotions and hemispheric specialization. In K. Hoppe (Ed.), *The psychiatric clinics of North America.* 11:3, Hemispheric Specialization. Philadelphia: W. B. Saunders.

MacKinnon, R., & Michels, R. (1971). *The psychiatric interview in clinical practice.* Philadelphia: W. B. Saunders.

Miller, L. (1988). Ego autonomy, creativity, and cognitive style. In K. Hoppe (Ed.), *The psychiatric clinics of North America.* 11:3, Hemispheric Specialization. Philadelphia: W. B. Saunders.

Peven, D., & Shulman, B. (1983). The psychodynamics of bipolar affective disorder: Some empirical findings and their implications for cognitive theory. *Individual Psychology, 39,* 2-16.

Rado, S. (1956). *Psychoanalysis of behavior: Collected papers.* New York: Grune & Stratton.

Rotter, J. (1975). Some problems and misconceptions related to the construct of internal versus external control of reinforcement. *Journal of Consulting and Clinical Psychology, 43*, 56-57.

Schildkraut, J., & Kety, S. (1967). Biogenic amines and emotion. In E. Wolpert (Ed.), *Manic-depressive illness: History of a syndrome.* New York: International Universities Press.

Sullivan, H. (1954). *The psychiatric interview,* edited by H. Perry & M. Gawel (Eds.). (Taken from two lecture series given in 1944-45 and 1945-46.) New York: W. W. Norton.

The Pendulum. (1990). *Newsletter of the Manic Depressive and Depressive Association of Chicago.* XI:1. Chicago.

Turns, D. (1978). The epidemiology of major affective disorders. *American Journal of Psychotherapy, 35*, 5-19.

Willerman, L., & Cohen, D. (1990). *Psychopathology.* New York: McGraw-Hill.

Winokur, G. (1975). Heredity in the affective disorders. In E. Anthony & T. Benedek (Eds.), *Depression and human existence* (pp. 7-20). Boston: Little, Brown.

Zuckerman, M. (1979). *Sensation seeking: Beyond the optimum level of arousal.* Hillsdale, NJ: Lawrence Erlbaum.

CHAPTER 5

DEPRESSIVE DISORDERS

Ronald J. Pancner, M.D.

When depression is discussed among mental health professionals, profound disagreements often emerge. Some profess that the use of somatic therapy (medication or electroconvulsive therapy) is unnecessary (if not deleterious) to outcome. They reason that depression emerges from limited coping techniques to meet life's challenges and one's perception about life and themselves. Those trained in medical settings (and thus more likely to work with inpatient populations) tend to treat those depressions that profoundly interfere with functioning. They will agree that medications and electroconvulsive therapy are highly effective treatments.

The polarity of these attitudes stems from various factors such as being trained by teachers who were heavily biased toward one approach or the other and later reinforced by selective perceptions of the therapist's experiences in practice. Another factor is the practice setting. Those who primarily have an outpatient practice will usually see fewer varieties of depression than the hospital-based practitioner deals with on an everyday basis. Since Adlerian psychology is an holistic psychology, the challenge to Adlerian practitioners is to keep all factors in perspective and to recognize that perception affects biochemistry and biochemistry affects perception in formulating an effective treatment approach and understanding of the patient.

Much of the psychiatric literature is devoted to research to try to help determine which depressions are most likely to respond to medications, identifying subgroups that will likely respond to specific classes of medications, and discovering the biochemical changes occurring in depression. The vast majority of psychiatrists, however, recognize the environmental and perceptual factors in the etiology and the importance of psychotherapy in successful treatment of depressions.

In any discussion of depression, several factors need to be kept in mind. The first is that depression is a universal affect. In other words, all human beings feel sad or depressed at times. The "feeling" of depression is not an illness. Only when the feeling of depression interferes with functioning does the condition qualify for a diagnosis or become a disease. Adler recognized this concept by citing that psychopathology exists when people avoid the life tasks. Avoidance is justified by individuals either claiming, "Yes, but I'm sick," if neurotic techniques are utilized or stating, "No" and utilizing their own private logic (perceptions without conceptual validation) to excuse themselves.

A second factor in any discussion of depression is that psychological, psychiatric, and Adlerian literature is often confusing. Older articles usually do not cite where the studied depressive patient group fits in the continuum of symptoms and functional incapacity. In other words, when depression is discussed, it is often not specified whether or not the symptoms fulfill the criteria of melancholia, major depression, dysthymia, or cyclothymia.

A third factor is that diagnostic criteria have changed markedly in this century and even in the last 10 years. The changes followed research that was conducted in the United States and United Kingdom regarding diagnostic concepts. In North America, schizophrenia and character disorder diagnoses were found to be unnecessarily broad (Cooper, Kendall, & Gurland, 1972). This led to extensive studies of diagnostic reliability and validity, ultimately resulting in the development of DSM-III. This led to supporting diagnostic decisions by (1) inclusion and exclusion criteria; (2) familial genetic history; (3) considerations of age of onset, premorbid course, and prospective follow-up; and (4) treatment response. In addition, laboratory tests that provide confirmatory evidence for affective diagnoses are being used increasingly in clinical practice (Akiskal, 1989; Carroll, Feinberg, Greden, et al., 1981).

The difficulty in the diagnosis and treatment of depression is that fundamental symptoms in the spectrum of depression remain very similar. From clinical observation and history alone, those conditions which are likely to respond to medications are often nearly impossible to differentiate. In the DSM-III-R are at least eight depressive diagnoses: normal sadness; normal bereavement; adjustment reaction with depressed mood; dysthymia; cyclothymia; atypical depression; major depression; major depression with melancholia and/ or psychosis; and bipolar disorder, mixed and depressed. The reason for accurate diagnosis is to minimize patient risk. As an example, now that we have a specific agent for treating bipolar disorder, no longer do these patients need to be exposed to antipsychotics with the risk of tardive dyskinesia. Many psychotic patients that were formerly diagnosed as schizophrenic are now found to fulfill the criteria of psychotic major depression. Many patients that previously were believed to be hypochondriacs, or were diagnosed as having a character disorder, are being found to have varieties of depressive illness and treated accordingly. The result has been the broadening of the boundaries of affective disorder (Akiskal & Lemmi, 1983).

Statistics: The Extent of the Problem

Depression is by far the most common psychiatric disorder in this country and is a major public health problem. Weissman, Klerman, Prusoff, Sholomskas, and Padian (1981) reported studying a community in Connecticut that at any one point in time, three percent of the population met the criteria of major depression with an approximate lifetime risk of up to 20%. Bipolar disorder was much less common, with only one percent lifetime risk. The lifetime prevalence for major depression in women is 59%, while men have approximately one-half that frequency at 24%. In any six-month period, four percent of all women and two percent of all men could be diagnosed as having major depression. In addition, an equal proportion could be diagnosed as having dysthymia. The highest prevalence for both sexes tends to be in the young and middle adult years with a drop-off in frequency after age 65 (Myers, Weissman, & Tischler, 1984; Weissman & Boyd, 1982).

No clear relationship exists between the syndrome of major depression and social class or race. The prevalence of bipolar disorder is less, 0.6 to 0.9 percent, with the male to female ratio as 1:1.2.

Several risk factors for major depression have been reported. The two most powerful risk factors for major depression are being female and having a family history of depressive illness (Hirschfeld & Cross, 1982). Studies of stressful life events have found that depressed patients tend to have an excess of negative events, particularly losses, in the six months prior to the onset of depression. Such events increase the relative risk of depression by a factor of 6.5 (Paykel, 1978). Loss of a parent because of death or separation during childhood, long considered a predisposing factor to a major depression, has not been substantiated by empirical research. Studies of recovered persons with major depression have often shown a dependent, emotionally unstable, and introverted personality (Hirschfeld, Klerman, & Clayton, 1983).

Mortality is high with an estimated 15% suicide risk for recurrent depressions (Robins & Guze, 1970). Moreover, studies indicate a high rate of cardiovascular disease in depressives. Depressives often utilize the health care system heavily, seeking relief for their often vague somatic distress such as stomachaches and headaches. The majority of depressives, however, are not treated. Only 33% are seen by physicians and mental health professionals, and only six percent are treated by psychiatrists. This is unfortunate, since many studies have shown that effective treatment is available.

Depression is one of the most common mental disorders, affecting an estimated 10 to 12% of the population in this country. This figure does not include normal bereavement and adjustment disorders with depressed mood.

Diagnosis—DSM-III-R

Depression can best be understood as a spectrum condition. The symptoms of depression can be a normal human condition designated in DSM-III-R as normal bereavement, for example when a loss occurs of a love object, such as the death or separation from a loved one, or loss of status or position. At the other end of the spectrum is major depression, where the person has marked impairment of functioning and may exhibit psychotic symptoms, such as delusions and halluci- nations, and marked physiological manifestations, such as psychomotor slowing or agitation and constipation. Accurate diagnosis is often difficult because the distinction among groups is often slight.

The category of major depression in all probability does not delineate one illness, but a symptom cluster as a manifestation of a group of illnesses. Probably several etiologies are involved in major depression. In DSM-III-R the criteria for major depressive episode include the presence of either depressed mood, which can express itself in irritability in children and/or adolescents, or markedly diminished interest or pleasure in almost all activities. One of these symptoms must be present.

Additional symptoms include a significant weight loss or weight gain when not dieting or decrease or increase in appetite, insomnia or hypersomnia, and psychomotor agitation or retardation. The symptom needs to be observed by others and not be merely a subjective feeling. A failure or loss of energy and/or feelings of worthlessness or excessive or inappropriate guilt may occur, which needs to be beyond merely self-reproach or guilt for being ill and may reach delusional proportions. Symptoms also may include a diminished ability to think or concentrate, indecisiveness, or recurrent thoughts of death, including recurrent suicidal ideation with or without a specific plan or a suicide attempt. The preceding symptoms need to be present most of the day nearly every day. A total of five of the above factors need to be present for the diagnosis of major depressive episode.

Exclusion criteria are that an organic factor cannot be established that would account for the initiation and maintenance of this disturbance, and secondly, that the disturbance is not a normal reaction to the death of a loved one (uncomplicated bereavement). However, a morbid preoccupation with worthlessness, suicidal ideation, impairment of function, or psychomotor retardation over a prolonged duration would suggest bereavement complicated by a major depression. At no time during the disturbance would delusions or hallucinations have been present for as long as two weeks in the absence of prominent affective symptoms.

Lastly, these symptoms are not superimposed on either schizophrenia, schizophreniform disorder, delusional disorder, or psychotic disorder not otherwise specified.

Major depression is a category that encompasses several conditions previously diagnosed separately such as involutional depression, psychotic depression, unipolar affective disease, and some more severe forms of psychoneurotic depressive reaction. Major depression can further be sub-classified into single episode, recurrent, melancholic, and/or psychotic. In addition, the term "double depression" is found in the literature. This pertains to those patients who have an underlying chronic depression with a superimposed major depressive episode. The prognosis for this group is relatively unfavorable, with remission of both chronic and acute symptoms being only one-half as likely as from major depression alone. Thirty-nine percent of double depressives recovered after two years, compared with 79% for depression alone. The relapse rate also is twice as frequent among those with double depression who do recover (Keller, Lavori, & Endicott, 1983).

Subtypes of Major Depression

The DSM-III-R was modified from DSM-III by adding seasonality and reformulating endogenous depression into a subheading of melancholia. This was done to eliminate etiologic implications.

The diagnostic criteria for the melancholic type of major depressive episode include at least five of the following: (1) loss of interest or pleasure in almost all activity; (2) lack of reactivity to usual pleasurable stimuli; (3) does not feel better even temporarily when something pleasurable happens; (4) the depression has diurnal variation, namely, the depressive feels worse in the morning; (5) has early morning waking at least two hours before the usual time of wakening; (6) psychomotor retardation or agitation is observable and not based solely on subjective complaints; (7) significant anorexia or weight loss occurs which equals more than five percent of body weight in a month; (8) one or more previous major depressive episodes followed by recovery; and (9) a prior good response to adequate somatic antidepressant therapy which includes tricyclic antidepressants, electroconvulsive therapy, monomine oxidase inhibitors, or lithium.

Exclusion criteria include the absence of significant personality disturbance before the first major depressive episode.

Obviously many of these symptoms are found in non-melancholic depressions as well. Those symptoms most characteristic of melancholia are the lack of reactivity and the psychomotor changes.

The diagnostic criteria for psychotic features requires delusions, hallucinations, or depressive stupor. These features need to be further categorized into either mood congruent or incongruent. Mood congruent psychotic depression requires a depressive stupor or delusions and/or hallucinations with mood congruent content. The themes of the delusions would be personal inadequacy, punishment, guilt, and/or annihilism. To receive a diagnosis of psychotic depression with mood incongruent features, the delusions and hallucinations must be inconsistent with a depressed mood. Examples are thought broadcasting, thought projection, and delusions of persecution.

Those patients who are psychotic have recovery rates essentially the same as nonpsychotic, depressed patients. However, they tend to recover more slowly and have lower short-term (six-month) recovery rates (Coryell, Lavori, & Endicott, 1984).

Dysthymia (or Depressive Neurosis)

Dysthymia is not synonymous with the traditional definitions of neurotic depression. Many of the previous neurotic depressions would now be classified according to the DSM-III-R as major depression. Dysthymia also includes a portion of a condition that was previously classified as cyclothymia.

DSM-III-R criteria require at least a two-year history of continual or numerous episodes of depressive symptoms that, while characteristic of major depression, do not meet full severity or duration criteria for the syndrome. Thus, dysthymia is a chronic condition whose age of onset varies from the mid-teens to late life. Dysthymics are at high risk to develop other psychiatric disorders such as alcohol and drug dependence and major depressive episodes.

The criteria for dysthymia include depressed mood (which can express itself as irritable mood in children and adolescents) for most of the day more days than not, as indicated either by subjective account or the observation of others, for at least two years (one year for children and adolescents). During this period individuals are not without the symptoms of depression or irritable mood for more than two months at a time. While depressed, at least two of the following must be present: (1) poor appetite or overeating, (2) insomnia or hypersomnia, (3) low energy or fatigue, (4) low self-esteem, (5) poor concentration or difficulty making decisions, and (6) feelings of hopelessness.

Exclusion criteria are (1) no evidence of an unequivocal major depressive episode during the first two years of the disturbance (one year for children and adolescents); (2) never a manic episode or hypomanic episode; (3) the lack of symptoms being superimposed on a chronic psychotic disorder such as schizophrenia or delusional disorder; and (4) failure to establish that an organic factor initiated and maintained the disturbance, such as prolonged administration of an anti-hypertensive medication.

One should note that a previous major depressive episode may have occurred prior to the diagnosis of dysthymia if a full remission had been present for six months before development of the dysthymia. In addition, if the patient fulfills the criteria for dysthymia, a superimposed episode of major depression may be present; in that case, both diagnoses are given. This is the "double depression" previously mentioned.

Depression also can exhibit itself in various "unusual" affective presentations (Akiskal & Lemmi, 1983). These include grief that progresses to melancholia, and melancholia with anxious presentations in which the primary presentations are panic, fear of death, breathlessness, profuse sweating, and nightmares. Also included are somatic presentations in which the person primarily complains of vague somatic complaints such as headache, abdominal discomfort, weakness, and dizzy spells without associated medical findings. Characterological presentations of recurrent affective disorder include repeated romantic or marital failure, substance abuse, job instability, and dilettantism. Pseudodemented presentation of retarded depression may be diagnosed in some elderly subjects who present with confusion, disorientation, and memory difficulties. They may actually suffer from irreversible affective disorder which responds to antidepressants or electroconvulsive therapy. In presentation of affective psychosis (schizophreniform), some severe depressions show classical schizophrenic symptoms.

Many depressives show obsessive-compulsive symptoms, and some resort to alcohol or other mind-altering drugs for relief. This compounds and complicates the clinical picture and patients' problems. From the complexity of symptomatology and the overlapping with other psychiatric conditions, one can easily understand why considerable research is being done to try to find trait markers and state markers for various depressive syndromes so that the most effective and least risky medication can be utilized.

An additional sub-classification of dysthymia was proposed by Akiskal (1983). One subgroup includes a characterological depression in which the dysthymia appears to be based on temperament. Another subgroup is composed of a dysthymia which is secondary to an incapacitating physical or non-affective psychiatric disorder, and retains chronic residual symptoms of the late-onset depression.

Seasonal Affective Disorder (SAD)

The seasonal nature of moods has long been known to man, and references to that phenomenon can be found in ancient writings. Modern-day evidence demonstrates that attacks of mania are more frequent in the summer, while hospitalizations for depression are relatively more common in the late spring. Only in recent years has this syndrome been investigated systematically (Rosenthal, Sack, & Gillin, 1984). The onset appears to occur in the second and third decades of life and the patients appear to be predominately women with the symptoms of bipolar II illness (depression with hypomanic episodes). Depressions usually begin in October or November and have atypical depressive symptoms such as hypersomnia, carbohydrate craving, lack of energy, and weight gain, along with typical features of hopelessness, suicidal thoughts, decreased libido, and social withdrawal. Usually considerable functional impairment is associated.

This syndrome seems to have a higher prevalence in the northern latitudes and less in the sunnier southern latitudes. Successful treatment of this syndrome includes exposure to high intensity, full-spectrum lighting for two hours in the morning.

Differential Diagnosis

The diagnosis of depression is an extremely complicated process. Not only can depression be superimposed on other psychiatric illnesses such as panic disorder or schizophrenia, but it is also found frequently with substance abuse, particularly in the withdrawal from alcohol and cocaine. Moreover, depression accompanies many physical illnesses such as endocrine disorders, including those of the pituitary, adrenals, and thyroid; vitamin and mineral deficiencies and excesses; infections, such as hepatitis and tuberculosis; neurological disorders, such as multiple sclerosis; collagen disorders, such as systemic lupus erythematosus; cardiovascular disease, such as myocardial infarction or cerebral ischemia; and also some malignancies.

Further complicating this picture is the presence of several classifications of medications which frequently produce depressive reactions. These include the hormones estrogen and progesterone; the antihypertensives, such as reserpine, propranadol (Inderal), clonadine, and methyldopa; the corticosteroids, such as cortisone; anti-cancer medications, such as Vincristine and Vinblastine; anti-tuberculins, such as cycloserine; and the anti-Parkinsonian medications, such as Levodopa, Carbidopa, and Amantadine.

In addition, except for a history of mania or hypomania, the depressive symptoms of major depression and dysthymia are indistinguishable from those of the bipolar disorders. Obtaining a family history may be helpful to make this differentiation because of genetic predisposition.

Accurate diagnosis is important in ascertaining which treatment is most likely to be effective. The medication armamentorium has multiplied dramatically. The utilization of proper medication when indicated can dramatically shorten the length of suffering and perhaps prevent the dire complication of suicide (Hirschfeld & Goodwin, 1988).

Genetic Studies

Mounting evidence has been that some forms of depression have a genetic factor. Affective disorders which have been the most closely studied genetically, and the most impressive, are those studies of bipolar (manic depressive) illness. A large twin study was accomplished by Bertelson, Harvald, and Hauge (1977) which showed that monozygotic (74%) twin pairs are significantly more likely to be concordant for bipolar illness than dizygotic (17%) twin pairs. Recently a specific gene location of bipolar disorder was found on the short arm of chromosome 11 in a large Amish pedigree (Egeland, Gerhard, & Pauls, 1987); however, these findings are questioned. The conclusion reached from these data by many researchers is that a genetic factor is responsible for bipolar illness and that bipolar disorder is a specific illness, in contrast to major depression, which is a group of disorders.

Research data also include a high concordance rate in unipolar depression: 43% for monozygotic twins and 19% for dizygotic twins. However, these data are not considered conclusive evidence of the presence of a genetic factor (Bertelson, Harvald, & Hauge, 1977). More recent studies have shown consistently that identical twins are far more concordant for major affective disorder (65 to 75%) than are fraternal twins (14 to 19%). This strongly supports the genetic contribution to vulnerability. Additional evidence from adoption and family pedigree studies confirm these findings. However, the etiology of affective illness is still unknown (Pancner, 1985).

BIOCHEMICAL THEORIES

Biogenic Amine Hypothesis

The biogenic amine hypothesis arose from observations of the effect of various pharmacological substances on patients. Theoretically, depression is linked with disorders in the functioning of two major amine neurotransmitter systems: norepinephrine and serotonin. This theory developed from observations that reserpine caused a depressive syndrome in 10 to 15% of patients, that the medications deplete brain monoamine stores, and that ipronazid medication used to treat tubercular patients elevated their mood. It is a monomine oxidase inhibitor and thus increases brain monomine concentration. In addition, tricyclic antidepressants (Tofranil, Pamelor, Norpramine, etc.) block the reuptake of neuro-transmitters into the presynaptic neurons, and Lithium Carbonate, which is effective in bipolar affective disorders, facilitates monomine reuptake.

Studies have been made on the relationship of serotonin, norepinephrine, and dopamine levels in cerebral spinal fluid (CSF) and human behavior. A study performed by Traskman, Asberg, Bertilsson, and Sjostrang (1981) on patients who were treated in a hospital emergency room after a suicide attempt found that those who had low serotonin levels in their spinal fluid had a 20% mortality rate by suicide within a year. Depression was more closely related to low levels of the dopamine metabolite, homovanillic acid (HVA). Although psychoanalytic theories have suggested an integral association between aggression and depressed states (Freud, 1953), an important point to remember is that not all suicide victims suffer from depression.

Those persons in the psychiatric unit of a naval hospital with diagnosed personality disorders had a robust inverse correlation between aggression and suicide and levels of a serotonin metabolite, 5-HIAA. In other words, those persons who were admitted because of aggressive behavior and suicide attempts had low serotonin levels, again suggesting a link between aggression and central serotonin mechanisms (Brown, Ebert, & Goyer, 1982).

Low levels of CSF 5-HIAA have been reported in other psychiatric conditions such as alcoholism (Ballenger, Goodwin, & Major, 1979) and obsessive-compulsive disorder (Thoren, Ansberg, & Bertilsson, 1980). These findings may indicate that low levels of the serotonin metabolite are associated with increased vulnerability to a spectrum of psychiatric disturbances and to suicidal behavior, and not associated with any specific illness. Depending upon genetic predisposition and/or environmental circumstances, aggressive impulses can lead to psychopathic behavior, excessive drinking, murder, or violent suicide (Georgotos, 1983).

BIOLOGIC TESTS

Whenever a depressed patient is seen, the question is raised, "Is this a biologically-based condition accompanied by a chemical abnormality, or is this a method of coping with a life challenge or loss?" Currently, no lab tests or x-ray imagery that conclusively determine depressive diagnoses are available; nonetheless, several tests have recently been applied to this question.

Dexamethasone Suppression Test (DST)

The most studied and currently utilized test is the *Dexamethasone Suppression Test (DST)*. DST abnormalities imply the existence of an imbalance in the hypothalamic-pituitary-adrenal axis (H-P-A). The neurotransmitters implicated in depression, norepinephrine and serotonin, have an effect on hypothalamic hormones. Dexamethasone is a potent glucocorticoid that suppresses ACTH and cortisol production for up to 24 hours. Failure of a single dose to suppress cortisol secretion indicates overactivity of the H-P-A axis. The DST is not a trait marker; it is abnormal only when the person is depressed. An abnormal finding is considered 95% valid in diagnosing a major depression; however, the test only detects 50% of those persons diagnosed as a major depression based on symptom criteria.

Other studies (Targum, 1983) have pointed out that eight percent of non-depressed patients and seven percent of persons diagnosed schizophrenic also have positive *Dexamethasone Suppression Tests.* Similarly, recent studies by the collaborative depression program at the National Institute of Mental Health indicate that the *Dexamethasone Suppression Test* for depression has not been found to have diagnostic specificity. Eight of 77 controls were non-suppressors, with eight of 16 manic patients, 10 of 37 bipolar patients, and 20 of 74 unipolar depressions demonstrating non-suppression.

A helpful feature of the test is that a person's improvement is reflected in the normalization of the abnormal DST. Those patients who appear to improve clinically, but whose DST is still abnormal, are at high risk of relapse if treatment is discontinued, and their prognosis is poor.

Some medications and disease states interfere with the results of the DST, among which are alcoholism during and after withdrawal, hemodialysis, diabetes mellitus, anorexia nervosa, anticonvulsant medication, and high doses of the benzodiazepines (Valium and related medications). However, for the majority of the population, it remains a useful tool.

Jenike (1982) in a summary article concluded that the use of the DST may aid in diagnosis, treatment, and follow-up of patients with depressive illness. In the absence of either medical illness or medication that affects the DST, escape of dexamethasone suppression strongly suggests the presence of major depressive disorder; however, as mentioned previously, it does not rule out such a disorder. The DST is useful in both pediatric and elderly patients. In those elderly patients with severe dementia, however, the value is unclear because some data indicate dementia alone may produce abnormal DST results.

Thyrotropin Releasing Hormone Test

More recently, a correlation between depression and thyroid function has been found. The usual tests that most physicians utilize to test for thyroid dysfunction are within the normal range in depression. *Thyrotropin releasing hormone (TRH)*, which is an hypothalamic tripeptide, regulates the release of *thyroid stimulating hormone (TSH)* from the anterior pituitary. Normally, giving TRH to a person will stimulate production of large amounts of TSH; however, in patients with major depression this response is blunted.

Thirty percent of depressed patients are positive to both the DST and TRH tests; 34% are abnormal on the TRH test alone, and 20% are abnormal only on the DST. The two tests together confirmed 84% of the major unipolar depressive patients with a diagnostic confidence greater than 95% (Gold, Pottash, Extein, & Sweeney, 1981). Only a few false positive results are obtained, excluding alcoholics in withdrawal and hyperthyroidism (Loosen, Prange, Wilson, Lara, & Pettus, 1977).

Although the neurochemical mechanisms for these and other widely-reported neuroendocrine abnormalities in major depression await explanation and do not prove causality, the diagnostic tests described are useful today. Sachar, Asnis and Halbreich (1980) stated that an abnormal DST can assist in diagnosis, provide information about genetics, and predict treatment response to medication or electroconvulsive therapy. Furthermore, these same tests repeated after treatment can help document response to treatment and help in determining whether the underlying disease is in remission or in an active state, which would leave the patient extremely vulnerable to relapse if medication were to be stopped.

Serum Antidepressant Levels

In the last few years serum levels of the antidepressants have been available to clinicians. Studies have found that only 15 to 25% of the depressed patients referred to psychiatrists have had the proper medication prescribed in adequate doses. A Columbia University study treated depressives with dosages usually considered adequate: 200 mg. for females; 250 mg. for males. The study found 40% of patients were below what was considered therapeutic levels. Moreover, in the elderly, small quantities of medication can produce high serum levels and often toxic symptoms which resemble depression and psychosis. Other studies have shown that 60 to 70% of patients respond to tricyclic medications after two weeks or more, but another 15 to 16% improve if the serum level is adjusted (Pancner, 1985).

Polysomnography

Abnormalities of polygraphically-monitored sleep have been reported consistently in major depression; specifically, the short latency in time from the beginning of sleep to the onset of rapid eye movement (REM); the increased frequency of rapid eye movement during REM sleep (increased REM density); reduced slow wave sleep; a shift in the temporal distribution of REM sleep so that more of it occurs in the early part of the night (shorter REM latency and longer first REM periods); and reduction of sleep which includes longer latency intermittently awakening at night, early a.m. wakening, and therefore decreased sleep efficiency (Hirschfeld & Goodwin, 1988). However, most of these abnormalities lack diagnostic specificity.

Interestingly, well-established studies have shown that total sleep deprivation (Pflug & Tolle, 1971) or deprivation of sleep in the second half of the night (Schilgen & Tolle, 1980) is able to induce remissions in depressed unipolar and bipolar patients temporarily. In fact, shifting the timing of sleep also appears to influence mood. Bipolar and unipolar patients who went to sleep five or six hours earlier than usual are at times relieved of depressive symptoms (Sack, Nurnburger, & Rosenthal, 1985). Such a remission can be sustained for one to two weeks.

CHILDHOOD FORERUNNERS
OF DEPRESSION

Alfred Adler studied the interpersonal aspect of depressive symptoms. He viewed psychological symptoms as a way of coping with social demands. The development of a depressive style as a method of coping with life's challenges theoretically begins in early childhood when children try to master their environment. The process of learning occurs when children try various methods of obtaining their desires. When a method is found to be successful, the children will utilize the method repeatedly. Moreover, after these behaviors are found to be useful, they may then be utilized in later life to reach goals (A. Adler, 1956, p. 288).

In 1914, Adler wrote:

> The discouraged child finds that he can tyrannize best by tears will be a crybaby; the direct line of development leads from the crybaby to the adult depressed patient. Tears and complaints—the means which I have called "water power"—can be extremely useful weapons for disturbing cooperation and reducing others to a condition of "slavery." (A. Adler, 1956, p. 288)

In another article, Adler stated that:

> Melancholia develops in individuals whose method of living has from early childhood been dependent upon the achievement and support of others. Such individuals will always try to lean on others and will not scorn the use of exaggerated hints at their own inadequacy to force the support, adjustment, and submissiveness of others . . . Their self-esteem from childhood on is clearly low as can be concluded from their unceasing attempts to achieve greatest importance. (A. Adler, 1956, p. 319)

Adler theorized that several types of children are in danger of developing neuroses, psychoses, and personality disorders. The commonality was that they tended to concentrate too much on themselves and too little on other people; their development of social interest *(Gemeinschaftsgefühl)* was limited. He outlined three reasons for why a child might become so self-focused. First, the child might have organ inferiorities, such as being lame or stuttering. These problems, he theorized, would require so much of the child's attention to master that little time was left to develop positive relationships with other people except to depend on them.

Second, some children develop a pampered style of life. This state does not necessarily require actual pampering of children, but rather that children interpret life to mean that they should get everything without any effort on their part, that everyone should be supportive and that children should be catered to by everyone. To such persons, their often unconscious goal in life is to take from others, to be in a superior position in order to better exploit others. The attitude may be modeled after a parent or taught by concepts such as "You better get it while you can." It may have been learned from people who always gave material gifts, attention, or accolades to the depressive. Because of receiving throughout life, some people expect such treatment as adults and feel entitled (Mosak, 1985).

The third category of children in danger of developing such difficulties later in life are those who were neglected or even hated. These are children who never have experienced a loving, friendly relationship, nor ever had a loving, friendly relationship modeled for them. They usually have the misconception that getting from others or manipulating others into giving to them represents the main goal in life. Children who are more active will tend to enter more easily into delinquency, crime, and those behavior disorders which utilize threatening and coercive methods. The more passive children tend to use alcohol or other substances or develop symptoms of psychoses or neuroses (K. Adler, 1978).

When confronted with rejection, neglect, or refusal of their wishes, children who become depressed adults are more likely to crawl under the bed and daydream of finding their real parents (the stepchild fantasy), a passive way of criticizing and depreciating their parents. Some children, however, also develop a method of hurting themselves in order to hurt the opponents. Children have many ways of hurting themselves in order to strike out against a parent and thus gain revenge or establish dominance. A refusal to eat is one such method that is usually successful in centering attention on the child while the parents become irritated and upset. Another method might be lying on a cold stone floor refusing to get up, thinking, "It will serve her right if I get pneumonia. Then she'll be sorry for not letting me have my way." The extent of this pattern of hurting self in order to affect others can be viewed as a forerunner to the utilization of suicidal threats, ideation, gestures, and attempts in later life (K. Adler, 1980).

Adler did not believe that any event in childhood was causal of any particular symptom or psychological illness. Rather, when people develop a "neurosis," they bring up from memory events long past to give explanation to their current position (A. Adler, 1956, p. 289).

PSYCHODYNAMICS

Adler believed neurosis was not a disease in the sense of a medical illness, but a "mistaken way of living." The patient is not viewed as a victim of symptoms; rather, the symptoms are viewed as purposeful and chosen for some unconscious goal. The symptoms of depression are chosen because of life-style predisposition; specifically, the convictions which are formed from our interpretation of life experiences as we develop. The depressive unconsciously decides to meet life challenges with depressive symptoms.

Mosak (1985) stated that depressives can be grouped into two categories. The first group focuses on feelings of guilt. These people attribute all their ills to what they have done in the past or should have done, but didn't. They feel that they are failures and create a litany of how their acts have resulted in negative consequences. They depreciate themselves, verbalizing guilt for their shortcomings or what they consider evil actions in their past. They seem to hold themselves responsible for unfortunate happenings within the family, within the neighborhood, and, as their thinking becomes psychotic, for disasters in the nation and the world.

The second group attributes their feelings to something external that happened to them; some past misfortune. They create a litany about how life defeats them, is unjust, and how they never have been given a "fair shake." They have a feeling of hopelessness and helplessness about their situation.

Adler stated that:

> Neurosis and psychosis have the ultimate purpose (unconscious) of safeguarding people from a clash with life tasks—that is with reality—and of sparing them the danger of having the dark secret of their inferiority (or inadequacy) revealed to themselves and to others. (K. Adler, 1978, p. 14)

Whenever they are confronted with a problem for which they have not been sufficiently prepared, their mind, their feelings, and much of their body will strain to find a way to deal with this unexpected difficulty which would threaten to expose inadequacy to deal with the situation. Therefore, they will apply those methods of safeguarding self-image and self-esteem that they found effective as children. They usually will adhere to these techniques tenaciously, even when to all observers they are inappropriately and ineffectively dealing with the problem. Adler termed these methods **safeguarding devices.** Twelve years later Freud introduced the term **defense mechanisms** for this phenomenon (K. Adler, 1978, p. 14).

Depression is a special safeguarding device with specific characteristics. However, the individual seldom demonstrates all the psychodynamic manifestations of depression, since all individuals are creative and develop other defenses such as phobias, compulsions, or withdrawal, depending upon their previous learning and experience (K. Adler, 1961).

A description of the interrelatedness and various purposes of symptoms was explored by Mosak and Shulman (1967) and Mosak (1968).

The depressive tries to be better than others in some way in an attempt to overcome inferiority feelings and gain superiority (defined as moving from a perceived minus to a felt plus). This is often demonstrated by a lack of "social interest" or caring about other people and lack of cooperation. It is also manifested in intense competition in what has been described as vertical striving, focusing on who is better and who is a winner or a loser, rather than extending oneself to fellow human beings as an equal and a contributor.

This attitude of superiority, which is just under the surface of depressives, can be seen more clearly in the depressives who become psychotic. For example, they often claim to be the *worst* sinner, or the personification of the devil. They strive to be number one in a negative direction. This phenomenon has been described as downward ambition.

Mosak (1985) postulated that depressive symptomatology is chosen because of problems in the self-ideal and themes in the life-style. The depressives have the mistaken convictions that in order to have a place, to belong, to be significant, they should get, they should be good, and they should control or be in control. These convictions exist in various proportions in many people, but with the depressives, the problem is compounded because the "shoulds" become the imperative, "I must always." And if they do not or others do not provide, they then feel worthless and without significance.

The first theme, "having to get," becomes a demand that the world should give to them. If the world does not, then something is wrong and the world is blamed. As the person becomes angry, life is then accused of being unfair and inconsistent. Moreover, the demand includes that life should provide what is wanted on schedule; thus, the depressive is impatient.

These people also want "good things," not "bad things." Because of this factor, anger is not expressed, because if they expressed anger, others or life may not like them and may retaliate and then they may not get what they want. Further, these persons are trained or have trained themselves to do only in order to get. Since they rely on others to provide for them, they are poor problem solvers; thus, when life provides difficulties they often become discouraged, resigned, and give up. They have learned that if they create a good appearance, smile, and are enticing, the world will rescue them. This maneuver is also known as "learned helplessness" (Seligman & Maier, 1967).

The second theme, "I should always be good," is linked to perfectionism and can be seen as an "aspiration for sainthood." These people are often in a dilemma about doing what is good because people define "good" differently: should they do what they think is good or what others think is good? Often they are in conflict about "Which is the higher good?" or "Which is the lesser of two evils?" The result is vacillation and doubt. Therefore, they seek guidelines and standards and often are attracted to the study of philosophy and to churches that emphasize dogma. Since goodness is an imperative demand, being good 99% of the time is not sufficient. They strive for absolute perfection. Thus, any transgressions perpetrated in the past are constantly in their thoughts.

Individuals so engrossed with being good and perfect often find that people tend to stay away from them because they do not permit others to live their own lives. They moralize and tell others how to live better lives. "It is difficult living with a saint." They compensate by trying to convert others to their point of view in an attempt to have companionship.

The third central theme is wanting to control others or not wanting life to control them. Again, the key element is the imperative "always." In this particular theme, the person appears to aspire "to be God." Since the task is impossible as no one can be in control of everything all the time, the demand is frustrating. They begin to view the world as unfair and unjust and as an adversary (a place where one must be careful; otherwise, without vigilance, adversity can "sneak up on you"). Thus, these people are always on guard. They fear any sort of physical disability, even of a short duration like the flu, because they lose control. They also fear loss of control of their minds. They often state that they are afraid they are "going crazy" or "losing their minds." They also often verbalize fear of death and dying. This is based on the inability to control death; death will control them. Death is the realm of the unknown; thus, it is impossible to control.

Since these themes coexist in various proportions, they often interact and cause conflict within individuals. The "chocolate bar conflict" illustrates the interaction between the themes, "I should be good" and "I should always get." In this scenario, those who believe they need to always be good have a chocolate bar. They decide they would like some chocolate, but they are with a friend. In order to be "nice and good," they should share. So, they break the bar in half only to quickly note that the bar is not broken exactly in half. As a getter, they tell themselves they have to take the bigger piece; but to be good, they should take the smaller piece. If they are good, however, they will reason that they were "suckers" not to get the most. Thus, they put themselves into a "double bind" in which either choice will result in distress.

The next scenario is a conflict between "I should be good" and "I should control." This is known as the "cookie jar conflict." The persons in this instance want cookies that are in a jar. As they grasp as many of the cookies as they can, they discover the narrow opening stops them as they try to extract their hands. Thus, they perceive a loss of control. To drop some cookies places them in the dilemma of not getting as much as they want. Either way, they find themselves in another "double bind."

The last scenario involves the themes of having to be in control and "I have to be good." This Mosak (1985) called the "stoplight conflict." In this instance, people driving through a bad neighborhood at night stop at a stoplight. An assailant comes and starts smashing the window in order to gain access to the car. The companion asks why they don't drive away and they point to the red light. If they obey the law and be good, they are not in control of the situation; however, if they gain control and drive away, they will be rule violating and therefore not be good. They again are in a "double bind" because of the imperative "always" they impose on themselves.

These themes also are a contributing factor to the choice of depressive symptomatology. People who are nice and good do not give themselves permission to express anger to register a protest. When life doesn't permit the depressives to be in control, they will not allow themselves to express anger either because they are afraid of losing control, or they fear the consequences of their expression of anger. "If I lose my temper, someone may get hurt." The theme of getting will inhibit the expression of anger because of the fear that if anger is expressed, they may not like what they get or retaliation may occur, thus resulting in the holding back of further receiving.

Not only do the depressives not allow themselves to demonstrate anger, they deny anger and avoid acknowledging the emotion. When asked about anger they will often respond, "No, I am depressed." When asked further, they may reply that they are annoyed or they sometimes resent certain actions or they feel hurt. They refuse to use the word "angry." One reason for this avoidance is that if they acknowledge anger, then they might have to do something about the situation or the person provoking the anger. However, if *they* are hurt, then all they need to do is to deal with themselves rather than with the external problem. Thus, they develop a "sideshow" of depressive symptoms to "cloud the issue." Their ruminations about how they have to change themselves because they are failures and bad persons give them an excuse not to deal directly with the life task that is presenting a challenge. This is in contrast with the well-known concept of depression as aggression turned inward. Depression is better described as "a silent temper tantrum" or protest about the way life is proceeding (Mosak, 1985).

Desperation, Exploitation, and Guilt

Adler believed that neurotics are like people who believe they are drowning. Their focus is entirely on saving themselves. In such a situation they cannot appreciate the beautiful scenery around them. When others come to help them and try to save them, they will frantically try to clutch at them, jeopardizing everybody's lives. If they could cooperate with those who want to be of help, they could be saved. Similarly, neurotics are like people who feel constantly in danger of drowning and of succumbing to the dangers of life. They depreciate those who are trying to help them by proving them either incapable or not willing to try hard enough to help them (K. Adler, 1978).

The depressives' method of attaining superiority is not easily detected from their self-debasing statements. But the goal can be ascertained from examining the effect these verbalizations have on those who care about them. They worry about the depressives constantly; they reassure the depressives of their devotion and love. Because of the depressive's inability to function, they become forced into the person's service at great personal sacrifice. The net outcome is that the depressives are placed at the center of attention, their importance to others is reinforced, and they are relieved of obligations and given license to do whatever they want. "Only in fairy tales can a prince or princess command such a privileged position" (K. Adler, 1961, pp. 56-67).

Since they are unaware of the hidden purpose of gaining superiority, yet aware of how much others are doing for them, they express guilt feelings about exploiting others and being such a burden. Such guilt feelings are viewed as a prestige enhancer in which the depressives elevate themselves to a position of judges of their own behavior. In so doing, they profess even higher moral "goodness" than their behavior demonstrates. Guilt feelings have been described as an expression of "good intentions which one does not have" (Dreikurs, 1950, pp. 12-21).

In many cases the feelings are verbalized when the person does not want to end the morally-violating behavior, but still wants to appear good. An example would be married patients verbalizing depression and guilt because they have been having an affair for the past two or three years. Solutions are sought such as deciding which one of the partners is to be discarded by the patients who profess love for both, and depressives utilize guilt feelings as proof of their high moral character, in spite of their rule-violating behavior. "Adler explained their purpose and function as a device for appearing to oneself and others as noble and socially minded while persistent in exploitive actions (K. Adler, 1961, p. 57). Alfred Adler wrote, "In depression, the patient contents himself with merely expressing the sense of guilt while he would never think of exercising active contrition in the form of improved behavior" (A. Adler, 1956, p. 307).

Depreciation

When depressives are relatively free of symptoms, ambition compels them to pursue achievements where little risk for failure exists and where little effort is required. Whenever failure looms, however, they tend to shrink from the task and claim that, as usual, they are failures. They repeat to themselves and to all others who are willing to listen a litany of pessimism. The repetition of pessimistic self-defeating ideation, of course, leads them to fulfill their own prophecy as they further undermine their self-confidence. Indirectly, however, the failure is often blamed on relatives or friends who somehow did not fulfill their obligations, the method by which they were reared, some "biochemical imbalance," and/or heredity (A. Adler, 1979b, p.249). They depreciate those trying to help by not responding, proving them incapable or not trying hard enough to help. They are usually unaware of how their thinking and actions are actually contributory or generating the depression. Pessimistically, they anticipate dire outcomes from which they cannot be saved or helped, nor can they help or save themselves.

Depressives tend to catastrophize. They become preoccupied with the thought of how miserable they will become if the undesired occurs. Alfred Adler stated:

> That dynamic can best be observed in depressed or melancholic individuals who live as if the misfortune has already happened (A. Adler, 1956, p. 283). The categorical imperative of melancholia is "act, think, feel in such a way as if the horrible fate that you have conjured up had already befallen you and was inevitable." (A. Adler, 1956, p. 321 also A. Adler, 1979b, p.250)

Proving Illness and Maintenance of Symptoms

The suffering of depressed persons is genuine, although usually exaggerated. The depressives want relief and sincerely want to give up their symptoms. However, since symptoms were generated as a protection against a loss of prestige and self-esteem, depressives are prevented from relinquishing symptoms because they fear the consequences. As Alfred Adler stated, it is "The danger of death through loss of prestige" (A. Adler, 1956, p. 266).

In their attempts to certify their illness, patients' continuous ruminations over misfortune, hopelessness, helplessness, and inadequacy affect their whole body. The depressives begin to neglect themselves and their outward appearance, sleep becomes disordered, they do not care about eating and may actually lose weight, and even bodily functions, such as bowel movements, are disturbed. An interesting point to note is that Adler remarked, "We want to stress especially that toxins are released by the endocrine glands through the effect of rage and grief by way of the vegetative nervous system" (K. Adler, 1961, p. 59). The result of all these obvious signs of deterioration and physical complications is definite proof to all that a truly serious condition exists that needs care and assistance from others, and that they must be relieved from all obligations to occupation, social relations, and marriage (K. Adler, 1961).

In addition, a depressive has to maintain his/her symptoms. For this purpose several mechanisms are utilized. One is not to take responsibility for the symptom, to believe that the symptoms spontaneously recur and remit and that nothing can be done to change the pattern. The second mechanism is to fight against the symptoms and, by fighting against them, actually reinforce the symptoms. The third is to feel sorry for oneself constantly for having the symptoms and endlessly search for the cause or worry about the dire consequences if the symptoms continue.

Sometimes recognition of the success of their suffering is evidenced by the occasional slight secret smile observed on the faces of depressives when they count the extent others have tried to help because of their depression or how frustrated others are about the situation. Kurt Adler (1961, p. 61) cited a Viennese playwright, Mestroy, as recognizing this phenomenon years ago through a character who states, "If I could not annoy people with my melancholia I wouldn't enjoy it at all."

If the patients actually did enjoy suffering the symptoms, it would mean that they had lost contact with the ties of social interest and "the logical reason that binds us all," and thus have become psychotic. Some depressives do develop delusions and hallucinations. This theoretically occurs when inferiority feelings are so great and the overambitious idealized goals are so lofty that distortion of reality is the only possible protection (K. Adler, 1961).

Suicide

A common symptom that occurs with depressives is that of suicidal ideation, intent, or attempts. The childhood forerunners of such symptoms have been previously discussed as a method of revenge and protest. Similar motives can be suspected in adults. Sometimes suicidal patients will even admit that they fantasized family and friends crying and feeling guilty for what they had done to or not done for the patient. This also reveals the aggressive, hostile, unconscious motivation of the act against significant others.

The attempt to commit suicide may seem a contradiction to the theme of "being good"; however, depressed individuals use various techniques to justify such an action. They may just give up and decide that the possibility of being good all the time is impossible; therefore, they might as well give up and no longer be good and decide to end their lives. Others, however, rationalize suicide as being an altruistic act. They state that their friends and family will be better off without them, that the family will collect insurance and be able to clear up many debts they accrued because of the way they have failed.

Suicide can have other interpersonal dynamics. As an example, some people have a difficult time admitting they need help because of fear of loss of prestige or sometimes because of a self-concept or family concept that to seek help means weakness. In these situations the suicide attempt may be a cry for help. It forces people to recognize the desperation of patients and places patients in a position where they can be legally "forced" to receive treatment. In many suicide attempts, patients finally arrange the opportunity to discuss dissatisfactions with their lives or their marriages when previous attempts to do so were unsuccessful.

Threats of suicide also have been used as a form of coercion and "blackmail." Perhaps the most common example would be the lover who is using coercive tactics to continue a relationship: "If you leave me, my life is not worth living; I'll kill myself." Threats of suicide have been effective in preventing parents from insisting that a child in the mid-twenties or older become employed or leave home. Similarly, suicide attempts can be used as an escape from a potentially disgraceful situation. As an example, a college student facing final examinations with insufficient preparation and high personal goals for achievement may make a suicide attempt in order to be hospitalized and thus have an excuse not to take the finals.

Even in the escape motivation, an element of revenge due to perceived unfairness is often visible with the refrain as stated by Kurt Adler (1961, p. 60), "See what you have driven me to do; now you will suffer for the rest of your life for it. Missing me you will realize what a rare and sensitive person I was." Perhaps the statement needs to be made again that these interpersonal dynamics are usually unconscious; the patient is usually unaware of the hidden motivations for such an action.

INTEGRATION OF SOMATIC AND PSYCHOLOGICAL THERAPIES

Although Adler believed firmly that the medical model was not valid for neuroses (and to some extent psychoses) and believed them to be "mistaken ways of living," he nevertheless acknowledged that physicians were the ones who were best trained for the supervision, if not for the actual treatment, of neuroses and psychoses because of their understandings of the diseases associated with depressive symptoms, the somatic concomitants of mental disorders, and the differential diagnosis that was necessary to ascertain where an organic, physical factor was present (K. Adler, 1980). However, he also wrote that some mental disorders, specifically psychosis, epilepsy, melancholia and schizophrenia, might have an organic etiology: although " here, too, a part is played by the exogenous situation" (A. Adler, 1979a, p. 230).

Since many somatic treatments can offer significant relief of suffering within two to eight weeks, an essential first step in any therapy process is to conduct an active differential diagnosis to ascertain whether the depressive's symptoms are partially or completely correctable by medications or electroconvulsive therapy.

Since Individual Psychology is an holistic, not a reductionistic psychology, many have taught that diagnosis can interfere with understanding the dynamics of a patient and the therapeutic process. With the dissemination of recent depression research to the public and the demands of third-party payors, this position is increasingly untenable. The reductionistic process of accurate diagnosis is imperative in establishing whether the person is likely to respond to a somatic therapy and what treatment approach is most likely to benefit the patient.

The proof of any theory, whether it be psychodynamic, genetic, or biochemical, is its usefulness. One benefit of somatic theories is that they alleviate guilt feelings which prevent improvement. The blockage that guilt produces is often removed with the discovery of a physical cause of depression, such as a probable genetic basis or abnormal cortisol levels. Patients are then free to learn how to manage their illness and use all the treatment modalities that are available. Often they are then more open to learn psychological techniques that will lessen the probability of relapse and lead more positively productive lives.

Trying to treat a psychotic depression or even a non-psychotic melancholic depression with psychotherapy alone is somewhat similar to trying to use psychotherapy with an intoxicated alcoholic or an alcoholic going through withdrawal. A certain amount of supportive dialogue is essential to explain what is being done and to establish a positive relationship. However, often an impairment of concentration and memory and a preoccupation with current physical symptoms occur to such an extent that to establish meaningful insight is difficult. Once acute withdrawal is completed and less organic disruption of cognitive functioning is present, the patient is not only more open to learn, but also better able to learn. A parallel can be made to the depressive. During melancholic stupor or when psychotically depressed, to develop psychological insight is difficult. Once the major symptoms are cleared with medication or ECT and a determination is made as to whether or not psychological symptoms persist, the more insight-oriented therapies can be very helpful. The previously described psychodynamics fit some depressed patients. What remains to be ascertained is to which diagnostic categories they are applicable. We can speculate that they are more apt to fit the characterological depressives, although some dysthymics and major depressives also can demonstrate these psychodynamics. Moreover, these traits can be seen in some non-depressive patients.

Kurt Adler (1983) stated that in evaluating the biochemical findings we must ask, what is really proved? Can these biochemical changes such as low serotonin levels in people who have made suicide attempts be brought about by attitudes, ways of looking at life, as well as some biochemical deficiency? Every time a person sees, hears, feels, tastes, thinks, the biochemistry of the body is changed, the endocrine output is changed. As an example, if something is said to bring a blush to a person's face, the blush is a reaction to what was heard and how it was interpreted. The person's thinking affects this feeling and produces an endocrine biochemical change that results in the dilation of blood vessels in the face. Blushing requires an endocrine reaction to be transmitted. With medication, often

> the patient feels amelioration of the symptoms that accompany depression. The patient feels encouraged and psychotherapy will often be more accepted by the patient. When I give some of my patients antidepressant drugs, and I do with some, not many, patients, I usually tell

them that this drug will ameliorate their physical symptoms and they may find that they can live without depression. But, we have to work very hard together to find for what purpose they always create depression, how they develop the idea that this was the best way to achieve significance. Because only they can make the depression. (K. Adler, 1983, p. 298)

A recent multi-center study comparing two psychotherapies with an antidepressant (Imipramine) and a placebo demonstrated that for less severely depressed patients (*Hamilton Rating Scale for Depression* total score less than 20) all the therapies, including the placebo with case management, produced significant improvement. Moreover, they did not differ significantly from each other. However, for the subgroup of patients who were more severely depressed and functionally impaired, Imipramine was much more effective than the placebo and the two psychotherapies fell between those treatments in effectiveness. Several surprises came from these findings, namely that the placebo in clinical management was unexpectedly effective in the mildly depressed patients. Apparently encouragement, attention, and empathy may be more therapeutic than previously thought. One limitation of the study was that the patients were all relatively well-educated outpatients who were non-psychotic (Elkin et al., 1989).

These results corroborate many of the points made earlier, that depression is a complex group of disorders for which a variety of effective interventions exist. Since criteria on effective treatment for specific subgroups have not yet been established, factors such as patient's goals, time, financial limitations, sensitivity to side effects, and severity of symptoms will have to be considered in deciding which intervention to utilize.

ADLERIAN PSYCHOTHERAPY
OF DEPRESSION

Change can transpire in many ways. To discuss comprehensively the procedure of Adlerian psychotherapy is beyond the scope of this chapter. The reader is referred to Dreikurs' (1967) and Mosak's (1984) discussions of the process.

However, some specific applications of techniques will be outlined.

Generally, the Adlerian therapist is a teacher, and the teacher shares what he/she knows about the illness. Thus, if the symptoms include a melancholic or psychotic aspect, the biochemical and genetic theories of the illness are explained, as well as references to readings designed for the layperson. When psychological issues are identified, the steps of self-understanding through the gathering of life-style data and the purpose of psychotherapy are discussed with the patient.

At the beginning of treatment, both Alfred and Kurt Adler advocated avoiding conflicts or battle with patients. Depressive patients are already irritable, angry, ready for battle. The recommendation is that the therapist establish with patients the fact that the therapist is completely powerless without patients' cooperation. To people who have developed patterns of depending upon others for assistance and expect the "doctor" to miraculously save them from their symptoms, this approach often comes as a shock. The second tactic is to make clear to patients that nothing is demanded or expected from them. "Never do anything you don't like" (A. Adler, 1956, p. 346). This tactic has several effects. First, it relieves depressives of pressures of having to perform. The depressive is given a status to do as he/she wants, free from social pressure and restraint. The therapist thus removes him/herself as an adversary. This tactic can be further enhanced by initially advising relatives that the patients are too ill to fulfill their usual roles and responsibilities and that they will need several weeks to recover.

The process of psychotherapy is compared, on occasion, with Dorothy's quest in the *Wizard of Oz* (Pancner & Pancner, 1988). Parables and fables are utilized to illustrate various crucial dynamics found in the patient's behavior or thinking (Pancner, 1978). For example, to illustrate how we maintain symptoms by fighting against them, we use the fable of the king who gave one-half of his kingdom for the power to turn lead into gold; however, he was informed after making the agreement that the ability would only be present if he would not think about the word "crocodile." And, of course, with that requirement, he would dwell on how not to think about. crocodile and thus constantly think about crocodiles.

The antidote to this dilemma is the technique of "antisuggestion" as described by Ervin Wexberg, later named **Paradoxical Intention** by Victor Frankl (1960). In this technique, instead of fighting the symptoms, the person is encouraged to act out the symptoms and try to create them even more often. Adler utilized paradox in treatment, calling it "prescribing the symptoms." He utilized this technique when patients indicated they wanted to stay in bed all day. Adler agreed that this was what patients needed to do. When patients complained of being in bed all day, they would be reminded of the rule of not doing anything they disliked doing; thus, they were free to get up from bed if they so wished.

To deal with the areas of distrust of others and competitiveness, Adler (A. Adler, 1956, p. 347) utilized the statement, "You can be cured in 14 days if you will follow my prescription to try to think every day, 'How I can please someone.'" This can be further magnified by actually assigning the task of doing something to be helpful to another on a daily basis. Adler stated:

> All my efforts are devoted to increasing social interest of a patient. I know that the real reason for his malady is lack of cooperation, and I want him to see it too. As soon as he can connect himself with his fellow men on an equal and cooperative footing, he is cured. (A. Adler, 1956, p. 347)

Another useful modality for attaining this goal is the therapeutic group, particularly with other depressives with whom identification can easily occur. This imparts a feeling of belonging, of not being alone, not being unique, and eventually more courage and increased self-esteem.

Adlerian therapy was systemized by Dreikurs (1967) as consisting of four essential overlapping stages in the therapeutic process. First, establish a rapport between the therapist and client. In this relationship, mutual trust, cooperation, and respect need to develop. An agreement as to goals and objectives for the relationship is essential. In the second stage the patient's current behavior is examined in relationship to their perceptions which have been developed. Specifically, the current life situation is examined in the light of the life-style assessment (Mosak, 1958; Mosak & Gushurst, 1972). The possible purpose of the current symptoms is identified. The emphasis in this process is an investigating, uncovering, and seeking to perceive life from the patient's point of view.

In the third stage, the therapist extracts from these personality characteristics an underlying behavior pattern and explains the dynamics to the patient. They learn about their self-concept or self-ideal, their view of their environment, what people are like, what life is like, what their ethical convictions are, how they believe they should act and others should act, and their method of operation for attaining their goals. In addition, they are made aware of their mistaken apperception, those convictions that somehow interfere with their optimal functioning.

In therapy, patients' distorted perceptions and pessimistic predictions must be pointed out and patients convinced that they are produced for a purpose, the purpose being to avoid assuming responsibility because of the crippling perceptions about themselves and the world that formed in childhood. With more optimistic anticipation they can recognize the strengths within their personalities. They will then enjoy entering into cooperative relationships with others, removing the need to attempt to dominate others since people will no longer seem so hostile and threatening.

In the last stage, clients are encouraged to implement these insights into changing their behavior. The hope is that patients will learn to recognize patterns of the past and how they tend to recur persistently. They first learn to catch themselves on the verge of repeating the pattern; then patients are asked to make a decision whether to do things differently. If they try a new method and it is successful, then with support they are urged to continue the new method until it becomes comfortable. With successful practice of the new methods, their perceptions on life are influenced and changed (Nikelly, 1971).

Throughout treatment the therapist needs to demonstrate to patients that they are held in high esteem, that recognition is made that some of their actions and perceptions are based on childhood perceptions. Their misperceptions can be corrected through education and their effort. As they develop their human potential they will discover how this experience is gratifying and expanding.

Mosak (1985) advocated the use of the "pushbutton technique" to demonstrate to patients that they don't have to remain unhappy. In this exercise patients are asked to recall some positive and pleasant event, then to picture the experience in their minds and enjoy the feelings that came from the situation. Next, they are asked to do the same with an episode that was unpleasant. When they have opportunity to picture, project, and feel those emotions, they are again assigned to pick a positive incident and repeat the process. Mosak then asks patients if they noticed anything during the exercise. They usually respond that they felt happy and enthusiastic during the first and third exercises. This technique is utilized to illustrate to them that when they think about disasters and unpleasant experiences, they are going to feel badly. It further demonstrates that what one thinks has a large effect on how one feels, leading to the conclusion that patients create their feelings and also maintain them. Once that is discovered, they often no longer feel as helpless or hopeless (Mosak, 1985).

THE PREVENTION OF SUICIDE

Perhaps the most critical psychological treatment situation is the emergency brought forth by suicidal ideation or attempt. Kurt Adler (1980, p. 173) advocated treating suicidal, depressed patients with vigorous, open confrontation to uncover the hidden rage, hostility, and revenge. This is necessary because the patients try to hide their inner motives by noble motives such as to relieve others of the burden of having to care for them. When the therapist exposes the rage, hostility, and revenge motives against those whom they profess to love, patients have difficulty in maintaining the illusion that their pretended high and noble motives will be believed. Thus, patients' hope that suicide will make them appear noble and well-meaning disappears. Moreover, when faced with the anger and revenge interpretation, suicide becomes ego-dystonic, and the act of suicide will not be consistent with the idealized self-image.

Kurt Adler (1980) tells patients that the revenge motive of suicide is well-known, that people hide suicides, do not talk about them, and try to forget them as quickly as possible. Many religions do not permit suicides to be buried with the faithful because the deviousness of the act is such common knowledge. He points out that, contrary to some glorified notions and stories to indicate that suicide is a heroic act which requires courage, escape from one's problems shows a lack of courage. Suicide is doing exactly that—running from one's problems.

To counter the rationale that, "This is my life and my decision as to whether or not I want to live or die," Adler would tell them that they fool themselves, but they cannot fool him as to why they consider suicide. They are actively thinking of someone else who they want to punish, make feel guilty, and make suffer. He then further adds that the suffering of the significant other is not a certainty, that they may be relieved to finally be rid of the burden of the relationship. He tries to put a doubt in their minds that the suicide will fulfill their goal of making their significant other suffer. In the attempt at making suicide ego-alien, he emphasizes that they will not look noble, but by committing suicide, they will look hateful, mean, and stupid.

For those who profess a love so strong that they cannot live without their chosen other, Kurt Adler (1980, p. 174) again counters strongly, telling them,

> not to make such phony pretenses; everyone can see that they want their mates to feel guilt and want to punish them for leaving. The main drive is not love, but hatred and lust for revenge. Since when is blackmailing a person proof of undying love?

To those depressives who are suicidal professing that they want to free their relatives to whom they are a burden, he again confronts sharply, stating that their purpose is only to show relatives how noble-minded they are while the relatives are low-minded. Their inner motive is for relatives to suffer guilt for the rest of their lives, which is an unloving act, a tactic which again makes suicide ego-alien.

Kurt Adler (1980) believed that although these tactics may seem unfair and even cruel, this is justified in such an emergency. Strong, quick action has to be taken to smash the illusions under which a suicidal depressive operates, making it virtually impossible for them to attempt suicide. He stressed the importance, however, of first having convinced patients that while they are valued by the therapist, their actions or manipulations are not (K. Adler, 1961). Patients are advised that their actions are understandable, that they stem from attitudes and techniques that were learned in early childhood, and that they have utilized these tactics without realizing their self-defeating aspects (K. Adler, 1980). It also can be pointed out that other ways exist to express dissatisfaction and anger to others that have a much greater chance of succeeding and bringing about significant change and that they have the capability to learn these new techniques and ways of coping with life's challenges.

CONCLUSION

An important point is to conceptualize major depressive illness holistically, to view the process as a function of many factors. The genetic, biochemical, and organic factors are probably activated by the level of stress in most cases. The level of stress is determined by individuals' perception of life events. Stress can be reduced by certain positive factors such as the individuals' extent of competence or capacity to cope, their self-esteem, and their support system. Mental illness from all indications is not attributable to simple "cause and effect," but is the product of an interplay of many factors.

Bernard H. Shulman (1983) has pointed out that it would be a mistake to diagnose on the basis of the biochemical tests alone, and to make etiological inferences about any biochemical tests is a mistake. A test is a measurement at a certain point in time of what is happening in a certain process. Tests are useful for suggesting that depression should be considered and that the patient may respond to certain types of antidepressant medication. While the organic theorist will tend to view abnormal tests as causal, the psychodynamic theorist will tend to perceive them only as a correlation or possibly as a consequence of psychological events inside the person rather than cause.

Adlerian theory is a psychodynamic theory, but also recognizes the existence of constitutional factors.

> It gives us direction for research, for re-examining the old Adlerian ideas of "organ inferiority" or the constitutional diathesis. Are people who suffer from depression more inclined to do so because they are born with a tendency in that direction, or are they more likely to become depressed because they have been exposed to certain life experiences, have come to certain conclusions about them, and on the basis of their creative selves have devised a method of response and attitude toward life which we would call a tendency to become depressed when life becomes difficult? It is difficult to determine how much is learning, how much is the creative self, how much is in the constitutional diathesis.
>
> The challenge of these discoveries is to bring together what we are learning about the body and what we believe psychodynamically and fit them together. After all, Adlerian theory says that the body and mind work together and if Adlerian theory cannot make the mind and body work together we will have to invent a new theory. (Shulman, 1983)

Acknowledgement

I am deeply grateful to Kurt Adler and Harold Mosak, whose lectures and presentations provided most of the concepts for the psychodynamics of this chapter. I am also indebted to Robert Doyal and Ann Wheeler for their editorial assistance.

REFERENCES

Adler, A. (1956). H. Ansbacher & R. Ansbacher (Eds.), *The Individual Psychology of Alfred Adler*, pp. 239-349. New York: Harper & Row.

Adler, A. (1979a). *Superiority and social interest* (3rd ed). H. Ansbacher & R. Ansbacher (Eds.). New York: W.W. Norton.

Adler, A. (1979b). Melancholia and paranoia (1914). In *Practice and theory of Individual Psychology*, pp. 246-262. Patterson, NJ: Littlefield Adams.

Adler, K. (1961). Depression in the light of Individual Psychology. *Journal of Individual Psychology, 17*, 56-67.

Adler, K. (1978, March). *The contribution of Individual Psychology to the mental health professions.* Lecture delivered at Kean College of New Jersey.

Adler, K. (1980). Depression and suicide as they relate to intimacy and communication. *Modern Psychoanalysis, 5*(2), 167-176.

Adler, K. (1983, May). Discussant at symposium presented at the North American Society of Adlerian Psychology, Boulder, CO.

Akiskal, H.S. (1983). Dysthymic disorder psychopathology of proposed chronic depressive subtypes. *American Journal of Psychiatry, 140*, 11-20.

Akiskal, H.S. (1989). New insights into the nature of heterogeneity of mood disorders. *Journal of Clinical Psychiatry, 50*, (Suppl: 6-10).

Akiskal, H.S., & Lemmi, H. (1983, March). Clinical, neuroendocrine, and sleep EEG diagnosis of "unusual" affective presentations: A practical review. In *Psychiatric Clinics of North America, 6*(1), 69-83.

American Psychiatric Association. (1987). *Diagnostic and statistical manual of mental disorders* (3rd ed., revised). Washington, DC: Author

Ballenger, J.C., Goodwin, F.K., & Major, L.F. (1979). Alcohol and central serotonin metabolism in man. *Archives of General Psychiatry, 36*, 224-227.

Bertelson, A., Harvald, B., & Hauge, M. (1977). A Danish twin study of manic-depressive disorders. *British Journal of Psychiatry, 130*, 330-351.

Brown, G.L., Ebert, M.H., & Goyer, P.F. (1982). Aggression, suicide, and serotonin: Relationships to CSF amine metabolites. *American Journal of Psychiatry, 139*, 6.

Carroll, B.J., Feinberg, M., Greden, J.F., et al. (1981). A specific laboratory test for the diagnosis of melancholia. Standardization, validation, and clinical utility. *Archives of General Psychiatry, 38*, 15-22.

Cooper, J.E., Kendall, R.E., & Gurland, B.J. (1972). *Psychiatric diagnosis in New York and London: A comparative study of mental hospital admissions.* (Institute of Psychiatry, Maudsley Monograph No. 20). London: Oxford University Press.

Coryell, W., Lavori, P., & Endicott, J. (1984). Outcome in schizophrenia, affective, psychotic and nonpsychotic depression course during a 6- to 24-month follow-up. *Archives of General Psychiatry, 41*, 787-791.

Dreikurs, R. (1950). Guilt feelings as an excuse. *Individual Psychology Bulletin, 8*, 12-21.

Dreikurs, R. (1967). *Psychodynamics, psychotherapy and counseling.* Collected Papers. Chicago: Alfred Adler Institute.

Egeland, J.A., Gerhard, D.S., & Pauls, D.L. (1987). Bipolar disorders linked to DNA markers on chromosome II. *Nature, 325*, 783-787.

Elkin, I., Shea, M.T., Watkins, J.T., Imber, S.D., Stotsky, S.M., Collins, J.F., Glass, D.R., Pilkonis, P.A., Leber, W.R., Docherty, J.P., Fiester, S.J., & Parloff, M.B. (1989). National Institute of Mental Health treatment of depression collaborative research program. *Archives of General Psychiatry, 46*, 971-982.

Frankl, V. (1960). Paradoxical intention: A logotherapeutic technique. *American Journal of Psychotherapy, 14*, 520-535.

Freud, S. (1953). Mourning and melancholia. In *Complete Psychological Works*, standard ed., vol. 14. London: Hogarth Press.

Georgotos, A. (1983). Monoamine metabolites in CSF and suicidal behavior. *Intelligence Reports in Psychiatric Disorders, 2*, 15.

Gold, M.S., Pottash, L.C., Extein, I., & Sweeney, D.R. (1981). Diagnosis of depression in the 1980s. *Journal of the American Medical Association, 245*, 1562-1564.

Hirschfeld, R.M.A., & Cross, C.K. (1982). Epidemiology of affective disorders: Psychosocial risk factors. *Archives of General Psychiatry, 39*, 35-46.

Hirschfeld, R.M.A., & Goodwin, F.K. (1988). Mood disorders. *Textbook of Psychiatry.* J.A. Talbott, R.E. Hales, & S.C. Yudofsky (Eds.). Chapter 13, 403-441. Washington, DC: American Psychiatric Press.

Hirschfeld, R.M.A., Klerman, G.L., & Clayton, P.J. (1983). Personality and depression: Empirical findings. *Archives of General Psychiatry, 40*, 993-998.

Jenike, M.A. (1982). Dexamethasone suppression: A biological marker of depression. *Drug Therapy, 7*, 73-82.

Keller, M.B., Lavori, P.W., & Endicott, J. (1983). "Double depression": Two-year follow-up. *American Journal of Psychiatry, 140*, 689-695.

Loosen, P.T., Prange, A.J., Jr., Wilson, I.C., Lara, P.P., & Pettus, C. (1977). Thyroid stimulating hormone response after thyrotropin releasing hormone in depressed schizophrenic and normal women. *Psychoneuroendocrinology, 2*, 137-148.

Mosak, H.H. (1958). Early recollections as a projective technique. *Journal of Projective Techniques, 22*(3), 302-311.

Mosak, H.H. (1968). The interrelatedness of the neurosis through central themes. *Journal of Individual Psychology, 24*, 67-70.

Mosak, H.H. (1984). Adlerian psychotherapy. In R. Corsini and Contributors (Eds.), *Current psychotherapies* (3rd ed.) (pp. 56-107). Itasca, IL: F.E. Peacock Publishers, Inc.

Mosak, H.H. (1985). *The assumptive universe of the depressive.* Paper presented at the meeting of the North American Society of Adlerian Psychology, Atlanta, GA.

Mosak, H.H. & Gushurst, R.H. (1972). Some therapeutic uses of psychologic testing. *American Journal of Psychotherapy, 26* (4), 539-546.

Mosak, H.H., & Shulman, B.H. (1967). Various purposes of symptoms. *Journal of Individual Psychology, 23*, 79-87.

Myers, J.K., Weissman, M.M., & Tischler, G.L. (1984). Six-month prevalence of psychiatric disorders in three communities. *Archives of General Psychiatry, 41*, 959-967.

Nikelly, A.G. (Ed.). (1971). *Techniques for behavior change: Applications for Adlerian theory.* Springfield, IL: Charles C. Thomas.

Pancner, K.L. (1978). The use of parables and fables in Adlerian psychotherapy. *The Individual Psychologist, 15*, 19-29.

Pancner, K.L., & Pancner, R.J. (1988). The quest, gurus, and the yellow brick road. *Individual Psychology, 44*, 158-166.

Pancner, R.J. (1985). Impact of current depression research on Adlerian theory and practice. *Individual Psychology, 41*, 289-301.

Paykel, E.S. (1978). Contribution of life events to causation of psychometric illness. *Psychol Med, 8*, 245-253.

Pflug, B., & Tolle, R. (1971). Disturbance of the 24-hour rhythm in endogenous depression and the treatment of endogenous depression by sleep deprivation. *International Pharmacopsychiatry, 6*, 187-196.

Robins, E., & Guze, S.B. (1970). Suicide and primary affective disorder. *American Journal of Psychiatry, 126,* 107-111.

Rosenthal, N.E., Sack, D.A., & Gillin, J.C. (1984). Seasonal affective disorder: A description of the syndrome and preliminary findings with light therapy. *Archives of General Psychiatry, 41,* 72-80.

Sachar, E.J., Asnis, G., & Halbreich, U. (1980). Recent studies in the neuroendocrinology of major depressive disorders. *Psychiatric Clinics of North America, 3,* 313-326.

Sack, D.A., Nurnburger, J., & Rosenthal, N.E. (1985). The potentiation of antidepressant medications by phase-advance of the sleep-wake cycle. *American Journal of Psychiatry, 142,* 606-608.

Schilgen, B., & Tolle, R. (1980). Partial sleep deprivation as therapy for depression. *Archives of General Psychiatry, 37,* 267-271.

Seligman, M., & Maier, S. (1967). Failure to escape traumatic shock. *Journal of Experimental Psychology, 74,* 1-9.

Shulman, B.H. (1983, May). Discussant at meeting of the North American Society of Adlerian Psychology, Boulder, CO.

Targum, S.D. (1983). Neuroendocrine challenge studies in clinical psychiatry. *Psychiatric Annals, 13,* 385-395.

Thoren, P., Ansberg, M., & Bertilsson, L., (1980). Clomipramine treatment of obsessive-compulsive disorder: II. Biochemical aspects. *Archives of General Psychiatry, 37,* 1289-1294.

Traskman, L., Asberg, M., Bertilsson, L., & Sjostrang, L. (1981). Monoamine metabolites in CSF and suicidal behavior. *Archives of General Psychiatry, 38,* 631-636.

Weissman, M.M., & Boyd, J.H. (1982). The epidemiology of affective disorders, rates and risk factors. In L. Grinspoon (Ed.), *American Psychiatric Association Annual Review* (Vol. 2) (pp. 406-428). Washington, DC: American Psychiatric Press.

Weissman, M., Klerman, G.L., Prusoff, B.A., Sholomskas, D., & Padian, N. (1981). Depressed outpatients. *Archives of General Psychiatry, 38,* 51-55.

PART III

ANXIETY, SOMATOFORM, AND DISSOCIATIVE DISORDERS

OVERVIEW

Prior to the publication of DSM-III in 1980, a distinction was made between psychotic and neurotic disorders. The first section of this book dealt with what used to be called the psychoses. This section deals with what used to make up the neuroses. Whereas Adler (1956) considered psychosis to be a "No!" in response to the challenges of life, he believed:

> Neurosis is always behavior which can be expressed in two words, the words "Yes—but." This is the best and easiest definition because it distinguishes a neurosis from all other types of failure and the neurotic from the normal person. (p. 302)

When faced with challenges, Adlerians believe "normal," that is, socially interested people, will respond with a "Yes—I can" attitude. These people will focus not upon themselves and their own prestige (i.e., inferiorities), but upon the task at hand. They are task-oriented rather than prestige-oriented. Psychotics will respond with a "No!" attitude, refusing to even acknowledge the request or demand. Neurotics will acknowledge the demand (the "Yes" part of the response), but they will hesitate and attempt to excuse themselves (the "but" portion of the response): "Yes, I know what to do, but I can't, because of . . . fears . . . pains . . . etc."

Dreikurs (1967), in differentiating neurotic from psychotic disorders psychodynamically, noted that whereas psychotics discarded common sense in favor of their private logic, neurotics had a firmly developed common sense that they hoped to disqualify. Neurotics followed their private logic, but they maintained enough of their common sense to at least act as if they were outwardly compliant. Unlike the psychotics, they at least acknowledged the challenge.

Sperry, in Chapter 6, begins this section with "Anxiety Disorders I," a discussion of the Panic, Obsessive Compulsive, and Agoraphobic Disorders. He discusses the biopsychosocial components of each condition, along with latest research into treatment strategies.

In Chapter 7, "Anxiety Disorders II" by O'Connell and Hooker, are discussed the Post-Traumatic Stress Disorder, Generalized Anxiety Disorder, and Social Phobia. This chapter presents O'Connell's unique interpretation of Individual Psychology and his many years of experience working with very troubled individuals from a multiplicity of life experiences, ranging from such common occurrences as being worried about attending social gatherings to the horrors and devastation involved in being in a combat zone, fighting for survival.

Mays, in Chapter 8, elaborates upon the "Somatoform Disorders and Psychological Factors Affecting Physical Conditions." He introduces the Adlerian concept of organ jargon and analyzes from the vantage point of the holistic hypothesis in order to understand and intervene in conditions that, by definition, "speak through the body."

Chapter 9, the final chapter in this section, deals with the rather infrequently discussed topic of "Dissociative Disorders." Sperry, in a truly integrative fashion, reviews the works of not only Adler but also Janet, Freud, and Prince in order to illuminate what have traditionally been some of the most elusive of all conditions to conceptualize and treat.

REFERENCES

Adler, A. (1956). *The Individual Psychology of Alfred Adler*. H. L. Ansbacher & R. R. Ansbacher (Eds.). New York: Basic Books.

Dreikurs, R. (1967). *Psychodynamics, psychotherapy, and counseling*. Chicago: Alfred Adler Institute.

CHAPTER 6

ANXIETY DISORDERS I

Len Sperry, M.D., Ph.D.

The anxiety disorders are perhaps the most common clinical conditions diagnosed and treated by mental health professionals. The designation Anxiety Disorders in DSM-III-R refers to seven discrete clinical entities: Panic Disorders, Agoraphobia, Simple Phobia, Social Phobia, Obsessive Compulsive Disorder, Post-traumatic Stress Disorder, Generalized Anxiety Disorder, and an eighth category Anxiety Disorders Not Otherwise Specified (NOS). Previously these disorders were classified in DSM-I and DSM-II as neuroses or neurotic disorders.

The terms fear and anxiety have been variously defined, but in this chapter we will utilize the definitions of Beck and Emery (1985). They distinguished anxiety from fear by defining fear as a cognitive assessment of a threatening stimuli, while anxiety is an emotional reaction to that assessment. As anxiety is experienced, a number of physiological reactions, particularly symptoms associated with the autonomic nervous system, may occur simultaneously. When we speak of the anxiety disorders, we can differentiate the variety of manifestations of anxiety. For instance, overwhelming anxiety is either the predominant disturbance as it is manifested in Panic Disorders and Generalized Anxiety Disorders, or anxiety experienced as a person attempts to master symptoms, as when confronting a dreaded object or situation in phobic disorders. However, when the anxiety is manifested when resisting an obsession or a compulsion, then an Obsessive Compulsive Disorder would be diagnosed.

A few generalizations are in order about the anxiety disorders. With a possible exception of Social Phobia, these disorders develop most frequently in young women and generally have a poor prognosis and a chronic unremitting course when appropriate treatment is not provided. These disorders occur relatively frequently. The most comprehensive epidemiological study of mental illness in the United States, the *Epidemiologic Catchment Area* (ECA) study, reported high lifetime problems rates between 10% and 25% (Robins, Helzer, & Weissman, 1984). Even though the prevalence rate is quite high, only a small percentage of individuals with these disorders is ever treated by a professional therapist. This chapter will describe three anxiety disorders: Panic Disorder, Obsessive Compulsive Disorder, and Agoraphobia. The next chapter will focus on other Phobias, Generalized Anxiety Disorder, and Post-traumatic Stress Disorder. The plan for this chapter is to present each disorder descriptively or phenomenologically, including DSM-III-R criteria, a clinical formulation in terms of Adlerian theory, and a brief section on treatment goals and methods. Also, a case study is provided that exemplifies each disorder.

PANIC DISORDER

Panic attacks are the cardinal feature for panic disorders. The panic or anxiety attack has dramatic, acute symptoms lasting minutes to hours and is usually self-limited. Symptoms are perceived by the individual as medical in nature and are characterized by strong autonomic nervous system discharges: heart pounding, chest pains, trembling, choking, sweating, and dizziness. Individuals also may experience feeling disorganized, confused, as well as a sense of impending doom. The Panic Disorder is primarily recurrent and episodic, rather than chronic in nature. The panic attacks are clearly separate incidents, but the anxiety experienced is not a response to a phobic stimuli or to any event that is very dangerous in reality. The terror experiences are not unlike "free-floating anxiety," which has been described as an experienced anxiety with the inability to specify any source of reason. It is probably for this reason that Freud combined two forms of anxiety, panic attacks and chronic anxiety, under the rupert of the anxiety neurosis. This convention was followed in both DSM-I and DSM-II. However, researchers found that the tricyclic antidepressant imipramine produced remission of panic symptoms in anxiety individuals without altering the severity of their generalized anxiety (Klein, 1980). This finding suggested the panic attacks might distinguish a Panic Disorder from a Generalized Anxiety Disorder. Subsequently DSM-III and DSM-III-R adopted this distinction introducing the diagnoses of Panic Disorder and Generalized Anxiety Disorder.

DSM-III-R Criteria

In the DSM-III-R is offered specific criteria for Panic Disorder with Agoraphobia (300.21) or without Agoraphobia (300.01). For a diagnosis of Panic Disorder either one or more attacks must occur within a month of persistent fear of another attack, or at least four panic attacks within a month. These panic attacks cannot be a response to naturally anxiety-arousing stimuli, heavy physical exertion, phobic stimuli, or a situation in which the person becomes the focus of another's attention. This diagnosis also requires the presence of at least four of the following symptoms during most of the attack: dyspnea, palpitations, chest discomfort, choking or smothering sensations, dizziness, feelings of unreality, paresthesia, hot or cold flashes, sweating, faintness, trembling, nausea or abdominal distress, or fears of going crazy, losing control, or dying. During the attack, at least four of these symptoms develop suddenly and increase in intensity within 10 minutes of the appearance of the first symptom. Some individuals attempt to cope with these panic attacks with an anticipatory fear of helplessness and by becoming increasingly reluctant to leave the comfort and familiarity of their homes. If this fear increases, the diagnosis will likely change to Panic Disorder with Agoraphobia. With the panic disorder it is *important* to rule out physical disorders which mimic panic attacks such as hypoglycemia and hyperthyroidism, withdrawal symptoms from alcohol or other drugs, or mitral valve prolapse, which cause approximately 40% of all panic episodes.

Course of the Disorder

Typically, Panic Disorder begins with a spontaneous panic attack, that is an anxiety attack with no environmental precipitant. Most frequently, this panic attack occurs in the third decade of life and within six months of a stressful life event such as a marital separation or death of a parent. Generally, when individuals experience this first panic attack they misinterpret its significance, frequently believing that they are dying of a heart attack or going crazy.

Psychosocial factors can significantly affect the course of the panic disorder. As mentioned earlier, adverse life events are associated with the onset of the disorder and probably with the course of the panic symptoms. Individuals with panic disorders tend to display poor problem-solving ability. Coexisting personality disorders or traits such as the dependent, avoidant, or histrionic personality disorders are present in approximately 50% of panic patients. The presence of an Axis II personality disorder tends to worsen treatment prognosis. Hypersensitivity to bodily sensations and cognitive distortions tend to exacerbate symptoms, and tend to increase the risk of complications.

Under very stressful circumstances, usually following an illness or a loss of sleep, an individual often will experience an anxiety attack. In the normal individual, no progression in terms of frequency or severity will occur to meet the DSM-III-R criteria. However, in the biologically and psychologically predisposed individual, panic episodes tend to continue with sufficient severity and frequency to meet DSM-III-R criteria within two months or so of the first panic attack. In the first year after the onset of panic symptoms, most patients will develop anticipatory anxiety and agoraphobia (Breier, Charney, & Heninger, 1986). About 20% of individuals with panic also have histories of alcoholism. Panic-disordered individuals often use alcohol as a self-treatment for their panic attacks.

The lifetime prevalence of panic disorders is in the range of 0.4% and 2.5% according to the ECA (Robins, Helzer, & Weissman, 1984). Panic symptoms were shown to be two to three times more frequent in women, mainly because men use alcohol to self-treat their panic and subsequently are given a diagnosis of alcoholism rather than panic disorder. In both men and women panic is most prevalent in the second through fourth decades and decreases in frequency thereafter.

AGORAPHOBIA

Literally, agoraphobia means a fear of the marketplace or of being in open spaces. Clinically, agoraphobia is a fear of being trapped in such places as crowded theaters, traffic jams, bridges, and elevators. Typically, agoraphobia develops in individuals already experiencing panic attacks. A useful procedure is to think of agoraphobia as a learned fear response to panic attacks. Following the onset of agoraphobia, individuals generally begin avoiding the setting of anxiety attacks. This avoidance generalizes as a disorder and becomes more severe, thus resulting in the individual becoming housebound.

Agoraphobics develop a strong sense of helplessness and anticipate that panic will set in at any time, leaving them without any means of control. Their ultimate fear is that they will be trapped, left alone, and overwhelmed with panic attack. The increasing incidence of agoraphobia may reflect increasing interpersonal alienation, increasing competitiveness, as well as the rising divorce rate, the breakdown of the family unit, and high levels of social and geographic mobility. These changes in demands increase the likelihood that the individual will experience being alone in the face of change and stress.

These stresses and changes are often first noted in adolescence, though they may have been preceded by attacks of separation anxiety and occurrences of school phobia in childhood. Social and vocational role changes can make the individual particularly vulnerable to agoraphobia. Thus, women in a traditional housewife role who are experiencing menopause at the same time their children are leaving home are likely to be vulnerable to agoraphobia. Housebound agoraphobics are noted for their manipulative behaviors toward significant others. These individuals may, with time, become bothersome to those around them, and subsequently depression will complicate their agoraphobia. Needless to say, the agoraphobic who utilizes alcohol or other drugs to diminish his/her anxieties has a high propensity toward substance addiction. The lifetime prevalence of this disorder is approximately five percent.

DSM-III-R Criteria

The two specific DSM-III-R diagnoses are Agoraphobia without history of panic attack (300.22) and Panic Disorder with Agoraphobia (300.21). Agoraphobia is defined as the avoidance of any situation, particularly being alone, where individuals fear they could not be helped or get in touch with help in the event of sudden incapacitation. These fears pervade their world, and as a result, they avoid being alone in public or open spaces where help may not be available if an emergency occurs. Subsequently, their normal behavior patterns and experiences are disrupted.

Developmental Antecedents

Although Panic Disorder and Agoraphobia with panic episodes usually begin in early adulthood, they can be preceded by childhood anxiety or psychological trauma. Individuals with Panic Disorder report more childhood fears, recall being more anxious as children, and have more disturbed childhood environments than individuals with Generalized Anxiety Disorder. Females with agoraphobia and panic attacks are increasingly likely to have experienced childhood separation anxiety. Several studies have confirmed this history of separation anxiety (Aronson & Logue, 1987). The development of phobias in individuals with Panic Disorders is also associated with the history of childhood depression, Obsessive Compulsive Disorder, and Overanxious Disorder. Individuals with such a history of separation anxiety do show an earlier onset of panic attacks. Since separation anxiety is not a significant feature of individuals with Panic Disorder without Agoraphobia, a history of childhood separation experiences or a formal diagnosis of Separation Anxiety Disorder appears to be a marker for Agoraphobia.

The history of childhood fearfulness in anxiety disorders in agoraphobics may represent an earlier manifestation of the same disorder or a predisposing factor increasing their vulnerability to panic and other phobias. This increasing vulnerability to agoraphobia suggests a temperamental difference. The agoraphobic individual was most likely an overanxious and clinging child who experienced parental withdrawal which contributed to the development of this disorder.

OBSESSIVE COMPULSIVE DISORDER

The Obsessive Compulsive Disorder is distinguished by its two cardinal features: obsessions and compulsions. Obsessions are persistent, unwanted ideas or impulses that cannot be easily overcome by logic or reason. Compulsions are persistent, repetitive, and intrusive urges to perform an action that is contrary to one's wishes and standards. Compulsions may be performed in response to an obsession or without a clear percipient. Obsessions may be distinguished from delusions by the retention of reality testing which permits the sufferer to recognize the intrusive thought as irrational, excessive or uncharacteristic. For example: "I know I just washed my hands, but I keep thinking that they're dirty." Obsessions also may be distinguished from depressive ruminations which are characteristically "owned" by the person. For example: "I'm worthless because I lost my job." Compulsions are rarely confused with symptoms of other diagnoses.

The most common obsessions are fears of contamination such as by dirt, toxins, or germs. Other common obsessions involve aggression or violence, doubts about self, religion, or duties. The most common compulsions include checking behaviors, handwashing, and repetitive actions. The Obsessive Compulsive Disorder does not include compulsions to perform behaviors that are in themselves pleasurable such as alcohol use or overeating. Even though the users of alcohol or food may not be able to control these behavior patterns they are not ego-alien. In fact, these behaviors are inherently pleasurable and thus would not be considered compulsions.

Individuals diagnosed with Obsessive Compulsive Disorder give a history of subclinical ritualistic behaviors dating back to early childhood. Avoiding stepping on cracks in the sidewalk, touching a lucky chair or book when walking into a room, or rubbing objects or a particular part of their bodies in a repetitive almost mechanical way are examples of these subclinical rituals. The usual onset for the Obsessive Compulsive Disorder is late adolescence or early adulthood. By the age of 25 years, the majority of individuals who will be diagnosed with this disorder will have already expressed clinical symptoms.

The Obsessive Compulsive Disorder syndrome occurs proportionately more often in middle- and upper-class individuals. In a culture that highly values achievement, individuals with compulsive patterns are often quite efficient and productive and are likely to have been rewarded for their compulsiveness. Obsessive-compulsive individuals tend to be brighter than individuals with other anxiety disorders. This is probably because obsessions are basically intellectual coping strategies to reduce anxieties.

The Obsessive Compulsive Disorder was considered relatively uncommon. However, the recent ECA study found the lifetime prevalence of Obsessive Compulsive Disorder to be two to three percent which was approximately 20 times more than had previously been thought (Robins, Helzer, & Weissman, 1984). Males and females appear to be approximately equally affected with Obsessive Compulsive Disorder, although the childhood form of this disorder appears to develop more frequently in males.

A high incidence of major depression occurs in individuals with Obsessive Compulsive Disorder. Typically, depressive symptoms appear after the Obsessive Compulsive Disorder has already produced functional impairment. Also, Obsessive Compulsive Disorder may exist concurrently with panic disorder as well as Tourette's syndrome. The belief was that the Obsessive Compulsive Disorder and the Obsessive Compulsive Personality Disorder were either one and the same, or that individuals who exhibited the Axis I Obsessive Compulsive Disorder would exhibit an Axis II Obsessive Compulsive Personality Disorder. This belief was fostered, in large part, by Freud's case of "The Rat Man." The Rat Man displayed an Obsessive Compulsive Personality Disorder as well as the obsessions and rituals characteristic of the Obsessive Compulsive Disorder. The ego-alien quality discriminates the Obsessive Compulsive Disorder from the personality disorder. If the personality-disordered individual does engage in occasional rituals, these compulsions are ego-syntonic; that is, they are not viewed as conflictual. Based on research data (Jenike, Baer, & Minichiello, 1986; Rappoport, 1989) Obsessive Compulsive Personality Disorder is noted in less that 40% of individuals with the Obsessive Compulsive Disorder.

DSM-III-R Criteria

Based on criteria in DSM-III-R, evidence of obsessions and/or compulsions are required. In addition, the individual must be distressed and recognize the irrationality of these behaviors. Furthermore these obsessions or compulsions must occupy at least one hour of the day or significantly disrupt the individual's life. The diagnosis cannot be given unless other syndromes which are accompanied by obsessions or compulsions are ruled out. These include Schizophrenia, Organic Mental Disorder, or a Major Depressive Episode.

AN ADLERIAN INTERPRETATION OF PANIC DISORDER, AGORAPHOBIA, AND OBSESSIVE COMPULSIVE DISORDER

Adler (1964) taught that anxiety is utilized to create distance between the individual and life tasks so as to safeguard self-esteem when the individual feels defeat. Adler considered the neurotic individual as an ambitious person who had lost his or her courage and so lived in constant dread of his or her weaknesses being discovered by others. Adler would say that the neurotic has a "hesitating attitude" or a "yes-but" response to life. The anxious individual postpones decisions and tries to keep a safe distance from others and difficult tasks.

> Agoraphobia, anxiety neurosis, and all the forms of phobia may originate at this point (the individual's unwillingness to admit his defeat), but, whichever may be, it fulfills its purpose of blocking the way to further activity. Thus, what was desired is obtained—namely, the ordeal is evaded without disclosing, even to its owner, the hated feeling of inferiority. All other symptoms, such as compulsions, ideas, fits, fatigue, sleeplessness, functional disturbances such as neurotic

heart, headaches, migraines, and so on, develop out of
thc scvcrc tcnsion of this very difficult concealment. (Adler,
1964, p. 11)

These neurotic patterns are laid down in early childhood.
Because pampered children are ill prepared to perform the
tasks of life, they find their courage taxed when another child
is born, school life begins, or a major change takes place
in their environment, such as a move to another neighborhood
or the death of a parent. The first anxious symptoms often
take the form of organ dysfunction, such as abdominal pains,
respiratory symptoms, anuresis, or temper tantrums. Their
purpose is to compel the parents to give into their children
and relieve them of certain responsibilities. Dreikurs noted
that these symptoms are among the first weapons children
use to get their way (Dreikurs, 1950).

Like Freud, Adler did not distinguish the Panic Disorder
from Agoraphobia or from the other anxiety disorders. On
the other hand, Adler (1964) described the Obsessive Compulsive
Disorder in considerable detail. In fact, he considered the
Compulsive Neurosis as the prototype of all mental disorders.

Adler delineated at least eight features of the Compulsive
Neurosis. First, there is a striving for personal superiority
which is diverted into easy channels. This striving for personal
superiority is encouraged in the child by excessive parental
pampering. The onset of the Compulsive Neurosis occurs in
the face of actual situations where the dread of a blow to
vanity through failure leads to the "hesitating attitude." The
compulsive symptoms then provide a means of relief. And
once fixed upon, they provide the individual with an excuse
for failing. The construction of the compulsive neurosis as
seen by Adler is identical with that of the life-style. Adler
was careful to point out that the compulsion did not reside
in the compulsive actions themselves, but originated in the
demands of social living that represented a menace to the
individual's prestige and courage. The life-style of the compulsive
neurotic adopted only those forms of symptom expression
that suited its purpose while rejecting other forms of expression.
And finally, the ever-present guilt feelings experienced by

the compulsive neurotic were efforts to kill time in order to gain time. This then is a summary description of the dynamics of the Obsessive Compulsive Disorder formulated by Adler and his followers. Parenthetically, Leon Salzman's formulation in the book, *Obsessive Personality* (1968), is consistent with Adler's formulation.

TREATMENT CONSIDERATIONS

Treatment of Panic and Agoraphobia

Biological and psychosocial factors have a significant effect on the time of onset, course, treatment, and response of Panic and Agoraphobic Disorders. For this reason, these factors need to be considered in the treatment of Panic Disorder and Agoraphobia. Therefore, assessment of an individual with Panic Disorder should include careful attention to Axis II features, major coping strategies used, life-style convictions and the cognitive interpretation of the significance of panic symptoms, history of childhood disorders, and recent or impending life changes. Many individuals, especially those with Axis II personality disorder diagnoses, poor coping skills, or significant cognitive distortions will require psychotherapy in addition to medication for panic and agoraphobic symptoms. Antidepressant and/or anxiolytic medications such as Xanax and Tranzene have been shown to quickly abate and prevent panic attacks. Psychotherapy will be most helpful if it is targeted specifically for the person's current deficits and includes cognitive restructuring techniques and psychoeducation about effective problem solving. Common issues in the therapy of panic and agoraphobia include dependency, autonomy, and defensive overcontrol.

In the course of treatment individuals can learn to identify, anticipate, and deal with some of their adverse life changes that have exacerbated their illness in the past. Encouragement and education are important in helping individuals with their first panic attacks, especially if they are concerned about life-threatening illnesses or "going crazy." These concerns, as well as a history of childhood anxiety, indicate a need for encouragement from the therapist to help these individuals confront feared situations and avoid the development of agoraphobia. Treatment of individuals with established agoraphobia must include careful attention to significant interpersonal relationships.

Treatment of Obsessive Compulsive Disorder

Surprisingly, treatment of the Obsessive Compulsive Disorder is moderately successful, with approximately 70 to 80% of individuals reporting resolution of their symptoms. Medication has been found to be particularly useful in this disorder. Drugs like Prozac and Anafranil and other drugs with serotonergic properties like Desyrel are most likely to reduce symptoms. Behavior therapy also has been found particularly helpful. For ritualizers, the most effective combination of behavioral interventions is *exposure therapy* and *response prevention.* In *exposure therapy,* the individual is exposed to the fearful situation, while in *response prevention* the compulsive response is blocked or prevented from occurring. For individuals who experience obsessions only, two behavioral methods are recommended. They are *imaginal exposure* and *thought stopping.* In *imaginal exposure,* the individual is helped to mentally experience the dreaded situation and become systematically desensitized, and in time the fear is extinguished. In *thought stopping* the therapist, and then later the individual, interrupts obsessional thoughts by either seeing the word "stop" mentally on a large T.V. screen or billboard, whispering the word "stop," or shouting it out at the moment the obsessional thought comes to consciousness. Since this disorder is not solely a biological dysfunction, not surprisingly a combination of medications and psychotherapy results in significant improvement. Therapeutic issues, particularly life-style convictions about control and feeling avoidance, are the focus of insight-oriented therapy. Readers are referred to Salzman's book on *Treatment of the Obsessive Personality* (1980) or his more recent article for a review of the psychotherapy of obsessions and compulsions (Salzman, 1985).

CASE EXAMPLES

Case of Mr. Z

Mr. Z is a 41-year-old claims adjuster who was referred by his family doctor for psychological evaluation. He related a six-month history of recurrent bouts of extreme fear of sudden onset, accompanied by sweating, shortness of breath, palpitations, chest pain, dizziness, numbness in his fingers and toes, and the fear that he was going to die. His family physician had given him a complete medical workup and could not find an organic cause for these symptoms. Mr. Z and his wife had been married for eight years and have no children. He had served with distinction in the military before his marriage. Afterwards, he began working at a large insurance company during the day while going to college at night to complete a bachelor's and master's degree in business administration. He was quite successful and well-liked at his place of employment. He and his wife generally got along quite well and had an active social life. Because of the attacks, which occurred unexpectedly and in a variety of situations several times a week, Mr. Z started to avoid driving his car and going into shops and office buildings fearing he might have an anxiety attack. He convinced his wife to accompany him on all errands; and during the last four weeks, he had felt comfortable only at home with his wife. Finally, he could not face the prospect of leaving home to go to his office and applied for a medical leave of absence. While at home, he experienced only occasional "twinges" of chest pain and slight numbness in his fingers, but no full-blown anxiety attacks. When asked about circumstances surrounding the onset of his attacks, Mr. Z noted that he and his wife had discussed buying a home and moving from their apartment. He admitted that the responsibilities of owning a home intimidated him and related the significance of the move to similar concerns his parents had that had prevented them from ever buying a house.

This case exemplifies the DSM-III-R diagnosis of Panic Disorder with Agoraphobia (300.21). Mr. Z's recurrent, unexpected anxiety attacks in the absence of an organic cause indicate Panic Disorder. Agoraphobia developed as Mr. Z increasingly constricted his normal activities because of a fear of being in situations from which escape would be difficult or embarrassing, or where help might not be available in the event of a panic attack. For Mr. Z, the significant life change event was the anticipation of home ownership. Having similar concerns as his parents, Mr. Z's "hesitating attitude" about assuming the added financial and day-to-day responsibilities for owning a home resulted in his panic and agoraphobic symptoms. These symptoms effectively safeguarded Mr. Z from having to move into a home he owns. Ironically, the symptoms, particularly the agoraphobia, "force" Mr. Z to remain in his apartment.

Case of Mrs. A

For an example of the Obsessive Compulsive Disorder, we return again to the case of Mrs. A that was described in some detail in this book. The reader will recall that Mrs. A was a housewife with two children who presented with a dysphoric mood, a cleaning compulsion, a night phobia, and a fear of seriously harming her younger son. She also experienced significant marital and other family problems. Her obsessions and compulsions progressively worsened in the 18 months following a terrifying dream in which angels surround a coffin. About this time she had problems with her neighbors and difficulty with her husband to such an extent that she moved out of her home, took her children, and returned to live with her parents. During this time her husband experienced a "nervous breakdown" and begged for her to return to care for him. After returning, her obsessive thoughts and compulsive behaviors incapacitated her to such an extent that she sought psychotherapy. Her faulty life-style convictions include the following: Mrs. A viewed life as hostile, unfair, and overcontrolling. She saw herself as a victim who expected to be humiliated, but also believed she was entitled to be treated differently. Therefore, she demanded that others take care of her. Furthermore, she utilized obsessions, compulsions, and threats of harming herself and her children to ensure that her husband and family continued in their caretaking roles. In short, Mrs. A utilized interpersonal relationships as a means of gaining dominance and resisting submission. For her, cooperation was construed as conquest and defeat rather than mutual helpfulness and social interest.

SUMMARY

This chapter focused on three anxiety disorders: Panic Disorder, Agoraphobia, and Obsessive Compulsive Disorder. Each disorder was described with DSM-III-R criteria, an Individual Psychology formulation, treatment goals and interventions, and a case example. The next chapter focuses on other phobic disorders, Generalized Anxiety Disorder, and Post-traumatic Stress Disorder.

REFERENCES

Adler, A. (1964). *Problems of neurosis*. New York: Harper Torchbooks.

American Psychiatric Association. (1987). *Diagnostic and statistical manual of mental disorders* (3rd ed., revised). Washington, DC: Author.

Aronson, T., & Logue, H. (1987). On the longitudinal course of panic disorder: Developmental history and predictors of phobic complications. *Comprehensive Psychiatry, 28*, 344-355.

Beck, A.T., & Emery, G. (1985). *Anxiety disorders and phobias*. New York: Basic Books.

Breier, A., Charney, D.S., & Heninger, G.R. (1986). Agoraphobia with panic attacks. *Archives of General Psychiatry, 43*, 1029-1038.

Dreikurs, R. (1950). *Fundamentals of Adlerian psychology*. New York: Greenburg Publishers.

Jenike, M.A., Baer, M., & Minichiello, W.E. (1986). *Obsessive-compulsive disorders: Theory and management*. Littleton, MA: PSG Publishing.

Klein, D. (1980). Anxiety reconceptualized. *Comprehensive Psychiatry, 21*, 411-427.

Rappoport, J.L. (Ed.). (1989). *Obsessive-compulsive disorder in children and adolescents*. Washington, DC: American Psychiatric Press.

Robins, L.M., Helzer, J.E., Weissman, M.M., et al. (1984). Lifetime prevalence of specific psychiatric disorders in three sites. *Archives of General Psychiatry, 41*, 949-958.

Salzman, L. (1968). *Obsessive personality: Origins, dynamics, and therapy.* New York: Science House.

Salzman, L. (1980). *Treatment of the obsessive personality.* New York: Jason Aronson.

Salzman, L. (1985). Psychotherapeutic management of obsessive-compulsive patients. *American Journal of Psychiatry, 39,* 323-330.

CHAPTER 7

ANXIETY DISORDERS II

Walter E. O'Connell, Ph.D.
Elizabeth Hooker, Ph.D.

> The honest psychologist cannot shut his eyes to social conditions which prevent the child from becoming a part of the community and from feeling at home in the world, and which allow him to grow up as though he lived in enemy country. Thus the psychologist must work against nationalism when it is so poorly understood that it harms mankind as a whole; against wars of conquest, revenge, and prestige; against unemployment which plunges peoples into hopelessness; and against all other obstacles which interfere with the spreading of social interest in the family, the school, and society at large. (Adler, 1956, p. 454)

This chapter will cover the Adlerian diagnosis, understanding, and treatment of three DSM-III-R categories of the anxiety disorders (American Psychiatric Association, 1987). These are: Post-traumatic Stress Disorder (PTSD), Generalized Anxiety Disorder (GAD), and Social Phobias (SP). Diagnosis, understanding, and treatment of these problem patterns of inner and outer movement will follow the insightful conceptualizations of Alfred Adler. His wisdom is summarized succinctly in the above-mentioned quotation originally published in 1933.

Psychological trust, according to the Adlerian view, is expressed by those inner and outer movements which maximize experiences of **self-esteem** (SE), **social interest** (SI), and the **sense of humor** (SH). Anxiety, on the other hand, is the cause and effect of the negative certainty that the future is out of control. Powerful negative forces, it is feared, will overwhelm the spurious solid, permanent separateness of the psyche. These negative inner and outer threats must be resisted and/or denied to maintain this tremulous ego trance state (O'Connell & Gomez, 1990). Of course, the anxiety-ridden person does not express these self-defeating assumptions and purposes with any psychic distance and subsequent humor. Popular certainties of solid, permanent, and separateness must be threatened by such negative misconceptions for tension to be reframed into an habitual set of objectless fears.

A precursor to distress is the normal shock of an unexpected overwhelming stimulation which subsequently cannot be shared without "awfulizing." This shock reaction follows from the abrupt realization that one is mortal and not able to predict perfect control over persons and events. This perception of mortality and limited control over persons and events stimulates psychic and physical reactions. When such out-of-control states are resisted and catastrophized, they are called "anxiety." Strong persons, those who generate SE, SI, and a buoyant SH, recover their psychic balance quickly. That is, such actualized and individuated persons resist the temptations to identify with guilt and other subsequent negative judgments of the discouraging ego identity. The hallmark of ego identity movements (see Figures 7.1 and 7.2) is perceptions of separation and boundaries, feelings of deprivation, anxiety and guilt. Stimulating and believing such negative perceptions will guarantee anxiety. And, of course, no anxiety is possible without this central belief that one is weak and isolated, and therefore "out of control."

(Continued on page 189)

GUILT FEELINGS: Negative judgments of person and events, mainly unconscious . . . "Worthless . . . now and forever . . . because of what was done or not done."

1. Focus on guilt feelings does not stimulate positive changes in behavior.

2. Guilt feelings diminish self-esteem (SE), social interest (SI), and the sense of humor (SH).

3. Guilt feelings have gluttonous and grandiose purposes:

   a. Gluttonous guilt feelings grab all the blame by ignoring the influence of other persons and events.
   b. Grandiose guilt feelings are negative certainties about the future (selective perceptions, provoked reactions).

4. Guilt feelings can be projected (dumped on others). And so, we have prejudices and wars.

5. "Guilt Gluttons" unconsciously seek *and* fear punishment at the same time.

6. Guilt feelings can be used to gain minimal power (ego esteem through social influence) while neglecting strength (SE, SI, SH). These are the useless social goals of attention, special service, excitement, being boss, getting even, and displaying disability (Dreikurs, 1972).

7. Once weakened by guilt-addiction, the Guilt Glutton becomes the dumping ground for the projected guilt of others. Note the magnetic attraction of the Guilt Dumper and Guilt Glutton which makes for Gruesome Twosomes in marriages.

8. Guilt feelings grow out of the horrible confusion between judgment of worth of persons and events, and judgment of worth of actions. All persons are *more than* their actions.

Figure 7.1. The constrictive power of guilt feelings.

The learned ego-delusions that worth and belonging depend upon taking seriously (or otherwise attempting to make virtuous) are the following vices, with their hidden commands:

1. **AWFULIZING ATTITUDES**—"It wasn't only a happening. It was an awful, terrible catastrophe."

2. **BOUNDARY BUILDING**—"I must fragment, with impenetrable walls, certain thoughts, acts, and persons."

3. **CONTROL**—"I must be the boss of thoughts, events, and persons."

4. **ACTIVE COMPETITION**—"If I am not number one, in competitive combat, I am nothing."

5. **DEPENDENT COMPETITION**—"I need the perfect person or belief . . . ," to give a (pampering) fix for worthlessness and isolation.

6. **PASSIVE COMPETITION**—"I will do my secret avoid-dance and remove myself by depreciating any learning situation in which I am not the perfect master."

7. **DOUBLE DENIAL**—Two negative certainties, one at the beginning and the other much later, in the neurotic struggle with anxiety: initial denial of the ego defenses, followed later by denial of the necessity for self-training.

8. **DISTANCING**—"Stay out of my territory, or I'll waste you."

9. **FUTILE FORCE**—"Only a cowardly wimp would be too scared to use force to teach any lessons."

10. **SELF-GUILT**—The core and kingpin of the ego identity movements. "I am worthless, now and forever, for what I did and did not do." All facts of ego identity illustrate ego-diminishments. Subsequent social movements to restore worth and belonging conditionally make for dependency.

11. **PROJECTED GUILT**—This distrusting stance is an interpersonal reaction to basic guilt and depression. Substitute specific others for the "I" in the Self-guilt formula above. Self-guilt destroys passionate SE. Paranoia destroys compassionate SI.

12. **INVIDIOUS COMPARISONS**—Comparisons designed to stimulate the learning of excellence is fine. "Invidious" means judgment of persons and events negatively, and so guarantees misery-making.

13. **PERFECTIONISM**—The dualism of antithetical thinking. "I am perfect or else I am nothing." Perfectionism devalues persons.

14. **RESISTANCE**—"Stop essential change at all costs" is the ego's motto: Clinging, grasping, and hanging onto, clinging, grasping, and hanging on.

15. **TIME ADDICTION**—Keep the past alive with guilt, and vice versa. Anticipate future catastrophic failures of worth and belonging for anxiety's sake. Watch the images, words, and sensations. BASH for self-cure of ego-induced diseases and pretensions. (see p.196)

Figure 7.2. The pull of ego-gravity.

POST-TRAUMATIC STRESS DISORDER (PTSD)

Persons with the diagnosis of PTSD have been faced with experiences which have shattered their sense of personal identity (worth and belonging). The physical or psychic disabling or death, actual or implied, of oneself and/or one's significant others can seriously disrupt perceptions of significance and continuity. The absurd and excessive, meaningless violence of our times (in multiple contexts) threatens the existence of ideals, connectedness, and purposes of living. Traumatic termination, linked to sudden, shocking outer events, is the essence of the PTSD phenomenology.

The presence of PTSD is reflected by persistent re-experiencing of the traumatic event. Habitual attempts are made to avoid stimuli connected with the negativized and resisted happening. Increased arousal also reflects the presence of the PTSD syndrome. Excessive reexperience, arousal, and avoidance must be inferred from at least one, two, and three actions, respectively. Persistent **reexperiencing** is inferred from the presence of at least one of the following four movements: harrowing recollections, dreams, symbolizations, or expectations of the reliving of the traumatic event. At least two activities assumed to show the presence of increased **arousal** need to be reported: sleep disturbances, anger, excessive vigilance, overreactions to symbolic connections, and the inability to concentrate. The criteria for **hyperavoidance** are at least three of the following actions: resistances to thoughts or feelings or memories of the traumatic event; feelings of detachment or loss of interest; restriction of interest range; or the sense of an impending finish to one's future.

GENERALIZED ANXIETY DISORDER (GAD)

Persons diagnosed as suffering from GAD have persistent, excessive, irrational, ruminating, agonizing, and obsessing thoughts about two or more life situations for at least six months ("bothered more days than not").

For a GAD diagnosis, the candidate must report at least one-third of the following 18 symptoms when experiencing "anxiety." The four **motor tension** movements are trembling, muscular complaints, restlessness, and fatigue. **Autonomic hyperactivity** is marked by nine bodily complaints. These are feelings of being smothered, palpitations, sweating, dry mouth, vertigo, abdominal distress, flushes or chills, excessive urination, and "lump-in-throat." **Hypervigilance** has five characteristics: "keyed up," exaggerated startle response, blank mind, irritability, and sleep disturbances. From that wide range of emotional reactions, at least six are required for the GAD diagnosis.

Generalized anxiety is a manifestation of the individual's inability to cope. The primary source of the fear is often not conceptualized, and the individual is consistently in a state of high anxiety. Almost every person and event can be a serious threat to well-being, work, and belonging, depending on the extent of the lowering and narrowing of SE, SI, and SH. Even when the fear has generalized to a broad range of people, places, and/or things, the source of the fear/anxiety is not perceived as being related to misery-making ego demands.

SOCIAL PHOBIA (SP)

The person with the diagnosis of SP experiences chronic intense anxiety in social situations. Social phobics irrationally believe that they are being critically judged by others. Consequently, they "know" that they will perform acts of commission or omission by which their tenuous worth and belonging will be severely threatened.

When exposed to the negative social stimuli, the person reacts with the feared symptoms of anxiety. Such displays or signs of loss of control are especially repugnant to social phobics. They usually endure phobic situations without any self-disclosure of anticipatory anxiety. Social phobics believe their suffering is excessive, irrational, and often crippling to vocational goals.

Social phobias are another way the individual conserves energy and obtains psychic distance from the problem by externalizing the object of the fear. The ego identity is defended by focusing on a specific target rather than generalized fear ("It is only this specific situation in which I am not acceptable"). Externalizing the fear can be seen as a creative, laudable coping mechanism (like all learned movements), for which the client deserves congratulations. However, if one framed symptoms as "necessary safeguard skills," those symptoms would cease to be hated, and would disappear. Symptoms owe their painful existence to ego resistance and negativization of happenings.

Social phobias can serve the purpose of giving structure to the individual's fear and at least a limited sense of power and control. A sense of power and control is an essential element in avoiding, alleviating, or forestalling the learned helplessness of depression. With a sense of control, even if this is judged as delusional, the person is able to remove himself/herself from the position of being helpless and thus hopeless. Any level of control, even pseudo-control, allows the person to keep hope alive, the remote but possible chance of being happy. One temporary value of social phobias is that the certainty of total worthlessness and inherent isolation is not generalized indiscriminately. People practicing and clinging to social phobias are considerably more tragicomic than most of us. Their awkward "avoid-dances," seen as so unnecessary to the disinterested observer, is the stuff of comedy. Their monumental misery-making triggers acute sadness in those aware of their inner struggles. Social phobias do not make sense: panic and "avoid-dances" are sad and mad, in the absence of life-threatening situations.

The phobic sufferer lacks self-esteem and social interest. It is the psyche that invites and fights the death threat. What we call psychopathology or mental "dis-ease" is a perceived threat to ego-esteem (or the ability to get strokes from other folks). Ego-esteem feels like self-esteem, but the risks involved in addiction to it are tremendous. Just as Arab oil "feels" like Texas oil, so ego-esteem feels like self-esteem. However, the ever-present danger is of being cut off for not performing up to the ego demands of the other. Ego-esteem is, as we all know, a pleasant experience. Esteem or worth gives the impetus to move about, carry on, and take risks. But to rely on ego entirely for the energy of esteem is a grievous error.

Another important point to be made is that ego-esteem is tied to a certain role. For example, if I have adequate ego-esteem as a doctor, I may show plenty of confidence and feel significant in the doctor's office. Unfortunately I may feel guilty and grossly inferior as a father. To avoid these feelings in the father's role, I may try to compensate by repeating behaviors I trust to "work"—those behaviors I am comfortable with and know well. Therefore as a father, I will "act" the same way I do as a "good doctor." For obvious reasons, I will be without much success. Self-esteem, on the other hand, is self-generated from within. In this state the images, words, and bodily tensions of guilt and anxiety are noted and let go. Meditative practices and conscious efforts to give oneself strokes for effort, uniqueness, and simply "food-for-being" lead to the experience of unconditional expansive worth (SE). Practice in interpersonal encouragement stimulates cooperation-as-equals (active social interest). Self-training in cooperation-as-equals makes for anxiety-free persons, in any role in life. The twin keystones are the experience of worth (SE) and belonging (SI) while helping others to develop this capacity fully (O'Connell, 1984b).

In Adlerian terms, often mistaken social goals are involved in the maintenance of the mislabeling and avoidance stance toward anxiety, for example, attention, power, revenge, and the display of inadequacy (Dreikurs, 1972). Yet, social phobias are a result of the individual's discouragement and mistaken belief that he/she is somehow imperfect and unable to live up to self- or other-imposed standards. For example, the most common social phobia, the fear of speaking in public, usually has an identifiable premorbid incident in which the messages of "not good enough" were given and/or "heard" by the person plagued by this social phobia. The ego-imposed guilt ("worthless-now-and-forever") is persistently experienced, but by an uncompleted projection: the originator of the judgement is "the other" in social phobias. We believe that in more "skilled" projections, the self-guilt affect disappears. In such a paranoia, "the other" is forever unworthy. Hence, the popularity of prejudices.

Although it may seem contradictory, a person with this phobia may not be phobic of all forms of public speaking. In fact, she or he could be paralyzed with fear of extemporaneous speaking, but be perfectly comfortable in a play, speaking memorized lines. Another possibility is for the individual to be phobic of addressing or making a presentation to peers or those vital to his/her welfare, but perfectly at ease when she or he is "the authority" or when addressing a non-threatening audience. Once again, the specific area of phobic involvement often can be traced to an earlier incident in which the individual's ego-esteem was damaged, but the present state of worth and belonging is far more crucial for change.

PTSD, GAD, SP:
SIMILARITIES AND DIFFERENCES

The Adlerian approach to anxiety (the copeless appraisal of future catastrophic failure) is immensely promising. The precipitating external conditions which stimulate the internal appraisal and coping incapacities may be varied. External stimuli may be symbolically widespread GAD. They may be more limited to competitive social environments which can be avoided (SP) at the cost of even more ego punitiveness. (The fear of negative evaluation is the best long-term predictor of the behavior of the social phobic, for example.) Or, the anxiety might arise from the perceptions of helplessness/hopelessness after one's identity has been shattered by an overwhelming experience with death. In all cases, the disordered person needs to develop an orderly way to create esteem, belonging, and a playful switch to alternative perceptions. Trower and Gilbert (1989) detail this necessary movement from the atonic (competitive) to a hedonic (cooperation, equality, and mutual support) sense of relatedness.

In essence, what they are saying is that the therapist needs to model and reinforce the "hedonic" style of life and " . . . give people a (sometimes prolonged) exposure to a hedonic relationship in which the therapist always respects . . . never attacks, puts down or ridicules the client" (p. 32). We believe that the state-of-art diagnosis and treatment of anxiety disorders has roots in the Adlerian philosophy of healing, no matter what the label used.

The Adlerian psychotherapist knows that psychotherapy, and the progression of other maturity as well, moves faster and surer when the motivation of therapist, patient, and the patient's social surroundings is toward the experience and understanding of self-identity. This self-identity is more intensely curative the more SE, SI, and SH energize inner and outer movements. Foremost with our thinking is the ability of therapist (healer, teacher, leader) to be an encourager (O'Connell & Gomez, 1990). The encourager takes literally the old cliche of "loving the sinner and hating the sin," both simultaneously and wholeheartedly. Institutions do not foster this kind of enchantment and enthusiasm. Institutions create images, but forego the actual healing. Institutions move as if impelled by a giant ego identity (see Figure 7.2).

The anxiety-ridden patient's tongue sings a litany of change, but the feet move in tune with ego identity demands. Anxiety patients are suffering from starvation of SE, SI, and SH, but do not know it. They are focused upon disruptions of external supports (ego "props" or "fixes") which they cannot control. Anxiety patients learn to identify bodily sensations with the negative certainty that some events that they cannot control will render them helpless and hopeless. In this ego-induced state, the "victim" does not think of his or her part in the wellness of others (SI). What would happen if we had culturally-approved anxiety contests in which the anxiety client became a pop artist? If the client received adulation for symptoms, the guilt (worthlessness) and isolation would be hard to create. And, without resisting and negativizing the tensions, reexperiences, avoidances, arousals, and numbing, they would be harder to produce. When we imagine these overstatements, we imagine the laughable. We might then have patients having anxiety over not having anxiety (O'Connell, 1987)!

Adler believed that the therapist who could not teach happiness was a charlatan. We also see the SE, SI, and SH of the therapist—the qualities never taught in medical and graduate schools—to be the most crucial elements of the healing equation. Like Adler, we perceive the diagnosis of the patient to be less crucial by far than the encouragement of the healer. In our diagnoses, we find the symbols and metaphors of discouragement in overwhelming force. The inner and outer ways in which the client loses the struggle for security and satisfaction are noted in our diagnoses. The breadth and depth (intensity, certainty) of discouragement are seen, along with the client's discouraging ways of fighting discouragement. At the same time, we can gauge in our diagnoses the extent of the client's knowledge of the struggle and the discouraging ways that this knowledge does not lead to SE, SI, and SH.

We always give students two aphorisms to contemplate initially. When they begin to understand them, they begin to be real healers. These are, "Never diagnose unless you treat" and, "Don't even treat anyone here: Just understand them." After all, a diagnosis is just a diagnosis. But with Adlerians, a diagnosis also can be a true treatment for discouragement.

To us, the DSM-III-R categories reflect the various erosions of esteem, belonging, and inflexibility of ego-mindset. The inner and outer unsuccessful compensatory movements for weaknesses are likewise part of the diagnostic function. In brief, we could say that the categories show similarity of movements which *create* and *maintain* discouragement. The therapist must use compassion, knowledge, and adroitness to have the strength to keep encouraging strength.

What are the differences suggested between diagnoses? The psychic pain of SP is in the lust for certain others to confirm clients' worth and belonging. The tragicomic twist is that clients are the ones who unwittingly decide between the movements of "strokes" and the movements of "slights" from others. Initially, clients never believe that when they banish ego identity and become socially responsible, they will find the energy to fuel encouragement within themselves.

GAD inlcudes ego-fighting and ego-winning by misery-making. The client fights symptoms (rejects, denies, awfulizes, negativizes, resists them), but eventually uses them for useless power (attention, be boss, revenge, be let alone). Motor tension, autonomic hyperactivity, apprehensive expectation, and hyperalertness generate more of the same. The flight from crises and challenges into labeling negatively (as a passive victim: "Anxiety makes me miserable") is the start of the tragicomic journey into the land of chemical addiction. Anxiety, like most psychic symptoms, is a big tar baby. The more it is fought as a hated enemy, the more it sticks and grows (O'Connell, 1984b).

Would PTSD be prevalent in a society which welcomed and honored awareness and sharing of death (O'Connell, 1981b)? Would suicide be such an epidemic if death lost its sting and thereby its useless power? In PTSD we see the loss of control over life suddenly erupting into a consciousness where that issue of death is never allowed easy entry. If we had no guilt (neither self-blame nor its sequel, other-blame), we would not have PTSD, with regression into psychoses or character disorders. The abrupt loss of control (with death as its extreme) wreaks havoc with the life-style that is unprepared to live fully (SE, SI, SH focus) and die fully (without guilt). Once feelings of unworth, isolation, and superseriousness become foremost, so do the defenses against the multi-meanings and occasions of anxiety. Healers of combat-related PTSD wish that the angry, defensive veteran could continue as a warrior, but a warrior of peace (Blackburn, O'Connell, & Richman, 1984; Egendorf, 1985; Lifton, 1985). The same type of emotional logic would be involved in wishing that each anxiety victim would develop an anxiety dictum: Anxiety can be a blessed message showing our defective (inner and outer) movements. After accepting this **blessing,** there is a lifetime of being **aware, sharing, honoring,** and **humoring.** This **BASH**-dance is the prologue to the creation of a full and happy life in a discouragenic, but not necessarily discouraging, world (O'Connell, 1981a, 1984b, 1988).

CASE EXAMPLE OF SOCIAL PHOBIA

Case of Jimmy

Jimmy's Joke: Smiling in phobic relationships with phobias. Jimmy has been a chronic disease carrier. His symptomatic social phobias have contributed to narrow circumscribed lives for his wife, Jane, and daughter, Mary. Jane has had chronic colitis throughout most of their 40-year marriage. Surgery and increasing use of tranquilizers have narrowed the ambience of her quiet desperation. The 30-year-old daughter has been under psychiatric care for a score of years for "hatred toward men."

Jimmy only felt good ego-esteem when his favorite football team (the Dallas Cowboys) won. He videotaped victories and went into depression when they lost. Jimmy and the wife, Jane, attended a weekly group for six months 12 years ago with the Adlerian therapist. They were satisfied that Jimmy learned to be happy (when he was praised by the boss and the Cowboys actually won). Jane believed the marriage was saved when her anger toward her symptoms, toward Jimmy, and toward the daughter, Mary, disappeared. However, encouragement (how to solve life's tasks with SE, SI, SH) was never reached. Jimmy returned to the therapist (now 150 miles away from Jimmy's home) when he could not tolerate retirement (no strokes from bosses) and the Cowboys' losing season.

Jimmy's early recollections all could be summed up as "Poor Little Jimmy": a dethroned older brother whose only connection with his younger sibling was the shared family value of "Everything's horrible and will only get worse." Jimmy's father deserted the family in infancy. His mother never remarried. Jimmy, in effect, has been her henpecked husband, even at a distance. Jimmy believed he had never succeeded at anything. He had even faked getting himself fired at his work in sales, and failed that too. He never stopped competing (and losing in his mind) with every other salesman. He made invidious comparisons with every quality constantly. Then, he would avoid giving presentations before groups at all costs (faking sicknesses, deaths, etc.), yet he would occasionally make a presentation for which he never credited himself.

The therapeutic relationship became positive from the first session, since the therapist readily predicted how Jimmy would make himself miserable, and gave him credit for the effort and success at failure. Jimmy now had a new father figure, the therapist, who stroked for effort. He was confirmed as being wonderful, even at the creation of the numbing control that Jimmy put on all feelings in an effort to avoid "catastrophes" (failures which the excessive effort successfully brought about). Jimmy wanted rituals and strokes from bosses. He got them, in line with Adler's implied dictum of encouraging the display of a symptom, provided it's performed (paradoxically) with SI (O'Connell, 1975). In this way, behavior which is not negativized and resisted and is done for practice of human expansion (SE, SI, SH) is no longer symptomatic of disorders.

Jimmy now has a ritualistic time for work-play. He plays Adlerian tapes of theory, relaxation, and letting go meditations (O'Connell, 1984a, 1988). He had a tape made for him by the therapist of his favorite sounds, images, thoughts, and bodily sensations. He also has a personalized tape bringing awareness of avoided words, images, and feelings, with practice at letting them go (without negative judgements). In therapy he laughs at the therapist's *Reductio Ad Absurda*. These remarks are relevantly overstated irreverences such as: "How many centimeters must the boss' mouth turn upward?" and "How many seconds before *you* will allow yourself to feel loved?"

According to our way of thinking, transforming anxiety into positive challenges follows identification with the encouraging therapist who is able to perceive and reinforce a nimbus of light in even the most discouraged, anxiety-ridden, anxiety-avoider (O'Connell & Gomez, 1990).

TREATMENT FOR ANXIETY DISORDERS

Creative Cooperation-as-Equals
for Treatment of Anxiety Disorders

We perceive ourselves, others, and the world according to the goals of our life-style premises (Adler, 1956, 1964).

In short, believing is seeing. Our common nonsense renders certain psychiatric diagnoses easier to relate to than others. Most people have had direct or indirect experiences coping with an irrational avoiding of harmless persons or in temporarily being overwhelmed with torrents of anxiety, SP, and GAD. Far fewer people, however, have the creativity of imagination to empathize with youth who have faced months or even years of death-threatening experiences under the domination of senseless authorities and contradictory goals (Veninga & Wilmer, 1985; Wilmer, 1989). Further traumata to the life-style (ego-identity ideals) came with the killing of women and children who at unpredictable times were friends or enemies. These youth fought in an unpopular war in an inhospitable climate, where drugs were easy to obtain as self-medication for the effects of guilt and isolation. A mechanical dehumanized technique was used to avoid psychiatric casualties caused by losing friends in combat. These boys were flown in alone to battle and given a personal date of expected departure. Within hours of firefights, they arrived suddenly at home, again alone. Courageous leadership and even older role models were rare. The murdering of officers ("Fraggings") was far worse than in any other American army. Covert operations were often dishonest, stupid, and just plain evil. When the youth found comrades in their shared repeated battles and withdrawals over the same bit of land, the composite of this camaraderie was interracial at a time when the home front was afire with interracial riots. The boy soldiers were too often targets of hostility, attacked and spat upon as baby-killers and dope-fiends. And, of course, no parades were given to the losers. The boy soldiers, wielders of the most tremendous power of destruction the world has ever known, had been beaten by skinny, small persons in "pajamas," often armed with homemade and foraged weaponry.

The Adlerian orientation, with its emphasis on the guiding fictions of life-styles and embedded in ironclad logic of communal living, related empathically to the inner needs of such youth for esteem and belonging or encouragement (Blackburn, O'Connell, & Richman, 1984). References to worthlessness, isolation, and purposelessness as precursors for disturbed and disturbing life-styles are recorded throughout Adlerian literature. Lifton (1985) noted comparable pathological processes of disintegration, disconnectedness, and stasis (purposelessness). His finding also concurred with studies of PTSD from other disciplines (Baritz, 1985; Egendorf, 1985; Manchester, 1979; Veninga & Wilmer 1985). Combat-related PTSD is simply, yet destructively, an intense magnification of the shocking confrontation with psychic and physical death. From the Adlerian perspective, the death that terrorizes is the feared death of inner guiding fictions: goals, conscious or unconscious, presumed to generate esteem and belonging (O'Connell, 1981a, 1981b, 1984b, 1988).

Delayed and chronic PTSD presents problems for professionals who are not of Adlerian frame of reference. Adlerians see the "delay" of the disorder more in terms of thresholds of attention which fail to note the initial losses of worth, belonging, and humor. The PTSD victim (and victimizer) intensifies his or her safeguarding tendencies, with movements patently doomed to fail (antithetical thought, deprecation, overcompensation, power strivings, isolation). Accelerated disturbed and disturbing actions ensue. As the communal ideal of cooperation-as-equals disappears, both individual and social tension increase drastically.

The failure to relate losses (or fear of losses) in shared ways with others, perceived as equal and similar, keeps restorative grief out of awareness. Violence is a popular cultural choice to cover this grief-denial. Once again, Adlerian theory and practice provides the frame of understanding and treatment. Diagnosis here is the identifying of the breadth and intensity of movements which constrict the experiences of unconditional worth (SE) and universal belonging (SI). Treatment is aimed at promoting such awareness without more negative attitudes or constrictions. Treatment moves from initial learning how to cooperate as equals (with all participants) to learning how to let go of one's own negative certainties by helping others to do so. Professionals soon learn that Adlerians do not view monadic catharsis ("release of bottled up emotions") as a treatment goal. Emotions are seen as energies devoted to goal-fulfillment and are therefore socially purposive. No units of *one* are in the Adlerian open system of creative community existence. One is not automatically victimized by the past, present, or future. All determinisms are "soft," decided by goals of one's guiding fictions rather than external factors alone. What other therapists might see as healthy catharsis, the Adlerian would see as an example of social responsibility, admitting hidden goals without negativity.

Adlerians excel at uniting the poles of "living concepts" (O'Connell & Gomez, 1990). From his early writings, Adler (1956, 1964) did not isolate the social conditions of tailors from their subsequent diseases, or the neuroses of children from the movements of teachers and classroom peers. In fact, this Adlerian method is neither boundary-ridden subjectivity nor objectivity, but "phenomenological operationalism" (Ansbacher, 1965), an interaction of subjective guiding fictions and goals with overt behavior. The patient who represses **awareness** of hostility does show hostile **behavior** (e.g., depreciation of self and others). According to the Adlerian emphasis on both polar opposites, living concepts, social units, and ends of any stick are not without polar opposites. An overemphasis on one role ("no hostility") may be in the service of the disowned polar opposite (subtle violence).

Such Adlerian dialectics pioneered paradoxical and strategic therapies (Mozdzierz, Marchitelli, & Lisiecki, 1976; O'Connell & Gomez, 1990). In Adler's dialectics, one-sided behavior often reflected the deflected energy of a disowned pole of a living concept. "Too much" or "too little" movement (awareness) of the polar opposites of living concepts destroys the experience balance. A balanced encouraging life-style has a "both/and" orientation, not an "either/or" dichotomy. For example, take angry depreciatory tendencies of the chronic severe PTSD victim-victimizer. Violence can hide the soft, sad, impotence of loss of person and symbols which gave life positive meaning. The pole where we feel the most vulnerability (of worth and belonging) is the pole where the defenses are stacked. An Adlerian would understand the need to share the grieving process. Such a helper would see the symptom as a painful blessing, showing us where our "weaknesses" are and how they are hidden and become blocks to community. Honoring happenings without blame and humoring blame away is part of the healing process. In healing, a distancing exists from *identification* with constricting symptoms, to an identification with universal community. ("I am more than my negative fears. I am always in community," *sub specie aeternitatis*.)

Allopathic Quietment for Anxiety Disorders

One of the discouraging fallacies of allopathic psychiatry is the implied ease of optimal development. In the allopathic framework, good living follows automatically upon freedom from the symptoms of mental disease. However, in Adlerian terms, good living and freedom from mental disease are anchored in the processes of courage and encouragement. Adler (1956) made a distinction between courage and social interest. *Courage* is *active* social interest. Courage is a distinct step beyond the more passive acceptance of others "as if" they are equals, sharing in the human need to experience unconditional worth (SE) and purposive belonging (SI). Courage is *active*, risk-taking (SI) (O'Connell, 1975). Courage reflects the strength of the individual (SE, SI) as well as knowledge of and skill with the encouragement process. To Adler (1956, 1964), the mother's task was to stimulate the appearance of the search for similarities and extend it broadly to others. That role is a similar goal for the Adlerian therapist with the courage to give feedback and self-disclosure (O'Connell, 1984a).

We see the physician identified with allopathic model premises to be the shadow-opposite of the Adlerian healer. The latter is a rare occurrence in institutional settings (O'Connell, 1983). Allopathic psychiatrists often have not expanded their narrow training of search-and-destroy of symptoms into concerns about the processes of spirit and soul as did Jung, Adler, and Milton Erickson (O'Connell & Gomez, 1990). If the goal is immediate reduction of symptoms, no emphasis is upon cooperation-as-equals between peers. The serious allopaths deal only with the abstract logic world of so-called "solid" facts (Weil, 1983). Like the madman, this hard determinist acknowledges no doubt. On the other hand, the Adlerian healer can play, guessing without the lack of certitude, in a world of changing perceptions, possibilities, and attitudes. Allopathic understanding and treatment can be dehumanized to following geometric models of "fitting" chemical receptors with "blocking" locks. Then, the human needs of spirit (SE) and soul (SI) are victims of reductionistic regression. The growth possibility of reframing negative emotions as complementary challenges which develop character (when resistance and negativity cease) is not acknowledged in the standard allopathic model of quick quietment (Weil, 1983).

In our estimation, the orthodox allopathic model in psychiatric institutions is hostile to treatments whose metaphors are more congruent with psychospiritual pilgrimages, developing athletic prowess, or skill games than with reductionistic and isolated physical focus. Adlerians would be on the side of treatment for chronic and severe PTSD, rather than simple allopathic quietment of symptoms by chemical constraints. Adlerian therapy for anxiety disorders of all types would be more similar to homeopathic medicine (Weil, 1983). That is, the inner state of the sufferer would be strengthened (SE, SI, SH) using individualized, "diluted injections" of the events labeled "traumatic." Putting the patient back into a psychodramatic simulation of the stressors (O'Connell, 1975), now encouraged with Adlerian knowledge and trusting democratic relationships, is a fine example of Adlerian treatment (O'Connell, 1987).

Psychiatrists doing research for the Pentagon are still enamored with the goal of inventing a "Brave Pill" to overcome the physical fatigue and fear of dying and killing connected with absurd round-the-clock violence (Gabriel, 1987). Such institutional ego-thinking does not take into consideration the human needs for integrity, connectedness, and inspiring goals, which are affected by the encouragingly or discouragingly, caring or careless actions of others. Institutional thinking ignores the power (social influence) of psychic weakness which is seen in the belief of the necessity of guilt. It is the dimuniting actions and useless reactions of living with the unlimited technology of absurd death that promotes wartime PTSD (Lifton, 1985). Perceiving the absurdity of ego identity in the context of a shattered self-identity equals severe PTSD. Most humans would go to their deaths without PTSD if that death would guarantee the continued existence of idealized goals and persons. The trauma of PTSD is the result of experiencing the death of worth, belonging, and humor. Similarly, PTSD follows the death of integrity, connectedness, and movement, an equivalent process translated by Lifton (1985) as "Death Anxiety." One can be ego-sustaining in the face of pervasive death and dying as long as the dead are no more than external objects. But such unfortunate and shocking sadnesses can be opportunities for expansive growth when **BASH**ed (seen as **b**lessing with **s**hared **a**wareness, while **h**onored and **h**umored). However, if what are dying are inner values (SE, SI, SH), no immediate possibility exists of positive transformation of life-style (Blackburn, O'Connell, & Richman, 1984).

Individual psychologists who perceive mental illness as stemming from deficiencies of SE, SI, and SH as did Alfred Adler (1956, 1964), are concerned with the *uses* of diagnoses. The diagnosed are not perceived by Adlerians as passive victims or malicious monsters. The diagnostic process, in Adlerian terms, needs to highlight the inner and outer movements of *how* innate worth (SE) and belonging (SI) are *not* realized and experienced. Diagnostic concepts are our guiding fictions to understand how the client constricts perceptions and experiences of well-being. The Adlerian therapist must create mutual trust, relate to, interpret discouraging movements, and offer corrective experiences of cooperation-as-equals. The discouraging diagnosis and quietment of wartime PTSD in institutions is proof positive that diagnoses are allied to guiding fictions, used to either discourage or encourage. Diagnoses are not palpable essences, reliable and valid for all persons, for all social conditions diagnoses.

Our observations of hundreds of combat-era patients and scores of diagnosticians and healers lead us to believe that the manner in which a hospitalized psychiatric patient is diagnosed and treated for PTSD depends as equally on the life-style of the mental health professional as on that of the patient. PTSD is a relatively new diagnosis. When given the choice, some diagnosticians will resist acknowledging that diagnosis. Moreover, the diagnostic change which accompanied inclusion of PTSD in DSM-III de-emphasized the longstanding contention that predisposition was essential for the presence of psychiatric casualties. PTSD could be a delayed reaction, another change in the traditional time frame of immediate reaction and past predispositions. But, a hidden ambivalence exists about the limits of life-threatening (and psychic identity) stress upon the life-style. By arbitrary definition of many practitioners, one can contract an *anxiety* disorder from life-threatening stress, but not a *psychotic* disorder. So while contemporary stress is given more importance as an independent factor in anxiety reactions of PTSD by most therapists, often an arbitrary ceiling is placed on its allowed severity. PTSD is "only" an anxiety disorder. If your identity is extremely shattered, if life (or psychic) threat is severe enough to precipitate a psychotic reaction, then PTSD is often ruled out of the diagnostic picture.

An alarming example of what happens to a chronic and severe combat-related PTSD (all of whom are now middle-aged "youths") follows. We believe that the orthodox diagnosis of PTSD requires a knowledge of the interaction between individual preconditions and the perception of threat of the stressors. In a recent case of ours, a local district attorney sought to establish a morbid precondition by finding relatives who confessed to engaging in incestuous homosexual activities with the defendant when he was young. She also said the defendant could not be diagnosed as being "under stress" since he was not now in combat. (She saw "stress" in terms of counting, weighing, and measuring current firepower. Destruction to the life-style from two combat tours and eight years in prison did not count as "stress" now.)

The district attorney did not investigate the psychiatric hospitalization and documented dissociative states experienced by this individual while he was in Vietnam. She stated her reasons for ignoring these highly relevant facts as being "irrelevant" because they did not "explain" current violence toward women whose behavior contributed to the defendant's self-perceived helplessness. The defendant himself muddied the waters with his emphasis on causative "flashbacks" rather than his decompensated life-style. His defense lawyer would not accept the validity of flashbacks because the defendant was not reexperiencing the externals of combat. It appears that the defendant used the slang of his youth in Nam, but no one understood the meaning. Therefore, no one empathized with the one who was capable of crimes of violence toward females. Using these irrational arguments, punishment of imprisonment rather than treatment for PTSD was initiated. When O'Connell could not offer long-term treatment under locked ward conditions, the defendant's fate was sealed. Unfortunately, only a few institutional and instrumental treatments for PTSD exist.

HOW ANXIETY DISORDERS CAN BECOME CHRONIC CHARACTER DISORDERS

Si Me Disturbes, Te Occidero (which when translated means, "If you hassle me, I'll waste you"). When a group of PTSD Nam vets were moving as if they would trust the intentions of the therapist, had at least an intellectual understanding of ego and self-identity, and were learning to work-play their way to self-awareness, the above "humorous" quotation was written on the blackboard in the ward by the therapist. It was a dignified Latin rendition of a common threat by chronic and severe PTSD combat veterans. In essence, this Latin inscription is a succinct statement of how to change a neurosis into a character disorder. The same theme was often incorporated into the belief systems of gullible boys as early as basic training. Particularly during the Vietnam era, the drill instructors' goal seems to have been to transform scared kids into disciplined killers with admonitions such as: "Whenever you get scared, kill!" Given the isolation, confusion, anxiety, and art of weaponry of the Vietnam conflict, the killing was prodigious indeed. And, the fragmenting and negativizing of the ego identity (called "delayed") under conscious and unconscious guilt was harrowing.

The Adlerian practitioner can readily understand the self-destructive course and discouraging outcome of prolonged intense negativity and isolation. One criticism of DSM-III-R is that PTSD remains under the classification of anxiety. For everyone except chronic saints, the lack of encouraging models leads to progressive dehabilitation of unconditional worth (SE) and SI. Even the narrower and conditional ego-esteem and dependent interests fade away in threatening, discouraging atmospheres.

Given only a community of violent discouragement, the constricted PTSD can resemble more of a character disorder (little or no social interest and too much ego-esteem). If treatment participants have the hidden goals of ego-esteem *without* SI and the therapist is unaware of how to counter with encouraging movements (quality of SE, SI, SH), no therapy is likely. The most to hope for is narrow SI, confined to an in-group, with hostility against the rest of the universe. True social interest means cooperation-as-equals, *sub specie aeternitatis* (O'Connell, 1984b). We now know that some of the best therapy with PTSD Nam vets was through using World War II veterans, in empathic sharing relationships (O'Connell, 1975, 1987). Beyond creating helpfulness in identifying and moving beyond constrictions, the World War II veteran demonstrated in his misery that time and external assets would not likely cure the chronic and severe PTSD life-style (ego identity).

We have noted a crucial difference between those veterans whose PTSD remained on an anxiety level (resisting, negativizing) and those who dumped this diminuting guilt on others. For the latter, youth who went on to develop character disorder-type behavior, moving against others, in one form or another, became an addiction. "Justified" hostility toward those now regarded as worthless and less-than-human became acts calculated to show masculine "overcoming" of fears. "Love thy neighbor" became "Hassle me and I'll waste you" in a world peopled with competitive dissimilarities.

In Figure 7.3 are our views on the emergence of two types of PTSD. They often become pronounced following the existential crises of prolonged exposure to the unlimited and absurd violence of modern combat. Type A, the more neurotic variety, is emphasized in DSM-III-R. Type B reflects the unacknowledged choice to continue killing (actually or psychic-symbolically). This striving for power (ego-esteem) through degrees of violence contributes to the development of psychopathic, borderline character types. Veterans in this more disturbing category are less amenable to treatment. In fact their ego-justified and wide range of hostility ("joking" verbal to provoking physical) makes them a chronic disease carrier. Type B's extraverted disturbing style stimulates burnout epidemics in any program which does not contain encouragement training for staff (O'Connell, 1983).

(Continued on page 210)

		Type A—"Neurotic"	Type B—"Psychopathic"
1.	Basic attitude	Introverted	Extroverted
2.	Hostility	Narrow, with concern for friends: "I should have 'fragged' that ignorant bastard who led the squad into that ambush."	Wide toward all authority: "You bastards can never know what we went through."
3.	Guilt	Lacerating. Numbing of all affects: "I am worthless, now and forever, because of what I did/ did not do."	Projected on others: "You are no good, now and forever, because of what you did/did not do."
4.	Sleep disturbances	Chronic, severe, witnessed by others	Quality of controlled purposiveness: In service of ego image (top macho). Usually not seen by others.
5.	Combat memories	Repressed. Traumatic rearousal may accompany sharing.	Excellent memory for details. Dotes on atrocity nuances.
6.	Symptomatology	Disturbed, depressive	Disturbing, paranoid
7.	Reactions to symptoms	Expresses need to eradicate symptoms.	Uses symptoms to create and maintain actively competitive image.
8.	Safeguarding tendencies	Avoid-dance	Power ploys
9.	Ego-esteem	Low esteem Lifton's (1985) stasis (little movement)	High ego esteem: Brittle sense of worth. Manipulates environment for worth and belonging.
10.	Social interest	Present, but restricted to narrow range of people and situations.	Very little and temporary if any at all.
11.	Prognosis toward SE, SI, SH	Good, with friendly firm encouragement.	Poor because close personal relationships are rejected and disdained.

Figure 7.3. Main reactions to shock of unlimited absurd violence of modern combat.

Figure 7.3. Continued.

Addendum to Figure 7.3

These observations of drastic (but necessary—at the time) reactions to inner and outer extreme violence were made on hundreds of PTSD patients in our (VA) drug and PTSD treatment programs. Veterans on entering the PTSD ward were given the opportunity to design their treatment programs, which varied from medications only to combinations of medication, individual and group therapies, psychodrama, art therapy, and a PTSD "rap" group. The veteran was offered all these treatment possibilities. In true Adlerian fashion, the patients' diagnosis (and prognosis) depended on the extent to which they would fight or invite encouragment. The Type B reaction to violent and absurd killing was, as a rule, in an intense and habitual avoid-dance. With the B type PTSD, the possibilities of positive change and renewed relationships with others (who did not obsess and ruminate on the impossibility of change) were resisted and negativized. Type B dedication is toward maintaining and enhancing negative certainties of "Once a trauma, always a trauma" and "Hassle us, and we'll waste you."

The Axis I diagnosis for most program patients included PTSD. However, the Type B patterns often had (or at least deserved) the Axis II code of personality disorders. Such disorders, "characteristic of the individual's current and long-term functioning," were seen more in the habitual rejection of training in worth, belonging, and humor (Natural High Theory and Practice). Guesses about possible disorders based on patients' reports of early childhood and combat experience were not as predictive of outcome as were the patients' movements of foot and tongue when presented with an opportunity to fight for encouragement.

Both patient Types A and B, in our opinion, overestimate the importance of externals of combat and underestimate the importance of friendly, firm affection in creating prognoses for their own futures. We believe, on the other hand, that *psychic* deaths (numbing and lacerating of esteem and belonging) lead directly to the deep discouragement of the worthless, isolated, super-serious candidate for violence and other useless addictions.

CASE EXAMPLES OF PTSD

Case of Sammy S.

Sammy S. was an actively competitive ex-Marine. His ego identity (of which he was unaware) was to be praised as the best in every task he undertook. His desired image was that of Ultra-Masculine, always in command, taking "no crap" from anyone, especially males he competed with. He was a well-conditioned boxer and dancer and excelled in martial arts. He was hospitalized for seizures (as well as for PTSD) and heavily medicated on standard medications for epilepsy. Sammy was discouraged about this condition. He was certain that he would have his physical defects all his life and was told that he was totally and permanently disabled by more than one allopathic physician. Moreover, the useless power he had acquired through his sick role of ten years was tremendous. He was compensated "100%— permanent and total," since his first seizures appeared in combat conditions. Along with Social Security payments, Sammy received over $1,500.00 monthly plus room and board during hospitalization. Sammy had the useless luxury of being able to talk of his potential without ever risking the loss of ego-esteem by undertaking training. That training at government expense was automatically ruled by Sammy's receipt of a "total and permanent" rating. Even if the disability was lessened, the fact of reported seizures remained, although none had ever been seen during his frequent hospitalizations.

Sammy was seeing himself as a passive victim of an insufferable fate which reluctantly and paradoxically rewarded him for taking on the sick role so readily. He was considered a "good patient," therefore, doctors and nurses could easily see themselves as good professionals. Sammy was being schooled in trained incapacity in the vital areas of social responsibility (love, cooperation-as-equals, work). He loved to complain about his chronic social rejection as a Vietnam vet and obsessed about having his compensation tragically reduced some day. One of the dangers of forming groups exclusively for Vietnam veterans is that once out of total isolation, the group's social interest will not advance beyond the "us against them" competitive stance.

Veterans like Sammy were pampered, but rejected as persons capable of being trained to fulfill life-style tasks of social, vocational, and loving commitments. They were trained in quietment and discouragement. In quietment, no acceptance is made of the primacy of expanding one's identity (SE), which is made strong through learning the technology of spirit and soul (SI) growth. Treatment of the human identity requires empathic therapists who will model and reinforce the striving for loving worth (SE) and universal belonging (SI). Treatment for combat PTSD in *Natural High Therapy* has psychoactive drugs at times but only as facilitators for learning encouragement in the face of deeply intense discouragement.

Sammy moved into and through the grief, which signals letting go of useless power. But he did so only through the loving care of equals who accepted, without ridicule, his diminuting, depreciatory tendencies. At the same time, participants in Adlerian psychodrama (O'Connell, 1975) urged Sammy to reexperience the content which he hid under the cloak of isolating violence. The key incident was the killing of a Vietnamese boy whom he loved. Sammy was certain that the boy was moving toward him with a concealed grenade. Such incidents were becoming commonplace with his unit at that time. In actuality, the child was hiding a gift carving he had made for Sammy. With the help of a fellow PTSD patient who played the "wasted" boy, Sammy, with hesitant back and forth movements, reenacted the scene while shaking and sobbing violently. He wanted to retreat to the nursing station to take his standing (PRN) order for dilantin. He admitted that he wanted to avoid an emotional "female" out-of-control experience. However, staff dialogued with Sammy to show the courage to express "weakness" and shake without guilt. Sammy did it enveloped in a circle of staff who hummed his favorite tune ("The Rose"). This incident in itself was not "curative" catharsis, but was a giant step to shared SI and the courage to admit imperfections without guilt. The incident was then available for giving Sammy strokes for effort, free from negative judgments. Today, Sammy is a teacher of meditation and a college student. He has long been discharged from the hospital and is now married to a fellow student of recreational therapy.

Case of Tim

The diagnostic ambivalence of the case of Tim certainly contributed something to his habitual look of confusion. His working diagnosis on the VA hospital ward was PTSD, delayed, severe. But the VA rating board, which decides if a psychiatric condition is worthy of financial compensation, considered him to have the disease of schizophrenia, paranoid type, without service connection.

Tim's bearing was always military. He dressed and moved as if always on inspection. Tim's upright frame moved at a brisk pace, as though he had an important secret mission. During all of his frequent hospitalizations, Tim was never known to miss a ward or therapy group meeting. He was also never known to speak spontaneously except during Natural High Walkabouts (Blackburn, O'Connell, & Richman, 1984) in which he voluntarily, briskly, and rapidly expressed his angry frustrations about the diagnostic confusions.

The staff of the psychiatric section believed Tim deserved compensation and treatment for delayed and severe PTSD. Since no one knew for certain the reasons for his claim rejection, rumors abounded. A social worker held that some rating boards wanted to know and evaluate the intensity of enemy action in places where patients served. The ward psychiatrist noted that Tim's diagnosis was made in 1976, before the diagnosis of PTSD became officially recognized in 1980. And, once a patient is diagnosed, changing it is difficult, especially if subsequent psychiatrists "Didn't believe that PTSD was a real disease." O'Connell, the ward psychologist, lamented that many psychiatrists had no idea of the connections between guilt (both lacerating and numbing), the ego identity, and paranoid reactions. An Adlerian would be far more likely to see that self-guilt ruins feelings of worth (SE), belonging (SI), and joy (SH).

Such grandiose overcompensations cannot succeed in the ironclad law of communal living as equals (Salzman, 1968). To O'Connell, Tim was certainly paranoid, but more numbed in SI than ego inflated with grandiosity. Tim even may have had predispositions toward paranoid reactions, but would not likely have had "irrational" discouragement (low SE, narrow SI, super-seriousness) without lacerating and numbing guilt: "I am no good now and forever because of what I did not do." Without a doubt Egendorf (1985) and Lifton (1985) would agree with O'Connell's contentions that Tim's "paranoid" death fears and fear of punishment were dynamically related to his continuing guilt. This inner weakness resulted from deflation of esteem and belonging, and disappearance of humor. Tim identified more and more with negative images, words, and bodily sensations of discouragement (O'Connell, 1975, 1988).

Tim's case is not uncommon in the diagnosing and treating of combat-related PTSD. Tim did not fire a gun at the enemy, nor was he fired upon. He took on too much responsibility for perfection and control in a futile effort to prove his worth and belonging. Even as he drove his fire-fighting and rescue trucks at his air base, Tim dreamed of burning pilots and awoke in fear and panic for years. Tim's sense of patriotic pride and duty, his ignorance of psychic matters, and his lack of introspection kept him from reporting to a psychiatrist in Vietnam, if he could have found one. Like many of the Vietnam veterans, Tim had the flashbacks, arousals, numbings, reexperiences, and avoidances after traumatic events (outside the range of usual human experience). However, symptoms were "delayed" in the sense that they were not recorded in official documents until Tim believed that help was available and reported to that location.

Tim still wallows in self-guilt because he believes that officials regard him as "unworthy of PTSD." He projects his worthlessness outward and now evil "others" are responsible for his weaknesses. That delusional set is not systemic and specific. Tim expects and fears punishment. Because of his unworthiness and the presence of evildoers, Tim stays in the past with images, words, and sensations which are not shared, honored, and humored. This weakness and self-loathing of guilt set Tim up for anticipatory anxiety of the future. Tim feels so weak, inept, and inadequate that he knows he will be victimized in the future by things out of his control. The success of other Vietnam veterans in securing the payments for compensation and rehabilitation only accentuates his unsuccessful competition and guilt. His invidious comparisons with fellow vets create more paranoid distrust.

While Tim repeats his predictable tragicomic scenarios from day to day, his future gets bleaker. Instrumental PTSD programs in institutions were always rare, but now are exceedingly rare. One reason is that PTSD veterans upset authorities with their intense and direct "hostile" demands toward them. Another is that with all of their overt re-experiencing, arousing, avoiding, and numbing, these veterans are not apt candidates for traditional institutional quietment. A third reason is that successful PTSD treatment requires helper-experts who stimulate, allow, and share the natural lows of grief (O'Connell, 1981a, 1987) which are so necessary for the letting go of hostility (O'Connell, 1983, 1984a, 1984b). Cultural and economic pressures and ego needs to reframe problems of living into easy medicalized solutions have also contributed to the early demise of authentic and effective PTSD treatment programs in institutions (O'Connell, 1983).

And so, Tim marches on, losing his few empathic encouragers as non-allopathic PTSD treatment fades away. Soon he will be engulfed by chronic schizophrenics, lost on an orthodox quietment ward. He will be distinguished from the others only by his brisk upright parade step, as if on a confusing mission of tragicomic proportions.

FLASHBACK: CAUSE OR EFFECT?

An Adlerian psychotherapist would not regard "flashbacks" as an explanatory concept necessary to understand human behavior. Popular media and a number of ill-advised veterans have misused the descriptive metaphor of flashbacks as "the cause" of untoward actions. In psychotherapy, the chronic PTSD client learns to "let go" of the negativity and resistance toward being aware of and sharing the actual or feared loss. He or she begins to lose the "John Wayne: numbed but violent" defensiveness as the necessary grief work proceeds. At the same time, work-play continues on concentrating (contemplating) previously unacknowledged strength (SE) and belonging (SI) ("I'm learning now that I've always been more than my old need to show super-toughness, which eventually cracked"; "I never knew that we are all so weak. Maybe real strength is in sharing our mutual human defects . . . "; "I now know that he who laughs—without anger—lasts").

Another quality that changes (often automatically) with the unfolding of the natural low of grief and the construction of strength is the reframing of "flashbacks." What becomes obvious to those who work closely with chronic and severe PTSD clients, like the Nam vets, is the misuse for power (SI) of flashbacks and violence. The threat of violence frightens others and gets the user the attention, special service, power over others, revenge, and/or avoidance of social responsibility he or she misperceives as necessary (Dreikurs, 1972). The threat of violence protects the weak, brittle macho overcompensation, which continues to generate increasingly disturbed, or disturbing behaviors (e.g., violence toward authority). In therapy, flashbacks are reframed as similes, ways of hiding the avoidance of responsibility ("I didn't want to attack that woman. The flashbacks made me do it"). Similes add the "like" (symbolic) dimension to a metaphoric statement: "It seems, at times, *like* the flashbacks make me do things." In successful life-style changes, the patient becomes aware (while sharing, honoring, and humoring) of a previously hidden, denied, and disguised sequence. That perception is the unwanted perceived helplessness (seen as negative and resisted) triggering the out-of-control panic. Then the images, words, and bodily sensations hit. The client has lacked the psychic distance and *becomes* the feared weakness, equivalent to psychic death (Lifton, 1985). Helplessness and loss of control—which have been repressed, negativized, resisted—now are that person. The chronic and severe PTSD patient who learns to evolve beyond quietment of symptoms into an encouraging life-style ceases to resort to violence and flashbacks to protect ego-esteem and ego interests. In the cure of all psychic disorders, the direction is the same: increase of unconditional worth, belonging, and joy. This task becomes harder with increase of disintegration, disconnection, and stasis (lack of psychic movement), the more chronic and severe the death anxiety.

GROUP TECHNOLOGY FOR NATURAL HIGH THERAPY FOR ANXIETY DISORDERS
(Order-for-disorder)

" . . . childlike foolishness is the calling of mature men. Just this way, Rank prescribed the cure for neurosis: as the 'need for legitimate foolishness.' The problem of the union of religion, psychiatry and social science is contained in this one formula" (Becker, 1973, p. 202).

A *strong* ego in effect disappears. That is, the identification with the lacks and desires of the weak ego "wants" (see Figure 7.1) is at least temporarily defused. Distance from ego demands means that one no longer judges persons and events negatively, on a contingency basis for allowing the experience of values of worth and belonging. All striving for external proof of esteem and belonging (the basis of ego-identity standards) is then seen as absolutely crazy-making! When the person is strong enough (SE, SI, SH) to break out of all forms of ego addictions (enslavement to externals for the "feel-goods"), he or she is in touch with the natural birthright of self-identity: unlimited worth and belonging, the universal free gift. Self-identity is never contingent upon what others do, say, think, or feel. In fact, once a person is afflicted with that "spell," the enthusiasm, inspiration, and enchantment of encouraging living pops like a bubble. Now, you can see the purpose of metaphoric images of fairy tales (spells, "rationally" incomprehensible connections), games (teamwork, conditioning, arbitrary rules), and psychospiritual pilgrimages (searches beyond the ego addictions).

Following this way of imaging, the orthodox allopathic medical model can be seen with its "evil" pole. When transposed beyond medical emergencies and physical illnesses, the allopathic model can be the losing game, or a blatant sin for optimal psychic and spirit-soul development (Weil, 1983). To avoid this discouraging medicalized existence, one must be self-trained for skills in the sport of unconditional worth (SE), universal belonging (SI), and psychic dialectics (SH). The allopathic model in psychiatry, which emphasizes reductionism and hard determinism, has no place for the type of courageous play which is needed.

COMBAT AND NON-COMBAT PTSD: SIMILARITIES AND DIFFERENCES

The individual experiencing and exhibiting the symptomatology of PTSD resulting from events which are not combat related likewise has suffered from overwhelming, absurd violence over which she or he has had no control. Combat and non-combat PTSD manifest many of the same symptoms. These include **hypervigilance, exaggerated startle reaction, somatization,** and the **exclusive use of specific coping mechanisms**—ones which once were successful, but which now contribute to the maintenance of the problem (Hooker, 1985).

A common pattern in both etiologies of PTSD is perceived or actual lack of power and inability to control the situation; little or no sense of belonging, resulting in low SI; lack of, or inability to access past successes, resulting in low SE; and scarcity of potential resources which the individual could marshal in order to cope with, or make sense of, the situation. The level or intensity of each of these impacts the way the individual will internalize and respond to the initial and any subsequent trauma. For example, individuals who have been victimized, yet experience/internalize the traumatic event as less severe than those whose experience results in PTSD symptomatology, are theorized to have some mitigating factor. Perhaps the individual was able to exert control in a situation which resulted in higher SE. Perhaps supportive, protective siblings banded together, resulting in feelings of belonging and higher SI. These same factors contribute to the recovery prognosis.

Flashback, Selective Repression, and Use of Dissociation

In the non-combat PTSD patient/client, the principle differences are in the **flashbacks, selective repression,** and **use of dissociation** as survival tools while the trauma is occurring. These differences are noted as flashbacks, memory loss, and/or regression during a flashback.

> **Flashbacks**—Less frequently one of the earlier manifestations of the disorder. Because the use of denial and/or repression of the memory are preferred defense mechanisms with non-combat PTSD, considerable energy is required to break through that block. When a flashback does occur, it is often in the form of a nightmare in which the face of the perpetrator is

distorted, demonic, blank, or dark and blurred. Such dreams, especially initially, tend to be symbolic rather than realistic portrayals of the event. Flashbacks are frequently fragments at first, with the person remaining consciously in the here and now, rather than reliving the trauma.

With PTSD of both types, when the individual totally returns to the trauma and loses contact with the present time, a danger is that of the individual remaining locked in the memory, unable to return to the present. When this happens, the event is diagnosed as a psychotic break. Temporary flashbacks have also resulted in this diagnosis, particularly in individuals where exposure of the trauma would jeopardize someone more influential.

Memory Loss—The individual reports periods of time which are unexplainably lost. These periods may be days, months, or as extensive as a number of years. Although these time periods are no longer part of the person's conscious memory, the individual continues to relive and to have his or her decisions influenced by the experience, at the unconscious level.

Regression During a Flashback—In cases where the trauma being reexperienced occurred when the individual was young, during the flashback or reliving of the memory the individual appears to "become" that age. With especially severe and/or chronic trauma, care needs to be taken to keep the bridge between past and present open for "safety" and to prevent a "psychotic" break in which the individual could become developmentally "stuck" or fixed at that age. Many PTSD patients have a great fear of "going crazy," due in part to previous occurrences of such flashbacks, and having no other label or frame of references with which to "make sense" of the flashback experience.

One coping or survival mechanism often selected while PTSD-inducing trauma is occurring is to *mentally dissociate.* This psychological distancing leaves the memory of the trauma unavailable to the *conscious* mind. However, the trauma continues to be reality for the unconscious. Another complication is that trauma, particularly chronic, creates a block or impasse beyond which the individual cannot proceed with subsequent developmental tasks (Erikson, 1963). The outcome is a person who is developmentally arrested, often both emotionally and mentally. (Hooker, 1985, discussed the effects of trauma on the person's ability to access to intellectual resources due to the mental drain of obsessively reliving the experience or reviewing the tape, so to speak, which in turn affects his or her ability to focus on the here and now.) This means that the individual who experiences trauma resulting in PTSD symptomatology will often have both the complication of memory loss, and of being psychologically frozen at the age/stage when the debilitating trauma occurred. When this is the case, expect an increasing disparity between the person's chronological age and the behaviors she or he is exhibiting. Some people with high natural intelligence are very creative in hiding this. However, if even a hint or glimpse of behavior does not correspond with the "rest of the picture," consider exploring the possibility of early trauma.

Once the decision is made that remembering the event could jeopardize the individual's survival, the flashback/repression cycle is put in place. This means the individual then will be unable to consciously access or verbalize memories or feelings concerning the event. Repression of the memory will continue until the individual, often with the help of an encouraging therapist, is able to somehow perceive the ego strength as sufficient to risk remembering some portion of the event without total destruction. The exception to this is, of course, the flashback. One criteria of PTSD is that the traumatic memory(s) is powerful enough to force through the wall of repression and reach the consciousness, that is, the flashback. A major problem here is that the flashback occurs *spontaneously*—before the ego strength has improved sufficiently for the necessary psychological distance to be obtained, and for the guilt and shame surrounding the original trauma to be assigned appropriately.

Another problem that arises with the flashback is that the same emotions and intensity are experienced. (When dissociation was the coping mechanism used to survive, the individual may be consciously experiencing these emotions for the first time.) For example, during a flashback, the physical pain of a violent act will be felt. The individual may go into shock, scream, faint, become hysterical—anything that would have been appropriate at the time but may or may not have been options for the individual when the event occurred.

If the trauma occurred at an early age, during therapy the client's attempts to verbalize or express the feelings connected with the event often result in moans, guttural viscular cries, or an inability to produce any sound, even while the entire body is positioned to scream. That is, the body is tense, the head is back, the chin is up, the mouth is open, the face is contorted in a grimace, but the person is still unable to produce any sound. This silent scream is most prevalent in the individual initially traumatized under the age of six and not allowed to make a sound even when in great pain, or in the person who was told not to let anyone know.

Individuals suffering from non-combat-related PTSD report periods of mental confusion, emotional numbness, frequent dissociation or taking a mental "trip," with the accompanying inability to focus on present events or remain in the here and now. These symptoms intensify when the person is under stress. This includes therapy when the individual is working to recall the traumatic event/memory. Typically, a client who mentally **checks-out** will have the most difficulty staying in the present time when a mental connection is made between what is being said and the trauma. This connection may be made with information that seems totally unrelated to an outsider, and often to the person with PTSD.

Several factors are at work to produce this effect. First, because PTSD-invoking trauma is intense, **extensive gener-alization** can take place quickly, and the connections made during the generalization will remain in effect until the power of the trauma is somehow diminished or negated. Second, due to the intensity of the emotions at the time, and the high levels of energy involved in repressing the memory, a great deal of power is brought to bear anytime the wall of repression/denial is threatened. Although what is being said may, in reality, have no connection with the event, the fear of discovery will be so strong that the most effective *coping mechanism* will be utilized and at an extremely high level. One patient would go to sleep during lectures about the possibility of changing or in a small group when the subject of incest or any form of abuse was being discussed or disclosed. Discovering the memory is particularly frightening with sexual abuse and/or incest, especially when the child has been told not to tell and/or has been threatened with terrible consequences if she or he does tell. Typical threats are the child's death and/or the harm or death of a loved one.

Treatment Techniques

In therapy, a clue that the memory is beginning to surface is when the client reports having had a disquieting dream, or recalling a recurring nightmare she or he had as a child. Asking the client what the dream meant to him or her and allowing the *client* to do the **interpreting** is the most effective tool. This includes the times when the therapist is completely sure of the meaning, and the client "doesn't have a clue." The important procedure is for the client to do the discovering work so he or she can take the credit.

If an impasse has been reached, with the client unable to bring the memory to consciousness, one tool is to ask the client to draw or write what happened, with his or her non-dominant hand. The non-dominant hand seems to have access to the visual memories. If therapists are comfortable working with the inner child, this is a tool to access the inner child's memory. Drawing and writing also circumvent the "don't tell" injunction.

This is a terribly frightening time, and leaving therapy is an inviting alternative. Leaving is often judged the safest course of action. Although the client may or may not verbalize this fear, as memories begin to surface, one can expect the client to threaten to or actually leave therapy. This is a time when bonding or level of trust will be critical. To offer safety and encouragement, to be completely nonjudgmental, and to convey these attributes to the client sufficiently so that she or he will trust the therapist to provide these at all times and in all circumstances are very important. **Safety, encouragement,** and **nonjudgmentalness** are scarce commodities for PTSD survivors. This is one reason the Adlerian approach is so effective in working with PTSD.

At times, the client may report having a flashback much like a snapshot that appears briefly, often is incomplete, and may seem nonsensical. These fragments may take the form of a sound, a partial view of a room, an article of clothing, a weapon, a color, something the person was looking at or focusing on while the trauma occurred, or a symbolic image.

The therapist can be helpful by *framing* these as "trial runs" or "tests" which the unconscious is using to see if the individual is now strong enough to remember the event and survive. The Adlerian practitioner should also encourage the client with statements such as, "You are safe. You can trust that regardless of what you remember, you will be able to deal with it. If not, it would not have come up at this time." If the initial memories do not prove too frightening and are accepted, owned, and honored, another fragment will be supplied. If not, the repression and denial mechanisms will be reinstated. These pieces of the jigsaw may be given in various patterns, for example, one fragment one day, with the next one in two weeks, the next day, or an hour later. Again, what surfaces and the timing are determined by the way in which the person accepts and deals with each one. Denial is commonly the first defense. When denial is being used, the client will say things such as, "I'm making this all up. It never did happen. It was just a bad dream," or "I wanted to be loved and special to my Dad and that's why I had the dream. It was just a fantasy. I feel awful for telling you those things. None of them were true. I lied, Daddy would never do anything to hurt me. He loves me."

The Adlerian practitioner also congratulates the client for any mental confusion, numbness, and inability to remain in the present. This is done by telling the client the truth: "These coping mechanisms allowed you to survive." The individual used these as a way to protect himself/herself from a reality that was too severe, too punishing, too traumatic to have been tolerated otherwise. The fact that he or she still uses these familiar devises as protective mechanisms also can be a source of encouragement. One can remind the person that she or he is continuing to use the techniques that "worked," which is very wise. The therapist then helps the client see that although these mechanisms worked very well and served a useful purpose initially, they are no longer necessary to protect him or her in this way. Helping the client learn new ways to protect himself/herself, and deal more effectively with situations which are or have been anxiety producing, is the logical next step.

One useful technique is to have the client *congratulate the inner child* (the part of the psyche that experienced and endured the trauma), to thank the inner child for his or her continuing help, and then assure the child that she or he no longer needs to protect the *adult self* from the truth, that the adult self is now strong enough to protect them both. In this process, the child self is not discounted and thus discouraged. Rather, the inner child is encouraged through praise and is thanked for all his or her hard and diligent work. Even the most negative client, one who is unable to accept praise or thanks at the adult, conscious level, is often able to thank the inner child, thereby indirectly raising his or her SE, as well as feelings of worthiness and belonging (SI).

Psychological Distance

Another basic difference between the combat veteran and the person with PTSD is the inability to establish and maintain psychological distance. The combat veteran is subjected to intense, continual, real, and/or anticipatory anxiety. In combat, no relief occurs from this. The proximity, the intensity, and the lack of control all contribute to the inability of the individual with combat-related PTSD to establish and maintain appropriate, necessary, healthy, survival-essential, psychological distance.

On the other hand, the non-combat sufferer of PTSD who has been able to maintain his or her sanity has found a way to obtain this distance. Being able to establish this distance is critical. The individual's way of getting this distance may seem dysfunctional or even "crazy," yet the therapist needs to recognize that establishing distance is an essential survival technique for the trauma survivor. Basically, we have encountered four ways this distance is established: **denial** of the perpetrator's identity or the full extent of the trauma, **repression, dissociation,** and **self-blame.** For example, a victim of sexual abuse such as incest with multiple perpetrators may recall and/or admit that sibling incest occurred, but deny that a parent was involved as well. The victim of the abuse may remember that "something bad" happened, but remember monsters, grotesque faces, demons as being present and/or responsible for what happened (again, having memory of the event at one level, while maintaining denial of the actual perpetrator's identity).

Repression as a safeguarding tendency frequently occurs with abuse victims with PTSD. When repression is being used as a coping/defense mechanism, amnesia of the event may be total. At the conscious level, the individual is unaware the traumatic event occurred. This type of client may report reacting or behaving in strange ways for no apparent reason. The person will be genuinely puzzled by his or her actions which are residual effects of the traumatic event which has been repressed.

Dissociation in one form or another, especially when reinforced later by repression, is the most common and most effective method of dealing with non-combat trauma which results in PTSD. Dissociation may take one of several forms. One, an **out-of-body experience** where the person views the scene as an observer rather than a participant. Two, **imploding,** which is going **inside,** resulting in a complete shutting down of all sensations and thoughts. This is a state in which the person actually does not feel or experience the physical pain involved, nor hear, on the conscious level, the verbal abuse. Third, the individual may create a **pseudo-self** to take the place of the real self (during the experience). For example, one victim of incest assumed a different identity by "becoming" one of her dolls during the actual sexual intercourse with her father. The girl had a large doll collection, each of which had a different name. The ritual was that when her father entered the room, she would say, "Hello, my name is Melanie."

Her father would then refer to his daughter as "Melanie" during the act. The next day, the child would bury the "bad" doll who died the night before. In this way, the child established the psychological distance needed to survive. This is not to say that this is a mentally healthy way to establish psychological distance, but it did work.

Lastly, the individual may mentally **check-out,** to absent himself/herself from the scene completely. Although on the surface this may seem safer and more effective, in some ways this form of dissociation is more dangerous. The dissociation is so complete that it becomes extremely appealing and addictively alluring to the individual using it. The greatest danger of the use of this dissociative technique of mental numbing or blanking out of all reality is that it is so effective that the therapist has difficulty convincing the client that the use of this defense mechanism is no longer necessary. The client often is not aware of doing it. The other reason this form of dissociation is so dangerous is that its use results in behavior and a mental state which is frighteningly close to a psychotic break. Individuals who have consistently used this escape or coping mechanism as children often report having lost years of time. As adults these same people report having difficulty concentrating and staying in the here and now in any situation, but especially when any type of stressor is present.

CASE EXAMPLES

Case of Bill

When any form of dissociation is used, the individual will report lost time or disjointed, partial, fragmented memories. For example, one patient who we will call "Bill" reported feeling as if he was in a piece of a room. He said there was a pair of shoes in the room and nothing else, then everything disappeared and the "bad" thoughts (thoughts of becoming violent) started. When queried about the feelings, Bill became emotional and screamed, "I didn't feel anything! I never feel anything. There was nothing there. There never is anything there. It is all in my head. Nothing is real." He was very uncomfortable during the entire time he was recounting what he called "this fragment" but did have the courage to continue.

At one point during the session, Bill looked directly at the therapist and said, "I have thoughts like wanting to stick my fist through your face and knock the back of your head off." The therapist calmly assured Bill that such feelings of rage and powerlessness were a natural result of the childhood abuse he suffered. The therapist then said to Bill, "I want you to look at me for a minute, and listen." As soon as eye contact was established, the therapist immediately said, "You are not crazy. You are not going to go crazy. You are safe. It is safe to remember what happened and feel your feelings. You are strong enough to hear the truth and deal with the past. You have strength to work through anything that surfaces."

Encouraging clients in this way is helpful. Tell him or her not to worry if the memories are not complete or clear immediately. Reassure the client that as the scared part feels safer, more memories will surface; that some of what happened may never be remembered, and that is fine; that it is not necessary to remember everything in order to be free of the past. Ask the client when he or she gets scared to say, "I am safe. I will never be given any memory that is more than I can deal with. I will never be confronted with anything that will make me lose control and go crazy. I have the power and strength to deal with anything from the past."

Perceived inability to control or predict either the level or the timing of the violence of future events remain key elements in the prognosis of individuals with PTSD. Were the individual able to predict or control the level of violence in future similar events, he or she would be able to avoid the continuing feelings of powerlessness and worthlessness (low SE), which are integral parts of the belief system of a person experiencing the residual effects of trauma or PTSD.

Changing the person's internal belief system regarding the ability to control future events; *addressing* and correctly assigning responsibility for the original trauma; and *absolving* the victim of trauma-connected shame and guilt (which have often been assumed as ways of gaining some feeling of control;

that is, being able to change, stop, avoid, or lessen past and future trauma) are all essential. Changing the belief system and dealing with the past help end the necessity of recreating or reliving the event. When an individual keeps reexperiencing similar traumatic events, not always with the same perpetrator or victimizer, it may be an attempt by the unconscious to "correct the error" and change the script. Mentally replaying the video tapes of the event is often an attempt to find this perfect answer. The reason for seeking the "right way" is to regain the power lost during the trauma; to be able to protect one's self; to abolish the constant fear connected with being revictimized and the need for hypervigilance; and to stop the cycle of fear and pain, the continuous mental (and frequently physical) reenactment of the trauma, looking for clues. Adler's dynamic of "clinging to the shock effects" may be a manifestation of this: an attempt to make sense of insanity or this time to "get it right" in order to erase the "fatal flaw" and thus deserve to belong (SI) and finally to feel better about one's self (SE).

Case of Female Incest Victim

Phobias can often be tied to a traumatic event. In one case, a female incest victim came into therapy complaining of nervousness and an intense though "foolish" fear of bugs. In the course of therapy, it was discovered that her perpetrator was her grandfather, with whom she was living, and the sex act always took place where a number of bugs were. As a survival tool she associated the pain and the terror with the bugs. To fear and hate bugs was easier (safer). They were not responsible for her well-being or survival. Her grandfather was. Her grandfather also gave her love and affection, praise and self-worth. So naturally, bugs had to be what were "bad," not Papa. Papa loved her.

Feelings of **emptiness,** being **worthless,** overwhelming **isolation,** and poorly defined, undefined, or generalized irrational **fear** (anxiety and/or phobic responses) are also frequently reported feelings when the client is asked to recall what it was like to grow up in his/her family.

Assuming the blame/guilt or self-blame affords the individual a pseudo though inaccurate feeling of power and/or the ability to control the situation and thus, to prevent future similar traumatic events from occurring. By assuming responsibility or blame for causing the event, the individual feels in control. She or he obtains a feeling of having some power—real or not—over the situation and his or her life. Any amount, any level, of power is a crucial factor in preventing the debilitation of helplessness and the despair of hopelessness in the individual.

GLOBAL APPROACH TO TREATMENT

Two of the most crucial factors in Adlerian treatment of PTSD are the practitioner's ability to help the client reconnect with his/her intrinsic value/worth (SE) and sense of belonging to the wider community (SI). Increasing the client's SI (which includes a sense of worthiness to belong to the community and therefore basic worth as a person who is a capable, important, and necessary member of society) is also related to the psycho-spiritual healing phase that completes the integration of all levels—body, mind, and spirit. Healing at any of these levels is important and necessary, but in and of itself, insufficient to accomplish reestablishment of wholeness and ultimate reconnectedness of the integrated and thus "healthy" individual with the community (at the universal level). Integration, a sense of worth and belonging, across all levels of the psyche is implicit in the definition of adjustment and/or mental "health" in the Adlerian sense. This **global approach** of total reintegration may seem grandiose. However, to these writers, this global approach remains both the ultimate and minimal criteria for true healing.

Adlerians believe that the client's level of discouragement or displayed damage to SE predetermines or predisposes the individual's expressed symptomatology as well as which therapeutic approach(es) might be most helpful. We agree. For example, the person who has been discouraged since childhood with resulting low SE and little SI would have a great deal of difficulty tackling, much less chance of accomplishing, a task/challenge designed to help teach a client whose SE and SI have sustained only recent damage/

trauma. With the former, basic trust issues (Erikson, 1963) need to be addressed. Rudimentary teaching of techniques, such as stroking for strength and use of affirmations, is required. Clients with longstanding histories of rejection (or perceived rejection) by others have learned not to trust, and trust is the basic building block of self-esteem (SE), followed by SI. With the chronically discouraged client, joy, a sense of humor (SH), and feelings of connectedness and worthiness to be/ feel connected are notably absent. Our experience has been that joy—a sense of humor (SH)—and zest for living and life are the first casualties in the PTSD victim's life-style, belief system, and drama. O'Connell (1981a) addressed this need to restore SH and SI in his work on psycho-spiritual healing.

SEPARATING DISCOURAGING EVENTS FROM BASIC WORTH

Most non-combat, and many combat, PTSD victims have a great deal of difficulty separating the discouraging event(s) from their basic worth (SE). It is not unusual to hear clients with a PTSD diagnosis assuming the guilt and/or blame for the event. For example, the client will say, "If I hadn't been there . . . dressed that way . . . looked at him like that . . . said what I did," "It would never have happened . . . I knew better . . . I knew what would happen . . . It's all my fault." These messages are not always created without help from others. Many incest and/or rape victims and battered women and children are told, "It's your fault. You provoked him/her" or "You should have stopped it. You knew better" or "If that was going on, why did you go back? You knew what would happen. It's your own fault it kept going on. You wanted it to go on or else you wouldn't have kept going back" or "You let it happen" or "Why didn't you tell me?" which corroborates the myth that if the victim had told, then magically some help would have been forthcoming or that the parent or protector would have been there for them, giving aid, assistance, protection, and love. Again, the underlying message is that what happened is the victim's fault and responsibility, the same type of message the victim has been giving himself/herself all along. Victims mentally abuse or beat themselves up using discouraging messages, such as assuming the blame (Hooker, 1985).

One client assumed the blame for a violent rape. Her reasoning? "I knew better than to pick up my car alone after office hours." Unfortunately, this client's belief that she had been solely to blame for the rape was reinforced by several hours of interrogation by police officers while she sat in ripped, blood-stained clothes, unable even to shower because she had not yet been "permitted" to go to the county hospital for a medical examination to see if indeed a rape had occurred. This sense of being to blame, somehow responsible, was compounded by the victim's husband's and mother's tirades. Her husband accused the victim of lying about the rape— using it to cover up an extramarital affair. Her mother insisted that the daughter put herself in the position of "asking for it" by picking up her car after working hours (and that she had probably had on a dress that was too tight or in some way provocative). Mother went on to say that under no circumstances was the daughter ever to tell her father because "the shame would kill him." This client carried the shame of her "guilty secret" and therefore her intrinsic lack of worth for over 20 years before ever sharing it. The facts about the rape came out in therapy after the client began to trust and as a result was able to begin releasing the discouraging, negative aspects of the past and then start building and accepting her true worth.

SUMMARY

The level of self-acceptance (SE) affects one's ability to tolerate change, to recognize the power to initiate and make needed changes. The individual who can accept personal responsibility for all his or her actions and decisions, particularly positive ones (because victims seem to instinctively assume responsibility for everything negative), is well on his or her way to mental health and integration. As teachers, Adlerian practitioners should know that *accepting responsibility, seeing challenges instead of obstacles,* the *ability to laugh at oneself, knowing that "I belong,"* and *this is the way it should be* are all goals of treatment and/or therapy. To move the client to this point of *acceptance,* or as close to it as possible, is our mission. Some Adlerians are crusaders. We are often considered the "outsiders," the ones who are out of step, but we know the truth. Adlerian therapy makes a difference with Generalized Anxiety Disorder, Social Phobias, and Post-traumatic Stress Disorder because we encourage, teach, and model change and bring about integration, hope, and acceptance of our human imperfections. We see our flaws and challenges as a chance to humor ourselves as we "laugh-dance" through the reality we have created in our lives.

Natural High Haiku

Discouragement grasps
separation, fear and guilt.
Humor lets them go.

O'Connell

REFERENCES

Adler, A. (1956). *The Individual Psychology of Alfred Adler*. H. R. Ansbacher & R. R. Ansbacher (Eds.) New York: Basic Books.

Adler, A. (1964). *Problems of neurosis*. New York: Harper Torchbooks. (originally published 1929)

American Psychiatric Association. (1987). *Diagnostic and statistical manual of mental disorders* (3rd ed., revised). Washington, DC: Author.

Ansbacher, H. (1965). The structure of Individual Psychology. In B. Wolman (Ed.), *Scientific psychology* (pp. 340-364). New York: Basic Books.

Baritz, L. (1985). *Backfire: A history of how American culture led us into Vietnam and made us fight the way we did*. New York: William Morrow.

Becker, E. (1973). *Denial of death*. New York: Free Press.

Blackburn, A., O'Connell, W., & Richman, B. (1984). Post-traumatic stress disorder, the Vietnam veteran, and Adlerian Natural High Therapy. *Individual Psychology: The Journal of Adlerian Theory, Research, and Practice, 40*, 307-332.

Dreikurs, R. (1972). Technology of conflict resolution. *Journal of Individual Psychology, 28*, 203-206.

Egendorf, A. (1985). *Healing from the war: Trauma and transformation after Vietnam.* Boston: Houghton Mifflin.

Erikson, E. (1963). *Childhood and society.* New York: Norton.

Gabriel, R. (1987). *No more heroes: Madness and psychiatry in war.* New York: Farrar, Straus and Giroux.

Hooker, B. (1985). *Rx for victims: A clinician's guide to recognizing and treating victim behavior.* Dallas, TX: Thompson Publishing.

Lifton, R. (1985). *Home from the war.* New York: Basic Books.

Manchester, W. (1979). *Goodbye, darkness.* Boston: Little, Brown.

Mozdzierz, C., Marchitelli, F., & Lisiecki, J. (1976). The paradox in psychotherapy. *Journal of Individual Psychology, 32,* 169-184.

O'Connell, W. (1975). *Action therapy and Adlerian theory: Selected papers by Walter O'Connell.* Chicago: Alfred Adler Institute.

O'Connell, W. (1981a). Natural high therapy. In R. Corsini (Ed.), *Handbook of innovative psychotherapies* (pp. 554-568). New York: Wiley.

O'Connell, W. (1981b). Spirits in thanatology. *Death Education, 4,* 397-409.

O'Connell, W. (1983). The impossible dream: Institutionalized actualization of self-esteem and belonging. In R. Steffenhagen (Ed.), *Hypnotic techniques for increasing self-esteem* (pp. 163-180). New York: Irvington.

O'Connell, W. (1984a). Letting go and hanging on: Confessions of a Zen Adlerian. *Individual Psychology: The Journal of Adlerian Theory, Research, and Practice, 40,* 71-82.

O'Connell, W. (1984b). Cutting edges: PTSD. *V.A. Chief Psychologist, 7* (2), 18.

O'Connell, W. (1987). Natural high theory and practice: The humorist's game of games. In W. Fry & W. Salameh (Eds.), *Handbook of humor and psychotherapy: Advances in the clinical use of humor* (pp. 55-79). Sarasota, FL: Professional Resource Exchange.

O'Connell, W. (1988). Natural high theory and practice: A psychospiritual integration. *Journal of Integrative and Eclectic Psychotherapy, 7* (4), 81-94.

O'Connell, W., & Gomez, E. (1990). Dialectics, trances, and the wisdom of encouragement. *Individual Psychology: The Journal of Adlerian Theory, Research, and Practice, 46,* 431-442.

Salzman, L. (1968). *Obsessive personality: Origins, dynamics, and therapy.* New York: Science House.

Trower, P., & Gilbert, P. (1989). New theoretical conceptions of social anxiety and social phobias. *Clinical Psychology Review, 9,* 19-35.

Veninga, J., & Wilmer, H. (1985). *Vietnam in remission.* College Station, TX: Texas A & M University Press.

Weil, A. (1983). *Health and healing.* Boston: Houghton Mifflin.

Wilmer, H. (1989). *Evil and the American shadow: Lessons from Vietnam.* Dallas, TX: Isthmus Institute, February 4.

CHAPTER 8

SOMATOFORM DISORDERS AND PSYCHOLOGICAL FACTORS AFFECTING PHYSICAL CONDITION

Mark Mays, Ph.D., J.D.

Somatoform disorders are those psychological conditions in which the focus is upon physical functioning, the *soma.* In these conditions, patients perceive themselves as physically ill, describe health symptoms, or describe worries about health, but they are without actual organic pathology. The diagnosis of "psychological factors affecting physical condition" refers to those conditions in which actual organic pathology is present, yet psychological factors are seen to trigger, intensify, or maintain the physical distress. In all of these conditions, the focus is on the body. In all of these conditions, patients define themselves as physically ill, in whole or in part. In all of these conditions, their physician disagrees partially or entirely with them.

HYPOCHONDRIASIS

Hypochondriacal patients are concerned about their health. Often they have had some experience which has made them unsure about the security of good health, or life itself. To them, the world is full of worries. The satisfactions and enjoyments that come with good health may be gone forever. The ultimate loss is just a heartbeat, or lack thereof, away. Life to them seems somewhat gray and often unenjoyable, but worth holding on to. For them to know how completely to rely upon physicians is difficult, since their doctors' concerns are not as great, their worries not as intense, their personal investment not so high. Perhaps they have overlooked something? Perhaps some condition exists that they know about but aren't disclosing? Support often seems lacking, both from doctors and nurses as well as friends and family who don't seem to understand how serious all of this is and how great the consequences might be.

The physical body and the world of physical enjoyments are to them a source of frustration rather than satisfaction. The world of thought or caring matters more. Movement and energy are diminished in an attempt to control one's safety, all of which requires skills which they fear may not be available.

In a more objective sense, the hypochondriacal patient starts off with the assumption that ill health is a likelihood and interprets ambiguous events as indicating serious pathology. Much like an Alice in Wonderland, in which a "sentence first, trial later" occurs, the hypochondriacal patient assumes physical disease or ill health, sometimes catastrophic, and gathers data to support this assumption.

DSM-III-R defines *hypochondriasis* as follows:

300.70 Hypochondriasis (or Hypochondriacal Neurosis)

A. Preoccupation with the fear of having, or the belief that one has, a serious disease, based on the person's interpretation of physical signs or sensations as evidence of physical illness.

B. Appropriate physical evaluation does not support the diagnosis of any physical disorder that can account for the physical signs or sensations or the person's unwarranted interpretation of them, and the symptoms in A are not just symptoms of panic attacks.

C. The fear of having, or belief that one has, a disease persists despite medical reassurance.

D. Duration of the disturbance is at least six months.

E. The belief in A is not of delusional intensity, as in Delusional Disorder, Somatic Type (i.e, the person can acknowledge the possibility that his or her fear of having, or belief that he or she has, a serious disease is unfounded).

SOMATIZATION DISORDER

Patients with a somatization disorder are those who are long-suffering, act helpless, and feel physically out of control. To them, the world is truly a frightening place. They fear they may not be up to dealing with some of the challenges of life themselves. Security for them resides outside themselves, and only a helpful "other" such as a doctor or medicines can hold any hope for reducing the distress and suffering. Even these only help a little. People often don't seem to understand how much more is necessary.

The world is full of things that they might wish to do but feel unable to do because physical symptoms preclude full participation in life. If all of these symptoms didn't exist, my, but the world would be full and rich. As of now, they feel they need to settle for second best and to only hope that help in the form of a caretaker is down the road. Since for them power resides outside of one's self, an essential way of life for them is to please and avoid the disapproval of others who may hold the keys to some improvement of or hope for betterment in the future. They feel dragons are out there far bigger than any one person, and they must find the knight to rescue them. They believe one must avoid pain of any kind.

Indeed, the **somatization disorder,** by definition, has numerous physical symptoms. These may include **conversion like phenomena,** in which physical symptoms cannot be explained by organic or physical dysfunction, or by those mechanisms that affect the body, such as medicines or alcohol. The somatization disorder patient usually *complains of pain* and is clear to present himself/herself as long-suffering. Things are generally "all in a mess" without a singular focus for physical concern or symptomatology. These patients *feel sick.* Regardless of what their physicians say, and they usually have numerous physicians, they believe they have the proof through their subjective distress. Unlike the hypochondriacal patient, who is concerned about possible medical illness, the somatization disorder patient actually has *numerous symptoms.* These persist over time, and, given their physical basis, the patient is convinced of their physical cause. Unlike the hypochondriacal patient who has reached a "sentence" of illness before the actual "trial," the person with the somatization disorder has vast and prolific evidence they offer to prove their point.

DSM-III-R defines the **somatization disorder** as follows:

300.81 Somatization Disorder

A. A history of many physical complaints or a belief that one is sickly, beginning before the age of 30 and persisting for several years.

B. At least 13 symptoms from the list below. To count a symptom as significant, the following criteria must be met: (1) no organic pathology or pathophysiologic mechanism (e.g., a physical disorder or the effects of injury, medication, drugs, or alcohol) to account for the symptom or, when there is related organic pathology, the complaint or resulting social or occupational impairment is grossly in excess of what would be expected from the physical findings; (2) has not occurred only during a panic attack; (3) has caused the person to take medicine (other than over-the-counter pain medication), see a doctor, or alter life-style.

Symptom list:

Gastrointestinal symptoms:

1. vomiting (other than pregnancy)
2. abdominal pain (other than when menstruating)
3. nausea (other than motion sickness)
4. bloating (gassy)
5. diarrhea
6. intolerance of (gets sick from) several different foods

Pain symptoms:

7. pain in extremities
8. back pain
9. joint pain
10. pain during urination
11. other pain (excluding headaches)

Cardiopulmonary symptoms:

12. shortness of breath when not exerting oneself
13. palpitations
14. chest pain
15. dizziness

Conversion or pseudoneurologic symptoms:

16. amnesia
17. difficulty swallowing
18. loss of voice
19. deafness

20. double vision
21. blurred vision
22. blindness
23. fainting or loss of consciousness
24. seizure or convulsion
25. trouble walking
26. paralysis or muscle weakness
27. urinary retention or difficulty urinating

Sexual symptoms for the major part of the person's life after opportunities for sexual activity:

28. burning sensation in sexual organs or rectum (other than during intercourse)
29. sexual indifference
30. pain during intercourse
31. impotence

Female reproductive symptoms judged by the person to occur more frequently or severely than in most women:

32. painful menstruation
33. irregular menstrual periods
34. excessive menstrual bleeding
35. vomiting throughout pregnancy

CONVERSION DISORDER

The person with the conversion disorder experiences a loss or alteration in physical functioning suggesting a physical disorder, but psychological factors cause this. Such symptoms as paralysis, loss of sensory functioning in one or more areas, or the like, initially appear to have a physical cause, but adequate medical evaluation eliminates a physical basis.

The phenomenology of the conversion disorder patient is generally that of *resigned acceptance.* Their world is one in which there are losses, sometimes irretrievable losses. One can only deal with this by the quiet acceptance of situations that are beyond control. Since life seems full of loss, they feel that all that one can do now is to attempt to avoid further loss. Feeling disabled and impaired, helpless to change things beyond one's control, they try to look on the bright side and try to make the best of things. Fortunately, others are often helpful and seem to understand the sad blow that fate has dealt them. Others "understand" that they can do nothing to change things, except to help and try to make it a bit better. If medical illness is a prison, they attempt to be a trustee.

From a more objective point of view, conversion disorder patients seem to have accommodated all too well to their current difficulties. They seem to have little insight or understanding regarding the possible psychological rewards for their distress. Often these environmental supports or rewards are quite notable, but the patient treats all of this with an almost automatic emotional response of generally bland indifference. They appear to be a rider in the car, with physical symptoms clearly driving. Their symptomatology is consistent over time, and they clearly are not malingering or consciously attempting to deceive others. Their own experience is that of having no control over aspects of their physical functioning.

DSM-III-R defines a **conversion disorder** as follows:

300.11 Conversion Disorder (or Hysterical Neurosis, Conversion Type)

A. A loss of, or alteration in, physical functioning suggesting a physical disorder.

B. Psychological factors are judged to be etiologically related to the symptom because of a temporal relationship between a psychosocial stressor that is apparently related to a psychological conflict or need and initiation or exacerbation of the symptom.

C. The person is not conscious of intentionally producing the symptom.

D. The symptom is not a culturally sanctioned response pattern and cannot, after appropriate investigation, be explained by a known physical disorder.

E. The symptom is not limited to pain or to disturbance in sexual functioning.

Specify: Single episode or recurrent.

PSYCHOLOGICAL FACTORS

Psychological factors affecting physical condition is the diagnosis given when actual organic pathology is present, but psychological stressors, causes, or stimuli serve to start or exacerbate the physical process. Such problems as **ulcers, migraine headaches, arthritis, allergic reactions, dermatological conditions,** and many other such conditions may have a psychosocial aspect. In fact, some very interesting research suggests that many health issues may have more of a psychosocial aspect than has been previously thought. Research studies suggest, for example, that psychosocial factors may affect the rate of cancer growth, may correlate with the onset of certain forms of cancer, may affect the resiliency of the immune system, or may affect physical functioning in a variety of other ways. While intriguing, these considerations are beyond the specific diagnostic criteria of psychological factors affecting physical condition. *Here a psychologically meaningful stimuli must be related in time to the initiation or intensification of a specific physical disorder.* While such correlations between psychosocial factors and more general health maintenance may, in fact, exist, this is a more *general* question regarding holistic theories of physical well-being and beyond the more *particular* diagnostic questions raised by this DSM-III-R category.

Patients who have this diagnosis *experience physical distress.* They know that they are ill, and can point to X-rays, laboratory studies, and the like. They are sick, and come with portfolios and credentials.

From their point of view, physical pain and physical deterioration are realities, often frightening realities. Resources must be marshalled to avoid further loss, stress, and even risk of loss. They often *feel powerless* to control what occurs with their bodies, and *feel a sense of helplessness* and powerlessness over other aspects of life as well. Life to them is stimulating but sometimes in painful ways. The focus on life is on outer stimuli rather than on inner stimuli, since *satisfaction for them is generally found externally.* It's hard for them to predict or plan in a world which seems unpredictable and occasionally chaotic, a world they believe is best controlled by attempts to deal with problems in a rational and orderly way without the intrusion of disruptive emotion. Things feel out of control enough, they believe, so it is best not to further this with impulsive or expressive actions or to cause further distress by focusing on unpleasant aspects of life.

From a more objective point of view, these patients clearly have illness, participate in continuing care for their illness, but are often only getting treated, rather than getting better. Medical treatment focuses on the more visible threads of the tapestry of the illness syndrome, often neglecting the "binding weave" of psychological and physical factors into the holistic tapestry of human functioning. The range of conditions and the slightly differing dynamics behind these conditions makes it hard to distinguish any specific syndrome or psychological mechanism. Further, psychological assessment is sometimes complicated by the context of health care delivery. These patients may have changed somewhat as a result of kinds of treatment that they have received, either defining themselves as more passive participants in their own health process or becoming exceptionally frustrated with the lack of notable exchange that has occurred through their medical interventions. These contextual factors may complicate the patient's presentation and should be considered in understanding them.

DSM-III-R defines **psychological factors** as follows:

316.00 Psychological Factors Affecting Physical Condition

A. Psychologically meaningful environmental stimuli are temporally related to the initiation or exacerbation of a specific physical condition or disorder (recorded on Axis III).

B. The physical condition involves either demonstrable organic pathology (e.g., rheumatoid arthritis) or a known pathophysiologic process (e.g., migraine headache).

C. The condition does not meet the criteria for a Somatoform Disorder.

ADLERIAN APPROACH

A variety of ways exists to conceptualize these psychological conditions. The DSM-III-R, with which we are primarily concerned here, divides them into the previously noted four classifications. The ICDA (International Classification of Diseases Adapted for Use in the United States), an international system of nomenclature, has defined them somewhat differently, referring to two categories; *physical conditions with tissue injury,* and *physical conditions without such tissue injury.* Previous diagnostic categories in the prior edition (DSM-III) referred to *psychophysiological reactions.* Prior to that, *psychosomatic disorders* was the appropriate diagnosis.

The history of changes in diagnostic criteria and conceptualization shows how psychiatric medicine has attempted to deal with a dichotomy between mind and body. Today's DSM-III-R implies this dichotomy of mind and body, with the criteria of psychological stimuli "triggering" organic pathology, and the distinction between psychological and physical events. Although Adlerian theory is quite helpful in understanding psychosomatic disorders, regardless of how labeled, a theoretical assumption in the current diagnostic conceptualization hints at some incompatibility with Adlerian theory, sometimes complicating communication with those of a dissimilar theoretical framework.

One similarity among all of these conditions is the patient's presentation of physical symptoms or concerns which have a psychological aspect. From an Adlerian point of view, in which all behavior is social, this would mean a social-communicative value, a meaning, exists to all such conditions.

(Continued on page 246)

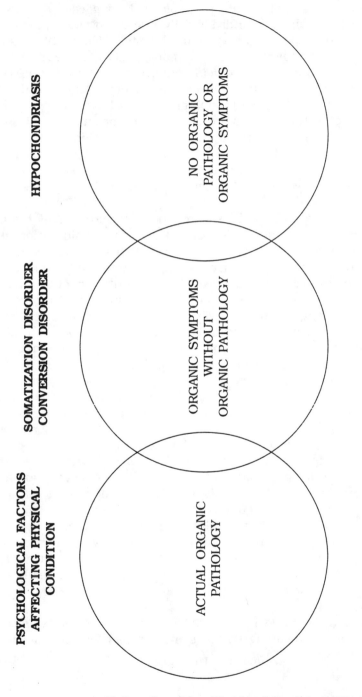

PSYCHOLOGICAL FACTORS
AFFECTING PHYSICAL
CONDITION

SOMATIZATION DISORDER
CONVERSION DISORDER

HYPOCHONDRIASIS

ACTUAL ORGANIC
PATHOLOGY

ORGANIC SYMPTOMS
WITHOUT
ORGANIC PATHOLOGY

NO ORGANIC
PATHOLOGY OR
ORGANIC SYMPTOMS

Figure 8.1. Psychological/physical continuum.

In effect, the definition of "psychological" suggests the social context within which an individual lives and moves and interacts with their own personal goals and life-style. Here, this results in a reaction or disruption of psychological "movement" which is reflected in a physiological symptom or condition. This is one of the strengths of Adlerian theory. Adlerian theory is a holistic and phenomenological *social* psychology. This allows exploration and understanding of an individual from a variety of perspectives. It allows consideration of the host of different levels of systems in which psychological movement occurs. These range from the cultural to the social to the familiar to the psychological as depicted in Figure 8.2.

Adlerian psychology allows for an understanding of human movement that accounts for or takes into consideration not only the person, but also the social fields in which he or she moves and the contributing holistic interaction of subsystems which form a psychological entity. In other words, Adlerian theory can "make sense" of an individual's personal and social situation more easily than can other theories since it takes into account the person's social context. **Psychoanalytic** attempts to interpret or infer generalized psychodynamics behind varying conditions have not been supported in the research literature. Psychoanalytic formulations employ a metaphor of human functioning that is biological, rather than social psychological. These theories attempt to look at animalistic urges in conflict with external social forces. The focus remains intrapsychic, rather than one that takes into complete account the ecology in which an individual lives and functions. The social psychological "pay-off," or benefit, for psychosomatic conditions in other theories is seen as secondary, as is clear in the concept of "secondary gain." The primary gain, or psychological benefit, is a resolution of an unconscious conflict, according to traditional psychoanalytic theory. Unfortunately for the psychoanalyst, these quite difficult-to-research theoretical positions have often been found wanting, both in analytical and empirical studies.

Adlerian theory looks at individuals in their social situation. We look at the meaning that a symptom has for an individual,

(Continued on Page 248)

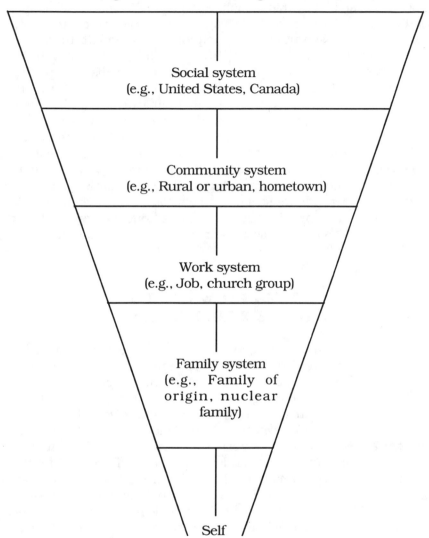

Cultural system
(e.g., Judeo-Christian, Anglo-American)

Social system
(e.g., United States, Canada)

Community system
(e.g., Rural or urban, hometown)

Work system
(e.g., Job, church group)

Family system
(e.g., Family of origin, nuclear family)

Self

Figure 8.2. Different levels of systems in which psychological movement occurs.

the anticipated reactions of others, the social psychological "role" that an individual maintains by being medically ill, and a life-style in which such exaggerated goals as claiming, getting, avoiding, or revenge can play a role in contributing to a patient's symptoms. We explore the context to see in which ways an individual's life-style might be served by symptoms. Adlerian therapy is also helpful in terms of exploring the psychological meaning of being medically ill within our culture. Depending upon one's background and social circumstances, the role of the medical patient may have some profound implications and rewards. Some good things can happen when a person is sick. Friends and family pay attention. The rigors and demands of work and contributory activity can be avoided in a face-saving manner. Sometimes special favors are given, and social expectations shift when one is sickly. As most people view situations, one is expected not to have any "say so" over their medical condition and the consequences of it.

SOCIAL ROLE GAINED
BY MEDICAL ILLNESS

Anthropologists have explored the social role of the medically ill in differing cultures. For example, a rather intense symptomatology response was commonly expected to "the change in life." Swooning, fainting, and being incapacitated were all fairly normative, understood, and, given the general understanding of the syndrome, condoned. In the latter part of the 20th century in America, perhaps following the rise of the feminist movement and an increase of women in the workplace, such expectations have diminished, and a woman who swoons and faints in response to "the change of life" would be viewed askance by males and females alike. A social role for what is accepted and expected of the medical patient is an anthropological variable. It shifts over time, it varies among subcultures, and it certainly plays a role in a person's symptoms.

For example, an individual might develop a psychological paralysis of the vocal cords immediately preceding an audition for the opera. The psychoanalyst might see this as a reflection of rage directed towards a harsh and introjected father figure who has compelled excessive devotion to the precision of musical and operatic training, with a secondary psychological pay-off of solicitousness from friends. One with a more physiological bent might see this as a laryngeal spasm secondary to heightened arousal, with psychological distress secondary to this, such distress reflecting itself in the most vulnerable organ system, coincidentally, that of the voice. A behaviorist might see subvocalization and intense muscular tension secondary to performance distress as contributing to a build-up of lactic acid and resultant muscular discontrol.

An Adlerian, on the other hand, would explore a person's life-style and the social context, exploring what occurred as a result of the physical symptom without a physical cause. The Adlerian would look at the anticipated effect as well as the actual one, and the meaning of this to the individual. Here an Adlerian would wonder if this reflects discouragement, and might hypothesize that such an individual was discouraged and developing a "face-saving" way to avoid social evaluation, evaluation which her/his discouragement and pessimism might make the person wish to avoid. The development of a physical symptom, something consensually seen in our culture as beyond an individual's volitional or voluntary control, takes the person "off the hook." The individual, therefore, can say "I would have if I could have." Self-definition remains intact, and the person can see self, and, likely mistakenly, believe that others see her/him as still possessing such skill that, were it not for fate, would certainly reflect itself with an opening at the Met.

Although this is one hypothesis that such a symptom picture might reflect, the Adlerian therapist looking at a patient's unique and individual approach to situations might find a variety of different dynamics. It might not be quite so simple as avoidance of a psychologically threatening situation. It might well be, for example, that the individual was a woman and was raised in a subculture in which, for example, the "good Mormon girl" deferred to her husband's directives, relinquished leadership to the husband, and would not wish to "overshadow" her spouse as such success might cause to happen. The life-style of such an individual might be that of one who had an exaggerated need to do what was right, or an individual who had martyristic tendencies, gaining superiority through "righteous suffering."

This might also be, for example, an individual who wished to use physical symptoms to put others in one's service, reflecting a life-style of dominance more than avoidance. In one case, the situation might be analogous to the discouraged child who wishes to be left alone. In another case, it might be more akin to the individual who gets greater attention from family for frailties ("a bird in the hand") than she/he anticipates would occur following an audition in which fears are present that she/he might not have the skills to triumph over others.

In making a diagnosis, the Adlerian would look at individuals' life-styles and how this interacts with the social context and consequences to produce a creative solution to personal problems. Psychological symptoms always are an individual's creative attempt to resolve a conflict between his/her own life-style and the social demands for cooperative living. The solution is a mistaken and a socially useless one, yet a creative one nonetheless.

In fact, the Adlerian practitioner can often shift the social psychological meaning of a symptom by reframing the symptom's meaning. For example, frequent nocturnal headaches might serve the purpose of distancing a wife from sexual contact with her spouse. A notable change might occur in symptom presentation if both she and her husband were told by a credible and authoritative resource, such as a family doctor, that her headaches were the result of muscle tightness, suggesting the need for emotional release, and that nothing would be better for this than sexual climax. This might cause the headaches to lead to the consequence of sexual activity, rather than distancing one's self from it. The symptom might well change, and another "solution" sought.

BRIDGE BETWEEN SOCIAL AND INDIVIDUAL

This bridge between the social psychological and the individual is fairly unique to Adlerian thought. This allows for the contributions of both the systems theorist and the personality theorist. Goal-directed behavior in a social context is an understanding that Adlerians possess, yet a conceptual omission in many other theories of psychotherapy.

Meaning

But what does all of this mean in real life? One result is that patients are referred to us who define themselves as medically ill. This often means that they are moving towards a personal goal of seeing themselves as ill and wishing to be seen by others as physically ill. If this is their goal, one could expect that attempting to move them away from their goal would result in some notable lack of cooperative activity. The Adlerian therapist would either need to initially "make friends" with the private logic of a patient, or challenge or change the patient's mistaken goals. Telling an individual who wishes to be seen as physically ill that "there is nothing wrong with you. It's all in your head" would often result in the individual seeking another, "more understanding" psychologist or therapist. A patient who is told that "Your stomach problems are psychological in nature" might likely find this counter to his or her own experience, and certainly at great disharmony with his or her private goals of being seen as medically ill. One so diagnosing would likely be disbelieved, disregarded, or dismissed. Such patients are, however, quite comfortable with the diagnosis of "functional bowel syndrome," a label which implies the same condition, but still hints at physiology rather than personal motivation as being the cause or culprit in the patient's difficulties. A medical diagnosis such as this might be quite compatible with an individual's mistaken goals of, for example, being taken care of, suffering, avoiding, or getting from others as a result of their distress. A "psychological" diagnosis might not move one towards those goals. This makes treatment of such patients an art, demanding tact, timing, trust, and rapport.

Development

So how does it all come about? Within Adlerian psychology, no specific antecedent leads directly and causally to these conditions. This is the beauty and elegance of Individual

Psychology, an idiographic study of personality. Individuals' creativity is reflected in their choice of symptom, with the commonality being a lack of social interest and exaggerated or mistaken personal goals displayed in their life-style and current circumstances.

Some predecessors are more common than others, however. Often the individuals who reflect physical disorders have aspects of their personality which are quite dependent. They wish to get from others or to be taken care of. These are more often youngest children. Overprotection on the part of parents may leave one with a discouraged perception of self as frail and unable to deal with life's hardships. Family constellations in which another sibling died often result in an overconcern and attentiveness to health on the part of family members. Early recollections of death, disease, injury, or medical treatment often are reflective of such a family focus. Chronic medical disabilities on the part of anybody in the family, elderly grandparents living at home, physically dangerous parental vocations, and the like, all might result in a family more attentive to health than the average.

Early recollections may show situations in which misfortune allowed an avoidance of stressful situations, or ways in which symptoms, physical or situational, put others in one's service. These also are quite compatible with somatoform disorders or psychological factors affecting physical condition. Early recollections which display a focus on kinesthetic processes, such as enjoying swinging, moving, tumbling, and the like, suggest a preference for kinesthetic representational systems, often associated with physical forms of communication as occur in these diagnostic groups. Individuals who have a heightened need for control often find the ultimate circumstance in which they lack control, that of death and life itself, as posing a particular stress for them. Hypochondriacal patients often have such an exaggerated need for control. Those who seek stimulation excessively, or who are "getters" in their early recollections (Adler, 1957), may often be those who are vulnerable to prescription medicine dependence and somatoform dysfunction. Those who have experienced sexual abuse also may be more at risk for chronic pain syndromes or somatoform disorders. Deductions based on research would suggest that this may play more of a role in female chronic pain patients than was previously thought. This would certainly suggest that early recollections in which physical aspects of life, or physical attractiveness, resulted in any unfortunate outcomes could certainly be consonant with a symbolic expression of distrust of physical forms of relating to the world. Those in occupations which emphasize physical activity, such as athletes, physical therapists, physical education teachers, dancers, and the like, may reflect a very positive way of relating to the world physically. Disruptions and discouragement in such vocational arenas may result in physical symptomatology, a more socially useless way of dealing with kinesthetic communicative systems.

TREATMENT
Somatoform Disorders and Psychological Factors

In treating such patients, an essential procedure is to examine the individual dynamics. A strong recommendation to pursue assessment on both a medical and a psychological dimension is in order with suggestive findings (Ford, 1983; Taylor, 1982). The diagnosis of the somatoform disorders implies the absence of physical pathology or other effects upon physical functioning, as can be found in drug misuse, alcohol abuse, and the like. Some researchers have suggested that many patients thought to have a somatoform disorder are, in fact, misdiagnosed; they are medically ill patients (Ford, 1983; Taylor, 1982). Such conditions as early presentation multiple sclerosis, endocrine disorders, certain neurologic conditions, environmental agents, and a host of other situations may appear similar to these psychological conditions. This makes it essential not only to gain a thorough medical understanding of the patient, but also to have a life-style or psychological assessment which seems to "make sense" of the patient's symptoms. Both should be present for these diagnoses to occur.

Such physical symptoms also can occur as an individual attempts to express indirectly and metaphorically certain unacknowledged private goals. Attentiveness to such indirect communication is helpful, since this may reflect a patient's misguided effort to solve a personal problem. For example, individuals whose life-styles cause difficulty for them being emotionally expressive, assertive, or confrontive to problematic individuals might develop functional neck pain which metaphorically reflects frustration and discomfort with a personal situation. Likely such a person would know immediately the answer to the question, "Who is the pain in your neck?" Some patients with functional bowel symptoms or ulcerative colitis with a psychogenic aspect often wish to rid themselves of something, their life-style inhibiting them from expressing this directly. Treatment which focuses on understanding, clarifying, and resolving life-style restrictions on full cooperative expressiveness aids in the resolution of such physical symptoms.

Individuals also may have as a private and unacknowledged goal to be like another person, an individual who has similar symptoms. Identification can occur upon occasion in somatic disorder, and an exploration of others with similar syndromes who have been significant to a patient, may provide insight.

Dreikurs (1954) recommended the use of the **Question technique.** He asked patients how their lives would be different if one could wave a magic wand and take away all of these symptoms, exploring what they could do then that they cannot do now. He believed that this provided some examples of the psychological gains or benefits which accrue from the symptom. This technique is frequently helpful. Some believe that the absence of such changes tends to suggest a physical cause, with notable changes suggesting a psychosocial component. A helpful procedure is to ask individuals with physical symptoms what it says about them to have such symptoms, how others understand and respond to them and their symptoms, if they have known anyone who has such symptoms, and if they can describe their symptoms metaphorically, asking what their symptoms are like or similar to. These are helpful expansive questions which can explore alternative ways in which an individual's life-style and personal movement can result in physical symptoms.

Treatment strategies focus on helping the patient understand and gain greater control over physical functioning, while gradually building up other aspects of social embeddedness and social interest so that physical symptomatology erodes and fades away as it becomes unnecessary. Encouragement, greater understanding of mistaken goals in life, an increased feeling of social interest, and a less self-absorbed approach to life all tend to be good antidotes to these physical conditions.

CASE EXAMPLES

Case of Ethel

Ethel is 59 years old and a widow on her second marriage. Her first husband left her rather well-off financially, and she and her second husband spend leisure time in their apartment, interacting marginally with a few longstanding friends. Ethel is the youngest of four children, having three older brothers. She described herself as "daddy's little girl." Her family was visible and highly regarded, if not wealthy, and she grew up in the family as the "young princess," a person much taken care of by her older siblings.

Always concerned with fashion, she prided herself on doing well and opened up a small boutique, financed in large part by her first husband, a physician quite older than her. Following her husband's death, the boutique began to fail and soon closed. She ultimately married a disabled laborer who frequented the coffee shop next to her store. Mildly depressed, she was referred to a psychiatrist for treatment and eventually became sexually involved with him during the course of treatment. When this relationship ended she sought further care from a counselor who was supportive and saw her three times a week for several years until his retirement. Following his retirement, she developed episodes in which she had left-sided paralysis. Her husband, alarmed, referred her for neurological evaluation, but extensive studies were normal. Hospitalization showed muscle tone to continue, and irregularities of her presenting problems were noted that did not coincide with known medical processes. Her symptoms would vary over time, becoming acutely worse when her husband would have to spend time with his volunteer veterans association, ultimately necessitating his abandoning this effort to spend time with her. Ethel was diagnosed as having a conversion disorder.

Case of Ingrid

Ingrid is a 42-year-old obese female referred by her internist for a psychological evaluation. He notes numerous medical problems, including bizarre sensory experiences, gastrointestinal difficulties, pain, and symptom complaints that cover virtually every organ system. He is concerned about her prescription medicine dependence and notes that extensive medical exploration has not revealed a physiological basis to account for her symptoms. He notes that she is a long-term patient of the clinic, seen by his former partner. She reports a history of having been adopted and raised in a foster home. She was removed at an early age by Child Protective Services workers as a result of neglect and abuse on the part of her alcoholic custodians. She has little information regarding her biological parents, but reports them also to have been alcoholics. Her early recollections start at age seven, and include rocks thrown at her by an older boy, and having had her gloves and coat stolen by a school mate. She has been unable to maintain consistent employment as a result of her health status and is supported by her husband, a sergeant in the air force who is frequently on remote assignment in his role of a safety instructor. She arrived at the clinic with a big handbag filled with all her medicines, assuming she would be asked about her health history, and prepared for the social aspect of the interview by wearing thick blue eye shadow and heavy make-up. She is diagnosed as having a somatization disorder.

Case of Robert

Robert is a salesman for a tobacco company and has a large regional sales route. With recent health concerns the tobacco industry has been increasingly competitive. The quotas from the home office have become increasingly hard to meet. Demoralized by the difficulties he experiences, concerned about his rather notable debt to support his indulgent life-style, he has taken on an additional sales territory which causes him to be absent from home and family even more frequently.

He notices that he has migraine headaches which seem to preceed his monthly sales meetings and also correlate with his contacts with large accounts. These sometimes prohibit his making trips, but, more generally, he continues with his activities but believes his performance has diminished as a result of his physical distress. He is diagnosed as having psychological factors which affect his physical condition.

Case of Henry

Henry is a 29-year-old only living son of a family with three children. One of his brothers died at infancy; the other was an alcoholic killed in an automobile accident. He has profound concerns about his health, concerns so pronounced as to make it difficult for him to concentrate on his academic activities. He has missed classes for medical appointments. The oldest of these three children, he wishes to be a success in his career field of accounting, feeling that likely he will need to support his parents as they age. He finds that his health concerns distract him from attending to his school activities, inhibit his dating, and are an almost constant source of worry. He takes his blood pressure regularly, has complete physical exams twice a year, and is diagnosed as having hypochondriasis.

Case of Karen

Karen is a laboratory technician at a local hospital, having previously worked professionally in the ballet. Her family constellation shows a family of three children, with Karen the middle sibling, and generally positive recollections and descriptions of her siblings and parents. Her early recollections show energy and physical movement and the involvement of others. She is referred for an evaluation of numerous physical complaints, including dizziness, problems with balance, and lapses of concentration and memory. Her family physician could not find a medical cause and referred her for psychological evaluation. An exploration of her life-style showed a high degree of social interest and involvement and no suggestion of psychopathology. Her referral back to her physician resulted in an ultimate diagnosis of exposure in the workplace to toxic levels of formaldehyde, which resulted in her symptoms. She received no psychiatric diagnosis.

SUMMARY

The variety of somatic problems with a psychological basis has been described and discussed. These clinically challenging diagnoses seem to be especially well-suited to Adlerian formulation and treatment. The hope is that further research and study in this will yield even more effective clinical intervention.

REFERENCES

Adler, A. (1957). *Understanding human nature* (W. B. Wolfe, trans.) Greenwich, CT: Premier Books. (Originally published, 1918).

Dreikurs, R. (1954). The psychological interview in medicine. *American Journal of Individual Psychology, 10,* 99-122.

Ford, C. (1983). *The somatizing disorders: Illness as a way of life.* New York: Elsevier Biomedical.

Taylor, R. L. (1982). *Mind or body: Distinguishing psychological from organic disorders.* New York: McGraw-Hill.

CHAPTER 9

THE DISSOCIATIVE DISORDERS

Len Sperry, M.D., Ph.D.

The Dissociative Disorders represent a class of disorders that have come to be considered so rare that some texts omit or limit their discussion. The reader should note that in older texts, as well as in DSM-I (1952) and DSM-II (1968), these disorders were often termed Hysterical Neurosis-Dissociative type. Hysteria seems to have been highly prevalent among the leisure class of the late 19th century. Ellenberger (1970) believed this was due to cultural factors such as affectation and theatricality as well as a puritanical ethos which fostered repression as a mechanism of defense or a neurotic safeguard. The change to a more compulsive, work-oriented culture in the early and middle part of the 20th century may have accounted for the virtual disappearance of hysteria/dissociative disorders. However, the apparent reappearance of this class of disorders, influenced by the "me" and "now" generation of the 1960s and a shift to a more narcissistic ethos, suggests their inclusion in this text.

Dissociation is a phenomenon that is commonly defined as a temporary alteration in the normally integrative functions of consciousness, identity, or memory (Yaeger,1989). Dissociation involves a splitting of thoughts, feelings, or behaviors that are ordinarily closely connected. Thus, thoughts can be dissociated from behaviors or from feelings. Dissociative phenomena are not necessarily associated with psychopathology. These phenomena may occur spontaneously, can be sought after, or can be induced for therapeutic purposes. The belief is that the ability to have such experiences is related to the same phenomenon that underlies hypnotizability. Hypnosis requires concentrated focal alteration with a relative reduction in awareness of stimuli (Spiegel & Spiegel, 1978).

Dissociation is a continuous rather than a singular or discrete phenomenon. Beahr (1982) referred to the "dissociative continuum" ranging from milder, more common forms of dissociation to pathological dissociative states which are included in the DSM-III-R category of Dissociative Disorders. Commonplace dissociative. events include daydreaming and absorption in reverie such that one can drive past one's freeway exit or not hear one's name being called by a class instructor. For the three-year-old child, having an imaginary playmate would be considered normal, as would a college student learning and practicing one of the many forms of meditation. Our culture tacitly supports and reinforces some degree of dissociation. In the process of becoming socialized, an American child is taught to take on a variety of roles that exist simultaneously but are expressed sequentially, depending on the demands of the situation. Among adults, the "part self" nature of the psyche has been. easily accepted by the lay public, and is a favorite theme in literature and the arts. We tacitly understand that we are not homogeneous, "singleminded" organisms, that conflict, diversity, and disparity within the self-structure are central features of being human.

The dissociative states are pathological forms in which complex behavior takes place outside the awareness of one's predominate consciousness and include trances, blackouts, psychogenic amnesia, psychogenic fugue, depersonalization disorder, and multiple personality disorder (MPD). Although the etiology of dissociative states is usually thought to be functional or psychological, these states can have an organic etiology. Yaeger (1989) noted that blackouts—periods of amnesia—can be caused by alcohol or other substance intoxication as well as by head trauma. And, Yaeger also noted that dissociative states including MPD have been noted in individuals with temporal lobe epilepsy or partial complex seizures.

BRIEF HISTORY OF THE CONCEPT OF DISSOCIATION

The phenomenon of dissociation has enthralled as well as puzzled philosophers, clinicians, and the lay public since the beginning of recorded history. For instance, the early Greeks employed dissociation in their "sleep therapy." Medical interest in dissociative disorders was reported beginning in the late 19th century with systematic studies of hysteria and hypnosis. Janet is credited with introducing the term "dissociation" (Vander Kolk & Vander Hart, 1989). He hypothesized a model of idea complexes existing outside of consciousness as the cause of hysterical symptoms, as well as the basis for hypnotic and post-hypnotic phenomena. Janet used the term dissociation to describe a split in consciousness. He also believed that dissociation was the result of neuropsychological weakness.

Freud and Breuer, in their *Studies on Hysteria* (1955), claimed that thoughts that were kept out of conscious awareness to ward off painful affects could cause hysterical symptoms. Freud used the term repression rather than dissociation as a label for this phenomenon of thoughts kept out of consciousness. Unlike Janet, Freud's dissociation referred to both the observation of the split in consciousness and the mechanism of defense, that is, repression. Furthermore, Freud preferred a psychological rather than an organic explanation for dissociation. Finally, Freud's patients tended to be diagnosed as patients suffering from hysteria without a clear organic cause.

Prince also developed a theory of dissociation similar to Janet's in which different conscious states could exist in a person without awareness since his or her attention was not focused on them. He described co-consciousness as an explanation for phenomenon seen in both hysterical symptoms and multiple personality. Like Janet, Prince primarily studied patients with amnesia, fugue, gomnabulism, and multiple personality.

Freud and Prince had considerable impact on subsequent researchers and theorists on hysteria and multiple personality, and the result has been that dissociative symptoms tend to be attributed to the existence of a split in consciousness, not to organic etiologies. Furthermore, even though Freud reported his observations on a more limited and distinct population—hysterical neurotics—than did Prince, the fact that both postulated "dissociation" as the underlying mechanism led many investigators to "lump" observations on the phenomena of amnesia, fugue, multiple personality, and hysteria together. This unwarranted assumption and consequent lumping of clinical presentations has led to diagnostic confusion. One result of this was that *DSM-III* and *DSM-III-R* approached diagnosis on the basis of similarities of signs and symptoms or known organic etiologies rather than on postulated psychological mechanisms. This change in focus has meant that cases described in the literature as psychogenic fugue would be considered psychogenic amnesia in DSM-III and DSM-III-R. Or, whereas the main character in Hannah Green's *I Never Promised You a Rose Garden* (1964) was diagnosed and treated by her psychiatrist as a schizophrenic, today she would be classified as a multiple personality. For these and perhaps other reasons, considerable skepticism exists about dissociation and the dissociative disorders in the mental health profession. In the past 15 years, a resurgence of interest has occurred in the multiple personality disorder. A small but vocal group believes that the diagnosis of MPD was overlooked, leaving untold numbers of patients undiagnosed or not adequately treated if they received a different diagnosis. This group has championed the diagnosis and developed its own organization, journal, and numerous workshops. A much larger group of mental health professionals believe that MPD is very rare, if it exists at all. A recent issue of the *Journal of Nervous and Mental Disorders* (1988, vol. 176, 9) was devoted to this "split" in the profession. These professionals are convinced that any increase in the number of reported cases of MPD represents a resurgence of interest in mental health professionals who in turn have influenced suggestible patients that they have this disorder. Furthermore, they contend that hypnosis is an introgenic treatment in that it probably induces the disorder.

DIAGNOSTIC FEATURES AND DSM-III-R CRITERIA

With some background of the convoluted history of the phenomenon of dissociation and its diagnosis, we now turn to a description of the features and diagnostic criteria for the five disorders listed in DSM-III-R. These five are psychogenic amnesia, psychogenic fugue, depersonalization disorder, multiple personality disorder, and dissociative disorder NOS. A growing number of researchers and clinicians believe that the Post-traumatic Stress Disorder (PTSD), particularly the chronic form, is also a dissociative disorder, even though *DSM-III* and *DSM-III-R* assigned it to the Anxiety Disorders category. It is speculated that PTSD will be relocated to the Dissociative Disorders category in *DSM-IV*.

PSYCHOGENIC AMNESIA

Psychogenic Amnesia is described as the sudden but temporary loss of ability to recall important personal information. This loss of memory can involve information about a specific topic or memories of the immediate or distant past. This memory loss is too extensive to be explained by ordinary forgetfulness, and it cannot be due to an organic etiology such as amnesia following a head injury, alcohol-induced blackouts, or amnesia associated with a seizure disorder or induced by electroconvulsive therapy (ECT). Unlike the common portrayal of amnesia in T.V. shows and movies, psychogenic amnesia very rarely involves a total loss of recall.

Epidemiologically, this disorder is most commonly diagnosed in female adolescents and young adults. It is also seen in young males under combat conditions. It is rarely observed in the elderly. Since the disorder is relatively rare, the rate of prevalence is unknown.

The etiology of psychogenic amnesia involves dissociation usually secondary to severe psychosocial trauma or intrapsychic conflict. Unexpected loss is the most common catalyst for this disorder.

A hallmark of psychogenic amnesia is that both the onset and termination of amnesia are rapid, and complete recovery of amnesia secondary to organic etiologies tends to be gradual and rarely is complete. Four subgroupings of psychogenic amnesia are listed. **Localized amnesia** is the most common and refers to loss of memory for events during a circumscribed period of time. **Selective amnesia** involves loss of memory for *certain* events during a circumscribed period of time. **Generalized amnesia** is a total failure to recall all of one's past. Finally, **continuous amnesia** is loss of recall of events subsequent to a certain time up to and including the present. Generalized and continuous amnesia are rare.

DSM-III-R criteria require evidence of sudden memory failure for important personal information that is too extensive to be explained by ordinary forgetfulness. Secondly, this memory loss cannot be due to organic causes or multiple personality.

The differential diagnosis of Psychogenic Amnesia includes organic mental disorder, psychoactive substance-induced intoxication, alcohol amnestic disorder, postconcussion amnesia, epilepsy, catatonic stupor, multiple personality disorder, malingering, and factitious disorder.

Appropriate assessment of amnesia requires a complete psychosocial evaluation including psychosocial stressors, history of drug use, trauma, tasks of life, and life-style convictions. Referral for a medical evaluation must be considered to rule out physical trauma, neurological disease, and metabolic or drug-induced causes as primary or contributing factors.

Case Example—Mr. M

Mr. M was 21 years of age when he was found wandering along a busy freeway by a highway patrol officer. He did not appear to know who he was, and could not account for his whereabouts prior to being picked up. He did not acknowledge the driver's license and credit cards in his wallet as his own, nor did he recognize members of his family when they arrived at the highway patrol office where he was being held. He appeared confused and perplexed about these circumstances. Mr. M's family reported that he returned home early from a date with his steady girlfriend of three years, complained of a headache, and had gone to bed early. He awakened the next morning, appeared rather withdrawn, and said little to anyone. He left home and was found later that day about nine miles from home. Gradually, over a period of days, he recovered his awareness of his identity and his life prior to the onset of amnesia. Upon investigation, what was learned was that on the day prior to leaving home, his best friend observed Mr. M's girlfriend with another man. When Mr. M confronted her, she told him she wanted to be free to date other men. A discussion of the amnestic period with a consulting psychologist prompted Mr. M's own spontaneous recollection. After a brief attempt to deny the loss of his girlfriend, he became dysphoric and briefly suicidal. Thereafter, he was able to grieve her loss and profited from short-term psychotherapy.

PSYCHOGENIC FUGUE

Psychogenic Fugue is a specific form of amnesia in which the individual is unable to recall the essentials of his or her previous personality. The key features of this disorder are sudden, unplanned travel away from home or workplace and the assumption of a new identity, with the inability to recall one's previous identity.

The course of this disorder is variable. However, in the majority of cases the fugue lasts for hours or days, though in rare cases it may continue for months. Recovery tends to be rapid and recurrences are rare. After recovery, generally no recollection is made of what occurred during the fugue.

Epidemiologically, this disorder is considered very rare. Its incidence and prevalence are unknown. The age of onset is variable, and it does not appear to be more common in women than in men. The etiology of this disorder is similar to psychogenic amnesia. It often occurs as a reaction to a severe psychosocial stressor, such as the unexpected loss of a job, breakup of a marriage, or other serious disappointment. A history of heavy alcohol and substance use when combined with the above named psychosocial stressors can greatly facilitate the expression of this disorder. In addition, conflicts over money, sex, and aggressive behavior frequently coexist with this disorder.

DSM-III-R criteria requires evidence that the individual suddenly assumed a new identity either partially or fully. Also, the individual must engage in unexpected travel away from the normal home or workplace and cannot recall his or her previous life. Finally, this condition cannot be due to an organic etiology or multiple personality.

The differential diagnosis of Psychogenic Fugue includes organic mental disorder, temporal lobe epilepsy or partial complex seizure, psychogenic amnesia, malingering, multiple personality disorder, and factitious disorder.

A comprehensive assessment of fugue states requires a full psychosocial evaluation with emphasis on psychosocial stressors, history of drug and alcohol use, trauma, interpersonal difficulties, life tasks, and life-style convictions. Referral for a medical evaluation must be considered to rule out physical trauma, neurological disease, and metabolic and alcohol- or drug-induced causes as primary or contributing factors.

Case Example—Dr. B

The family of Dr. B filed a missing person's report with the Chicago police two days after his mysterious disappearance. Two weeks later, a Mr. S was found sleeping on a park bench in San Diego. When questioned by the San Diego police, he appeared confused as to where he was and what he was doing, as nothing around him appeared familiar. He had no memory for Mr. S but insisted he was a physician, Dr. B, from Chicago. In running a description check, the San Diego police learned that he fit the description of the missing Dr. B. Mrs. B was contacted and immediately flew to San Diego and confirmed the man's identity. She explained that for six months prior to his disappearance, her husband had been very worried over a pending medical malpractice suit and had been considered troubled by two physicians leaving his group practice.

Previously an easygoing, affable person, he had recently become moody, irritable, and critical of his family. The last straw seemed to have been a phone call from his only child, a daughter, whom he believed would go to medical school and join him in his practice upon completion of training. She had called to say she was dropping out of her freshman year of college to enter a commune. This call seems to have precipitated Dr. B.'s fugue.

DEPERSONALIZATION DISORDER

The Depersonalization Disorder is unlike the other *DSM-III-R* Dissociative Disorders in that consciousness is never actually segmented nor is significant memory loss a factor. In fact, it bears little semblance to any *DSM-III-R* category. Probably, because it includes the feature of dissociation and "fits" even less well with other major *DSM-III-R* categories, it was assigned to the Dissociative Disorders.

Depersonalization is usually described as an alteration in the individual's perception of self. In this altered perception, individuals perceive and experience being estranged from themselves, feeling as though they were separate observers of the self. Meditators and users of hallucinogens have reported "out of body" experiences, which is a form of depersonalization. The estimate is that 30 to 70% of young adults have had some experience of dissociation, suggesting that it is a very common phenomenon. In fact, some systems of meditation insist that the ability to regularly achieve a dissociative state in meditation is a marker of progress toward enlightenment. Since depersonalization is experienced by many individuals who are not bothered by it, the criteria for a diagnosable disorder then depends on its frequency or the extent of distress brought about by the experience. A corollary phenomenon, called **derealization,** refers to alterations in one's perception of one's environment or object; it is as if it were alien or unreal. Derealization frequently accompanies Depersonalization. Depersonalization is a symptom that is present in a number of psychiatric syndromes, particularly panic disorder, partial complex seizures, and schizophrenia.

Epidemiologically, the incidence and prevalence of Depersonalization Disorder are unknown. Some studies have suggested that it is more common in females than males, but other studies have shown no gender differences. Since this disorder emphasizes the experiences of a changing identity, not surprisingly it occurs most often during adolescence, whereas onset after the age of 40 is very rare.

The etiology of Depersonalization is uncertain. A number of investigators, following Janet, have postulated a biological basis. Others have suggested that depersonalization follows the attempt to repudiate a self-image associated with unacceptable drives or alterations of ego boundaries, while others point to interpersonal influences. In addition to purely biological and psychological explanations, Putnam (1985) believed that data on severe social stressors and life-threatening circumstances demonstrate that dissociation has a social basis. Perhaps a biopsychosocial explanation better explains and predicts this disorder as well as suggests treatment directives.

The course of the disorder is generally chronic and marked by remissions and exacerbations. The degree of impairment is minimal but can be exacerbated by anxiety or the fear of becoming insane. In that sense, it is similar to the conditioned anxiety response that many argue is the cause of the flashbacks occurring with certain drug experiences. Not surprisingly, abuse of alcohol or other substances facilitates the development and expression of this disorder. Other predisposing factors can be hypnotic induction, fatigue, and severe stress such as an accident, natural disaster, or combat experience. *DSM-III-R* criteria requires substantial indication of an episode of depersonalization sufficiently severe and persistent to cause significant distress, though reality testing remains intact. Furthermore, a persistent experience must be present of either being outside of or detached from one's body, or feeling as if one were an automaton or in a dream. Finally, the conditions cannot be caused by organicity, schizophrenia, mood, or anxiety disorders.

The differential diagnosis of Depersonalization Disorder includes schizophrenia; panic disorder or agoraphobia without a history of panic disorder; organic mental disorders, especially intoxication or withdrawal; personality disorders; and temporal lobe epilepsy.

Case Example—Mr. P

Mr. P was a 21-year-old college student when he sought evaluation at the University Student Health Service, reporting he was losing his mind. Having begun to doubt his own reality, he felt he was living in a dream in which he saw himself from without, neither feeling connected to his thoughts or his body. Through his own eyes, he perceived his body parts as distorted, in that his hands and feet seemed extraordinarily large. In addition, he thought people might be robots. He also had begun to ruminate about the recent onset of dizzy spells, thinking he might have a brain tumor. During the psychiatric evaluation he was observed to be somewhat confused, moderately dysphoric, and given to obsessional brooding. He admitted spending so much time thinking about his circumstances that he had lost contact with all feelings except for a pervasive discontent about his predicament. In a follow-up session, he was preoccupied with the perception that his feet had grown too large for his shoes and fretted about breaking up with his girlfriend, as he also had begun to perceive her in a distorted manner. A thorough medical and neurological evaluation ruled out an organic etiology. Various trials of medication were without significant effect. Yet, over the course of two years of weekly psychotherapy, his symptoms gradually diminished. Although his obsessive-compulsive style remained, he now experiences himself and external reality more accurately.

MULTIPLE PERSONALITY DISORDER

Multiple Personality Disorder (MPD) is characterized by the presence of two or more distinct identities or "alter egos" within the same individual. Each alter is dominant at a particular time. Because a large number of alters can occur, MPD individuals can be difficult to detect and diagnose, especially early in the course of the disorder. Putnam, Guroff, & Silberman, et al. (1986) noted that the average duration of psychological treatment prior to the proper diagnosis of MPD is over six years. Because of the waxing and waning character of this disorder and the innumerable permutations of symptoms, an MPD patient may present differently on different occasions. Thus, these patients usually have a history of being given several diagnoses. Kluft (1985) noted that this variable clinical picture is characteristic of 80% of MPDs.

Individuals with MPD usually enter psychotherapy for any number of concerns from anxiety to sleep disorders. In the course of treatment, these individuals may complain of new concerns like the sudden onset of dizziness, difficulty finding their parked car, inordinate indecision about which clothes to wear, or denial of actions that were clearly observed by others. Upon further investigation, a different personality emerges or is discovered in the course of treatment. In some cases, alters continue to be produced. This may result from the indirect suggestion of the clinician, or through formal means like hypnotic induction or amytal interview.

Auditory hallucinations and some features of thought disorder are commonly noted in MPD, as are sudden mood swings. In fact, depression is the most commonly identified symptom of MPD. The more severely dysfunctional MPDs engage in para-suicidal behavior including self-mutilation. Horevitz and Braun (1984) found that 70% of simple MPD cases met the *DSM-III* criteria for Borderline Personality Disorder. Finally, amnesia is considered the pathogenomonic sign of MPD.

Epidemiologically, MPD is more common in females, accounting for 70 to 90% of all cases. Though the actual prevalence rate is unknown, recent research based on studies by Horevitz and Braun suggest that this disorder is not as rare as was once believed.

Etiologically, a predisposing factor appears to be a history of repeated childhood abuse or trauma for which the child responded by dissociating; 97% have been found to have a repeated and severe history of physical and/or sexual abuse as children (Putnam et al., 1986). For the MPD patient, dissociation becomes the predominant or only adaptive coping style.

The onset is usually in early childhood, and the course tends to be more chronic than for any of the other dissociative disorders. The individual develops as many alters as are necessary to cope. Block (1988) noted that the alters have names that reflect their functions. Most common are the Protector, the Whore, the Little Girl (Child), and the Angry One. In their review of hundreds of confirmed diagnoses of MPD, Putnam et al. (1986) found an average number of 10 alters with a median of 7 and a mode of under 5.

Most MPD are diagnosed between late adolescence and early middle age. As they enter their late 50s, the majority begin to spend an increasing amount of time in one resilient personality with a wide range of functions. Some personalities may even integrate spontaneously. The ultimate goal of therapy becomes to reintegrate the personality. Fortunately, recent developments in therapy tailored to MPD suggest that individuals with MPD may be quite responsive to therapy.

DSM-III-R criteria for MPD requires the individual be consecutively dominated by at least two separate and distinct personalities that determine separate behavior patterns. At least two of these personalities must alternately take full control of the individual's behavior.

Case Example—Ms. Y

Ms. Y is a 23-year-old undergraduate female who was admitted to the acute care psychiatric teaching unit at a university hospital with bandaged wrists that had required several stitches to close the self-inflicted horizontal lacerations.

She reported that the day prior to admission she had found herself "waking up" in a liquor store check-out line with two bottles of scotch. This surprised and puzzled her since she never drank. She explained that she had lost track of time after leaving class that morning, and could not account for her whereabouts between then and being in the liquor store later that afternoon. With some hesitation, she also admitted she had been experiencing nightmares for the past three nights. These involved watching her dead father lying in a casket while she held a knife in her hands. In addition, information was elicited that her father had died one year prior to her current admission.

Ms. Y admitted that she had previously been hospitalized once before for a "panic attack" and that she currently was in therapy with a counselor at the University Student Health Services. Academically, she was a junior although this was her fifth year in college. She gave a history of being repeatedly physically abused as a child by both her parents and being molested by an older male cousin who lived next door.

During the initial psychiatric evaluation, she responded that she experienced episodes of depersonalization and derealization. And when asked about her memory and the amnestic experience of the previous day, she noted that she often could not find where she had parked her car, and that she would sometimes not recognize people who said they knew her. She volunteered that she had always been a daydreamer and was easily able to enter trance-like states. Upon hypnotic induction, two "personalities" presented themselves.

DISSOCIATIVE DISORDER
NOT OTHERWISE SPECIFIED (NOS)

This catch-all category is intended for those disordered presentations in which dissociation is the predominant feature but does not meet criteria for one of the four aforementioned Dissociative Disorders. Some examples include derealization unaccompanied by depersonalization, fugues in which the presence of a second identity cannot be documented, dissociated states following brainwashing in prison camps, and duress associated with hostage situations or indoctrination in cults. **Ganser's Syndrome,** which involves responding with "approximate answers" to questions and is associated with amnesia, conversion symptoms, or disorientation, is another disorder that merits the diagnosis of Dissociative Disorder NOS.

ADLERIAN VIEW OF DISSOCIATION

Alfred Adler wrote relatively little about dissociation, and to the best of my knowledge, nothing about the dissociative disorder. What accounts for this? Of course, we do not know, but we can speculate. First of all, prior to *DSM-III,* the Dissociative Disorders were usually known as Hysterical Neuroses-Dissociative type to distinguish them from the Conversion type of the Hysterical Neuroses. In that regard, Ellenberger (1970) noted that Freud tended to limit his practice to the treatment of higher functioning, upper middle-class patients who for the most part presented with Hysterical Neuroses of both types. Adler, on the other hand, reportedly treated a wider variety of patients, many of lower functioning working-class individuals with obsessive compulsive and characterological features. Thus, Adler may have had little or no therapeutic contact with dissociative disordered patients.

Second, Adler did at least once allude to the term "dissociation" as synonymous with "the apparent double-life of the neurotic" (Adler, 1925/1968, p. 21). He was fond of discussing daydreams, which are a form of dissociation (Adler 1956, 1964). His basic view of daydreams, and presumably of other dissociative phenomenon, was consistent with his overall theory of psychopathology: "The findings of Individual Psychology point to the fact that all behavior of a human being fits into a unit and is an expression of the individual's style of life" (Adler, 1956, p.358). In discussing the retrogressive movement of the neurosis, Adler does mention psychogenic amnesia as one such manifestation (Adler, 1925/1968).

Finally, Adler's aversion to hypnosis should be noted (Adler 1925/1968, pp. 161-2). Since hypnosis has and continues to be a basic diagnostic and treatment method of dissociative disorders, then it is unlikely that Adler or his protegees and later followers would focus much of their theoretical, clinical, and research efforts on the dissociative disorders. A review of the published Adlerian literature seems to support this observation.

At the present, some indications are that this trend might be changing. As more and more dissociative disordered individuals present for treatment, more and more clinicians, including Adlerians, are "gearing up" to meet this therapeutic challenge. A recent rediscovery of the pioneering efforts of Janet holds considerable promise for those clinicians who were unconvinced or uncomfortable with the prevailing theories based on Freud's formulation (Vander Kolk & Vander Hart, 1989). Not only does Janet's formulation of dissociation provide a broad integrative framework for understanding and unifying elements for other theories, but it is quite compatible with Adlerian thinking (Shulman, 1990).

Essentially, Janet proposed a broad theory of perceptive and cognitive processes and memory that is now being validated by research in the neurosciences. Janet hypothesized that consciousness consisted of a unified memory of all psychological facets related to a particular experience and that memory was an act of creation rather than a passive and static recording of events. He speculated that memories were synthesized into a perceptual system that provided a matrix for categorizing and integrating subsequent data into what we would today call cognitive schemas. Janet believed that dissociations were sentiments of incompleteness or idea complexes that were split off or existed outside of consciousness. He believed that therapy is a process of bringing these split-off ideas into consciousness and that his process would be curative. For Adler, therapy was likewise a process of bringing these mistaken and missing ideas into consciousness. Of course, the "missing" element is social interest (Shulman, 1990).

TREATMENT OF THE
DISSOCIATIVE DISORDERS

The goal of treatment for both psychogenic amnesia and psychogenic fugue is to recover lost memories and identity and to integrate the traumatic antecedent event(s) into the patient's consciousness. Regardless of the clinician's theoretical orientation, the general treatment strategy is to **elicit the history** in a supportive manner and **listen empathetically.** A **supportive environment** may be sufficient for spontaneous resolution to occur, and may be all that is needed in some cases. More active measures to recover missing memories are **hypnosis, free association, suggestion, amytal interviews,** and **abreactive techniques.** These methods are often utilized in conjunction with ongoing psychotherapy.

The literature on the treatment of Depersonalization Disorder is scant and inconclusive. Since the Dissociative Disorder is as much identity development disorder as it is a dissociative phenomenon, *the goal of treatment is a fuller integration of the personality and correlatively a more accurate perception of self and external reality.* Treatment approaches which hold promise include **hypnosis** (especially for those of high hypnotizability), **imagery techniques,** and **cognitive-behavioral approaches.** The medications **clozapine** and **phenazapam** have been reported to be useful, especially when introduced shortly after the onset of the disorder (Nuller, 1982).

The treatment of MPD tends to be long, demanding, and painful. *The initial goal is to establish a trusting relationship and the intermediate goal is to optimize the patient's functioning and potential. The ultimate goal,* of course, *would be the achievement of total integration of the alters into one personality.* However, a reasonable degree of conflict-free collaboration among the personalities may be the only realistic goal for some patients. Generally speaking, medications have been ineffective for the disorder, although they have been of some use with targets such as symptomatic depression, insomnia, and panic symptoms. Treatment success has been reported with **hypnotherapy, psychoanalytical psychotherapy, group therapy** with and without videotaping, and **sodium amytal** (Wilbur & Kluft, 1989). Braun (1986) has described a 13-step treatment protocol which has been found useful regardless of the clinician's treatment orientation.

SUMMARY

Once considered quite rare, the Dissociative Disorders are commonplace today. This is particularly true for the Multiple Personality Disorder. The media, including television and movies, have been enamored by MPD, probably because of its unusual and varied manifestations. In this chapter has been reviewed the concept of dissociation, the criteria for the various Dissociative Disorders, and the emphasis on the Adlerian formulation of this class of disorders. Various reasons are suggested for why Adler wrote little about these disorders. Nevertheless, Adler's view is quite similar to that of Janet.

REFERENCES

Adler, A. (1956). *The Individual Psychology of Alfred Adler.* H. L. Ansbacher, & R. R. Ansbacher (Eds.). New York: Basic Books.

Adler, A. (1964). *Superiority and social interest: A collection of later writings.* H. L. Ansbacher & R. R. Ansbacher (Eds.). Evanston, IL: Northwestern University Press.

Adler, A. (1968). *The practice and theory of Individual Psychology.* (P. Radin Trans.) Totawa, NJ: Littlefield, Adams and Co. (Original work published 1925)

American Psychiatric Association. (1952). *Diagnostic and statistical manual of mental disorders.* Washington, DC: Author.

American Psychiatric Association. (1968). *Diagnostic and statistical manual of mental disorders* (2nd ed). Washington, DC: Author.

American Psychiatric Association. (1986). *Diagnostic and statistical manual of mental disorders* (3rd ed, rev). Washington DC: Author.

Beahr, J. (1982). *Unity and multiplicity: Consciousness of self in hypnosis, psychiatric disorder and mental health.* New York: Brunner/Mazel.

Block, J. (1988). Clinical assessment of multiple personality disorder. In P. Keller & S. Heyman (Eds.), *Innovations in clinical practice: A source book.* Sarasota, FL: Professional Resource Exchange.

Braun, B. (1986). Issues in the psychotherapy of multiple personality disorder. In B. Braun (Ed.), *Treatment of multiple personality disorder.* Washington, DC: American Psychiatric Press.

Ellenberger, H. (1970). *The discovery of the unconscious.* New York: Basic Books.

Freud, S., & Breuer, J. (1955). Studies on hysteria. In J. Strachey (Ed.), *The pre-standard edition of the complete psychological works of Sigmund Freud.* London: Hogarth Press.

Green, H. (1964). *I never promised you a rose garden.* New York: Holt, Rinehart, Winston.

Horevitz, R., & Braun, B. (1984). Are multiple personalities borderline? *Psychiatric Clinics of North America, 7,* 69-88.

Kluft, R. (1985). The natural history of multiple personality disorder: A study of thirty-three cases. In R. Kluft (Ed.), *Childhood antecedents of multiple personality.* Washington, DC: American Psychiatric Press.

Nuller, Y. (1982). Depersonalization—symptoms, meaning, therapy. *Acta Psychiatrica Scandanavica, 66,* 51-458.

Putnam, F. (1985). Dissociation as a response to extreme trauma. In R. Kluft (Ed.), *Childhood antecedents of multiple personality.* Washington, DC: American Psychiatric Press.

Putnam, F., Guroff, J., Silberman, E., et al. (1986). The clinical phenomenology of multiple personality disorder: Review of 100 recent cases. *Journal of Clinical Psychiatry, 47,* 285-293.

Spiegel, H., & Spiegel, D. (1978). *Trance and treatment.* New York: Basic Books.

Shulman, B. (1990). Personal communication.

Vander Kolk, B., & Vander Hart, O. (1989). Pierre Janet and the breakdown of adaptation in psychological trauma. *American Journal of Psychiatry, 146,* 1530-1540.

Wilbur, C., & Kluft, R. (1989). Multiple personality disorders. In *Treatment of psychiatric disorders: A task force report of the American Psychiatric Association. (Vol. 3).* Washington DC: American Psychiatric Press.

Yaeger, J. (1989). Manifestations of psychiatric disorders. In H. Kaplan & B. Sadock (Eds.), *Comprehensive textbook of psychiatry* (5th ed.). Baltimore: Williams and Wilkins.

PART IV

ADJUSTMENT REACTIONS, PERSONALITY DISORDERS, ADDICTIONS, AND SEXUAL DYSFUNCTIONS

OVERVIEW

Adler (1956) noted that all life-styles are adequate until life or other people present a challenge for which the individual is unprepared. At those times the life-style is tested, and the amount of social interest which is present is displayed. This section deals with a variety of conditions listed in DSM-III-R which can be summarized according to one overriding dynamic: The life-styles of individuals with these conditions have generally been sufficient to meet the tasks of life until an event or series of events occurs which severely taxes individuals, and their dysfunctional patterns come to the attention of others (be it law enforcement personnel, employers, or spouses).

The first chapter, by Carlson, is on the "Adjustment Disorders and V Codes." He explores various types of conditions and responses individuals make to life's stresses and the effects those responses have upon self, family, and others.

Sperry and Mosak in the next chapter explore the "Personality Disorders" in general, and Sperry and Ansbacher explore the "Narcissistic Personality Disorder" in specific in the chapter that follows. Dreikurs (1967) noted that psychodynamically, psychotics discard common sense; neurotics acknowledge it but look for excuses in order to not follow it. What he referred to as character disorders might now be known as personality disorders. He noted that individuals with character disorders never fully developed common sense. For them, their private logic was intimately fused with a distorted common sense, so that the distinction between the two was hard to make. When confronted with a challenge, these people responded with a "Yes—But I'll do it my way" approach. In other words, they felt that their way of solving the challenges of life was the way to solve it. Sperry presents an in-depth, biopsychosocial exploration of the 11 DSM-III-R personality disorders, along with an integrative analysis of the Narcissistic Personality Disorder based upon the works of Adler and Kohut.

Lewis and Carlson next explore "Psychoactive Substance Use Disorders." They make the useful distinction between use, abuse, and dependence, and discuss the Adlerian perspective, which they note has quite a bit to offer current treatment intervention strategies, particularly with regards to some fundamental Adlerian concepts such as the social context of behavior, an awareness of life-style, and the purposefulness of symptoms.

"Antisocial Personality Disorder and Addictions" is the subsequent chapter by Lombardi. It explores the Antisocial Personality Disorder in greater depth, and relates fundamental attitudes of such individuals to addictions such as alcoholism, drugs, gambling, and food.

The last chapter in this section is by Peven and deals with "The Individual Psychological Viewpoint of the Psychosexual Disorders." Adler (1978) long ago noted the interrelatedness of sexuality to personality, and felt that an individual's sex life could be one of the key barometers of the individual's amount of social interest. After a thorough review of DSM-III-R criteria, Peven describes the relationship of the various disorders to life-style convictions and attitudes, noting not only Adler's early emphasis upon the social inequality of the sexes, but also the current status of women and men in their interpersonal and sexual relationships.

REFERENCES

Adler, A. (1956). *The Individual Psychology of Alfred Adler*. H. L. Ansbacher & R. R. Ansbacher (Eds.). New York: Basic Books.

Adler, A. (1978). *Co-operation between the sexes: Writings on women, love and marriage, sexuality and its disorders*. H. L. Ansbacher & R. R. Ansbacher (Eds.). New York: Doubleday.

Dreikurs, R. (1967). *Psychodynamics, psychotherapy, and counseling*. Chicago: Alfred Adler Institute.

CHAPTER **10**

ADJUSTMENT
DISORDERS
AND
V CODES

Jon Carlson, Psy.D., Ed.D.

Controversy continues as to whether or not adjustment disorders and V codes should be contained within the diagnostic description. Many clinicians believe the symptoms associated with adjustment disorders and V codes will take care of themselves with time and therefore do not need treatment. Critics indicate that adjustment disorders are, by definition, time-limited and to treat them wastes the clients' time, money, and effort. Additionally, intervention interferes with the natural recovery process, leaving the clients believing they are not able to take care of their own problems.

Adjustment disorders and V codes are very common and are a large part of clinical practice. Psychologists enjoy working with these conditions as they are often successfully treated and seem to respond well to traditional therapeutic intervention strategies designed for higher functioning individuals. Due to the high functioning nature of the clients, they not only resolve their disrupting and distressing situation, but many are able to become even healthier and stronger as a result of this problem. Successful treatment builds self-confidence and skill development, making therapy a growth-promoting situation for most clients.

Both adjustment disorders and V codes are at the least severe end of Axis I problems. However, an important point to note is that people with these diagnostic categories have problems that are more severe than normal problems in living.

DESCRIPTION

Adjustment disorders are more severe and less common than V code conditions. According to the DSM-III-R (American Psychiatric Association, 1987), the essential feature of this disorder is a maladaptive reaction to an identifiable psychosocial stressor or stressors that occurs within three months of the onset of the stressor(s) and has persisted for no longer than six months (p. 329). Stressors may be single events, such as death, divorce, or birth, or continuous circumstances, such as marital discord, financial problems, or chronic illness. All, however, are within the normal realm of experience and would not meet the criteria for post-traumatic stress disorder. According to Maxmen (1986), the most common stressors for adults are marital difficulties, divorce or separation, and relocation, while for adolescents they are school-related problems, parental conflict, and substance abuse. In the DSM-III-R are specified nine types of adjustment disorders.

309.24 Adjustment disorder with anxious mood. Predominant manifestations are symptoms such as nervousness, worry, and trouble falling asleep.

309.00 Adjustment disorder with depressed mood. Predominant manifestations are symptoms such as depressed mood, feelings of worthlessness, and decreased self-esteem.

309.30 Adjustment disorder with disturbance of conduct. Violation occurs of the rights of others or violation of age-appropriate norms and rules. The predominant manifestations are symptoms such as truancy, fighting, or reckless driving.

309.40 Adjustment disorder with mixed disturbance of emotions and conduct. The predominant manifestations are a combination of emotional symptoms such as those found in adjustment disorder with anxious or depressed mood concurrent with behavior found in adjustment disorder with disturbance of conduct.

309.28 Adjustment disorder with mixed emotional features. The predominant manifestations are a combination of emotional symptoms such as those found in adjustment disorders with anxious and depressed moods.

309.82 Adjustment disorder with physical complaints. The predominant manifestations are physical symptoms such as headache, backache, and lethargy.

309.83 Adjustment disorder with withdrawal. The predominant manifestation is social withdrawal without a significantly depressed or anxious mood.

309.23 Adjustment disorder with work (or academic) inhibition. The predominant manifestation is inhibition of work or academic function that occurs in a person whose previous performance was adequate.

309.90 Adjustment disorder not otherwise specified. A maladaptive reaction to psychosocial stress with a symptom or symptoms not classified by the other adjustment disorders. For example, a patient who is diagnosed with cancer but denies the diagnosis and is non-compliant with treatment recommendations.

These nine different types of adjustment disorders are classified according to their predominant symptoms. The diagnostic criteria for adjustment disorders of all types is as follows:

A. A maladaptive reaction to an identifiable stressor or stressors that occurs within three months of the onset of the stressor(s).

B. The maladaptive reaction is manifested by either (1) impairment in occupational (or school) function, social activities, or interpersonal relationships; or (2) symptoms in excess of a normal and expected reaction to the stressor(s).

C. Not merely one instance of a pattern of overreaction to stress or an exacerbation of a mental disorder.

D. The maladaptive reaction has persisted no longer than six months.

E. Disturbance does not meet criteria for a specific mental disorder and does not represent uncomplicated bereavement.

Kaplan and Sadock (1985) reported that adjustment disorders are experienced by 10 to 15% of the population. Maxmen (1986) indicated that these disorders are even more prevalent and typically more severe in adolescents with as many as one-third experiencing adjustment disorders. However, because many people with adjustment disorders do not seek treatment, the number may be considerably higher than the above estimates.

FORMULATION

Nearly everyone has experienced an adjustment disorder or a V code condition or both. These disorders are often triggered by the normal life transitions that we all face. The transitions may be positive, such as the birth of a child or graduation from school, or negative, such as the loss of a job or the death of a loved one. These problems also may reflect and be related to the normal problems of living such as job dissatisfaction, marriage problems, and the care of an elderly or aging parent. To go through life without experiencing this type of problem seems almost impossible. However, people with effective coping mechanisms and ways of effectively handling stress are less troubled by these life transitions.

Adjustment disorders will therefore occur in all types of people. They are likely, however, to be more prevalent in people who have limited resources and support systems, undeveloped coping mechanisms, or little experience in dealing effectively with previous stressful events and multiple stressors. Adlerians would view adjustment problems as resulting from faulty beliefs or life-style convictions. Likely individuals, due to early family learnings, have developed inferiority feelings and unrealistic goals and need assistance and education in learning healthier, more adaptive responses to the demands of life. Many need to learn the courage to be imperfect and to live in an imperfect world. Most clients with adjustment disorders have had a high level of previous functioning and are usually capable of handling the stressors themselves, but they have somehow lost self-esteem and need to be encouraged to increase their levels of confidence.

INTERVENTION STRATEGIES

Psychologists need to express confidence in clients with adjustment disorders and often by providing support and direction can help clients solve these problems themselves. An optimistic attitude will strengthen the clients' self-esteem and encourage them to face the stressors in their lives.

As previously indicated, adjustment disorders often improve spontaneously without treatment. However, therapy can facilitate recovery. It can hasten improvement, provide coping skills and adaptive mechanisms to avert future problems, and minimize poor choices and self-destructive behaviors (Maxmen, 1986).

Many experts believe that the goals of therapy should be two-fold: (1) to help the client return to baseline level, and (2) to capitalize on the emotional turmoil and to change longstanding maladaptive patterns to stress and to develop more useful and satisfying ones. The therapy then would be more likely to be called a flexible crisis intervention approach. This approach focuses both on relieving the acute symptoms and helping the clients to learn more adaptive coping strategies. Therapy will use encouragement and support the clients' strengths and minimize or play down past problems unless a pattern is identified. Education and information are often a large part of treatment. This allows clients to look realistically at their situations, realize they are not alone, and become aware of resources that might be useful and helpful to them.

Often therapeutic interventions need to be tailored depending on the predominant symptoms. For example, if the client presents with depressive symptoms, cognitive techniques are often useful, while those with anxiety will probably benefit best from stress reduction procedures, while those who have academic or career problems often respond best to a more behavioral approach (Brown & Brown, 1990).

Due to the diversity of presenting problems, a variety of interventions are appropriate. Many therapists have found environmental change useful. Moving to a safer neighborhood, applying for a new job, or receiving further education are often useful. Bibliotherapy, or the use of books and reading material, seems to be an important part of treatment. Adlerian parenting materials (Dinkmeyer & McKay, 1989), marriage materials (Dinkmeyer & Carlson, 1984), career development materials (Bolles, 1989), etc. are often important tools. Many psychologists use inventories such as the Kern (1986) *Lifestyle Scale* and the *Millon Clinical Multiaxial Inventory* (Millon, 1984) to help clients understand why they are having difficulties with particular situations and on what resources they might draw and what options they have.

Therapy needs to be supportive, active, flexible, and goal-directed working within a time-limited context (Sperry, 1989). The brief therapy model seems particularly well-suited to problems of acute onset experienced by clients who have had good prior adjustment and who can relate well to others and engage in a therapeutic relationship. Often such patients are very highly motivated toward treatment. Some researchers have found group therapy to be a useful adjunct to treatment, as well as family interventions. Such interventions provide a support system and can be used to teach and reinforce coping mechanisms, improve self-esteem, and provide alternative solutions to problems. Many clients have found groups composed of people going through similar life circumstances such as divorce, separation, and death of a loved one to be particularly helpful. Although group therapy doesn't provide the crisis intervention necessary to resolve the urgency of such a problem, it does provide a good support base and is often used in conjunction with individual approaches.

Medication is seldom used with adjustment disorders. However, in rare cases time-limited prescriptions are provided for anxiety or sleep problems.

Adjustment disorders have a tendency to reoccur (Donovan, Bennett, & McElroy, 1981). Therefore, therapists need to be particularly vigilant with regards to treatment compliance and relapse. A useful procedure is to schedule follow-up appointments for 18 months following intervention in order to prevent future reoccurrence of this situation.

SPECIFIC SUGGESTIONS FOR
ADJUSTMENT DISORDERS

Anxious Mood

In addition to the previous principles, the client needs to be reassured that the symptoms are transient and that the psychologist and client together can alleviate them. Unobtrusive support, crisis intervention techniques, relaxation, meditation, self-hypnosis, and/or biofeedback may be used by therapists experienced in any of these techniques. Temporary anti-anxiety medications such as a benzodiazepine may be considered. The emphasis needs to be on the client's ability to weather the stress, as well as encouragement for their ability to strengthen coping mechanisms.

Depressed Mood

Clients with depressive symptoms are often more uncomfortable than those with any other adjustment disorder. They may actually appear disabled and have undergone considerable behavioral change such as sleep disturbance and lack of energy. Some even present with suicidal ideation. Most likely, this client will not need medication. If medication is warranted, adjustment disorder is likely to be the wrong diagnosis. This client will benefit from the support and reassurance of the therapist that the experience is short-term. Simple and often practical suggestions for problems of sleeplessness and energy show good results. The client should be questioned about any suicidal thoughts and these should be pursued seriously. Most likely, however, these thoughts are more anxiety-producing than real. Nevertheless, the therapist needs to discuss this topic thoroughly and take whatever precautions seem warranted.

Disturbance of Conduct

The therapist, the client, and often the client's family need to understand the difference between this diagnosis and a more chronic antisocial personality disorder. The therapist needs to recognize that the treatment for these problems is often preventive of future antisocial symptoms. The therapist needs to make sure that a harsh approach is not taken with these clients in spite of the problems that they may have caused others. Acceptance and attempts to have the client understand their symptoms as just characteristics of having a difficult time adjusting, rather than some deep-seated problem, is very important. This will allow the client to see treatment as something logical and accomplishable. Another important point is to stress that the client needs to take responsibility and consequences for his/her own actions. The therapist's acceptance of the client and reassurance of the person's fragile condition do not really imply acceptance of the behavior, but rather of the person.

Disturbance of Emotions and Conduct

This category should be treated using a combination of the principles already mentioned.

Mixed Emotional Features

The principles outlined earlier in this chapter also cover this disorder.

Physical Complaints

The previous treatment principles will apply to this disorder. The therapist needs to acknowledge the presence of physical complaints along with the dysphoria they generate without elevating these problems to Axis III disorders. Once the therapist is confident, i.e., via medical examination, that no organic problem is present, this type of intervention should be limited. Psychologists working with this type of client often find the procedures mentioned in the somatoform/somatization disorders chapter very helpful. Therapy needs to focus on emotional issues and feelings rather than the physical complaints. This can help the client attend to the real issues, clarify stressors, and improve coping skills and emotional adaptation.

Withdrawal

The therapist needs to be aware that withdrawal lends itself to isolation from sources of growth and support and that this disorder might evolve into a chronic avoidance or depression pattern. This client should receive considerable encouragement and prescriptions to have considerable contact with other people. Therapists also find contacting the client's family to provide additional reassurance helpful.

Work or Academic Inhibition

General principles previously mentioned or indicated work with this disorder. Assistance often is needed because an adjustment disorder with work or academic inhibition will endanger or postpone one's career or academic progress. Therapists usually find brief, supportive, goal-directed counseling such as that found in many student health centers or employee assistance programs useful. These programs should include encouragement to discuss current difficulties with the teacher or employer in person. This may clarify any misperceptions about the way the person is being treated and help them separate real world situations from the distressing fantasies. If this problem continues and does not respond to these interventions, likely the diagnosis needs to be changed.

Not Otherwise Specified (NOS)

Disorders that fall into this residual category should be treated according to the previously listed suggestions. The presenting symptoms, the temporary or chronic stressors involved, and the environmental and psychodynamic characteristics are likely to have an influence upon the eventual resolution of the condition.

V CODES

V codes is the name given for conditions that are not attributable to a mental disorder and are the focus of attention or treatment. These conditions are on a continuum less severe than those encountered in an adjustment disorder. These conditions are not mental disorders nor have they resulted from mental disorders. These clients may or may not have coexisting and unrelated mental disorders, but the diagnosis of a V code implies that the focus of treatment will be on this condition, rather than on any presenting mental disorder. In the DSM-III-R are listed the following 13 V code conditions.

V62.30 Academic Problem

V71.01 Adult Antisocial Behavior

V40.00 Borderline Intellectual Functioning (Note: This is coded on Axis II)

V71.02 Childhood or Adolescent Antisocial Behavior

V65.20 Malingering

V61.10 Marital Problem

V15.81 Noncompliance with Medical Treatment

V62.20 Occupational Problem

V61.20 Parent-Child Problem

V62.81 Other Interpersonal Problem

V61.80 Other Specified Family Circumstance

V62.89 Phase of Life Problem or Other Life Circumstance Problem

V62.82 Uncomplicated Bereavement

As one can see from the above list, these are problems of living that are experienced by most people. Usually these disorders go untreated, and people somehow manage to deal with them with varying degrees of success. The conditions are seldom troubling for long periods of time nor do they cause extreme and persistent emotional pain. Typically clients with a V code diagnosis have good reality contact, and their reactions are consistent with the stressors or life experiences that they are experiencing. However, clients are experiencing considerable unhappiness and dissatisfaction with their lives and therefore often benefit greatly from therapy.

V codes are often diagnosed in fairly healthy clients with good ego strength and self-esteem. Traditionally these are what have been called YAVIS (Young Attractive Verbal Intelligent Social) clients.

INTERVENTIONS

Therapists intervene in a very similar fashion to the treatment for adjustment disorders. Clients respond best to therapists who are supportive and flexible, but also challenge the clients to grow and develop. Therapists need to encourage clients to take responsibility for their own treatment, and, although non-directive strategies work very well, at times therapists need to prescribe resources and information as needed. Therapists usually have no difficulty maintaining a positive, optimistic attitude and anticipating short-term involvement.

Adlerians seem to be especially helpful treating clients with V code problems through encouragement and helping clients to understand the universal nature of their problems. Clients tend to not feel abnormal and feel empowered to make the changes necessary to successfully cope with their problems.

Support groups and self-help groups are often available for most V problems. Often these support groups are all a client will need.

Prognosis for V codes, as well as adjustment reactions, is very good, although the wide variety of conditions and clients who fit these diagnoses makes one cautious in terms of generalizing. Likely clients who have high levels of self-efficacy (Bandura, 1987) will have the highest prognosis of success. Clients with self-efficacy have high self-concepts and have had previous success at life-style changes.

CASE EXAMPLE

Case of Jim

Jim is a 30-year-old businessman who was referred by his family doctor because Jim wanted to talk to someone about his unhappy marriage. During the eight years of courtship and four years of marriage, there have been repeated problems that have usually been initiated by his overall dissatisfaction. Although he and his partner share many interests and have had an acceptable sexual relationship, he feels that his wife is too self-centered and cold. He is upset that she has no real concern about him, his work, or his interests. He is extremely upset with her and does not want to raise a family with her. His dissatisfaction periodically builds up to a point that leads to verbal fights, temporary separations, and then apologies. This leaves Jim feeling lonely, and he then comes crawling back to her. Jim appears to be in therapy looking for support to help him make a permanent break from his partner. Although he is currently in acute distress due to his marital situation, no evidence is noted of any of these difficulties in other aspects of his life. During the course of the intake interview, Jim often held back tears, had a voice that cracked, and reported having difficulty sleeping.

Diagnosis

Axis I: V61.10 Marital Problem

Axis II: None

Axis III: None

Axis IV: 3; marital discord

Axis V: Current GAF: 80; Highest GAF Past 12 Months: 80

In interviewing the client, he revealed that he and his wife had just had a very serious fight and today he felt pretty convinced that the marriage is over. The therapist's hypothesis was that the client's resolution probably will not continue. Discussion ensued in which he described that both his parents and his wife's parents had stormy relationships that were characterized by a family life with considerable ups and downs. Although both he and his wife do not like the current way of living, neither seem to know how to make it effectively different. Although he indicated that he was doubtful as to the prognosis of marriage therapy, he was more than willing to invite his wife to come in for conjoint sessions. Conjoint marital therapy was followed using the strategies developed by Sperry and Carlson (1991). The treatment was supplemented utilizing bibliotherapy with the TIME program materials (Dinkmeyer & Carlson, 1984). The couple was seen weekly for ten weeks, and then the sessions switched to monthly meetings. Both report increased satisfaction in the marriage and decreased conflict. Providing treatment to this type of client is rewarding because the progress is so readily observable.

SUMMARY OF
TREATMENT RECOMMENDATIONS

Seligman (1990) has developed an effective procedure entitled "DO A CLIENT MAP" that effectively summarizes the recommendations for adjustment disorders and V code conditions.

Diagnoses. Adjustment disorders and V codes for conditions not attributable to mental disorder.

Objectives. Relieve symptoms, improve coping, restore at least prior level of functioning.

Assessments. Generally none, although measures of transient anxiety, depression, and stress might be helpful.

Clinician. Flexible yet structured. Present oriented. Optimistic.

Location. Outpatient.

Interventions. Crisis intervention. Brief psychodynamically oriented psychotherapy, stress management. Other short-term active approaches.

Emphasis. Encouragement client responsibility. Moderately supportive. Probing only when relevant to current concerns with focus determined by specific precipitant and response.

Nature. Individual therapy and/or peer support group. Possibly some family sessions.

Timing. Brief duration, rapid pace.

Medication. Rarely needed.

Adjunct services. Inventories to clarify goals and direction. Education and information very important. Possibly environmental manipulation.

Prognosis. Excellent, especially when no underlying mental disorder is present. (pp. 73-74)

REFERENCES

American Psychiatric Association. (1987). *Diagnostic and statistical manual of mental disorders.* (3rd ed., rev.). Washington, DC: Author.

Bandura, A. (1987-May). Self-efficacy. *University of California-Berkeley Wellness Letter,* pp. 1-2.

Bolles, R.N. (1989). *The 1989 what color is your parachute?* Berkeley, CA: Ten Speed Press.

Brown, D., & Brown, L. (1990). *Career choice and development.* San Francisco, CA: Jossey-Bass.

Dinkmeyer, D., & Carlson, J. (1984). *Time for a better marriage.* Circle Pines, MN: American Guidance Service.

Dinkmeyer, D., & McKay, G.D. (1989). *Systematic training for effective parenting.* Circle Pines, MN: American Guidance Service.

Donovan, J.M., Bennett, M.J., & McElroy, C.M. (1981). The crisis group: Its rationale, format, and outcome. In S.H. Budman (Ed.), *Forms of brief therapy* (pp. 283-303). New York: Guilford Press.

Kaplan, H.I., & Sadock, B.J. (1985). *Modern synopsis of comprehensive textbook of psychiatry.* Baltimore, MD: Williams and Wilkins.

Kern, R. (1986). *Lifestyle scale.* Coral Springs, FL: CMTI Press.

Maxmen, J.S. (1986). *Essential psychopathology.* New York: W. W. Norton.

Millon, T. (1984). *Millon clinical multiaxial inventory.* Minneapolis, MN: National Computer System.

Seligman, L. (1990). *Selecting effective treatments.* San Francisco: Jossey Bass.

Sperry, L. (Ed.). (1989). Special issue: Varieties of brief therapy. *Individual Psychology, 45,*(1/2).

Sperry, L., & Carlson, J. (1991). *Marital therapy: Integrating theory and technique.* Denver, CO: Love Publishing Company.

CHAPTER 11

PERSONALITY DISORDERS

Len Sperry, M.D., Ph.D.
Harold H. Mosak, Ph.D.

Personality can be defined as enduring patterns of thinking, feeling, and behaving and relating to the environment and oneself in a consistent manner and in various social contexts. When specific traits such as orderliness, rigidity, thriftiness, and emotional constriction cluster together they can be referred to as a *personality style.* For instance, the four traits noted above would be labelled the obsessive compulsive personality style. When these personality styles become inflexible and maladaptive so as to cause significant impairment in occupational or social functioning, or result in great subjective distress, the criteria in DSM-III-R would cause them to be labelled as *personality disorders* and assign them Axis II codes. In the example above, the classification would be obsessive compulsive personality disorder, 301.40. While everyone exhibits a personality style, not everyone manifests a personality disorder or disorders. Personality disorders indicate the existence of a longstanding, maladaptive pattern of attitudes and behaviors of the way one relates to, perceives, and thinks about the environment and oneself that is of sufficient severity to cause either significant impairment in adaptive functioning or subjective distress. The manifestations of personality disorders are usually recognizable by adolescence and continue throughout most of life. According to DSM-III-R, the pattern must be present by early adulthood (American Psychiatric Association, 1987).

The purpose of this chapter is to overview the 11 personality disorders described in DSM-III-R and related information about their diagnostic, clinical, and treatment formulations. Before beginning this undertaking, we will clarify the place of personality disorders within the five axes system of DSM-III-R and a few other classification systems. Unlike other chapters that describe one or two disorders, this chapter provides an overview of 11 disorders. Because of space limitations, each disorder is described and elaborations are made for the various summary Figures provided.

Why distinguish between Axis I and Axis II? **Axis II** personality disorders are conditions which are chronic and longstanding patterns of dysfunctional behavior. On the other hand, **Axis I** disorders tend to be acute, symptomatic, or episodic. Personality disorders are conditions which represent a more basic and chronic dysfunction than the superimposed Axis I symptom or syndrome. Another way of thinking about personality disorders is as the psychological vulnerability for an Axis I syndrome. In addition, Axis II disorders are much more resistant to change than a symptom or syndrome. Finally, personality disorders are **ego-syntonic,** which means that individuals are relatively comfortable with their behavior and usually are unwilling to enter treatment or to change once in treatment. This contrasts with Axis I disorders which are **ego-dystonic** and more distressing. Here treatment is usually sought by the clients in order to relieve distress.

According to DSM-III-R, personality disorders are listed on Axis II. If no personality disorder is present, the clinician is encouraged to indicate the presence of personality style, traits, or features on Axis II. In addition, specific defense mechanisms that have been elicited can be likewise noted.

Earlier in this book, the analogy of pneumonia was presented to clarify multi-axial diagnoses. In terms of DSM-III-R, Axis I and III represented all the individual symptoms of pneumonia whether they be physical, mental, or emotional. The bacteria eliciting pneumonia symptoms were represented by Axis IV—stressors—and Axis II represented the person's biological vulnerability or compromise of immune functioning. You will recall that treatment for pneumonia—Axis I—was quite aggressive if the patient was older, sickly, and immunosuppressed (had a disease like AIDS). Treatment was less aggressive or shorter term if the patient was an otherwise healthy, young college student. The first instance would be analogous to a severe personality disorder, while the second a personality style. In terms of psychological treatment, knowledge of the Axis II disorder or style can be prognostic regarding symptom expression as well as motivation for and compliance with treatment. For instance, the individual presenting with an Axis I adjustment disorder with depressed mood and an Axis II dependent personality style is likely to manifest a stable and mild course of symptoms and might be quite motivated and compliant with treatment. On the other hand, the same Axis I presentation with an Axis II passive-aggressive personality disorder would likely present with a more fluctuating and severe course of symptoms, and the individual would likely be uncooperative with treatment.

Adler did not discuss the personality disorders per se but did advance a two-dimensional theory of personality structure which was the basis for other Adlerians to develop personality typologies consistent with DSM-III-R categories. Adler (1935) described two variables or dimensions: Social interest or usefulness (cooperative to uncooperative) and activity (active to inactive). These resulted in a four-fold personality typology: The ruling type (high active, low social interest); the avoiding type (low active, low social interest); the getting type (low active and high social interest); and socially useful, ideal type (high active, high social interest). Mosak (1968, 1979) expanded Adler's four-fold typology to eight types which he correlated with DSM-II diagnostic codes. Mosak (1988) described the psychodynamics of personality disorders listed in DSM-III-R.

CLASSIFICATION OF PERSONALITY DISORDERS

In DSM-III-R are listed 11 distinct personality disorders that are grouped into three clusters. The clusters are Cluster A—odd or eccentric personality disorders (Paranoid, Schizoid, and Schizotypal); Cluster B—dramatic, emotional, or erratic personality disorders (Antisocial, Borderline, Histrionic, and Narcissistic); and Cluster C—anxious and fearful personality disorders (Avoidant, Dependent, Obsessive Compulsive, and Passive Aggressive). This classification of DSM-III-R clusters is intuitive rather than being based on empirical data.

At least two other sets of groupings have been proposed. Based on a theoretical model Millon (Millon, 1981; Millon & Everly, 1985) proposed grouping the 11 personality disorders into two large clusters: mild and severe personality disorders. Mild personality disorders are arranged on a four-by-two matrix. The four main types are ambivalent personalities, dependent personalities, detached personalities, and independent personalities. These four types are then subdivided as either active or passive. For instance, the active form of the independent personality would be the Antisocial Personality Disorder, while the passive form would be the Narcissistic Personality Disorder. Millon believed that the severe personality disorders are syndromal extensions and decompensations of the mild personality disorders (Millon, 1981).

Shea (1988) described an approach to grouping the personality disorders based on client-clinician interactions. His three categories are anxiety-prone, poorly empathic, and psychotic-prone. These three Axis II classification schemes of Millon, Shea, and DSM-III-R are listed in Figure 11.1.

Finally, note that DSM-III-R criteria include the designation and coding "Personality Disorder NOS" for listing disorders of personality functioning that are not classifiable as a specific personality disorder because the full criteria for one or more disorders cannot be met. When the features of one or more disorders are present, however, this diagnostic designation is to be used. In DSM-III-R are listed two other personality

(Continued on page 304)

Millon	Shea	DSM-III-R
Ambivalent	**Anxiety-Prone**	**Cluster C**
Obsessive Compulsive	Obsessive Compulsive	Obsessive Compulsive
Passive Aggressive	Passive Aggressive	Passive Aggressive
Dependent	Dependent	Avoidant
Dependent	Avoidant	Dependent
Histrionic	**Poorly Empathic**	**Cluster B**
Detached	Histrionic	Histrionic
Avoidant	Schizoid	Borderline
Schizoid	Narcissistic	Narcissistic
Independent	Antisocial	Antisocial
Narcissistic	**Psychotic-Prone**	**Cluster A**
Antisocial	Schizotypal	Paranoid
Severe/Psychotic-Prone	Borderline	Schizoid
Schizotypal	Paranoid	Schizotypal
Borderline		
Paranoid		

Figure 11.1. Three Axis II classification schemes.

disorders for Axis II. Since the DSM-III-R Committee could not agree about the Self-defeating and Sadistic Personality Disorders (partly because of considerable outside pressure from lobbying groups), these two diagnoses were not included in the regular section on personality disorders but were given the status of entry into Appendix A. The diagnosis of either of these two disorders must be made with the "Personality Disorder NOS" classification and code.

CLINICAL PRESENTATION AND DEVELOPMENTAL ETIOLOGICAL FACTORS IN PERSONALITY DISORDERS

We began this chapter by defining personality as enduring patterns of thinking, feeling, and behaving/interacting. In the 11 personality disorders to be described, each disorder will be described in terms of its pattern of clinical presentation and its underlying predisposition or its etiological and developmental features.

The clinical presentation will be described by the observable pattern of the disorder in terms of its behavioral and inter-personal style, its thinking or cognitive styles, and its feeling or emotional style. This section also includes specific DSM-III-R diagnostic criteria for each disorder.

The section on developmental and etiological features describes how the personality style and disorder developed and are maintained. A biopsychosocial framework will form the basis of this section. A biopsychosocial formulation is an integrative effort to combine biological, psychological, and social data to explain and predict behavior. Biological factors can include predispositions associated with temperament, heredity, and central nervous system functioning. Temperament can be thought of as the biologically determined subset of personality. Each individual enters the world with a distinctive pattern of response, dispositions, and sensitivities. Thomas and Chess (1977, 1984) have described infant and child temperament patterns, while Burks and Rubenstein (1979) have described the application of these temperament types in adults, particularly adults in psychotherapy.

Psychological factors that influence personality development can be described in cognitive, dynamic, or behavioral terms. We will utilize the cognitive and dynamic approach of Individual Psychology to explain psychological development. Specifically, life-style convictions which refer to the individual's view of self, world, and life goals will be described (Mosak, 1954). In addition, levels of social learning and skill training will be noted.

Social factors will be described in terms of parenting style, parental injunction, as well as sibling, peer, and family relationship. In addition, those factors within the individual and the individual system and environment which reinforce and reconfirm this pattern and clinical presentation will be described.

DEPENDENT PERSONALITY DISORDER

DSM-III-R Description and Criteria

The Dependent Personality Disorder is characterized by a pervasive pattern of dependent and submissive behaviors. Those with this disorder are excessively passive, insecure, and isolated individuals who become abnormally dependent on one or more persons. While initially acceptable, this dependent behavior can become controlling, appear hostile, and even blend into a passive-aggressive pattern. This disorder is more common in females (2:1 females to males). In females the dependent style often takes the form of submissiveness, while in males the dependent style is more likely to be autocratic, such as when the husband and boss depends on his wife and secretary to perform essential tasks which he himself cannot accomplish. In either case, this disorder is likely to lead to anxiety and depression when the dependent relationship is threatened.

As in the case of all personality disorders, this pattern begins by early adulthood and can be noted across a variety of situations and circumstances. To make this DSM-III-R diagnosis, individuals must meet at least five of nine criteria: are unable to make everyday decisions without an excessive amount of advice or reassurance from others; allow others to make most of their important decisions; agree with others even when the individuals believe the others are wrong out of fear of being rejected; have difficulty initiating projects or doing things on their own; volunteer to do things that are unpleasant or demeaning in order to get other people to like them; feel uncomfortable or helpless when alone, or go to great lengths to avoid being alone; feel devastated or helpless when close relationships end; are frequently preoccupied with fears of being abandoned; and, are easily hurt by criticism or disapproval of others.

Clinical Presentation

The clinical presentation of the Dependent Personality Disorder can be described in terms of behavioral and interpersonal style, thinking style, and feeling style.

Their behavioral and interpersonal styles are characterized by docility, passivity, and nonassertiveness. In interpersonal relations, they tend to be pleasing, self-sacrificing, clinging and constantly requiring the assurance of others. Their compliance and reliance on others lead to a subtle demand that others assume responsibility for major areas of their lives.

The thinking or cognitive style of dependent personalities is characterized by suggestibility. They easily adopt a Pollyannish attitude toward life. Furthermore, they tend to minimize difficulties, and because of their naïveté are easily persuadable and easily taken advantage of. In short, this style of thinking is uncritical and unperceptive.

Their feeling or affective style is characterized by insecurity and anxiousness. Because they lack self-confidence, they experience considerable discomfort at being alone. They tend to be preoccupied with the fear of abandonment and disapproval of others. Their mood tends to be one of anxiety or fearfulness, as well as having a somber or sad quality.

Developmental and Etiological Features

In this section is described a biopsychosocial formulation of the development of the dependent personality. Biologically, these individuals are characterized by a low energy level. Their temperament is described as melancholic. As infants and young children they were characterized as fearful, sad, or withdrawn. In terms of body types, they tend to have more endomorphic builds (Millon, 1981).

Psychologically, Dependent Personality Disorders can be understood and appreciated in terms of their view of themselves, their world view, and their life goal. The self view of these individuals tends to be a variant of the theme: "I'm nice, but inadequate (or fragile)." Their view of self is self-effacing, inept, and self-doubting. Their view of the world is some variant of the theme: "Others are here to take care of me, because I can't do it for myself." Their life goal is characterized by some variant of the theme: "Therefore, cling and rely on others at all cost."

The social features of this personality disorder can be described in terms of parental, familial, and environmental factors. The dependent personality is most likely to be raised in a family in which parental overprotection is prominent. It is as if the parental injunction to the child is: "I can't trust you to do anything right (or well)." The dependent personality is likely to have been pampered and overprotected as a child. Contact with siblings and peers may engender feelings of unattractiveness, awkwardness, or competitive inadequacy, especially during the preadolescent and adolescent years. These can have a devastating impact on the individual, and further confirm the individual's sense of self-deprecation and doubt. The Dependent Personality Disorder becomes self-perpetuating through a process that involves a sense of self-doubt, an avoidance of competitive activity, and the availability of self-reliant individuals who are willing to take care of and make decisions for the dependent person in exchange for the self-sacrificing and docile friendship of the dependent personality. A summary of characteristics of Dependent Personality Disorder is provided in Figure 11.2.

(Continued on page 309)

1.	Behavioral Appearance:	Docile Passive Nonassertive Lack of self-confidence
2	Interpersonal Behavior:	Pleasing, Self-sacrificing Clinging, compliant Expect others to take respon- sibility for them
3.	Cognitive Style:	Suggestible; Pollyannish about interpersonal relations Overprotective—the "too good parent"
4.	Feeling Style:	Pleasant, but anxious, timid or sad when stressed
5.	Parental Injunction/ Environmental Factors:	"You can't do it by yourself."
6.	Biological/Temperament:	Low energy level; fearful, sad or withdrawn during infan- cy; melancholic
7.	Self View:	"I'm nice, but inadequate or fragile." Self-doubting
8.	World View:	"Others are here to take care of me." (Because I can't do it myself)
9.	Self & System Perpetuant:	Avoidance of competitive acti- vities Self-deprecation

Figure 11.2. Characteristics of Dependent Personality Disorder.

Treatment Considerations

The differential diagnoses for the Axis II personality disorder include the Histrionic Personality Disorder and the Avoidant Personality Disorder. Common Axis I diagnoses that are associated with the Dependent Personality Disorder include the Anxiety Disorders, particularly Simple and Social Phobias, and Panic Disorders with or without Agoraphobia. Other common DSM-III-R disorders include Hypochondriasis, Conversion Disorders, and Somatization Disorders. The experience of loss of a supportive person or relationship can lead to a number of affective disorders including Dysthymia and Major Depressive episodes. Finally, because Dependent Personality Disorders can have lifelong training in assuming the "sick role" they are especially prone to the Factitious Disorders.

In general, the long-range goal of psychotherapy with a dependent personality is to increase the individual's sense of independence and ability to function interdependently. At other times, the therapist may need to settle for a more modest goal, that is, helping the individual become a "healthier" dependent personality. Treatment strategies typically include challenging the individual's convictions or dysfunctional beliefs about personal inadequacy, and learning ways in which to increase assertiveness. A variety of methods can be used to increase self-reliance. Among these are providing the dependent person directives and opportunities for making decisions, being alone, and taking responsibility for his or her own well-being.

Case Example: Ms. A

Ms. A is a 34-year-old single, female with a two-year history of partially treated panic attacks and major depression. Her panic symptoms began approximately three years previously and consisted of symptoms of hyperventilation, palpitations, lightheadedness, and a feeling of dread while she was working around her apartment. Because she believed she was having a heart attack, she called for an ambulance and was taken to the emergency room of a local hospital. A heart attack was ruled out, and she was referred to her personal physician to be treated for anxiety symptoms. Over the course of the next several months, she was treated with Valium, and the physician insisted she get psychotherapy. She did not, however, follow up with the recommendation for psychotherapy until 19 months after her first symptoms occurred, and because of anticipatory anxiety of further panic attacks, she became increasingly homebound and agoraphobic. Over this period of time she became more moody, irritable, fatigued, and tearful, and she had difficulty with initial insomnia as well as early morning awakening.

She is the younger of two siblings. Her brother was described as a successful attorney. Her parents were both alive, and since the panic attacks had begun, Ms. A moved back into her parents' home. She described both her parents as caring, concerned, and "my best friends." Ms. A had graduated from college and went on to complete a master's degree in education. Subsequently, she worked for four years as an elementary school teacher before her first symptoms occurred. Since then she had taken an indefinite leave of absence from her job. Ms. A reported being sickly as a young child and being taken by mother from doctor to doctor for various minor ailments. Even though she was a good student at school and had some friends, she preferred to come home after school and help mother around the house with the house cleaning and chores.

The following early recollections were reported:

> At age six she remembers her first day of going to school by herself. "I was proud. My mother said I could walk to school by myself. But when I turned the corner, I saw her out of the corner of my eye, following me." Ms. A recalls looking over her shoulder and seeing her mother behind a tree and feeling flustered and anger, and at the same time relieved that her mother was there. She remembers thinking, "Why can't she let me do this by myself?"

> She remembers at age four getting her first puppy. "It was a mixed collie and a shepherd. Little Fluffy couldn't make it down the driveway on its own. When I tried to take him for a walk his legs just collapsed

and he began to pant. So Fluffy became dependent on everyone. I had to pick him up and I said, 'He's too tired to do it by himself.'" She recalls bending down and picking up her dog and thinking, "He's too tired" and feeling love for her puppy, and love and appreciation from him.

At age five she recalls her mother asking her to go to the corner store to get some stamps. "She gave me instructions on how to cross the street, get change from the cashier, and put the money in the stamp machine. But when I went over to the stamp machine, I couldn't reach the coin slot because it was too high off the ground." Ms. A recalls standing in front of the machine and trying to get it to work, but not being able to reach the coin slot, and feeling puzzled and nervous, wondering if someone would see her and try to help her.

Ms. A's presenting symptoms, her early childhood and family history, and her early recollections are all suggestive of the clinical presentation and dynamics of the Dependent Personality Disorder. Not only was Ms. A overly dependent on her parents, she also became quite dependent on the Valium that she was prescribed for panic symptoms. The case of Ms. A is prototypic of many individuals who present with panic, agoraphobia, and depressive features. That is, the Dependent Personality Disorder is the most common Axis II presentation in individuals presenting with panic and agoraphobic symptoms.

HISTRIONIC PERSONALITY DISORDER

DSM-III-R Description and Criteria

Histrionic personalities may initially seem charming, likable, energetic, and seductive, but as time passes they are likely to be seen as emotionally unstable, immature and egocentric. This personality style and disorder predominates in females, and presents with a caricature of femininity in dress and manner. The Histrionic Personality Disorder is characterized by a pervasive pattern of excessive emotionality and attention-seeking. At least four of eight criteria are needed to make the DSM-III-R diagnosis: constantly seeking or demanding reassurance, approval or praise; being inappropriately sexually seductive in behavior or appearance; being overly concerned with physical attractiveness; expressing emotion with inappropriate exaggeration; being uncomfortable in situations in which they are not the center of attention; displaying rapidly shifting and shallow expression of emotions; being self-centered and having no tolerance for the frustration of delayed gratification; and having a style of speech that is excessively impressionistic and lacking in detail.

Clinical Presentation

The clinical presentation of the Histrionic Personality Disorder can be characterized with the following behavioral and interpersonal style, thinking style, and feeling style.

The behavioral style is characterized as charming, dramatic, and expressive, while also being demanding, self-indulgent, and inconsiderate. Persistent attention-seeking, mood lability, capriciousness, and superficiality further characterize their behavior. Interpersonally, these individuals tend to be exhibitionistic and flirtatious in their manner, with attention-seeking and manipulativeness being prominent.

The thinking or cognitive style of this personality can be characterized as impulsive and thematic, rather than being analytical, precise, and field-independent. In short, their tendency is to be non-analytic, vague, and field-dependent. They are easily suggestible and rely heavily on hunches and intuition. They avoid awareness of their own hidden dependency and other self-knowledge, and tend to be "other-directed" with respect to the need for approval from others. Therefore, they can easily dissociate their "real" or inner self from their "public" or outer self. Their emotional or affective style is characterized by exaggerated emotional displays and excitability, including irrational outbursts and temper tantrums. Although they are constantly seeking reassurance that they are loved, they respond with only superficial warmth and charm and are generally emotionally shallow. Finally, they are exceedingly rejection-sensitive.

Developmental and Etiological Features

The following biopsychosocial formulation may be helpful in understanding how the Histrionic Personality Disorder develops.

Biologically and temperamentally, the Histrionic Personality Disorder appears to be quite different from the Dependent Personality Disorder. Unlike the dependent personality, histrionic personality is characterized by a high energy level and emotional and autonomic reactivity. Millon and Everly (1985) noted that histrionic adults tended to display a high degree of emotional lability and responsiveness in their infancy and early childhood. Their temperament then can be characterized as hyperresponsive and externally-oriented for gratification.

Psychologically, Histrionic Personality Disorder has the characteristic view of self, world view, and life goal. The self view of the histrionic will be some variant of the theme: "I am sensitive and everyone should admire and approve of me." The world view will be some variant of: "Life makes me nervous so I am entitled to special care and consideration." Life goal is some variant of the theme: "Therefore, play to the audience, and have fun, fun, fun."

In addition to biological and psychological factors, social factors such as parenting style and injunction, and family and environmental factors influence the development of the histrionic personality. The parental injunction for the histrionic personality involves reciprocity: "I'll give you attention, if you do X." A parenting style that involves minimal or inconsistent discipline helps insure and reinforce the histrionic pattern. The histrionic child is likely to grow up with at least one manipulative or histrionic parent who reinforces the child's histrionic and attention-seeking behavior. Finally, the following sequence of self and system perpetuants are likely to be seen in the Histrionic Personality Disorder: denial of one's real or inner self; a preoccupation with externals; the need for excitement and attention-seeking which leads to a superficial charm and interpersonal presence; and, the need for external approval. This, in turn, further reinforces the dissociation

(Continued on page 315)

1.	Behavioral Appearance:	Charming/excitement-seeking Labile, capricious, superficial
2.	Interpersonal Behavior:	Attention-getting/manipulative Exhibitionistic/flirtatious
3.	Cognitive Style:	Impulsive, thematic, field-dependent Avoid awareness of their hidden dependencies Dissociate "real" from "public" self
4.	Feeling Style:	Exaggerated emotional display
5.	Parental Injunction/ Environmental Factors:	"I'll give you attention when you do what I want." Manipulative/histrionic parental role models; minimal or inconsistent disciplining
6.	Biological/Temperament:	Hyperresponsive infantile pattern externally-oriented for gratification
7.	Self View:	"I need to be noticed"; externally-oriented for gratification
8.	World View:	"Life makes me nervous, so I'm entitled to special care and consideration."
9.	Self & System Perpetuant:	Preoccupation with external/repression Denial of shadow and inner life Reinforcement of need for approval

Figure 11.3. Characteristics of Histrionic Personality Disorder.

and denial of the real or inner self from the public self, and the cycle continues. Characteristics of Histrionic Personality Disorder are provided in Figure 11.3.

Treatment Considerations

The differential diagnosis of the Histrionic Personality Disorder includes the Narcissistic Personality Disorder and the Dependent Personality Disorder. In addition, in Axis II is combined the Histrionic-Borderline Disorder which is a decompensated version of the Histrionic Personality Disorder. Also according to Millon (1981) is the Histrionic-Antisocial Personality Disorder. Associated DSM-III-R Axis I diagnoses are in order of occurrence: Dysthymia; Acute Anxiety Syndromes such as Simple and Social Phobias; and the Somatoform Disorders, particularly Conversion Reactions and Hypochondriasis. Other disorders are the Obsessive Compulsive Disorder and the Dissociative Disorders, particularly Fugue States. Finally, Major Depression and Bipolar Disorders are common in the decompensated Histrionic Personality Disorder.

The treatment of the Histrionic Personality Disorder may present a considerable challenge to the clinician. For the purposes of this discussion, we will limit ourselves to some general considerations about treatment goals, limits, and medications. General treatment goals include helping the individual integrate gentleness with strength, moderating emotional expression, and encouraging warmth, genuineness, and empathy. Because the histrionic personality can present as dramatic, impulsive, seductive, and manipulative with potential for suicidal gestures, the clinician needs to discuss the matter of limits early in the course of therapy regarding professional boundaries and personal responsibilities. Some histrionic personalities, particularly those that bear some resemblance to "hysteroid dysphoria," respond to certain antidepressant agents, particularly Parnate and Nardil (Liebowitz & Klein, 1979). Otherwise, unless a concurrent acute psychotic or major depressive episode is present, psychotherapy is the principal mode of treatment.

Case Example: Ms. J

Ms. J. is a 19-year-old female undergraduate student who requested psychological counseling at the University Health Services for "boyfriend problems." Actually, she had taken a nonlethal overdose of minor tranquilizers the day before coming to the Health Services. She said she took the overdose in an attempt to kill herself because "life wasn't worth living" after her boyfriend had left the afternoon before. She was an attractive, well-dressed woman adorned with makeup and nail polish, which contrasted sharply with the very casual fashion of most coeds on campus. During the initial interview she was warm and charming, maintained good eye contact, yet was mildly seductive. At two points in the interview she was emotionally labile, shifting from smiling elation to tearful sadness. Her boyfriend had accompanied her to the evaluation session and asked to talk to the therapist. He stated the reason he had left the patient was because she made demands on him which he could not meet, and that he "hadn't been able to satisfy her emotionally or sexually." Also, he noted that he could not afford to "take her out every night and party."

NARCISSISTIC PERSONALITY DISORDER

Although often symptom-free and well functioning, the Narcissistic Personality Disorder is chronically unsatisfied due to a constant need for admiration and habitually unrealistic self-expectations. The narcissist is impulsive and anxious, has ideas of grandiosity and "specialness," becomes quickly dissatisfied with others, and maintains superficial, exploitative interpersonal relationships. Under stress and when needs are not met, the narcissist may become depressed, develop somatic symptoms, have brief psychotic episodes, or display extreme rage.

DSM-III-R Description and Criteria

The Narcissistic Personality Disorder is characterized by a pervasive pattern of grandiosity, lack of empathy, and hypersensitivity to the evaluation of others. At least five of the following nine criteria must be met: reacting to criticism with feeling of rage, shame or humiliation; being interpersonally exploitative; having a grandiose sense of self-importance; believing that his or her problems are unique and can be understood only by other special people; being preoccupied with fantasies of unlimited success, power, brilliance, beauty, or ideal love; having a sense of entitlement; requiring constant attention or admiration; lacking empathy; and, being preoccupied with feelings of envy.

Clinical Presentation

The narcissistic personality is characterized by the following behavioral and interpersonal style, cognitive style, and affective style.

Behaviorally, narcissistic individuals are seen as conceited, boastful, and snobbish. They appear self-assured and self-centered, and they tend to dominate conversation, seek admiration, and act in a pompous and exhibitionistic fashion. They are also impatient, arrogant, and thin-skinned or hypersensitive. Interpersonally, they are exploitative and use others to indulge themselves and their desires. Their behavior is socially facile, pleasant, and endearing. However, they are unable to respond with true empathy to others. When stressed, they can be disdainful, exploitative, and generally irresponsible in their behavior.

Their thinking style is one of cognitive expansiveness and exaggeration. They tend to focus on images and themes rather than on facts and issues. In fact, they take liberties with the facts, distort them, and even engage in prevarication and self-deception to preserve their own illusions about themselves and the projects in which they are involved. Their cognitive style is also marked by inflexibility. In addition they have an exaggerated sense of self-importance and establish unrealistic goals of power, wealth, and ability. They justify all of this with their sense of entitlement and exaggerated sense of their own self-importance.

Their feeling or affective style is characterized by an aura of self-confidence and nonchalance which is present in most situations except when their narcissistic confidence is shaken. Then they are likely to respond with rage at criticism. Their feelings toward others shift and vacillate between overidealization and devaluation. Finally, their inability to show empathy is reflected in their superficial relationships with minimal emotional ties or commitments.

Developmental and Etiological Features

The following biopsychosocial formulation may be helpful in understanding how the Narcissistic Personality Disorder is likely to have developed.

Biologically narcissistic personalities tend to have hyperresponsive temperaments (Millon, 1981). As young children they were viewed by others as being special in terms of looks, talents, or "promise." Often as young children they had early and exceptional speech development. In addition, they were likely keenly aware of interpersonal cues.

Psychologically, the narcissists' view of themselves, others, the world and life's purpose can be articulated in terms of the following themes: "I'm special and unique, and I am entitled to extraordinary rights and privileges whether I have earned them or not." Their world view is a variant of the theme: "Life is a banquet table to be sampled at will. People owe me admiration and privilege." Their goal is, "Therefore, I'll expect and demand this specialness." Common defense mechanisms utilized by the narcissistic personality involve rationalization and projective identification.

Socially, predictable parental patterns and environmental factors can be noted for the narcissistic personality. Parental indulgence and overevaluation characterize the narcissistic personality. The parental injunction was likely: "Grow up and be wonderful—for me." Often they were only children and, in addition, may have sustained early losses in childhood. From an early age they learned exploitative and manipulative behavior from their parents. This narcissistic pattern is confirmed, reinforced, and perpetuated by certain individual and systems factors. The illusion of specialness, disdain for

(Continued on page 320)

1.	Behavioral Appearance:	Conceited, boastful, snobbish Self-assured, self-centered, pompous Impatient, arrogant, thin-skinned
2.	Interpersonal Behavior:	Disdainful, exploitative, irresponsible Socially facile but without empathy Use others to indulge themselves
3.	Cognitive Style:	Cognitive expansiveness and exaggeration Focus on images and themes: takes liberties with facts Persistent and inflexible Defense: projective identification
4.	Feeling Style:	Self-confidence—narcissistic rage
5.	Parental Injunction/ Environmental Factors:	"Grow up and be wonderful, for me." Parental indulgence and over-evaluation Learned exploitative behavior "Only child" status, early losses
6.	Biological/Temperament:	Special books, talents, or "promisc" Early and exceptional language development Keenly aware of interpersonal cues
7.	Self View:	"I'm special and unique, and I'm entitled to extraordinary rights and privileges whether I've earned them or not."
8.	World View:	"Life is a banquet table to be sampled at will. People owe me admiration and privilege. Therefore, I'll expect and demand this specialness."
9.	Self & System Perpetuant:	Illusion of specialness (+) disdain for others' views (+) entitlement → underdeveloped social interest and responsibility → increased self-absorption and reinforcement of narcissistic beliefs.

Figure 11.4. Characteristics of Narcissistic Personality Disorder.

others' views, and a sense of entitlement lead to an underdeveloped sense of social interest and responsibility. This, in turn, leads to increased self-absorption and confirmation of narcissistic beliefs. The characteristics of Narcissistic Personality Disorder are provided in Figure 11.4.

Treatment Considerations

Included in the differential diagnosis of the Narcissistic Personality Disorder are these other Axis II personality disorders: Histrionic Personality Disorder, Antisocial Personality Disorder, and Paranoid Personality Disorder. The most common Axis I syndromes associated with the Narcissistic Personality Disorder are Acute Anxiety Reactions, Dysthymia, Hypochondriasis, and Delusional Disorders.

In terms of treatment goals, a decision needs to be made as to whether the treatment is short-term and crisis-oriented or long-term and focused on personality restructuring. Crisis-oriented psychotherapy usually focuses on alleviation of the symptoms such as anxiety, depression, or somatic symptoms associated with the narcissistic injury or wound. This injury occurs when others fail to respond to the narcissist's sense of entitlement and specialness. Empathic mirroring or reflection and soothing are the treatments of choice (Kohut, 1971). The goals of longer term therapy involve the restructuring of personality. These goals include increasing empathy, decreasing rage and cognitive distortions, and increasing the individual's ability to mourn losses. Treatment methods and strategies include empathic mirroring (Kohut, 1971), anger management, cognitive restructuring and empathy training, as well as interpretation. When marital issues are involved, couples therapy has been shown to be a useful treatment modality (Feldman, 1982). Medication management is directed only at treatable Axis I conditions (Reid, 1989). Clinicians have noted that the majority of narcissistic personalities who present for treatment are interested only in having the narcissistic wound soothed; then they leave treatment.

Case Example: Mr. E

Mr. E is a 32-year-old male who presented for therapy after his wife of six years threatened to leave him and because his employer was pressuring him to resign his position as a sales executive for a condominium project. Apparently, Mrs. E had told her husband that he loved himself "a hundred times more than you love me." Mr. E dismissed this by saying he needed to buy $600 suits because his job demanded that he look his best at all times and that he was "tall, dark, handsome and sexy, all any woman could want in a man." Mr. E denied that he used scare tactics, exaggerated claims, or other pressure selling techniques with customers. "Sure, I'm a bit aggressive, but you don't get into the 'Millionaire's Club' by being a wimp." He added that his employer would "go belly up without me," and that he was too important to be dismissed for such petty reasons.

THE ANTISOCIAL PERSONALITY DISORDER

DSM-III-R Description and Criteria

Antisocial behavior tends to begin in childhood or early adolescence and is characterized by aggressiveness, fighting, hyperactivity, poor peer relationships, irresponsibility, lying, theft, truancy, poor school performance, runaway behavior, inappropriate sexual activity, as well as drug and alcohol abuse. As adults, assaultiveness, self-defeating impulsivity, hedonism, promiscuity, unreliability, and continued drug and alcohol abuse may be present. Criminality may be involved. These individuals fail at work, change jobs frequently, tend to receive dishonorable discharges from the military, are abusing parents and neglectful spouses, have difficulty maintaining intimate relationships, and may be convicted and spend time in prison. Antisocial Personality Disordered persons are frequently anxious and depressed and show both conversion symptoms and factitious symptoms. Antisocial behavior often peaks in the late adolescence and early twenties and lessens in the late thirties. This is primarily a diagnosis of males with a prevalence rate being approximately 6:1 males to females.

According to DSM-III-R criteria, an individual must be 18 years of age and have evidence of a conduct disorder before age 15. This disorder is characterized by irresponsible and antisocial behavior since the age of 15 and must include at least four of ten criteria: inability to sustain consistent work behavior; failing to conform to social norms with respect to lawful behavior; irritability and aggressiveness; repeatedly failing to honor financial obligations; impulsivity in failing to plan ahead; lying or "conning" others for personal profit or pleasure; being reckless regarding own or other's personal safety; lacking ability to function as a responsible parent or guardian; never having sustained a totally monogamous relationship for more than one year; and, lacking in remorse.

Clinical Presentation

The Antisocial Personality Disorder is recognizable by the following behavioral, and interpersonal style, cognitive style, and emotional style.

As previously noted with the DSM-III-R criteria, the behavioral style of antisocial personalities is characterized by irresponsible parenting, poor job performance, repeated substance abuse, persistent lying, delinquency, truancy, and violations of others' rights. Antisocial Personality Disordered individuals also are noted for their impulsive anger, hostility, and cunning. They are forceful individuals who regularly engage in risk-seeking and thrill-seeking behavior. Their interpersonal style is characterized as antagonistic and belligerent. They tend to be highly competitive and distrustful of others and thus poor losers. Their relationships may at times appear to be "slick" as well as calculating. The flavor of this DSM-III-R diagnosis still retains much of the "criminal" diagnostic category. Yet, these criteria also can characterize the behavior of successful businessmen, politicians, and other professionals who could be described as ambitious, hard-driving, and successful.

The cognitive style of the antisocial personality is described as impulsive and cognitively inflexible as well as externally-oriented. Because they are contemptuous of authority, rules, and social expectations, they easily rationalize their own behavior.

Their feeling or emotional style is characterized with shallow, superficial relationships that involve no lasting emotional ties or commitments. They avoid "softer" emotions such as warmth and intimacy because they regard these as signs of weakness. Guilt is seldom if ever experienced. They are unable to tolerate boredom, depression, or frustration and subsequently are sensation-seekers. They are callous toward the pain and suffering of others and show little guilt or shame over their own deviant actions.

Developmental and Etiological Features

The following biopsychosocial formulation may be helpful in understanding how the antisocial personality is likely to have developed.

Biologically, antisocial personalities manifested "difficult child" temperaments (Thomas & Chess, 1977). As such their patterns were unpredictable; they tended to withdraw from situations, showed high intensity, and had a fairly low, discontented mood. This ill-tempered infantile pattern has been described by Millon (1981) as resulting in part from a low threshold for limbic stimulation and a decrease in inhibitory centers of the central nervous system. Their body types tend to be endomorphic and mesomorphic (Millon, 1981).

Psychologically, the antisocials' view of themselves, others, the world, and life's purpose can be articulated in terms of the following themes. They tend to view themselves with some variant of the theme: "I am cunning and entitled to get whatever I want." In other words, they see themselves as strong, competitive, energetic, and tough. Their view of life and the world is a variant of the theme: "Life is devious and hostile, and rules keep me from fulfilling my needs." Not surprisingly their life's goal has a variant of the theme: "Therefore, I'll bend or break these rules because my needs come first, and I'll defend against efforts to be controlled or degraded by others." Acting out and rationalization are common defense mechanisms used by the antisocial personality.

Socially, predictable parenting styles and environmental factors can be noted for the Antisocial Personality Disorder. Typically, the parenting style is characterized by hostility and deficient parental modeling. Or, the parents might have provided such good modeling that the child could not or refused to live up to high parental standards. The parental injunction is that, "The end justifies the means." Thus, vindictive behavior is modeled and reinforced. The family structure tends to be disorganized and disengaged. The antisocial pattern is confirmed, reinforced, and perpetuated by the following individual and systems factors: The need to be powerful and the fear of being abused and humiliated lead to a denial of "softer" emotions plus uncooperativeness. This, along with the tendency to provoke others, leads to further reinforcement of antisocial beliefs and behaviors. (See Figure 11.5 for characteristics of Antisocial Personality Disorder.)

Treatment Considerations

The differential diagnosis for Antisocial Personality Disorder includes other Axis II personality disorders such as the Narcissistic Personality Disorder and the Paranoid Personality Disorder. The most common Axis I syndromes associated with the Antisocial Personality Disorder are Substance Abuse and Dependence, Acute Anxiety States, Delusional Disorders, and Factitious Disorders.

In terms of treatment goals, these individuals are usually not interested in presenting for treatment or are resistant to treatment if they are forced by the courts, employers, or other agencies. Individual therapy, in and of itself, has proved to be remarkably ineffective with these individuals. However, special residential treatment programs have shown some promise (Reid, 1989). If the antisocial personality is able to engage in psychotherapy, a clear sign of progress is noted with the appearance of depressive features.

Case Example: Mr. Z

Mr. Z is a 24-year-old male who presented late in the evening to the emergency room at a community hospital complaining of a headache. His description of the pain was vague and contradictory. At one point he said the pain had been present for three days, while at another point it was "many years." He indicated that the pain led to violent behavior and described how, during a headache episode, he had brutally

(Continued on page 326)

1. Behavioral Appearance:	Impulsively angry, hostile, cunning Forceful, risk-taking, thrill-seeking Temper, verbally or physically abusive Avoid "softer" emotions such as warmth and intimacy = weakness
2. Interpersonal Behavior:	Antagonistic to belligerent "Slick" but calculating Highly competitive and poor losers Distrustful of others
3. Cognitive Style:	Impulsive, inflexible, and externally-oriented → hard-nosed, realistic, and devious Defense: Acting out
4. Feeling Style:	Glib, shallow, superficality
5. Parental Injunction/ Environmental Factors:	"The end justifies the means." Parental hostility → learned vindictive behavior (+) deficient authority figure Disorganized family and/or subculture system
6. Biological/Temperament:	Ill tempered infantile pattern Low threshold for limbic stimulation and inefficient inhibitory centers (+) Mesomorpic-endomorphic body types (Subclass) Adult ADD—Residual
7. Self View:	"I'm cunning and I'm entitled to get what I want." They view themselves as strong, competitive, self-reliant, energetic, and tough
8. World View:	"Life is devious and hostile and rules keep me from fulfilling my needs. Therefore, I'll bend or break them because my needs come first and I'll defend any efforts to be controlled or degraded."
9. Self & System Perpetuant:	Need to be powerful (+) fear of being abused/humiliated → denial of tender feelings and unwillingness to cooperate (+) tendency to provoke others → reinforcement of antisocial style.

Figure 11.5. Characteristics of Antisocial Personality Disorder.

assaulted a medic while he was in the Air Force. He gave a long history of arrests for assault, burglary, and drug dealing. Neurological and mental status examinations were within normal limits except for some mild agitation. He insisted that only Darvon—a narcotic—would relieve his headache pain. The patient resisted a plan for further diagnostic tests or a follow-up clinic appointment, saying unless he was treated immediately "something really bad could happen."

SCHIZOID PERSONALITY DISORDER

DSM-III-R Description and Criteria

Individuals with Schizoid Personality Disorder are seclusive individuals who have little desire or capacity for interpersonal relationships and derive little pleasure from them. Yet, they can perform well if left alone. For instance, they make excellent night watchmen and security guards. They have little emotional range, they daydream excessively, and appear to be humorless and aloof. Research evidence does *not* confirm the belief that the schizoid personality has an increased risk of developing a schizophrenic pattern (Grinspoon, 1982).

In the DSM-III-R criteria the Schizoid Personality Disorder has a pervasive pattern of indifference to relationships and restricted emotional expression. It is diagnosed if at least four of seven criteria are present: neither desiring nor enjoying close interpersonal relationships; choosing solitary activities almost exclusively; rarely, if ever, claiming or appearing to experience strong emotions; indicating little if any desire to have sexual experiences with other persons; being indifferent to the praise and criticism of others; having no close friends nor confidants other than first-degree relatives; and, displaying constricted affect.

Clinical Presentation

The Schizoid Personality Disorder is characterized by the following behavioral and interpersonal styles, thinking or cognitive styles, and emotional or affective styles.

The behavioral pattern of schizoids can be described as lethargic, inattentive, and occasionally eccentric. They exhibit slow and monotonal speech and are generally non-spontaneous in both their behavior and speech. Interpersonally, they appear to be content to remain socially aloof and alone. These individuals prefer to engage in solitary pursuits, they are reserved and seclusive, and they rarely respond to others' feelings and actions. They tend to fade into the social backdrop and appear to others as "cold fish." They do not involve themselves in group or team activity. In short, they appear inept and awkward in social situations.

Their thinking style can be characterized as cognitively distracted. That is, their thinking and communication can easily become derailed through internal or external distraction. This is noted in clinical interviews when these patients have difficulty organizing their thoughts, are vague, or wander into irrelevance such as the shoes certain people prefer (Millon, 1981). They appear to have little ability for introspection, nor ability to articulate important aspects of interpersonal relationships. Their goals are vague and appear to be indecisive.

Their emotional style is characterized as being humorless, cold, aloof, and unemotional. They appear to be indifferent to praise and criticism, and they lack spontaneity. Not surprisingly, their rapport and ability to empathize with others are poor. In short, they have a constricted range of affective response.

Developmental and Etiological Features

The following biopsychosocial formulation may be helpful in understanding how the schizoid personality develops.

Biologically, the schizoid personality was likely to have had a passive and anhedonic infantile pattern and temperament. Millon (1981) suggested that this pattern results, in part, from increased dopaminergic postsynaptic limbic and frontal lobe receptor activity. Constitutionally, the schizoid is likely to be characterized by an ectomorphic body type (Sheldon, Dupertius, & McDermott, 1954).

Psychologically, schizoids view themselves, others, the world, and life's purpose in terms of the following themes. They view themselves by some variant of the theme: "I'm a misfit from life, so I don't need anybody. I am indifferent to everything." For schizoid personalities, the world and others are viewed by some variant of the theme: "Life is a difficult place and relating to people can be harmful." As such, they are likely to conclude, "Therefore, trust nothing and keep a distance from others and you won't get hurt." Alexandra Adler (1956) further described these life-style dynamics. The most common defense mechanism utilized by them is intellectualization.

Socially, predictable patterns of parenting and environmental factors can be noted for schizoids. Parenting style is usually characterized by indifference and impoverishment. It is as if the parental injunction was: "You're a misfit," or, "Who are you, what do you want?" Their family pattern is characterized by fragmented communications and rigid, unemotional responsiveness. Because of these conditions, schizoids are grossly under-socialized and develop few if any interpersonal relating and coping skills. This schizoid pattern is confirmed, reinforced, and perpetuated by the following individual and systems factors: Believing themselves to be misfits, they shun social activity. This plus social insensitivity leads to reinforcement of social isolation and further confirmation of the schizoid style. In Figure 11.6 are listed characteristics of Schizoid Personality Disorder.

Treatment Considerations

Included in the differential diagnosis of the Schizoid Personality Disorder are the following Axis II personality disorders: The Avoidant Personality Disorder, Schizotypal Personality Disorder, and the Dependent Personality Disorder. The most common Axis I syndromes likely to be associated with the Schizoid Personality Disorder are Depersonalization Disorder, the Bipolar and Unipolar Disorders, Obsessive Compulsive Disorder, Hypochondriasis, Schizophreniform, and Disorganized and Catatonic Schizophrenias.

(Continued on page 330)

1. Behavioral Appearance:	Speech: slow and monotonous Lethargic, inattentive, non-spontaneous
2. Interpersonal Behavior:	Minimal "human" interests and friends "Cold fish," fades into social background Rarely responds to feelings or actions of others, isolate Content to remain aloof
3. Cognitive Style:	Cognitively distracted—thoughts and communications are easily derailed and tangential or loose, absent minded Minimally introspective Defense: intellectualization
4. Feeling Style:	Aloof, indifferent
5. Parental Injunction/ Environmental Factors:	"Who are you, what do you want?" Rigid, emotionally unresponsive family of origin Fragmented family communications Under-socialized in interpersonal skills
6. Biological/Temperament:	Passive and anhedonic infantile pattern Excessive dopaminergic post-synaptic limbic and frontal lobe receptors Ectomorphic build
7. Self View:	"I'm a misfit from life, so I don't need anybody." "I'm indifferent to everything."
8. World View:	"Life is a difficult place and can be harmful. Therefore, trust nothing and keep distance from others and you won't get hurt."
9. Self & System Perpetuant:	Infrequent social activity (+) social insensitivity → reinforcement of social isolation.

Figure 11.6. Characteristics of Schizoid Personality Disorder.

Schizoid personalities rarely volunteer for treatment unless decompensation is present. However, they may accept treatment if someone, like a family member, demands it. Treatment goals are focused on symptom alleviation rather than on restructuring of personality. Treatment strategy involves a crisis and supportive approach, as well as providing a consistent and supportive therapeutic interaction. Medications, particularly the neuroleptics, do not appear to be useful with schizoid personality unless some psychotic decompensation has been noted (Reid, 1989).

Case Example: Mr. S

Mr. S is a 19-year-old freshman who met with the director of the introductory psychology course program to arrange an individual assignment in lieu of participation in the small group research project course requirement. Mr. S told the course director that because of a daily two-hour commute each way, he "wouldn't be available for the research project," and that he "wasn't really interested in psychology and was only taking the course because it was required." Upon further inquiry, Mr. S disclosed that he preferred to commute and live at home with his mother, even though he had the financial resources to live on campus. He admitted he had no close friend nor social contacts and preferred being a "loner." He had graduated from high school with a "B" average, but did not date or participate in extracurricular activities, except the electronics club. He was a computer science major, and "hacking" was his only hobby. Mr. S's affect was somewhat flattened, and he appeared to have no sense of humor and failed to respond to attempts by the course director to make contact through humor. No indication was noted of a thought nor perceptual disorder. The course director arranged for an individual project for the student.

AVOIDANT PERSONALITY DISORDER

DSM-III-R Description and Criteria

Avoidant personalities are seemingly shy, lonely, hypersensitive individuals with low self-esteem. Although they are desperate for interpersonal involvement, they avoid personal contact with others because of their heightened fear of social disapproval and rejection sensitivity. In this regard, they are quite different from the schizoid personality who has little if any interest in personal contact.

In DSM-III-R criteria the avoidant personality is characterized by a pervasive pattern of social discomfort, timidity, and fear of negative evaluation by others. To make this diagnosis, at least four of seven criteria must be met: being easily hurt by criticism or disapproval; having no more than one close friend or confidant other than first-degree relatives; being unwilling to get involved with people unless certain of being liked and accepted; avoiding social or occupational activities that involve significant interpersonal contact; being reticent in social situations because of a fear of saying something that would be inappropriate or foolish, or of being unable to answer a question; fearing embarrassment by blushing, crying, or showing signs of anxiety in front of other people; and, exaggerating the potential difficulties, physical dangers, or risk involved in doing something ordinary but outside of their usual routine.

Clinical Presentation

The Avoidant Personality Disorder is characterized by the following behavioral and interpersonal style, thinking or cognitive style, and emotional or affective style.

The behavioral style of avoidant personalities is characterized by social withdrawal, shyness, distrustfulness, and aloofness. Their behavior and speech are both controlled and inactive, and they appear apprehensive and awkward. Interpersonally, they are rejection-sensitive. Even though they desire acceptance by others, they keep distance from others and require unconditional approval before being willing to "open up." They guardedly "test" others to determine who can be trusted to like them.

The cognitive style of avoidants can be described as perceptually vigilant; that is, they scan the environment looking for clues of potential threat or acceptance. Their thoughts are often distracted by their hypersensitivity. Not surprisingly, they have low self-esteem because of their devaluation of their own achievements and their overemphasis of their own shortcomings.

Their affective or emotional style is marked by a shy and apprehensive quality. Because they are seldom able to attain unconditional approval from others, they routinely experience sadness, loneliness, and tenseness. At times of increased distress, they will describe feelings of emptiness and depersonalization.

Developmental and Etiological Features

The following biopsychosocial formulation may be helpful in understanding how the Avoidant Personality Disorder is likely to have developed.

Biologically, the avoidant personality was likely to have been a hyper-irritable and fearful infant. In Thomas and Chess's classification (1977), the avoidant would likely exhibit the "slow-to-warm-up" infant temperament. Millon and Everly (1985) suggested that avoidant personalities often experience maturational irregularities as children. This, as well as a hyper-irritable pattern, is due in part to a low arousal threshold of the autonomic nervous system.

Psychologically, avoidants view themselves, others, the world, and life's purpose in terms of the following themes. They tend to view themselves by some variant of the theme: "I'm inadequate and frightened of rejection." They see themselves as chronically tense, fatigued, and self-conscious, and they devalue their achievements by their self-critical attitude. They tend to see the world as some variant of the theme: "Life is unfair—people reject and criticize me—but, I still want someone to like me." As such, they are likely to conclude, "Therefore, be vigilant, demand reassurance, and if all else fails, fantasize and daydream about the way life could be." The most common defense mechanism of the avoidant personality is that of fantasy.

Socially, predictable patterns of parenting and environmental factors can be noted for the Avoidant Personality Disorder. The avoidant personality is likely to have experienced parental rejection and/or ridicule. Later, siblings and peers will likely continue this pattern of rejection and ridicule. The parental injunction is likely to have been, "We don't accept you, and probably no one else will either." They may have had parents with high standards and worried that they may not have or would not meet these standards and therefore would not be accepted.

This avoidant pattern is confirmed, reinforced, and perpetuated by the following individual and systems factors: A sense of personal inadequacy and a fear of rejection lead to hypervigilance, which leads to restricted social experiences. These experiences, plus catastrophic thinking, lead to increased hypervigilance and hypersensitivity, leading to self-pity, anxiety, and depression, which lead to further confirmation of avoidant beliefs and styles.

Treatment Considerations

Included in a differential diagnosis of the Avoidant Personality Disorder are other Axis II personality disorders: Schizoid Personality Disorder, Schizotypal Personality Disorder, Borderline Personality Disorder, and Dependent Personality Disorder. The most common Axis I syndromes associated with the Avoidant Personality Disorder are Generalized Anxiety Disorder, Dysthymia, Major Depressive episode, Hypochondriasis, Conversion Disorder, Dissociative Disorder, and Schizophrenia. Next to the Borderline Personality Disorder, the Avoidant Personality Disorder is the most labile and likely to decompensate (Reid, 1989).

In terms of treatment goals and strategies, very little research has been reported on treating the avoidant personality. However, the goal of therapy should be to increase the individual's self-esteem and confidence in relationship to others and to desensitize the individual to the criticism of others. Desensitization techniques appear to be much more useful and expedient in this regard. Assertiveness training and shyness

(Continued on page 335)

1. Behavioral Appearance:	Shy, mistrustful, aloof Apprehensive, socially awkward Controlled, underactive behavior Feelings of emptiness and deperson- alization
2. Interpersonal Behavior:	Guardedly "tests" others Rejection sensitive as self-protectant Desires acceptance but maintains distance Have interpersonal skills, but fear using them
3. Cognitive Style:	Perpetual vigilance Thoughts easily distracted by their hypersensitivity Defense mechanism--fantasy
4. Feeling Style:	Shy and apprehensive
5. Parental Injunction/ Environmental Factors:	"We don't accept you, and probably nobody else will either." Parental rejection and/or ridicule Later, peer group alienation
6. Biological/Temperament:	Hyperirritable infantile pattern Low arousal threshold for autonomic nervous system
7. Self View:	"I'm inadequate and frightened of rejection." Chronically tense, fatigued, self- conscious Devalue their achievement, self- critical
8. World View:	"Life is unfair, people reject and criticize me, but I want someone to like me. Therefore, be vigilant, demand reassurance, and, if all else fails, fantasize and daydream."
9. Self & System Perpetuant:	Fear of social rejection and humil- iation →hypervigilance → restricted social experiences (+) catastro- phizing → increased hypervigilance and hypersensitivity → increased self pity

Figure 11.7. Characteristics of Avoidant Personality Disorder.

training are reported very effective with the avoidant personality pattern (Turkat & Maisto, 1985). As with other personality disorders, medication is only useful for diagnosable Axis I conditions associated with the avoidant pattern.

Case Example: Ms. W

Ms. W is a 24-year-old female graduate student who contacted the College Counseling Service for help with "difficulty concentrating." She indicated that the problem started when Ms. W's roommate of two years precipitously moved out to live with her boyfriend. Ms. W described herself as being "blown away and hurt" by this. She noted that she had no other close friends and described herself as being shy and having had only one date since high school. Since then, she had foiled attempts by men to date her because of being rejected when she was a freshman by a guy who had dated her for a month and never contacted her again. On examination, she had poor eye contact with the admissions counselor and appeared very shy and self-conscious.

PASSIVE AGGRESSIVE PERSONALITY DISORDER

DSM-III-R Description and Criteria

Individuals with the Passive Aggressive Personality Disorder are irritating, oppositional, resentful, and controlling. Thus, they tend to have few friends and a significantly impaired social and occupational functioning. Their hostility is expressed passively through intentional inefficiency, negativism, stubbornness, procrastination, forgetfulness, and somatic complaints. They are, on the one hand, overly dependent on other persons and institutions, while at the same time resist demands made on them.

To meet the DSM-III-R diagnosis, the person needs to exhibit a pervasive pattern of passive resistance to demands for adequate social and occupational performance. To meet the DSM-III-R diagnosis, at least five of nine of the following criteria must be met: procrastinating; becoming sulky, irritable or argumentative when asked to do something they do not want to do; seeming to work deliberately slowly or doing a bad job on tasks that they really do not want to do; protesting, without justification, that others make unreasonable demands on them; avoiding obligations by claiming to have "forgotten"; believing they are doing a much better job than others think they are doing; resenting useful suggestions from others concerning how they can be more productive; obstructing the efforts of others by failing to do their share of the work; and, unreasonably criticizing or scorning persons in positions of authority.

Clinical Presentation

The Passive Aggressive Personality Disorder is usually characterized by the following behavioral and interpersonal style, cognitive style, and affective style.

Behaviorally, passive aggressive persons are characterized by passive resistance to adequate performance by such means as stubbornness, forgetfulness, tardiness, deliberate inefficiency, or procrastination. Their behavior is basically oppositional and provocative in nature. They are the perennial "sour pusses." Interpersonally, they are uncooperative and quickly dampen others' enthusiasm. They easily induce guilt in others, and Mosak (1988) called them "injustice collectors." In relation to others, they appear to be socially ambivalent. On one hand, they appear to be insecure, dependent, and victimized, while on the other hand, they present themselves as provocative, independent, and oppositional.

The thinking style of passive aggressives is characterized as conflictual. They quickly fluctuate between an assertive or defiant stance and a pleasing or reliant stance. For example, the self-talk of the passive aggressive personality is typically: "He has no right to do that to me . . . I'll retaliate." (This is the direct aggressive and defiant stance.) "But, he'll really get me, then." (This is the passive aggressive or reliant stance.) Passive aggressive individuals have little awareness that their behavior is responsible for generating negative feelings and responses in others. Furthermore, their cognitive style encompasses a fault-finding type of cynicism, befitting their deeply pessimistic outlook on life.

Emotionally, passive aggressive individuals do not show anger directly. Instead, they have a tendency toward sulking and sullenness. As children, temper tantrums were common, while temper outbursts are rarely seen in the passive aggressive adult.

Developmental and Etiological Features

The following biopsychosocial formulation may be helpful in understanding how the Passive Aggressive Personality Disorder is likely to have developed.

Biologically passive aggressive individuals were likely to have exhibited the "difficult child" temperamental style (Thomas & Chess, 1977). Their behavior as children, adolescents, and adults was typically characterized by affective irritability. Millon and Everly (1985) suggested that low stimulation thresholds in the limbic structures of the brain probably account for this biological pattern.

Psychologically, passive aggressives' views of themselves, others, the world, and life's purposes can be articulated in terms of the following themes. They tend to view themselves by some variant of the theme: "I am competent, but not competent," and other such contradictory appraisals. They tend to view life by some variant of the theme: "Life is a big bind. It's unfair, unpredictable, and unappreciative" or "People try to push you around." As such, they are likely to conclude: "Therefore, vacillate, temporize, oppose, and anticipate disappointment and betrayal" or "It is better to be stubborn and get some satisfaction than to take the risk of losing everything." The Irish saying, "The devil you know is better than the devil you don't know," nicely characterizes this conviction. The most likely defense mechanism utilized by these personalities is displacement.

Socially, predictable patterns of parenting and environmental factors can be noted for the passive aggressive personality. Passive aggressive individuals were most likely exposed to a parenting style noted for its inconsistency. As such, they experienced severe and harsh discipline for a particular infraction at one time, while at other times little or no discipline was given for the same infraction. Communication patterns were likewise inconsistent and contradictory. Family schisms and sibling rivalry are common features of this disorder. The passive aggressive individual was likely to have experienced being cut-off and displaced from his parents' affection at the time of a birth of a younger sibling, resulting in ambivalence of feelings and behavior for this individual. Sometimes the passive aggressive individual was chosen to play a moderator or peacemaker role in a conflicted family. In general, contradictory thinking and behavior was reinforced in the family of origin. Learned vacillation and role-switching were the family's legacy to the passive aggressive individual.

This passive aggressive pattern was confirmed, reinforced, and perpetuated by the following individual and systems factors: Self view of contradictory appraisals plus unpredictability and inconsistency led to learned vacillation and role-switching behavior. The reinforcement of this ambivalent and contradictory behavior then provoked rejection by others, which led to further ambivalence and role-switching, leading to further confirmation of passive aggressive beliefs and behavior. In Figure 11.8 are listed characteristics of Passive Aggressive Personality Disorder.

Treatment Considerations

Included in the differential diagnosis of Passive Aggressive Personality Disorder are other Axis II personality disorders: Self-defeating Personality Disorder, the Antisocial Personality Disorder, and the Avoidant Personality Disorder. Those most common Axis I syndromes associated with the Passive Aggressive Personality Disorder are Generalized Anxiety Disorder; Dysthymia; Cyclothymia; and, various Somatoform Disorders, particularly Hypochondriasis, Somatization Disorder, and Psychophysiological Disorders. In addition, Factitious Disorders are seen with this Axis II condition.

Treatment goals are similar to those of the Dependent Personality Disorder. They are to increase the individual's

(Continued on page 340)

1. Behavioral Appearance:	Indecisive, procrastination, tardy
	Oppositional, forgetful, mistrustful
	Pessimistic, envious, "sour puss"
2. Interpersonal Behavior:	Uncooperative, dampen other's enthusiasm
	Socially ambivalent (impulsive role-shifting)
	Insecure, dependent, victimized
	Guilt peddling, injustice collecting
3. Cognitive Style:	Conflict: assertive (defiant) vs. pleasing (reliant)
	"He has no right to do X—I'll retaliate (direct anger)—But he'll really get me then."—(passive anger)
4. Feeling Style:	"Smiling" resistance, resentful
5. Parental Injunction/ Environmental Factors:	"Don't count on things staying the same." Moderator/Switcher role in conflicted family sibling rivalry: replaced by younger sib
6. Biological/Temperament:	"Difficult Infant"
	Affective irritability, Hormonal/premenstral syndrome
7. Self View:	"I'm competent but not competent." (and other contradictory appraisals)
8. World View:	"Life is a big bind. It's unfair, unpredictable and unappreciative. Therefore, vacillate, temporize, and anticipate disappointment and betrayal."
9. Self & System Perpetuant:	Learned vacillation re: role-switching
	Reinforcement of ambivalent behavior
	Ambivalent behavior provokes inconsistency and rejection leading to more ambivalence.

Figure 11.8. Characteristics of Passive Aggressive Personality Disorder.

ability to think and act independently and interdependently. Common consensus among clinicians would support the treatment of the Passive Aggressive Disorder individual is much less rewarding and more frustrating than working with most of the other mild to moderate personality disorders. The treatment strategy involves clarifying rules and expectations for treatment. With some patients, the suggestion is that these rules and expectations be specified in writing to stave off the kind of oppositionalness, "forgetfulness," and argumentativeness that are frequently involved as they test treatment limits. Methods of treatment involve both direct and indirect techniques. Insight-oriented psychotherapy has been shown to have relatively limited utility in the treatment of this disorder. Behavioral techniques, however, such as assertiveness training, have been shown to be quite promising (Reid, 1989). In addition, the use of indirect strategies and methods such as paradox have been shown to be particularly useful in "neutralizing" oppositionalness and hostile dependency.

Case Example: Ms. F

Ms. F is a 32-year-old female who was referred for counseling to a community mental health clinic by her family physician after his workup for abdominal pain was negative. She appeared for her first therapy appointment 20 minutes late, stating she had trouble finding a place to park. She stated she had abdominal pains for years and that "none of those doctors could help me." Ms. F had had custody of her two children—now both teenagers—for the ten years she had been divorced. She had been fired from five jobs due to chronic tardiness and forgetfulness. She smiled throughout most of the session and appeared compliant and cooperative, yet she indicated that she tried counseling once before but did not continue "because I didn't think it was all in my head like they tried to tell me."

OBSESSIVE COMPULSIVE PERSONALITY DISORDER

DSM-III-R Description and Criteria

Obsessive Compulsive Personality Disordered individuals are described as inhibited, stubborn, perfectionistic, judgmental, overconscientious, rigid, and chronically anxious. Character-istically, they are people who avoid intimacy and experience little pleasure from life. They may be successful, but at the same time are indecisive and demanding. Often they are perceived as cold and reserved. Unlike the Axis I Obsessive Compulsive Disorder, ritualistic compulsions and obsessions do not characterize this personality disorder. According to DSM-III-R criteria, the Obsessive Compulsive Personality Disorder is characterized by a pervasive pattern of perfectionism and inflexibility in various situations and circumstances. The diagnosis of this disorder is made if five of nine criteria are met: perfectionism that interferes with task completion; preoccupation with details, rules, lists, order, organization or schedules to the extent that the major point of the activity is lost; unreasonable insistence that others submit to exactly their way of doing things, or unreasonable reluctance to allow others to do things because of the conviction that they will not do them correctly; obsessive devotion to work and productivity to the exclusion of leisure activities and friendships; indecisiveness; overconscientiousness, scrupulousness, and inflexiblity about matters of morality, ethics, or values; restricted expression of affection; lack of generosity in terms of money, time, or gifts when no personal gain is likely to result; and, inability to discard worn-out or worthless objects even when they have no sentimental value.

Clinical Presentation

The Obsessive Compulsive Personality Disorder can be recognized by the following behavioral and interpersonal style, cognitive style, and emotional style.

Behaviorally, this disorder is characterized by perfectionism. Individuals with this disorder are likely to be workaholics. In addition to dependability, they tend to be stubborn and possessive. They, like passive aggressive disordered individuals, can be indecisive and procrastinating. Interpersonally, these individuals are exquisitely conscious of social rank and status and modify their behavior accordingly. That is, they tend to be deferential and obsequious to superiors, and haughty and autocratic to subordinates and peers. They can be doggedly insistent that others do things their way without an appreciation or awareness of how others react to this insistence. At their best they are polite and loyal to the organizations and ideals they espouse.

Their thinking style can be characterized as constricted and rule-based. They have difficulty establishing priorities and perspective. They are "detail" people and often lose sight of the larger project. In other words, they "can't see the forest for the trees." Their indecisiveness and doubts make decision making difficult. Their mental inflexibility is matched by their nonsuggestible and unimaginative style, suggesting they have a restricted fantasy life. Like passive aggressive individuals, the obsessive compulsives have conflicts between assertiveness and defiance, and pleasing and obedience.

Their emotional style is characterized as grim and cheerless. They have difficulty with the expression of intimate feelings such as warmth and tenderness. They tend to avoid the "softer" feelings, although they may express anger, frustration, and irritability quite freely. This grim, feeling-avoidant demeanor shows itself in stilted, stiff relationship behaviors.

Developmental and Etiological Features

The following biopsychosocial formulation may be helpful in understanding how the Obsessive Compulsive Personality Disorder is likely to have developed.

Biologically, these individuals were likely to have exhibited an anhedonic temperament as an infant (Millon, 1981). Firstborn children have a greater propensity for developing a compulsive style than other siblings (Toman, 1961).

Psychologically, these individuals view themselves, others, the world, and life's purpose in terms of the following themes. They tend to view themselves with some variant of the theme: "I'm responsible if something goes wrong, so I have to be reliable, competent, and righteous." Their world view is some variant of the theme: "Life is unpredictable and expects too much." As such, they are likely to conclude, "Therefore, be in control, right, and proper at all times."

Socially, predictable patterns of parenting and environmental conditioning are noted for this personality. The parenting style they experienced could be characterized as both consistent and overcontrolled. As children they were trained to be overly responsible for their actions and to feel guilty and worthless if they were not obedient, achievement-oriented, or "good." The parental injunction to which they were most likely exposed was, "You must do and be better to be worthwhile."

This obsessive compulsive pattern is confirmed, reinforced, and perpetuated by the following individual and systems factors: Exceedingly high expectations plus harshly rigid behavior and beliefs, along with a tendency to be self-critical, lead to rigid rule-based behavior and avoidance of social, professional, and moral unacceptability. This in turn further reconfirms the harshly rigid behaviors and beliefs of this personality. In Figure 11.9 are listed characteristics of Obsessive Compulsive Personality Disorder.

Treatment Considerations

Included in the differential diagnosis of the Obsessive Compulsive Personality Disorder are two other Axis II personality disorders: the Dependent Personality Disorder and the Passive Aggressive Personality Disorder. The most common Axis I syndromes associated with the Obsessive Compulsive Personality Disorder are: the Obsessive Compulsive Disorder, Simple Phobias, Generalized Anxiety Disorder, and Dysthymia. Other Axis I syndromes are Hypochondriasis, Somatization Disorder, and Psychological Factors Affecting Physical Condition. Occasionally, a Brief Reactive Psychosis may be noted in the decompensated obsessive compulsive.

The Obsessive Compulsive Personality Disorder has a long tradition of treatment dating back to Freud's case of the "Rat Man" and Adler's "Case of Mrs. A." Note that OCD is an Axis I disorder while the Obsessive Compulsive Personality Disorder is an Axis II disorder. Since the "Rat Man" exhibited both Axis I and II disorders, many who have read Freud's account of this case and its treatment have incorrectly assumed that both disorders are the same and

(Continued on page 345)

1. Behavioral Appearance:	Workaholic/dependable Stubborn/possessive Procrastination/indecisive Perfectionistic
2. Interpersonal Behavior:	Feeling avoidance Autocratic to peers/subordinates Obsequious to superiors Polite, loyal
3. Cognitive Style:	Constricted—rule-based, unimaginative Conflict-assertive (defiance) vs. pleasing (obediance)
4. Feeling Style:	Grim and cheerless
5. Parental Injunction/ Environmental Factors:	"You must do/be better to be worthwhile." Consistent parental overcontrol. Training in being overresponsible/guilty
6. Biological/Temperament:	Anhedonic temperament Firstborn
7. Self View:	"I'm responsible if something goes wrong." Sees self as reliable, competent, righteous
8. World View:	"Life is unpredicctable and expects much. Therefore, be in control, right, and proper."
9. Self & System Perpetuant:	Very high expectations (+) harshly rigid behavior and beliefs (+) tendency to be self-critical → rigid rule-based behavior and avoidance of social, professional unacceptablity → passive-aggressive behaviors

Figure 11.9. Characteristics of Obsessive Compulsive Personality Disorder.

are treated the same. They are not the same disorder, but in about one-third of cases, both disorders have been shown to be present (Jenike, Baer, & Minichiello, 1986). When both disorders are present together, treatment has been shown to be much more challenging than if only OCD is present.

The goals of treatment include increased cognitive constriction and increased feeling expression, so that a more reasonable balance can be obtained between thoughts and feelings. Treatment strategies for the Obsessive Compulsive Personality Disorder usually involve long-term insight-oriented therapy. Unlike the Obsessive Compulsive Disorder, where antidepressants plus behavior therapy can result in amelioration of obsessions and compulsions in a relatively short period of time, the Obsessive Compulsive Personality Disorder does not lend itself to short-term treatment outcomes. However, Salzman (1968) and Turkat and Maisto (1985) offered dynamic and cognitive behavior intervention that has proved effective. Medication is usually not needed with this disorder if the restitution of the accompanying Axis I condition is attained.

Case Example: Mr. Q

Mr. Q is a 37-year-old male business executive who wanted to begin a course of psychotherapy because his "whole world was closing in." He gave a history of longstanding feelings of dissatisfaction with his marriage which had worsened in the past two years. He described his wife's increasing demands for time and affection from him, which he believed was a weakness she had. His professional life also had become conflicted when his partner of ten years wanted to expand their accounting firm to another city. Mr. Q believed this proposal was fraught with dangers and had come to the point of selling out his share of the business to his partner. He knew he had to make some decisions about his marriage and his business but found himself unable to do so. He hoped therapy would help with these decisions. He presented as neatly dressed in a conservative three-piece gray suit. His posture was rigid and he spoke in a formal and controlled tone with constricted affect. His thinking was characterized by preoccupation with details and was somewhat circumstantial.

The reader is referred to the Case of Mrs. A, one of Adler's (1969) most famous, for a detailed description and formulation of the Obsessive Compulsive Disorder. It so happened that Mrs. A manifested a moderately severe borderline personality disorder.

PARANOID PERSONALITY DISORDER

DSM-III-R Description and Criteria

Paranoid personalities are aloof, emotionally cold individuals who display unjustified suspiciousness, hypersensitivity, jealousy, and a fear of intimacy. In addition they can be grandiose, rigid, contentious, and litigious. Because of their hypersensitivity to criticism and tendency to project blame on others, they tend to lead isolated lives and are often disliked by others. Millon (1981) conceived of the Paranoid Personality Disorder as a pathological syndromal continuation of the Narcissistic Personality Disorder, the Antisocial Personality Disorder, or the Obsessive Compulsive Personality Disorder. As a result, the clinical presentation of the paranoid personality takes on characteristics of these three respective precursors.

In DSM-III-R the Paranoid Personality Disorder is characterized as the pervasive and unwarranted tendency to interpret others' actions as deliberately demeaning or threatening. To meet the DSM-III-R diagnosis at least four of seven criteria must be present: expecting, without sufficient basis, to be exploited or harmed by others; questioning, without justification, the loyalty or trustworthiness of friends or associates; reading hidden meaning or threatening meaning into benign remarks or events; bearing grudges or being unforgiving of insults or slights; being reluctant to confide in others because of unwarranted fears that the information will be used against them; being slighted and quick to react with anger or counterattack; and questioning, without justification, the fidelity of a spouse or sexual partner.

Clinical Presentation

The Paranoid Personality Disorder is characterized by the following behavioral and interpersonal style, cognitive style, and emotional style.

Behaviorally, paranoid individuals are resistive of external influences. They tend to be chronically tense because they are constantly mobilized against perceived threats from their environment. Their behavior also is marked by guardedness, defensiveness, argumentativeness, and litigiousness. Interpersonally, they tend to be distrustful, secretive, and isolative. They are intimacy-avoiders by nature, and repudiate nurturant overtures by others.

Their cognitive style is characterized by mistrusting preconceptions. They carefully scrutinize every situation encountered and scan the environment for "clues" or "evidence" to confirm their preconceptions rather than objectively focus on data. Thus, while their perception may be accurate, their judgment often is not. The paranoid personalities' prejudices mold the perceived data to fit their preconceptions. Thus, they tend to disregard evidence that does not fit their preconceptions. When under stress their thinking can take on a conspiratorial or even delusional flavor. Their hypervigilance and need to seek evidence to confirm their beliefs lead them to have a rather authoritarian and mistrustful outlook on life.

The affective style of the paranoid personalities is characterized as cold, aloof, unemotional, and humorless. In addition, they lack a deep sense of affection, warmth, and sentimentality. Because of their hypersensitivity to real or imagined slights, and their subsequent anger at what they believe to be deceptions and betrayals, they tend to have few, if any, friends. The two emotions they experience and express with some depth are anger and intense jealousies.

Developmental and Etiological Features

The following biopsychosocial formulations may be helpful in understanding how the Paranoid Personality Disorder is likely to have developed.

Biologically, a low threshold for limbic system stimulation and deficiencies in inhibitory centers seem to influence the behavior of the paranoid personality. The underlying temperament can best be understood in terms of the subtypes of the paranoid disorder. Each of three subtypes are briefly described in terms of their underlying temperament, and correlative parental and environmental factors. In the narcissistic type, a hyperresponsive temperament and precociousness, parental overevaluation and indulgence, as well as the individual's sense of grandiosity and self behavior probably result in deficits in social interest and limited interpersonal skills. The antisocial type of the paranoid personality is likely to possess a hyperresponsive temperament. This plus harsh parental treatment probably contribute to the impulsive, hedonistic, and aggressive style of this type. In the compulsive type, the underlying temperament may have been anhedonic. This, as well as parental rigidity and overcontrol, largely accounts for the development of this type. Finally, a less common variant is the paranoid-passive aggressive type. As infants, these individuals usually demonstrated the "difficult child" temperament, and later temperament characterized by affective irritability. This plus parental inconsistency probably account in large part for the development of this type (Millon, 1981).

Psychologically, paranoid individuals view themselves, others, the world, and life's purpose in terms of the following themes. They tend to view themselves by some variant of the theme: "I'm special and different. I'm alone and no one likes me because I'm better than others." Life and the world are viewed by some variant of the theme: "Life is unfair, unpredictable and demanding. It can and will sneak up and harm you when you are least expecting it." As such, they are likely to conclude, "Therefore, be wary, counterattack, trust no one, and excuse yourself from failure by blaming others." The most common defensive mechanism associated with the paranoid disorder is projection.

Socially, predictable patterns of parenting and environmental factors can be noted for the Paranoid Personality Disorder. For all the subtypes, the parental injunction appears to be, "You're different. Don't make mistakes." Paranoid personality disordered individuals tend to have perfectionistic parents who expose these children to specialness training. This plus the parental style that has been articulated for the subtypes of the disorder and parental criticism lead to an attitude of social isolation and hypervigilant behavior. To make sense of the apparent contradiction between being special and being ridiculed, the children creatively conclude that the reason they are special and that no one likes them is because they are better than other people. This explanation serves the purpose of reducing their anxiety and allowing them to develop some sense of self and belonging.

This paranoid pattern is confirmed, reinforced, and perpetuated by the following individual and systems factors: A sense of specialness, rigidity, attributing malevolence to others, blaming others, and misinterpreting motives of others lead to social alienation and isolation, which further confirms the individual's persecutory stance. In Figure 11.10 are listed characteristics of Paranoid Personality Disorder.

Treatment Considerations

Included in the differential diagnosis of the Paranoid Personality Disorder are the following Axis II personality disorders: Antisocial Personality Disorder, Narcissistic Personality Disorder, Obsessive Compulsive Personality Disorder, and Passive Aggressive Personality Disorder. The most common Axis I syndromes associated with the Paranoid Personality Disorder are Generalized Anxiety Disorder, Panic Disorder, and Delusional Disorder. If a Bipolar Disorder is present, an irritable manic presentation is likely. Decompensation into Schizophrenic reaction is likely. The Paranoid and Catatonic subtypes of Schizophrenia are most commonly noted.

Until recently, the prognosis for treatment of the Paranoid Personality Disorder was considered guarded. Today more optimism prevails in achieving these goals of treatment: increasing the benignness of perception and interpretation of reality, and increasing trusting behavior. The social skills training intervention described by Turkat (1985) focuses on changing the internal processes of attention, processing, response emission, and feedback from a pathological to a non-pathological mode of perceiving and thinking. In essence, individuals are taught how to reduce their perceptual scanning and attending to inappropriate cues to attending to more appropriate cues; and rather than using idiosyncratic logic and misinterpretation

(Continued on page 351)

1. Behavioral Appearance:	Guarded and defensive to hyper-vigilant Resistive of external influence Chronically tense because constantly mobilized against perceived threats Restricted affect, jealous
2. Interpersonal Behavior:	Distrustful, secretive, isolate, blaming Provocative, counterattacks, hypersensitive Testing others' loyalty, searching for hidden motives, cynical
3. Cognitive Style:	Mistrusting, preconceptions—tendency to disregard evidence to the contrary May become conspiratorial or delusional under stress
4. Feeling Style:	Aloof humorless; easily provoked
5. Parental Injunction/ Environmental Factors:	"You're different. Don't make mistakes." Perfectionistic parent(s) (+) Specialness training (+) parental/peer criticalness → isolation (+) vigilant attitude
6. Biological/Temperament:	Low threshold for limbic system stimulation and deficient inhibitory centers Narcissistic type: hyperresponsive temperament (+) parental over-evaluation and indulgence → deficits in cooperation and interpersonal skills (+) grandiosity/selfishness aggressiveness style Compulsive type: anhedonic temperament (+) parental rigidity and control Passive-Aggressive type: affective irritability (+) parental inconsistency
7. Self View:	"I'm so special and different. I'm alone and no one likes me because I'm better than others."

Figure 11.10. Characteristics of Paranoid Personality Disorder.

Figure 11.10. Continued.

8. World View:	"Life is unfair, unpredictable, and demanding. It will sneak up and harm you. Therefore, be wary, counteract, trust no one, and excuse yourself from failure by blaming others."
9. Self & System Perpetuant:	Rigidity and interpersonal suspicion (+) blaming and attributing malevolent motives to others → social alienation and isolation → confirmation of persecutory stance

to process their cues, they learn to use more common logic and a more benign interpretation of cues. In so doing they are able to respond in a more socially graceful fashion and are more likely to interpret feedback, including criticism, as constructive. This social skills intervention approach can be combined with insight-oriented therapy to achieve positive therapeutic outcomes. Medication, particularly lower dose neuroleptics, has been shown useful for decreasing anxiety secondary to loss of control (Reid, 1989).

Case Example: Mr. Z

Mr. Z is a 59-year-old male referred for psychiatric evaluation by his attorney to rule out a treatable psychiatric disorder. Mr. Z had entered into five lawsuits in the past two and one-half years. His attorney believed that each suit was of questionable validity. Mr. Z was described as an unemotional, highly controlled male who was now suing a local men's clothing store "for conspiring to deprive me of my consumer rights." He contends that the store manager had consistently issued bad credit reports on him. The consulting psychiatrist elicited other examples of similar concerns. Mr. Z had long distrusted his neighbors across the street and regularly monitors their activity since one of his garbage cans disappeared two years ago. Mr. Z took an early retirement from his accounting job one year ago because he could not get along with his supervisor, whom he believed was faulting him about his accounts and paperwork. Mr. Z contends he was faultless. On examination, Mr. Z's mental status is unremarkable except for constriction of affect and for a certain hesitation and guardedness in his response to questions.

BORDERLINE PERSONALITY DISORDER

DSM-III-R Description and Criteria

Individuals with borderline personalities present with a complex clinical picture including diverse combinations of anger, anxiety, intense and labile affect, and brief disturbances of consciousness such as depersonalization and dissociation. In addition, their presentation includes chronic loneliness, a sense of emptiness, boredom, volatile interpersonal relations, identity confusion, and impulsive behavior that can include self-injury or self-mutilation. Stress can even precipitate a transient psychosis. The borderline personality is a heterogeneous diagnosis which may be related to schizophrenia or the mood disorders. This personality disorder remains controversial and first appeared in DSM-III. Some conceptualize this disorder as a level of personality organization rather than as a specific personality disorder (American Psychiatric Association, 1987).

In DSM-III-R criteria, the Borderline Personality Disorder is characterized as a pervasive pattern of unstable mood, interpersonal relations, and self-image. As with other personality disorders, the Borderline Personality Disorder will be manifested in early adulthood, and at least five of eight of the following criteria are needed to make the diagnosis: (1) a pattern of unstable and intense interpersonal relationships characterized by vacillation between the extremes of overidealization and devaluation; (2) impulsiveness in at least two areas that are potentially self-damaging—spending, sex, substance abuse, shoplifting, reckless driving, or binge drinking; (3) affective instability manifested by marked shifts from baseline mood to depression, irritability or anxiety, lasting a few hours and only rarely more than a few days; (4) inappropriate, intense anger or lack of controlled anger; (5) recurrent suicide threats, gestures, or behavior, or self-mutilating behavior; (6) marked and persistent identity disturbance manifested by uncertainty about at least two of the following five—self-image, sexual orientation, long-term goals or career choice, type of friends desired, or preferred values; (7) chronic feelings of emptiness or boredom; and (8) frantic efforts to avoid real or imagined abandonment.

Clinical Presentation

The borderline personality is characterized by the following behavioral and interpersonal styles, cognitive style, and emotional style.

Behaviorally, borderlines are characterized by physically self-damaging acts such as suicide gestures, self-mutilation, or the provocation of fights. Their social and occupational accomplishments are often less than their intelligence and ability warrant. Of all the personality disorders, they are most likely to have irregularities of circadian rhythms, especially of the sleep-wake cycle. Thus, chronic insomnia is a common complaint.

Interpersonally, borderlines are characterized by their paradoxical instability. That is, they fluctuate quickly between idealizing and clinging to another individual to devaluing and opposing that individual. They are exquisitively rejection-sensitive, and experience abandonment depression following the slightest of stressors. Millon (1981) considered separation anxiety as a primary motivator of this personality disorder. Interpersonal relationships develop rather quickly and intensely, yet their social adaptiveness is rather superficial. They are extraordinarily intolerant of being alone and they go to great lengths to seek out the company of others whether in indiscriminate sexual affairs, late night phone calls to relatives and recent acquaintances, or late night visits to hospital emergency rooms with a host of vague medical and/or psychiatric complaints.

Their cognitive style is described as inflexible and impulsive (Millon, 1981). Inflexibility of their style is characterized by rigid abstractions that easily lead to grandiose, idealized perceptions of others, not as real people, but as personifications of "all good" or "all bad" individuals. They reason by analogy from past experience and thus have difficulty reasoning logically and learning from past experiences and relationships. Because they have an external locus of control, the borderlines usually blame others when things go wrong. By accepting responsibility for their own incompetence, borderlines believe they would feel even more powerless to change circumstances. Accordingly, their emotions fluctuate between hope and despair because they believe that external circumstances are well beyond their control (Shulman, 1982). Their cognitive style is also marked by impulsivity, and just as they vacillate between idealization and devaluation of others, their thoughts shift from one extreme to another: "I like people, no I don't like them"; "Having goals is good, no it's not"; "I need to get my life together, no I can't, it's hopeless." This inflexibility and impulsivity complicate the process of identity formation. Their uncertainty about self-image, gender identity, goals, values, and career choice reflects this impulsive and inflexible stance. Gerald Adler (1985) suggested that borderlines have an underdeveloped evocative memory, such that they have difficulty recalling images and feeling states which could structure and soothe them in times of turmoil. Their inflexibility and impulsivity are further noted in their tendency toward "splitting." Splitting is the inability to synthesize contradictory qualities, such that the individual views others as all good or all bad and utilizes "projective identification," that is, attributing his or her own negative or dangerous feelings to others. Their cognitive style is further characterized by an inability to tolerate frustration. Finally, micropsychotic episodes can be noted when these individuals are under a great deal of stress. These are ill-defined, strange thought processes especially noted in response to unstructured rather than structured situations, and may take the form of derealization, depersonalization, intense rage reactions, unusual reactions to drugs, and intense brief paranoid episodes. Because of difficulty in focusing attention and subsequent loss of relevant data, borderlines also have a diminished capacity to process information.

The emotional style of individuals with this disorder is characterized by marked mood shifts from a normal or euthymic mood to a dysphoric mood. In addition, inappropriate and intense anger and rage may easily be triggered. On the other extreme are feelings of emptiness, a deep "void," or boredom.

Developmental and Etiological Features

The following biopsychosocial formulation may be helpful in understanding how the borderline personality pattern is likely to have developed.

Biologically, borderlines can be understood in terms of the three main subtypes: borderline-dependent, borderline-histrionic, and borderline-passive aggressive. The temperamental style of the borderline-dependent type is that of the passive infantile pattern (Millon, 1981). Millon hypothesized that low autonomic nervous system reactivity plus an overprotective parenting style facilitate restrictive interpersonal skills and a clinging relational style. On the other hand, the histrionic subtype was more likely to have a hyperresponsive infantile pattern. Thus, because of high autonomic nervous system reactivity and increased parental stimulation and expectations for performance, the borderline-histrionic pattern was likely to result. Finally, the temperamental style of the passive-aggressive borderline was likely to have been the "difficult child" type noted by Thomas and Chess (1977). This pattern plus parental inconsistency mark the affective irritability of the borderline-passive aggressive personality.

Psychologically, borderlines tend to view themselves, others, the world, and life's purpose in terms of the following themes. They view themselves by some variant of the theme: "I don't know who I am or where I'm going." In short, their identity problems involve gender, career, loyalties, and values while their self-esteem fluctuates with each thought or feeling about their self-identity. Borderlines tend to view their world with some variant of the theme: "People are great, no they are not"; "Having goals is good, no it's not"; or, "If life doesn't go my way, I can't tolerate it." As such they are likely to conclude, "Therefore keep all options open. Don't commit to anything. Reverse roles and vacillate thinking and feelings when under attack." The most common defense mechanisms utilized by Borderline Personality Disordered individuals are regression, splitting, and projective identification.

Socially, predictable patterns of parenting and environmental factors can be noted for the Borderline Personality Disorder. Parenting style differs depending on the subtype. For example, in the dependent subtype, overprotectiveness characterizes parenting, whereas in the histrionic subtype, a demanding parenting style is more evident, while an inconsistent parenting style is more noted in the passive-aggressive subtype. But because the borderline personality is a syndromal elaboration and deterioration of the less severe Dependent, Histrionic, or Passive Aggressive Personality Disorders, the family of origin in the borderline subtypes of these disorders is likely to be much more dysfunctional, increasing the likelihood the child will have learned various self-defeating coping strategies. The parental injunction is likely to have been, "If you grow up and leave me, bad things will happen to me (parent)."

This borderline pattern is confirmed, reinforced, and perpetuated by the following individual and systems factors: Diffuse identity, impulsive vacillation, and self-defeating coping strategies lead to aggressive acting out, which leads to more chaos, which leads to the experience of depersonalization, increased dysphoria, and/or self-mutilation to achieve some relief. This leads to further reconfirmation of their beliefs about self and the world as well as reinforcement of the behavioral and interpersonal patterns. In Figure 11.11 are listed characteristics of Borderline Personality Disorder.

Treatment Considerations

Included in the differential diagnosis of the Borderline Personality Disorder are these other Axis II personality disorders: Passive Aggressive Personality Disorder, Histrionic Personality Disorder, Dependent Personality Disorder, and the Schizotypal Personality Disorder. The most common Axis I syndromes associated with the personality disorder are Generalized Anxiety Disorder, Panic Disorder, and Dysthymia. In addition, other syndromes may be Brief Reactive Psychoses, Schizoaffective Disorder, Hypochondriasis, or the Dissociative Disorders, especially Psychogenic Fugue.

The Borderline Personality Disorder is becoming one of the most common Axis II presentations seen in both the public

(Continued on page 358)

1. Behavioral Appearance:	"Hemophiliacs" of emotion Resentful, impulsiveness, acting out Helpless, dysphoric, empty "void" Irregular ciradian rhythms (sleep-wake, etc.)
2. Interpersonal Behavior:	Paradoxical—idealizing and clinging vs devaluing and oppositional Rejection sensitivty → abandonment depression Separation anxiety as prime motivator Role reversal
3. Cognitive Style:	Inflexible—rigid abstracting → gran- diosity and idealizations, splitting Reasons by analogy; doesn't learn from experience External locus of control → blaming Poorly developed evocative memory
4. Feeling Style:	Extreme lability of mood and affect
5. Parental Injunction/ Environmental Factors:	"If you grow up, bad things will happen to me (parent)." Overprotective or demanding or inconsistent parenting
6. Biological/Temperament:	Dependent type: passive infantile pattern → low autonomic nervous system reactivity (+) parental over- protectiveness → restrictive inter- personal skills and pleasing, clinging style parental stimulation and demand for child to "perform." Passive Aggressive type—"difficult" infantile pattern → affective irri- tability (+) parental inconsistency
7. Self View:	"I don't know who I am or where I'm going." Identity problems involving gender, career, loyalties, and values Self-esteem fluctuates with current emotion

Figure 11.11. Characteristics of Borderline Personality Disorder.

Figure 11.11. Continued.

8. World View:	"People are great, no they're not. Having goals is good, no it's not. If life doesn't go my way, I can't tolerate it. Therefore, keep all options open. Don't commit to anything. Reverse roles when under attack."
9. Self & System Perpetuant:	Self-defeating coping strategies: particularly "reversal" (i.e.) from submissiveness to aggressiveness → more chaos → depersonalization, brief psychotic episodes, increased dysphoria and/or self-mutilation to achieve relief → reconfirmation

sector and in private practice. It can be among the most difficult and frustrating conditions to treat. Clinical experience suggests that it is important to assess the individual for overall level of functioning and for subtype. The higher functioning borderline-dependent personality has a higher probability for collaborating in psychotherapeutic treatment than the lower functioning borderline-passive aggressive personality. Higher functioning borderlines possibly may be engaged in insight-oriented psychotherapy without undue regression and acting out. Masterson (1976) suggested that rather than using traditional interpretation methods with borderlines, the therapist should utilize confrontational statements in which borderlines are asked to look at their behavior and its consequences.

With lower functioning patients, treatment goals may be much less limited. Here, the focus of treatment would be on increasing day-to-day stable functioning. Treatment strategies and methods are varied for the treatment of borderline subtypes. Strategies range from long-term psychotherapy, lasting two or more years, to rather short-term formats in which sessions are scheduled biweekly or even monthly, except when crises arise. Task-oriented group therapy has been shown to be a useful adjunct, as well as a primary treatment in and of itself (Linehan, 1987). The rationale for group therapy with the borderline is that the intense interpersonal relationship that forms between the therapist and the patient and serves as the nidus for so much acting out is effectively reduced in a group format. Whether seen individually or in a group format, the therapist does well to clearly articulate treatment limits and objectives. For the lower functioning borderlines and the histrionic and passive-aggressive subtypes, a particularly useful procedure is to employ a written treatment contract. Medications are often used with borderline patients and are particularly aimed at target symptoms such as insomnia, depression, or anxiety disorders. Low dose neuroleptics are often utilized as well.

Case Example: Mr. T

Mr. T is a 29-year-old unemployed male who was referred to the hospital emergency room by his therapist at a community mental health center after two days of sustained suicidal gestures. He appeared to function adequately until his senior year in high school, when he became preoccupied with Transcendental Meditation. He had considerable difficulty concentrating during his first semester of college and seemed to focus most of his energies on finding a spiritual guru. At times, massive anxiety and feelings of emptiness swept over him, which he found would suddenly vanish if he lightly cut his wrist enough to draw blood. He had been in treatment with his current therapist for 18 months and became increasingly hostile and demanding as a patient, whereas earlier he had been quite captivated with his therapist's empathy and intuitive sense. Lately, his life seemed to center on these twice-weekly therapy sessions. Mr. T's most recent suicidal thoughts followed the therapist's disclosure that he was moving out of the area.

SCHIZOTYPAL PERSONALITY DISORDER

DSM-III-R Description and Criteria

In addition to having features similar to that of the Schizoid Personality Disorder, the schizotypal disorder is characterized by eccentric behavior and peculiar thought content. Schizotypals describe strange intrapsychic experiences, think in odd and unusual ways, and are difficult to engage. Yet none of these features reach psychotic proportions. It has been suggested that the schizotypal personality is one of the schizophrenic spectrum disorders because schizophrenia occurs with increased frequency in family members of the schizotypal.

In DSM-III-R the schizotypal personality is characterized by a pervasive pattern of interpersonal deficits and peculiar ideation, appearance, and behavior. At least five of nine criteria must be met for this diagnosis to be made: ideas of reference; excessive social anxiety; odd beliefs or magical thinking which influence behavior and are inconsistent with cultural norms; unusual perceptual experiences; odd or eccentric behavior or appearance; no close friends or confidants other than first-degree relatives; odd speech that is impoverished, digressive, vague, or inappropriately abstract, but that is not incoherent or characterized by loosening of associations; inappropriate or constricted affect; and, suspiciousness or paranoid ideation.

Clinical Presentation

The Schizotypal Personality Disorder is typically recognized by the following behavioral and interpersonal style, cognitive style, and emotional style.

Behaviorally, schizotypals are noted for their eccentric, erratic, and bizarre mode of functioning. Their speech is markedly peculiar without being incoherent. Occupationally, they are inadequate, either quitting or being fired from jobs after short periods of time. Typically, they become drifters, moving from job to job and town to town. They tend to avoid enduring responsibilities and in the process lose touch with a sense of social propriety.

Interpersonally, they are loners with few if any friends. Their solitary pursuits and social isolation may be the result of intense social anxiety which may be expressed with apprehensiveness. If married, their style of superficial and peripheral relating often leads to separation and divorce in a short period of time.

The cognitive style of schizotypals is described as scattered and ruminative, and is characterized by cognitive slippage. Presentations of superstitiousness, telepathy, and bizarre fantasies are characteristic. They may describe vague ideas of reference and recurrent illusions of depersonalizing, derealizing experiences without the experience of delusions of reference, or auditory or visual hallucinations.

Their affective style is described as cold, aloof, and unemotional with constricted affect. They can be humorless and difficult individuals to engage in conversation probably because of their general suspicious and mistrustful nature. In addition, they are hypersensitive to real or imagined slights.

Developmental and Etiological Features

The following biopsychosocial formulation may be helpful in understanding how the Schizotypal Personality Disorder is likely to have developed.

This personality disorder is described by Millon (1981) as a syndromal extension or deterioration of the Schizoid or the Avoidant Personality Disorders. As such, a useful procedure is to describe the biological and temperamental features of both of these subtypes. The schizoid subtype of a schizotypal personality is characterized with a passive infantile pattern, probably resulting from low autonomic nervous system reactivity and parental indifference that led to impoverished infantile stimulation. On the other hand, the avoidant subtype is characterized by the fearful infantile temperamental pattern (Millon, 1981). This probably resulted from the child's high autonomic nervous system reactivity combined with parental criticalness and deprecation that was further reinforced by sibling and peer deprecation. Both subtypes of the schizotypal personality have been noted to have impaired eye tracking motions, which is a characteristic shared with schizophrenic individuals.

Psychologically, the schizotypals view themselves, others, the world, and life's purpose in terms of the following themes. They tend to view themselves by some variant of the theme: "I'm on a different wave length than others." They commonly experience being selfless; that is, they experience feeling empty, estranged, and disconnected or dissociated from the rest of life. Their world view is some variant of the theme: "Life is strange and unusual, and others have special magical intentions." As such, they are likely to conclude, "Therefore, observe caution while being curious about these special magical intentions of others." The most common defense mechanism utilized by them is undoing, the effort to neutralize "evil" deeds and thoughts by their eccentric, peculiar beliefs and actions.

Socially, predictable patterns of parenting and environmental factors can be noted for the Schizotypal Personality Disorder. The parenting patterns noted previously of the cold indifference of the schizoid subtype or the deprecating and derogatory parenting style and family environment of the avoidant subtype are noted. In both cases, the level of functioning in the family of origin then would be noted in the Schizoid Personality Disorder or the Avoidant Personality Disorder. Fragmented parental communications are a feature common to both subtypes of the Schizotypal Personality Disorder. The parental injunction is likely to have been, "You're a strange bird." In Figure 11.12 are listed characteristics of Schizotypal Personality Disorder.

Treatment Considerations

Included in the differential diagnosis of the Schizotypal Personality Disorder are three other Axis II personality disorders: Schizoid Personality Disorder, Avoidant Personality Disorder, and the Borderline Personality Disorder. The most common Axis I syndromes associated with Schizotypal Personality Disorder are the Schizophrenias, particularly the Disorganized, Catatonic and Residual types. Other disorders noted are the Anxiety Disorders, the Somataform Disorders, and the Dissociative Disorders.

The Schizotypal Personality Disorder finds it very difficult to engage and remain in a psychotherapeutic relationship. Rather than attempting personality restructuring, the realistic treatment goal for the schizotypal personality is to increase the individual's ability to function more consistently even though on the

(Continued on page 364)

1. Behavioral Appearance: Eccentric, erratic, bizarre

Speech: markedly peculiar but not incoherent

Occupational: dropouts, drift from job to job

2. Interpersonal Behavior: Socially isolative, peripheral relationships

Intense social anxiety → apprehension or apathy

Marriage: superficial relating → separation, divorce

3. Cognitive Style: "Cognitive slippage," scattered, ruminitive

Magical thinking, superstitiousness

Defense: Undoing (neutralize "evil" deeds, thoughts)

4. Feeling Style: Hypersensitive, hostile and aloof

5. Parental Injunction/Environmental Factors: "You're a strange bird."

Cold or derogatory family environment

Fragmented parental communications

6. Biological/Temperament: Schizoid type: passive infantile pattern → low autonomic reactivity RA's activity (+) impoverished infantile stimulation/parental indifference

Avoidance type: fearful infantile pattern → hypersensitive RA's activity (=) parental/peer deprecation

Impaired smooth (eye tracking) pursuit

7. Self View: "I'm on a different wavelength than others."

Experience of being "self-less," empty, estranged, depersonalization, dissociation

8. World View: "Life is strange and unusual and others have special magic intentions. Therefore, observe caution while being curious."

9. Self & System Perpetuant: Dependency training → social isolation → Self-insulation which further reinforces social isolation and differentness

Figure 11.12. Characteristics of Schizotypal Personality Disorder.

periphery of society. Some reports have been of utilizing long-term insight and dynamically-oriented therapies with the schizotypal. Those that have been successful report incorporating some psychoeducational or social skills training along with supportive psychotherapeutic methods. Reid (1989) noted that if these patients can remain in long-term treatment, they may be able to increase their ability to function more consistently and with less disease. Reid reported that homogeneous groups can occasionally be a useful adjunct to individual treatment. In terms of medication, low dose neuroleptics have been found to be useful for the schizotypal personality even in the absence of psychotic features. Yet, it should be noted that medication compliance is particularly a problem with the Schizotypal Personality Disorder.

Case Example: Ms. B

Ms. B is a 46-year-old single female who was referred to a community mental health clinic by her mother because Ms. B had no interests, friends, or outside activities and was considered by neighbors to be an "odd duck." Ms. B's father had recently retired, and because of a limited pension, the parents were having difficulty in making ends meet since Ms. B had been living with them for the past eight years after she had been laid off from an assembly line job she had held for about 10 years. The patient readily admitted she preferred to be alone but denied that this was a problem for her. She believed that her mother was concerned about her because of what might happen to the patient after her parents' deaths. Ms. B was an only child who had graduated from high school with average grades but had never been involved in extracurricular activities while in school. She had never dated, and mentioned she had a female friend whom she had not talked with in four years. Since moving back with her parents, she stayed in her room preoccupied with books about astrology and charting her astrological forecast. On examination, she was an alert, somewhat uncooperative female appearing older than her stated age, with moderately disheveled hair and clothing. Her speech was monotonal and deliberate. She achieved poor eye contact with the examiner. Her thinking was vague and tangential, and she expressed a belief that her fate lay in "the stars." She denied specific delusions or perceptual abnormalities. Ms. B's affect was constricted except for one episode of anger when she thought the therapist was being critical.

SUMMARY

Unlike the rest of the disorders surveyed in this book, the personality disorders are listed on Axis II according to DSM-III-R. By definition, Axis II reflects personality structure rather than more acute symptomatology which would be assessed by Axis I criteria. The 11 personality disorders of DSM-III-R were reviewed in terms of nine biopsychosocial variables: behavioral appearance, interpersonal behavior, cognitive style, feeling style, parental injunction and environmental factors, biological/temperament, self-view, world view, and self and system perpetuant. The Adlerian formulation for each disorder, specific treatment goals and methods, along with a case example were provided for all 11 disorders.

REFERENCES

Adler, Alexandra. (1956). Problems in psychotherapy. *American Journal of Individual Psychology, 12*,12-24.

Adler, Alfred. (1935). The fundamental views of Individual Psychology. *International Journal of Individual Psychology, 1*(1), 5-8.

Adler, Alfred. (1969). *The case of Mrs. A: The diagnosis of a life style* (2nd ed. with commentary by B. Shulman). Chicago: Alfred Adler Institute.

Adler, G. (1985). *Borderline psychopathology and its treatment.* New York: Jason Aronson.

American Psychiatric Association. (1987). *Diagnostic and statistical manual of mental disorders* (3rd ed., revised), (DSM-III-R). Washington DC: Author.

Burks, J., & Rubenstein, M. (1979). *Temperament styles in adult interaction: Applications to psychotherapy.* New York: Brunner/Mazel.

Feldman, L. (1982). Dysfunctional marital conflict: An integrative interpersonal-intrapsychic model. *Journal of Marital and Family Therapy, 8*,417-428.

Grinspoon, L. (Ed.). (1982). The schizophrenic disorders. In *Psychiatric Update, Vol. 1, 82-255.* Washington, DC: American Psychiatric Press.

Jenike, M., Baer, L., & Minichiello, M. (1986). *Obsessive-compulsive disorder.* Littleton, MA: PSG.

Kohut, H. (1971). *The analysis of the self.* New York: International Universities Press.

Liebowitz, M., & Klein, D. (1979). Hysteroid dysphoria. *Psychiatric Clinics of North America, 2,* 555-575.

Linehan, M. (1987). Dialectical behavior therapy: A cognitive behavioral approach to parasuicide. *Journal of Personality Disorders, 1*(4), 328-333.

Masterson, J. (1976). *Psychotherapy of the borderline adult: A developmental approach.* New York: Brunner/Mazel.

Millon, T. (1981). *Disorders of personality: DSM-III—Axis II.* New York: John Wiley and Sons.

Millon, T., & Everly G. (1985). *Personality and its disorders: A biosocial learning approach.* New York: John Wiley and Sons.

Mosak, H. (1954). The psychological attitude in rehabilitation. *American Archives of Rehabilitation Therapy, 2,* 9-10.

Mosak, H. (1968). The interrelatedness of the neurosis through central themes. *Journal of Individual Psychology, 24* (1), 67-70.

Mosak, H. (1979). Mosak's typology: An update. *Journal of Individual Psychology, 35* (2), 92-95.

Mosak, H. (1988). "Personality disorders" in course syllabus outline. *Psychodynamics of psychopathology I and II.* Chicago: Alfred Adler Institute.

Reid, W. (1989). *The treatment of psychiatric disorders: Revised for the DSM-III-R.* New York: Brunner/Mazel.

Salzman, L. (1968). *The obsessive personality: Origins, dynamics and therapy.* New York: Science House.

Shea, S. (1988). *Psychiatric interviewing: The art of understanding.* Philadelphia, Pa: W.B. Saunders.

Sheldon, W., Dupertius, C., & McDermott, E. (1954). *Atlas of men: A guide for somatotyping the adult male at all ages.* New York: Harper & Row.

Shulman, B. (1982). An Adlerian interpretation of the borderline personality. *Modern Psychoanalysis, 7*(2), 137-153.

Thomas, A., & Chess, S. (1977). *Temperament and development.* New York: Brunner/Mazel.

Thomas, A., & Chess, S. (1984). *Origins and evolution of behavior disorders.* New York: Brunner/Mazel.

Toman, W. (1961). *Family constellation: Theory and practice of a psychological game.* New York: Springer.

Turkat, I. (1985). Formulation of paranoid personality disorder. In I. Turkat (Ed.), *Behavioral case formulation.* New York: Plenum.

Turkat, I., & Maisto, S. (1985). Personality disorders: Application of the experimental method to the formulation and modification of personality disorders. In D.H. Barlow (Ed.), *Clinical handbook of psychological disorders.* New York: Guilford.

CHAPTER 12

THE CONCEPT OF NARCISSISM AND THE NARCISSISTIC PERSONALITY DISORDER

Len Sperry, M.D., Ph.D.
Heinz L. Ansbacher, Ph.D.

According to Greek mythology, Narcissus fell in love with his reflection as he gazed into a reflecting pond. Unable to tear himself away from his reflection, he died of languor. While the story is usually told in this way, it omits the following larger context that is most significant from the Adlerian viewpoint as will be seen later. Echo, a beautiful nymph, loved Narcissus but failed to win him. All the other nymphs who loved him also were shunned by him. One nymph prayed that Narcissus might sometime himself feel what it was to love and be rejected. In response to this prayer, he was made to fall in love with his own image reflected in a pond, which led to his demise (Bulfinch, 1989).

The term narcissism was apparently introduced toward the end of the nineteenth century simultaneously by Paul Nacke and by Havelock Ellis. Freud first used the term in 1910. In 1925 Waelder detailed the "narcissistic personality." The Narcissistic Personality Disorder received formal recognition as a clinical entity with its inclusion into DSM-III in 1980. Today, the concept of narcissism has been fully assimilated into common parlance aided by the mass media, advertising, and best-sellers like *The Culture of Narcissism* (Lasch, 1978) and *The Self-Seekers* (Restak,1982). The "me generation" and Yuppies further popularized and reified narcissistic aphorisms such as "having it all," "have it your way," and "greed is good." Among mental health professionals, the concept of narcissism and discussion of treatment of the narcissistic personality have gained high visibility as witnessed by the spate of books, articles, and workshops on self psychology and Narcissistic Disorders.

The designation of self psychology and Narcissistic Disorders has become almost synonymous with the late psychoanalyst Heinz Kohut (1971). Although Alfred Adler never used the term "narcissistic personality," his description of the neurotic personality is strikingly similar to that of a consensus of many contemporary writers (Ansbacher, 1985). Adler's psychology, which he proposed some 70 years ago, is strikingly similar to the self psychology of Kohut's.

The present paper reviews the concept of narcissism and the psychology of Adler. It also discusses the DSM-III-R criteria and those of others and Kohut and of the Adlerian formulation for the Narcissistic Personality Disorder. A case study is also included.

Concept of Narcissism and Kohut's Self Psychology

Narcissism can be described as an investment or concentration of energy or interest in the self. For Freud, narcissism referred to the withdrawal of libido and an investment in the self. In Kohut's thinking, narcissism implied the development of self-esteem through a relationship with a self-object. For Kohut, narcissism was normal and healthy. Furthermore he believed narcissism had its own line of development separate from Freud's structural line of id, ego, and superego development (Kohut, 1971). Kohut believed that narcissism can be fixated at certain points and, thus, had its own form of pathology requiring its own form of treatment (Kohut, 1977).

Kohut's self psychology emphasizes the structure and constituents of the self as well as the subjective conscious and unconscious experience of selfhood. He described the constituents of the self in terms of two poles: one from which emanates the basic strivings for power and recognition, and the other which maintains the guiding ideal. The arc of tension between these two poles activates the individual's basic talents and skills. This view of self is remarkably similar to Adler's formulation, which is detailed later in this paper.

The core of Kohut's theory involves the experiential relationship between the self and the empathic "self-object." Self-object is Kohut's term for the child's partially fused view of self and others. It is the child's internal perception of persons in his/her environment who serve functions that, if development proceeds normally, will later be performed by the individual's own psychic structure. Kohut believed a normal child grows up in an empathic-responsive environment peopled by others who are in tune with his/her psychological needs and wishes. As a result, the child experiences a merger with the all-powerful self-object. When the self-object is calm and collected, the child's needs, anxieties, and rage are calmed such that he/she begins to experience the rudiments of a stable, cohesive self. Over the course of time, the child will experience disappointment and frustration or "empathic failure." To the extent that his/her "failure" does not exceed the child's capacity to manage it, maturation continues. But if the empathic failure occurs too early or too violently, the stability of the self is compromised, leading to loss of self-esteem and diminished capacity to function in the world. Kohut postulated that the self disorders, particularly the Borderline and Narcissistic Personality Disorders, result from early empathic failure on the part of the parents, particularly the mother. Repeated empathic failures result in a lack of cohesion in the child's sense of self. In adult life, the sequelae of these failures are typically rage, depression, substance abuse, splitting, projective identification, thrill-seeking, and sexual perversion. Kohut and his self psychology colleagues agreed that treatment of narcissistic disorders is based on resolution of developmental deficits that interfere with the adult's capacity to deal with the frustrations of everyday life.

Kohut stressed the importance of the mother's mirroring and empathy out of which the infant and young child internalize a stable and cohesive sense of self. In Adler's psychology, the empathic/unempathic mother was not emphasized as much as the child's adaptiveness to his/her family environment.

Adler emphasized the child's initial adaptations to the significant persons in his/her environment, usually the parents' response. Adler focused on affective values in the parental response to the young child and the child's perception of the parents' response. When the child felt secure and loved, Adler believed the child felt worthwhile and a sense of belonging. When the child's feeling toward the parents reflected insecurity, the child experienced a sense of inferiority and would resort to neurotic safeguards to ward off inferiority feelings. This was Adler's formulation of the neurotic personality in general, rather than of the narcissistic personality in particular.

Both Adler's and Kohut's formulations of self are radical departures from Freud's drive-reduction psychology. There are close similarities between Adler's and Kohut's formulations of self. Unfortunately, recognition of these similarities has not been forthcoming. In a somewhat obscure 1972 paper, Kohut did acknowledge some debt to Adler, and that was in regard to the concept of "organ inferiority" (Stepansky, 1983). Eagle (1984) criticized Kohut for failing to acknowledge the influences of predecessors. For instance, Eagle noted the striking parallels between Kohut and Carl Rogers on empathy, but, like so many other commentators, failed to mention Kohut's parallels with Adler.

NARCISSISM AND INDIVIDUAL PSYCHOLOGY

Freud's paper, "On Narcissism: An Introduction," published in 1914, was important as it marked the beginning of his ego psychology. Adler had challenged the basis of Freud's libidinal theory and notions of infant sexuality in Adler's paper on "masculine protest" published in 1911 (Adler, 1980). Freud's paper was his attempt to offer an alternative to Adler's masculine protest and to Jung's non-sexual libido.

For Adler, the masculine protest was the basic neurotic motive, rather than the libidinal drive that Freud had promulgated. Freud criticized Adler's formulation saying that the masculine protest was "nothing other than fear of castration." Later, he faulted Adler for offering only an ego psychology and for basing masculine protest on a social valuation. Instead, Freud proposed the concept of narcissism in which libido was directed toward the self as the basis of neurosis. This revised formulation marked the beginning of Freudian ego psychology.

Adler's concept of masculine protest is poorly understood by many. Even authoritative reference works have limited or misguided definitions. Typically, masculine protest is described as a compensatory process by which women overcome their feelings of inferiority by striving to gain the power of men (Walrond-Skinner, 1986). Adler indicated that masculine protest was tied to self-esteem. In 1912 he wrote, "The neurotic purpose is the enhancement of self-esteem, the simplest formula of which can be recognized in the exaggerated masculine protest. This formula, 'I wish to be a real man' is the guiding fiction in every neurosis" (Adler, 1912/1917). Masculine protest was a starting point in Adler's goal-oriented value psychology in which the self was central.

The term "masculine protest" in this broad sense was soon replaced by such terms as will to power, striving for an exaggerated personality ideal, for superiority, conquest, security, perfection, completion, success as subjectively defined, or for overcoming. All these are value terms denoting a movement from minus to plus toward enhancement of self-esteem or its preservation, an impetus which never ceases. They imply an actively striving individual, self, or ego, rather than one dominated by some other primary process. "Striving upward from below. . . represents the fundamental fact of our life. . . ." Complementary to this, "The supreme law" of life is that "the sense of worth of the self shall not be allowed to be diminished" (Adler, 1956).

Freud made primary narcissism the basis of self-esteem and so gave the concept a positive connotation, whereas previously it had been regarded negatively. In psychoanalytic circles, various forms of narcissism have been described: "normal," "primary," "secondary," "healthy," and "pathological." These different meanings of narcissism have been criticized by a number of psychoanalysts, particularly Balint (1960), as being of confusing and questionable meaning.

Adler's critique of psychoanalytic interpretations of narcissism predated the criticism of Balint and others. Adler maintained that the crucial feature in narcissism is not self-love, but rather the exclusion of others. "In the conception of narcissism the most important part has been overlooked: the continuous exclusion of others, the narrowing of the sphere of action. This . . . signifies a lack of social interest." This lack in turn is to be attributed to a lack of self-confidence, "a feeling of weakness which originated from a feeling of inferiority. . . This feeling seeks compensation through seemingly making the situation easier" (Adler, 1931/1979, p. 208).

The original Narcissus myth as described at the beginning is quite in accord with Adler's understanding of the exclusion of others as the crucial part of narcissism, the myth presenting the fatal self-love of Narcissus as punishment for his exclusion of others.

Adler believed that the decisive basic difference between his psychology and that of Freud was that Freud starts with the assumption that by nature man only wants to satisfy his drives—the pleasure principle—and must, therefore, from the viewpoint of culture, be regarded as completely "bad." By contrast, Adler held that "the indestructible destiny of the human species is social interest. In Individual Psychology this is the truth; in psychoanalysis it is a trick. Individual Psychology maintains that . . . the human being is inclined toward social interest, toward the good" (Adler, 1931/1979).

NARCISSISTIC PERSONALITY DISORDER

The Narcissistic Personality Disorder (NPD) has been described variously by different authors. For Wolf (1988) and other followers of Kohut, the NPD is viewed as one of several "self disorders" in which a significant failure of the self has occurred in achieving cohesion. Psychosis and Borderline States are self disorders in which serious damage to the self is either permanent or protracted, whereas the Narcissistic Behavior Disorders and NPD are less serious.

Wolf (1988) described the NPD as a self disorder in which damage to the self is temporary and restorable through appropriate psychoanalytic treatment and where the symptoms express the tensions associated with damage to the self or the tensions of autoplastic attempts to restore self-object functioning. He indicated that hypochondrias, depression, and hypersensitivity are examples of autoplastic attempts to restore functioning.

Kernberg (1975) offered another psychoanalytic perspective on the NPD which is quite different from Wolf's or Kohut's. Kernberg believed that narcissism is not a separate line of development, as Kohut claimed, but an elaboration of psychosexual development and drive theory. Kernberg drew upon Freud and the object relations and development theories of Klein, Jacobson, Fairbairn, and Mahler to provide a systematic view of narcissism and the NPD. Kernberg concluded that narcissism is essentially pathological, and included the NPD within the wider category of the borderline personality disorder and conditions.

From a biopsychosocial perspective and based on psychometric data, Millon and Everly (1985) described persons with a narcissistic personality as passive-independent individuals who "possess an inflated sense of confidence and self-worth." Narcissistic personalities believe that they need merely be themselves to be secure and content. Their self-esteem is based on a blind assumption of superiority. Their behavior is often motivated by a desire to achieve the things they feel they deserve because of their "superiority." Millon and Everly described the NPD much less dysfunctionally than does *DSM-III-R*. Millon also noted that the descriptions of the NPD in Kohut (1977) and Kernberg (1975) are different than *DSM-III-R*. Finally, Millon and Everly noted that both Kernberg and Kohut described the NPD as a composite of both *DSM-III-R* Narcissistic and Passive Aggressive Personality Disorders.

From a psychiatric perspective, Ludwig (1986) described the NPD in terms of cognitive, behavioral, and emotional styles or features. The cognitive style of the NPD reflects an exaggerated sense of self-importance as well as unrealistic goals of power, wealth, and ability. It also reflects a sense of entitlement and self-deception or prevarication to preserve self-illusions. The behavioral style of the NPD suggests an individual who strives to be the center of attention, dominates conversations, and seeks admiration. Further, this individual can be interpersonally exploitative, supercilious, and lacking humility. The emotional style of the NPD is characterized by a lack of empathy with others, ragefulness following criticism, as well as feelings toward others that shift from overidealization to devaluation. Furthermore, affection will be largely directed toward the self while projecting an aura of nonchalance, except when the individual's narcissistic confidence is shaken.

These criteria are quite similar to those of *DSM-III-R* (American Psychiatric Association, 1987) where the NPD is described as a pervasive pattern of grandiosity in either behavior or fantasy as well as a lack of empathy and a hypersensitivity to others' criticism. In *DSM-III-R* also is specified that this disorder is present from early adulthood and is manifested in all aspects or contexts of the individual's life. At least five of nine criteria are required to make this diagnosis: (1) reacting to criticism with narcissistic rage, shame, or humiliation; (2) being interpersonally exploitative; (3) exhibiting a grandiose sense of self-importance; (4) believing that their problems are unique and can only be understood by a special person; (5) being preoccupied with fantasies of unlimited success, power, beauty, etc; (6) having a sense of entitlement; (7) lacking empathy; (8) demanding constant attention and admiration; and, (9) being preoccupied with feelings of envy (349-351).

Akhtar and Thompson (1982) offered an expanded view of the NPD that is a composite of *DSM-III* criteria, the object relations and self psychology views of Kernberg and Kohut, and social and existential perspectives. They described the NPD as consisting of overt and covert deficits in six areas of functioning: (1) self-concept; (2) interpersonal relationships; (3) social adaptation; (4) ethics, standards, and ideals; (5) love and sexuality; and (6) cognitive style.

Shea (1988) noted the *DSM-III-R* criteria for NPD houses two rather distinctive types: the stable and unstable NPD. He described individuals with stable NPD as usually the product of a spoiled upbringing in which sharing was uncommon. As both children and adults they find it difficult to view others as having needs, since they believe the world revolves around themselves. Their view of others may shift rapidly from idealizing others to devaluing them depending on how others meet or fail to meet their needs. According to Shea, stable narcissists are able to lead reasonably happy lives, especially if they are talented. Typically, they are difficult people to get along with. When they do not receive the adulation and subservience they believe they are entitled, they may pout, stomp about, or become depressed.

In contrast, the unstable NPD tends to inhabit a more hostile world. Since their sense of self is less developed and less cohesive, life is viewed as a constant threat. They experience themselves as worthless and constantly need to project a grandiose style. Few people are trusted and bitterness becomes a way of life. They are easily wounded, and when this occurs, they immediately react with narcissistic rage, projective identification, and cognitive distortions. Tantrums and rages are second nature to them. To please them is nearly impossible, and they are prone to severe depressive episodes, substance abuse, and sexual perversions if their needs are not met. In addition, they may be prone to micropsychotic episodes. These unstable NPDs are often not successful in life since their self-absorbed behavior prevents advancement, and their labile moods and anger make consistent work efforts difficult. At other times, they can demonstrate appropriate impulse control on the job or in public. This characterization of unstable NPD seems close to Wolf's description of the severe Self Disorders: the Psychotic and Borderline States. Shea's stable

NPD more closely resembles Wolf's Narcissistic Personality and Behavior Disorders.

Finally, Bach (1985) described the NPD in terms of two types: Type I and II. Type I patients are well described by *DSM-III-R* criteria. However, Type II patients present primarily with feelings of inferiority as well as insecurity, boredom, hypersensitivity, uncertainty, and chronic idealizations followed by disillusionment.

INDIVIDUAL PSYCHOLOGY FORMULATION OF THE NARCISSISTIC PERSONALITY

Alfred Adler described the neurotic personality as stemming from childhood experiences characterized by either overprotection or neglect, or a confusing admixture of both. From these experiences, the young child develops a set of psychological opinions about self, the world, and life goals. These opinions are reinforced and confirmed by the child's family and outer environment. These opinions help or hinder the person's ability to cope and master the tasks of life. Again, Adler did not describe the NPD per se. Yet as Ansbacher (1985) found, the prevailing view of NPD is reasonably consistent with Adler's general description of the neurotic personality. Ansbacher (1985) matched Akhtar and Thompson's description of deficits of functioning with Adler's description of the neurotic personality. Ansbacher noted that Adler's characterizations of the disorder as overestimation of self, hypersensitivity, superiority complex, burning ambition, deprecation tendency, idealization, predestination complex, envy, prestige, as well as pampered life-style and lack of social interest are akin to *DSM-III* and other descriptions of the NPD.

The life-style opinions, or to use Shulman's term "convictions," can be expressed in terms of I am _____ (self-view); life is _____ (world view); therefore _____ (life goal) (Shulman, 1973). For the NPD the self-view is likely to be some variant of the theme: "I'm special and unique, and I'm entitled to extraordinary rights and privileges whether I've earned them or not." The world view is likely to be a variant of the theme: "Life is a banquet table to be sampled at will. People owe me admiration and privilege." The life goal or pattern will be some variant of the theme: "Therefore, I'm entitled to have things my way, and I'll expect and demand this specialness. When I don't get what I demand, others will bear the brunt of my rage" (Sperry, 1990).

TREATMENT CONSIDERATIONS

The goals of treatment of the NPD depend in large part on the expectations and needs of the patient. The goals of treatment for reactive or superficial symptoms such as a reactive depression, marital discord, or acute anxiety symptoms are typically addressed with symptom-reduction methods. Treatment methods that salve and support the narcissistic injury are all that most NPDs want and expect. Often after symptoms have reduced, the narcissistic individual will leave or be unwilling to continue in longer-term psychotherapy. When longer-term therapy is indicated and desired by the patient, treatment goals will vary depending on the therapist's theoretical orientation. For psychoanalytically-oriented clinicians who emphasize the patient's narcissistic vulnerability and reaction to empathic failures, restructuring therapy is proposed. The goals of restructuring therapies are increased empathy for others and toward the self; decreased regression in the face of rebuff, failure, or separation; a capacity for flexible detachment and distancing oneself; the ability to feel gratified when working alone; the ability to give without personal gain; and the capacity to truly mourn an important loss (Nurnberg, 1984).

The Individual Psychology perspective tends to focus longer-term treatment of the NPD on the goals of increasing social interest, specifically by reversing life-style convictions about entitlement, self-absorption, and specialness, and by developing alternatives to angry, rageful, and demanding behaviors. The Individual Psychologist might combine dynamic interpretations with cognitive restructuring and behavioral interventions. Among the behavioral interventions that have been shown effective with narcissistically-focused patients are empathy training, cognitive awareness training, and anger management (Feldman, 1982).

CASE EXAMPLE

Case of Marilyn Monroe

Occasionally, the lives of public figures lend themselves well as case examples. Such was the life of Marilyn Monroe. She died of an overdose of sleeping pills at age 36. Ansbacher (1974) has previously demonstrated the application of Adlerian theory to understanding both the dynamics of Marilyn's life and untimely demise the following being a brief summary of this analysis.

Marilyn was born to a lower-class mother in Los Angeles. Her mother had previously divorced and had two other children from that marriage, but these children were not in her custody. For much of her early years, Marilyn was reared in what appears to have been relatively stable foster homes. Yet, her natural mother visited her weekly, and her maternal grandmother likewise visited Marilyn until grandmother was committed to a mental institution. Later Marilyn's mother was also committed. In addition to this family history of unspecified psychiatric illness, an uncle reportedly committed suicide, further predisposing Marilyn to personality dysfunctioning.

As a child, Marilyn described herself as a tomboy who was quite good at athletics but uninterested and unskilled in feminine ways. Her earliest ambition was to be an actress, and her favorite pastime was movie matinees in which she would imagine herself on the big screen.

She became an actress after being discovered by an army photographer while she was working as a supervisor in a munitions factory during WWII. She became an overnight sensation, making 23 films before being dismissed by her studio for unjustified absences during filming. At the height of her career, she received 5,000 fan letters a week. Two months after her dismissal, and two years after her divorce from playwright Arthur Miller—her third husband—she took her life on August 5, 1962. She never had children, even though she had two miscarriages. When under stress she reportedly became sick to her stomach. Over the course of her career, and up until the time of her death, she had seen several psychoanalysts, with little apparent therapeutic success.

Colleagues described her as warm, likeable, good-humored, witty, and generous. Yet, they also noted she was self-absorbed much of the time, as well as had a bad temper shown in rages and private furies.

Some of Marilyn's early recollections (ER) have been reported in various biographical sketches. We will describe and analyze two of them as suggestive of her narcissistic personality.

> ER 1. She related the following childhood dream: "When I was maybe 6 or 7, I dreamed I was standing up in church without any clothes on, and all the people there were lying at my feet on the floor, and I walked naked, with a sense of freedom, being careful not to step on anyone."

Here we learn how her dream reflected her preoccupation with fantasies of unlimited success and beauty. She stands up like a goddess and everyone is lying at her feet in adoration, suggesting a grandiose self. Marilyn regarded herself as outside of this world. In the world she was just "poor little me" who should be protected and admired. But outside this world, at least her body could be immortal (Ansbacher, 1974). Twenty-five years after her death, books of photo-essays of Marilyn continue to be successfully published as the older generations worship and reminisce and a new generation becomes enamored of her beguiling charm.

> ER 2. From the time she was 11 she remembered: "The whole world which was always closed to me suddenly opened up. Even the girls paid attention to me because they thought, 'She is to be dealt with.' I had this long walk—2 1/2 miles to school, 2 1/2 miles back—it was sheer pleasure. Every fellow honked his horn. . . The world became friendly. All the newspaper boys when they delivered the paper would

come around to where I lived. I used to hang from a limb of a tree, and I had a sort of a sweatshirt on. . . Here they'd come with their bicycles and I'd get these free papers and the family liked that and they'd all pull their bicycles up around the tree and I'd be hanging. I was a little too shy to come down. I did get down to the curb. . . mostly listening. . . I used to laugh so loud and so gay. . . It was just this sudden freedom, because I would ask the boys, 'Can I ride your bike now?' and they'd say, 'Sure.' Then I'd go zooming, laughing in the wind, riding down the block, and they'd all stand around, and wait till I came back, but I loved the wind; it caressed me."

Marilyn had become the center of constant attention and admiration. Furthermore, her sense of entitlement is obvious: Girls must "deal with her" and every guy must honk his horn. This recollection also reflects her desire to be pampered. She receives newspapers and bicycle rides free. And without giving anything in return, she takes off on her own. That others would expectantly wait on her to return further suggests her pampered, special, and entitled status. In the recollection no indication is present of Marilyn's ability to be empathic. Rather than responding to her admirers, she "loved the wind; it caressed me."

Neither of these ERs, nor the other six reported by Ansbacher (1974), indicate that Marilyn believed life's goals could be obtained through cooperation and social interest. In the two ERs noted above, she is either above others (1&2) or getting something for nothing (2). With such underdeveloped social interest and elevated sense of narcissism, we could expect that Marilyn would have approached life situations from a self-centered viewpoint rather than one of mutuality.

In summary, Marilyn Monroe was an active person with extraordinary ambition and little thought of others. Although she spent considerable time in foster care, no indication is found that she was abandoned by her mother or grandmother. In fact, she probably was a rather pampered child. She was rewarded by our society out of all proportion through her overnight stardom. After her death, her mystique appears to have actually increased. A review of biographical material and reported early recollections clearly suggests that she meets the *DSM-III-R* criteria for Narcissistic Personality Disorder, as well as the dynamic "criteria" for this disorder. Specifically, her view of herself, of the world, and of goals is similar to the views of other individuals who would be considered narcissistic personalities. In addition, based on biographical material on Marilyn, the suggestion is of some Borderline and Dependent personality features or traits.

SUMMARY

The narcissistic personality has become one of the most prominent personality types today in the Western world. Psychoanalytic formulations of the narcissistic personality have evolved over the past several decades to closely parallel Adler's original description of the neurotic personality. Although not specifically using the term narcissistic personality, Adler's description of the neurotic personality and a recent Adlerian formulation are quite consistent with DSM-III-R and other descriptions of the NPD.

REFERENCES

Adler, A. (1912/1917). *The neurotic constitution: Outlines of a comparative individualistic psychology and psychotherapy.* (B. Glueck, & J.E. Lind, Trans.). New York: Moffat, Yard.

Adler, A. (1931/1979). The difference between individual psychology and psychoanalysis. In H.L. Ansbacher & R.R. Ansbacher (Eds.), *Superiority and social interest.* New York: W.W. Norton.

Adler, A. (1956). *The Individual Psychology of Alfred Adler.* H.L. Ansbacher & R.R. Ansbacher (Eds.). New York: Harper & Row.

Adler, A. (1980). Masculine protest and a critique of Freud. In H. Ansbacher & R. Ansbacher (Translators and editors), *Cooperation between the sexes.* New York: Jason Aronson.

Akhtar, S., & Thompson, T.A. (1982). Overview: Narcissistic personality disorder. *American Journal of Psychiatry, 139,* 12-20.

American Psychiatric Association (1987). *Diagnostic and statistical manual of mental disorders* (3rd. ed, revised). Washington, DC: Author.

Ansbacher, H. L. (1974). Goal-oriented Individual Psychology. In A. Burton (Ed.), *Operational theories of personality.* New York: Brunner/Mazel.

Ansbacher, H. L. (1985). The significance of Alfred Adler for the concept of narcissism. *American Journal of Psychiatry, 142* (2), 203-207.

Bach, S. (1985). *Narcissistic states and the therapeutic process.* North Vale, NJ: Jason Aronson Press.

Balint, M. (1960). Primary narcissism and primary love. *Psychoanalytic Quarterly, 29,* 6-23.

Bulfinch, T. (1989). *The age of fable or beauties of mythology,* (rev.ed.). J.L. Scott (Eds.). Philadelphia: David McKay

Eagle, M. (1984). *Recent developments in psychoanalysis: A critical evaluation.* New York: McGraw-Hill.

Feldman, L. (1982). Dysfunctional marital conflict: An integrative interpersonal-intrapsychic model. *Journal of Marital and Family Therapy, 8,* 417-428.

Freud. S. (1914/1949). On narcissism: An introduction. In *Complete psychological works, standard edition (ed.),* Vol. 14. London: Hogarth Press.

Kernberg, O. (1975). *Borderline conditions and pathological narcissism.* New York: Jason Aronson.

Kohut, H. (1971). *The analysis of the self.* New York: International Universities Press.

Kohut, H. (1977). *The restoration of the self.* New York: International Universities Press.

Lasch, C. (1978). *The culture of narcissism.* New York: Norton.

Ludwig, A. (1986). *Principles of clinical psychiatry* (2nd ed.). New York: Free Press.

Millon, T., & Everly, G.S. (1985). *Personality and its disorders.* New York: John Wiley & Sons.

Nurnberg, H. (1984). Survey of psychotherapeutic approaches to narcissistic personality disorders. *Hillside Journal of Clinical Psychiatry, 6* (2), 204-220.

Restak, R. (1982). *The self-seekers.* Garden City, NY: Doubleday.

Shea, S.C. (1988). *Psychiatric interviewing.* Phildelphia: W.B. Saunders.

Shulman, B. (1973). Confrontation techniques in Adlerian psychotherapy. In B. Shulman (Ed.), *Contributions to Individual Psychology*. Chicago: Alfred Adler Institute.

Sperry, L. (1990). Personality disorders: Biopsychosocial description and dynamics. *Individual Psychology, 46,* 193-202.

Stepansky, P. (1983). Perspectives on dissent: Adler, Kohut, and the idea of psychoanalytic research tradition. In *The annual of psychoanalysis, Vol. XI*. New York: International Universities Press.

Walrond-Skinner, S. (1986). *A dictionary of psychotherapy*. London: Routledge & Kegan Paul.

Wolf, E. (1988). *Treating the self: Elements of clinical self psychology*. New York: Guliford Press.

CHAPTER **13**

PSYCHOACTIVE SUBSTANCE USE DISORDERS

Judith A. Lewis, Ph.D.
Jon Carlson, Psy.D., Ed.D.

The use of psychoactive substances is so prevalent in our society that its negative effects have become impossible to overlook.

> Thirty-two million Americans smoke marijuana at least once a year; twenty million smoke it at least once a month. Annual cocaine users number over twelve million. Several million others take hallucinogens, stimulants, sedatives, and tranquilizers without medical supervision. And of course these figures are dwarfed by the number of people who use legal drugs, including alcoholic beverages (125 million) and tobacco cigarettes (70 million). (Polich, Ellickson, Reuter, & Kahan, 1984, p. v)

At least in the case of alcohol, an ample body of research indicates that a relationship exists between the general level of consumption among members of a population and the number of substance-related problems that can be expected to occur (Grant, 1986). Thus, the fact that substance use is widespread means that therapists are very likely to be confronted by drug- or alcohol-related problems with great frequency. Therapists need to understand, however, that a vast difference exists between substance *use* and substance *abuse* or *dependence*. One of the most useful contributions of the DSM-III-R has been to highlight these distinctions. The manual's guidelines make clear that psychoactive substance use is considered a disorder only when the individual demonstrates an inability to control his or her use despite the appearance of cognitive, behavioral, and physiologic symptoms. Mere use of a substance that modifies mood or behavior is not considered a substance abuse problem unless the user's functioning is clearly affected.

PSYCHOACTIVE SUBSTANCE USE DISORDERS: THE DSM-III-R

In the DSM-III-R the pathological use of psychoactive substances is classified in terms of two categories: Psychoactive Substance Dependence and Psychoactive Substance Abuse. Regardless of the specific substance used by individual clients, they are diagnosed as *dependent* only if at least three of the following nine symptoms are present (American Psychiatric Association, 1987, pp. 167-168):

> Substance often taken in larger amounts or over a longer period than the person intended.

> Persistent desire or one or more unsuccessful efforts to cut down or control substance use.

> A great deal of time spent in activities necessary to get the substance (e.g., theft), taking the substance (e.g., chain smoking), or recovering from its effects.

> Frequent intoxication or withdrawal symptoms when expected to fulfill major role obligations at work, school, or home (e.g., does not go to work because hung over, goes to school or work "high," intoxicated while taking care of his or her children), or when substance use is physically hazardous (e.g., drives when intoxicated).

Important social, occupational, or recreational activities given up or reduced because of substance use.

Continued substance use despite knowledge of having a persistent or recurrent social, psychological, or physical problem that is caused or exacerbated by the use of the substance (e.g., keeps using heroin despite family arguments about it, cocaine-induced depression, or having an ulcer made worse by drinking).

Marked tolerance: need for markedly increased amounts of the substance (i.e., at least a 50% increase) in order to achieve intoxication or desired effect, or markedly diminished effect with continued use of the same amount.

Characteristic withdrawal symptoms.

Substance often taken to relieve or avoid withdrawal symptoms.

The diagnostic criteria also require that symptoms have persisted for at least one month or have occurred repeatedly over a longer period of time. If criteria for substance dependence are met, the disorder is categorized as **mild** (few symptoms beyond those required for the diagnosis; no more than mild impairment in social or occupational functioning), **moderate,** **severe** (many symptoms in excess of those required to make the diagnosis; marked impairment of social/occupational functioning), **in partial remission** (some symptoms during the last six months), or **in full remission** (during the past six months, either no use of the substance or use of the substance with no symptoms of dependence).

Psychoactive Substance Abuse is a diagnosis reserved for individuals who have shown maladaptive patterns in their use of a particular substance but who have never met the criteria for dependence on the substance.

The maladaptive pattern of use is indicated by either (1) continued use of the psychoactive substance despite knowledge of having a persistent or recurrent social, occupational, psychological, or physical problem that is caused or exacerbated by use of the substance or (2) recurrent use of the substance in situations when use is physically hazardous (e.g., driving while intoxicated). (American Psychiatric Association, 1987, p. 169)

Like the substance dependence diagnosis, the substance abuse diagnosis requires that the symptoms have persisted for at least one month or have occurred repeatedly over a longer period of time.

In the DSM-III-R, nine classes of psychoactive substances are associated with both abuse and dependence: alcohol; amphetamine or similarly acting sympathomimetics; cannabis; cocaine; hallucinogens; inhalants; opioids; phencyclidine or similarly acting arylcyclohexylamines; and sedatives, hypnotics, or anxiolytics. A tenth substance—nicotine—has a dependence diagnosis but not an abuse diagnosis. Each class of substances has its own code number.

303.90 Alcohol Dependence and 305.00 Alcohol Abuse

Alcohol dependence and abuse are very common in the United States, with approximately 13% of the adult population having had one of these disorders at some time in their lives (American Psychiatric Association, 1987, p. 174). The behavior of people with either diagnosis may be characterized by a pattern of regular daily intake, of heavy drinking limited to weekends, or of periods of drinking limited to weekends, or of periods of sobriety interspersed with binges. The diagnosis depends on the role of alcohol in the individual's life, the presence of symptoms of tolerance or withdrawal, and the degree of impairment in social and occupational functioning.

304.40 Amphetamine or Similarly Acting Sympathomimetic Dependence and 305.70 Amphetamine or Similarly Acting Sympathomimetic Abuse

Substances in this category are nervous system stimulants, with patterns of dependence or abuse including either chronic, daily use, or episodic use tending to be followed by unpleasant "crashes." Many amphetamine users also abuse alcohol or sedatives in an attempt to alleviate their symptoms. Psychological and behavioral changes include depression, irritability, anhedonia, anergia, and social isolation.

304.30 Cannabis Dependence and
305.20 Cannabis Abuse

The DSM-III-R suggests that Cannabis Dependence is usually characterized by daily, or almost daily, use of the substance (marijuana, hashish, or purified THC), while Cannabis Abuse involves episodic use with evidence of maladaptive behavior. Impairment tends to be less severe than is the case with alcohol, cocaine, and heroin, but Cannabis is often used in combination with other substances. Cannabis Dependence may be characterized by such symptoms as lethargy, anhedonia, and attentional and memory problems.

304.20 Cocaine Dependence and
305.60 Cocaine Abuse

The mode of administration is an important factor in Cocaine Dependence or Abuse. Smoking and intravenous administration tend to be associated with rapid progression to abuse or dependence, while intranasal administration tends to engender problems much more gradually. Over time, the individual tends to show a marked increase in tolerance, so that vastly increased doses are needed to create the desired euphoria. Use may be chronic or episodic, with episodic binges being followed by very unpleasant crashes.

304.50 Hallucinogen Dependence and
305.30 Hallucinogen Abuse

Hallucinogen Abuse is much more common than Hallucinogen Dependence. Use is generally episodic rather than chronic, with users taking "time out" to experiment with the substances and generally being successful in obtaining remission without treatment.

304.60 Inhalant Dependence and
305.90 Inhalant Abuse

Individuals diagnosed as inhalant dependent or abusing become intoxicated by inhaling volatile substances that are available commercially. The disorder is frequently found in children and adolescents and is often associated with other life problems and with abuse of other substances.

305.10 Nicotine Dependence

The DSM-III-R does not include a classification of Nicotine Abuse because maladaptive use of nicotine is virtually always associated with dependence. Among Nicotine Dependent individuals, attempts to stop use are frequent and the relapse rate very high. Although social or occupational impairment is small, serious physical complications are associated with smoking.

304.00 Opioid Dependence and
305.50 Opioid Abuse

This group of psychoactive drugs includes natural opioids, such as heroin and morphine, and synthetics that produce similar effects. Although some individuals may develop Opioid Dependence or Abuse based on use of prescription drugs, the more frequent pattern involves use of illegal opioids. In the United States, this problem may be exacerbated by long-term involvement in a drug-using subculture associated with violence and illegal activity.

304.50 Phencyclidine (PCP) or
Similarly Acting Arylcyclohexylamine Dependence and
305.90 Phencyclidine (PCP) or
Similarly Acting Arylcyclohexylamine Abuse

The most common of this group of substances, PCP, has a euphoric effect and is usually used in episodic binges. Abuse or Dependence develops very quickly, but the presence of physical withdrawal symptoms or tolerance has not been proven.

304.10 Sedative, Hypnotic, or Anxiolytic Dependence and 305.40 Sedative, Hypnotic, or Anxiolytic Abuse

Drugs in this group may be taken as treatment for anxiety or insomnia. Some individuals develop Abuse or Dependence patterns after increasing the frequency or dose of prescribed drugs. Others may use substances illegally, either to obtain euphoria or in an attempt to balance the stimulant effects of cocaine or amphetamine. Heavy daily use and vastly increased tolerance are common.

304.90 Polysubstance Dependence

This diagnosis is reserved for individuals who have used at least three categories of psychoactive substances, but with no single substance predominating.

Diagnosis of the Disorder

In the DSM-III-R the definition of Substance Dependence has greatly expanded in comparison with that found in the DSM-III. The DSM-III reserved the diagnosis of Substance Dependence for individuals showing symptoms of physiological addiction (withdrawal symptoms and increased tolerance). Now, difficulties in controlling use, daily activities revolving around the substance, and the presence of social and psychological problems are considered signs of Dependence even in the absence of characteristic withdrawal symptoms. In both the DSM-III and the DSM-III-R, the term **psychoactive substance use disorder** denotes the presence of maladaptive behaviors associated with the regular use of substances. (Related nervous system effects are categorized as Substance-induced Organic Mental Disorders. For instance, Alcohol Intoxication, Alcohol Withdrawal Delirium, Alcohol Hallucinosis, and Dementia Associated with Alcoholism are all categorized as Alcohol-induced Organic Mental Disorders and described in a separate section.) Clearly, recognition of a client's pattern of substance use as pathological depends on the presence of a complex interaction of individual behaviors and social context. Diagnosis of the disorder thus requires an understanding of the individual's life situation; an awareness of the social, legal, and occupational difficulties associated with the substance use; and an assessment of the centrality of the drug to the individual's life goals.

CONTRIBUTIONS OF ADLERIAN THOUGHT

The DSM-III-R's description of the range of symptoms that can be associated with substance dependence or abuse makes it clear that the diagnostic and treatment processes are complex. Traditionally, many substance abuse treatment providers have oversimplified their assessments, especially when dealing with alcohol dependence. Their erroneous belief that alcoholism is a unitary disease affecting all individuals in the same way has frequently led them to assume that, once a diagnosis has been made, a standardized course of treatment could be prescribed.

> The unitary concept assumes that there is a distinct class of persons who have the specific disease of alcoholism, who are substantively different from problem drinkers, heavy drinkers, prodromal alcoholics, and prealcoholics . . . Most scientific authorities in the field of alcoholism now concur that the construct of alcoholism is most accurately construed as a multivariate syndrome. That is, there are multiple patterns of dysfunctional alcohol use that occur in multiple types of personalities, with multiple combinations of adverse consequences, with multiple prognoses, that may require different types of treatment interventions. (Pattison & Kaufman, 1982, p.13)

Understanding the special needs and goals of a highly varied client population is equally important in the treatment of other drug problems. As Brill (1981) pointed out,

> It is now generally accepted that nonmedical drug users comprise a great diversity of individuals who are drug dependent in different ways and degrees, use drugs to meet different needs, have different socio-economic backgrounds, are of both sexes, and represent a wide range of ages, races, and ethnic groups. No single treatment response will work for all: we need to match a particular approach to each individual. (pp. 5-6)

Effective treatment of substance use disorders can be provided only if therapists address these complexities, comprehending the social factors in substance abuse and using a holistic approach to understanding the individual client. Adlerian conceptualizations such as the social context of behavior, holism, encouragement, and teleology can provide a sorely-needed alternative to "generic, global, diffuse, and nonspecific treatment of such singularly different dimensions of change as drinking behavior, psychological function, social interaction, physical function, and vocational competency" (Pattison, 1982, p. 225).

Social Context

Adlerians know that people cannot be understood in isolation from the social environment of which they are a part.

> Adler viewed man as embedded in the community of his fellowman, which furnishes both the resources and the problems of his life . . . He knew that a person can overcome his fear of life only if he has a stable relationship to his human environment and that a person's all-powerful feeling of inferiority can be assuaged only when the voice of the community has begun to resound within him. (Rattner, 1983, p. 24)

One of the reasons that substance use disorders are difficult to treat is that, for many addicts, the "voice of the community" has long since been silenced. In fact, the community of fellow substance abusers may provide for them the only feeling of belonging that they know. Adolescent initiation into drug use has been termed a "group phenomenon" (Polich et al., 1984), as has maintenance of substance-abusing life-styles among adults. Stephens (1985) described a "street addict subculture" with an accompanying role that may be highly valued by heroin-dependent individuals.

> The role is highly prominent (almost to the exclusion of all other roles), has a very great level of social support from other junkies, provides both intrinsic and extrinsic social and psychological rewards and can be enacted successfully in most social situations. (p. 437)

Individuals who have become drug dependent spend more and more time with other addicts and learn to avoid non-substance-using friends and relatives.

Substance abusing individuals frequently lack "the feeling of being a part of a larger social whole, the feeling of being socially embedded, the willingness to contribute in the communal life for the common weal" (Mosak, 1989, p. 66). Whether this lack of social interest is part of the etiology of the substance abuse problem or simply the result of years of drug use, the individual's recovery depends on his or her ability to rekindle the sparks of social reciprocity. Without Gemeinschaftsgefühl, long-term sobriety becomes a difficult proposition at best. Among the most important factors affecting recovery from drug and alcohol problems are family and marital resources, positive work environments, and community support networks (Moos, Cronkite, & Finney, 1982). Encouraging the client to re-enter the social environment and find a place in it must be one of the therapist's first priorities.

Holism

Adlerian conceptualizations reject the reductionistic division of the individual into parts in favor of a holistic orientation that sees the person as a unity (Mosak, 1989). Similarly, the most realistic approaches to substance abuse recognize that "social, cultural, biological, and psychological factors interact reciprocally in both the etiology and the resolution of substance-related problems" (Lewis, Dana, & Blevins, 1988, p. 17). In addressing adolescent drug use, for instance,

> Efforts toward prevention and rehabilitation aimed at changing adolescent alcohol and drug use may not be maximally effective if they are limited in focus to the use behavior itself or to an isolated domain of the adolescent's life. Instead, interventions should focus simultaneously on multiple domains. The multidimensional approach is also advisable because alcohol and drug use is intertwined with many issues and problems confronting adolescents, often to the extent that focusing solely on establishing the "cause and effect" relationship between substance abuse and life problems obscures the path to a successful intervention. (Pandina & Schuele, 1983, p. 971)

Some treatment providers mistakenly believe that they can address substance abuse problems in a vacuum, focusing solely on the drug issue and ignoring the interwoven concerns that make up the individual's life. In fact,

The client's substance abuse must also be considered in the context of other life problems, although not necessarily in terms of causality. Substance abuse tends to be associated with a variety of social, psychological, family, and financial problems. The counselor does not need to determine whether these problems are a cause of or a result of substance abuse. Each of a client's major concerns should be addressed as part of the counseling process under the assumption that a favorable outcome involves rehabilitation across several life domains. (Lewis, Dana, & Blevins, 1988, p. 11)

As Mejta (1988) has pointed out, "We need to think of a person who happens to have a drug problem, not a drug problem that happens to be expressed in this person."

Encouragement

The field of substance abuse treatment has a long history of controversy over the degree of responsibility that clients should assume for their problems and for the solution to those problems. The disease concept has helped clients to understand that they should avoid self-blame for what were essentially involuntary behaviors (Fingarette, 1983). Unfortunately, the recognition that individuals' behavior was not under their own control may have brought with it an assumption of powerlessness.

It is ironic that the major strength of the disease model, absolving the addict of personal responsibility for the problem behavior, may also be one of its major shortcomings. If alcoholics come to view their drinking as the result of a disease or physiological addiction, they may be more likely to assume the passive role of victim whenever they engage in drinking behavior if they see it as a symptom of their disease . . . Relapse is the turning point where the disease model is likely to backfire. If an alcoholic has accepted the belief that it is impossible to control his or her drinking . . . then even a single slip may precipitate a total, uncontrolled relapse. Since drinking under these circumstances is equated with the occurrence of a symptom signifying the reemergence of the disease, one is likely to feel as powerless to control this behavior as one would with any other disease symptom. (Marlatt & Gordon, 1985, pp. 7-8)

Treatment would be enhanced in its effectiveness if therapists replaced the negative messages frequently given to clients ("you are unable to control your behavior") with positive, encouraging messages ("through self-understanding, you can learn and change"). Through the encouragement process, treatment can begin to focus on enhancing the client's feeling that personal mastery is possible and desirable.

> In essence any psychological treatment is an attempt to increase the patient's self-confidence and to encourage him directly or indirectly. The Adlerian approach is characterized by its deliberate efforts to encourage the patient. Even exposure of the fraud which underlies the contradiction between what the patient "wants" to do and what he "can" do, between his apparent intentions and incapacity to give them effect, ultimately helps to encourage him. He sees that his failures have not been due to any weakness of character or equipment, but that he has been mistaken as to the nature of his intentions. (Dreikurs, 1953, p. 88)

Teleology

Adlerian psychology replaces the reductionism of over-simplified cause-and-effect relationships with a teleological orientation that sees behavior as a function of its goal.

> Alfred Adler stresses the fact that all living things move, and that every movement must have a goal. So, according to Adler, all living things seek a goal. With regard to man in particular, Alfred Adler declares that it is impossible for us to understand his behavior and actions unless we know their goal. (Dreikurs, 1953, p. 11)

In the substance abuse field, decades of searching for "the cause" of substance use disorders have been fruitless. A combination of many physiological, psychological, and social factors may contribute to the development of substance abuse problems. The ultimate resolution of these problems, however, depends on the client's understanding of the purpose that the psychoactive substance has performed in his or her life. Until the individual finds other ways to meet his or her life goals—and makes appropriate life-style changes—maintenance of behavior changes may prove illusory.

> Addicts improve when their relationships to work, family, and other aspects of their environment approve. Addicts

have come to count on the regular rewards they get from their addictive involvement. They can give up these rewards when they believe they will find superior gratifications from other activities in the regular fibre of their lives. (Peele, 1985, p. 154)

GENERAL TREATMENT STRATEGY

Whether the issue at hand is substance dependence or any other dysfunction, the therapist's first priority needs to be the establishment of a helping relationship. Some substance-abuse treatment providers overlook the importance of this factor, moving quickly into direct confrontation and attempting to force each client into an acceptance of the therapist's point of view on the existence or seriousness of the problem. A more appropriate strategy is to establish a relationship based on the notion that the therapist can help the individual to reorient his or her thinking but that the decision to change or not to change is the client's. Miller's (1983) motivational interviewing approach, for instance, treats the substance dependent client as a responsible adult, based on a belief in "the individual's inherent wisdom and ability to choose the healthful path given sufficient support" (p. 490). *The substance-abuse treatment provider walks a thin line, providing very active support and encouragement but refusing to take responsibility for the client's behavior.*

With the formation of a trusting relationship, the process of change can begin. Cooley (1983) suggested that formal life-style work should not begin too early in the client's recovery. In the early months of recovery, the client's attention needs to focus on the attainment of abstinence in the present. Once behavior changes have become established, the client can begin to understand the nature of the faulty conclusions that have affected his or her life-style and use this knowledge to prevent relapse. This approach complements Washton's (1989) conceptualization of the stages in substance abuse treatment. In Stage 1 (stabilization and crisis intervention), clients are helped to resolve immediate crisis situations, break off contacts with the drug world, stop all drug and alcohol use, and establish a connection to the treatment program. Stage 2 (early abstinence) involves learning about addiction, establishing support systems, and achieving stable abstinence. In Stage 3 (relapse prevention), clients learn about relapse and its prevention, start to identify and handle negative feelings, learn how to deal with problems, and make some beginnings in the direction of permanent life-style changes. Stage 4 (advanced recovery) involves deeper, more lasting changes in attitude, life-style, and behavior. At this stage, which is open-ended, the client is ready to examine the convictions upon which his or her life-style has been based, to recognize the faulty goals that have influenced his or her behaviors, and to deepen his or her involvement in the social milieu. Through this difficult but crucial process, the possibilities of long-term recovery can be enhanced.

CASE EXAMPLE

The Case of Harold "Hal" Willis

Diagnosis:

Axis I:	303.90 Alcohol Dependence
	291.80 Uncomplicated Alcohol Withdrawal
Axis II:	301.81 Narcissistic Personality Disorder
Axis III:	Early liver disease; early heart disease
Axis IV:	Psychosocial stressors: loss of job, estrangement from son, marital discord.
	Severity: 3 (Moderate). Loss of job an acute event; family stressors (enduring circumstances).
Axis V:	Current GAF: 55
	Highest GAF past year: 70

Hal Willis is an engineer whose alcohol dependence was not recognized until he was in his mid-40's. Harold, who was the oldest of three children, has always suspected that his father, who died when Hal was quite young, was an alcoholic. Hal himself had only one serious alcohol-related episode in his youth, during a particularly stressful period in college.

After graduation from the university, Hal did not drink for well over 20 years. He married his college sweetheart immediately after graduation, and they led a quiet life, with Harold concentrating on his career and achieving considerable success. At that point, Harold became acutely aware of something missing in his marriage and asked for a divorce.

Hal continued to feel guilty about leaving his wife, whom he knew was dependent on him, and depressed that his son severed his relationship with him. When Hal later married Mildred, 15 years his junior, he vowed that he would make this marriage work.

Mildred, too, was counting on the success of this marriage, but it was because she felt that Harold—sober, responsible, and mature—would be able to rescue her from her own alcohol problems. Instead, Hal found himself stymied in his attempts to stop or control his wife's drinking and began to join her. He started going on binges almost immediately after his social drinking began. He and Mildred checked into hotels for binges of up to a week in duration, with Harold calling his office to say he was ill. The episodes occurred more and more frequently; after the last few episodes, the only way he was able to return to work at all was to spend several days being detoxified in an inpatient setting. During the last year of his drinking, he lost his job. He was able to find another position, but despite his competence, this job too was in jeopardy. During Hal's last stay at a detoxification facility, he was told by a physician that he was beginning to show early signs of heart disease and liver malfunction. At this point, Harold made a decision to try to change.

As important as this decision was, it was just a first step. When he returned home, he recognized that his own recovery was jeopardized by Mildred's continued drinking. When she began to drink, he drove her immediately to the treatment center, telling her he would stay with her only when she was sober. After another solitary episode on Mildred's part, she, too, began the process of recovery.

At this point, Hal and Mildred were ready to assess their lives together. Both began attending Alcoholics Anonymous meetings several times a week, allowing them to participate in a positive social milieu for the first time. Mildred began working, which enabled her to become less dependent on her husband, while he, too, worked to reestablish himself in his profession. Hal began to reach out to his son and to his family of origin in an attempt to bridge his isolation. A therapist helped Hal and Mildred to reexamine their relationship and develop a family life based on shared responsibility. In the long run, Harold was able to bring about permanent changes only when he recognized the importance of changing his life-style from one of striving to overcome inferiority and maintain power over others to one in which he was able to concentrate on the real tasks he needed to address.

RECOMMENDED READING

Kaufman, E., & Kaufman, P. (Eds.). (1979). *Family therapy of drug and alcohol abuse.* New York: Gardner Press.

A classic collection of papers related to substance abuse and family systems.

Lewis, J. A., Dana, R. Q., & Blevins, G. A. (1988). *Substance abuse counseling: An individualized approach.* Pacific Grove, CA: Brooks/Cole.

An introduction to substance abuse counseling based on the recognition that substance abusers and their families are members of a heterogeneous population and must be treated from an individualized perspective. Describes the methods best supported by current research.

Marlatt, G. A., & Gordon, J. R. (1985). *Relapse prevention: Maintenance strategies in the treatment of addictive behaviors.* New York: Guilford Press.

Applications of Marlatt's well-established relapse prevention model to several substance abuse related issues.

Miller, W. E., & Heather, N. (1986). *Treating addictive behaviors: Processes of change.* New York: Plenum Press.

A collection of readings based on a comprehensive model of change; discusses approaches to addictive behaviors at the stages of contemplation, action, and maintenance.

Miller, W. E. (1985). *Alcoholism: Theory, research, and treatment.* Lexington, MA: Ginn Press.

An overview of empirically-validated approaches to alcoholism treatment. Includes reprints and original papers by Miller and others.

REFERENCES

American Psychiatric Association. (1987). *Diagnostic and statistical manual of mental disorders* (3rd ed., rev.). Washington, DC: Author.

Brill, L. (1981). *The clinical treatment of substance abusers.* New York: Free Press.

Cooley, H. (1983). Alcoholism and drug dependency: Some mistakes we can avoid. *Individual Psychology, 39* (2), 144-155.

Dreikurs, R. (1953). *Fundamentals of Adlerian psychology.* Chicago: Alfred Adler Institute.

Fingarette, H. (1983). Philosophical and legal aspects of the disease concept of alcoholism. In R. G. Smart, F. B. Glaser, Y. Israel, H. Kalant, R. E. Popham, & W. Schmidt (Eds.), *Research advances in alcohol and drug problems.* New York: Plenum.

Grant, M. (1986). From contemplation to action: The role of the World Health Organization. In W. R. Miller & N. Heather (Eds.), *Treating addictive behaviors: Processes of change* (pp. 51-57). New York: Plenum Press.

Lewis, J. A., Dana, R. Q., & Blevins, G. A. (1988). *Substance abuse counseling: An individualized approach.* Pacific Grove, CA: Brooks/Cole.

Marlatt, G. A., & Gordon, J. R. (1985). *Relapse prevention: Maintenance strategies in the treatment of addictive behaviors.* New York: Guilford Press.

Mejta, C. (Speaker) (1988). Treatment. In *Substance abuse: Current concepts.* Videocassette series. University Park, IL: Governors State University.

Miller, W. R. (1983). Motivational interviewing with problem drinkers. In W. R. Miller (Ed.), *Alcoholism: Theory, research, and treatment,* (pp. 484-503). Lexington, MA: Ginn Press.

Moos, R. H., Cronkite, R. C., & Finney, J. W. (1982). A conceptual framework for alcoholism treatment evaluation. In E. M. Pattison & E. Kaufman (Eds.), *Encyclopedic handbook of alcoholism* (pp. 1120-1139). New York: Gardner Press.

Mosak, H. H. (1989). Adlerian psychotherapy. In R. J. Corsini & D. Wedding (Eds.), *Current psychotherapies* (4th ed.) (pp. 65-118). Itasca, IL: F. E. Peacock.

Pandina, R. J., & Schuele, J. A. (1983). Psychosocial correlates of alcohol and drug use of adolescent students and adolescents in treatment. *Journal of Studies on Alcohol, 44*, 950-973.

Pattison, E. M. (1982). Decision strategies in the path of alcoholism treatment. In W. M. Hay & P. E. Nathan (Eds.), *Clinical case studies in the behavioral treatment of alcoholism* (pp. 251-274). New York: Plenum.

Pattison, E. M., & Kaufman, E. (1982). The alcoholism syndrome: Definitions and models. In E. M. Pattison & E. Kaufman (Eds.), *Encyclopedic handbook of alcoholism* (pp. 3-30). New York: Gardner Press.

Peele, S. (1985). *The meaning of addiction.* Lexington, MA: Lexington Books.

Polich, J. M., Ellickson, P.L., Reuter, P., & Kahan, J. P. (1984). *Strategies for controlling adolescent drug use.* Santa Monica, CA: Rand Corp.

Rattner, J. (1983). *Alfred Adler.* New York: Frederick Ungar.

Stephens, R. C. (1985). The sociocultural view of heroin abuse: Toward a role-theoretic model. *Journal of Drug Issues, 15*, 433-446.

Washton, A. M. (1989). *Cocaine addiction: Treatment, recovery, and relapse prevention.* New York: W. W. Norton.

CHAPTER **14**

ANTISOCIAL PERSONALITY DISORDER AND ADDICTIONS

Donald N. Lombardi, Ph.D.

The purpose of this article is to present the essence of Personality Disorders, Antisocial (Psychopathic) Personality, and the Addictive Disorders from points of view of (1) DSM-III-R (American Psychiatric Association, 1987) and (2) Individual Psychology. Evolving from this double-barreled presentation will come an awareness of the relationship between DSM-III-R and Individual Psychology in regard to these disorders.

ACCORDING TO DSM-III-R

Personality Disorders were earlier known as Character Disorders (Zax & Cowen, 1976). Implicit in this conceptualization was the idea that the individual suffered a weakness of the will. Pinel named it *manie sans delire* and later in 1935, a British psychiatrist, J. C. Pritchard, introduced the term "moral insanity" (McCord & McCord, 1964). It was not until the appearance of DSM-I in 1952 that Personality Disorders were recognized. DSM-I (1952) distinguished three different types of personality disturbances: personality pattern disturbances, personality trait disturbances, and sociopathic personality disturbances.

In DSM-II, which appeared in 1968, ten Personality Disorders are listed but one category was rarely used (Asthenic Personality) and two others (Cylothymic Personality and Explosive Personality) were later not classified among the Personality Disorders (DSM-III, 1980). In DSM-III (1980), Personality Disorders, coded on Axis II, were comprised of personality traits that are inflexible and maladaptive, causing either significant impairment in social or occupational functioning or subjective distress. The diagnosis of a Personality Disorder is made only when the characteristic features are typical of the individual's long-term functioning and are not limited to discrete episodes of illness. Twelve different Personality Disorders are grouped into three clusters. In DSM-III is stated that diagnosis of more than one Personality Disorder should be made if the individual meets the criteria for more than one (DSM-III, 1980).

According to the most recent *Diagnostic and Statistical Manual of Mental Disorders ([DSM-III-R]* of the American Psychiatric Association, 1987), the following organization of Personality Disorders exists:

Cluster A—Paranoid, Schizoid, Schizotypal Personality Disorders.

Cluster B—Antisocial, Borderline, Histrionic, Narcissistic Personality Disorders.

Cluster C—Avoidant, Dependent, Obsessive Compulsive, Passive Aggressive Personality Disorders.

Two additional Personality Disorders (Self-defeating and Sadistic) are listed under the heading "Proposed Diagnostic Categories Needing Further Study" in the appendix to the manual. Frequently, associated features are with Personality

Disorders. Disturbances of mood, frequently involving depression or anxiety, are common and even may be the person's chief complaint (American Psychiatric Association, 1987).

ANTISOCIAL (PSYCHOPATHIC) PERSONALITY

The Personality Disorder that is probably best researched and understood is Antisocial Personality Disorder. In DSM-III-R (1987) are listed a number of diagnostic criteria that must be met for this disorder. They include evidence of a Conduct Disorder with onset before age 15 and a pattern of irresponsible and antisocial behavior since the age of 15.

One of the more popular abnormal psychology textbooks, *Abnormal Psychology and Modern Life* (Eighth Edition) (Carson, Butcher, & Coleman, 1988), lists the following characteristics as typical of Antisocial Personality Disorders:

1. Inadequate conscience development and lack of anxiety and guilt.

2. Irresponsible and impulsive behavior; low frustration tolerance.

3. Ability to put up "a good front" to impress and exploit others, projecting blame onto others for their own socially disapproved behavior.

4. Rejection of authority and inability to profit from experience.

5. Inability to maintain good interpersonal relationships.

Etiological explanations range from biological factors through disturbed family relationships to sociocultural considerations. A variety of therapeutic approaches have been utilized but none found to be too successful. The general topic of Personality Disorders, including Antisocial Personality, is confusing and an enigma from the point of view of etiology, dynamics, and treatment.

ADDICTIVE DISORDERS

Addictions are not found in the DSM-III-R index. Alcohol and drug dependence and abuse are found in the chapter on Psychoactive Substance Use Disorders. Pathological Gambling is under the heading, Impulsive Control Disorders Not Elsewhere Classified. Obesity is not in the section on Eating Disorders. Instead it is reserved for Psychological Factors Affecting Physical Condition (American Psychiatric Association, 1987).

The *Abnormal Psychology and Modern Life* textbook (Carson, Butcher, & Coleman, 1988) has a chapter on Substance Use and Other Addictive Disorders. Included in this chapter are alcohol abuse and dependence, drug abuse and dependence, extreme obesity, and pathological gambling. In another widely used text, *Abnormal Psychology* (Rosenhan & Seligman, 1984), drug and alcohol problems are treated in one chapter and obesity in another chapter under childhood disorders. No mention is made of pathological or compulsive gambling in either the index or the table of contents.

The classification and organization of mental disorders, especially Personality and Addictive Disorders, are a very confusing state of affairs. This is true historically and currently. Personality Disorders are often a factor in other disorders such as alcohol and drug problems, pathological gambling, and sexual deviations (Carson, Butcher, & Coleman, 1988). For example, Gilbert and Lombardi (1967) found a high incidence of psychopathic traits among heroin addicts.

FROM THE POINT OF VIEW
OF INDIVIDUAL PSYCHOLOGY

Before examining the syndromes from an Adlerian viewpoint, a number of basic concepts will be presented and explained first. These concepts are critical in understanding and appreciating Alfred Adler's Individual Psychology. It is so-called because the emphasis is on the uniqueness of each person. The striving is in a social context in a goal-directed manner. Individual Psychology is an idiographic science (Ansbacher & Ansbacher, 1956).

Teleology

Teleology is concerned with the aim, purpose, or goal of human behavior. The prefix "tele" in derivation literally means distant, far, or end. A telephone is an instrument used to talk over a distance; a telescope can be used to view a distant or far object. In other words, in trying to understand behavior from a teleological point of view, the concern is with goals for which one is striving. The emphasis is not on the past antecedents of behavior. The traditional and Freudian approaches in psychology are to look to the past for the explanation of behavior occurring in the present. However, *teleology looks to the present and the future, not from where one is coming but to where one is going.* Ask why the rat in a Skinner box presses the bar and the respondent usually answers that the rat will get food. The answer is not in terms of past learning, although it certainly is where the original learning took place. The point is that behavior is strategy and has an intention or purpose. It is designed to accomplish a goal.

In a very real sense, behavior may be said to have less to do with cause and more to do with purpose. This can be seen when examining the concept of habit. A habit is usually defined as an acquired response which is easily elicited and relatively invariable. It is a fixed behavior which occurs easily and automatically because it has been repeated frequently and requires decreased attention. Although a habit was learned in the past, it continues to serve a purpose in the present. A habit would cease to exist if it served no purpose (Beecher & Beecher, 1966).

Psychology of Use

A psychology of use can be contrasted with a psychology of possession (Ansbacher & Ansbacher, 1956). A psychology of possession states that you are what you are because of what you possess. This may be genetic endowment or environmental or social influence. A psychology of use means that you are what you are because of the use you make of what you possess, whether it be physical/genetic or social. Two people may have the same height or handicap or environment but make use of and live with it differently. Adler once expressed "Do not forget the most important fact that not heredity and not environment are determining factors. Both are giving only the frame and the influence which are answered by the individual in regard to his styled creative power" (Ansbacher & Ansbacher, 1956, p. xxiv). The raw material provided the individual is molded and shaped in his or her own way. It is not what you have, but generally the use you make of what you have that makes all the difference.

The relationship between a psychology of use and psychotherapy and psychopharmacology is beyond the scope of this paper, but an issue which must be addressed. It was a topic of focus at the 36th Annual Convention of the North American Society of Adlerian Psychology, NASAP '88 (Mays, Sperry, Pancner, & Shulman, 1988). Regarding the matter of the relationship between DSM-III-R and Individual Psychology, Sperry (1989a, 1989b) has examined the two systems. He contrasts DSM-III-R based on the disease model and a psychology of possession with the Adlerian approach based on the growth model and a psychology of use. But Sperry also sees similarities and points of convergence between these two systems. Earlier, Mosak (1968) interrelated eight life-style themes with 19 DSM-I diagnostic categories for the neuroses.

Unitary Concept of Motivation

From an Adlerian point of view one basic dynamic force is behind all human activity, a striving from a felt minus situation towards a plus situation, from a feeling of inferiority towards superiority, perfection, totality (Ansbacher & Ansbacher, 1956). In his or her own way, the individual is trying to overcome a subjectively felt sense of weakness and looking for a feeling of worth and place in the sun. In his or her unique way, each person is trying to belong and find personal significance (Lombardi, 1975). People are trying to overcome the difficulties of their lives and put themselves in a position of advantage so they feel a sense of security. But we must be aware that people in their overcoming felt weakness and searching for significance can do it in either the right (well-adjusted) or wrong (mistaken) way. However, one's interpretations and style of living are unique. Everyone is the same in wanting to feel significant, but different in the ways of achieving that goal.

Life-style

This is one of Adler's major contributions. It is a series of opinions and conclusions that are come upon early in one's life, probably about the age of six. The three major components of life-style are (1) view of self, (2) view of others and the world, and (3) way of fitting oneself into life as one finds it. Once the life-style is formed, the inclination is to see and do things from that vantage point. Each person's life-style is patterned, organized, and consistent. It gives the individual a distinctive character and flavor. This is much like the modus operandi characteristic of an artist or criminal whose style of painting or criminal activity is easily detected and recognized.

To say that one's life-style is unique is a most important statement with many implications. To be unique means that you are one of a kind, unlike anybody else. When you were born, the mold was broken. There never has been, nor will there be, anyone just like you living with your exact genetics in your unique circumstances in this place and time. Even if you have an identical twin, you and your twin are not exactly alike. For example, one twin is born before the other and they do not always have identical fingerprints. People who live in the same family do not have the same familial environment. This is because you are not in your own environment. For example, Mary and John are brother and sister in the same family. Mary has a younger brother (John), but John does not have a younger brother (himself). Instead he has an older sister. Thus, their environments are quite different from each other.

As was brought out above, people may have erroneous ideas and faulty notions and conclusions which become the basis for and support mistaken life-styles. This happens all too often resulting in a great variety of problems and disorders. You cannot understand a person on the basis of generalities but must always look at the individual case. A nomothetic approach in science must be supplemented with an idiographic approach (Allport, 1960). A concern has to be with a science of the individual person and an appreciation of not only commonalities but also individual differences.

Early Childhood Training and Family Dynamics

The family for the young child is the world in miniature. It provides the child with a basic training for life. Each member of the family constellation has distinctive traits and characteristics. The important relationships within the family are between parents, parent-child relationships, and sibling relations.

Another of Adler's major contributions is his calling attention to the importance of family dynamics and ordinal or birth position upon personality and life-style development (Adler, 1958). Much has been written and researched on this topic in the Adlerian literature (Dreikurs & Soltz, 1987; Leman, 1985; Watkins, 1986). Many probability statements can be made about a given birth-order position. For example, the oldest child is likely to be the most responsible, reliable, dependable, and somewhat of a perfectionist. Again, however, caution must be taken regarding any general statement that applies to everyone, in this case, oldest children. More importantly, attention must be paid to the unique circumstances of a particular person.

The important point here is that growing out of the family experience, the child develops values, beliefs, opinions, and conclusions about ever so many things. This includes a self-concept, view of authority, the opposite sex, others, and the world. Out of the experience of living in a particular place (which includes one's family, neighborhood, culture) with a particular body (which includes heredity and physical makeup) one reaches certain conclusions, and the nucleus of life-style is formed. This summary set of conclusions grows out of one's experience, and is affected by heredity, environment, family constellation, relationships, and birth-order dynamics. These opinions, conclusions, and cherished values are the foundation of life-style and serve as a basis for living our lives. But so many ideas, opinions, and conclusions are mistaken certaintudes that make living our lives intelligently difficult to say the least.

Unitary Concept of Psychopathology

A dynamic similarity exists to all clinical psychopathology regardless of the classification and names that are used to describe them. These people can best be understood by an idiographic assessment, not a classification system. All the various psychopathologies (syndromes, abnormal behavior patterns) are efforts to find personal significance, but these individuals go about it in the "wrong way" with mistaken life-styles. As Adler would put it, they live on the useless side of life (Ansbacher & Ansbacher, 1956). A person's symptoms or syndrome are less important than the fact that he or she has erroneous ideas, a mistaken life-style, and is moving in the wrong direction in life. Such a person is a discouraged individual, without common sense and lacking in self-confidence. As I learned from Willard Beecher, my mentor and friend for a period of 15 years, a symptom is simply a person's unique way of falling apart.

A great many classification systems and typologies have been put forth by personality theorists and mental health professionals. However, when considered in its most basic form, just two broad ways of living exist which go in opposite directions. One is living with reality on its terms in a well-adjusted manner. The other is living with maladjustment of one kind or another, with private logic that makes no sense to anyone but to oneself. One makes for life, love, creation, and joy; the other for death and destruction. Either one feels adequate to life or not. One is either a giver and a maker or a taker and a breaker. A person is either a lover with good will toward others or a hater who displays hostility. Instead of live and let live, one's philosophy is kill or be killed.

Social Interest and Cooperation

Life is relationship. We are social organisms embedded in a social matrix. Our lives are filled with social activities of all kinds. Social interest in others and in all things that pertain to humankind, as well as the need for social cooperation, are necessary. In fact, they are absolutely indispensable. Social cooperation is essential for personal well-being and is also the key to the solution of the problems of humankind.

If the task is too great for one and beyond his or her capabilities, then cooperation is the answer. What one cannot do alone can be done in concert and cooperation with others. As has been recognized and exclaimed, in unity is strength. Since social embeddedness is the reality of life, an important aspect is to be able to get close to people and to work with them for the common good and welfare. Social relationships without cooperation, friendship, and love will raise havoc.

Before one can cooperate with others, the person must first be independent and self-sufficient. Self-reliance is a prerequisite for social cooperation (Beecher & Beecher, 1966). A dependent person cannot cooperate. One has to be able to carry one's own weight and hold up one's end of the bargain before entering into a social situation where teamwork and cooperation are necessary.

The more of an ego one has, in the sense of wanting recognition and to make an impression, the less social interest the person has. Ego spurs on competition and makes cooperation difficult, if not impossible. Ego makes task centeredness difficult because the individual is more concerned about looking good, or at least not looking bad. The alternative to possessing an ego is to have self-esteem. This means liking yourself at all times with no contingencies or strings attached. Liking yourself is independent of winning or losing, succeeding or failing, or other people liking you (Beecher & Beecher, 1966). As Dreikurs pointed out, if you don't like yourself now the way you are, you will probably never like yourself (Terner & Pew, 1978).

Diagnosis and Treatment

The purpose of diagnosis is not simply classification on the basis of symptoms. A more basic purpose is the understanding of personal and social dynamics. When a clear and adequate understanding exists, a prescription for action is known. Seeing is the action and knowing is the doing.

This theme is very much a part of the teaching and writing of Jiddu Krishnamurti (1960, 1972, 1976, 1983). The ideas of Adler and Krishnamurti are very compatible.

The purpose of Adlerian psychotherapy includes the following:

> learning to live with reality on its terms rather than on one's own terms;
>
> getting rid of mistaken certaintudes;
>
> seeing reality as it is and coping with it as one finds it;
>
> increasing self-reliance and lessening dependency;
>
> gaining self-confidence;
>
> increasing courage (the willingness to put oneself at risk and take a chance—to not be afraid to make a mistake or fail);
>
> getting rid of ego or the need to impress others;
>
> having genuine self-esteem in that one likes oneself at all times no matter how things are going and what others think of you; and
>
> increasing social interest and expanding the aptitude for social cooperation.

The interested reader can find much information about the theory and techniques of Adlerian therapy in other sources (Corsini, 1979; Dreikurs, 1973; Ford & Urban, 1963; Nikelly, 1971).

Adler once expressed the idea that the best we can hope to gain from therapy is to learn to make smaller mistakes. One should keep in mind the Chinese proverb that states that the start of a ten thousand mile journey is but a single step. The concern is with movement in the right direction and improvement, not perfection, and is with a strong sense of realism and optimism.

AN ADLERIAN INTERPRETATION OF
ANTISOCIAL PERSONALITY

Dreikurs (1973) distinguished among neurosis, psychosis, and psychopathy on the basis of a structural differentiation. This differentiation is based on the solution to the inner conflict between the spirit and the flesh. Adler spoke in terms of the conflict between common sense and private sense. Common sense refers to thinking that is general to the group, how one should act. However, note needs to be taken that common sense is not determined by the general consensus. It is dictated by the demands of reality. Usually the wise solution is generally known, but not always. Private sense conflicts with the general rules of common understanding and the needs of reality. Dreikurs expressed this well in the single sentence "I know how one should act, but this is only true for others; I myself gain more if I act differently" (p. 124).

Dreikurs (1973) explained how the neurotic, psychotic, and psychopath solve their conflict between common and private sense differently. "The neurotic person meets the conflict by hiding his private sense from his own consciousness, but not admitting his own tendencies when they conflict with his conscience, his common sense. He looks for alibis to excuse his social shortcomings" (p. 124).

The psychotic resolves . . .

> his inner conflicts by changing, temporarily or indefinitely, his recognition of the common sense. Through delusions or hallucinations, he can impress himself with an assumed reality, which then conforms with his private sense. He lives in a world of his own; in which his personal goals finds complete justification. He no longer adheres to the logic of life; he has his own logic shared by none. (Dreikurs, 1973, p. 125)

The psychopath,

> . . . unlike the neurotic, has no inner conflict. He has
> failed to develop sufficient common sense. He denies the
> logic of others, never accepts their values and morals, and
> considers his own interests as the only motivation which
> counts. Therefore, he needs no alibis and flaunts his own
> interests and tendencies. (Dreikurs, 1973, p. 125)

The neurotic is the only one of the three who is aware of
the conflict between private sense and common sense. The
psychotic avoids the realization by adjusting his or her common
sense. The psychopath has never developed common sense.

Case of Tom

In the DSM-III Casebook, an historical case is presented
(Spitzer, Skodol, Gibbon, & Williams, 1981). It is the case
of Tom, extracted from the book *The Mask of Sanity* by Hervey
Cleckley (1976). Tom is 21 years old. His manner and appearance
are pleasing and he creates a favorable impression. To reconcile
his appearance and manner with what one knows about his
extensive maladjustment and problems is hard to do. His
family and legal authorities were in hope that if some psychiatric
disorder could be discovered he might escape a jail sentence
for stealing. His maladjustment was evidenced in childhood.
He could never be counted on to keep at any task and was
frequently truant from school. Though he was generally provided
for, he stole from home and from others. He lied, made excuses,
and did not for long identify himself with others. At 14 he
became involved in stealing automobiles. At one point, as
part of a therapeutic maneuver, a car was bought for him.
Tom was also involved with forgery. He was sent to a federal
institution and underwent a program of rehabilitation. He
was impressive with his efforts to change his old ways and
was released. Some time afterward, his deceitful and
irresponsible behavior cmerged and continued. He has been
arrested and imprisoned approximately 50 times. On 150
other occasions, his family came to the rescue and made
good his small thefts, damages, and paid fines for him. He
never formed any substantial attachment for another person,
including the other sex.

Cleckley's diagnosis of Tom was Psychopathic Personality. The DSM-III diagnosis was Antisocial Personality Disorder (301.70) on Axis II (Spitzer, Skodol, Gibbon, & Williams, 1981).

Discussion

The comments by Dreikurs about the psychopath are very apropos to the case of Tom. As an Adlerian psychologist, I would like to know about family constellation and birth-order dynamics and to elicit early recollections and memories if possible (Adler, 1958; Lombardi, 1975). These memories serve as an express route to the identification of life-style. Even with the limited information about the case, one can easily become aware of several important matters. Tom is impatient and impulsive with extremely low frustration tolerance, a central trait of Antisocial Personality and Personality Disorders generally. He has low social interest and is more concerned with his interests and needs. Likely he has a very pampered personality and does not wish to defer the gratification of his needs. Tom is a hedonistic individual who does not feel guilty about what he does. He is quick to have an explanation or alibi/excuse for everything and projects blame to others so that he is always free from blame. No wonder he is so recidivistic in his behavior, and cannot maintain good interpersonal relationships. He has a big ego in that he lacks genuine self-esteem and is selfish with no concern or regard for others. He has a consistency of irresponsible behavior from childhood through his adult years, which is an important diagnostic consideration for DSM-III-R (American Psychiatric Association, 1987).

THE ADDICTIONS

At this point let us examine four addictions—alcoholism, drug addiction, pathological gambling, and obesity. In each situation a case is presented to illustrate an Adlerian interpretation.

Alcoholism

Case of Bill. Bill was in a hospital for detoxification, then in residence for a month in an Alcohol Rehabilitation

Program. As an oldest child, he had a lot of obligations and responsibility placed on him. He was a hard worker in and out of school, helpful, considerate, and a conforming and pleasing person. He assumed the mantle of parent as a teenager. Bill was a serious person for whom success and accomplishment were important. He was an achievement-oriented person. He is a perfectionist and likes to be in control and on top of things. He is idealistic in wanting things to be correct and done the right way. He has a strong fear of failure and, at times, he suffers from indecision. Bill has low self-esteem. He wishes he was very wealthy and is envious of others and their success. He does not like the unknown and unfamiliar. At one point in his life, he was confused and lacked direction; he started drinking at that time.

When an individual has involvement with a number of different therapists and programs, as Bill did, it is likely that one could receive several different diagnoses at different times. A review of his case history data reveals this to be the case. Diagnostic classifications are provided for Obsessive Compulsive Personality Disorder (301.40), Generalized Anxiety Disorder (300.02), and Alcohol Dependence in Remission (303.93) according to DSM-III (1980).

Discussion. A person does not always fit into a mold or classification schema. From social psychology we know that a stereotype does not allow for the exception to the rule nor take into consideration the fine points and nuances. A particular theory or test may not capture the essence of the person. This is not surprising since each individual has a unique quality and aspect. Generalities are limited, and allowances have to be made for seeing the uniqueness and individuality of a given case. Understanding psychodynamics and group dynamics must be a part of any diagnostic effort and classification system. The understanding of individuality cannot be avoided.

As is widely known, alcohol is not a stimulant; it does not exhilarate. Instead it dulls the mind and critical faculty. The human cortex has the cognitive function of memory, learning, and judgement. The cortex remembers, compares, and classifies. Alcohol knocks out the cortex, also called the "fault finder." It makes one less critical, and much of our misery stems from comparison. Alcohol is a convenient pain killer. Pain can come from many sources, including the hurt from frustrated ego needs. One of the reasons people get drunk is to kill the irritation, envy, and humiliation that comes from being unable to cope with the reality of what is here and now. Alcohol is the poor man's self-medication to combat anxiety, depression, envy, and other kinds of hurt. The normal state of functioning requires alertness, consciousness, and activity. Alcohol reduces this state and brings calm. Increased consumption brings stupor and sleep. The final stage of this anesthetic process is death. If an alcoholic has to confront anything that is painful without this anesthetic, he or she relapses and experiences what is commonly called the dry jitters.

Drug Addiction

Case of Harry. Harry grew up as a youngest child in a family of many achievers. The father was a highly successful professional person. The older siblings each had their claims to fame. The oldest child was a superstar whose picture was frequently in the newspapers. Harry was always in the shadow of stardom and felt insignificant, especially compared to the oldest child who was the family favorite. Growing up, Harry was pampered, spoiled, and babied by his mother. He got everything he wanted from his parents and older siblings. He felt no one ever really took him seriously. During childhood he was in a continuous parade of trouble and difficulties. Before the age of 15, he was classified as having a Conduct Disorder (American Psychiatric Association, 1987).

After the age of 15, his irresponsible and antisocial behavior increased in frequency, intensity, and seriousness. His mother felt he was weak and easily influenced by his peers. Harry had a charming personality, at least average intelligence, and was very popular with his friends. He was heavily involved with a criminal element. Compounding his difficulties was a serious drug problem. He used and experimented with many different kinds of drugs. His progression of drug use started with the weekend drinking of beer. He went to cough medicine, and onto pills and snorting, skin popping and mainlining heroin (which was his favorite drug). He did not like to use marijuana or other psychedelic drugs. Several drug overdoses were a part of his drug history. Harry was in numerous drug rehabilitation programs and spent many years of his life in jail and behind bars. His reputation as a drug addict and criminal was well known. Within the scenario of his family, if he could not be first best, he would be first worst. One of his outstanding traits was an extremely low frustration tolerance. Despite his horrible life experience and several broken marriages, Harry's case has a happy ending. He is now happily married, with a family, a well-paying job, and living a constructive life.

Discussion. Thomas Szasz (1974) stated

> Powerful "addictions"—whether to smoking cigarettes or injecting heroin—are actually both very difficult and very easy to overcome. Some people struggle vainly against such a habit for decades; others "decide" to stop and are done with it; and sometimes those who have long struggled in vain manage suddenly to rid themselves of the habit. How can we account for this? Not only is the pharmacology of the so-called addictive substance irrelevant to this riddle, but so is the personality of the so-called addict. What is relevant is whether "the addiction"—smoking, drinking, shooting heroin—is or is not a part of an internally significant dramatic production in which the "patient-victim" is the star. So long as it is (and if it is, the struggle to combat the addiction is only a part of the play), the person will find it difficult or impossible to give up his habit; whereas once he has decided to close down this play and leave the stage, he will find the grip of the habit broken and will "cure" himself of the "addiction" with surprising ease. (pp. 72-73)

From the point of view of a unitary concept of psychopathology, all abnormal behavior, not only addiction, is a mistaken and erroneous way to achieve a semblance of personal significance, save face, and avoid a painful clash with reality (Lombardi, 1975). Some people do bizarre things to get attention. Some people will do any number of things to be viewed and considered a star or a hero, even at the high price of self-destructive behavior. Some of the facets of drug addiction have been spelled out elsewhere (Gilbert & Lombardi, 1967; Lombardi, 1969, 1971, 1973; Lombardi

& Angers, 1967; Lombardi & DiPeri, 1965; Lombardi & Isele, 1967; Lombardi, O'Brien, & Isele, 1968).

Essentially, drug use and abuse are to be viewed as symptomatic of more basic and underlying problems. The extent of drug use indicates the degree of the underlying problem just as a thermometer indicates the degree of temperature in the body. Addiction and drug use are merely a sideshow activity, a way of avoiding the problems of everyday living (Beecher & Beecher, 1966). As I learned from Willard Beecher, there are no addicting substances, only people. Of course, some drugs like heroin produce physical dependence and tolerance, but the more important concept is psychological dependence. The problem is not a drug problem but a people problem. Drugs have no real power over people. To deal with the physical problem of addiction is relatively easy, but to cope with its psychological aspects is much harder. Also, like all other abnormal behaviors, addiction is an achieved disability. Work and effort are necessary to become what one is. Addiction is not without its purpose and gives the addict a sense of comfort, an alibi, and a semblance of significance and security.

Obesity

Case of Joan. Joan is hyper-obese, that is to say, more than one hundred pounds overweight. She is an only child and growing up she was pampered, indulged, and spoiled. Nothing she ever wanted was denied her. Her birthday was celebrated not yearly, but monthly. When she was single and living at home, her father made sure that her car was always filled with gas and washed. In the winter, he would start the car, and let the engine and interior warm up before his daughter drove it. This symbolizes the kind of care and child rearing she experienced.

Joan came into counseling because she was having personal and marital problems. She would like to lose weight but is not ready to stop indulging herself with the repetitive pleasure of eating. She is a very impatient person who cannot tolerate irritation or annoyance. Her preference is to eat something that does not have to be prepared or cooked. She prefers a candy bar to a steak dinner; and candy, cake, bread, and ice cream are her nemeses. Pleasure is important to her and she is a hedonistic person who relishes attention. She has an insatiable hunger for recognition and likes to have her way. Joan is very sensitive and quick to have her feelings hurt. She has practically no frustration tolerance and cannot stand delay or hassle of any kind. This is a hallmark trait of her personality. She often feels that she has been cheated, or at least not given due consideration. She likes to be active, dominant, and ascendant. People are not always compatible with her needs and wishes. She operates on the basis of greed, not need. Eating lessens her deprivation, dulls her hurt, soothes her envy, and makes her feel happy and good.

Discussion. With regard to the etiology of Joan's obesity, a major consideration is her wanting to be fussed over and catered to by others. The root cause of the problem is her belief that she has value and personal significance only when she is the focal point of attention and has whatever she wants or desires. Essential psychodynamics revolve around Joan's efforts to satisfy these needs. Whenever she feels frustrated and irritated, she looks for a quick fix to make things better.

Therapeutic goals that must be met in order to help Joan are as follows: increase patience and frustration tolerance, learn to place emphasis on we rather than me, become task centered instead of self-centered, and learn to live as an equal rather than a privileged person. Understanding the psychodynamics provides a prescription for therapeutic action to be taken. However, these are difficult goals to achieve and one can only move gradually in the right direction. In Adlerian psychotherapy the emphasis is on making smaller mistakes and striving for improvement, not perfection. Joan feels defeated and deprived and alienated from the world. With such frustrations, the desire is for instant rewards. And a fat person is an angry person because no one wants to be that fat. With a sensible approach in therapy, the prognosis is brightened with an element of optimism.

Pathological Gambling

Case of Frank. Frank was the second oldest of seven children, but the oldest boy growing up. He took charge of the younger siblings and is an individual who tends to dominate and be in control. He was very intelligent, independent, and somewhat rebellious with a mind of his own. The family lived in a poverty-stricken area. The house in which he lived was small. Instead of friends coming to his house to visit, he would go to their homes. His house had little space and poor facilities. His father had a small business, but Frank thought that his father was afraid to take chances to increase business. As an adult Frank was not at all conservative with either business or gambling. His preference is to gamble big or not at all. In the span of a few years, he has lost in excess of a million dollars.

He will not let anyone dominate or intimidate him. He wants to win and does not like to lose in anything he does or undertakes. He will put himself at risk, take a chance, and is not afraid to lose. He is confident that he will make good. In the past this attitude has served him well, but as so often happens in life, what is an asset can turn out to be a liability. Frank has a supreme ego in that the odds pertain to other people but not to him. He knows he is intelligent and unafraid, and thinks he has a special claim to fortune. He feels that he can do anything to which he puts his mind. For him money is important (he never had any when he was young); with money, he believes, you can do anything. It is security, and gambling provides an opportunity to show how smart and clever he is. He feels that he is insignificant as a person and has nothing, but with money he has power.

Discussion. In talking about the other addictions, the point was made that the basic problem is in the person, not in the substance used. If an obese person overeats food, this is not because food has some magical power or control over him or her. The problem is with the person, not the food. The same is true with all addictions, and this can be more easily seen with the problem of pathological gambling. The horseplayer doesn't get that way from eating horse meat.

REFERENCES

Adler, A. (1958). *What life should mean to you.* New York: Capricorn Books. (Original work published 1930)

Allport, G. W. (1960). *Personality and social encounter.* Boston: Beacon Press.

American Psychiatric Association. (1952). *Diagnostic and statistical manual of mental disorders (DSM-I).* Washington, DC: Author.

American Psychiatric Association. (1968). *Diagnostic and statistical manual of mental disorders (DSM-II).* Washington, DC: Author.

American Psychiatric Association. (1980). *Diagnostic and statistical manual of mental disorders (DSM-III).* Washington, DC: Author.

American Psychiatric Association. (1987). *Diagnostic and statistical manual of mental disorders (DSM-III-R)* (3rd ed. revised). Washington, DC: Author.

Ansbacher, H. L., & Ansbacher, R. R. (1956). *The Individual Psychology of Alfred Adler.* New York: Harper & Row.

Beecher, W., & Beecher, M. (1966). *Beyond success and failure.* New York: The Julian Press.

Carson, R. C., Butcher, J. N., & Coleman, J. C. (1988). *Abnormal psychology and modern life* (8th ed.). Glenville, IL: Scott, Foresman & Company.

Cleckley, H. (1976). *The mask of sanity* (5th ed.). St. Louis: C. V. Mosby.

Corsini, R. J. (Ed.). (1979). *Current psychotherapies.* Itasca, IL: F. E. Peacock.

Dreikurs, R. (1973). *Psychodynamics, psychotherapy and counseling.* Chicago: Alfred Adler Institute. (Original work published 1967)

Dreikurs, R., & Soltz, V. (1987). *Children: The challenge.* New York: E. P. Dutton. (Original work published 1964)

Ford, D. H., & Urban, H. B. (1963). *Systems of psychotherapy.* New York: John Wiley and Sons.

Gilbert, J. G., & Lombardi, D. N. (1967). Personality characteristics of young male narcotic addicts. *Journal of Consulting Psychology, 31* (5), 536-538.

Krishnamurti, J. (1960). *Commentaries of living* (3rd series). Wheaton, IL: The Theosophical Publishing House.

Krishnamurti, J. (1972). *You are the world.* New York: Harper & Row.

Krishnamurti, J. (1976). *Krishnamurti's notebook.* New York: Harper & Row.

Krishnamurti, J. (1983). *The flame of attention.* San Francisco: Harper & Row.

Leman, K. (1985). *The birth order book.* New York: Dell Publishing.

Lombardi, D. N. (1969). The special language of the addict. *Pastoral Psychology, 20* (195), 51-52.

Lombardi, D. N. (1971). Self-reliance and social cooperation. *Journal of Drug Education, 1* (3), 279-284.

Lombardi, D. N. (1973). The psychology of addiction. In H. H. Mosak (Ed.), *Alfred Adler, his influence on psychology today* (pp. 71-75). Park Ridge, NJ: Noyes Press.

Lombardi, D. N. (1975). *The search for significance.* Chicago: Nelson-Hall.

Lombardi, D. N., & Angers, W. P. (1967). First memories of drug addicts. *Individual Psychologist, 5* (1), 7-13.

Lombardi, D. N., & DiPeri, J. B. (1965). Heroin and God. *The Catholic Psychological Record, 3* (1), 35-38.

Lombardi, D. N., & Isele, F. W. (1967, February). The young drug addict. *NJEA Review,* pp. 28-29.

Lombardi, D. N., O'Brien, B. J., & Isele, F. W. (1968). Differential responses of addicts and non-addicts on the MMPI. *Journal of Projective Techniques and Personality Assessment, 32* (5), 479-482.

Mosak, H. H. (1968). The interrelatedness of the neuroses through central themes. *Journal of Individual Psychology, 24* (1), 67-70.

Mays, M., Sperry, L., Pancner, R. J., & Shulman, B. (1988, May). *Psychotherapy and psychopharmacology: A challenge for Adlerian therapy and theory.* Symposium conducted at the annual meeting of the North American Society of Adlerian Psychology, Seattle, Washington.

McCord, W., & McCord, J. (1964). *The psychopath.* New York: Van Nostrand Company.

Nikelly, A. (Ed.). (1971). *Techniques for behavior change.* Springfield, IL: Charles C. Thomas.

Rosenhan, D. L., & Seligman, M. E. P. (1984). *Abnormal psychology.* New York: W. W. Norton.

Sperry, L. (1989a). DSM-III-R and Individual Psychology: A case summary. *NASAP Newsletter, 22* (2), 1-3.

Sperry, L. (1989b). Differential therapeutics and IP: The case of Mrs. A. revisited. *NASAP Newsletter, 22* (3), 3-6.

Spitzer, R. L., Skodol, A. E., Gibbon, M., & Williams, J. B. W. (1981). *DSM-III casebook* (1st ed.). Washington, DC: American Psychiatric Association.

Szasz, T. (1974). *The second sin.* Garden City, NY: Anchor Press/Doubleday.

Terner, J., & Pew, W. L. (1978). *Courage to be imperfect.* New York: Hawthorn Press.

Watkins, C. E. (1986). A research bibliography theory. *Journal of Individual Psychology, 42* (1), 123-132.

Zax, M., & Cowen, E. L. (1976). *Abnormal psychology* (2nd ed.). New York: Holt, Rinehart and Winston.

CHAPTER 15

THE INDIVIDUAL PSYCHOLOGICAL VIEWPOINT OF THE PSYCHOSEXUAL DISORDERS

Dorothy E. Peven, M.S.W.

General observation leads us to the conclusion that much sexual behavior has motives that are not primarily sexual and often occurs for a great number of nonsexual reasons. Because the sexual act is a social function, it requires a significant amount of human cooperation. Furthermore,

> . . . It is hedged around with taboos, and it makes a demand for a degree of intimacy uncomfortable to many . . . [thus] all the factors involved in human relationships can often be found in full regalia . . . [and] sex becomes an arena in which many desires and strivings interpose and influence the sexual behavior itself. (Shulman & Peven, 1971, p. 28)

For example, one may offer sexual opportunities to another in order to gain an advantage, or sexual intercourse can be forced on an unwilling partner for the purpose of establishing dominance. In both cases the principle is unmistakable: The motive behind the sexual behavior is not at all a sexual one.

For the Individual Psychologist, the use of sex for purposes other than intimacy and pleasure is considered "neurotic" (Ansbacher & Ansbacher, 1978, p. 187). Neurotic behavior is designed to create distance between people and life's challenges, and all sexual disorders are to be understood as distance-keeping behavior. Such behavior is used by those who are not prepared for cooperation and feel too uncertain about themselves to take risks. Neurotic people look for guarantees, they "hesitate," find detours, and create imaginary obstacles in order not to "expose" themselves. Such people look for sexual situations in which their fictional superiority, security, and status will be preserved. Often, this leads to sexual behavior which appears incomprehensible to the observer since the behavior has so little to do with the sentiments of affection and closeness we usually associate with sex.

Adler was one of the first to understand that many sexual behaviors did not have a primarily sexual purpose. He especially pointed out that certain sexual behaviors like dominance and submission, or conquest and resistance, are "political" behaviors concerned with strivings for power and authority. Sexual conflicts, said Adler, were concerned with prestige and status, and he suggested that perhaps all sexual conflicts were really dominance conflicts. He observed that male dominance and female submission were socially determined and that the masculine protest was women's answer. He believed male/female relationships are a function of culture rather than a set of biologically determined behaviors. Not penis envy, but patriarchy and the superior position of the male in society leads to the masculine protest. The masculine protest is the compensatory behavior demonstrated by both men and women in response to the cultural tendency to overvalue masculinity and depreciate femininity.

Freud, on the other hand, believed all behavior was motivated by the libidinal energy of the id, and sexual disorders are the result of inadequately repressed libidinal urges which are expressed in ways repulsive to civilized societies. (Das Id unleashed!)

Earlier, Kraft-Ebbing (1939) had advanced the proposition that sexual disorders were "illnesses." It was not until the 1960s that Masters and Johnson (1966) reintroduced the topic of sex to the medical field.

Kinsey (1948) also made a contribution to the understanding of sexual behavior when, in the 1940s, he published a report that verified what many had long suspected; certain sexual behaviors which had previously been considered perversions were quite common, such as masturbation and adultery.

By 1980 those who study human sexual behavior had come to understand that some sexual disorders were of physical origin; for example, certain medications can produce penile erectile dysfunction (Kaplan, 1974). But others understood sexual dysfunctions as psychological in origin. Thus, the *Diagnostic and Statistical Manuals I, II,* and *III* all had/have sections called Psychosexual Disorders; that is, sexual disorders which have a psychological etiology.

This paper is devoted to a discussion of the Psychosexual Disorders as listed in the *Diagnostic and Statistical Manual of Mental Disorders, (Third Edition-Revised)* (American Psychiatric Association, 1987) with an emphasis on the views of Individual Psychology.

ADLER'S VIEWPOINT

At a time in medical and psychological history when the cycle swings toward chemical and physiological explanations for human behavior, a worthwhile procedure is to examine the ideas of a philosopher/psychologist who understood all behavior, including the language of the body, in psychological terms.

Adler said, "While we do take the organic foundations of eroticism fully into account, we must assert that the individual attitude is decisive for the erotic direction and shortcomings" (Ansbacher & Ansbacher, 1978, p. 183). He took for granted the existence of the sexual drive, understood that it could be disturbed by organic factors, but also believed that the expression of sexuality is indistinguishable from the personality. The manner and mode in which people choose to express their sexual inclinations are to be considered reflections of life-style phenomena.

Adlerians, with their belief in the ultimate perfection of society, also look at sex from an ethical point of view and ask for what purpose is the sexual behavior used. The criterion by which the act is judged is the social purpose for which it is used (Shulman, 1967). Sex is not only something that happens to people, it is something that they *do*, and they use sex in ways that are related to their own personal opinions about sex and life.

When sexual behavior is used to promote pleasure and love, to increase feelings of belonging, and leads to conjunctive emotions, it is socially "useful." Such sexual behavior is prosocial and brings people closer together.

Sexual behavior which is antisocial leads people away from the group, produces social isolation, is exploitative, and produces dysjunctive emotions. Antisocial sexual behavior promotes suffering in others and is considered socially "useless" behavior. According to Individual Psychologists, all destructive and unethical sexual behavior is socially useless (Shulman, 1967).

Human beings will reflect in their sexual behavior their own propensities. If they are competitive, they will be likewise in sex. If they are antisocial in nature, the sexual behavior will be self-seeking and exploitative. Those who have intoxicated themselves with thoughts of power, control, and dominance over others will use sexual behavior to reflect such purposes. Those who are not ready for the cooperation and mutuality of sex will often use one of the sexual paraphilias as their mode of sexual expression.

THE PSYCHOSEXUAL DISORDERS

The *Diagnostic and Statistical Manual of Mental Disorders* (3rd ed., rev.) (American Psychiatric Association, 1987) (DSM-III-R) in the section of Psychosexual Disorders cautions the clinician that the listed disorders are of psychological origin. The Disorders are divided into four groups.

1. The Gender Identity Disorders which are characterized by the individual's feelings of discomfort about his or her anatomic sex.

2. The Paraphilias which are characterized by arousal in response to sexual objects or situations that are not part of normative arousal-activity patterns.

3. The Psychosexual Dysfunctions which are typified by inhibitions in sexual desire or the psychophysiological changes that characterize the sexual response cycle.

4. A residual class of Other Psychosexual Disorders which shall not be discussed in this paper.

Gender Identity Disorders

These disorders include Transsexualism and Gender Identity Disorder of Childhood. The essential feature of the disorder is an incongruence between anatomic sex and gender identity. These people experience a sense of discomfort and inappropriateness about their anatomic sex.

The desire to be like the other sex is to be understood as a failure to identify oneself completely with the given heredity. It is a repudiation of nature. Jealousy of the role of the other, competitiveness, and an obsessive preoccupation with the idea that "something is wrong with me" indicate an attempt to turn life into a one-sided idea, a struggle to get the "ungettable." People who always want to be what they are not are people who find life uncomfortable and hostile, a place where there is difficulty fitting in since they are neither fish nor fowl nor good red herring. They are in the never-never land of Nowhere.

To always feel miserable and unhappy with the givens of life ("I am a man." "I am a woman.") lends itself to an excuse for avoiding responsibilities. Work is avoided, love is avoided, sex is avoided since " . . . the problems encountered in attempting to live in the desired gender role lead to extensive life difficulties" (American Psychiatric Association, 1980).

Paraphilias

The essential feature of these disorders is that unusual or bizarre imagery or acts are *necessary* for sexual arousal to occur. In the absence of paraphiliac imagery, sexual excitement or orgasm is not attained. The acts are "involuntary," repetitive, and involve the following:

1. preference for the use of a nonhuman object for sexual arousal;

2. repetitive sexual activity with humans involving real or simulated suffering or humiliation; and

3. repetitive sexual activity with nonconsenting partners, statistically, male related.

Because some of these disorders are associated with nonconsenting partners, the paraphiliacs are often in conflict with society. The behavior has legal significance. In DSM-III also is pointed out that often " . . . impairment in the capacity for reciprocal affectionate sexual activity and psychosexual dysfunctions are common" (American Psychiatric Association, 1980).

The Individual Psychologist is not surprised to find paraphiliacs in conflict with society, for these are antisocial people who go through life on the useless side. Their behavior is destructive and exploitative.

In DSM-III (American Psychiatric Association, 1980) is stated that virtually all reported cases of paraphilias are males, with the exception of sadism and masochism, which are still, however, reported more commonly in males. Individual Psychology understands this behavior as primarily culturally determined; that is, paraphiliac behavior is a manifestation of the Masculine Protest in the male. The onus of "performance" is usually on the male, and some men respond to this demand with behavior that means, "I don't *want* to perform the prescribed male role. I don't *want* to service women. Leave me alone!" And off they go on a neurotic, often "crazy" detour, away from "reciprocal affectionate sexual activity . . . " (American Psychiatric Association, 1980).

These are men who suffer from exaggerated feelings of inferiority. They see themselves as not capable of or not interested in "normal" sexual acts. Often, their self-image is "I'm weird" which enables them to claim a "disability grant": "Don't expect anything normal (like love and marriage) from me. I'm disqualified because I'm bizarre." Paraphiliacs demonstrate to the utmost degree the lack of preparation and willingness to join with others for mutually satisfying relationships.

Fetishism. Fetishism is the use of nonliving objects (fetishes) as the preferred or exclusive method of achieving sexual excitement. Fetishes tend to be articles of clothing such as female undergarments, shoes, boots, or, more rarely, parts of the female anatomy such as breasts.

When a man, rather than make a date with a woman, steals her shoe and masturbates into it, he is, in fact, disparaging and devaluing the female. Some unimportant detail is given sexual rank and dignity, such as the shoe. The female partner becomes object, not person; she is reduced to a pair of panties or a breast rather than a living, breathing human being with interests and feelings of her own.

Adler said the fetishist is dependent on incidentals for he or she displaces sexual pleasure onto the fetish. These fetishists have freed themselves from dependency on a partner for they "fear and [have a] feeling of weakness toward the other sex" (Ansbacher & Ansbacher, 1978, p. 180).

Exhibitionism and Voyeurism. The essential feature of exhibitionism is the repetitive act of exposing the genitals to an unsuspecting stranger for the purpose of achieving sexual excitement. No attempt is made at further sexual activity, only a desire to surprise and shock. While the voyeur gets sexually aroused by repeatedly looking at unsuspecting people who are naked, disrobing, or engaging in sexual activity, he or she also enjoys thinking about the observed people as being helpless and feeling humiliated if they knew they were being seen.

Adler suggested that both the exhibitionist and the voyeur are visual-types who sexually do not get beyond showing and looking.

> . . . the cowardliness and low degree of activity of these persons can be readily observed also in their other life relationships . . . Exhibitionism . . . always contains a battle against the norms of society. Furthermore, the urge to frighten and corrupt children through exposure of oneself, and to depreciate others by exposing them, places their deviation close to sadism. (Ansbacher & Ansbacher, 1978)

Zoophilia, Necrophilia, and Pedophilia. *Zoophilia* is the use of animals as the preferred or exclusive method of achieving sexual satisfaction. *Necrophilia* is intercourse with the dead. *Pedophilia* is achieving sexual satisfaction with prepubescent children.

Adler said people who commit sexual acts with animals are demonstrating an "extreme form of discouragement and despair regarding sexual possibilities" (Ansbacher & Ansbacher, 1978, p. 182). In these perversions there is no human partner with whom to interact; the partner is devalued into the form of an animal. Necrophiliacs, according to Adler, demonstrate a desire for the complete defenselessness of the partner and the "relief" from no obligations and no consequences. In this paraphilia, a complete renunciation occurs of the mutuality of sexual pleasure and an easily attained feeling of "unrestrained domination" over the partner. Like many paraphiliacs, the zoophilic, the necrophilic, like the pedophile, get a great deal of sexual satisfaction from the utter defenselessness of their victims. The pedophile also exploits the innocence and naiveté of children.

These people have completely failed at the challenge of relationships, have given up all hope of equal relationships, and have rejected society and the social field entirely. They seem to have lost all hope of mutually satisfying cooperative sexual pleasure. Their stance is distance, their belief is they cannot make it like others do, and so they choose the mistaken method of striving for dominance in "cheap" ways that are repulsive to society.

Sexual Sadism and Sexual Masochism. *Sadists* are people who become sexually aroused through inflicting physical or psychological suffering on another person. One of the following conditions must prevail if a diagnosis of sadism is to be made.

1. The sadist has inflicted suffering on a nonconsenting partner.

2. With a consenting partner, sexual excitement is achieved with humiliation or mildly injurious bodily suffering.

3. Body injury that is extensive, permanent, or possibly mortal is inflicted on a consenting partner for the purpose of sexual arousal.

Masochists are people whose preferred mode of producing sexual arousal is to be beaten, humiliated, bound, or dominated. Also possibly the masochist has intentionally participated in an activity in which she or he was physically harmed or life was threatened. The diagnosis is made only if the person engages in masochistic sexual acts, not merely fantasies.

What is to be said of people who derive their sexual pleasure from torturing others and watching them suffer? Adler said biographical accounts of these people show a

> . . . long history of erroneous training . . . [and that] the development of sadism and masochism always has an understandable history . . . the goal remains constant: the careful elimination and depreciation of the normal . . . [and] the continuous attempt to harden oneself against initial inhibitions, and to learn to love abnormalities and horrors and to elaborate on them. (Ansbacher & Ansbacher, 1978, p. 174)

Adler reasoned that sexual perversions had nothing to do with any innate abnormality of drives or instincts, and that paraphiliacs moved easily from sadism to masochism and " . . . from homosexuality into masochism or sadism [because] in every person are traits of defiance and obedience, cravings for dominance and submission, that serve the striving for significance" (Ansbacher & Ansbacher, 1978, p. 174).

Again and again the Individual Psychologist will point to the "cowardliness" of the sexual deviate, especially the sadist and pedophile. In fear of defeat before the challenge of sexual relationships and egalitarian love, they choose children or defenseless people for they see the least resistance as a threat to a very precarious self-esteem. Sadism is the quest for power in an "easy way" by people lacking the courage to meet the real problems of life. Sadists and pedophiles are people looking for " . . . the semblance of power, of a secret, often unconscious supermanliness in a situation of uncontested superiority" (Ansbacher & Ansbacher, 1978, p. 373).

The upward movement of all life in the direction perceived as superiority (significance) is seen by Adler even in the masochist. He said, "Even . . . in masochism, there is always a compensatory line upward, as when in flagellation the individual seeks a ridiculous justification in thoughts of penance." Adler thought that " . . . the partner falls under the dictates of the masochist . . . [and that] while the sadist is the triumphant vanquished, the masochist becomes the vanquished conqueror. (Ansbacher & Ansbacher, 1978, p. 373).

Even while discussing nonsexual behavior Adler pointed out that obedience, submission, and humility were meant to "capture and conquer the other." He saw the "feeling of weakness" as a weapon which secured dominance over the environment (Ansbacher & Ansbacher, 1978, p. 373). Haley, quoted by Ansbacher and Ansbacher, agreed and said that helpless behavior influences other people as much if not more than authoritarian behavior (Ansbacher & Ansbacher, 1978, p. 375) and gives the suffering victim control over what happens in a relationship. Dreikurs used to call this "the power of passivity" (R. Dreikurs, personal communication).

Shulman and Peven (1971) also believed that sadism is a perversion in which the desire to dominate is the most important issue.

> In DeSade's writings he constantly deals with what is, to him, the main issue in sex or in life; namely, one person gaining complete control over another. Sex is merely one vehicle for achieving this goal. The sadist is excessively concerned with the issue of personal domination, but it also seems he must reduce his [victim] . . . to the status of an object so he can use the object without having to enter into a relationship between equals (Shulman & Peven, 1971, p. 31).

They also pointed out the paradox brought up by Adler; that is, who dominates whom?

> When a man pays a prostitute to whip him until he is aroused, who is dominant? When a girl can only achieve orgasm if her partner brutalizes her, which one is dominant? Many sadomasochistic relationships are really cooperative endeavors in which, often, the masochist is the one who calls the tune (Shulman & Peven, 1971, p. 31).

Shulman and Peven (1971) also suggested that people who want to dominate others are those who are discouraged about the possibility of egalitarian relationships. Such people want to establish authority over others because they do not trust or believe in democratic relationships. They make themselves bigger by trying to make others smaller and feel threatened if they cannot dominate.

Homosexuality. Homosexuality is not listed as one of the paraphilias nor is it even listed in DSM-III-R (American Psychiatric Association, 1987) as a dysfunction (except when it is ego-dystonic). However, Adler wrote a great deal about homosexuality, and it seems appropriate to at least mention his views in a paper that discusses the Individual Psychological views on sexual behavior.

Adler firmly believed homosexuality is psychological in origin and that the reason for a considerable public sentiment against homosexuals is not because homophobics have repressed their own homosexuality, but because " . . . the logic of man's living together, the urge to preserve the human race—in short, the inherent communal feeling in man—is what compels people toward the energetic rejection of homosexuality" (Ansbacher & Ansbacher, 1978, p. 150).

According to Adler, homosexuals are those who early on decide that they are inadequately equipped for "normal" sexual behavior and have been inadequately prepared either because of improper education or faulty upbringing for the customary sexual role. Adler saw homosexuality as an " . . . expression of great discouragement and hopeless pessimism, states in which one is satisfied with life in a small circle, far from the other sex" (Ansbacher & Ansbacher, 1978, p. 155).

Adler also made the profound observation that throughout history, whenever an increase has occurred in the emancipation of women (as in Greek culture), an increase also has occurred in homosexual trends. Men, in an escape from feelings of insecurity, attempt to put distance between themselves and women; they take flight from females into exclusively male society.

The Psychosexual Dysfunctions

Psychosexual dysfunctions are characterized by inhibition in the appetitive or psychophysiological changes that characterize the complete sexual response cycle:

1. appetitive—the desire for sexual activity;

2. excitement—physiological changes;

3. orgasm—the release of sexual tension; and

4. resolution—the sense of general relaxation.

Usually disturbances are in both the subjective sense of desire and objective performance. The dysfunction must be both recurrent and persistent to be given a designation although some dysfunctions may be short-lived or episodic.

Other features included in the dysfunctions are fear of failure and "spectatoring" (the experience of dissociation, watching oneself during the sexual experience and judging the performance).

The psychosexual dysfunctions are as follows:

1. Sexual desire disorders

   a. hypoactive sexual desire disorder

   b. sexual aversion disorder

2. Sexual arousal disorders

   a. female sexual arousal disorder

   b. male erectile disorder

3. Orgasm disorder

   a. inhibited female orgasm

   b. inhibited male orgasm

   c. premature ejaculation

4. Sexual pain disorders

   a. dyspareunia

   b. vaginismus

5. Not elsewhere classified

   a. feelings of inadequacy

   b. distress (sexual orientation, repeated sexual conquests "Don Juanism")

Adler said bodily symptoms often contained an organ dialect, a nonverbal statement that reflects an internal attitude. "Adler considered all kinds of sexual dysfunction . . . impotence, frigidity, premature ejaculation, etc., forms of 'organ dialect.' 'While the patient's words, his thoughts and desires express his longing, his body, his sexual organs, speak another language, expressing his cowardliness'" (Ansbacher & Ansbacher, 1978, p. 376).

Behavior is understood as nonverbal language reflecting the apperceptive mode, the assumptive world — the life-style. All body functions are influenced by the style-of-life. The expression of the sexual urges are indistinguishable from the personality. "While we do take the organic foundations of eroticism fully into account, we must assert that the individual attitude is decisive for the erotic direction and shortcomings" (Ansbacher & Ansbacher, 1978).

Sexual dysfunctions are, therefore, psychological, and it is the meaning and the function of the disorder which is to be examined: what is being said in the language of the body by each particular dysfunction. Those who demonstrate failure, for example, may be saying "I can't do this correctly," or "I'm incompetent in this important area of life." Sexual dysfunctions are the unconscious expressions of deep feelings, beliefs, and values: the grammar of the genitals.

Those who fail to function sexually are making statements about their sexuality. Their "failure" has a purpose. The impotent male unconsciously says, "Go do it yourself, bitch!" and the woman suffering from frigidity just as unconsciously answers, "You leave me cold, Mister."

Adler said,

> In sexual impotence the patient's faintheartedness is materialized in a main line of life. He evades the very aggression that he longingly desires. While his word, his thoughts, and his desires express his longing, his body, his sexual organ, speaks another language, expressing his cowardliness. (Ansbacher & Ansbacher, 1978, p. 189)

Those who suffer from sexual dysfunctions rarely understand what their body is telling them. Men experiencing premature ejaculation feel as if they cannot restrain themselves: as if they have no control over their body functions. Yet one gentleman client explained his "quickie" by saying, "I was in a hurry." Most others explain their dysfunction by claiming inability to inhibit orgasm, "I tried but I couldn't control myself," or, as one unconsciously hostile client said when his wife complained, "I didn't time it."

Adler believed that women with vaginismus (an involuntary spasm of the vagina that interferes with intercourse) showed " . . . tendencies toward isolation, aversion against the feminine role . . . and a fear of loss of one's own value, of depreciation and disappointment . . . a passive resistance" (Ansbacher & Ansbacher, 1978, p. 186). They are saying "No!" to men.

The hostility inherent in the dysfunctions is part of the hostility of all neurotics, the negativistic, pessimistic view of life, the fear of failure, the demand for service from others, the desire to win without putting out effort. However, in the sexual dysfunctions, the body reveals the truth: They are not willing to perform under these circumstances no matter how much they protest their good intentions.

Sex requires cooperative endeavor and the failure to understand this is at the core of the sexual dysfunctions. Those who suffer are often concerned with themselves and their performance to the exclusion of all else. Oblivious to the desires, feelings, and messages of other, they concentrate on "How am I doing?" and forget the "what" in "What am I doing?" (Dreikurs, personal communication).

When people are self-absorbed, fearful of making a mistake, cower before "normal" interpersonal activities, afraid that others will find out what they are really like, is it any wonder that they falter before the sexual task? Sexual gratification with a loving partner requires cooperation and self-revelation, a risk of exposure to the eyes of another, for all imperfections are open to inspection. Therefore, all sexual disorders are to be understood as distance-keeping behavior, " . . . a self-imposed distance from the other sex" (Ansbacher & Ansbacher, 1978, p. 380) in those who are generally neurotically disposed, who experience discouragement about their sexual role or gender, and who have trained themselves in their disorders.

ETIOLOGY

According to Adler, those suffering from psychosexual disorders are neurotic. Neurotic people are those who live their lives in a mistaken manner; they compete rather than cooperate as they strive for personal superiority over others. Neurotic people lack social interest, do not contribute to the community, lean on others, and take no responsibility for their behavior. When faced with situations calling for increased courage, they feel a threat to their self-esteem, to their fictitious goal of superiority. Many neurotic people develop disabling symptoms which serve as "excuses" for failures (real or imagined) and the general unwillingness to move forward into life.

The psychosexual disorders are understood as neurotic symptoms because they are part of an arrangement enabling retreat from the challenge of love. Those people who have trained themselves from childhood on to falter before a challenge develop psychosexual disorders.

Adler recognized the possible organic factors which lead to sexual disorders and believed that "organ inferiority" is one possible factor in the developmental history of sufferers. Thus, some men may imagine their penis too small and develop feelings of inferiority vis-a-vis their genitalia. Any exaggeration of normal inferiority feelings can lead to a neurotic lifeline and the avoidance of intimacy and love.

In the case of sadism and masochism, Adler observed that some children experience sexual excitement during situations that create anxiety. He thought that in some children, an organ inferiority of the nervous system leads to sexual arousal as well as " . . . excitation of the intestines, bladder, etc., [and that] this mind-body connection holds a strong temptation to get oneself into threatening, prohibited situations, and to provoke them in reality or fantasy" (Ansbacher & Ansbacher, 1978, p. 175).

Pampering and neglect are also important etiological factors in the developmental history of neurotic people and, therefore, in the history of those with psychosexual disorders. Pampered children are those who have managed to secure for themselves a position in which everything comes easily and people do for them. All wishes and desires are quickly granted. These pampered children often grow up to be discouraged adults for they have never learned to take care of themselves. When the time comes (as it must to everyone) to face up to responsibility they respond with, "Who me? I've never had to do it before; why are you asking me now?" Never having developed their social interest, these children grow up to be ill-prepared and ill-equipped to deal with life-situation challenges.

Neglected children, on the other hand, may have never had the nourishing experience of the feeling of belonging and being cared for. Often no one has been available as a guide to the adult world to encourage these children to feel comfortable and at home in the world. Such children seldom develop feelings for others, they have never been loved themselves, and when the task of love appears they often do not understand how to behave. No guiding lines have been available.

Training and self-training play an important part in the development of the psychosexual disorders, for there could be " . . . no sexual deviation without training" (Ansbacher & Ansbacher, 1978, p. 393). The sexual disorders represent training from childhood on of people discouraged about their ability to function in a normal, gender-related role. The possibility of "exposure" is avoided by using devious modes of sexual expression.

Another factor in etiology is early sexual education. Adler believed that of the three life tasks, we are the least prepared for the task of love and marriage, and suggested education in preparation for the task of marriage with a special emphasis on training for "equality" (equal worth between the genders).

The first five/six years of life will, according to Individual Psychologists, determine the life-style. Since sexual disorders are an expression of the life-style attitude about sex and intimacy, the Individual Psychologist will look there for indications of developmental disorders. Obviously, the more cooperation is modeled in the home, the more prepared the child will be for relationship tasks as they arise throughout life. If mother and father model a harmonious marriage endeavor, their children will likely meet the task of marriage more easily. Other important early environmental factors include the relationship between the siblings and the family values as well as the parental models, family atmosphere, and cultural norms. Then, with the givens of heredity and environment, children will create their life-plan which, includes all gender-related concepts as well as psychosexual role-related behaviors.

TREATMENT

The concept of accepting responsibility for the creation of our own lives carries with it the implication that, once aware of our fictitious goals, we can choose to make changes. The task of the Individual Psychologist is to convince clients to make these changes and discover for themselves that life can be different, better, and more comfortable. The therapist's job is to listen, understand, analyze, illuminate, and, most of all, encourage.

In a discussion of treatment of sexual disorders, Adler suggested that the outcome was highly dependent on the ability of the therapist to encourage, thus, to rid the client of the always "erroneously created" psychological inhibitions. "The supreme remedy is change of the personality into a courageous, self-confident fellow man. Such a transformation should be carried out in a clear, deliberate manner, preferably according to the principles of Individual Psychology" (Ansbacher & Ansbacher, 1978, p. 191).

The treatment of paraphilia is difficult and little, if any, literature is available on it. If therapy is going to succeed, according to Adler, an essential component is to destroy the tie between anxiety and sexual arousal. He suggested that paraphiliacs train themselves to increase the connection between anxiety arousal and sexual excitement, and said paraphiliacs had to be encouraged to give up this "thrill" in order for therapy to be successful.

Based on the pioneering work of Masters and Johnson (1966, 1970), treatment of the psychosexual dysfunctions has evolved in the last few decades using a combination of behavior modification techniques as well as psychotherapy. A psychosexual history and anamnesis is taken, and on the basis of these psychological findings, a set of sexual techniques are prescribed. To describe each treatment developed for each sexual dysfunction is, however, beyond the scope of this paper. Therefore, the reader is referred to Kaplan (1974) and Masters and Johnson (1970) for a full description of the treatment for psychosexual dysfunctions.

CASE EXAMPLE

Case of a Divorced Woman

The following is a case study described by a psychoanalyst in Kaplan's book (1974, p. 142) but not to be construed as a recommended analysis by Kaplan (Kaplan, 1974, p. 144).

> The patient, a divorced woman of 40, sought help for the treatment of orgasmic dysfunction. She has great difficulty in achieving orgasms in the presence of a partner. Although she has sex frequently, she has climaxed with a man only on one . . . occasion of sexual intercourse. However, she is orgastic, albeit with some difficulty, on masturbation when she is alone. During masturbation she usually fantasizes scenes of a small girl being seduced by an older man. She is only attracted to men who are attached to other women or unavailable to her for some other reason.
>
> According to an analytic formulation, she is fixated at the oedipal phase. A married man evokes a father "transference." The man unconsciously reminds her of the ardently desired father she could never seduce, and her relationship with this man represents an attempt to *undo* or compensate for this original childhood traumatic defeat and frustration. However, old oedipal taboos inhibit her orgasm and if she succeeds in seducing the man away from her rival, she is gratified for a little while only before quickly losing interest. Her real unconscious goal, to finally seduce her father and thereby to humiliate her mother as she had felt humiliated as a child by her mother's dominant position, has only been attained symbolically. In fact, after she really succeeds in involving the man, her unconscious fantasy that he is her father is destroyed and she now becomes angry with him for "deterring" her from her quest for her "daddy." For this reason she ultimately destroys each new relationship. The patient's life is dominated

by this dynamic, which prevents her from enjoying orgasms and, more important, from forming a realistic and satisfying relationship with a man. In addition, anxiety, depression and inhibitions in other areas of life trouble this patient. (Kaplan, 1974, p. 142)

The Freudian psychoanalyst understands this case according to the belief that oedipal conflicts are universal and contain the idea

. . . that early incestuous experiences are the *only* causes of sexual conflict and that sexual dysfunctions are *always* caused by unconscious conflict, which is the *only* etiologic factor, and that *cure* must be predicated on *resolution* of these specific underlying conflicts (Kaplan, 1974, p. 144). Kaplan did not agree. (Kaplan, 1974)

The Individual Psychologist understands this woman in an entirely different way. Although no actual history is given, there appears to have been a struggle for power between this woman (when a child) and her mother. Apparently, the mother won, and the woman developed the idea that all relationships are a question of power and authority; that is, who will tell whom what to do and when. Her attraction to "unavailable" men is understood as a striving for dominance as she tries to prove her sexual prowess through cheap and easy flirtatious conquests.

The fantasy of a small girl being seduced by an older man demonstrates the woman's interest in dominance and submission. For, as Adler said, all behavior can be seen from an antithetical point of view; those who dominate are also those who desire submission. Perhaps the fantasy about the girl and the man *is* about the woman and her father, in which case we see this woman as one who wants to have everything, even the impossible, or to get the ungettable.

If this woman truly wanted her father sexually as a child and in her present fantasies, one can surmise she was a pampered child who believed nothing should be denied her. A hunch suggests she was the only child or the oldest as she is so interested in power and winning out over others.

The expression of sexuality in this woman is clearly one of keeping distance from the "other." Her *modus vivendi* is one of conquest and then disdain. She never enters a relationship as a full functioning partner willing to cooperate to the mutual advantage of both parties. She consistently demonstrates her unwillingness to share herself with another for fear of losing her power, her potency. Her orgasmic failure with men is her body's way of saying "No!" to full commitment. If orgasmic, she would feel she had capitulated in her battle with the world, would have "submitted" to the power of another.

The Individual Psychologist is not surprised to discover the woman suffers also from anxiety and depression as she is ill-prepared for the "ironclad logic of social living," and her life-style does not include enough feeling for her fellows for her to be able to live successfully and comfortably in any areas of her life.

For sexual gratification the woman uses masturbation. Even then she has difficulty attaining an orgasm. Everything about her screams loudly that *she will not give in* without a struggle, even to her own body. Her life-style is that of a person who must stay on top, who must always attain the semblance of superiority even if she uses devious methods. She has a mistaken opinion of herself and what it takes to be of significance, and her sexual dysfunction is designed to guard her opinion of herself as one who cannot be manipulated to submit. She thinks only of personal power over others and fails to understand the comfort in social interest, the feeling of belonging to the community.

Most likely this woman demonstrates the masculine protest in an invidious form. The overvaluation of the male and the undervaluation of the female leads many women to compensatory behavior. Some women become "Southern Belles" or superfeminine stereotypes of helpless women acting passive and seeking dependence. Others create an Annie Oakley response: "Anything you can do I can do better," and some become very angry and hostile and move against men by keeping their distance from them. To keep up the show of superiority and dominance over men, the woman in the case study has tried to eliminate men completely; she masturbates and she does it alone. What better way of telling men they are not needed, at all, for anything?

No doubt the woman tells herself she is trying; she sees men often and has relations with them. Her hostility is a secret from herself, and it is unconscious, for if it were brought into the light of common logic she would not be able to sustain it.

The Individual Psychologist would treat this woman as neurotic and understand her to be living according to her mistaken ideas about herself, life, and other people. Her sexual problems are the expression of her style-of-life. This should be explained and illuminated in the most friendly, encouraging way to help this woman increase her capacity to enjoy others, especially men, reduce the unresolved conflict with mother (if there was one), and arouse her interest in a life of equality and cooperation between the sexes—a life on the horizontal plane. The Individual Psychologist would like to help her end the frustrating, unhappy way she has been living.

CONCLUSION

Adler believed that because humanity is divided into two sexes there is an " . . . eternal compulsion toward one another" (Ansbacher & Ansbacher, 1978, p. 321), and it is possible to recognize the amount of courage and the capacity to cooperate by observing interactions between the sexes. Those who falter before the sexual challenge develop psychosexual disorders and are "neurotic." Psychosexual disorders are an attempt to run away from sexual obligations because neurotic people are hypersensitive and have developed limited social interest. From the Individual Psychological point of view, the sexual deviations are compensatory efforts created to alleviate a feeling of inferiority vis-a-vis sexuality and to exclude sexual commitment.

According to Adler, the sexual drive is the means by which men and women join together for the good of society. The interests of society, in general, are best served when the two sexes learn to cooperate in their sexual relationships, marry, and fulfill their obligations to society.

Ethical behavior is an important consideration for Individual Psychologists, as behavior is seen as either socially useful (for the greater good) or socially useless (without the interests of society). Adler looked at sexuality sub species aeternae (from the viewpoint of eternity) and said: "Love is the equal partnership between a man and a woman - where two are merged into one, a human dyad, reconciling the sex urge of each individual with the biological needs of the race and the demands of society" (Ansbacher & Ansbacher, 1978, p. 321).

REFERENCES

American Psychiatric Association. (1980). *Diagnostic and statistical manual of mental disorders* (3rd ed.). Washington, DC: Author.

American Psychiatric Association. (1987). *Diagnostic and statistical manual of mental disorders (Third Edition-Revised)*. Washington, DC: Author.

Ansbacher, H., & Ansbacher, R. (Eds.). (1978). *Alfred Adler: Cooperation between the sexes: Writings on women, love and marriage, sexuality and its disorders*. New York: Anchor Books, Doubleday & Co.

Kaplan, H.S. (1974). *The new sex therapy: Active treatment of sexual dysfunctions*. New York: Brunner/Mazel.

Kinsey, A. C. (1948). *Sexual behavior in the human male*. Philadelphia: W. B. Saunders.

Kraft-Ebbing, R. von. (1939). *Psychopathia sexualis: A medical forensic study*. New York: Pioneer.

Masters, W. H., & Johnson, V. E. (1966). *Human sexual response*. Boston: Little, Brown.

Masters, W. H., & Johnson, V. E. (1970). *Human sexual inadequacy*. Boston: Little, Brown.

Shulman, B. H. (1967). The uses and abuses of sex. *Journal of Religion and Health, 6* (4).

Shulman, B. H., & Peven, D. E. (1971). Sex for domination. *Medical Aspects of Human Sexuality, 5* (10).

PART V

CHILDHOOD AND ADOLESCENT DISORDERS

OVERVIEW

Adler (1930a, 1930b, 1930/1963) was very concerned with the welfare of children and, unlike Freud, worked with children and families quite extensively throughout his professional career. He strongly stated that:

> In the rearing of children there are some things which the parent or teacher must never allow to discourage him. He must never grow hopeless . . . he must not anticipate defeat . . . nor must he permit himself to be influenced by the superstition that there are gifted or ungifted children. Individual Psychology claims that the effort should be made with all children to stimulate their mental faculties by giving them more courage, more faith . . . by teaching them that difficulties are not . . . insurmountable obstacles, but as problems to meet and conquer. (Adler, 1930a, p. 227)

Individual Psychologists have continued this effort and philosophy, working with children and families to provide education, guidance, and therapy in numerous formats across a wide variety of settings (Mosak & Maniacci, in press). The three chapters in this section explore a variety of conditions.

Myers and Croake in Chapter 16 provide an extensive discussion of "Major Depressive Disorder During Childhood." They explore the relationship of childhood depression to adult depression, and present guidelines for working with these issues as well as conduct disorders. They provide an excellent, in-depth review of the current literature and research.

Croake and Myers in Chapter 17 provide an extensive discussion of "Attention-Deficit Hyperactivity Disorder and Specific Developmental Disorders." After an in-depth, broad review of the literature and current research in the field, they provide an Adlerian interpretation of the management and treatment strategies needed to deal effectively with such conditions. They highlight the interrelatedness of medication, family therapy, and psychological assessment in the treatment of these disorders.

Carlson in Chapter 18 presents the final chapter in this section, entitled "Eating Disorders." He reviews the various theoretical perspectives and integrates these with the Adlerian notions of purposiveness, sideshows, and the use of weakness in order to gain power.

REFERENCES

Adler, A. (1930a). *The education of children.* (E. Jensen & F. Jensen, Trans.). South Bend, IN: Gateway Editions.

Adler, A. (1930b). *The pattern of life.* New York: Cosmopolitan Book Corporation.

Adler, A. (1963). *The problem child.* New York: Capricorn Books. (Original work published 1930)

Mosak, H. H., & Maniacci, M. P. (In Press). Adlerian child psychotherapy. In R. J. Morris and T. R. Kratochwill (Eds.), *Handbook of psychotherapy with children.* Elmsford, NY: Pergamon Press/McMillon.

CHAPTER 16

MAJOR DEPRESSIVE DISORDER DURING CHILDHOOD

Kathleen M. Myers, M.D., M.P.H., M.S.
James W. Croake, Ph.D.

PURPOSE

The purpose of this chapter is to review the syndrome of Major Depressive Disorder (MDD) in children. The syndrome will be reviewed specifically according to diagnostic criteria of DSM-III-R (American Psychiatric Association, 1987), and more generally with respect to phenomenology. MDD during childhood is an example of a disorder which is usually observed during adulthood, but which may have an onset during earlier life as well. In this respect, Childhood-onset Major Depressive Disorder (COMDD) may be considered an example of a less common childhood disorder by DSM-III-R criteria.

HISTORICAL

The diagnosis of MDD in children has aroused controversy. Early observations of young children separated from their mothers suggested that they developed a depressive disorder. Many institutionalized infants appeared devoid of interest in the outside world, apathetic, inconsolable, with poor developmental progression, sleep disturbances, and weight loss. They were termed "anaclitically depressed" (Spitz, 1946). Anaclitic depression in infants is a rare disorder, probably limited to infants who have been institutionalized early in life. A syndrome suggestive of a depressed state was also described in young children separated from their parents during wartime (Freud & Burlingham, 1974). Many of their features resembled a grieving process. However, the persistent and disabling course of their affective responses was similar to a depressed state. Other young children whose mothers were depressed were also observed to reciprocate their mothers' depressive affect (Freud, 1946). A developmental schema of separation, protest, and despair has been proposed to account for the depressive affects noted in these children (Bowlby, 1980). Initially, these young children protest separation from their parents with crying; later they despair that they will ever return; and finally they detach themselves from human bonding. This response is less likely to develop if the young child receives personal substitute parenting.

However, these infantile disorders associated with parental separation have never been accepted as constituting the same depressive syndrome which is observed in later life. In the 1960s the argument was that children could not develop the full syndrome of depression, despite their ability to sustain a depressed affect (Rie, 1966). The development of a full depressive disorder purportedly required psychological structures that were not developed until adolescence. Depressive affects were attributed to normal developmental processes. Piaget's studies lend credence to this theory, since "formal operations" in cognition do not become well developed until adolescence (Croake & Catlin, 1986).

By the 1970s the terms "masked depression" and "depressive equivalents" were used to conceptualize depression in children (Lefkowitz & Burton, 1978). Conduct problems, hyperactivity, and multiple other maladaptive behaviors were thought to represent behavioral manifestations of an underlying depression. According to this idea children could become depressed, but they displayed their depression through typical childhood misbehaviors. The affective components were obscured by the behavioral components. The phenomenology of childhood depression then would differ from adult depression. Under this schema childhood depression was also overdiagnosed.

By 1980 several authors noted that depressive symptomatology could be distinguished from overlying "masking" behaviors when both occurred concurrently. They suggested applying to children the same criteria used to diagnose MDD in adults. The past decade has shown a growing consensus that children can experience an MDD syndrome which is consistent with adult diagnostic criteria, and which is distinct from self-limited depressive symptoms (Carlson & Cantwell, 1980a, 1980b; Kovacs, Feinberg, Crouse-Novak et al., 1984a; Mitchell, McCauley, Burke, & Moss, 1988; Puig-Antich, 1980). Other disorders may occur with the depression and may appear to "mask" depressive symptomatology, but these disorders are diagnosed separately.

In DSM-III-R (American Psychiatric Association, 1987) are delineated criteria for diagnosing Major Depressive Disorder (MDD) without reference to developmental period. If an infant, child, teen, or geriatric individual presents signs and symptoms that meet DSM-III-R criteria for MDD, then the diagnosis may be made, regardless of other coexisting diagnoses, symptoms, or behaviors. The application of DSM-III-R criteria to childhood psychopathology has led to the recognition and general acceptance of Childhood-onset Major Depressive Disorder (COMDD).

Nevertheless, controversy persists. Specific questions include whether COMDD represents a common nonspecific pathway during childhood to various adult Axis I or Axis II disorders? Alternatively, could it represent a self-limited syndrome phenomenologically similar to Adult-onset Major Depressive Disorder (AOMDD), which children will "outgrow"? Or does it represent an early-onset form of AOMDD syndrome? If the latter, does such early onset of MDD herald a more severe life course of the disorder? Current research is geared toward elucidating whether COMDD is the same disorder that at least 10% of men and 20% of women will experience at some time during their lives (Kaplan & Sadock, 1985), and how COMDD affects the holistic course of childhood development.

DSM-III-R CRITERIA AND
PHENOMENOLOGY OF COMDD

DSM-III-R Diagnostic Criteria

The diagnostic criteria for Major Depressive Disorder (MDD) are listed in Figure 16.1. A pervasively depressed or anhedonic state must be present in addition to four other signs and symptoms.

Mood. Most COMDD children will report a depressed mood. However, many may report a predominantly irritable mood, without a depressed one. This is the only developmental concession made in DSM-III-R to establish the diagnosis of MDD during the life span. The irritable mood may represent children's lesser ability to conceal the anger implicit during depressive episodes. Anger is even more commonly reported by MDD children than MDD adults (Mitchell, McCauley, Burke, et. al., 1988). It may also represent less discouragement. They have not withdrawn totally from others, but continue to seek interpersonal contact, however negative.

Children often do not recognize feeling depressed, especially if they have been depressed for a long time. Their current mood may be perceived as normal because they have lived with it for as long as they can remember. Hence, they can not identify a premorbid state. Inquiry into related symptoms like sadness, gloominess, crankiness, or unhappiness may elicit unequivocal confirmation of a depressed or irritable mood. About one-half of the time children cannot identify a reason for feeling so bad. It just seems to overcome them. They do not describe it as a reaction to life events. Other times they may offer a reason for their difficulties. Identifying a possible cause for the depression does not exclude the diagnosis. Many children who develop a depressed mood in response to a psychosocial stressor will not have a complete MDD syndrome, but rather will meet DSM-III-R criteria for

(Continued on page 464)

Note: A "Major Depressive Syndrome" is defined as criterion A below.

A. At least five of the following symptoms have been present during the same two week period and represent a change from previous functioning; at least one of the symptoms is either (1) depressed mood, or (2) loss of interest or pleasure. (Do not include symptoms that are clearly due to a physical condition, mood-incongruent delusions or hallucinations, incoherence, or marked loosening of associations.)

    1. depressed mood (or can be irritable mood in children and adolescents) most of the day, nearly every day, as indicated by subjective account or observation by others

    2. marked diminished interest or pleasure in all, or almost all, activities most of the day, nearly everyday (as indicated either by subjective account or observation by others of apathy most of the time)

    3. significant weight loss or weight gain when not dieting (e.g., more than 5% of body weight in a month), or decrease or increase in appetite nearly every day

    4. insomnia or hypersomnia nearly every day

    5. psychomotor agitation or retardation nearly every day (observable by others, not merely subjective feelings of restlessness or being slowed down)

    6. fatigue or loss of energy nearly every day

    7. feelings of worthlessness or excessive inappropriate guilt (which may be delusional) nearly every day (not merely self-reproach or guilt about being sick)

    8. diminished ability to think or concentrate, or indecisiveness, nearly every day (either by subjective account or as observed by others)

    9. recurrent thoughts of death (not just fear of dying), recurrent suicidal ideation without a specific plan, or a suicide attempt or a specific plan for committing suicide

B.   1. It cannot be established that an organic factor initiated and maintained the disturbance

    2. The disturbance is not a normal reaction to the death of a loved one (Uncomplicated Bereavement)

Figure 16.1. Diagnostic Criteria for Major Depressive Disorder. Reproduced by permission from DSM-III-R, American Psychiatric Association, 1987.

Figure 16.1. Continued.

C. At no time during the disturbance have there been delusions or hallucinations for as long as two weeks in the absence of a prominent mood symptoms (i.e., before the mood symptoms developed or after they have remitted).

D. Not superimposed on Schizophrenia, Schizophreniform Disorder, Delusional Disorder, or Psychotic Disorder Not Otherwise Specified (NOS).

Major Depressive Episode codes: fifth-digit code numbers and criteria for severity of current state of Bipolar Disorder, Depressed, or Major Depression:

1. Mild:
Few, if any, symptoms in excess of those required to make the diagnosis, *and* symptoms result in only minor impairment in occupational functioning or in usual social activities or relationships with others.

2. Moderate:
Symptoms or functional impairment between "mild" and "severe."

3. Severe, without Psychotic Features:
Several symptoms in excess of those required to make the diagnosis, *and* symptoms markedly interfere with occupational functioning or with usual social activities or relationships with others.

4. With Psychotic Features:
Delusions or hallucinations. If possible, specify whether the psychotic features are *mood-congruent* or *mood-incongruent.*

Mood-congruent psychotic features:
Delusions or hallucinations whose content is entirely consistent with the typical depressive themes of personal inadequacy, guilt, disease, death, nihilism, or deserved punishment.

Mood-incongruent psychotic features:
Delusions or hallucinations whose content does not involve typical depressive themes of personal inadequacy, guilt, disease, death, nihilism, or deserved punishment. Included here are such symptoms as persecutory delusions (not directly related to depressive themes), thought insertion, thought broadcasting, and delusions of control.

5. In Partial Remission:
Intermediate between "In Full Remission" and "Mild," and no previous Dysthymia. (If Major Depressive Episode was superimposed on Dysthymia, the diagnosis of Dysthymia alone is given once the full criteria for a Major Depressive Episode are no longer met.)

Figure 16.1. Continued.

---

6. In Full Remission:
    During the past six months no significant signs or symptoms of the disturbance.

0. Unspecified

    Specify chronic if current episode has lasted two consecutive years without a period of two months or longer during which there were no significant depressive symptoms.

    Specify if current episode is *Melancholic Type.*

Diagnostic Criteria for Melancholic Type:

The presence of at least five of the following:

1. loss of interest or pleasure in all, or almost all, activities

2. lack of reactivity to usually pleasurable stimuli (does not feel much better, even temporarily, when something good happens)

3. depression regularly worse in the morning

4. early morning awakening (at least two hours before usual time of awakening)

5. psychomotor retardation or agitation (not merely subjective complaints)

6. significant anorexia or weight loss (e.g., more than 5% of body weight in a month)

7. no significant personality disturbance before first Major Depressive Episode

8. one or more previous Major Depressive Episodes followed by complete, or nearly complete, recovery

9. previous good response to specific and adequate somatic antidepressant therapy, e.g., tricylics, ECT, MAOI, lithium

---

an Adjustment Disorder with Depressed Mood. However, others will meet the full diagnostic criteria. Lack of an identifiable stressor is not part of the diagnostic criteria. Whether or not a stressor is identified, COMDD children usually report that their depressed or irritable mood lacks reactivity, i.e., their mood does not improve in response to positive external events (Mitchell, McCauley, Burke et al., 1988). The disturbance seems pervasive to them. Parents, however, may note objective evidence of a favorable response to positive events.

Careful differentiation must be made of these mood states from the transitory unhappiness demonstrated by all children at stressful times during development. Such transitory unhappiness often reflects Goal I, attention getting, or Goal II, desire to dominate the adult, misbehavior. Depression communicates greater discouragement and more frequently communicates Goal III misbehavior, in which the child feels hurt and wants to hurt back, or Goal IV misbehavior, in which the child wants to be left alone without the burden of expectations (Dreikurs, 1958).

Anhedonia. Anhedonia does not appear to occur any more frequently in children than in adults, but it seems more striking (Mitchell, McCauley, Burke et al., 1988). Adults are not accustomed to children lacking interest in any activities. Children are often better able to identify anhedonia than a depressed mood in themselves. They easily can understand feeling bored, not wanting to do anything, and that nothing is fun anymore. Sometimes they will state that they do have interests, but do not feel like pursuing them. They may expect others to provide them with interesting activities. Parents often feel that they are supposed to entertain their depressed children. Some children do continue to participate in activities, but with less fervor or pleasure. Others, especially eldest children, may continue with their perceived "obligations," especially if they hold positions of responsibility within their families. Their enjoyment of these activities must be determined. Care also must be taken to not confuse anhedonia with passivity, or with Goal IV misbehavior (Dreikurs, 1973).

Other Diagnostic Symptoms. Depressed or irritable mood and anhedonia are necessary but not sufficient criteria to diagnose the MDD syndrome. A total of five signs and symptoms of the nine listed in DSM-III-R must be present. Compared to adults children endorse significantly more guilt and have more suicide attempts, although the rate of suicidal ideation appears the same (Mitchell, McCauley, Burke et al., 1988). Often these children will express their guilt as feeling responsible for things they did not do. Suicide attempts are typically of mild severity, but the children clearly identify wanting to die, not just wanting to hurt themselves. Some make serious attempts, like hanging. However, usually these attempts are made with an adult nearby. Frequently, they are enacted impulsively. Reasons given often typically include reprimand by a parent, feeling unloved, or feeling ridiculed by peers. Frequently, they state that they do not know why they made an attempt.

COMDD children endorse decreased appetite, weight loss, and early morning awakening, or terminal insomnia, significantly less frequently than adults (Mitchell, McCauley, Burke et al., 1988). Difficulty in getting to sleep, called initial insomnia, is common in MDD children and occurs at a rate comparable to MDD adults. Unlike AOMDD adults, children do not typically report their mood to be at its lowest ebb upon awakening and improving as the day progresses. Children do not generally describe any pattern of diurnal variability of their mood. Rather they describe a more consistently unhappy mood regardless of the time of day. Some children may state that their mood worsens during school hours. Careful inquiry must be made as to whether this is also true on weekends and whether their mood improves if they stay home from school. If the worsening of mood is related to school attendance, it is not considered a diurnal variation.

Psychotic Symptoms. DSM-III-R specifies that Major Depressive Episode, With Psychotic Features is diagnosed if the individual experiences delusions or hallucinations during the depressive episode. Approximately 25% of AOMDD is of the psychotic subtype (Spitzer, Endicott, & Robins, 1978). The presence of such psychotic symptoms indicates greater severity of the depression and, therefore, greater self-absorbance and lower social interest. They do not feel that they have a place in society. The delusions are further categorized as congruent or incongruent with the depressive mood. Mood-congruent delusions are consistent with the depressive themes of personal inadequacy, guilt, death, nihilism. Mood-incongruent delusions are those which emphasize thought control, paranoia, and other nondepressive themes. They are more commonly endorsed in schizophreniform psychoses.

Psychotic symptoms may occur during a COMDD episode (Chambers, Puig-Antich, Tabrizi et al., 1982; Freeman, Poznanski, Grossman et al., 1985; Mitchell, McCauley, Burke et al., 1988). However, hallucinations are the only commonly reported psychotic symptom. These hallucinations are generally mild in severity, and frequently nondistressing, but may include self-destructive commands. COMDD children rarely report the mood-congruent delusions, mood-incongruent delusions, or other psychotic symptoms which characterize psychotically depressed adults.

Because psychotic disorders occur frequently in the parents of children who hallucinate, regardless of their diagnosis, (Del Beccarro, Burke, & McCauley, 1988), COMDD children who hallucinate may be expressing a psychotic proclivity (Kemph, 1987). However, hallucinations are endorsed by children with various psychopathologies and even by normal children (Kotsopoulos, Kanigsberg, Cote, & Fiedorowicz, 1987). This nonspecificity of childhood hallucinations, their mild nature, and the lack of delusional thinking suggests that COMDD hallucinosis falls short of the psychotic depression syndrome which is observed in adults. However, according to DSM-III-R, COMDD children who endorse hallucinations, and especially hallucinations with depressive themes such as self-destructive acts, should be considered to meet criteria for Major Depressive Episode With Psychotic Features.

Phenomenologically, hallucinations reported by COMDD children represent greater discouragement. Psychotically depressed children are demonstrating even greater reluctance to meet their life tasks than those COMDD children without psychotic features.

Sources of Information for Establishing a Diagnosis. Information from both the child and parents is crucial to making the diagnosis. Children better describe subjective distress which their parents often underestimate, since they just can not imagine that their children feel as discouraged as they do. Parents, however, better describe objective behavioral signs which the children underreport, since children are usually not aware of the distress their misbehaviors cause others (Herjanic, Herjanic, Brown et al., 1975; Herjanic & Reich, 1982). When they are aware, they often feel guilty. This contrasts with childhood disturbances in which children do not seem to care how they affect others. Adjunctive information from auxiliary sources such as daycare, school, friends, or other family members is also helpful in establishing the diagnosis of MDD in children. In particular, teachers often have a better opportunity than parents to observe the MDD child's behavior around peers. Since depressed children feel alienated and withdraw from social activities even more than children with other psychiatric disorders, teachers can provide perspective on the extent to which the child is meeting responsibility to the life tasks of work, friendship, and community.

Related Signs and Symptoms

Cognitive Symptoms. In addition to the DSM-III-R criteria, other symptoms typically characterize the depressed state in adults, contributing to MDD phenomenology. Depressed adults demonstrate a characteristic cognitive schemata in which they recurrently interpret themselves, their experiences, and the future in a negative manner (Kovacs & Beck, 1978). In Adlerian language they lack courage, are overambitious and pessimistic.

Courage is the willingness to continue making efforts toward positive goals. *Overambition* is the opposite of self-confidence, characterized by the setting of unrealistic goals. *Pessimism* is the conviction that whatever one attempts to accomplish, it will not come to a happy ending.

Depressed children may be similarly discouraged. They set unattainable goals, become increasingly self-absorbed, and give up on themselves and life. Like depressed adults, these children also may express negative views of themselves, and exaggerate negative aspects of themselves, others, and the environment. Frequently, they see success as external to themselves and unpredictable. They do not feel in control of their fate. They harshly criticize themselves. As a result, depressed children feel hopeless, without self-control, and with little self-esteem compared to children with other psychiatric disorders (Haley, Fine, Marriage, Moretti, & Freeman, 1985; Kazdin, Unis, & French, 1983; McCauley, Mitchell, Burke, & Moss, 1988). The impaired self-esteem is profound and much more frequently endorsed by MDD children than MDD adults (Mitchell, McCauley, Burke et al., 1988). This probably reflects children's lack of previously established cognitive mechanisms to mitigate the depressed state. However, lowered self-esteem is common to many childhood psychiatric disorders and may not be specific to the depressed state. Rather, the pervasiveness of the impaired self-esteem may be that which characterizes depression. Maturation does not appear to make matters better. Depressed adolescents report even lower self-concept and greater depressive attributional style than depressed children (McCauley, Mitchell, Burke, & Moss, 1988).

These cognitive distortions, or negative self-talk, which result in mistakes relative to self and others, appear to resolve upon recovery from MDD, suggesting specificity to the depressed state. They do not necessarily characterize the life-style. In this respect, the cognitive distortions resemble the Four Goals of Misbehavior. There is no such thing as Goal I, Goal II, Goal III, or Goal IV children. Rather discouraged children demonstrate any of the Goals of Misbehavior to take unfair advantage of others at the moment. Similarly, negative self-talk is a *junctim,* a thought used to intensify an emotion, that guides children away from the life task that they are confronting at that instant (Adler, 1956).

This ability to "catastrophize" (Ellis, 1973) is what many cognitively-oriented theorists view as a necessary prerequisite to the development of depression. The idea assumes that one can only take the depressive mental stance by going beyond the present moment and thinking to past apperceived negative situations and assuring oneself that the future will be even worse. The particular way in which one abstracts beyond the moment is in accord with one's life-style, one's characteristic pattern of movement.

Consistent with the Adlerian notion of holism, as the individual becomes discouraged, cognitive abilities are recruited into the movement toward depression. Children use their developing cognitive abilities to confirm their discouraged perception of life. Teens can emphasize their greater abstraction and conceptual ability to further show the ways in which they can be discouraged. All movement is toward an individual life-style goal, one's reason to be.

Somatic Symptoms. One-quarter to one-third of AOMDD individuals present with somatic complaints and deny a depressed mood (Katon, Kleinman, & Rosen, 1982a, 1982b). These adults minimize the affective and cognitive components of their depression, while selectively emphasizing somatic symptoms (Katon, Kleinman, & Rosen, 1982a, 1982b).

Somatic complaints are also frequently reported by COMDD children (McCauley, Carlson, & Calderon, 1991). Children are much more likely to endorse somatic complaints than are adults or children with other psychiatric disorders (Mitchell, McCauley, Burke et al., 1988). They may deny depression, stating that pain is the only thing distressing them (Hershberg, Carlson, Cantwell, & Strober, 1982; Hughes, 1984; Kashani, Lababidi, & Jones, 1982; Mitchell, McCauley, Burke et al., 1988). Some may endorse both depression and physical symptoms. Hypochondriasis, however, is uncommon. The somatic complaints appear specific to the depressed state, since they resolve with remission of the MDD (Mitchell, McCauley, Burke et al., 1988). This somatization may lead to low level discomfort that minimally interferes with life activities, or to severe pain that interferes with most activities, especially with regular school attendance. The most common types of physical symptoms endorsed are abdominal pain, headaches, and chest pain.

The physical symptoms communicate these children's discouragement with their perceived inferiority. They are inadequately prepared for life's tasks. In their families of origin they have found that the reporting of physical symptoms allows them to escape responsibilities of school, friendship, and community involvement. When they do participate in these life tasks, they heroically surmount their feelings of inferiority by going on in spite of their claimed disability.

Concurrent Diagnoses

Phenomenologically, AOMDD frequently coexists with other DSM-III-R diagnoses. The most common are Dysthymic Disorder (DD) and the Anxiety Disorders, specifically Panic Disorder (PD), Phobias, and Generalized Anxiety Disorder (GAD).

Overall, dual diagnoses are made in more than one-half of COMDD children (Kovacs, Feinberg, Crouse-Novak et al., 1984a; Mitchell, McCauley, Burke et al., 1988). As with AOMDD, the most common diagnoses concurrent with COMDD are DD and Anxiety Disorders, especially Separation Anxiety Disorder (SAD). GAD occurs less commonly. Children with dual diagnoses do more poorly in meeting their life tasks than children with MDD alone (Mitchell, McCauley, Burke et al., 1988).

Dysthymic Disorder. DD affects about 38% of COMDD children (Kovacs, Feinberg, Crouse-Novak et al., 1984a), which compares closely with the 26% reported in AOMDD patients (Keller & Shapiro, 1982). The DD may precede or follow an acute MDD episode, similar to the adult pattern. COMDD-DD children appear to have a poorer course than those with COMDD alone, consistent with the poor prognosis noted for adult "double depression" (Akiskal, 1983; Keller & Shapiro, 1982; Miller, Norman, & Dow, 1986). Their lives are experienced as constant disappointment with too many expectations which they believe they cannot meet (DD), and which will only get worse (MDD).

Anxiety Disorders. Moderate to severe anxiety complicates the course of approximately half of AOMDD adults (Breier, Charney, & Heninger, 1985; Fawcett & Kravity, 1983; Leckman, Merikangas, Pauls et al., 1983). DSM-III-R is an improvement over previous diagnostic manuals, but a deficit is its lack of a mixed depression/anxiety diagnosis to describe this group of individuals.

Similarly, more than one-half of COMDD patients report anxiety symptoms (Hershberg, Carlson, Cantwell et al., 1982; Puig-Antich & Rabinovich, 1986). SAD, the most common anxiety disorder in childhood, is diagnosed in approximately 40% of COMDD children (Kovacs, Feinberg, Crouse-Novak et al., 1984a; Mitchell, McCauley, Burke et al., 1988; Puig-Antich & Rabinovich, 1986). Other anxiety disorders occur much less frequently. It remains to be shown whether development may mediate the behavioral and experiential manifestations of anxiety. For example, Panic Disorder and Agoraphobia, which are frequently experienced by AOMDD adults, but rarely by COMDD children, may be adult expressions of earlier SAD (Orvaschel & Weissman, 1986).

Separation anxiety is children's distress at being away from a nurturant adult figure. Their anxiety serves to control this significant other. They overcompensate feelings of inferiority by demonstrating how they can control another to their will. They demand the privilege of having their own mentor. They have learned that in their families the expression of such anxiety brings the special place of having no expectations placed on them (Goal IV misbehavior).

Conduct Disorders. Many COMDD children, particularly COMDD boys, misbehave sufficiently to meet diagnostic criteria for Conduct Disorder (CD) (Kovacs, Feinberg, Crouse-Novak et al., 1984a; Marriage, Fine, Moretti, & Haley, et al., 1986; Mitchell, McCauley, Burke et al., 1988; McGee & Williams, 1988; Puig-Antich, 1982). Because CD is a childhood diagnosis, a direct comparison of COMDD-CD children with AOMDD adults is not possible. CD is a precursor to Antisocial Personality Disorder (APD) in adulthood (Robins, 1978). Whether the co-occurrence of COMDD with CD also leads to adult APD or moderates the outcome is unknown.

Children who develop CD concurrently with MDD will often stop their CD misbehaviors upon recovery from depression (Puig-Antich, 1982), suggesting that CD may be an expression of MDD in some children. On the other hand, some COMDD children's depression develops secondary to a well-established CD (Anderson, Williams, McGee, & Silva, 1987). Other children appear to develop CD subsequent to a MDD episode (McGee & Williams, 1988). These sequences suggest that some COMDD-CD children may be evolving primary character disturbances (Axis II psychopathology) with secondary depression.

In adults 40% of AOMDD occurs secondary to another psychiatric disorder (Spitzer, Endicott, & Robins, 1978; Weissman, Pottenger, Kleber et al., 1977). Some COMDD children develop their depression secondary to Axis III medical illnesses as diabetes mellitus; or Axis I disorders as substance abuse or Attention-deficit Hyperactivity Disorder (Akiskal, Downs, & Jordan, et al., 1985; Anderson, Williams, McGee et al., 1987; Biederman, Munir, Knee et al., 1987); or Axis II Specific Developmental Disorders. COMDD secondary to an evolving Axis II character disorder is also possible. DSM-III (American Psychiatric Association, 1980) did not allow character disorders to be diagnosed in children, precluding consideration of such a diagnostic schema. A character disorder represents deficits in personality. But personality is not fully developed in children. DSM-III reasoned that a character disorder could not, therefore, be appropriately diagnosed in children. However, DSM-III-R has empirically removed this limitation, since many children and adolescents do demonstrate sufficiently dysfunctional personality structure to be considered characterologically impaired. Continuity between childhood and adulthood psychopathology, as observed between CD and APD, further supports the validity of diagnosing personality disorders at earlier developmental stages (Robins, 1978).

How the co-occurrence of MDD affects outcome of CD is unknown. It may attenuate Axis II Cluster B personality disorders away from APD toward other Cluster B disorders such as Borderline Personality Disorder (BPD). In adults, BPD is frequently associated with episodic MDD (Akiskal, 1981). Several studies have reported that COMDD-CD children meet criteria for BPD (Greenman, Gunderson, Cane et al., 1986; McManus, Lerner, Robbins et al., 1984).

COMDD-CD children believe that the world owes them. They are not constrained by the usual social mores. COMDD children with other concurrent diagnoses continue to make some movement toward meeting their life tasks, albeit within the constraints of their private logic. COMDD-CD children, however, make no movement toward meeting their life tasks. They do not feel part of the larger human community. They want the world to grant them special exemption.

Physiology and Organ Inferiority

Multiple studies have demonstrated physiological abnormalities in the neuroendocrine system of AOMDD adults during the depressed state. Three major areas of functioning are involved. First, sleep is disrupted, particularly the onset of rapid eye movement (REM) sleep. These abnormalities are well documented with sleep electroencephalography (S-EEG) (Gillin, Duncan, Murphy et al., 1981). Second, neuroreceptors which control the output of hormones and other neuroendocrine substances are blunted or "downregulated" during the depressed state. A failure to appropriately regulate output of these body chemicals results (Willner, 1985). Affected hormones and other circulating substances include, among others, growth hormone, cortisol, epinephrine (adrenalin), norepinephrine, serotonin, and beta-endorphin. Third, the hypothalamic-pituitary-adrenal axis (HPA), which controls basic bodily functions, is overactive during MDD resulting in excessive production of selected hormones (Arans, Baldessarini, & Ornsteen, 1985). These abnormalities are not present in all AOMDD adults. They probably reflect in part the severity of the depression and more endogenous features. An adult who develops these abnormalities during a severe depression that has gone untreated for some time may not develop them during another depression which has been treated early in its course. These neuroendocrine abnormalities are present during the depressed state, but not during recovery. Therefore, they reflect the acute depressed state, rather than preexisiting physiologic traits or organ inferiority.

However, the presence of an organ inferiority in MDD is supported by inheritance studies. Methods for investigating possible genetic transmission of psychological disorders have included twin studies, family history studies, direct family pedigree studies, and adoption studies. Most of these studies have been conducted with adults in order to allow affected individuals sufficient time to develop the disorder. MDD has a lifetime risk, unlike many other DSM-III-R disorders which have a limited age range for onset and usually are first demonstrated by young adulthood. Investigating children, teens, or young adults would not identify cases with later age-of-onset. All of these methodologies have supported a genetic component to the transmission of MDD (Nurnberger & Gershon, 1984; Wender, Kety, Rosenthal et al., 1986). They support the Adlerian concept of an underlying organ inferiority leading to the expression of a psychiatric disorder. How this genetic proclivity, or organ inferiority, relates to the observed physiological changes is not yet known. No studies have yet attempted to correlate physiologic abnormalities in the acute state with inherited risk for MDD. At present, some individuals appear to have an inherited organ inferiority predisposing them to depression. Some of these individuals develop the disorder, and others do not. Of those who do become acutely depressed, some demonstrate physiologic changes in their neuroendocrine system. These changes resolve with recovery from the depression. Due to an underlying organ inferiority, they remain at-risk for recurrence of the disorder at another time during their lives.

The occurrence of physiological abnormalities in children with COMDD has not been as well investigated. Preliminary evidence supports some alteration in biological functions, but not with the same frequency or with the same pattern as noted in AOMDD. Sleep disturbances are common complaints of COMDD children. However, the S-EEG abnormalities noted for adults have not been as strongly or consistently measured with children (Goetz, Puig-Antich, Ryan et al., 1987; Lahmeyer, Poznanski, & Bellur, 1983; Puig-Antich, Goetz, Hanlon et al., 1982, 1983; Young, Knowles, MacLean et al., 1982). They are more frequently observed with depressed adolescents than depressed children, and especially with older rather than younger depressed adolescents.

On tests that measure neuroendocrine functioning and integrity of the HPA axis, children have shown some abnormalities, but again not with the same sensitivity as depressed adults (Doherty, Madansky, Kraft et al., 1986; Freeman, Poznanski, Grossman et al., 1985; Petty, Asarnow, Carlson et al., 1985; Poznanski, Carroll, Banegas et al., 1982; Weller, Weller, & Fristad, et al., 1984, 1985). However, specificity of these abnormalities to the depressed state in children is high, similar to depression in adults.

Very few studies have investigated neuroreceptor control during COMDD. These few have reported that some children do show blunting, or downregulation, of neuroreceptors during COMDD, but less frequently than expected from adult studies (Cavallo, Holt, Hejazi et al., 1987; Puig-Antich, Goetz, Davies et al., 1984a, 1984b; Puig-Antich, Novacenko, Davies et al., 1984a; 1984b; Puig-Antich, Novacenko, Goetz et al., 1984). In particular, growth hormone and melatonin appear affected, but cortisol diurnal secretion does not.

Three conclusions relative to the phenomenology of COMDD have been proposed to account for these differences. First, children with COMDD may not develop physiological abnormalities during the depressed state as frequently as adults, because children may not become as severely depressed as adults. Second, children may not have the same disorder experienced by adults. In this case a different pattern of abnormalities would be expectable. Third, children may experience the same disorder, but the receptors mediating physiological dysfunction during depression may not be fully developed and so the abnormalities cannot be as reliably measured (Davis, Davis, Mathe et al., 1984; Gillin, Duncan, Murphy et al., 1981; Goetz, Puig-Antich, & Ryan, 1987). Receptor expression may accelerate with puberty, be completed with adulthood, and decline with senescence leading to a different pattern of physiological functioning at each developmental stage (Gillin, Duncan, Murphy et al., 1981). The development of neuroreceptor functioning in humans has not been well studied, and so this theory remains speculative.

Similar to adults, no studies have attempted to investigate these physiological abnormalities as a function of an underlying organ inferiority. However, several studies have shown that MDD in parents confers on their preadult children an increased risk of COMDD, as well as an increased risk of other psychopathology and of impairments in overall functioning (Beardslee, Bemporad, Keller et al., 1983; Keller, Beardslee, Dorer, Lavori, Samuelson et al., 1986; Weissman, Gammon, John et al., 1987; Weissman, Prusoff, Gammon et al., 1984). Conversely, parents of mood-disordered children and adolescents show high occurrence of mood disorders, but not higher than observed in the parents of children with other psychiatric disorders (Mitchell, McCauley, Burke, Calderon, Schloredt, 1989; Puig-Antich, Goetz, Davies et al., 1989). Transmission of an organ inferiority is suggested by these studies, but it may not be specifically related to disturbances of mood. In this respect, children of mood-disordered parents may demonstrate problems related to temperament, behavior, mood, and intellectual performance in the absence of any signs of a depressive disorder. Whether these children are demonstrating effects of parenting and environmental stressors or an underlying organ inferiority which places them at-risk for development of MDD is unknown.

All COMDD is a holistic movement. The building blocks of heredity and environment are present with everyone (Adler, 1956). The degree of influence from one or the other, from child to child is not known at this time. Further research is needed to determine whether this heterogeneous group of COMDD children with and without physiological abnormalities during the depressed state are differentiated by specific underlying organ inferiorities.

Demographic Phenomenology

Prevalence. As many as one-third of normal school-aged children report depressive symptoms at some time during elementary school years (Kaslow, Tannenbaum, Abramson et al., 1983; Seligman, Kaslow, Alloy et al., 1984). Feeling depressed appears to be a common problem for children. However, the full COMDD syndrome occurs much less frequently. Approximately 1-2% of all preteen children have experienced an episode of MDD (Anderson, Williams, McGee et al., 1987; Kashani, McGee, Clarkson, Anderson, Walton et al., 1983). Many children may never receive appropriate clinical evaluation. Those who do comprise from 13% to 34% of clinical samples (Carlson & Cantwell, 1980b; Hershberg, Carlson, Cantwell et al., 1982).

COMDD is probably underdiagnosed in younger children. Children under 10 years of age have difficulty identifying their affect and labelling problems, and parents frequently underestimate the subjective distress experienced by their young children. Therefore, depression is likely to be underdiagnosed in this age group (Herjanic, Herjanic, Brown et al., 1975; Kazdin, French, & Unis, 1983). By 10 years of age children do reliably endorse their depression, and reported rates are more accurate (Herjanic & Reich, 1982; Reich, Herjanic, Welner et al., 1982).

Age. Many independent centers have reported MDD in children as young as 7 years of age (Carlson & Cantwell, 1980a; Chambers, Puig-Antich, Hirsch et al., 1985; Kovacs, Feinberg, Crouse-Novak et al., 1984a; Mitchell, McCauley, Burke et al., 1988; Puig-Antich, Chambers, & Tabrizi, 1983). However, DSM-III-R criteria allow the diagnosis to be made in any age range, including infants. MDD-like states have been identified in preschoolers (Kashani & Carlson, 1987; Kashani & Ray, 1987), but the occurrence in toddlers and infants is not well documented.

Age-of-onset may be a variable which integrates COMDD and AOMDD into a single depressive disorder across the life span. Epidemiologic studies with adults indicate that earlier age-at-onset for AOMDD correlates with more severe dysfunction and with a more familial type disorder; and older age-at-onset correlates with more sporadic type depression (Mendlewicz & Baron, 1981). AOMDD is unique among DSM-III-R disorders in its cumulative risk throughout the life span. COMDD may represent the earliest end of a depression spectrum with increasing risk throughout the life span, and greater severity with younger age-at-onset.

Sex. The sex composition of AOMDD is complex. Higher rates of AOMDD for women are frequently reported (Myers, Weissman, Tischler et al., 1984; Robins, Helzer, Weissman et al., 1984). But marital status, presence of young children in the home, and differential patterns of help-seeking by sex may confound these reports (Radloff, 1975; Weissman & Klerman, 1977).

This issue is similarly complex with children. No sex differential has been established for COMDD (Carlson & Cantwell, 1980b; Kashani, McGee, Clarkson et al., 1983; Kovacs, Feinberg, Crouse-Novak et al., 1984a; Mitchell, McCauley, Burke et al., 1988); Puig-Antich, 1980). However, girls are overrepresented in clinical COMDD samples compared to other childhood DSM-III-R disorders and during adolescence increasingly outnumber boys in rates of MDD (Rutter, 1986). The role of sex in the expression of MDD in both adults and children remains unclear. Both sociocultural and biological factors are probably relevant to symptom expression. Females experience an inferior social status which they resent but are socially encouraged to maintain. Males enjoy superior social standing which they are encouraged to exert. These social mores may contribute to the greater rate of depression observed in females and of sociopathy in males (Kaplan & Sadock, 1985). Biological factors probably contribute as well, since testosterone is associated with higher levels of aggressiveness and estrogen with passivity in primates. Both nature and nurture may be invoked by the individual's private logic to support a life stance.

Course of the Disorder

Recovery from an episode of Major Depression during childhood and the risk of relapse is important to understanding the phenomenology of this disorder for three reasons. First, if this is not a serious illness comparable to adult-onset MDD, COMDD children might be expected to experience transient depressive states without significant morbidity. But if COMDD is comparable to AOMDD, then recovery and relapse patterns might be similar. This would portend a more serious life vulnerability to this disorder. Second, knowing the expected course would assist treatment planning for either a sporadic disability or a protracted impairment. Third, accurate determination of the onset and offset of the disorder is necessary to establish interepisode morbidity. For example, full recovery from an acute disorder is necessary in order to determine whether an underlying personality disorder is present, which may predispose to recurrence. Establishing remission of acute morbidity is the first step in beginning the evaluation for possible chronic morbidity.

Recovery. AOMDD used to be described as an episodic disorder with full recovery between episodes. Research over the past two decades, however, reveals more variability in the course of the disorder. Approximately two-thirds of AOMDD patients experience only a single MDD episode, while others develop recurrent episodes, and approximately 15% suffer a chronic nonremitting disorder (Robins & Guze, 1972; Weissman & Klerman, 1977; Zis & Goodwin, 1979). Some individuals with a recurrent disorder do fully recover between episodes, but others do not. Minor depression or Dysthymic Disorder (DD) may be present between AOMDD episodes, and may have preceded or followed the first AOMDD incident in natural history (Akiskal, 1983; Akiskal, King, Rosenthal et al., 1981). However, the range is large, from four weeks to several years.

Rates of recovery from MDD during childhood are not well established. However, preliminary evidence indicates that COMDD is not a transient disorder (Kovacs, Feinberg, Crouse-Novak et al., 1984a; McGee & Williams, 1988). The children are unlikely to recover within the first three months. Episodes average 32 weeks, with a range from 4 to 60 weeks (Kovacs, Feinberg, Crouse-Novak et al., 1984a). A later age-of-onset appears to correlate with faster recovery, but with a shorter interim well-time to recurrence. As with adults, DD frequently precedes COMDD or develops subsequently (Kovacs, Feinberg, Crouse-Novak et al., 1984a). More children seem to recover, and do so more rapidly, than adults. Only 50% of MDD adults reportedly recover by 12 months and 64% by 24 months (Akiskal, King, Rosenthal et al., 1981; Keller, Shapiro, Lavori et al., 1982a), compared to 92% of child subjects by 18 months (Kovacs, Feinberg, Crouse-Novak et al., 1984a). Children may have an advantage toward recovery.

However, the presence of concurrent DD negates this advantage. Adults with AOMDD superimposed on DD recover from the acute MDD episode more rapidly than adults with only AOMDD (Keller & Shapiro, 1982; Keller, Shapiro, Lavori et al., 1982a; Gonzales, Lewinsohn, & Clarke, 1985), but children with and without DD do not appear to demonstrate such a recovery differential (Kovacs, Feinberg, Crouse-Novak et al., 1984a). To date, COMDD appears to run a moderately long course comparable to AOMDD, but children have a better prognosis for recovery from MDD episodes. However, their course may be complicated by continuing behavioral problems, including overt Conduct Disorders or other behavioral deviance (McGee & Williams, 1988). Developmental factors influencing outcome are not yet known.

Recurrence. As indicated in Figure 16.1, MDD may be a single episode disorder, or it may be recurrent. Most, but not all, children initially presenting for help are usually experiencing their first episode, although it may be of long duration. Frequently, parents think that their children are going through a difficult period or will outgrow whatever is distressing them. They will then delay treatment. Over time, many of these children will experience a course with several recurrences.

The rate of recurrence is high (Kovacs, Feinberg, Crouse-Novak et al., 1984b; McCauley, Mitchell, Burke, Myers, Calderon, & Schloredt, 1988). The most current evidence ascertained from several independent studies suggests that 40% to 70% of COMDD children followed over three to five years will relapse at least once. Twenty-six percent may relapse within the first year of recovery (Kovacs, Feinberg, Crouse-Novak et al., 1984b). This compares with a one year relapse of 38% in adults (Keller, Shapiro, Lavori et al., 1982b). At two years, 40% of COMDD children relapse. If COMDD children also have a Dysthymic Disorder (COMDD-DD), the risk for one year recurrence increases from 9% (COMDD) to 43% (COMDD-DD) (Kovacs, Feinberg, Crouse-Novak et al., 1984b). This large differential is not shown by AOMDD adults with DD (44%) and without DD (38%) (Keller & Shapiro, 1982). However, both MDD children and MDD adults with DD appear to have their greatest rate of relapse during the first four weeks following full recovery. Dysthymic Disorder is also one of the strongest predictors of later MDD for individuals who have not yet had an MDD episode. Fifty percent of DD children and 36% of DD adults will experience an MDD episode within three to four years.

Longitudinal information contributes to the phenomenology of COMDD by demonstrating a propensity for recurrence, especially in the first year, similar to that observed in AOMDD. The similar courses strengthen the use of DSM-III-R criteria to diagnose the disorder in children. Unknown yet is whether the disability experienced by children with a recurrent disorder is comparable to that of adults. Recurrence suggests greater discouragement and increasing lack of social interest, a feeling that one is not a full member of society. However, knowing the disability incurred would reveal the direction of movement.

Greater disability might suggest a perceived helplessness (Goal IV misbehavior) which justifies reneging on one's life responsibilities. Lesser disability might suggest heroism, of rising above it all, and putting oneself above others.

ADLERIAN DYNAMICS

Constitutional Factors

Adoption studies established a heredity component to MDD (Kaplan & Sadock, 1985). Regardless of the family in which an individual is reared, depression is highly correlated among first degree biological relatives. Among identical twins separated at birth and reared in different families, a 65% concordance rate has been found for mood disorders. Therefore, a constitutional predisposition exists toward depression which Adler (1927) termed an "organ inferiority." The specificity of that organ defect is not known at this time.

Early Training

Adler (1961) believed that these children, in addition to having an organ inferiority, are pampered, hated or neglected. *Pampering* is doing for children that which they are capable of doing for themselves. This trains them to be overly dependent upon others and robs them of a normal, developmental self-confidence. Hating or neglecting children trains them to believe that others in the family are favored over them and the world is a hostile place.

This dependency upon others, most often mother (Kanoy & Miller, 1980; McDonald, 1980), becomes a generalized dependence upon others for support. These children rely on their parents' achievement rather than their own and believe that they are unable to attain the lofty recognition that they demand for themselves (Adler, 1969).

Life-style Themes

COMDD children are overambitious (Smith, 1981). The greater their depression, the greater their ambition. Mild depression shows itself in mild overambition. Severe depression is typified by extreme ambition (Adler, 1970). COMDD children want to give the impression that they are kind and noble. This exterior may appear to be humility, but it should never be taken as concern and consideration for others (Adler, 1961). Consideration is not extended toward others as can be seen by the self-pity which they demonstrate. Self-pity is not concern for others.

Anger

The absence of kindness and consideration for others is an expression of anger towards others. These children believe that they are not given the recognition that is due to them. They think that they have been unjustly cared for and have a right to be angry. They may recognize that they are treating others unkindly, but their private logic allows them to be unkind because others in the family have been favored in preference to them. Mosak (1971) repeats these children's private logic to them: "I may be wrong, but they are more wrong."

The hostility toward others is most often covert in the form of signs and symptoms of depression. Anyone who has lived with a depressed person knows how much everyone around the depressed person suffers. At times, the hostility will be more overt. Irritability is common. They may destroy property, including their own, and may verbally or physically attack others.

Pampering

Again, it is usually mother who is seen as the cause of their problems. Rather than allowing for normal successes and failures, the parents have protected them. The parents have pampered them in a misguided attempt to protect them. These children have not been allowed to assume increasing responsibilities with increasing age and ability. In an effort to be good parents they have not allowed their children to do whatever they could for themselves, to experience the successes as well as the failures that follow in normal growth and development.

The parents' overindulgence is increasingly seen as being "not enough consideration for me" by COMDD children as they find themselves to be less capable than others. Upon inquiry they can readily point to a sister, brother, relative, school mate, and so forth, who is better treated. They reason that this favored treatment has enabled these "anointed beings" to achieve where the depressed children feel incapable. They know that their parents could have done much more to help them succeed in a hostile world.

Life Tasks

COMDD children are not preparing to meet the tasks of life: community, occupation, and love (Adler, 1964). They demonstrate resentment toward others. They feel inferior to others and covertly desire to be above all others. They have not learned to cooperate with family members. They carry this lack of cooperation to peers, school, and the greater community as they age.

The pampering they receive does not allow them to master chores and develop a sense of competency which would later allow them to be willing and feel capable of making a contribution to self and others through useful work. They hesitate to fully involve themselves in school and other work even when they are talented. They do not experience the satisfaction that commitment to work affords.

Lacking in Cooperation

The successes that they do have are selfishly guarded and are used to momentarily feel superior to others. They begrudge the accomplishments of peers and siblings, and take another's achievement as a personal failure for themselves. They have not learned to cooperate.

This lack of cooperation is often first evident between children and parents. COMDD children may be demanding as infants, continue to wet the bed as they age, and even defecate on themselves. This self-soiling is a stealthy attack upon others who have to change the bedding, do extra washing, and put up with unpleasant odor and sanitation. It is a further example of their hostility. This hostility will carry over to dating and mating. They have not learned the value of cooperating as children but have learned to defeat others, to feel superior when others fail to succeed. They will use lovers for selfish gain. They do not know how to bond with others for the mutual good.

Recollections of punishment or unfairness are remembered and used as justification for not contributing, not trying, not treating others fairly, being angry or harming another. Revenge is most often demonstrated through self-destruction (e.g., poor posture, sleep, and eating problems). These are sideshows (Adler, 1961).

Obfuscation

Sideshows are sign and symptom production for the purpose of avoiding the life tasks, for not cooperating. These children become consumed with their problems and have no time, energy, or ability to get on with life, to make a contribution to the common welfare. Their bid for nobility translates into "no-ability."

Using Others

COMDD is a demonstration of learning to elicit concern and help from others by showing weakness, sadness, and helplessness. The more help that is offered in the form of pampering and indulgence, the greater the number and intensity of signs and symptoms of depression. In this way they defeat those who offer to help them. If self-esteem is low enough, the principal feelings of superiority come from being unique in that no one can make life better for them.

Giving suggestions, assuming responsibility for these children only meets with further defeat. To fall into this trap is very tempting, as COMDD children have mastered methods for gaining support from others. They seem so harmless and pitiful that others readily jump in and further the pampering.

This behavior continues until others feel so defeated and inadequate in their efforts that they detach themselves from the child. The human compassion that leads people to reach out to COMDD children with common sense methods of helping is an opportunity to turn the helper into a servant. No amount of common sense help is quite enough.

Overambition

COMDD children set goals which are impossible to attain. They will not settle for normal step-by-step progress which carries no assurance of success. They want it all, and they want it now. The hostile world is an ever-present opportunity to fail. This view leads to the idea that, "nothing ventured, nothing lost" (Mosak, 1971). Protecting their image of nobility and superiority becomes of paramount importance. They can not risk the possibility of failure. Those involved with them misinterpret this behavior as a lack of ambition and will mistakenly attempt to motivate them through common sense methods. The predictable result is that those doing the motivating end up defeated. Again, the COMDD child has triumphed and attained a feeling of superiority at the expense of another victim.

Attitude to Fail

These children have lofty, high standards, but effort toward tasks means opening themselves to possible defeat and perceived scorn by others. The hostility that they have for others is turned into imagined contempt from others if they were to try but fail in their attempt to achieve. The result is a replacement of the attempts toward achieving tasks with an intense contemplation of all the many ways that they might try but fail. By focusing on the many ways in which they might fail, the calamitous results; they attain the proper corresponding affect which connotes to themselves and the world that if it were not for their problems, they would be successful. In this stance toward the world, they feel hopeless.

They demand a guarantee of perfect results before they will take on a task. The fear of failure leads to an investment in pride rather than effort. The greater the pride, the less one has about which to be proud.

Appearance

The hostility and attempts to elevate themselves by defeating others is rarely in their consciousness. They are mostly aware of how bad they feel. As they mature, they offer increasing feelings of guilt when they demonstrate their selfishness and hostility. Appearing noble rather than acting noble becomes more and more characteristic of their pattern of behavior. This is most evident in suicidal ideation: "I just don't wish to be a further burden to my family."

Family Dynamics

The mother may be lacking in cooperation to a degree that she fails to bond with the child (Adler, 1956). Mother's self-absorption will not provide a secure attachment nor a model for useful involvement with others.

Competition between the parents is most easily seen in increasingly different interests. With time and devotion to common tasks, the expectation is that a salubrious marriage will result in more similarity of interests. This marital competition also sets the stage for competition between the children and is the basis for differences in life-style (personality) characteristics between the siblings, especially the dissimilarities between the first and second children (Dreikurs, 1958).

The other children in the family may appear to be better adjusted at the expense of the depressed child. So long as signs and symptoms of depression are maintained, they elevate themselves at the expense of their depressed sibling. They can further this elevation by being "helpful" and "feeling sorry" for their depressed sibling. This results in the depressed child feeling even more incapable while furthering the belief that "I have been done wrong and deserve special consideration to make up for this unfairness."

Firstborn children are most likely to develop depression for many reasons, including family expectations for successfully carrying on the family's perceived image, fulfilling the parental and other family member's ambitions, inability of the parents to allow these firstborns to be their own person, the desperate attempts of the oldest child to regain the focus of attention when the second child is born, feeling dethroned, believing achievement will result in regaining a favored position, and so forth.

More insidious is the tacit agreement of the parents to invest themselves in signs and symptoms of depression in their child as a method for avoiding looking at their dysfunctional marriage. The child's depression becomes a smoke screen for not moving forward with their love task. They too can appear to be nobly concerned; in this case "no-ability" to form a useful marital bond. The focus on their child provides them with an excuse for not attending to their marriage while elevating their "good parent" image. This parental behavior has the unfortunate result of modeling poor cooperation as well as making the child a scapegoat for their dysfunctional union.

Treatment Strategy

Therapy focuses on bringing to awareness the lofty ambition, the self-loathing, anger towards parents, and attempts to defeat others, particularly family members. The four goals of misbehavior (Dreikurs, 1958) are useful for detecting the immediate reason for maladaptive behavior and can guide one toward understanding the particular life-style which supports depression. The goals of misbehavior indicate the degree of discouragement and point to those adults who are the specific victims of these children.

Goals of Misbehavior

The children are asked in therapy if they could possibly be seeking attention (Goal I); or could they be attempting to demonstrate that they are more powerful than the adult in the situation (Goal II); or could it be that they are expressing their feelings of hurt by directly or furtively attacking the adult (Goal III); or could they be demonstrating their feelings of helplessness by demonstrating their inadequacy (Goal IV). With adolescents the questions are more pointed. "Everyone knows that depression is an expression of hostility and an effort to defeat people. Toward whom are you directing your anger?"

Self-pity

COMDD children believe that their situation is far worse than that of others, that too much is expected of them, that a constant demand to do for others is expected of them, and that too little is done for them. Asking them in counseling if it is possible that they are thinking these thoughts brings these attitudes to their and the family's awareness.

Fantasy

The reaction to revealing these private thoughts is often shock. The masquerade of nobility has been convincing to everyone. This can be further seen when a desire for fame has been revealed. The fame is characterized by fantasies of heroism. An extreme expression of this desire can be seen in suicidal ideation. These children may contemplate a TV program interruption bringing the late, breaking news of their death. This fantasy is followed by scenes of their family grieving.

A therapy question revealing this desire for heroism and notoriety is, "Would it be a fair statement to say that you want to be a hero (or that you desire to be famous)?" Adler (1927) termed this method of questioning as "spitting in the soup." These children and families have difficulty continuing to buy the apparent nobility and self-effacing image: they can continue to eat the soup, but it no longer is so appealing.

Family Therapy

The therapeutic setting of choice with children is with the entire family. This forum allows all members of the family to understand their roles in these dynamics. Adlerian family therapy is a systems approach with emphasis upon the family constellation. This approach considers the investment of the family in the depressive signs displayed by the identified child. Tactics such as focusing on potential problems of another family member who is seen as the best adjusted can be employed, as can other interventions familiar to family systems therapists.

Group treatment with peers, especially when adolescence has been attained, is also a good adjunctive therapy. The larger family is still an important involvement even when the focus is group therapy with peers. Parent education can also be an effective treatment method (Croake & Hinkle, 1983).

CASE VIGNETTE: JIMMY
ACUTE-ONSET MDD FOLLOWING RECENT SEVERE STRESSOR AND PRODROMAL COMPULSIVE BEHAVIORS

History

Jimmy was an 11-year-old boy who presented to the clinic due to trash collecting. He had been collecting trash for seven months and now had a disarrayed room full of it. Father's discovery of the malodorous trash motivated Jimmy's mother to seek treatment. Jimmy described feeling "sad" whenever he thought of throwing away any items. Multiple attempts by the family to dispose of the trash resulted in tearful, agitated tantrums. He always protested coming to therapy, although he always came. He would leave a session when we began to plan disposal of the trash. His mother insisted and Jimmy finally complied. However, he agreed to burn the trash only if he could keep the ashes near the house. In four weeks all of the trash was burned. The family was advised to check back four weeks after school began. They did not return, "since things were going well and we did not want to rock the boat."

The family returned to the clinic four months later. Jimmy was asking to see the doctor due to growing distress. He described an increasing anger especially directed toward one boy whom he felt received special treatment at school and who was harassing him. He wanted to kill this boy. He did not want to attend school anymore.

Jimmy felt like crying all the time, but did not endorse the sadness he had previously reported. His mother described him as constantly very irritable. He stated that he had great difficulty falling asleep, requiring one to three hours, but then slept well. He also reported wanting to eat all of the time and had gained 10 to 15 pounds. He had difficulty doing school work due to fatigue and decreased ability to concentrate. He tired very easily. Initially, he did not think of suicide. However, he did describe a desire to hurt himself or "to destroy something important to relieve the tension." He then began to scratch himself across the forehead with scissors which "released the tension." Later he became suicidal. When he broke items, they were only his own possessions. This did not relieve the tension sufficiently, and he feared breaking more important things. He lost interest in most activities. Additionally, Jimmy was reluctant to go out of his home unless with a family member, or with one friend who helped him by telling him what to do. He complained of several physical symptoms without detectable cause and often stayed home from school. He did not endorse any guilt, nor did he demonstrate any negative cognitive distortions. No endorsement of hallucinations or other psychotic symptoms was evident. He wanted to come to treatment as often as possible. Several unscheduled visits to the clinic were made.

Past Medical History. Jimmy had mononucleosis eight months previously. During this illness, he experienced a respiratory arrest. He was intubated to assist breathing and spent four days in the intensive care unit (ICU). He knew that he had almost died but stated that no one had discussed this with him.

Social History. Jimmy had always been an excellent student. He had an IQ in the superior range. His family was intact with no major family or marital problems endorsed. A 19-year-old sister lived at home while attending college. He had many friends, but was "shy." Father held stable employment as an engineer, and Mother as a special education teacher.

Family History. There was no significant medical or psychiatric history in first degree relatives. A distant relative had Bipolar Disorder.

Mental Status Examination and Observations

Jimmy was seen alone and with his family. The most notable observations were a very rationalized and intellectualized psychological style in all family members. They also appeared very guarded even after knowing the treating therapist for many months and having enjoyed success with the initial treatment program. Father and the sister kept particular distance and would not comply with recommended family treatment. Mother was described by her daughter as overinvolved with her son. Father did not object to being left out or not being told about the trash collecting.

Jimmy seemed more agitated and irritable than depressed on each evaluation. Although endorsing "uncontrollable anger," he seemed worried, anxious, sad, with a very blunted affect. His mood was anxious and irritable. Jimmy demonstrated great concern in play and drawings with armor, self-defense, danger, and dying.

Jimmy offered the following Early Recollection at the first clinic visit. "I was at my fourth birthday party. I was walking through the dining room and looking at the toy helicopter in my hand. My uncle gave it to me as a birthday gift." When asked for the most important scene and his feeling, Jimmy responded: "When I was looking at it." "I felt excited."

When seen four months later, Jimmy gave the same Early Recollection. He also described the same "most important scene." However, when asked for his feeling he replied, "I don't know; I can't tell what I feel."

Course of Treatment

Due to the previous episode of mononucleosis and his acute course, Jimmy received a comprehensive evaluation.

A CT scan of his head, an electroencephalogram, neuro-psychological testing, and projective testing revealed no indications of organicity or psychosis.

The father would not comply with regular family sessions, although he would attend sporadically. Due to the severity of Jimmy's depression with harm to himself and potential for harm to others, medication was started. The first medication chosen was ineffective and worsened his insomnia. Fluoxetine was then prescribed. This medication belongs to the alleged "serotonergic" medications, which have been efficacious for treating Obsessive Compulsive Disorder (OCD) as well as depression. Although Jimmy had no more compulsive behaviors, he still described many obsessional features, such as overfocusing on his schoolmate, constant thoughts of harming himself, worry about leaving the house, and overconcern with self-defense. He still collected, although the items were age-appropriate toys.

Jimmy improved steadily during six weeks of medication and sporadic family sessions. Goal diagnosis in the family session indicated Goal III and IV to be the most common misbehaviors directed toward both parents. "Could it be" questions to Jimmy clearly indicated that hostility and attempts to defeat mother were the purpose of many signs and symptoms.

Competition between the parents was addressed by having them agree to take one evening each week for an outing away from home where the two of them would have "fun." Obtaining mutual agreement for a strategy for dealing with Jimmy's signs of depression went a long way toward increasing marital cooperation. The older sister agreed to stop "mothering" Jimmy; albeit, she never did cease feeling sorry for him, but she would leave the house when those feelings came into her awareness.

Symptoms and signs persist, although significantly abated. In particular, he is no longer obsessed with the schoolmate, has no thoughts of hurting himself or breaking things, attends school regularly. He is playing baseball, his favorite sport. However, he joined the team only under the guidance of his trusted friend. His affect remains fairly blunted, although a sense of humor is returning. He remains concerned with self-defense and guns, but tolerates less frequent therapy sessions, since he is "too busy."

Comment

Jimmy's case is rather atypical due to the initial presentation of obsessive compulsive features. However, it is typical in other regards. Children may not demonstrate depression as the initial problem. A variety of symptoms may evolve over time to finally meet MDD criteria. Jimmy also demonstrated almost all of the criteria symptoms, plus the adjunctive symptoms of somatic complaints. His acute stress, which is coded on Axis IV, had recently changed from none or mild to extreme due to the respiratory arrest with invasive procedures and intensive care hospitalization. Family dynamics may have contributed to Jimmy's depression. However, this was a better functioning family than many. Jimmy's chronic level of stress, or the enduring circumstances also coded on Axis IV, was mild. Jimmy's family was stable and basically, although not optimally, supportive and showed improvement with family therapy. Jimmy was a very intelligent child with many strengths and had an apparent successful life adjustment prior to onset of depression.

Jimmy's early recollection was the same at each presentation and indicated liking to get things, or to be given to. He was a receiver. However, he changed his affect associated with receiving something from excited to confused. The positive affect reflected his concrete desire to collect and accumulate. With depression his goals were less clear to him; he felt confused because "getting" and "collecting" no longer contained his ambition and desire to have life his way.

DSM-III-R Diagnoses

> Axis I: 296.23 Major Depressive Disorder, Single Episode
>
> Axis II: No disorder but compulsive personality traits

Axis III: Status post mononucleosis and respiratory arrest

Axis IV: Psychosocial Stressors:

a) respiratory arrest and ICU hospitalization severity: 5-extreme (acute event)

b) chronic mild parental discord; overin-volvement of mother with son; underin-volvement of father severity: 2-mild (enduring circumstances)

Axis V: Current GAF: 35

Highest GAF Last Year: 92

CASE VIGNETTE: TIM
GRADUAL-ONSET MDD FOLLOWING
CHRONIC STRESS AND DYSTHYMIA

History

Tim was a 10-year-old boy who came for treatment following his destruction of fence posts with an axe at camp. He said that he used the axe in response to teasing by his peers. He had demonstrated impulsive behaviors in the past, but much more minor. He had broken small objects, walked out of class, and occasionally struck another student. Mostly Tim became very upset when teased. He would verbally berate his taunting peers and then run away crying. He had no friends. Despite these actions, Tim did not engage in antisocial activities, never bullied or teased others, and was generally well-behaved in class and elsewhere. He completed work in school and maintained average grades. His fraternal twin sister Taryn and older sister Kate (also a fraternal twin) described his teasing by others as due to his awkwardness with peers and his poor social presentation. Tim would often go to school in unkempt clothing, hair uncombed, and smelling of urine from not properly cleaning himself after nocturnal enuresis. He did not seem to know how to make small talk with peers. Mother and siblings described Tim as helpful, but mostly keeping to himself. Free time was spent around other adults or with his "big brother," who was assigned to Tim four hours per week. He had locked up his belongings to keep them from his older bother Ken who would take Tim's belongings, break them, or tauntingly hide them. Although Tim frequently protested to Mother, she stated she had no control over Ken.

Neither Tim nor the family noted any recent change in Tim's behavior. He was also always irritable and quick to blow up, but never showed any real tantrums. Between these sporadic episodes Tim was a calm and a "kind" boy. Detailed inquiry revealed a history of increased irritability with difficulty concentrating and difficulty getting up in the mornings. He always had insomnia, but this had increased recently. Both Tim and his mother attributed these problems to his change of schools the past September. Neither he nor his family endorsed depression. He had mentioned suicide a few times, but his mother thought that he was "discouraged from all the teasing."

Past Medical History. Noncontributory except for enuresis.

Family History. No known significant medical or psychological disorders.

Educational History. Regular education with average grades.

Social History. Tim's Mother was married and delivered her first set of fraternal twins, Kate and Ken. Tim and Taryn were born 18 months after the first set of twins. When the younger set of twins was 18 months old, the Father deserted the family leaving Mother with four preschool children. The family was on welfare for many years. Mother made several unsuccessful attempts to work after the children were all in school. She had successfully returned to work again eight months prior to Tim's referral to the clinic. She enjoyed her work, but reported many conflicts with supervisory figures. She left this job for another position one year after hiring. During their rearing the children had to fend for themselves. Mother reared the children to be "independent." They were very good at "odd jobbing" to make spending money. In fact, the adult relationships Tim made through "odd jobbing" were his main positive social contacts. These adults felt sorry for him and tried to help him. Mother was a proud woman. She appeared overwhelmed, but indicated that she had everything under good control. She had been very involved in organizing many social activities for the children who participated in multiple social organizations and activities. Mother often let the two boys work out their difficulties, but she intervened occasionally, which kept the conflict going between them. Ken escalated his harassment of Tim.

Mental Status Examination and Observations

Tim was initially seen with his family and then alone for evaluation. The family session was chaotic. All the children talked at once. They were evasive and seemed to play a game with the therapist. Mother sat back and just observed. She appeared overwhelmed, defensive, dysphoric, but not depressed. She seemed quite needy, but unable or unwilling to express this. She also wanted to control the direction of the sessions and recommendations. She would not allow the interviewer to focus on her or the overall family. Kate, the older girl, had a motherly role in the family and was the most "responsible." She also stuck up for Tim. She felt sorry for him. His brother Ken was uncooperative and sarcastic; and his twin Taryn gave the appearance of being oblivious.

Tim presented as a socially awkward but outgoing boy. He was very desirous of attention. He liked to talk about himself, especially his perceived accomplishments. However, these accomplishments were age-inappropriate simple acts, like tracing a logo onto a piece of paper. He presented this as artistic talent. Other exaggerations of ability were common, and he sought confirmation of his capabilities. He had a fixed smile on his face. Tim always wanted to extend sessions. Many times he asked to take something from the office with him when he left. He was never daunted when refused the items, and felt entitled to them. He seemed very vulnerable. Tim never spoke of his problems and tended to minimize them when addressed by the therapist, stating everything was going "fine." His scores on self-report questionnaires indicated severely impaired self-esteem, high level of anxiety, feelings of worthlessness, alienation from peers and family, negative distortions in his thinking, and suicidality. His scores were the worst the tester had seen in an outpatient setting. When carefully questioned he did endorse feeling depressed, and angry or irritable during part of every day. He felt guilty for what had happened to his mother in life. He also felt guilty about people starving in Ethiopia. He frequently thought about killing himself and occasionally about killing others. He took at least one hour to fall asleep at night, mostly because he felt worried. He had started to awaken during the night but did not have early morning awakening. Recent difficulty keeping his mind on schoolwork was endorsed. He was not anhedonic nor anorectic. He clearly noted that his mood was worse in the morning, even on weekends when he did not have to attend school. Despite Tim's strong endorsement of feeling "depressed," his mother did not believe he felt that way.

Course of Treatment

Mother did not want to involve herself or the family in treatment. She wanted individual treatment for her son. She would not allow a second family session. Tim's situation was critical. Antidepressant medication was started, since Tim continued to have difficulty regulating his affect with resultant disciplinary action at school. Mother's refusal to allow family therapy greatly curtailed treatment possibilities. Tim was enrolled in social skills training, and seen with his older sister who attended his school and was "popular." Sessions focused on bringing to awareness his skill at involving school children and his older brother in taunting him, the power he exerted by stimulating them to pick on him. Asking Tim in the family session and with his sister if it were possible that he elicited this harassment met with denial. However, when asked if he knew of anyone who knew how to better entice Ken to harass, he gave a recognition reflex (Dreikurs, 1958) by smiling proudly. The therapist's spitting in his noble, victimized soup effectively ended these behaviors. Tim quickly stabilized. However, many issues persisted. Mother was again requested to involve the entire family in treatment. At this point, she changed health policies and transferred Tim's care to another facility.

Comment

Tim's presentation typifies MDD in many children. Onset is frequently chronic with exacerbation of preexisting symptoms, rather than acute. The family and Tim did not perceive a change until a crisis developed. His symptoms included both depressed mood and irritability. Only the irritability was obvious, since it led to behaviors affecting others. He had grandiose ambitions for himself, but depended upon the success and support of his motherly sister. He had increasing insomnia, feelings of excessive guilt and worthlessness, diminished ability to concentrate, and suicidal thoughts. Neither his appetite nor weight changed. He was not fatigued nor anhedonic. Some psychomotor agitation existed. He did not meet criteria for other diagnoses concurrent with the depression. Despite his misbehavior, he did not demonstrate a Conduct Disorder. However, his longstanding depressive and irritable feelings did meet criteria for a preexisting Dysthymic Disorder.

Several factors delayed diagnosis. The irritability impressed others. Tim's feelings of depression were not so impressive. Tim's mother was overwhelmed and felt that life had been unfair to her. She was relatively inattentive to her children's needs. When Tim's needs could no longer be ignored, she was still unwilling to act in her children's best interests if it meant puncturing her own pride. Tim's psychological style was to avoid his problems in favor of impressing others. Depressive symptoms were elicited only with self-report questionnaires and careful individual interviewing. Most of his symptoms were chronic and so the increased intensity was discounted. Finally, because he had recently changed schools, an event could be identified to which change of symptoms could be attributed. Indications of a serious disorder were minimized by attributing them to "stress."

Diagnoses

Axis I: 296.2 Major Depressive Disorder, Single Episode

300.40 Dysthymia, Primary Type, Early-onset

307.60 Functional Enuresis, Primary, Nocturnal

Axis II: No disorder; but personality traits of grandiosity, self-involvement, intrusiveness, praise-seeking, entitlement, no close friends

Axis III: Deficits in personal hygiene

Axis IV: Psychosocial Stressors:

a) change of schools; mother takes job
severity: 2-mild (acute event)

b) welfare, abandonment by father, chronic single parent home with multiple siblings, socioemotional neglect by mother, harassment by brother, chronic ridicule by peers.
severity: 5-extreme (enduring circumstances)

Axis V: Current GAF: 40

Highest GAF Past Year: 50

REFERENCES

Adler, A. (1927). *The practice and theory of Individual Psychology*. New York: Harcourt, Brace, & Co.

Adler, A. (1956). *The Individual Psychology of Alfred Adler*. H.L. Ansbacher & R.R.Ansbacher (Eds.). New York: Harper Torchbooks.

Adler, A. (1961). Depression in the light of Adlerian psychology. *Journal of Individual Psychology, 17*, 56-57.

Adler, A. (1964). *Superiority and social interest*. H.L. Ansbacher & R.R. Ansbacher (Eds.). Evanston, IL: Northwestern University Press.

Adler, A. (1969). *The science of living*. Garden City, NY: Anchor Books.

Adler, A. (1970). *Problems of neurosis: A book of case histories*. Chicago: Henry Regnery.

Akiskal, H.S. (1981). Subaffective disorders: Dysthymic, cyclothymic, and bipolar II disorders in the borderline realm. *Psychiatric Clinics of North America, 4*, 25-46.

Akiskal, H.S. (1983). Dysthymic disorder: Psychopathology of proposed chronic depressive subtypes. *American Journal of Psychiatry, 140*, 11-20.

Akiskal, H.S., Downs, J., Jordan, P., et al. (1985). Affective disorders in the referred children and younger siblings of manic-depressives: Mode of onset and prospective course. *Archives of General Psychiatry, 42,* 996-1003.

Akiskal, H.S., King, D., Rosenthal, T.L., et al. (1981). Chronic depressions, Part I. Clinical and familial characteristics in 137 probands. *Journal of Affective Disorders, 3,* 297-315.

American Psychiatric Association. (1980). *Diagnostic and statistical manual of mental disorders* (3rd ed.). Washington, DC: American Psychiatric Association.

American Psychiatric Association, (1987). *Diagnostic and statistical manual of mental disorders* (3rd ed., rev). Washington, DC: Author.

Anderson, J.C., Williams, S., McGee, R., & Silva, P.A. (1987). DSM-III disorders in preadolescent children. Prevalence in a large sample from the general population. *Archives of General Psychiatry, 44,* 69-76.

Arans, G.W., Baldessarini, M.D., & Ornsteen, M. (1985). The dexamethasone suppression test for diagnosis and prognosis in psychiatry. *Archives of General Psychiatry, 42,* 1193-1204.

Beardslee, W.R., Bemporad, J., Keller, M.B., et al. (1983). Children of parents with major affective disorder: A review. *American Journal of Psychiatry, 140,* 825-832.

Biederman, J., Munir, K., Knee, D., et al. (1987). High rates of affective disorders in probands with attention deficit disorder and in their relatives. *American Journal of Psychiatry, 144,* 330-333.

Bowlby, J. (1980). *Attachment and loss: III. Loss, sadness, and depression.* New York: Basic Books.

Breier, A., Charney, D.S., & Heninger, G.R. (1985). The diagnostic validity of anxiety disorders and their relationship to depressive illness. *American Journal of Psychiatry, 142,* 787-797.

Carlson, G.A., & Cantwell, D.P. (1980a). Unmasking masked depression in children and adolescents. *American Journal of Psychiatry, 137,* 445-449.

Carlson, G.A., & Cantwell, D.P. (1980b). A survey of depressive symptoms, syndrome and disorder in a child psychiatric population. *Journal of Child Psychology and Psychiatry, 21,* 19-25.

Cavallo, A., Holt, K.G., Hejazi, M.S., et al. (1987). Melatonin circadian rhythm in childhood depression. *Journal of American Academy of Child and Adolescent Psychiatry, 26,* 395-399.

Chambers, W.J., Puig-Antich, J., Hirsch, M., et al. (1985). The assessment of affective disorders in children and adolescents by semistructured interview: Test-retest reliability of the K-SADS-P. *Archives of General Psychiatry, 42,* 696-702.

Chambers, W.J., Puig-Antich J., Tabrizi, M.A., et al. (1982). Psychotic symptoms in prepubertal major depressive disorder. *Archives of General Psychiatry, 39*, 921-927.

Croake, J.W., & Catlin, N. (1986). *A teleoanalytic approach to adolescence.* Seattle, WA: Seattle Institute for Adlerian Studies.

Croake, J.W., & Hinkle, D.E. (1983). Adlerian family counseling education. *Journal of Individual Psychology, 39*, 247-258.

Davis, K.L., Davis, B.M., Mathe, A.A., et al. (1984). Age and the dexamethasone suppression test in depression. *American Journal of Psychiatry, 141*, 872-874.

Del Beccarro, M., Burke, P., & McCauley, E. (1988). Hallucinations in children: A follow-up study. *American Academy of Child and Adolescent Psychiatry, 27*, 462-465.

Doherty, M.B., Madansky, D., Kraft, J., et al. (1986). Cortisol dynamics and test performance of the dexamethasone suppression test in 97 psychiatrically hospitalized children aged 3-16 years. *American Academy of Child Psychiatry, 25*, 400-408.

Dreikurs, R. (1958). *The challenge of parenthood.* New York: Hawthorn Books.

Dreikurs, R. (1973). *Psychodynamics, psychotherapy, and counseling.* Chicago: Alfred Adler Institute.

Ellis, A. (1973). *Humanistic psyhotherapy.* New York: McGraw-Hill Book.

Fawcett, J., & Kravity, H.M. (1983). Anxiety syndromes and their relationship to depressive illness. *Journal of Clinical Psychiatry, 44*, 8-11.

Freeman, L.N., Poznanski, E.O., Grossman, J.A., et al. (1985). Psychotic and depressed children: A new entity. *Journal of American Academy of Child Psychiatry, 24*, 95-102.

Freud, A. (1946). *The ego and the mechanisms of defense.* New York: International Universities Press.

Freud, A., & Burlingham, D. (1974). *Infants without families and reports on the Hamstead Nurseries 1939-1945.* London: Hogarth Press.

Gillin, J.C., Duncan, W.C., Murphy, D.L., et al. (1981). Age-related changes in sleep in depressed and normal subjects. *Psychiatry Research, 4*, 73-78.

Goetz, R.R., Puig-Antich, J., Ryan, N., et al. (1987). Electroencephalographic sleep of adolescents with major depression and normal controls. *Archives of General Psychiatry, 4*, 61-68.

Gonzales, L.R., Lewinsohn, P.M., & Clarke, G.N. (1985). Longitudinal follow-up on unipolar depressives: An investigation of predictors of relapse. *Journal of Consulting & Clinical Psychology, 53,* 461-469.

Greenman, D.A., Gunderson, J.G., Cane, M., et al. (1986). An examination of the borderline diagnosis in children. *American Journal of Psychiatry, 143,* 998-1003.

Haley, G.M.T., Fine, S., Marriage, K., Moretti, M.M., & Freeman, R.J. (1985). Brief reports: Cognitive bias and depression in psychiatrically disturbed children and adolescents. *Journal of Consulting & Clinical Psychology, 53,* 535-537.

Herjanic, B., Herjanic, M., Brown, F., et al. (1975). Are children reliable reporters? *Journal of Abnormal Child Psychology, 3,* 41-48.

Herjanic, B., & Reich, W. (1982). Development of a structured psychiatric interview for children: Agreement between child and parent on individual symptoms. *Journal of Abnormal Child Psychology, 10,* 307-324.

Hershberg, S.G., Carlson, G.A., Cantwell, D.P., & Strober, M. (1982). Anxiety and depressive disorders in psychiatrically disturbed children. *Journal of Clinical Psychiatry, 43,* 358-361.

Hughes, M.C. (1984). Recurrent abdominal pain and childhood depression: Clinical observations of 23 children and their families. *American Journal of Orthopsychiatry, 54,* 146-155.

Kanoy, K., & Miller, B. (1980). Children's impact on the parental decision to divorce. *Family Relations, 29,* 309-316.

Kaplan, H., & Sadock, B. (1985). *Synopsis of psychiatry.* Baltimore: Williams and Wilkins.

Kashani, J.H., & Carlson, G.A. (1987). Seriously depressed preschoolers. *American Journal of Psychiatry, 144,* 348-350.

Kashani, J., Lababidi, Z., & Jones, R. (1982). Depression in children and adolescence with cardiovascular symptomatology. *Journal of American Academy of Child Psychiatry, 21,* 187-189.

Kashani, J.H., McGee, R.O., Clarkson, S.G., Anderson, J.C., Walton, L.E., et al. (1983). Depression in a sample of 9-year-old children. *Archives of General Psychiatry, 40,* 1217-1223.

Kashani, J.H., & Ray, J.S. (1987). Major depression with delusional features in a preschool-age child. *American Academy of Child and Adolescent Psychiatry, 26,* 110-112.

Kaslow, N.J., Tannenbaum, R.L., Abramson, L.Y., et al. (1983). Problem-solving deficits and depressive symptoms among children. *Journal of Abnormal Child Psychology, 11*, 497-501.

Katon, W., Kleinman, A., & Rosen, G. (1982a). Depression and somatization: A review, Part I. *American Journal of Medicine, 72*, 127-136.

Katon, W., Kleinman, A., & Rosen, G. (1982b). Depression and somatization: A review, Part II. *American Journal of Medicine, 72*, 241-247.

Kazdin, A.E., French, N.H., & Unis, A.S. (1983). Child, mother, and father evaluations of depression in psychiatric inpatient children. *Journal of Abnormal Child Psychology, 11*, 167-180.

Kazdin, A.E., Unis, A.S., French, N.H., et al. (1983). Hopelessness, depression and suicidal intent among psychiatrically disturbed inpatient children. *Journal of Consulting & Clinical Psychology, 51*, 504-510.

Keller, M.B., Beardslee, W.R., Dorer, D.J., Lavori. P.W., Samuelson, M.A. et al., (1986). Impact of severity and chronicity of parental affective illness on adaptive functioning and psychopatholgy in children. *Archives of General Psychiatry, 43*, 930-937.

Keller, M.B., & Shapiro, R.W. (1982). "Double depression": Superimposition of acute depressive episodes on chronic depressive disorders. *American Journal of Psychiatry, 139*, 438-442.

Keller, M.B., Shapiro, R.W., Lavori, P.W., et al. (1982a). Recovery in major depressive disorder. Analysis with life table and regression models. *Archives of General Psychiatry, 39*, 905-910.

Keller, M.B., Shapiro, R.W., Lavori, P.W., et al. (1982b). Relapse in Major Depressive Disorder. *Archives of General Psychiatry, 39*, 911-915.

Kemph, J.P. (1987). Hallucination in psychotic children. *American Academy of Child and Adolescent Psychiatry, 26*, 556-559.

Kotsopoulos, S., Kanigsberg, J., Cote, A., & Fiedorowicz, C. (1987). Hallucinatory experiences in nonpsychotic children. *American Academy of Child and Adolescent Psychiatry, 26*, 375-380.

Kovacs, M., & Beck, A.T. (1978). Maladaptive cognitive structures in depression. *American Journal of Psychiatry, 135*, 525-533.

Kovacs, M., Feinberg, T.L., Crouse-Novak, M.A., et al. (1984a). Depressive disorders in childhood. A longitudinal prospective study of characteristics and recovery I. *Archives of General Psychiatry, 41*, 229-237.

Kovacs, M., Feinberg, T.L., Crouse-Novak, M.A., et al. (1984b). Depressive disorders in childhood. A longitudinal study of risk for subsequent major depression II. *Archives of General Psychiatry, 41*, 643-649.

Lahmeyer, H., Poznanski, E., & Bellur, S. (1983). EEG sleep in depressed adolescents. *American Journal of Psychiatry, 140*, 1150-1153.

Leckman, J.F., Merikangas, K.R., Pauls, D.L., et al. (1983). Anxiety disorders and depression: Contradictions between family study data and DSM-III conventions. *American Journal of Psychiatry, 140*, 880-882.

Lefkowitz, M.M., & Burton, N. (1978). Childhood depression: a critique of the concept. *Psychological Medicine, 85*, 716-726.

Marriage, K., Fine, S., Moretti, M., & Haley, G. (1986). Relationship between depression and conduct disorder in children and adolescents. *Journal of American Academy of Child Psychiatry, 25*, 687-691.

McCauley, E., Carlson, G.A., & Calderon, R. (1991). The role of somatic complaints in the diagnosis of depression in children and adolescents. *Journal of the American Academy of Child & Adolescent Psychiatry, 30*, 631-635.

McCauley, E., Mitchell, J., Burke, P., & Moss, S. (1988). Cognitive attributes of depression in children and adolescents. *Journal of Consulting & Clinical Psychology, 56*, 903-908.

McCauley, E., Mitchell, J., Burke, P., Myers, K., Calderon, R., & Schloredt, K. (1988). *Longitudinal assessment of depression in children and adolescents.* Paper presented at the annual meeting of the American Academy of Child & Adolescent Psychiatry, Seattle, Wa.

McDonald, G. (1980). Parental power and adolescents' parental identification. *Journal of Marriage and the Family, 42*, 289-296.

McGee, R., & Williams, S. (1988). A longitudinal study of depression in nine-year old children. *American Academy of Child and Adolescent Psychiatry, 27*, 342-348.

McManus, M., Lerner, H., Robbins, D., et al. (1984). Assessment of borderline symptomatology in hospitalized adolescents. *Journal of American Academy of Child Psychiatry, 23*, 685-694.

Mendlewicz, J., & Baron, M. (1981). Morbidity risks in subtypes of unipolar depressive illness: Differences between early and late onset forms. *British Journal of Psychiatry, 139*, 463-466.

Miller, I.W., Norman, W.H., & Dow, M.G. (1986). Psychosocial characteristics of "double depression." *American Journal of Psychiatry, 143*, 1042-1044.

Mitchell, J.R., McCauley, E., Burke, P.M., & Moss, S. (1988). Phenomenology of depression in children and adolescents. *American Academy of Child and Adolescent Psychiatry, 27,* 12-20.

Mitchell, J., McCauley, E., Burke, P., Calderon, R., & Schloredt, K. (1989). Psychopathology in parents of depressed children and adolescents. *American Academy of Child and Adolescent Psychiatry, 28,* 352-357.

Mosak, H. H. (1971). Lifestyle. In A. Nikelly (Ed.), *Techniques for behavioral change.* Springfield, IL: Charles C. Thomas.

Myers, J.K., Weissman, M.M., Tischler, G.L., et al. (1984). Six-months prevalence of psychiatric disorders in three communities: 1980-1982. *Archives of General Psychiatry, 41,* 959-967.

Nurnberger, J.I., & Gershon, E.S. (1984). Genetics of affective disorders. In R. Post & J. Ballenger (Eds.), *Neurobiology of mood disorders* (pp.243-266). Baltimore: Williams & Wilkins.

Orvaschel, H., & Weissman, M.M. (1986). Epidemiology of anxiety disorders in children: A review. In R. Gittelman (Ed.), *Anxiety disorders of childhood* (pp.168-176). New York: Guilford Press.

Petty, L.K., Asarnow, J.R., Carlson, G.A., et al. (1985). The dexamethasone suppression test—depressed, dysthymic, and nondepressed children. *American Journal of Psychiatry, 142,* 631-633.

Poznanski, E.O., Carroll, B.J., Banegas, M.D., et al. (1982). The dexamethasone suppression test in prepubertal depressed children. *American Journal of Psychiatry, 139,* 321-324.

Puig-Antich, J. (1980). Affective disorders in childhood. A review and perspective. *Psychiatric Clinics of North America, 3,* 403-424.

Puig-Antich, J. (1982). Major depression and conduct disorder in prepuberty. *American Academy of Child and Adolescent Psychiatry, 21,* 118-128.

Puig-Antich, J., Chambers, W., & Tabrizi, M. (1983). The clinical assessment of current depressive episodes in children and adolescents: Interview with parents and children. In D. Cantwell & G. Carlson (Eds.), *Affective disorders in children and adolescents. An update* (pp. 157-180). New York: Spectrum Press.

Puig-Antich, J., Goetz, R., Davies, M., et al. (1984a). Growth hormone secretion in prepubertal children with major depression. II. Sleep-related plasma concentrations during a depressive episode. *Archives of General Psychiatry, 41,* 463-466.

Puig-Antich, J., Goetz, R., Davies, M., et al. (1984b). Growth hormone secretion in prepubertal children with major depression, IV. Sleep-related plasma concentrations in a drug-free, fully recovered clinical state. *Archives of General Psychiatry, 41,* 479-483.

Puig-Antich, J., Goetz, D., Davies, M., et al., (1989). A controlled family history study of prepubertal major depressive disorder. *Archives of General Psychiatry, 46,* 406-418.

Puig-Antich, J., Goetz, R., Hanlon, C., et al. (1982). Sleep architecture and REM sleep measures in prepubertal children with major depression. *Archives of General Psychiatry, 39,* 932-939.

Puig-Antich, J., Goetz, R., Hanlon, C., et al. (1983). Sleep architecture and REM sleep measures in prepubertal major depressives: Sleep during recovery from the depressive episode in a drug-free state. *Archives of General Psychiatry, 40,* 187-192.

Puig-Antich, J., Novacenko, H., Davies, M., et al. (1984a). Growth hormone secretion in prepubertal children with major depression. I. Final report on response to insulin-induced hypoglycemia during a depressive episode. *Archives of General Psychiatry, 41,* 455-460.

Puig-Antich, J., Novacenko, H., Davies, M., et al. (1984b). Growth hormone secretion in prepubertal children with major depression. III. Response to insulin-induced hypoglycemia after recovery from a depressive episode and in a drug-free state. *Archives of General Psychiatry, 41,* 471-475.

Puig-Antich, J., Novacenko, H., Goetz, R., et al. (1984). Cortisol and prolactin responses to insulin-induced hypoglycemia in prepubertal major depressives during episode and after recovery. *Journal of American Academy of Child Psychiatry, 23,* 49-57.

Puig-Antich, J., & Rabinovich, H. (1986). Relationship between affective and anxiety disorders in childhood. In R. Gittelman (Ed.), *Anxiety disorders of childhood* (pp.204-216). New York: Guilford Press.

Radloff, L. (1975). Sex differences in depression: The effects of occupation and marital status. *Sex Roles, 1,* 249-269.

Reich, W., Herjanic, B., Welner, Z., et al. (1982). Development of a structured psychiatric interview for children: Agreement on diagnosis comparing child and parent interviews. *Journal of Abnormal Child Psychology, 10,* 325-336.

Rie, H.E. (1966). Depression in childhood: A survey of some pertinent contributions. *American Academy of Child and Adolescent Psychiatry, 5,* 653-686.

Robins, E., & Guze, S. (1972). Classification of affective disorders—the primary-secondary, the endogenous-reactive and the neurotic-psychotic dichotomies. In T.A. Williams, M.M. Katz, & J.A. Shield (Eds.), *Recent advances in psychobiology of the depressive illnesses* (pp.281-302). Washington, DC: U.S. Printing Office.

Robins, L.N. (1978). Sturdy childhood predictors of adult antisocial behavior. Replications from longitudinal studies. *Psychological Medicine, 8,* 611-622.

Robins, L.N., Helzer, J.E., Weissman, M.M., et al. (1984). Lifetime prevalence of specific psychiatric disorders in three sites. *Archives of General Psychiatry, 41,* 949-958.

Rutter, M. (1986). The developmental psychopathology of depression: Issues and perspectives. In M. Rutter, C.E. Izard, & P.B. Read (Eds.), *Depression in young people: Developmental and clinical perspectives* (pp. 12-14). London: The Guilford Press.

Seligman, M.E.P., Kaslow, N.J., Alloy, L.B., et al. (1984). Attributional style and depressive symptoms among children. *Journal of Abnormal Psychology, 93,* 235-238.

Smith, E.T. (1981). Adolescent agreement with perceived maternal and paternal goals. *Journal of Marriage and the Family, 43,* 85-94.

Spitz, R. (1946). Anaclitic depression. *Psychoanalytic Study of the Child, 2,* 313-342.

Spitzer, R.L., Endicott, J., & Robins, E. (1978). Research diagnostic criteria. Rationale and reliability. *Archives of General Psychiatry, 35,* 773-782.

Weissman, M.M., Gammon, G.D., John, K., et al., (1987). Children of depressed parents: Increased psychopathology and early onset of major depression. *Archives of General Psychiatry, 44,* 847-853.

Weissman, M.M., & Klerman, G.L. (1977). Sex differences and the epidemiology of depression. *Archives of General Psychiatry, 34,* 98-111.

Weissman, M.M., Pottenger, M., Kleber, H., et al. (1977). Symptom patterns in primary and secondary depression: A comparison of primary depressives with depressed opiate addicts, alcoholics and schizophrenics. *Archives of General Psychiatry, 34,* 854-862.

Weissman, M.M., Prusoff, B.A., Gammon, G.D., et al. (1984). Psychopathology in the children (ages 6-18) of depressed and normal parents. *Journal of American Academy of Child Psychiatry, 23,* 78-84.

Weller, E.B., Weller, R.A., Fristad, M.A., et al. (1984). The dexamethasone suppression test in hospitalized prepubertal depressed children. *American Journal of Psychiatry, 141,* 290-291.

Weller, R.A., Weller, E.B., Fristad, M.A., et al. (1985). A comparison of the cortisol suppression index and the dexamethasone suppression test in prepubertal children. *American Journal of Psychiatry, 142*, 1370-1372.

Wender, P.H., Kety, S.S., Rosenthal, D., et al. (1986). Psychiatric disorders in the biological and adoptive families of adopted individuals with affective disorders. *Archives of General Psychiatry, 43*, 923-929.

Willner, P. (1985). *Depression: A psychobiological synthesis*. New York: John Wiley & Sons.

Young, W., Knowles, J., MacLean, A., et al. (1982). The sleep patterns of childhood depressives: comparisons with age-matched controls. *Biological Psychiatry, 17*, 1163-1168.

Zis, A.P., & Goodwin, F.K. (1979). Major affective disorder as a recurrent illness. A critical review. *Archives of General Psychiatry, 36*, 835-839.

CHAPTER 17

ATTENTION-DEFICIT HYPERACTIVITY DISORDER AND SPECIFIC DEVELOPMENTAL DISORDERS

James W. Croake, Ph.D.
Kathleen M. Myers, M.D., M.P.H., M.S.

PURPOSE

This chapter reviews the syndrome of Attention-deficit Hyperactivity Disorder (ADHD). The discussion will focus on two areas. First, ADHD is presented as an example of a very common childhood disorder with onset during the earliest childhood years. Second, it is presented as a disorder affecting overall biopsychosocial development and significantly overlapping with Axis II Specific Developmental Disorders.

HISTORICAL

The current DSM-III-R description of the syndrome Attention-deficit Hyperactivity Disorder (ADHD) represents the most current conceptualization of a long-recognized disorder characterized by inattention, impulsivity, and excessive unfocused activity. The syndrome has been known by many different names over the past century. Still (1902) described a series of children with "defects in moral control." This term referred to his observation that these children had difficulty not only with attention, impulsivity, and hyperactivity, but frequently with socially appropriate behaviors as well.

Bradley (1937) reported a "paradoxical quieting effect" of amphetamines, which are stimulant medications, on children with these symptoms. He thought that they responded differently from normal children, and that this paradoxical response was part of an underlying brain dysfunction.

From the 1940s to the 1960s this disorder was referred to as Minimal Cerebral Damage or Minimal Brain Damage. These terms connoted the then prevalent concept that these behaviors arose from underlying brain damage. However, no structural or anatomical abnormalities have ever been documented. This designation was slowly discarded in favor of the term Minimal Brain Dysfunction (MBD) (Clements & Peters, 1962; Knobloch & Pasamanick, 1959). This terminology still suggested an underlying etiology. Structural brain damage was replaced by abnormality in brain functioning.

Attempts to define a syndrome accelerated in the mid 1960s to the 1970s. In DSM-II this same constellation of signs and symptoms was referred to as the Hyperkinetic Reaction of Childhood (American Psychiatric Association, 1968; Bakwin & Bakwin, 1966; Bender, 1975; Laufer & Denhoff, 1957; Safer & Allen, 1976). This term carried no reference to brain abnormalities or other possible etiology. In it was also described the one symptom which most distresses parents and teachers—hyperactivity.

Later in the 1970s and 1980s the core problem was conceptualized as a disorder of faulty attention and inhibitory control (Dykman, Ackerman, Clements, & Peters, 1971). Therefore, in DSM-III the disorder was designated as "Attention-Deficit Disorder, with or without Hyperactivity" (American Psychiatric Association, 1980). This approach specified three constellations of diagnostic symptoms: inattentiveness, impulsivity, and overactivity or restlessness. This threefold classificatory system impacted research and conceptualization of the disorder. However, it was short-lived.

In DSM-III-R this disorder was termed "Attention-Deficit Hyperactivity Disorder" (American Psychiatric Association, 1987). It reinstated hyperactivity in the diagnostic nomenclature and returned to an undifferentiated list of 14 diagnostic signs and symptoms without subtypes. Consistent with DSM-III-R's mandate to designate nomenclature descriptively and free from theoretical bias or potential etiology, no reference is made to etiology.

DIAGNOSTIC CRITERIA
AND PHENOMENOLOGY

Diagnostic Signs and Symptoms

DSM-III-R diagnostic criteria for ADHD are listed in Figure 17.1. These criteria include an undifferentiated list of 14 cardinal signs and symptoms. Any eight of these must be present to make the diagnosis. The undifferentiated list represents a shift to less rigid criteria from DSM-III's requirement that problem behaviors be present in all three categories: inattention, impulsivity, and hyperactivity. Operationally, the DSM-III-R schema would allow a child with features in only two of these three categories to be diagnosed as ADHD. This approach may overgeneralize and overdiagnose the disorder, producing a lower specificity. However, diagnostic reliability and sensitivity are improved. Experienced clinicians can identify ADHD children with a high degree of reliability, even though the symptoms predominating in any one child vary greatly. A hallmark of this disorder is its variability from child to child. The current approach, therefore, addresses the

(continued on page 513)

NOTE: Consider a criterion met only if the behavior is considerably more frequent than that of most people of the same mental age.

A. A disturbance of at least six months during which at least eight of the following are present:

(1) often fidgets with hands or feet or squirms in seat (in adolescents, may be limited to subjective feelings of restlessness)
(2) has difficulty remaining seated when required to do so
(3) is easily distracted by extraneous stimuli
(4) has difficulty awaiting turn in games or group situations
(5) often blurts out answers to questions before they have been completed
(6) has difficulty following through on instructions from others (not due to oppositional behavior or failure of comprehension), e.g. fails to finish chores
(7) has difficulty sustaining attention in tasks or play activities
(8) often shifts from one uncompleted activity to another
(9) has difficulty playing quietly
(10) often talks excessively
(11) often interrupts or intrudes on others, e.g., blurts into other children's games
(12) often does not seem to listen to what is being said to him or her
(13) often loses things necessary for tasks or activites at school or at home (e.g., toys, pencils, books, assignments)
(14) often engages in physically dangerous activities without considering possible consequences (not for the purpose of thrill-seeking), e.g., runs into street without looking

NOTE: The above items are listed in descending order of discriminating power based on data from a national field trial of the DSM-III-R criteria for Disruptive Behavior Disorders.

B. Onset before the age of seven.

C. Does not meet the criteria for a Pervasive Developmental Disorder.

Criteria for severity of Attention-deficit Hyperactivity Disorder:

Mild: Few, if any, symptoms in excess of those required to make the diagnosis *and* only minimal or no impairment in school and social functioning.

Moderate: Symptoms of functional impairment intermediate between "mild" and "severe."

Severe: Many symptoms in excess of those required to make the diagnosis *and* significant and pervasive impairment in functioning at home and school and with peers.

Figure 17.1. Diagnositic criteria for Attention-deficit Hyperactivity Disorder.

heterogeneity of the ADHD syndrome, while preserving its easily identifiable essence.

Representative Behaviors

The 14 different behaviors noted in Figure 17.1 represent developmentally inappropriate extremes in attention, impulsivity, and overactivity. Affected children generally display deficits in all three behaviors, although to varying degrees. The behaviors are pervasive, manifesting in most areas of functioning. They are not intermittent, but may wax and wane depending on environmental circumstances.

School Behaviors. Teachers' descriptions of attentional deficits generally involve ADHD children's difficulty following directions, completing work, staying on task, or being easily distracted by classroom noise. Impulsivity is demonstrated by blurting out answers, starting an assignment before the directions have been completed, not waiting a turn, being easily angered, or not being able to work in groups. In the schoolyard they may be involved in frequent fights. Hyperactivity is noted in their frequent fidgeting, inability to remain in their seats, dropping items, or constant running at recess or in the halls. Uninformed teachers may describe ADHD children as daydreaming, lazy, unmotivated, or uncooperative. Poor school performance affects the eventual level of academic attainment. The presence of fighting is a very negative indicator for future social adjustment.

Home Behaviors. At home, parents may describe difficulty getting ready for school in the morning, forgetfulness with chores or multiple commands, and inability to stick with tasks. They may break things accidentally by their rough play and impulsive acts. They are frequently accident-prone. Fighting with siblings goes beyond simple sibling rivalry. Since they act impulsively, they may act before having understood what is requested of them. Apparently good intentions go awry. Their hyperactivity is described as being constantly on the go, as having "their motor running." They lack age-appropriate judgement.

Unlike many psychiatric disorders where symptoms are described by the individual or parent as beyond usual day-to-day experience, ADHD symptoms are typical of most children at some time during development. Parents will tolerate their young children's inability to sit still, shifting from one activity to another, not listening, interrupting others, impulsive acts, and even aggression. However, they will not tolerate these same behaviors by older children. Additionally, most parents will describe their ADHD children as displaying these behaviors to a much greater extent than other children their age, even when the children are very young. The signs of ADHD, therefore, appear to represent the extreme on a continuum of motoric and cognitive behaviors.

Peer Behaviors. Peers frequently will not play with ADHD children. They cite reasons such as their not following rules of games, not listening, and immaturity. Impulsivity is evident in other children's complaints that they are bossy, disrupt games, do not wait their turn, risk dangerous activity, and generally get their peers into trouble. Their activity level is high in quiet games or unstructured activities and they talk too much. In more exciting activities they may become frenetic and appear out of control.

Observations of these ADHD children with peers indicate that they very easily become stimulated by peer interactions and have difficulty disengaging or calming down. Other children quickly pick out the ADHD children and label them as undesirable, even when watching silent videotapes of ADHD children playing with peers (Whalen, Henker, Castro, & Granger, 1987). It does not take long for these new peers to assess ADHD children, and rate them as negatively as their former peers rate them (Henker & Whalen, 1989). They become unpopular.

Purposiveness of Behavior. Their social difficulties do not arise because of poor intellectual capacity. ADHD children generally have normal intellect and information processing skills (Henker & Whalen, 1989; Milich & Dodge, 1984). They are as socially aware as their peers (Whalen & Henker, 1985). Their main deficit appears to be in self-regulation (Dykman, Ackerman, Clements, & Peters, 1971; Henker & Whalen, 1989; Laufer & Denhoff, 1957). Motivational factors play a central role, as indicated by their ability to attend and focus their activity when appropriately stimulated. ADHD may be described as an interpersonal disorder, that is, deficits in interfacing of the child with the social world (Henker & Whalen, 1989).

These behaviors may worsen in situations requiring self-application such as completing a task, or requiring sustained attention as listening to the teacher or sitting in church. Conversely, they may be minimized during novel activities, stimulating situations, individualized attention, strict control, or when receiving frequent reinforcement. Thus, adults will note that these children appear normal when they are examined at the clinician's office. Observations of their waiting room behavior provides a more diagnostic environment. They also do better when their desk is placed at the front of the room near to the teacher's desk. Finally, they may do very well with computers and stimulating computer games.

Primary vs. Secondary Syndrome

ADHD most frequently occurs as a primary syndrome, diagnosed in children with no other overt disorder to explain the symptoms. However, it may exist concurrently with or secondary to other abnormalities (American Psychiatric Association, 1987). Children who experienced earlier damage to their central nervous system, such as brain infections, head injuries, birth complications, or premature birth may later demonstrate signs consistent with ADHD. ADHD may be diagnosed in these children if the signs are excessive for the given condition. For example, if a mentally retarded child demonstrates symptoms of ADHD that are beyond the child's mental age, then ADHD is appropriately diagnosed. The frequent occurrence of ADHD in such cerebrally compromised children has contributed to etiologic theories of brain impairment.

Adjunctive Signs

The diagnostic criteria for ADHD reveal only a small part of the overall dysfunction experienced by these children and the impact they make on others. At this point in time, knowing whether impairments in the social, psychological, and physical domains are secondary to their inattention, impulsivity, and hyperactivity or whether all of these problems develop from a common developmental deficit is unclear. These adjunctive signs are the ones that are mostly distressing to parents and others who encounter ADHD children.

Social Development and Maladaptive Behavior

All four Goals of Misbehavior may be observed, and all within a very short time period. Dreikurs (1968) saw the purpose of children's misbehavior as falling into one of four categories: attention getting, power, power with revenge, and display of inadequacy. These are immediate goals of the situation which are aimed at the adults in the setting. With attention getting, the children are attempting to keep adults busy with them. Power is a statement of "I can do whatever I desire, and you can't stop me." Power with revenge is an indication that the child feels hurt and wants to hurt back. Display of inadequacy is a request to be left alone, to be free of expectations.

Power struggles of ADHD children with their parents are so common that even the smallest chores become major obstacles. They may be rigid, tolerating change poorly. They seem immature. Parents and teachers complain that the ADHD children do not learn from experience or from the consequences of their behavior. Praise and rewards are usually ineffective. They believe that punishment is the only recourse. They are convinced that they have to control their children. Peers exclude them. They may be enthusiastic and even charming so that they initially make friends, but they quickly antagonize these friends. Often they have no friends. They want their own way; they want what they want when they want it; they do not take no for an answer; they want to be the boss; and they play impulsively, often resulting in aggression. But they are not mean. Their violence often results from their impulsivity and other childen's negative response to their domineering ways.

The preceding profile indicates why ADHD is classified in the DSM-III-R with the Disruptive Behavior Disorders. The hallmark of ADHD and the other Disruptive Behavior Disorders is that the behaviors are usually more distressing to others than to the individual demonstrating them. For this reason, they have been termed "externalizing," as opposed to the "internalizing" symptoms seen with depression. ADHD children go through life apparently oblivious to the social codes and situational cues that guide others' behavior. They are often surprised to learn that others are very distressed by their behavior. Often they will blame their behavior and its consequences on others, taking no personal responsibility. The individual diagnostic signs and symptoms, therefore, do not convey the social disruption associated with this syndrome.

Emotional and Psychological Development

Three behavioral attributes seem to characterize the psychological profile of these children. Their moods are variable and unpredictable. They are fine one day, or even one minute, and impossible the next. Their moods also may be exaggerated. In pleasurable activities they may become overexcited so that they appear to lose control of themselves. They cannot "wind down." Secondly, they are generally irritable and easily frustrated. Their low frustration tolerance along with their impulsivity frequently leads to tantrums or temper outbursts. Thirdly, they seek stimulation. They may call attention to themselves, engage in novel activities, and even court danger. As part of their stimulus seeking, they are constantly unsatisfied and easily bored. Their impulsive behavior counters the boredom. They often have difficulty getting to sleep, perhaps reflecting their inability to "wind down" at the end of the day or their continued desire for stimulation. Many ADHD children do not appear affectionate, even as infants. Although attention-seeking, they are not affection-seeking.

Eventually, most ADHD children suffer impairments in their self-esteem. Usually this is evident by the second to fourth grade. They begin to recognize their social rejection; they feel different and may be very lonely. They may make statements about hurting themselves or wishing they were dead, and their impulsivity makes them a risk to incur some harm, either self-induced or by apparent accident. They are accident-prone. They may become depressed, and even if not depressed, they are often unhappy at a young age.

Physical and Neurological Development

Many, but not all, ADHD children demonstrate "soft neurological signs" (Werry, Minde, Guyman, Weiss, Dogan, & Hoy, 1972). These are observable neurological deficits of mild to moderate severity which are not localized to a specific part of the brain, but which indicate diffuse motoric dysfunction. The most common soft neurological signs are deficits in fine motor skills. Approximately half of ADHD children demonstrate such incoordination. In school these children may color or write very poorly, or be unable to cut with scissors. At home they may not be able to button their clothes, tie their shoes, or zipper their pants. They may have difficulty balancing themselves and therefore cannot learn to ride a bicycle. Others have poor hand-eye coordination, making them awkward at catching or throwing a ball, or at playing baseball or basketball. They tend to be clumsy and frequently break things accidentally. Some may not even respond to pain as robustly as other children. Gross motor skills are more frequently intact, so that even those children with fine motor deficits may still run and swim well, play soccer, or master martial arts. These gross motor activities can help them to focus some of their restlessness.

Related to incoordination is the inability to appropriately organize tasks. School papers appear disorganized, carelessly done. Test results show haphazard mistakes. They may miss easy questions and then correctly answer more difficult ones. They do not seem to plan their answers or problem solving. Chores at home are done poorly, if at all, without supervision. When they must work independently, they may not be able to organize the task to get started. They often do not have the skills that enable them to organize preparations for school in the morning. Continual parental supervision is typical.

CONCURRENT DISRUPTIVE BEHAVIOR DISORDERS

Approximately 50% of ADHD children also will meet criteria for other Disruptive Behavior Disorders, specifically Oppositional Defiant Disorder (ODD) or Conduct Disorder (CD) (Henker

& Whalen, 1989; Sandberg, Wieselberg, & Shaffer, 1980). The high concurrence of these diagnoses with ADHD results in part because criteria for the three disorders overlap (American Psychiatric Association, 1987; Biederman, Munir, & Knee, 1987; Reeves, Werry, Elkind, & Zametkin, 1987; Sandberg, Wieselberg, & Shaffer, 1980; Shapiro & Garfinkel, 1986; Werry, Reeves, & Elkind, 1987).

Oppositional Defiant Disorder

Oppositionally Defiant ADHD children demonstrate greater difficulty regulating mood and behavior. Presenting signs shift to anger, instead of just irritability as with ADHD, and increased power struggles instead of just disorganization and distractibility. These children will not only have difficulty remembering or sticking with tasks, they will adamantly refuse to do them or put up a struggle before doing them. Everything they do seems to say, "You can't make me." They seem to have a "chip on their shoulder." They seem provocative, resentful, and sometimes vindictive. They may treat others very poorly, being annoying and argumentative at the least to denigrating at worst. They disrespect parents especially, but authority figures in general. They are always showing that they are the boss. Other people are not as eager to reach out to help these children as the children with ADHD alone. Behavior is generally much worse at home, or around familiar people and situations. However, they do not generally break societal rules.

Conduct Disorder

Conduct Disordered ADHD children may have been diagnosed as having ODD when younger. CD supersedes ODD diagnostically, since the psychopathology is greater and ODD symptoms are generally present in CD youths. Basic age-appropriate societal rules are broken and the rights of others violated when ADHD children also demonstrate a CD. Such antisocial behaviors are not diagnostic of ADHD or ODD diagnoses without CD. Impairments of behavior are typically pervasive, occurring in most settings not just with authority figures, as is seen with ODD. Those ADHD children with better social skills are likely to develop the group type of CD, while those less skilled may develop the solitary aggressive type.

If a child does not present for therapeutic help until CD or ODD is present, parents will generally focus on these more disruptive and maladaptive behaviors. Careful assessment for underlying ADHD must then be undertaken and considered in treatment planning.

Mood Disorders

Some features of a Mood Disorder resemble symptoms of ADHD (Jensen, Burke, & Garfinkel, 1988). Both may demonstrate an irritable mood. The agitation of mood may resemble hyperactivity. Difficulty concentrating may be confused with inattention and distractibility. Both groups of children may display insomnia. Some of the mood lability seen in ADHD children suggests rapid cycling Bipolar Disorder. Therefore, Mood Disorders form part of the differential diagnosis of ADHD.

Additionally, ADHD children may develop a Mood Disorder subsequent to or concurrent with their ADHD. Major Depressive Disorder may develop. More commonly ADHD children will meet criteria for Dysthymia with either irritable or depressive mood (Anderson, Williams, McGee, & Silva, 1987; Jensen, Burke, & Garfinkel, 1988; McGee & Williams, 1988). The risk for a secondary Mood Disorder is increased by the increased rate of Mood Disorders in parents of ADHD children (Biederman, Munir & Knee, 1987; Lahey, Piacentini, McBurnett, Stone, Hartdagen, & Hynd, 1988). Some parents will have Mood Disorders undiagnosed prior to evaluation of their children's problems. Therefore, any symptomatic change of ADHD phenomenology must be reassessed with consideration of a Mood Disorder.

Specific Developmental Disorders

The Specific Developmental Disorders (SDDs) include academic skills disorders in arithmetic, expressive writing, and reading; language and speech disorders in articulation, expressive language, or receptive language; and motor skills disorders in coordination. Due to their large overlap with ADHD, a more comprehensive discussion is warranted.

Diagnosis. In DSM-III-R criteria for the various SDDs is the requirement that the individual's achievement in the particular developmental skill be "markedly below" what would be expected for the individual's age, schooling, and intellectual capacity. Additionally, the disturbance in the specific SDD must significantly interfere with academic achievement or activities of daily living related to that skill. Finally, the deficit in that SDD must not be due to any physical defect or other disorder. Also to be ruled out are psychosocial conditions that could lead to deprived educational opportunities. For example, children living in poverty or children from families where English is not the primary language need special consideration. The lack of appropriate motivation for learning also would preclude this diagnosis. In general, the SDD child is conceptualized as having average academic potential, but below-average academic performance, with academic difficulties resulting from a specific cognitive deficit, as language or perceptual-motor skills.

Diagnoses of the Academic Skills Disorders are made with tests that measure both the level of development of the impaired skill and the individual's intelligence. Additionally, the diagnosis of Developmental Expressive and Receptive Language Disorders requires that scores for these language skills be compared with scores for nonverbal intelligence. The Axis II Specific Developmental Disorders are unique among psychiatric disorders in that their diagnoses are dependent upon validating standardized tests; however, no comparable standardized tests are available to measure ADHD. However, ADHD children will generally demonstrate characteristic patterns on such testing that suggest inattention and impulsivity.

Detection. These SDDs are usually diagnosed by 8 years of age. Some children escape detection until later ages. Criteria in the DSM-III-R are vague. Multiple difficulties ensue when attempts are made to operationalize the definitions for SDDs, so that children may escape detection early in their schooling. Two major approaches have been used (Morris, 1988).

The first is an age-based definition which is most commonly used in educational settings. For children to be classified as SDD, schools require that children perform two years below their age or grade level in reading or other specific achievement area. This definition has many associated problems relating to the psychometric properties of scores, such as the use of age equivalents or grade equivalents (Reynolds, 1981).

The second approach has focused on the discrepancy between IQ and achievement measures, with a 1-standard-deviation difference being considered criterion to define a SDD child. The problem with such discrepancy-based classification relates to the use of standardized IQ tests, the choice of different achievement tests, and the definition of the skill being measured. Finally, the choice of the 1-standard-deviation discrepancy between IQ and performance is arbitrary. One of the most common uses of various discrepancy criteria is to control the number of children eligible for special services in relation to funding levels.

A final problem is the exclusionary criteria used in operationalizing definitions of SDD. Children with sensory/motor deficits, with psychiatric disorders, or from lower socioeconomic backgrounds would be excluded, although no operational criteria exist for identifying these problems which may contribute significantly to learning difficulties.

Current operationalized criteria group deficits in related skills as reading disorders, arithmetic disorders, or language disorders. However, such grouping assumes homogeneous symptomatology and implies a known etiology, as underlying brain dysfunction. However, the most current research does not support these conclusions. Great variability occurs within the SDD population. This heterogeneity may reflect individual differences or the occurrence of variable subtypes that differ in etiology, task performance, and prognosis (Morris, 1988). This heterogeneity has been largely ignored in theories of SDD as well as in the development of services to treat SDD children. New approaches to classification are now being investigated (Morris, 1988).

As summarized previously, these operational criteria for identifying SDD children are variable and inconsistently applied.

Definitions fail to acknowledge the multiple factors that influence academic development or the diversity of problems associated with academic handicaps (Taylor, 1988). As a result, many children who meet DSM-III-R criteria will not meet the school criteria and will therefore not be eligible for remedial services. Children with milder SDDs and shy children are especially vulnerable to being overlooked. By contrast, SDD children with concurrent ADHD or other Disruptive Behavior Disorders will be less likely to escape detection.

Prevalence. Individual SDDs affect approximately 2 to 11% of the general child population (American Psychiatric Association, 1987). Many children have more than one SDD. Among school-aged children, a prevalence rate of at least 10 to 15% is commonly reported for SDDs as a group (Heaton, 1988; Silver, 1989).

Different studies have variably reported that 20 to 40% of ADHD children have concurrent SDDs (Bashir, Wing, & Abrams, 1987; Denckla, 1978; Duane, 1985; Duffy, 1988; Forness, 1981; Halperin, Gittelman, Klein, & Rudel, 1984; Silver, 1981). This high overlap of the two disorders suggests a possible common etiology or predisposing factors. The inability to concentrate is a primary characteristic of perceptual dysfunction. A pupil who cannot focus and attend will have difficulty decoding sensory data efficiently. Achievement in all areas of learning will then be affected. ADHD children are prone to multiple developmental disorders. This makes them more easily identifiable but also makes academic achievement more difficult.

Maturation. Previously, these disorders were designated as learning disabilities or developmental delays. These designations are misleading, implying that maturation brings improvement. Some developmentally disordered children do improve their abilities with age; however, most do not. Children with more severe forms of these disorders are especially unlikely to attain skills comparable to their adolescent or adult peers.

Disorders of inadequate development may be more diagnostically descriptive. SDDs and ADHD share this historic conceptualization that the dysfunction results from delays of maturation and represents normal functioning for earlier developmental stages. This terminology persists in part because accurate prediction is not possible during preschool and school years as to which children will "catch up" and which will not. Whether these children will "catch up" relates not only to their academic success, but to their success with the life tasks.

Etiology. In general, SDD children vary in their academic, cognitive, and social abilities. No individual child has all of the deficits that have been associated with specific academic learning problems. Attempts to establish causality are therefore difficult, and the etiology of SDDs remains unknown. The current consensus is that the etiology is heterogeneous. Complex cognitive operations and neural factors are associated with children's ability to learn any skill. Learning is influenced by multiple factors including intelligence, academic skills, stimulation, social interest, effort, and encouragement. Each of these factors is affected by a wide range of emotional and environmental considerations. If any of these factors for success is missing, the risk of learning disability increases.

Traditional concepts of SDD have rested on two presuppositions: first, that SDDs are due to deficits in basic psychological processes; and second, that these processing deficits are, in turn, a reflection of an organ inferiority in biological-genetic or constitutional factors (Taylor, 1988). These concepts are being rethought in the light of new research.

Support for a genetic organ inferiority has been best established for Developmental Reading Disorder, or dyslexia (Pennington & Smith, 1988). Dyslexic children reportedly have a genetically influenced deficiency in single word recognition skills and the precursor to this deficit is in the domain of phonological processing skills (Pennington & Smith, 1988). Other SDDs have not been as well assessed for genetic influences. However, indicators of organ inferiority are supported by an association with biological markers such as positive family histories, electrophysiological abnormalities, and increased rates of pre- and perinatal complications (Taylor, 1988).

In the DSM-III-R no reference is made to any impairment of central nervous system organ inferiority or constitutional etiology. Such factors may be necessary, but they are not sufficient for the development of learning problems. The manifestations of these problems probably depend upon other factors, such as overcompensation, lack of encouragement, overambition, lack of social interest, as well as parental attitudes and educational approaches. "Encouragement" and "over-ambition" are technical terms in Adlerian theory. **Encouragement** is a willingness to go forth until the problem is solved. The opposite, **discouragement,** is characterized by not taking the sequential steps necessary for problem-solving. **Overambition** is the opposite of self-confidence. Overambition is a statement that "I am not enough." "I am unable to do the job."

Interpersonal Disturbances. The SDDs are, by definition, associated with impairment in academic functioning and also have been associated with impairments in daily living. The latter impairments are the ones that generally bring SDD children to clinical awareness (Hunt & Cohen, 1984).

An original problem such as reading will frequently generalize to other school subjects which rely heavily on written material. They are then considered unintelligent, since they cannot master age-appropriate language skills. These skills are not limited to academic subjects. They include the time taken to understand material as well as to associate it with old knowledge. Therefore, skills requiring wit and humor or creativity and intuition may be beyond these children in daily social interactions. To other children these children appear to "not get it." They are then excluded. These additional failure experiences are perceived by SDD children as further indication of their inferiority. SDD children then become further stigmatized by their peers.

Adlerian theory is holistic: A deficit in one aspect of being will necessarily show itself in all areas of functioning to a lesser or greater degree. It can take the form of overcompensation as in the classic case of Demosthenes who used pebbles in his mouth to overcome a speech impediment. His overcompensation resulted in his fame for great oration. Adler

(1956) saw all compensation as overcompensation. When one successfully strives to overcome a liability, the striving goes beyond a neutral position or average level of competence. Physical overcompensation is also seen. A broken bone heals stronger in the area of the wound than in the surrounding bone. Overcompensation requires courage, self-confidence, and optimism. Unsuccessful striving is characteristic of discouragement, a lack of self-confidence, and pessimism. These academic and functional impairments, interference with getting on with all aspects of life, are the bases for the inclusion of these disorders in psychiatric nomenclature. These children will go to extremes in their efforts to overcome their SDDs. They may fake a paragraph when it comes to their turn to read aloud. A "sour grapes" attitude can be a discouraged, unwillingness to try, response to confronting an academic task. Conduct Disorder will commonly be employed as a discouraged tactic in the avoidance of an academic challenge. A face-saving strategy obscures the fact that one cannot meet the academic requirements. All misbehaviors can be best viewed as an attempt to safeguard self-esteem. Overcompensation using misbehavior may bring admiration among some peers and give one a higher status position in certain circles. That method of attaining status will be an interference to achievement in academic areas where one might be successful. Coming to rely on misbehavior for finding one's place in the group can result in a life-long disability.

SDD children will often resist receiving special educational services because they are aware of the stigmatization that they will incur. Special education is an inferior station among peers. Special education encourages overcompensation in the direction of misbehavior because it sets these children in a socially inferior position. As Adler (1956) made clear, all striving is from a position of felt inferiority to a position of felt superiority. The child who believes that academic success is not possible will overcompensate, strive toward superiority which is not useful. Placing children with ADHD and SDD apart from their peers in any form is best avoided. Their striving for superiority will likely move in a negative direction if they are seen as different by peers.

Since many ADHD children have concurrent SDDs they face stigmatization by their peers even more than those with only ADHD. ADHD children are easily picked out by their peers as undesirable because of their disruptive behaviors. As seen above, ADHD-SDD children may additionally be considered stupid, socially inept, moody, and different.

Discouragement. Many studies have reported decreased self-esteem and social competence, poor social adjustment, emotional disturbances, and conduct and family problems (Rourke, 1988). As discussed, SDD children must deal with interpersonal environments that differ markedly from their normally achieving peers whether they are merely handicapped or further stigmatized with special education. They are often perceived by parents, teachers, and peers as less pleasant and desirable, and the recipients of more negative communications and discouragement from these sources. They may be ignored and rejected by teachers, and treated in a more punitive and derogatory manner by parents.

Dreikurs (1958) clarified the problem. Teachers and parents do not know how to encourage these children. Hence, they resort to discouraging tactics typically in the form of punishment.

Classmates describe SDD children as less socially competent regardless of their attempts to overcompensate. SDD children may also have difficulty perceiving and interpreting the affective states of others. They lack social interest; that is, they do not feel part of the group, perceive the environment as unfriendly, and then respond with socially useless behavior (Dreikurs, 1958). It is likely that social awareness and responsiveness vary markedly for subtypes of SDD children depending upon the central processing abilities and deficits, the specific task demands (Ozols & Rourke, 1985), as well as the degree of personal courage, self-confidence, optimism, and development of social interest.

The association of socioemotional disturbances with SDDs does not necessarily imply that they are consequences of the learning deficits. A causal connection has been proposed between particular patterns of central processing abilities and deficits on the one hand, and particular subtypes of learning disabilities and socioemotional functioning on the other (Rourke, 1988; Rourke & Fisk, 1981).

Idiographic. The Adlerian view is unwilling to compartmentalize brain functioning, behavioral manifestations, and interpersonal relationships. They are integral, an inseparable idiographic, and do not lend themselves to direction, specific stimulus-response predictability, nor individual prognosis even if all of the objective variables could be determined.

Long-term Functioning. The long-term outcome for SDD children is of relevance for interpersonal, occupational, and emotional adjustment as well as for the school, economic, and judicial systems of society. Early studies painted a bleak picture of the adolescent and adult outcomes for SDD children who did not overcome their learning disabilities (Critchley, 1964). Increased risk for an antisocial behavior pattern was emphasized. Intervention did not appear to affect outcome. Only if the child came from upper socioeconomic status (Schonhaut & Satz, 1983) or had superior intelligence (Robinson & Smith, 1962), did the prospect for academic skill development appear hopeful.

The current consensus is that SDDs persist into adulthood to some degree. The severity of academic deficits in adulthood is associated with the severity of the disability as a child (Spreen, 1988a, 1988b). Once children have fallen behind academically, they are susceptible to further delays with increasing disability (Kistner & Torgesen, 1987; Stanovich, 1986).

How intervention affects adult achievement remains unclear. Some studies report good success with specific intervention models (Kline & Kline, 1975), others have demonstrated only modest success with general interventions (Bruck, 1985; Spreen, 1988b), and others have not demonstrated any effect of intervention on outcome (Frauenheim, 1978). Nomothetically, the single best predictor of overall adult outcome is general intelligence (Muehl & Forrell, 1973; Rawson, 1968; Spreen, 1988a, 1988b). Similarly, the absence of neurological impairment is highly predictive of better outcome (Jaklewicz, 1982; Spreen, 1988a, 1988b; A. A. Silver, 1977). Occupational achievement appears lower for SDD children (Finucci, Gottfredson, & Childs, 1985; Jaklewicz, 1982; Spreen, 1988a). The father's occupational and educational status appear to predict SDD children's later occupational outcome better than many other relevant factors except general intelligence and lack of neurological impairment (Buerger, 1968; O'Connor & Spreen, 1988).

Socioemotional disturbances appear to peak in late adolescence and decrease somewhat in the third decade of life. Women appear to be more affected than men (Spreen, 1988a). SDD children with socioemotional disturbances continue to demonstrate problems as adolescents and adults, and may change the types of problems they have (Rourke, 1988). However, children without significant socioemotional disturbances are not likely to develop them later in life (Rourke, 1988).

ETIOLOGY OF ADHD

No structural or anatomical brain damage has been documented in ADHD. However, many studies over the past three decades have supported brain dysfunction in ADHD children; that is, an abnormality in how the brain functions rather than in tissue structure (Brown, Ebert, & Minichiello, 1985; Dykman, Ackerman, Clements, & Peters, 1971; Ferguson & Pappas, 1979; Hastings & Barkley, 1978; Levy & Hobbs, 1988; Rapoport, Buchsbaum, Zahn, Weingartner, Ludlow, & Mikkelsen, 1978; Rapoport & Ferguson, 1981; Satterfield, 1973; Werry, Minde, Guyman, Weiss, Dogan, & Hoy, 1972; Wender, 1971; Zametkin & Rapoport, 1987). This dysfunction is detected by psychophysiological and neuropsychological testing, and neurochemical assays, rather than by neurological examination or postmortem examinations of brain tissue. Recent developments in cerebral imaging techniques have revealed decreased blood perfusion of selected areas of brain tissue which may be associated with these functional deficits (Loh, Hendrickson, & Bruhn, 1984). The "soft neurological signs," such as fine motor control (Werry, Minde, Guyman, Weiss, Dogan, & Hoy, 1972), and the very frequent co-occurrence of SDDs with ADHD (Bashir, Wing, & Abrams, 1987; Denckla,

1978; Duane, 1985; Duffy, 1988; Forness, 1981; Halperin, Gittelman, Klein, & Rudel, 1984; Silver, 1981) also suggest underlying brain dysfunction.

Another line of thinking conceptualizes ADHD as a disorder of temperament with primary developmental deficits in self-control, interpersonal relatedness, and social transactions (Henker & Whalen, 1989; Wender, 1987). The high prevalence of personality disorders in adulthood and the enduring nature of ADHD deficits in those adults without personality disorders (Gittelman, Mannuzza, Shenker, & Bonagura, 1985; Hopkins, Perlman, Hechtman, & Weiss, 1979; Weiss & Hechtman, 1986; Weiss, Hechtman, & Perlman, 1978; Weiss, Hechtman, Perlman, Hopkins, & Wener, 1979) suggests an etiologic role for temperament.

DEMOGRAPHY

Prevalence

ADHD appears to affect approximately 3 to 5% of children in the United States (American Psychiatric Association, 1987; Lambert, Sandoval, & Sasone, 1981; Sandberg, Wieselberg, & Shaffer, 1980). It is the most common single disorder referred to child psychiatry (Safer & Allen, 1976). The onset of ADHD must be before 7 years old in order to meet DSM-III-R diagnostic criteria. If clinical assessment does not occur until after this age, the symptoms must still have been present before 7 years of age. Approximately half of ADHD children are diagnosed by age 4 years old (American Psychiatric Association, 1987). Most children are clinically identified by 10 years of age.

Masculine Protest

Males significantly outnumber females. In general population studies, the ratio approximates 3:1; but in clinical samples the ratio has been estimated between 6:1 and 10:1 (American Psychiatric Association, 1987; Lambert, Sandoval, & Sasone, 1981). The discrepancy probably reflects the differential misbehaviors demonstrated by boys and girls. Dreikurs (1968) suggested that this is a form of what Adler termed "the masculine protest." Striving from a position of felt inferiority toward superiority takes on the exaggerated caricature of masculinity. Misbehavior of an aggressive nature is supported by parents and culture as proof that one is a real man, and reassures the boy that even if he is not as capable in academic areas at least he is powerful in the male arena. Parents and culture do not desire feminine males. Hence, the misbehavior may result in referral for treatment because it is disrupting, but it is better than being a "sissy."

DEVELOPMENTAL CHANGE OF SYMPTOMS

ADHD children generally demonstrate different signs at various developmental periods. This variability may represent a true maturational change. Alternatively, parents and teachers may differentially respond to signs with advancing age. If children are overly active as toddlers, they may well be called hyperactive. But if they are unable to stay in their seats and bother other pupils when placed in a large stimulating classroom, their disruptiveness becomes a major problem. Expectations of children's behavior depends largely on established age-appropriate normative behaviors. The exact reasons for the shifting behavior pattern is not clear. Teachers are often better reporters of whether ADHD children are demonstrating inappropriate behaviors, due to their greater experience with these age-appropriate norms.

Preschool

Many ADHD children show their first signs as infants. They are irritable, not easily consoled, colicky, and sleep poorly. Some parents describe them as not wanting to be held. However, other parents note a normal infancy. As toddlers, the main complaints almost always center on their gross motor activity. ADHD children seem to be motorically ahead of their peers from the very first crawl they take. They are quickly into and on top of everything and seem fearless. They may wander away if not carefully supervised, not seeming to mind separation from mother. They are constantly on the go and tantrums continue throughout the preschool period. They also may be especially violent with head banging or serious injury to other children. If enrolled in preschool, social misbehaviors start to dominate the picture. They want all of the attention, talk incessantly, do not share, try to dominate, tantrum, do not nap, and are generally annoying and uncooperative.

School-age

At the start of school many children are first diagnosed who had escaped detection previously. Children who are smart and charming may be well tolerated by adults who can give extra time. In the classroom such individualized attention is not practical. Teachers complain of hyperactivity or restlessness, and of inattentiveness or distractibility. They may be aware of the social problems, even of the children's rejection by peers; but it is the inability to cooperate in class that is the most bothersome. Academic difficulties are usually noted in the first or second grade by an alert teacher but may be overshadowed by the social adjustment problems. Academic problems are seriously addressed around the fourth grade. By then ADHD children have sufficiently underachieved to warrant formal academic assessment. Specific developmental disorders may be first detected. Emphasis now centers on academic deficits. Aggression and antisocial behaviors may emerge around this time. Some children may be placed in special educational programs that further stigmatize them.

Adolescence

Adolescence often heralds a significant change (Lambert, 1988). Many ADHD children seem to grow out of the difficulties with inattention, hyperactivity, and impulsivity. This group has a relatively normal adolescence. Even specific developmental disorders may normalize. Another group no longer has hyperactivity, but continues to display inattentiveness and impulsivity. Academics remain problematic. A third group shows antisocial and self-destructive behaviors, including serious drug and alcohol abuse. They are at-risk to drop out of school or to enter the juvenile justice system. Their social problems receive much more attention than their persistent academic problems. Not all ADHD children display gross maladaptive behaviors at all stages; the pattern is quite variable. Perhaps another hallmark of this disorder is the inconsistency across groups of children and within individual children.

OUTCOME

Long-term Functioning

Early studies concluded that ADHD resolved at puberty. However, those studies focused on the hyperactivity. When the entire syndrome is assessed longitudinally, another picture emerges. Approximately one-third to one-half of ADHD children at puberty seem to have either resolved this disorder, or at least to have significantly mitigated it (Gittelman, Mannuzza, Shenker, & Bonagura, 1985; Hechtman, Weiss, Perlman, & Tuck, 1981; Lambert, 1988; Mannuzza, Klein, Bonagura, Konig, & Shenker, 1988; Minde, Weiss, & Mendelson, 1972; Weiss & Hechtman, 1986). They may have developed some problems with self-esteem, but generally do well with the tasks of life.

Another third continues to experience chronic interpersonal disharmony, restlessness, and impulsivity that have been only partially contained (Weiss & Hechtman, 1986; Weiss, Hechtman, & Perlman, 1978; Weiss, Hechtman, Perlman, Hopkins, & Wener, 1979). These may persist into the third and fourth decades of adulthood. The three main tasks of life, occupation, marriage, and community relationships pose conflicts, but do not totally preclude moderate interpersonal adjustment.

ADHD individuals in these first two groups who do attain some degree of social status, satisfying social ties, and stability may still have difficulty with social transactions and lack intimacy in their lives, as evidenced by lower participation in extracurricular and community activities (Mannuzza, Klein, Bonagura, Konig, & Shenker, 1988).

The last one-third of ADHD children as adults demonstrates serious problems throughout adolescence and adulthood (Wender, Reimherr, & Wood, 1981). These individuals experience significant failures in most domains of life. Multiple marriages and jobs fail. They frequently engage in antisocial activities and illicit substance usage. Incarceration is common. Their restlessness and impulsivity, chronic excitement-seeking, and rigidity indicate a lack of social interest and a serious failure with the tasks of life.

The decreased social interest of ADHD children in adulthood is further evidenced by an increased rate of personality disorders, particularly the DSM-III-R Cluster B of Antisocial, Borderline, and Narcissistic Personality Disorders (Hechtman & Weiss, 1986). These individuals are more likely to have had concurrent diagnoses of ODD or CD as youths.

Predicting Outcome

Early identification of those ADHD children who will eventually succeed with life tasks and those who will fail defies prediction at present. Some indication is available that those who will fare poorest are those most severely afflicted during childhood. They demonstrate the most social and academic maladjustment, and are usually diagnosed with other concurrent Disruptive Behavior Disorders (August & Holmes, 1984; August, Stewart, & Holmes, 1983; Gittelman, Mannuzza, Shenker, & Bonagura, 1985; Loeber & Schmaling, 1985; Loney, 1987; Milich & Loney, 1979; Walker, Lahey, Hynd, & Frame, 1987; Weiss, Hechtman, Milroy, & Perlman, 1985).

Their fathers appear to more frequently be antisocial, to use illicit substances, or to abuse alcohol (Cantwell, 1972; Lahey, Piacentini, McBurnett, et al., 1988; Stewart, DeBlois, & Cummings, 1980). Overall parental psychopathology appears higher. Factors such as general intelligence, soft neurological signs, Specific Developmental Disorders, and treatment history have not been shown to definitively affect outcome.

However, the prediction of outcome for ADHD children has been confounded by the heterogeneity of this disorder. Recent work has addressed the need to subtype ADHD children according to the concurrence of conduct problems and aggression (Loney, 1987; Loney, Langhorne, & Paternite, 1978; O'Leary & Steen, 1982). Children with only ADHD appear to meet the life tasks much more successfully than those ADHD children with other Disruptive Behavior Disorders.

Adlerian theory takes a different perspective. Outcome cannot be predicted because ADHD is not separable from the individual. It represents an idiographic. An ADHD individual's movement in life cannot be dissected into these discrete variables.

ADLERIAN DYNAMICS

Many dynamics addressed by Individual Psychology have been stated previously and will be further illustrated in the case vignettes. ADHD had not been a diagnostic entity when Adler was writing. Dreikurs, Adler's foremost student, was well familiar with the concept. Dreikurs (1968) believed that ADHD is a spurious diagnosis, as are most of the SDDs. The overrepresentation of males with these problems and the absence of hard diagnostic signs was evidence to him that these diagnoses are cultural artifacts. He agreed that intelligence is a strong influence with SDD. He further agreed that an optimal home and school environment will lessen the probability of any disorder developing. However, it is the masculine overemphasis discussed previously (masculine protest) that predominantly accounts for ADHD and the SDDs. Where no evidence of an organ inferiority is present, Dreikurs and Adler would have seen the cultural desire to be a real man as the largest culprit.

Organ Inferiority

As noted previously, the evidence is increasing that constitutional defects are present at birth in many children with ADHD and SDD diagnoses. Adler (1956) believed that any organ inferiority poses the possibility of risk for maladjustment. Parents and other family members may pamper these children, or worse, feel sorry for them. Pampering, doing for them that which they can do for themselves, is discouraging. It robs children of the confidence that comes with increasing skill development. It deprives them of learning opportunities and retards their emotional and intellectual development.

Feeling sorry for children (Dreikurs, 1958) teaches them that they have been short-changed by life, and now life owes them. They then expect that others will treat them special because they have been short-changed. They claim special exemption due to their disability. They learn not to maximize their striving, but to wait for life to come to them. Feeling sorry for these children provides them with evidence that they are inferior to others. Feelings of personal inferiority will result in a striving to be better than others. If that striving is not accomplished in culturally approved ways, for example, academics, it will take the form of misbehavior. Either way, striving for personal superiority is not social cooperation and can only be deleterious to the individual and others.

Competition

Parents who are unsure of their worth compete with each other for a place of significance. Their competition sets a model for the children to compete with them and with each other. If firstborn children are well behaved and academically successful, second children in these families are likely to misbehave and have academic problems. In other words, their ambition leads them to compete in areas not secured by the firstborn. If the "model child" position is occupied, a place for misbehavior and being the very best at failing is open and tempting to the second child. This competition can show in just the reverse. The first child can have the characteristics of the second child just described. Competition can also occur between any ordinal positions within the family (for example, between the first and third child). Competition is the key to diversity between siblings, whatever their ordinal position.

Life-style Theme

A representative life-style, pattern of behavior, might be as follows:

"I am less than others."

"I must be superior."

"Life is one big opportunity to fail."

"It is better not to try than to face the humiliation that comes with failure."

"If I don't put my neck out, no one will know that I can't succeed."

"My family expects too much of me."

"I have problems and they have to treat me differently."

"My siblings are favored and get all the breaks."

"My parents owe me and have to make up for what they should have done for me."

"I have been shorted by them and by life."

"Life is unfair."

"Too much is expected of me and too little has been given to me."

"If I can't be the best at that which is approved by my family, school and community, I'll be the best at being the boss."

"I'll show others that they can't tell me what to do or make me do anything."

"I can't find a place among my peers in academics, but I can gain their admiration by my defiance of adults."

"I feel superior when I defeat adults."

"Besides they deserve it for what they have done to me."

TREATMENT STRATEGIES

Medication Treatment

Comments regarding the medication management of ADHD children are warranted. Stimulant medication is the most prevalent and effective therapy used for ADHD. It is also the most carefully studied therapy of all childhood therapies (Henker & Whalen, 1989). Three stimulant medications are routinely used according to physician preference and the child's tolerance: methylphenidate (Ritalin), the most commonly prescribed stimulant; dextroamphetamine (Dexedrine); and Pemoline (Cylert). Medications other than stimulants are sometimes used. The most common is the tricyclic antidepressant imipramine or its metabolite desipramine (Pliszka, 1987). This medication is generally used if the child develops complications with the stimulants or has a concurrent Mood Disorder. Less frequently, antidepressants of the type termed monoamine oxidase inhibitors are chosen (Zametkin, Rapoport, Murphy, Linnoila, & Ismond, 1986; Zametkin, Rapoport, Murphy, Linnoila, Karoum, Potter, & Ismond, 1986).

Social Behaviors

Favorable stimulant-related changes are frequently immediate, dramatic, and multifaceted. They do not represent a placebo effect (Whalen, Henker, Swanson, Granger, Kliewer, & Spencer, 1987). The noted changes affect everyday life activities and may be noted by parents, teachers, and other adults interacting with the ADHD child. Parents note decreases in demanding, oppositional, and disruptive behaviors. The children cooperate better with family responsibilities, since they are less impulsive and excitable. Transitions, such as bedtimes, getting ready for school in the morning, or family outings proceed more smoothly. They are better able to engage in peer activities, such as scouts or athletic events.

Teachers note that they are better able to stay on-task during classroom assignments, more frequently complete assignments, and do not disrupt the class or get into as much trouble on the schoolyard. Their fine motor control, as evidenced in their handwriting or artwork, may improve. Improvements in learning disabilities also may be noted (August & Holmes, 1984; Gittelman, Klein, & Feingold, 1983; Richardson, Kupietz, Winsberg, et al., 1988).

Indirect benefits of the medication are observed in parents' and teachers' more positive and less controlling interactions with them (Barkley, 1985; Mash & Johnston, 1982; Whalen, Henker, & Dotemoto, 1980). They report that the child is more likeable and manageable. These improvements suggest that the negative family environment surrounding ADHD children may arise largely from the response of caretakers to these children's adverse behaviors. Containment of the children's symptoms may positively influence the family environment.

Less information has been obtained regarding peer relationships. Preliminary evidence is not encouraging. Some improvements in social standing may be realized, although still below that realized by their normal peers (Henker & Whalen, 1989). Their reputations and peer relationships do not seem to change, at least over the short-term (Cunningham, Siegel, & Offord, 1985; Pelham & Bender, 1982). Perhaps a longer time may be needed for these children to realize improved peer relationships. Alternatively, ADHD children taking stimulant medication may be better able to contain their adversive behaviors, but they may not replace these behaviors with more prosocial behaviors which build friendships. Achievement of social competence becomes the major focus of psychotherapeutic interventions (Henker & Whalen, 1989).

Cognitive Performance

Positive medication effects are also well-established on standardized neuropsychological measures (Campbell, Douglas, & Morgenstern, 1971; Sebrechts, Shaywitz, Shaywitz, et al., 1986), and classroom behavior (Brown & Sleator, 1979; Rapport, Stoner, DuPaul, Birmingham, & Tucker, 1985; Rapport, et al., 1988). The quantity, accuracy, and efficiency of completed classwork improves (Douglas, Barr, O'Neill, & Britton, 1986; Pelham, Bender, Caddell, Booth, & Moorer, 1986). Stimulant medication helps the children to focus, so that they make more effective use of their time and increase their speed and accuracy of response.

The larger question is whether stimulant medication facilitates these gains directly by improving information processing; or whether the enhanced performance results from changes in attitude, motivation, and self-regulation which allow ADHD children to cooperate and exert mental effort. The fact that stimulant treatment seems least effective in improving academic performance in children with learning disabilities, whether or not they also have ADHD, suggests that improved academic performance results from motivational and attitudinal change, rather than from changes in the basic cognitive processes (Henker & Whalen, 1989).

Despite these significant short-term effects, long-term effects have not been consistently documented in major areas of functioning, including scholarship. Many methodological factors may contribute to the lack of measurable long-term gains. However, stimulants may improve ADHD children's ability to discern social cues and modulate their behavior appropriately, but not provide the catch-up learning that many of these children may need. They also do not negate the effects of past experiences on ADHD children's motivation and self-perceived efficacy, nor the negative expectancies held by others for them (Henker & Whalen, 1989).

These long-term studies indicate that these ADHD children need more than just medication therapy. They need individualized programs in education, social skills, development, and parent education.

Psychosocial Treatment

Treatment involves the school and the family. Structure, predictable schedules, and adult disengagement from the child's misbehavior are useful. Building on strengths at school and home gives more opportunities for success. Focusing on misbehaviors and inadequate skills only furthers everyone's discouragement.

An organized environment which provides novel and stimulating activities aids attention in ADHD. Teachers are asked not to involve the parents in schoolwork. Parents assure the teachers that they will support decisions between the school and their child. Teachers do not advise the parents, and parents do not give advice to the teachers.

Stimulant medication typically assists attention, contains impulsivity, and decreases restlessness thereby allowing children to focus on more positive interactions. They become more educable. Hence, family therapy is facilitated, as well as peer, school, and home behavior. Family therapy is a structure that assists the initiation of family council meetings. An ability to listen to one another is learned in family therapy.

Family therapy gives an understanding to everyone as to the intent of misbehaviors. These misbehaviors may lessen upon recognition (Dreikurs, 1958), and provide valuable information to the therapist for parental recommendations, for example, parents leave the house when the child misbehaves. Parents of children diagnosed with ADHD are more ready to admit defeat, and they will more likely follow advice. The advice is basic to child rearing principles (Dreikurs & Soltz, 1964) and teaches the family methods of encouragement, mutual respect, winning cooperation, acting rather than speaking when it is time for discipline, refraining from pampering and overprotection, staying out of fights, stimulating independence, conducting family meetings for mutual problem solving, and emphasizing having fun together.

CASE EXAMPLES

Case of David: ADHD with
Specific Developmental Disorder and
Oppositional Defiant Disorder

Identified Patient. David is a 7.5-year-old boy living with his biological parents and 11-year-old sister. He is in the second grade.

Chief Complaint. "He just has a hard time coping."

History of Current Problem. David had been receiving special education services for moderately severe Specific Developmental Disorder in Reading since starting school. He had made progress but had developed behavioral problems related to reading. He was not completing reading assignments in class, and refused to do his reading homework. David had difficulty organizing work related to reading but not writing. He could compose sentences which were grammatically correct and had appropriate understanding of the structure of language. He exhibited a low frustration tolerance during his reading homework and frequently ripped up his papers. He berated himself and his teacher during these episodes. He alternately requested and then rejected his parents' help. Initially, his parents denied other problems. They were most concerned that he succeed in school.

A detailed history revealed other chronic problems which his parents attributed to David's personality. He was a demanding child who would not take "no" for an answer even when he was very young. When refused a request, he would verbally demand what he wanted. He would then attempt to defy his parents. For example, David would demand food just after finishing dinner or prior to bedtime. His parents would calmly try to divert him. David would loudly threaten to take the food. His parents would cut him off at the kitchen. He would berate them, and tell them "you can't stop me" (Goal II misbehavior). His parents would block the kitchen door. David would start to push them, and they would physically contain him. Both parents would sit their son in order to control his escalating tantrum. Strategies such as time-out had failed long ago. Inevitably they would escort him to his room and a physical confrontation would ensue. His parents felt confused. David had always been a difficult child requiring strict controls and did not seem to learn from his mistakes. However, he also could be charming and do well. He would then "become a terror" for no apparent reason. This would last for several days and then resolve. Parents could not predict the cycles.

Bedtimes were always difficult. He procrastinated, did not wash or brush his teeth (Goal IV was indicated). His mother would brush his teeth for him, while he fought her. He took one to three hours to fall asleep. He wet his bed regularly (Goal IV was indicated upon questioning). He took a very long time to get ready for school. He was easily distracted with other activities. Additionally, he could not tie his shoes or button his shirts correctly, and so he fought about which clothing to wear. At mealtime he was up and down from the table and had difficulty controlling his knife and fork when eating. Chores were problematic. He dawdled and forgot what he was supposed to do (Goal IV was indicated upon questioning). Sometimes he refused adamantly to do them. He opposed his parents on most requests. He usually wanted his own way. He had not learned how to cooperate, and he had not experienced the satisfaction of contributing to the family welfare.

Problems at school were not as serious. He had difficulty staying on task with reading, but not science or math. He was a "dreamer," but creative. He did fidget a lot, but so did some other first and second grade boys. He used to call out answers in class and not wait his turn. His handwriting was illegible. The greatest difficulty was on the schoolyard. He fought with other pupils who would set him up. He had few friends at school, but was accepted on his sports teams.

In his special education reading class he had more difficulty. He did not stick with the assignments. He did not receive as much attention due to the other students' similar needs. He would disrupt the class when he was not receiving the most attention. He intruded on other students and would annoy them willfully. He did comply with his teacher. However, he showed no tantruming behavior nor physical violence.

David also had many strengths. He was athletic, excelling at swimming and soccer. Recently he started skateboarding and did well. He had some difficulty in baseball with both batting and throwing the ball, but overall did average. He was the fastest runner on the team. He also excelled in science. He grasped science concepts quickly and received honors for his project at the school fair. He had encyclopedic knowledge about dinosaurs. Computers were easily mastered. His regular teacher liked him, and he behaved well in her classroom where his desk was next to hers.

Two weeks after their initial evaluation, David's parents called with a new problem. Twice David had climbed out of the window onto the ledge and had threatened to jump off if his parents did not comply with his requests. His father had pulled him in. His parents were scared. They felt bankrupt.

Developmental History. David suffered mild oxygen deprivation at birth due to a cervical umbilical cord. He did not like to be cuddled as an infant and slept poorly. However, developmental milestones were normal. In fact, he walked by 10 months. He was very active and into everything. He seemed very "curious," venturing where other preschoolers would not go, and getting lost. He did not seem to mind being away from his parents when young.

The oxygen deprivation may have resulted in an organ inferiority which contributed to his ADHD. However, the parents' handling of this early medical condition was helpful to David: they never considered it to be a problem.

Social History. Parents endorsed no major problems, including no marital dysfunction. Father was an academic scientist and worked long hours. Mother wanted to return to work, but was reluctant to do so due to her son's problems.

Family History. No major medical or psychiatric problems were endorsed. David's sister also had difficulty organizing her work. She presented some minor behavioral problems.

Mental Status Examination and Observations. During the initial three sessions, few unusual behaviors or family interactions were noted. In particular, David was able to attend well, was interactive and charming, and displayed no behavioral problems. He appeared to have good receptive and expressive language skills. He and his sister argued, but not inappropriately. David's father appeared anxious and bit his fingernails during the sessions. He generally deferred to his wife. David's mother was tearful on several occasions as she expressed concern for her son's welfare but was not depressed. She was reluctant to withdraw from her extensive role as social organizer and chauffeur for her son. She reasoned that he would not have positive outlets to counter his negative life experiences. She was also concerned that setting such limits would antagonize her son. In the sessions she did cue him frequently about his behavior.

The children were very verbal and outspoken. They chided their mother and mimicked her. Both complained that their mother wanted "perfection." She agreed that this might be so. The sister complained that the parents overprotected her. They described a series of activities in which their children could not engage. This included teen-like clothing and cosmetics for their daughter, and toy weapons for David. They monitored their children's activities and interests closely.

As David became more familiar with the therapist and treatment format he began to display his problematic behaviors.

He never became violent. However, he demonstrated restlessness and inattentiveness with longer family sessions. He would impulsively provoke his sister by going to her chair and annoying her. Then he could not understand why he was in trouble. He talked excessively. He easily became excited while describing mundane events and then had difficulty calming down again. Oppositional and defiant behaviors were not displayed during treatment. He was not depressed. Parents were fully compliant with treatment and began to model their interactions with David according to the way the therapist related to him.

Evaluation. Due to the history of birth hypoxia David received neuropsychological testing to supplement the testing given by the school for the purpose of determining his reading disability. An electroencephalogram (EEG) was also obtained. His testing showed deficits in tasks requiring concentration, and he made impulsive mistakes on easy material. He also demonstrated perceptual deficits. His intellect was in the above average range. Problem-solving skills were good. His EEG was normal and specifically did not reveal a static encephalopathy.

Medication Treatment. Stimulant medication is useful in the treatment of ADHD when combined with school and family consultation. The stimulant improves attention, often reduces impulsiveness, and makes it easier for the child to attend to new learning opportunities whether in school, home, or therapy sessions. The child demonstrates better self-control. *Medication without therapy is not recommended,* since it does not provide the family or child an opportunity to understand the purpose of the maladaptive behaviors and to develop greater social interest.

David was started on dextroamphetamine. The dosage was adjusted over 7 weeks to a therapeutic level and schedule. He did best using a long acting preparation in the morning and at lunch time. He generally did not require any late afternoon dose. However, if he had to participate in an activity requiring sustained attention or interactions with peers, such as scouts or church activities, then he took an additional low dose.

Immediate benefits were noted and sustained over the first year of treatment. Specifically, David was able to complete work at school and home. He was more patient at reading and no longer proclaimed that he "hated school." Fights were fewer. His handwriting improved dramatically. He mastered tying his shoes, buttoning his clothing, and controlling his fork at meals. He also was able to get to sleep in a much shorter time. He complied with his parents' requests more frequently and less oppositionally. He was less volatile. Some provocative, impulsive, and violent behaviors persisted. However, his parents stated that the medication "took the edge off." They felt that they could usually handle him. Mother felt more hopeful. David noted only that his handwriting was better, and that he might be getting teased less.

The medication was self-administered. The medication dosage was explained to David in his parents' presence. Because mother was most accessible, she kept the medication and it was up to David to request scheduled dosages from her. Neither she nor anyone else was to remind David when to take the medication. Frequently with ADHD, misbehaviors are attributed to "have you taken your medication." The goal of treatment was to put control in David's hands and remove the adults from potential power struggles.

School Intervention. To address David's inability to stay on task in the classroom, his impulsive behaviors were addressed in consultation with his teacher. Closer attention was paid to keeping on schedule. Math would always begin at 9:00 am, writing at 9:45, and so forth. She ignored his out-of-turn responses. She addressed his desire for control by frequently asking his advice and letting him know that she believed that he could work out a particular problem, find the answers, join in activities, wait in line, wait his turn, and so forth.

Conflict on the playground was reinterpreted to him in therapy sessions to indicate that he was controlling several other boys by his "cooperating" behavior. The other boys did not realize that he determined whether he would or would not provide them with a laugh. His playground interactions readily improved.

David's ability in sports was used as a strength upon which to build self-image and improved interactions. The suggestion was that he join the track club, attended by many of his peers at school, and participate in the relay team as well as short distance events. Peer recognition on the track team was immediate. He was given the nickname "rabbit" of which he was very proud. He was encouraged to participate in as many organized team sports as possible.

His science accomplishments were put in a perspective of greater social interest by suggesting that he represent his school, rather than himself, at the state fair. His class followed his project development closely. Also, his parents purchased a baseball statistics program for their home computer. Each week David entered statistics on the local minor league baseball team. He became a local expert on baseball, in addition to his previous reputation as a dinosaur expert. David knew all the esoteric statistics on the team. He was able to channel his attention through use of the computer. He compiled tables of statistics which the local paper published, bringing him community recognition.

Family Education and Therapy. The parents' feeling of bankruptcy in dealing with their son's escalating behaviors was a fortuitous therapeutic moment. ***"Bankruptcy," according to Dreikurs (1958), is the "teachable moment."*** The parents are ready to listen to advice and change their behavior. In this case Goal II misbehavior was determined in David's climbing out the window and threatening to jump. The parents were instructed to call the fire department whenever David went out on the ledge. They were not to make any contact with him. The fire department had to make only one visit to the home.

David's tantrums were addressed by instructing the parents to not encourage their son's self-destructive behaviors. The parents were to walk away from their son and to leave the house whenever he started any of these Goal III misbehaviors. They were very reluctant to do this, but complied. David quickly ceased tantruming.

The explanation to David of his control over peers who set him up seemed to have enlightened mother with respect to the ways in which her children set her up. She learned to go for a walk whenever she felt them baiting her. Disciplining the children was modeled in the therapy sessions. The parents had become fearful of "antagonizing" their son, since he might tantrum. They therefore tended to avoid addressing issues with him or exerting power over him. The therapist modeled discipline by "putting both children in the same boat" (Dreikurs, 1958). Both David and his sister were escorted to the waiting room by a coworker whenever David demonstrated misbehaviors with his sister. An arrangement was made prior to the second family session for another staff member to take both children to a waiting area if one of them misbehaved. Both children enjoyed the sessions: "I get treated as an adult," which helped to limit the times that they were removed. The therapist did not respond to David's request for explanations as to why he and his sister were removed.

Mother returned to work part-time and is requiring more cooperation from her husband and children in housework and schedules. She is no longer so involved with scheduling her son. They were all more encouraged. After these critical issues were addressed, family therapy focused on mother's demands for perfection from the family, and more so from herself. Parental intrusiveness into their children's lives was also addressed in response to the sister's complaints of overprotectiveness. Focus was gradually shifted from David to his sister. The strategy of focusing on the "good" child helps to achieve a more salubrious balance in the family. The parents genuinely become concerned about the other child when attention is diverted from the identified patient. This speeds the therapy process which Dreikurs and Stoltz (1964) noted: "I'll believe that the 'bad' one is getting better when the 'good' one gets worse." Dreikurs is pointing to the scapegoating function of the identified patient. This individual is the sign of a dysfunctional family interaction. Improvement can be seen when realignment is established within the family. This usually means strengthening the ties between the same generation, parent to parent and sibling to sibling, and weakening the ties between generations, parent to child. It has been shown that by focusing on parent education, improvement can be noted between the marital pair, even when the identified patient has a psychotic or mood disorder (Croake & Kelly, 1985; Croake & Kelly, manuscript in progress).

Diagnosis.

Axis I: 314.01 Attention-deficit Hyperactivity Disorder, moderate

313.81 Oppositional Defiant Disorder, moderate

307.60 Functional Enuresis, primary type, nocturnal

Axis II: 315.00 Developmental Reading Disorder

315.40 Developmental Coordination Disorder

Axis III: none

Axis IV: Psychosocial Stressors:

acute event: 2-mild
(recent move back to home state with change of schools)

enduring circumstance: 2-mild
(placement in special education; chronic teasing by peers)

Axis V: Current GAF: 55

Highest GAF past year: 60

Comment. David's case is especially relevant in showing how such a pervasively impairing disorder can develop in a child for no obvious "reason." David was a typical child with ADHD. His Developmental Reading Disorder was established early in life before he showed serious behavioral problems. Therefore, the school system was attuned to possible other needs. Nevertheless, his ADHD was neglected until his behavioral problems escalated necessitating intervention. David had an intact loving family. He had experienced no significant life stress. The family was readily amenable to therapeutic intervention.

Another asset of David's which helped him was his generally charming, attractive personality and good athletic skills. Others were, therefore, willing to extend themselves to him. He probably was more fortunate than many ADHD children in this respect. Most children would function well with these assets. The effects of ADHD are most impressive in a child with David's strengths.

Case of Cory: ADHD With Conduct Disorder

Identified Patient. Cory was an 11-year-old boy living with his divorced mother and attending 5th grade in the public school system.

Chief Complaint. "He needs a psychiatric evaluation before they will let him back into school."

History of Current Problem. Cory had been suspended from school for the third time during the current year. He was recurrently violent on the schoolyard and this time had bloodied a child's nose. He also started fights in other unstructured settings, such as walking home from school or in the lunchroom. These fights frequently developed after he had intruded into other children's activities and they did not want to include him. Other problems at school included stealing from his classmates and at least once from a teacher, destroying other pupils' belongings, and frequent lying about these and other activities. Teachers and the school psychologist described Cory as "mean": he seemed to be vindictive and take pleasure from the harm he inflicted. He did not go around with a gang, but rather was a loner. He was never truant from school. In fact, he liked school. His marks were good, although teachers said he was capable of much more if he would listen and settle down. They noted that he had difficulty concentrating on his work. He daydreamed and fidgeted constantly, which his teacher found annoying. He would impulsively respond to questions, wander about the class, and even leave the classroom. He generally blamed others for his misdeeds and took little responsibility for his behavior. He seemed to behave much better in structured settings where expectations were very clear and he could not act as impulsively. His teacher did not like him. The school had tried various programs, including denial of all unstructured activities, but to no avail. They had particular difficulty understanding Cory's behavior because he was quite bright and had no learning problems.

At home and outside of school Cory also had problems. He had not tortured animals but was cruel to pets. He had run away from home three times but went to a friend's house. He argued regularly with his mother and had shoved her several times. He reports that these were after she had shoved him, which mother confirmed. He refused to do anything around the house. He had stolen from his mother twice. Multiple projects were started but never completed due to his apparent disorganization and boredom. He was not using drugs nor alcohol.

Cory was excellent at skateboarding. He loved the excitement, and skated alone for hours. He wanted to compete nationally. Although athletically endowed, he hated team sports, and had been kicked off several teams for excessive violence and challenging the coaches. Anger was identified as a major problem wherever he went. Cory was aware of his problems and had expressed a desire to change.

Developmental History. This was not known. Cory was adopted at age 4 years. He had achieved appropriate milestones and continued normal development.

Family History. This was not well-known for the biological parents. His biological father had drug and alcohol problems and some legal infractions. His parents had never married. No major medical or psychiatric problems in the adoptive family.

Social History. Not much was known of Cory's early life except that he was physically abused by his mother and her boyfriend. Sexual abuse was suspected. His biological father was never involved with him. He had lived in a foster home for one year prior to adoption. Two years after his adoption his new parents divorced. This was reportedly in part related to the mother's recurrent depressions and dependency. Initially the adoptive father maintained contact with Cory, but had not seen him in the last two years. Mother worked steadily as an executive secretary. She had a few short-term relationships with men since the divorce but little other social life. An older biological daughter had moved away from home two years previously and had little contact with the family.

Mental Status Examination and Observations. Cory was seen for initial evaluation with his mother twice and alone once. His mother appeared depressed. With his mother, Cory was obviously inattentive and misunderstood several issues being discussed. He jumped to conclusions. He fidgeted constantly and changed chairs several times. He alternately was angry, blamed his mother, made self-deprecating remarks, and expressed a desire to have friends. He also cried about his situation, but then denied caring. Upon questioning, Goal III misbehavior was associated with his restlessness, anger, self-deprecation, and lack of friends. As the session progressed, he gradually moved his seat closer to the interviewer.

During his individual interview, Cory's presentation was similar, but moderated. He was less agitated. He blamed the therapist for making him miss school and threatened to leave, but did not. Blaming the therapist felt like Goal II misbehavior. The therapist received confirmation from Cory in the form of a recognition reflex (Dreikurs, 1958): He smiled when asked "Could it be that you want to show me that you are in charge here, that I cannot make you do anything?" Upon confirmation the therapist stated: "I cannot make you do anything and I will not try. You are too powerful." Cory seemed pleased with this confirmation. He calmed down and cried, stating that his life was miserable, nobody cared. He wanted to take self-defense classes, but asked not to tell his mother or "she would kill me." He asked if he could play a board game with the therapist and he played appropriately. He was obviously impulsive in his play strategy.

Course of Treatment. Cory had multiple problems. The violence obscured the underlying ADHD. He had made himself so unlikeable that others did not look further to understand his problems. To disentangle the effects of past environmental trauma, inadequate parenting by his mother, and his own possible organ inferiority is not possible. Clinic staffing of this family led to much controversy and an atmosphere of rejection.

Medication Treatment. A trial of a stimulant medication was initiated. At a moderate dosage of dextroamphetamine he became depressed. The medication exacerbated the depressive feelings he had shown during previous sessions. However, he also had demonstrated markedly improved ability to concentrate and to control his restlessness and temper. A different stimulant, pemoline, was tried and he did well. After eight weeks of treatment his impulsivity and fighting also decreased. Problems still persisted with difficulty making friends, blaming others, and anger. No recurrence of depression occurred.

Family Education and Therapy. Psychotherapy was initiated with Cory and his mother to maintain and enhance the gains noted. The first issue addressed was having fun together. Having fun together is a Dreikursian technique (Dreikurs, 1958). This method is commonly used with any family. It is not anticipated. Family members expect an immediate focus on the negative ADHD signs. An agreement and plan for an afternoon of fun for the coming weekend was planned in the session. The two of them selected an outing to the community swimming pool. Thereafter, Sunday afternoons were reserved as fun times based upon mutually agreed upon activities.

Next, Mother's depression, social isolation, overinvolvement with Cory, and tendency to self-defeating behaviors were addressed in relation to Cory's similar behaviors. Both were surprised at seeing the similarities. Mother seemed less overwhelmed at Cory's misbehavior when she could sympathize with her own discouragement. Recommended attendance at a parent study group (Dreikurs & Soltz, 1964) resulted in an improved relationship with Cory. Initiating a weekly family council meeting (Dreikurs & Soltz, 1964) relieved some of the pressure that mother felt about having to always be in charge. The family council meetings lasted about 15 minutes, consistent with Cory's attention span for such activities. These council meetings provided rules, regulations, and order for the two of them at home. Mutual decision-making resulted in much less desire by Cory to be the boss. Mother established two friendships with other women in the parenting group and was reserving one night each week for social activities with them.

Mother was unwilling to arrange martial arts classes for Cory. This training was recommended to teach discipline and self-regulation, as well as a cooperative atmosphere for educating Cory in getting along with others. Therapy is ongoing with Cory and his Mother.

Diagnosis.

Axis I: 314.01 Attention-deficit Hyperactivity Disorder, moderate

312.00 Conduct Disorder, solitary aggressive type

Axis II: depressive personality features

Axis III: none

Axis IV: Psychosocial Stressors:

a) acute events: none

b) enduring circumstances: 6-extreme (recurrent physical abuse as toddler, and possible sexual abuse; removal from biological parents; abandonment by adoptive father and sister; adoptive mother's depression).

Axis V: Current GAF: 40

Highest GAF Past Year: 55

Comment. Cory presented diagnostic pitfalls that are common with ADHD children who also display behavioral problems. ADHD signs are integrated with behavior into holistic movement. They are reflective of a probable organ inferiority (biological disposition) and interpersonal conflict. Perhaps the attention deficit and hyperactivity are biologically inherited and the misbehavior is learned within the family context. The latter is a discouraged attempt to interact with the adult in the situation.

Cory's movement kept others at a distance and created an environment of rejection. Therefore, ADHD was not considered in his school assessment and diagnosis was delayed. Additionally, Cory did not have any Specific Developmental Disorder. This further precluded him from any specialized services that many ADHD children receive.

Cory showed considerable depressive symptoms. They did not meet criteria for a Mood Disorder. However, both these depressive feelings and his early losses and abuse put him at-risk for a later depression. These depressive features may make him more amenable to treatment, since they may have related to his ability to establish a relationship with the therapist. However, depression in an impulsive child increases the risk of self-destructive behaviors.

For ADHD children treated with stimulants to develop an Organic Mood Disorder is not unusual. This disorder generally resolves with discontinuation of the stimulant. The occurrence of such a medication-induced Mood Disorder is not diagnostic of a proclivity for Mood Disorders.

Cory's vindictiveness and cruelty alienated others. His violence had resulted in punishment and rejection. Cory was so discouraged that he would not communicate his own dissatisfaction with his life. He had mostly given up on the idea of friendly relationships and was without skills for cooperation, and promoted alienation for himself. His adoptive family provided another model of discouragement. The parents had given up on their marriage, and Mother's depression indicated that she had lost heart. The tasks of life seemed overwhelming to her. She did not know how to parent. Her relationships with men were tenuous. She was not involved with her own family or the community. In Western culture the emphasis is upon vocational attainment. Cooperation with the other sex is poorly achieved for most people. Community involvement is somewhat better. Cory's Mother fit the rule and enjoyed success at her job.

Cory's lack of social interest places him at-risk for ongoing problems. Rejection by peers continues despite less anger and fighting. A peer group counseling forum aimed at social skill improvement is planned for Cory to increase his social interest, his sense of belonging, and having a place in life.

REFERENCES

Adler, A. (1956). *The Individual Psychology of Alfred Adler.* H.L. Ansbacher & R.R. Ansbacher (Eds.). New York: Harper Torchbooks.

American Psychiatric Association. (1968). *Diagnostic and statistical manual of mental disorders* (2nd ed.). Washington, DC: Author.

American Psychiatric Association. (1980). *Diagnostic and statistical manual of mental disorders* (3rd ed.). Washington, DC: Author

American Psychiatric Association. (1987). *Diagnostic and statistical manual of mental disorders* (3rd ed.,rev.). Washington, DC: Author.

Anderson, J., Williams, S., McGee, R., & Silva, P.A. (1987). The prevalence of DSM-III disorders in a large sample of preadolescent children from the general population. *Archives of General Psychiatry, 44,* 69-81.

August, G.J., & Holmes, C.S. (1984). Behavior and academic achievement in hyperactive subgroups and learning disabled boys: A six year follow-up. *American Journal of Diseases of Childhood, 138,* 1025-1029.

August, G.J., Stewart, M.A., & Holmes, C.S. (1983). A four year follow-up of hyperactive boys with and without conduct disorder. *British Journal of Psychiatry, 143,* 192-198.

Bakwin, H., & Bakwin, R.M. (1966). *Clinical management of behavior disorders in children.* Philadelphia: Saunders.

Barkley, R.A. (1985). The parent-child interaction patterns of hyperactive children: Precursors to aggressive behaviors? In M. Wolraich & D. Routh (Eds.), *Advances in developmental and behavioral pediatrics (Vol. 6)* (pp. 117-150). Greenwich, CT: JAI Press.

Bashir, A.S., Wing, E.H., & Abrams, J.C. (1987). Language disorders in childhood and adolescence. *Pediatric Annals, 16*, 145-156.

Bender, L.S. (1975). Career in clinical research in child psychiatry. In E.J. Anthony (Ed.), *Exploration in child psychiatry* (pp. 10-68). New York: Plenum Press.

Biederman, J., Munir, K., & Knee, D. (1987). Conduct and oppositional disorder in clinically referred childen with attention deficit disorder: A controlled family study. *American Academy of Child and Adolescent Psychiatry, 26*, 724-727.

Bradley, C. (1937). The behavior of children receiving benzedrine. *American Journal of Psychiatry, 94*, 577-585.

Brown, G.L., Ebert, M.H., & Minichiello, M.D. (1985). Biochemical and pharmacological aspects of attention deficit disorder. In L.M. Bloomingdale (Ed.), *Attention deficit disorder: Identification, course, and rationale* (pp. 106-154). New York: Spectrum.

Brown, R.T., & Sleator, E.K. (1979). Methylphenidate in hyperkinetic children: Differences in dose effects on impulsive behavior. *Pediatrics, 64*, 408-411.

Bruck, M. (1985). The long-term prognosis of childhood learning disabilities. In P. Gerber & K. Garnett (Eds.), *Adults with learning disabilities: An international perspective* (pp 165-178). New York: World Rehabilitation Fund.

Buerger, T.A. (1968). A follow-up of remedial reading instruction. *The Reading Teacher, 21*, 329-334.

Campbell, S.B., Douglas, V.I., & Morgenstern, G. (1971). Cognitive styles in hyperactive children and the effect of methylphenidate. *Journal of Child Psychology & Psychiatry, 12*, 55-67.

Cantwell, D.P. (1972). Psychiatric illness in the families of hyperactive children. *Archives of General Psychiatry, 27*, 414-417.

Clements, S.D., & Peters, J.E. (1962). Minimal Brain Dysfunction in the school age child. *Archives of General Psychiatry, 6*, 185-197.

Critchley, M. (1964). *Developmental dyslexia*. Springfield, IL: Charles C. Thomas.

Croake, J.W., & Kelly, D.F. (1985). Adlerian family therapy with depressed and schizophrenic patients. *Individual Psychology: The Journal of Adlerian Theory, Research, & Practice, 41, 302-310*.

Cunningham, C.E., Siegel, L.S., & Offord, D.R. (1985). A developmental dose-response analysis of the effects of methylphenidate on the peer interactions of attention deficit disordered boys. *Journal of Child Psychology & Psychiatry, 26*, 955-971.

Denckla, M.D. (1978). Minimal brain dysfunction. In J.S. Chall & A.F. Mirsky (Eds.), *Education and the brain* (pp. 23-54). Chicago: University of Chicago Press.

Douglas, V.I., Barr, R.G., O'Neill, M.E., & Britton, B.G. (1986). Short-term effects of methylphenidate on the cognitive, learning and academic performance of children with attention deficit disorder in the laboratory and the classroom. *Journal of Child Psychology & Psychiatry, 27*, 191-211.

Dreikurs, R. (1958). *The challenge of parenthood.* New York: Hawthorn Books.

Dreikurs, R. (1968). *Psychology in the classroom.* New York: Harper & Row Publishers.

Dreikurs, R., & Soltz, V. (1964). *Children: The challenge.* New York: Hawthorn Books., Inc.

Duane, D.D. (1985). Neurodiagnostic tools in dyslexic syndromes in children: Pitfalls and proposed comparative study of computed tomography, nuclear magnetic resonance, and brain electrical activity mapping. In G. Pavlidis & D. Fisher (Eds.), *Dyslexia: Its neuropsychology and treatment* (pp. 159-237). New York: Wiley.

Duffy, F.H. (1988). Neurophysiological studies in dyslexia. In F. Plum (Ed.), *Language, communication and the brain* (pp. 34-42). New York: Raven Press.

Dykman, R.A., Ackerman, P.T., Clements, S.D., & Peters, J.E. (1971). Specific learning disabilities: An attention deficit syndrome. In H.R. Myklebust (Ed.), *Progress in learning disabilities (Vol. 2)* (pp. 174-233). New York: Grune and Stratton.

Ferguson, H.B., & Pappas, B.A. (1979). Evaluation of psychophysiological, neurochemical, and animal models of hyperactivity. In R.L. Trites (Ed.), *Hyperactivity in children* (pp. 48-61). Baltimore: University Park Press.

Finucci, J.M., Gottfredson, L.S., & Childs, B. (1985). A follow-up study of dyslexic boys. *Annals of Dyslexia, 35*, 117-136.

Forness, S.B. (1981). *Recent concepts in dyslexia: Implications for diagnosis and remediation.* Virginia: ERIC Exceptional Child Education Reports.

Frauenheim, J.G. (1978). Academic achievement characteristics of adult males who were diagnosed as dyslexic in childhood. *Journal of Learning Disabilities, 11*, 476-483.

Gittelman, R., Klein, D.F., & Feingold, I. (1983). Children with reading disorders II. Effects of methylphenidate in combination with reading remediation. *Journal of Child Psychology & Psychiatry, 24*, 193-212.

Gittelman, R., Mannuzza, S., Shenker, R., & Bonagura, N. (1985). Hyperactive boys almost grown up. *Archives of General Psychiatry, 42*, 937-947.

Halperin, J.M., Gittelman, R., Klein, D.F., & Rudel, R.G. (1984). Reading-disabled hyperactive children: A distinct subgroup of attention deficit disorder with hyperactivity. *Journal of Abnormal Child Psychology, 12*, 1-14.

Hastings, J.E., Barkley, R.A. (1978). A review of psychophysiological research with hyperkinetic children. *Journal of Abnormal Child Psychology, 6*, 413-448.

Heaton, R.K. (1988). Introduction to the special series. *Journal of Consulting & Clinical Psychology, 56*, 787-788.

Hechtman, L., & Weiss, G. (1986). Controlled prospective 15-year follow-up of hyperactives as adults: Nonmedical drug and alcohol use and antisocial behavior. *Canadian Journal of Psychiatry, 31*, 557-567.

Hechtman, L., Weiss, G., Perlman, T., & Tuck, D. (1981). Hyperactives as young adults: Various clinical outcomes. *Adolescent Psychiatry, 9*, 295-306.

Henker, B., & Whalen, C.K. (1989). Hyperactivity and attention deficits. *American Psychologist, 44*, 216-223.

Hopkins, J., Perlman, T., Hechtman, L., & Weiss, G. (1979). Cognitive style in adults originally diagnosed as hyperactives. *Journal of Child Psychology & Psychiatry, 20*, 209-216.

Hunt, R.D., & Cohen, D.J. (1984). Psychiatric aspects of learning difficulties. *Pediatric Clinics of North America, 31*, 471-497.

Jaklewicz, H. (1982). Dyslexia: Follow-up studies. *Thalamus (International Academy for Research in Learning Disabilities), 2*, 3-9.

Jensen, J.B., Burke, N., & Garfinkel, B.D. (1988). Depression and symptoms of attention deficit disorder with hyperactivity. *American Academy of Child and Adolescent Psychiatry, 27,* 742-747.

Kistner, J.A., & Torgesen, J.K. (1987). Motivational and cognitive aspects of learning disabilities. In B.B. Lahey & A.E. Kazdin (Eds.), *Advances in clinical child psychology (Vol. 10)* (pp. 289-333). New York: Plenum Press.

Kline, C., & Kline, C. (1975). Follow-up study of 211 dyslexic children. *Bulletin of the Orton Society, 25,* 127-144.

Knobloch, H., & Pasamanick, B. (1959). Syndrome of minimal cerebral damage in infancy. *Journal of the American Medical Association, 170,* 1384-1387.

Lahey, B.B., Piacentini, J.C., McBurnett, K., Stone, P., Hartdagen, S., & Hynd, G. (1988). Psychopathology in the parents of children with conduct disorder and hyperactivity. *American Academy of Child and Adolescent Psychiatry, 27,* 163-170.

Lambert, M.N. (1988). Adolescent outcomes for hyperactive children: Perspectives on general and specific patterns of childhood risk for adolescent educational, social, and mental health problems. *American Psychologist, 43,* 786-799.

Lambert, M.N., Sandoval, J., & Sasone, D.M. (1981). Prevalence of hyperactivity and related treatments among elementary school children. In K.D. Gadow & J. Loney (Eds.), *Psychosocial aspects of drug treatment for hyperactivity* (pp. 10-15). Boulder, CO: Westview Press.

Laufer, M.W., & Denhoff, E. (1957). Hyperkinetic behavior syndrome in children. *Journal of Pediatrics, 50,* 463-474.

Levy, F., & Hobbs, G. (1988). The action of stimulant medication in attention deficit disorder with hyperactivity: Dopaminergic, noradrenergic, or both? *American Academy of Child and Adolescent Psychiatry, 27,* 802-805.

Loeber, R., & Schmaling, K.B. (1985). The utility of differentiating between mixed and pure forms of antisocial child behavior. *Journal of Abnormal Child Psychology, 13,* 315-336.

Loh, H.C., Hendrickson, L., & Bruhn, P. (1984). Focal cerebral hypoperfusion in children with dysphasia and/or attention deficit disorder. *Archives of Neurology, 41,* 825-829.

Loney, J. (1987). Hyperactivity and aggression in the diagnosis of attention deficit disorder. In B.B. Lahey & A.E. Kazdin (Eds.), *Advances in child psychology (Vol. 10)* (pp. 99-135). New York: Plenum.

Loney, J., Langhorne, J.E., & Paternite, C.E. (1978). An empirical basis for subgrouping the hyperkinetic/MBD syndrome. *Journal of Abnormal Child Psychology, 87,* 331-341.

Mannuzza, S., Klein, R.G., Bonagura, N., Konig, P.H., & Shenker, R. (1988). Hyperactive boys almost grown up II. Status of subjects without a mental disorder. *Archives of General Psychiatry, 45*, 13-18.

Mash, E.J., & Johnston, C. (1982). A comparison of the mother-child interactions of younger and older hyperactive and normal children. *Child Development, 53*, 1371-1381.

McGee, R., & Williams, S. (1988). A longitudinal study of depression in nine-year old children. *American Academy of Child and Adolescent Psychiatry, 27*, 342-348.

Milich, R.S., & Dodge, K.A. (1984). Social information processing in child psychiatric populations. *Journal of Abnormal Child Psychology, 12*, 471-489.

Milich, R.S., & Loney, J. (1979). The role of hyperactive and aggressive symptomatology in predicting adolescent outcome among hyperactive children. *Journal of Pediatric Psychology, 4*, 93-108.

Minde, K., Weiss, G., & Mendelson, N. (1972). A five-year follow-up study of 91 hyeractive school children. *Journal of American Academy of Child Psychiatry, 11*, 595-619.

Morris, R.D. (1988). Classification of learning disabilities: Old problems and new aproaches. *Journal of Consulting & Clinical Psychology, 56*, 789-794.

Muehl, S., & Forrell, E.R. (1973). A follow-up study of disabled readers: Variables related to high school reading performance. *Reading Research Quarterly, 9*, 110-123.

O'Connor, S.C., & Spreen, O. (1988). The relationship between parents' socioeconomic status and education level and adult occupational and educational achievement of children with learning disability. *Journal of Learning Disabilities, 21*, 148-153.

O'Leary, S.G., & Steen, P.L. (1982). Subcategorizing hyperactivity: The Stony Brook Scale. *Journal of Consulting & Clinical Psychology, 50*, 426-432.

Ozols, E.J., & Rourke, B.P. (1985). Dimensions of social sensitivity in two types of learning-disabled children. In B.P. Rourke (Ed.), *Neuropsychology of learning disabilities: Essentials of subtype analysis* (pp. 281-301). New York: Guilford Press.

Pelham, W.E., & Bender, M.E. (1982). Peer relationships in hyperactive children: Description and treatment. In K.D. Gadow & I. Bialer (Eds.), *Advances in learning and behavioral disabilities: A research annual* (Vol. 1) (pp. 365-436). Greenwich, CT: JAI Press.

Pelham, W.E., Bender, M.E., Caddell,. J., Booth, S.B., & Moorer, S.J. (1986). Methylphenidate and children with attention defiit disorder. *Archives of General Psychiatry, 42,* 948-952.

Pennington, B.F., & Smith, S.D. (1988). Genetic influences on learning disabilities: An update. *Journal of Consulting & Clinical Psychology, 56,* 817-823.

Pliszka, S.R. (1987). Tricylic antidepressants in the treatment of children with attention deficit disorder. *American Academy of Child and Adolescent Psychiatry, 26,* 127-132.

Rapoport, J.L., Buchsbaum, M.S., Zahn, T.P., Weingartner, H., Ludlow, C., & Mikkelsen, E.J. (1978). Dextroamphetamine: Cognitive and behavioral effects in normal prepubertal boys. *Science, 199,* 560-563.

Rapoport, J.L., & Ferguson, H.B. (1981). Biological validation of the hyperkinetic syndrome. *Developmental Medicine in Child Neurology, 23,* 667-682.

Rapport, M.D., Stoner, G., DuPaul, G.J., Birmingham, B.K., & Tucker, S. (1985). Methylphenidate in hyperactive children: Differential effects of dose on academic, learning, and social behavior. *Journal of Abnormal Child Psychology, 13,* 227-244.

Rapport, M.D., Stoner, G., DuPaul, G., Kelly, K.L., Tucker, S.B., & Schoeler, T. (1988). Attention deficit disorder and methylphenidate: A mutilevel analysis of dose-response effects on children's impulsivity across settings. *American Academy of Child and Adolescent Psychiatry, 27,* 60-69.

Rawson, M. (1968). *Developmental language disability: Adult accomplishment of dyslexic boys.* Baltimore, MD: Johns Hopkins University Press.

Reeves, J.C., Werry, J.S., Elkind, G.S., & Zametkin, A. (1987). Attention deficit disorder, conduct, oppositional, and anxiety disorders in children: II. Clinical characteristics. *American Academy of Child and Adolescent Psychiatry, 26,* 144-155.

Reynolds, C.R. (1981). The fallacy of "two years below grade level for age" as a diagnostic criterion for reading disorders. *Journal of School Psychology, 19,* 350-358.

Richardson, E., Kupietz, S.S., Winsberg, B.G., Richardson, E., Maitinsky, S., & Mendell, N. (1988). Effects of methylphenidate dosage in hyperactive reading-disabled children II. Reading achievement. *American Academy of Child and Adolescent Psychiatry, 27,* 78-87.

Robinson, H.M., & Smith, H.K. (1962). Reading clinic clients—Ten years after. *Elementary School Journal, 63,* 22-27.

Rourke, B.P. (1987). Syndrome of nonverbal learning disability: The final common pathway of white matter disease/dysfunction? *Clinical Neuropsychologist, 1,* 209-234.

Rourke, B.P. (1988). Socioemotional disturbances of learning disabled children. *Journal of Consulting & Clinical Psychology, 56,* 801-810.

Rourke, B.P., & Fisk, J.L. (1981). Socio-emotional disturbances of learning disabled children: The role of central processing deficits. *Bulletin of the Orton Society, 31,* 77-78.

Safer, D.J., & Allen, R.P. (1976). *Hyperactive children: Diagnosis and management.* Baltimore: University Park Press.

Sandberg, S.T., Wieselberg, M., & Shaffer, D. (1980). Hyperkinetic and conduct problems in a primary school population: Some epidemiological considerations. *Journal of Child Psychology & Psychiatry, 21,* 293-311.

Satterfield, J.H. (1973). EEG issues in children with Minimal Brian Dysfunction. *Seminars in Psychiatry, 5,* 35 46.

Schonhaut, S., & Satz, P. (1983). Prognosis for children with learning disabilities: A review of follow-up studies. In M. Rutter (Ed.), *Developmental neuropsychiatry* (pp. 542-574). New York: Guilford Press.

Sebrechts, M.M., Shaywitz, S.E., Shaywitz, B.A., Jatlow, P., Anderson, G.M., & Cohen, D.J. (1986). Components of attention, methylphenidate dosage, and blood levels in children with attention deficit disorder. *Pediatrics, 77,* 222-228.

Shapiro, S.K., & Garfinkel, B.D. (1986). The occurrence of behavior disorders in children: The interdependence of attention deficit disorder and conduct disorder. *American Academy of Child and Adolescent Psychiatry, 25,* 809-819.

Silver, A.A. (1977). Prevention. In A.L. Benton & D. Pearl (Eds.), *Dyslexia, an appraisal of current knowledge* (pp. 351-376). New York: Oxford University Press.

Silver, L.B. (1981). The relationship between learning disabilities, hyperactivity, distractibility, and behavioral problems. *Journal of American Academy of Child Psychiatry, 20,* 385-397.

Silver, L.B. (1989). Learning disabilities: Introduction. *American Academy of Child and Adolescent Psychiatry, 28,* 309-313.

Spreen, O. (1988a). Prognosis of learning disability. *Journal of Consulting & Clinical Psychology, 56,* 836-842.

Spreen, O. (1988b). *Learning disabled children growing up.* New York: Oxford University Press.

Stanovich, K. (1986). Cognitive processes and the reading problems of learning disabled children: Evaluating the assumption of specificity. In J. Torgesen & B. Wong (Eds.), *Psychological and educational perspectives on learning disabilities* (pp 87-131). Orlando, FL: Academic Press.

Stewart, M.A., DeBlois, C.S., & Cummings, C. (1980). Psychiatric disorder in the parents of hyperactive boys and those with conduct disorder. *Journal of Child Psychology & Psychiatry, 21,* 283-29.

Still, G.F. (1902). The Coulstonian lectures on some abnormal physical conditions in children. *Lancet, 1,* 1008-1012; 1077-1082; 1163-1168.

Taylor, H.G. (1988). Neuropsychological testing: Relevance for assessing children's learning disabilities. *Journal of Consulting & Clinical Psychology, 56,* 795-800.

Walker, J.L., Lahey, B.B., Hynd, G.W., & Frame, C.L. (1987). Comparison of specific patterns of antisocial behavior in children with conduct disorder with or without coexisting hyperactivity. *Journal of Consulting & Clinical Psychology, 55,* 910-913.

Weiss, G., & Hechtman, L. (1986). *Hyperactive children grown up*. New York: Guilford Press.

Weiss, G., Hechtman, L., Milroy, T., & Perlman, T. (1985). Psychiatric status of hyperactive adults: A controlled prospective 15-year follow-up of 63 hyperactive children. *Journal of American Academy of Child Psychiatry, 24*, 211-220.

Weiss, G., Hechtman, L., & Perlman, T. (1978). Hyperactives as young adults: School, employer, and self-rating scales obtained during ten year follow-up evaluation. *American Journal of Orthopsychiatry, 48*, 438-445.

Weiss, G., Hechtman, L., Perlman, T., Hopkins, J., & Wener, A. (1979). Hyperactives as young adults. A controlled prospective ten-year follow-up of 75 children. *Archives of General Psychiatry, 36*, 675-681.

Wender, P.H. (1971). *Minimal brain dysfunction in children*. New York: Wiley-Interscience.

Wender, P.H. (1987). *The hyperactive child, adolescent, and adult. Attention deficit disorder through the lifespan*. New York: Oxford University Press.

Wender, P.H., Reimherr, F.W., & Wood, D.R. (1981). Attention deficit disorder ("Minimal Brain Dysfunction") in adults. *Archives of General Psychiatry, 38*, 449-456.

Werry, J.S., Minde, K., Guyman, A., Weiss, G., Dogan, K., & Hoy, E. (1972). Studies on the hyperactive child VII. Neurological status compared with neurotic and normal children. *American Journal of Orthopsychiatry, 42,* 441-451.

Werry, J.S., Reeves, J.C., & Elkind, G.S. (1987). Attention deficit, conduct, oppositional, and anxiety disorders in children: I. A review of research on differentiating characteristics. *American Academy of Child and Adolescent Psychiatry, 26*, 133-143.

Whalen, C.K., & Henker, B. (1985). The social worlds of hyperactive children. *Clinical Psychology Review, 5*, 1-32.

Whalen, C.K., Henker, B., Castro, J., & Granger, D. (1987). Peer perceptions of hyperactivity and medication effects. *Child Development, 58*, 816-828.

Whalen, C.K., Henker, B., & Dotemoto, S. (1980). Methylphenidate and hyperactivity: Effects on teacher behaviors. *Science, 208*, 1280-1282.

Whalen, C.K., Henker, B., Swanson, J.M., Granger, D., Kliewer, W., & Spencer, J. (1987). Natural social behaviors in hyperactive children: Dose effects of methylphenidate. *Journal of Consulting & Clinical Psychology, 55,* 187-193.

Zametkin, A.J., & Rapoport, J.L. (1986). The pathophysiology of attention deficit disorder with hyperactivity: A review. In B.B. Lahey & A.E. Kazdin, *Advances in Clinical Child Psychology, 9,* 177-216, New York: Plenum.

Zametkin, A.J., & Rapoport, J.L. (1987). Neurobiology of attention deficit disorder with hyperactivity: Where have we come in 50 years? *American Academy of Child and Adolescent Psychiatry, 26,* 676-686.

Zametkin, A.J., Rapoport, J.L., Murphy, D.L., Linnoila, M., & Ismond, D. (1986). Treatment of hyperactive children with monoamine oxidase inhibitors I. Clinical efficacy. *Archives of General Psychiatry, 42,* 962-968.

Zametkin, A.J., Rapoport, J.L., Murphy, D.L., Linnoila, M., Karoum, F., Potter, W.Z., & Ismond, D. (1986). Treatment of hyperactive children with monoamine oxidase inhibitors II. Plasma and urinary monoamine findings after treatment. *Archives of General Psychiatry, 42,* 969-973.

CHAPTER 18

EATING DISORDERS

Jon Carlson, Psy.D., Ed.D.

Large portions of the world are faced with problems of malnutrition and starvation in their populations. However, more developed nations face problems of another form of eating problem: eating disorders. Eating disorders are characterized by a preoccupation with food. The shift in societal preference toward a thin physique has led to an increasing prevalence of dieting such that normal eating for North American women is now characterized by dieting. Anorexia and bulimia are conditions which involve disturbed eating behavior and distorted body image. They involve refusal to eat, overeating, impulse eating, and purging. Eating disorders are often a more passive form of rebellion combined with an exaggerated acceptance of society's idealized "perfect" image and are much more common in females than in males (Wadden & Stunkard, 1987; Ruderman, 1986). However, disorders seem to be increasing in males (Andersen, 1990). Actually in the DSM-III-R are listed five Axis I eating disorders.

307.10 Anorexia Nervosa
307.51 Bulimia Nervosa

307.52 Pica
307.53 Rumination Disorder of Infancy
307.50 Eating Disorder NOS

Of the five, pica and rumination usually occur during infancy and early childhood, while the others are predominantly an adolescent/early adulthood phenomenon. Simple obesity is a physical disorder and is not included in this chapter since it is not generally associated with any distinctly psychological or behavioral syndrome. However, when evidence is available that psychological factors are important in the course of a particular case of obesity, it is often noted under the category of psychological factors affecting physical condition.

Pica, which is the persistent consumption of non-nutritive substances such as dirt, plaster, hair, bugs, and/or pebbles, usually has an onset of between 12 to 24 months of age with remission in childhood. Pica rarely persists into adolescence or adulthood. ***Rumination Disorder of Infancy*** is a well-defined syndrome. Although it has been described in adult patients, it is much more common in children. The essential feature is a repeated regurgitation of partially digested food which is then chewed, spit out, or swallowed without nausea, retching, or other signs of gastrointestinal distress. The condition is potentially fatal because of weight loss or no weight gain and subsequent malnutrition. The purpose of this chapter is to concentrate on the two major categories, anorexia nervosa and bulimia nervosa.

Anorexia nervosa and bulimia nervosa may affect as many as 5 to 10% of young women. Morbidity and mortality rates associated with eating disorders are among the highest for any psychiatric disorder. The diagnostic criteria in DSM-III-R for ***Anorexia Nervosa*** (APA, 1987) are as follows:

Refusal to maintain minimum normal weight for age and height.

Weight maintained 15% or more below expected.

Fear of obesity or gaining weight.

Distorted body image.

Amenorrhea (absence of 3 cycles).

The diagnostic criteria in DSM-III-R for **Bulimia Nervosa** (APA, 1987) are as follows:

Recurrent binge eating (rapid consumption of large amounts of food: usually lasts less than 2 hours).

Fear of not being able to stop during binges.

Regular vomiting, taking of laxatives, dieting, or fasting to counteract binges.

A minimum of two episodes per week for three months.

Overconcern with body shape and weight.

Anorectics are fearful of becoming overweight and perceive themselves as being fat, despite being emaciated. They describe themselves as having felt moderately overweight as teenagers and therefore began to diet in early to mid teens which led to weight becoming an obsession. Seldom do anorectics come to treatment on their own, but are usually coerced by families, friends, employers, or physicians. **Denial is the hallmark of an anorectic.**

Anorectics may present for treatment with a variety of moods, from being full of energy and cheerful to being depressed and lethargic. At some point during the course of the illness, however, over one-half of these clients meet the criteria for major depression. This problem may begin quickly or gradually and its course can be chronic, self-limited, or cyclical.

As previously mentioned, bulimics binge on huge quantities of food, usually in private, followed by purging in order to produce weight loss or weight maintenance. Purging is accomplished through such methods as self-induced vomiting, laxative abuse, Ipecac abuse, diuretics, or restriction. Bulimics often will present for treatment feeling ashamed or distressed about their symptoms and are much more open about their problems than anorectics. The bulimics, in contrast to the anorectics, may look much better than they feel. They can appear strong, sociable, and assertive, but frequently are tormented by low self-esteem, fear of intimacy, and aggression. Physical signs of bulimia include a swelling of the parotoid glands, which produces a chipmunk-like appearance, scars on the back of the hand from vomiting, chronic hoarseness or throat problems, and a dryness of the mouth. Physiological reactions to the disorder include dental cavities and enamel loss, electrolyte imbalance, cardiac and renal problems, and esophageal tears (Agras, 1987).

Clients with anorexia often come from families where food has an important role. They are characterized as having been very well-behaved children and have a major role in holding the family together. Many have been parentified children in enmeshed families and have been overprotected and over-regulated. Clients with anorexia are often described as dependent, introverted, compulsive, stubborn, perfectionistic, asexual, and shy (Gutsch, 1988). These clients have low self-esteem and often use their eating disorder as a form of rebellion or a way to get attention from their families and therefore avoid having to be mature and responsible. Their disorder is generally classified as egosyntonic and they feel little hunger or discomfort with their symptoms.

Bulimic clients, however, tend to be anxious and depressed, self-critical, socially inhibited, secretive, and ashamed of their bulimia. According to Gutsch (1988), they have conflicted feelings about relationships and sex, feel angry and powerless, and have difficulty handling pain, loss, and conflict. Bulimics are characterized by their feeling out of control, and they often have a high incidence of other impulse control problems such as alcohol abuse, self-mutilation, and overexercising. Bulimic families are often low in cohesiveness with high levels of conflict. Unlike anorexia, bulimics tend to be egodystonic and experience considerable hunger and disappointment with their need to binge and purge. Bulimic binging episodes are often later in the day and tend to relate to mood change, stress, or unstructured time. According to Brotman and Herzog (1990), impaired psychological development may play a role in eating disorders. Impaired mother-child relationships have been described by psychoanalysts as central to the development of eating disorders. Self psychologists and proponents of feminist psychological theory have proposed that a history of sexual abuse is common in clients with eating disorders, and therefore, exploration of this subject during the initial evaluation would seem important. Many writers have tried to find a neurochemical explanation for both anorexia and bulimia. Researchers have often been frustrated by this, as neurochemical imbalances are often the result of the disorder and it is often hard to determine their etiology.

Although both bulimics and anorectics tend to have friends and have fairly successful life-styles, they also have a tendency towards isolation and social difficulties. It is likely that this was developed in their troubled and chaotic families. Additionally some researchers (Atwood & Chester, 1987) have noticed that they have a tendency to have mothers who doubt themselves and are unresponsive to their daughters and distant fathers who have high expectations for their daughters. Agras (1987) also has noticed that they have siblings and parents who have a high incidence of eating disorders and major depression.

TREATMENT FORMULATION

The anorectic personality is often described as submissive (although often stubbornly so), timid, duty-bound, rigidly disciplined, and achievement-oriented. Individuals also are quite moralistic and have underlying doubts and anxious hesitancy about social skills. In contrast to the typically shy anorectics, bulimics are more likely to be outgoing and friendly perfectionists who attempt to control the people around them by more direct means (Bruch, 1982; Agras, 1987). Bulimics generally show one of two patterns—either obsessive-compulsive or addictive features.

Several personality factors increase the tendency in adolescents to develop a bulimic pattern:

1. acceptance of a traditional feminine role,

2. middle- to upper-class social status,

3. attendance away at college or boarding school,

4. early physical maturation,

5. a lower metabolic rate,

6. higher stress,

7. tendency toward depression,

8. a high belief in the ability to control one's world,

9. a prolonged history of dieting attempts, and

10. a family that promotes psychological isolation from other people (Yager, Landsverk, & Edelstein, 1987; Striegel-Moore, Silberstein, & Rodin, 1986; Casper, Eckert, Halmi, Goldberg, & Davis, 1980).

The typical bulimic patient is Caucasian, female, single, in her mid-teens to mid-20s, well-educated, and close to her ideal weight. A binge episode usually is done in secret and commonly follows a sequence of stages including the following:

1. anticipation and planning,

2. anxiety,

3. urgency to begin,

4. rapid uncontrollable consumption of food,

5. relief, usually by purging and relaxation,

6. disappointment, and

7. shame or disgust.

Many theories attempt to account for eating disorders. Psychodynamic theories tend to see anorectics having a core conflict. Initially their core conflict was felt to be a fear of oral impregnation, while later analysts blamed domineering mothers for preventing the anorectic from completing the two chief psychosocial tasks of adolescence—individuating and separating. The theories are accurate in the fact that anorectics do fear sex, and they also demand independence while clinging to their mothers.

Family therapists have often noted that anorectics' fathers are ineffective, mothers overbearing, and both parents intrusive. The family system generally seems to be dysfunctional with the parents acting in inappropriate ways. (However, if one's daughter is starving to death, it's unlikely that any family would stay intact.)

Social theorists feel that the society places an inordinate value on thinness, beauty, proper behavior, diets, nutrition, exercise, health clubs, etc. This provides adolescents a way to rebel.

The biological research has been inconclusive; however, affective disorders seem to be closely correlated with eating disorders.

Adlerians tend to formulate eating disorders in a similar fashion to that of depression. Eating disorders are conceptualized as a result of overcontrolled behavior. Eating disorders are viewed as an expression of a combination of perfectionism and pessimism. Young girls are used by their parents in a way to live out unfulfilled ambitions. They are overprotected, overindulged, overcontrolled, with at least one parent having unrealistic hopes on her with the expectation of a perfect individual. The other parent and siblings indulge or compete in this arrangement, but never directly challenge it. The young girl then becomes discouraged about her own abilities, wants, and worth, and eventually develops a compliant attitude that says "I must be like my parents to be approved" or a complaining attitude that says "If I do what you want, I'm entitled to your approval." She is therefore trapped and finds her place in the family by being obedient.

As she gets older, her high degree of perfectionism without any of her own goals often leads toward disaster. The young woman is discouraged and both unwilling and perhaps unable to make an effort for herself. She is often a pessimist and believes that her efforts will not turn out well. She is overambitious and believes that she must be perfect and yet perfect by other people's standards.

Many theorists are puzzled why eating disorders affect primarily girls and surface as more of a behavioral rather than a mood disorder. Likely this relates to a young girl's close connection to a family, and this disorder can be a socially acceptable way to rebel against improper socialization. Also to have a physical problem is more socially acceptable than to have a mental illness or mood disorder.

In a controlled, strongly physically, vocationally, or socially competitive family, depression is effectively ruled out as a behavior which the family will tolerate. However, the family emphasis on eating or appearance can be selected as a vulnerable point by the child, or the refusal to eat or look good is a behavior reinforced in the family by their efforts to discourage it. Depression is not reinforced; it is not responded to (Slavik, 1990).

An adolescent girl seeking a more egalitarian place in this family, while still complying with family rules (and not face a father who speaks for most of them), must develop the whole repertoire of acceptable rebellious behaviors. A man in a similar family might develop a compulsive overwork schedule. The woman, however, has her body and her relationships. Her strategy might include stubbornness; a tendency to engage in power struggles; denial of body sensations and functions, hunger, and feelings, and an apparent inability to perceive how she appears to others; and obsessions, anxieties, and preoccupation with useless activities such as exercise. The anorectic woman has found the ultimate strategy to comply with all the family rules and still be most visible: a preoccupation with food yet refusing to eat. When these behaviors, obsessive plans, and vigilance begin to wear her down, then she may slip into depression. In an eating disorder, the woman chooses rebellion against the rules of appropriate performance. In depression, one rebels against the rules of appropriate affect. Both follow the family rules, and an eating disorder can thus easily be concurrent with depression (Slavik, 1990).

Adlerians, therefore, target therapy at how children are used for their parents' ambitions, children's profound discouragement, and their lack of skills and values. Often early recollections are a useful tool in order to enter into this process.

CLINICAL COURSE
AND COMPLICATIONS

Anorexia Nervosa

Anorexia nervosa often persists for years with active and inactive periods. Some clients, however, have stopped within 12 months and have not had reoccurrences. Physiologically, patients recover in two to three years from the nutritional deficits. However, many will continue to have menstrual problems, sexual and social maladjustment, weight fluctuations, disturbed appetite, and continued body and weight image problems. According to Hsu (1990), in terms of their overall prognosis, 40% are completely recovered, 30% are considerably improved, 20% are unimproved or severely impaired, and 5 to 10% prematurely die, usually by starvation, electrolyte imbalance (from vomiting or purging), or suicide.

How anorexia begins has little bearing on its course or outcome. Instead, predictors of a favorable outcome include a good premorbid level of functioning, more education, early age of onset, less weight loss, less denial of illness, overactivity, a greater psychosexual maturity, and feeling hunger when hospitalized. Indicators of a poor prognosis are the opposite of the above plus perinatal complications; binging, self-induced vomiting, and purging; longer duration of illness; longer delay in initially obtaining treatment; severe dysthymia; and obsessions and greater exaggeration of body width (Maxmen, 1986).

Bulimia

Bulimia occurs during the teenage years or early 20s, and rarely after the age of 30. It is a chronic disorder with fluctuating intensity and alternating periods of normal eating and binging. Sometimes normal eating does not occur, and the patient cycles between periods of binging and fasting. Bulimics generally improve and completely recover and seldom die. Connors, Johnson, and Stuckey (1984) found that 80% of the bulimic clients stopped their dysfunctional behavior in 10 weeks of treatment, 93% in 14 weeks. A positive prognosis is associated with good premorbid functioning, high educational level, early age of onset, feelings of hunger and low weight loss, short duration of disorder, acceptance of illness, overactivity, and psychosexual maturity (Seligman, 1990). Relapses are common and are often related to stressful life events. Therefore treatment should be extended through follow-up or support groups to prevent setbacks. Follow-up treatment also should be helpful in reducing the family, social, and occupational difficulties that often persist after the eating disorder has been eliminated. In addition to direct therapeutic follow-up, eating disorder assistance programs are available (Kapoor, 1988; Sandbek, 1986; Siegel, Brisman, & Weinshel, 1988).

THERAPIST CHARACTERISTICS

Clients presenting with eating disorders need considerable support and approval to make the difficult behavioral changes that are required. Engaging the client and developing strong rapport is an integral part of treatment. The individuality of these clients has often been denied in their families and that should not happen in therapy (Bruch, 1982). They need to be heard, encouraged, and helped to develop a separate identity. Treatment needs to be similar to that for clients with dependent personality features, with the therapist needing to encourage self-control and independence. Additionally, therapists will need to be firm and set limits in order to protect the client. Sometimes hospitalization will be necessary. Many writers also feel that women with eating disorders are uncomfortable with men and will prefer a female therapist or a male/female therapy team (Seligman, 1990).

According to Brouwers (1990), before counselors can ethically work on body image issues with their clients, they need to examine their own beliefs about weight and appearance. The worst thing to do with a bulimic client is to endorse the view that she must lose weight. The counselor's attitude is not only unhelpful, but actually colludes with the client in maintaining appearance-oriented attitudes that contribute to the bulimia. In the event that the client actually does need to lose weight for health reasons, the counselor must state clearly that bulimia is much worse for health than being overweight. Regardless of her appearance, the client must **accept herself as she is.**

"Fatism" is alive and well in our culture. Counselors owe it to themselves and to their clients to combat this form of prejudice. A counselor who believes the cultural indoctrinations that women must be thin to be happy, and that overweight people are lazy, lack willpower, or are less intelligent must seriously look at the effect that these beliefs are having on his or her own life and work. Counselors would do well to examine their own conscious and unconscious attitudes about appearance and work toward acceptance of their own bodies. Until a counselor works toward his or her own freedom from cultural slavery regarding appearance, he or she cannot work effectively with clients struggling with body image issues (Brouwers, 1990, p. 147).

TREATMENT

The client's initial evaluation should include a physical examination with a blood screen and a nutritional history in addition to a normal clinical intake (Garner & Davis, 1986). Because of these requirements, a treatment team consisting of a physician, therapist, nutritionist, and, in some cases, family therapist is often required (Bauer & Anderson, 1989a, 1989b; Bauer, Anderson, & Hyatt, 1986). Initially it is also necessary to have an initial treatment period where the client has behavioral treatment to help control the binging and purging and to closely monitor the weight. Fremouw, Wiener, and Seime (1987) have developed a useful set of forms for self-monitoring eating behavior. When the weight loss is severe or the client's medical condition is serious, hospitalization that includes a supervised eating program to prevent vomiting and laxative use and promote weight gain may be needed. However, an interesting point to note is that although hospitalization can stabilize a patient, most have eating problems after discharge (Agras, 1987). If the client does not seem to be in immediate danger, outpatient treatment is adequate as long as steps are taken to normalize weight and to stop self-damaging behaviors.

The treatment of eating disorders is often difficult because the clients and families tend to deny the illness. Premature termination of therapy frequently occurs. Power and control issues often inhibit the progress of therapy. Clients are resistant to changing behaviors that have served as coping mechanisms, even feeling as if they are giving up a part of themselves. The therapist needs to take control, yet to avoid triggering control issues or engaging in power struggles. This can be done in several ways (Schwartz, 1986; Sallas, 1985).

1. Therapists should allow clients to know that no one can make them change. The choice is one they can make. This reinforces that the client is in control and provides a sense of security so they can explore new behaviors.

2. Therapists should acknowledge that the evident goal (for the clients to be in control of their lives) is appropriate, but the methods for achieving the goal are inappropriate.

3. Therapists should presently suggest (occasionally through hypnosis) though not demand that the patient exercise some up-front and appropriate control over symptom behaviors.

4. Therapists should encourage the establishment of a support system for the patient by incorporating group therapy into the treatment plan.

5. Therapists should acknowledge that the symptom behaviors are important to the client and have functioned as part of their identity for a long time. This allows the client to be less defensive and more willing to seek alternative behaviors. The recognition of the interplay between physiology and psychology in the eating disordered client is imperative for successful treatment (Garner & Isaacs, 1986).

According to Seligman (1990), most treatment programs for clients with eating disorders tend to be relatively brief, 8 to 20 sessions, but sometimes include extended follow-up treatment. Therapy for clients with eating disorders, as for most clients with behavioral disorders, typically has several components. Behavioral therapy to promote healthy eating and to eliminate purging is the core of the treatment. Procedures usually include gathering baseline data on client's weight and related dysfunctional behaviors such as laxative use, establishment of goals, contingency contracting, monitoring of progress via diary or scale in the office if necessary, reinforcement and rewards for positive change, and relaxation strategies to reduce anxiety and improve self-image and sense of control. Other behavioral techniques, such as assertiveness, communication, and social skills training can enhance treatment, as can the development of leisure activities and improved relationships to provide alternatives to the dysfunctional eating (p. 192).

In order to help clients gain insight into the dynamics of the disorder, both cognitive and insight-oriented approaches have been useful. These approaches tend to improve the self-esteem, provide a sense of control, and contribute to the development of better eating. Therapists additionally need to deal with the conflicts that include the client's concurrent desire for autonomy and dependence and the need to be in complete control of a body that refuses to cease having appetites. During the course of treatment, attitudes and assumptions are identified, defined, and evaluated within a context of a firm yet supportive therapeutic relationship.

Many treatment programs are available in the literature that would be compatible with Adlerian thinking. These programs combine cognitive and behavioral interventions with some attention to affect in the structured format that could be used with either individuals or with groups. The psychoeducational aspects of treatment and the group dynamics are important. The programs basically shape diet, provide education, explore antecedents of the disorder, prevent vomiting, examine cognitions, teach problem solving and coping mechanisms, provide group support, and prevent relapse. Boskind-White and White (1983) found that group therapy with a male/female leadership team can be particularly helpful for bulimic women. Their approach to treating bulimia has the following elements:

1. Exploring affect, for example, shame, hostility, isolation, self-esteem, designed to clarify connection between emotions and eating.

2. Understanding relationships and the connection between intimacy and responsibility. Improvement of social skills.

3. Gaining awareness of eating patterns and cues to dysfunctional eating and purging.

4. Role-playing to develop assertiveness, communication, and other skills.

5. Developing coping strategies. Techniques such as the writing of autobiographies, feedback, values clarification, and self-disclosure also are used to help clients establish and work toward goals.

The eating disordered client also may need counseling regarding diet facts and simple control of eating behaviors, counseling of the type used with the more common problem of obesity and persistent eating disorders (Ruderman, 1986) such as the following:

1. A biological drive exists toward high fat and very sweet foods, so control should be directed toward "what" as much as "when" and "how much."

2. Weight loss is not hard to attain; keeping it off is.

3. More difficulty is experienced in losing weight during the second diet than the first.

4. Most diets are broken in the late afternoon.

5. If the activity level remains the same and a cessation of smoking occurs, a weight gain also will occur.

6. Changing exercise amounts and patterns are usually more effective in generating weight loss than changing diet amounts and patterns.

Many creative therapeutic approaches are used in treating eating disorders. O'Connor (1984) suggested a paradoxical intervention for bulimic clients. In this approach, clients are instructed to think obsessively about food for 30 minutes daily, to develop a mutually exclusive behavior such as shopping that they can engage in whenever they feel the urge to purge, and to binge on a schedule. This approach might be effective with clients who are highly resistant to straightforward treatment of their symptoms.

Madanes (1990) suggested a family intervention strategy where mass quantities of food that a bulimic would ordinarily eat are mixed on a table all together by the client with the family watching, and then ʌarried by hand and thrown into the toilet bowl all at one time and then having the father clean it out so that the toilet will work again. By exaggerating and bringing out into the open this behavior, Madanes has found that this often provides a quick stop to this problem.

In order to treat the negative thinking related to distorted body image, the counselor and client must first discover the self-defeating thoughts that the client holds about her body. Thoughts are examined in terms of associated feelings, rationality, and their connection with the eating behavior. The counselor then asks the client to generate alternative thoughts that encourage flexibility and self-acceptance (Ellis & Bernard, 1985). The client is encouraged to practice these alternative thoughts outside of the counseling office. Practice can involve writing them, saying them out loud to herself, or reminding herself quietly. In Figure 18.1 are listed examples of self-defeating thoughts, associated feelings, and alternative thoughts related to body image dissatisfaction (Brouwers, 1990).

(Continued on page 583)

Self-Defeating Thoughts	Associated Feelings	Alternative Thoughts
1. I am so fat and ugly.	1. Inadequate, Judged, Depressed.	1. My body is healthy and functional.
2. My thighs are disgusting.	2. Inadequate, Trapped, Judged.	2. This is the way my thighs are, and I accept them.
3. Fat people are gross and disgusting.	3. Fearful, Loathsome.	3. Overweight people are people with strengths and weaknesses. Their appearance has nothing to do with their value as human beings.
4. I should be able to control my appearance.	4. Anxious, Guilty, Inadequate.	4. My appearance is largely genetic, and I accept the way I look.
5. My boyfriend (husband, mother) wants me to be thin.	5. Angry, Fearful, Resentful.	5. I will not live to please others.
6. No one will like me if I'm fat.	Fearful, Inadequate, Anxious.	6. Appearance has nothing to do with being likeable.

Figure 18.1. Examples of thoughts and feelings associated with body image dissatisfaction. Reference: Browers, M. (1990).

Bauer and Anderson (1989a, 1989b) have discovered that individuals who suffer from bulimia nervosa share a characteristic pattern of thinking which needs to be understood if effective treatment is to take place. The following are the constructs and their corresponding beliefs.

1. Being or becoming overweight is the worst thing that can happen to me.

   a. Fat is disgusting and repulsive.

   b. To be fat is to be a failure.

2. Certain foods are good foods; other foods are bad foods.

   a. Good foods are "diet" foods; bad foods are fattening.

   b. Eating bad foods makes me a bad person; eating good foods makes me a good person.

   c. Bad food is turned directly into body fat.

3. I must have control over all of my actions to feel safe.

   a. Self-control is a sign of strength and discipline.

   b. Minor dietary indiscretions are indicative of a complete loss of self-control.

   c. Trying harder is the answer to my food problems.

4. I must do everything perfectly or what I do is worthless.

   a. I hold myself to standards that I would never apply to another individual.

   b. I feel bad regardless of performance. I could have done even better if I had tried harder.

   c. I negate accomplishments and dwell on failures.

5. Everyone is aware of and interested in what I'm doing.

   a. If I hear people laughing, I know it is about me.

   b. Other people watch and are critical of what I eat and know if I have gained weight.

6. Everyone must love me and approve of what I do.

   a. I must keep others happy regardless of the cost to me.

   b. I feel so unworthy of love that I attempt to buy it.

   c. I perceive rejection whether it is intended or not.

   d. I'm basically a bad person.

7. External validation is everything.

   a. Numbers are very important: calories, weight, grade point average, score on any type of competition.

   b. I take opinion polls every time I need to make a decision to be sure I am making the right choice.

8. As soon as I _____, I will be able to give up bulimia.

9. To be successful, a woman must combine the traditional values of women with the aggressive career orientation of men.

   a. I must be dependent and subservient like my mother.

   b. I must be aggressive and competitive like my father.

   c. I must be attractive and feminine but never sexual.

Some researchers (Bauer & Anderson, 1989a, 1989b) have found bizarre assignments designed to counter the perfectionism so integral to the personality of a bulimic to be highly effective. They suggest doing activities like balancing half a checkbook, leaving one corner of a bed unmade, or starting a letter and stopping in the middle of a sentence.

Andreas and Andreas (1989) believed that an important procedure is to help clients learn to think and respond the way naturally slender people do rather than wage a constant battle with food. These authors believed that to teach the following naturally slender eating method is important. This procedure helps people to learn and think how healthy people eat.

1. First, something makes me think of food. This might be seeing that it's time for lunch, hearing someone mention lunch, feeling hunger, or seeing food.

2. I check how my stomach feels now.

3. I ask myself "what would feel good in my stomach?"

4. I visualize a possible portion of food: a sandwich, a bowl of soup, a dinner salad, etc.

5. I imagine eating this food. I think of the taste of this food and then feel the food slipping into my mouth and get a feeling of how this amount of this food will feel in my stomach over time if I eat it now.

6. If I like this feeling better than how I will feel if I eat no food at all, I keep this food item as one possibility. If not, I discard it.

7. Next I visualize another food I might eat.

8. I imagine tasting this second item and feel how it feels as it goes into my stomach and stays in my system for some hours to come.

9. I notice how I like this feeling. Do I like it more than my first choice so far? I keep in mind the food item that makes me feel best to compare to my next choice.

10. Now I repeat steps 7, 8, and 9 as often as I want to, always keeping in mind the kind of food that I imagine would make me feel the best over time if I eat it. I compare each new possibility to that.

11. When I'm satisfied that I have considered enough options, I eat the food that I imagine would make me feel best over time so that I'll get to feel that good.

Other researchers have found family therapy (Root, Fallon, & Friedrich, 1986; Schwartz, 1987) to be very effective in the treatment of eating disorders, as well as an important adjunct to treatment. The classic study by Minuchin, Rosman, and Baker (1978) reported an 86% success rate with anorectics.

Many professionals are experimenting with the use of medications and eating disorders. It seems that at best medications will have a limited role in the current treatment of anorexia nervosa (Gitlin, 1990). The reasons for this are as follows.

First, anorexic patients, especially in the early stages of treatment when their weight is very low, are at a high risk to have a variety of metabolic and other biological disturbances from the self-induced starvation. Because of this, an increased danger exists in using any medication. Second, patients with anorexia nervosa are exceedingly sensitive to and intolerant of nondangerous medication side effects, both from the starvation effects and from their own sensitivity to unwanted feelings or changes in their bodies. Third, these patients often equate taking medication with losing control, further increasing the resistance to taking them (p. 141).

The most promising drug for anorexia nervosa is cyproheptadina (Periactin), which blocks the effect of serotonin.

While serotonin increases feelings of satiety (being full) through an effect in the hypothalamus, cyproheptadina stimulates appetite. Unfortunately, its major side effect is sedation.

In contrast to anorexia nervosa, medications, specifically antidepressants, have documented efficacy in decreasing the binge/purge cycle of bulimia (Walsh, 1987). The guidelines that a therapist should use before considering referral of a bulimic patient for possible antidepressant treatment are as follows.

1. It is important to acknowledge that medications are far from being the only well-documented treatment for bulimia. A variety of psychological approaches utilizing cognitive, behavioral, educational, psychodynamic, and supportive techniques in both individual and group formats have shown clear evidence of efficacy (Yagcr, 1988).

2. Studies comparing antidepressants to educational/cognitive/behavioral approaches are rare.

3. Medications are sometimes difficult to use in bulimic patients: side effects are often problematic, affecting compliance. Vomiting can cause erratic medication blood levels, making pharmacotherapy inconsistent, and the necessary dietary restrictions with the MAO inhibitors make these particular medications acceptable for only a subset of those with bulimia.

4. No established predictors are known for antidepressant responses with bulimic patients. Sincc the issues of control are so central to bulimia, patients often are frightened of being addicted to medications and are concerned that taking medication is an indication of lack of self-control. Bulimics also fear that the medications will make them fat (Edelstein, 1989).

CASE EXAMPLE

Case of Judy

Judy is a single 17-year-old who lives with her parents who insisted that she be seen by the counselor because of binge eating and vomiting. She achieved her greatest weight of 180 pounds at 16 years of age; her lowest weight since she reached her present height of 5'9" has been 150 pounds, and her present weight is about 160 pounds. Judy's parents are both professionals with advanced college degrees. Judy is the middle of three daughters.

Judy states that she has been dieting since the age of 12 and says that she has always been tall and chubby. At age 14 she started to binge eat and vomit. She was a serious competitive swimmer at that time and she felt it was necessary for her to keep her weight down in order to be the state champion that her father desired. She would deprive herself of food for a few days and then get an urge to eat. She could not control the urge and would raid the refrigerator and cupboards for desserts, potato chips, and whatever else caught her fancy. She would often do this in the evening when no one was looking and would eat everything in one sitting. While binging she knew that her eating was out of control but would only stop when she felt physical discomfort. She would then feel depressed and afraid of gaining weight and would self-induce vomiting by sticking a finger down her throat.

Judy has always been concerned about the effect this behavior was having on her weight and has constantly feared being overweight. Sometimes she would resort to laxatives to help her lose weight. When she was 15 she was having eating binges and vomiting four days per week. She has obtained very good grades in junior high school and high school and tends to be a student who works very hard.

Recently Judy has been drinking wine and beer on weekends. She drinks mostly with girlfriends. She dates infrequently, never getting very close to any boys, but Judy states that she wants to date. She feels ashamed of the way she looks and does not put herself in the right places at the right times. Four months ago she was hospitalized for two weeks in order to control her eating binges. During the time in the hospital she became very depressed, talked about suicide, and attempted to cut her wrist.

Judy is very well-dressed, well-oriented, and is able to answer questions with great psychological insight. During the interview, she indicates that she has a serious problem but feels hopeless about getting the behavior under control.

Diagnosis.

Axis I: 307.51 Bulimia nervosa

Rule out: Psychoactive substance abuse

Axis II: 301.83 Borderline personality disorder

Axis III: None

Axis IV: 3; eating disorder

Axis V: Current GAF: 65

Highest GAF Past 12 Months: 65

Initial Intake. Judy described herself as being "born fat" and always being a chubby kid, not really fat but somewhat overweight. She reports not liking this and having her mom and dad caring about the way she looked and always on her case about her weight. Her dad was always trying to get her to diet in order to be a better swimmer. Her parents often commented on everything she put in her mouth, making mealtime an awful experience. Her two sisters did not get it as bad as Judy. Actually, her sisters would even tell on her if they saw her eating stuff she wasn't supposed to.

Food issues are often the stated topic of power struggles between parents, though the subtext was typically a fight over who is in charge of the daughter's life. Therefore, one can easily see how a youngster such as Judy who was in the process of individuation is having a difficult time. Though Judy wants to please her parents and appear perfect on the outside, down inside she needs to rebel in order to establish her own identity.

Summary of the Family Constellation Information. Judy is the middle of three girls in a family with extremely high standards. These standards have led each girl to seek the goal of perfection. Judy's older sister has out-achieved Judy by being perfectly good and capable, while her younger sister acted out her perfect goals by being perfectly lousy. Judy supposed that father wanted a boy and tried to be a reasonable facsimile, and while she did gain some of her father's favor, doing so didn't give her a place with the power person in the family: her mom. By following an overachieving sister, she felt as though she had no ability, so she tried to win approval by trying to please her parents. Her academics and success in swimming were plays to accomplish this. However, as she approached adolescence and individuation, she began a war with herself.

Summary of Early Recollections.

"Life is a fight and dangerous."

"Everyone will give you a hard time unless you can remain perfect."

"People don't treat me the way that I should be treated."

Basic Mistakes.

1. She can't conceive of the possibility of good relationships.

2. She can do nothing to solve the situation except to look up to the upper dogs and down to the underdogs.

3. She sees life as a jungle and is so busy defending herself that she often provokes the battles.

4. She feels like Cinderella—a deprived princess in disguise.

Treatment. In order to help Judy with her problem, the therapist first received the medical records verifying that her medical condition was stable. Next, the therapist began individual therapy with a cognitive focus to look at many of the beliefs that Judy had that were getting in her way, particularly the beliefs of perfectionism and pessimism. The therapist helped to build up her self-esteem and to empower her. Instruction was provided in healthy eating and a consultation with a dietitian was arranged. A further suggestion was that Judy attend a local Overeaters Anonymous group and that her family contract to attend five sessions of family therapy focused on changing some of the family expectations.

CONCLUSION

Eating disorders are among the most challenging problems facing counselors/psychologists today. Their successful treatment involves a multimodal approach that seems to be well-suited to Adlerian orientation.

REFERENCES

Agras, W.S. (1987). *Eating disorders.* Elmsford, NY: Pergamon Press.

American Psychiatric Association. (1987). *Diagnostic and statistical manual of mental disorders (3rd ed.rev.).* Washington, DC: Author.

Andersen, A.E. (1990). *Males with eating disorders.* New York: Brunner/ Mazel.

Andreas, C., & Andreas, S. (1989). *Heart of the mind.* Moab, UT: Real Person Press.

Atwood, J.D., & Chester, R. (1987). *Treatment techniques for common mental disorders.* New York: Jason Aronson.

Bauer, B.G., & Anderson, W.P. (1989a). Bulimic beliefs: Food for thought. *Journal of Counseling and Development, 67,* 416-419.

Bauer, B., & Anderson, A. (1989b). Turning around bulimia with therapy. *Psychology Today*, September, 14.

Bauer, B., Anderson, A., & Hyatt, R. (1986). *Bulimia: Book for therapist and client*. Muncie, IN: Accelerated Development.

Boskind-White, M., & White, W.C., Jr. (1983). *Bulimarexia: The binge-purge cycle*. New York: Norton.

Brotman, A.W., & Herzog, D.B. (1990). Eating disorders. In S.E. Hyman & M.A. Jenike (Eds.), *Manual of clinical problems in psychiatry with annotated key references* (pp. 214-220). Boston: Little, Brown.

Brouwers, M. (1990). Treatment of body image dissatisfaction among women with bulimia nervosa. *Journal of Counseling and Development, 69*, 144-147.

Bruch, H. (1982). Anorexia nervosa: Therapy and theory. *American Journal of Psychiatry, 139*, 1531-1538.

Casper, R.C., Eckert, E.D., Halmi, K.A., Goldberg, S.C., & Davis, J.M. (1980). Bulimia. *Archives of General Psychiatry, 37*, 1030-1035.

Connors, M.E., Johnson, C.L., & Stuckey, M.K. (1984). Treatment of bulimia with brief psychoeducational group therapy. *American Journal of Psychiatry, 141*, 1512-1516.

Edelstein, C. (1989). *Mood disorders and eating disorders*. Presented at the 142nd American Psychiatric Association annual meeting, San Francisco, CA.

Ellis, A., & Bernard, M.E. (Eds.). (1985). *Clinical applications of rational emotive therapy*. New York: Plenum.

Fremouw, W.J., Wiener, A.L., & Seime, R.J. (1987). Self-monitoring forms for bulimia. In P.A. Keller & S.A. Heymen (Eds.), *Innovations in Clinical Practice and Sourcebook, 6*, 325-332. Sarasota, FL: Professional Resource Exchange.

Garner, D.M., & Davis, R. (1986). The clinical assessment of anorexia nervosa and bulimia nervosa. In P.A. Keller & L.G. Ritt (Eds.), *Innovations in Clinical Practice and Sourcebook, 5*, 5-28. Sarasota, FL: Professional Resource Exchange.

Garner, D.M., & Isaacs, P. (1986). The fundamentals of psychotherapy for anorexia nervosa and bulimia nervosa. In P.A. Keller & L.G. Ritt (Eds.), *Innovations in Clinical Practice and Sourcebook, 5*, 29-44. Sarasota, FL: Professional Resource Exchange.

Gitlin, M.J. (1990). *The psychotherapist's guide to psychopharmacology.* New York: The Free Press.

Gutsch, K.U. (1988). *Psychotherapeutic approaches to specific DSM-III-R categories.* Springfield, IL: C. C. Thomas.

Hsu, L.K.G. (1990). *Eating disorders.* New York: The Guilford Press.

Kapoor, S. (1988). *Bulimia: A program for friends and family members.* Springfield, IL: C. C. Thomas.

Madanes, C. (1990). *Metaphors and paradoxes.* San Francisco: Jossey-Bass.

Maxmen, J.S. (1986). *Essential psychopathology.* New York: W. W. Norton.

Minuchin, S., Rosman, B.L., & Baker, L. (1978). *Psychosomatic families: Anorexia nervosa in context.* Cambridge, MA: Harvard University Press.

O'Connor, J. (1984). Strategic individual psychotherapy with bulimic women. *Psychotherapy: Theory, Research, and Practice, 21,* 491-499.

Root, M.P., Fallon, P., & Friedrich, W.N. (1986). *Bulimia: A systems approach to treatment.* New York: W.W. Norton.

Ruderman, A. (1986). Dietary restraint: A theoretical and empirical review. *Psychological Bulletin, 99,* 247-262.

Sallas, R. (1985). Winning the war against eating disorders without doing battle. *The Journal of Psychiatric Research, 19,* 445-448.

Sandbek, T.J. (1986). *The deadly diet: Recovering from anorexia and bulimia.* Oakland, CA: New Harbinger Publications.

Schwartz, R. (1986). Eating disorders. *New England Journal of Medicine, 313,* 295-303.

Schwartz, R.C. (1987). Working with internal and external families in the treatment of bulimia. *Family Relations, 36,* 242-245.

Seligman, L. (1990). *Selecting effective treatments.* San Francisco: Jossey-Bass.

Siegel, M., Brisman, J., & Weinshel, M. (1988). *Surviving an eating disorder: New perspectives and strategies for family and friends.* New York: Harper & Row.

Slavik, S. (1990). *Speculations on eating disorders in Adlerian framework.* Mimeographed form, 4391 Torrington Place, Victoria, B.C. Canada V8N 4T3.

Striegel-Moore, R., Silberstein, L., & Rodin, J. (1986). Toward an understanding of risk factors for bulimia. *American Psychologist, 43*, 246-263.

Wadden, T., & Stunkard, A. (1987). Psychopathology and obesity. In R. Wurtman & J. Wurtman (Eds.), *Human obesity.* New York: New York Academy of Sciences.

Walsh, B.T. (1987). Psychopharmacology of bulimia. In H. Y. Meltzer (Ed.), *Psychopharmocology: The third generation of progress.* New York: Rabin Press.

Yager, J. (1988). The treatment of eating disorders. *Journal of Clinical Psychiatry, 49*(9), 18-25.

Yager, J., Landsverk, J., & Edelstein, C.K. (1987). A twenty-month follow-up study of 628 women with eating disorders. I: Course and severity. *American Journal of Psychiatry, 144*, 1172-1177.

RESOURCES FOR EATING DISORDERS

Organizations

American Anorexia/Bulimia Association, Inc.
133 Cedar Lane
Teaneck, NJ 07666
(201) 836-1800

National Association of Anorexia and Associated Disorders
Box 271
Highland Park, IL 60035
(708) 831-3438

Overeaters Anonymous—National Office
4025 Spencer Street, Suite 203
Torrance, CA 90504
(213) 542-8363

O-Anon
Check local listings

Publications

Eating Disorders Review
  P.O. Box 2468
  Van Nuys, CA 91404-9983

A bi-monthly publication providing current information to the professional treating eating disorders.

Hazledon Educational Materials
  Pleasant Valley Road
  P.O. Box 176
  Center City, MN 55012-0176

Publisher of many useful books and pamphlets in the 12 Step Tradition for compulsive overeaters. Catalog available upon request.

Carle Medical Communication
  611 West Park
  Urbana, IL 61801

Publisher of media on eating disorders for professionals and clients. Catalog available upon request.

Gurze Books
  P.O. Box 2238
  Carlsbad, CA 92008

The leading distributor of books and tapes on bulimia, anorexia nervosa, and compulsive eating. Catalog available upon request.

PART VI

A PRIMER
OF
INDIVIDUAL
PSYCHOLOGY

OVERVIEW

The primary goal of this book is to integrate both the descriptive, diagnostic features of DSM-III-R with the psychodynamic theories of Alfred Adler's Individual Psychology. In each chapter, the authors examine the various diagnostic categories and discuss the dynamics of each according to the holistic, phenomenological, socio-teleoanalytic perspective Individual Psychologists use in their case formulations. This chapter is designed to familiarize readers with the principles of Individual Psychology, particularly as they relate to psychopathology.

CHAPTER **19**

A PRIMER OF INDIVIDUAL PSYCHOLOGY

Michael P. Maniacci, Psy.D.

Adler (1956, 1964, 1978) received his medical training in Vienna at the turn of this century. Though initially an opthamologist, he soon turned his practice to general medicine, and shortly thereafter, psychiatry (only Jung received formal training in psychiatry—Freud was originally trained as a neurologist). Adler's assumptions about human nature and motivation differed considerably from Freud's, and subsequently, so did his conceptualizations about treatment. This discussion is intended to serve as an overview of Adler's theories; for a more complete presentation, interested readers are encouraged to see the texts by Adler (1956, 1964, 1978), Dreikurs (1953, 1967), Manaster and Corsini (1982), Mosak (1977, 1989), and Shulman (1973).

GENERAL DYNAMICS

Striving for Superiority

Adler conceptualized all life as engaged in movement from a perceived minus situation to a perceived plus situation. The minus situation received many different labels throughout Adler's writings, from feelings of inferiority, feeling worthless, insecure, in the one-down position, to feeling weak and discouraged. The plus situation was variously described as powerful, competent, secure, one-up, and superior. This movement is always intended to make the individuals feel better, to feel closer to perfection. What individuals define as minus varies; for some, they feel insecure and look to become secure or safe; while for others, they feel inferior, and look to become superior. The exact meaning of the minus situation is determined by individuals themselves, as is the meaning of the compensation chosen. All people will feel inferior in some area at some time in their lives (or weak, or helpless, or discouraged). The inferiority feelings themselves are not pathological; how the inferiority feelings are compensated for becomes important.

Social Interest

Adler used the phrase social interest to describe the sense of community feeling individuals have with each other. According to Adler, social interest was an innate potential that needed to be developed, something akin to the human infant's development of language, which too is an innate potential that needs to be developed. For Adler, all psychological problems were social problems, and individuals needed to be understood within their social field. People have three main challenges to meet throughout the life cycle: work, love, and friendship. These tasks of life require cooperation and a willingness to work with others in order for them to be met successfully. Healthy compensations were those compensations that allowed individuals to work with and for the greater good of those around them; unhealthy, that is, pathological compensations, were lacking in social interest. These latter compensations took place at the expense of others, not with them. Individuals who had greater degrees of social interest tended to share in the general welfare and possessed a sense of responsibility and useful participation with others.

Degree of Activity

Along with the amount of social interest individuals had, Adler examined the degree of activity they displayed. For Adler, individuals could be conceptualized as having either a high or low degree of activity. A high degree of activity and a low amount of social interest might lead a person to compensations which were useless (i.e., not socially useful, at the expense of others), as is sometimes seen in certain sociopaths who are very busy but not very socially adaptive. At the other extreme would be those whose degree of activity and social interest were low, such as is typically seen in depressed individuals. Adler conceptualized the degree of activity as being primarily a biological function that individuals adapted and used according to their goals.

Psychology of Use

Individuals' development is more than the result of heredity and environment. While important as to what they have and where they are born, the use they make of those givens is even more important. Adler believed that people will use their natural and learned traits and skills in ways that will further their movement from a minus to a plus. For example, a child is not conceptualized as being shy; the child is conceptualized as using shyness in order to move through life. Even in the case of biological abnormalities and what Adler referred to as organ inferiorities, individuals had the choice of how to react to those conditions. They could compensate usefully or uselessly; that is, they could use those conditions to gain service from others and to elevate themselves in self-centered ways, or they could become useful, cooperative individuals in spite of (or, in some cases with the overcompensations, because of) their problems. As examples, Adler often cited people who overcame their overcompensations, such as the Greek orator Demostheses who overcame stuttering, or Beethoven, who overcompensated for his ear afflictions and became a musical genius.

The Style of Life

Individuals will develop a consistent style of moving through life as they attempt to move from a minus to a plus situation. The goals they choose and the methods of attaining those goals are in part influenced by heredity and environment, but as mentioned previously, they also are influenced by the choices individuals make, by what Adler referred to as the creative self. Individuals with a high degree of social interest will move towards goals in ways which are socially useful and cooperative; individuals with a low degree of social interest will move in useless ways. Adler originally described four general styles of movement, which were classified according to the goals individuals selected and how they moved towards those goals. He spoke of the

Getting Type,
Ruling Type,
Avoiding Type, and
Ideal Type (Socially Interested Type).

The **Getting Types** will look to put others into their service in order to "get" as much as they can with as little effort as possible. The **Ruling Types** will look to dominate and control others. **Avoiding Types** will seek to steer clear of responsibility and challenges and will "avoid" effort and social interaction. The **Ideal Types** will be those whose goals and style of attaining them will take into consideration others and will operate as cooperative, egalitarian members of their social network. Contemporary Adlerians (e.g., Mosak, 1977; Shulman, 1973) have refined and elaborated upon the concept of life-style, conceptualizing it as a set of convictions individuals have about themselves, life, and others, such as

I am . . . worthy of special attention,

Life is . . . a stage on which people should perform,

Others are . . . there to appreciate me and make me feel good, and

Therefore . . . I will look to get others' attention and service through any means I can.

These beliefs will tend to produce the life-style of a "Star." If these people have a high degree of social interest, then they will fulfill their goals with others, perhaps bringing pleasure and enjoyment to others along the way. If their amount of social interest is low, they might become demanding, selfish, and difficult to get along with.

The Unity of Mental Disorders

As Adler often mentioned, all life-styles are adaptable until life presents challenges that individuals cannot meet. Life-styles that are high in social interest will generally find solutions to problems that are beneficial to all those involved. Life-styles in which social interest is low will be faced with challenges that demand cooperation, and in response, those individuals will react in uncooperative, self-serving ways. Life-style convictions that are too narrow, or too absolute (e.g., I *must always* be the best) are more likely to encounter situations in which the fundamental attitudes lead to interpersonal conflicts than are those that are more flexible (e.g., I would *like* to be the best, but I *don't have to be*). Individuals will react to life and others according to the life-styles and the amount of social interest they have.

What the particular manifestation of psychopathology is will depend upon a number of diverse factors, such as biological make-up, early family environment, self-training, life-style convictions, social interest, and choice. Whether the psychological problem is a Generalized Anxiety Disorder, Schizophrenia (catatonic type), or Alcohol Intoxication Disorder, Adlerians are interested in understanding the particular dynamics of each individual case in order to better grasp the life-style of the particular person. The symptoms of the particular disorder will be used according to the goals of the person. In general, Adler believed that all psychopathology served the purpose of creating distance from the demands of life which the individual felt compelled to meet. Life or other people present challenges which require cooperation and social interest; because of a particular life-style, the person feels incapable of meeting that challenge—hence, the person feels inferior. Because of a low amount of social interest, that person will attempt to create distance from the demands, while at the same time maintaining the appearance of cooperation, thereby preserving self-esteem. In effect, virtually all of DSM-III-R is a catalogue of socially useless attempts at compensations: a list of what Adler referred to as inferiority complexes—tactics designed to excuse the individual from meeting the challenges of life.

PSYCHOLOGICAL ASSESSMENT AND PSYCHOTHERAPY

Given the aforementioned dynamics, Adler placed special emphasis upon understanding the individual case and the life-style of the person. With that knowledge, the psychotherapist will understand the particular choice of symptomatology as a response to a situation the person felt unprepared (and hence inferior) to deal with. Such an understanding led to treatment which, while taking into account the symptoms and presentation of the case, focused upon the individual dynamics and life-style as well. Overall, the goal of psychotherapy is to increase the person's social interest, thereby allowing the person to solve the challenge in a socially useful way.

Family Constellation

Understanding the family constellation is one part of the process. Individuals grow up in an environment peopled by others. By examining the early family dynamics, psychotherapists can gain an understanding of the early social training of their clients. Part of the assessment of family constellation involves examining the childhood sibling relationships, the parental relationships to each other and the children, the early school and social environments, and the relevant biological and constitutional backgrounds of the family members (Shulman & Mosak, 1988). By assessing how clients found their place (i.e., strove for significance) in their early social microcosm, clinicians can gain some understanding of the vantage point clients adopt in the here and now.

Early Recollections And Dreams

Adler used early recollections and dreams in a way very different from Freud. Whereas Freud saw them as screen memories and attempts at wish fulfillment which were indications of unresolved childhood issues, Adler saw them as attempts to reinforce and facilitate movement towards subjectively determined goals. Early recollections are those memories individuals can visualize and report as happening at one specific time from their past. For example:

Age 6. "I remember my father put me on a horse. I was terrified. I thought I'd fall off."

This recollection of a 16-year-old girl is significant. Adlerians would ask why, of all the thousands of memories she could have remembered, she should choose to remember this one? The answer is it serves a purpose; the memory serves her goal of being cautious. She is very suspicious of men, and though she needs them to "elevate" herself in life, she is also "terrified" that by allowing them to do that, she will get hurt. She uses this memory as a reminder, as a way of keeping "on track" in her striving.

Dreams serve much the same purpose. Whereas early recollections are indicative of life-style goals (i.e., long-term personality goals), dreams are not necessarily so; they may be, but they also can be indicative of more immediate, short-term goals, which may or may not be related to life-style goals. Dreams serve many functions for the dreamer, including problem-solving, rehearsal for future actions, the generation of emotions which will then serve to facilitate movement toward goals (e.g., dreaming about fighting with a boss, waking up angry and irritable, and then going to work "looking" for an argument), and exploring new behaviors and attitudes.

Hidden Reasons, Immediate Goals, and Life-style Goals

Dreikurs (1973), clarifying and elaborating upon Adler's work, made the distinction between hidden reasons, immediate goals, and life-style goals. Understanding these distinctions will lead to an understanding of individuals' private logic.

Private logic (sometimes referred to as private intelligence by Adler) is beliefs, attitudes, and convictions which make every person unique. No two life-styles are identical. **Common sense** is the phrase Adler used to describe the shared thinking and attitudes found in the general population; common sense is based upon social interest. Individuals with social interest will develop a common language, a common way of seeing life and others that is found with people who feel "at home" with others, who can and are willing to see the interrelationship between others and the responsibility they need to take in solving problems cooperatively. **Private logic** is thinking based upon a purely individual, unshared perspective, but not necessarily pathological viewpoint. For example, a 38-year-old business executive might believe that in order to solve the life task of work, he or she has to be "The Boss." He or she accepts the common sense view that work is necessary, yet his or her private logic adds an extra dimension: to simply work is not enough. He or she has to be in charge. Again, that is not likely to lead to psychopathology; with enough social interest, he or she will be a fair, cooperative leader who will be well liked and productive. With less social interest, however, he or she may become a tyrant. In that case, as long as he or she maintains status as tyrant, the person will probably not manifest too much psychopathology; however, should the person not be able to maintain the status, then he or she may choose to compensate by being especially aggressive and vengeful (e.g., a Sadistic Personality Disorder), or deviant and crooked (e.g., an Antisocial Personality Disorder), or he or she may, if biologically loaded for it, become psychotic and choose to create in his or her fantasy the fiction that he or she is the ultimate "Boss": God (e.g., Schizophrenia, paranoid type, with delusions of grandeur being prominent).

Dreikurs (1973) discussed the difference between hidden reasons, immediate goals, and life-style goals. For Adlerians, the distinction between conscious and unconscious is not crucial, but between private logic and common sense. If the person's life-style goals are in line with common sense, he or she will be functioning relatively well. The more rigid, the farther away from common sense the private logic is, the greater the possibility of the person "running into" difficulty in his or her goal striving. **Life-style goals** are long-term personality goals, and successful psychotherapy either changes the goals themselves or the way the person moves toward them.

Immediate goals are those goals which individuals have that produce a more direct payoff. For example, several people may have the goal of "getting," that is, they are Getting Types.

That would be their long-range goal. The immediate goal may be to "get" attention, or love, or money, or so forth. **Hidden reasons** are the explanations individuals give to themselves for their behaviors. To continue the example of the 38-year-old executive, his or her long-range, life-style goal is to be "The Boss." In a given area of life, at a given time, his or her immediate goal may be to surround self with obedient, subservient employees. The hidden reason for the behavior, how his or her style is justified, may be something like this: "I pursue excellence, and only the best will do." This would be what the person tells self, what the self-statement or internal dialogue is. Successful psychotherapy can begin at any of these points: the life-style goals, the immediate goals, or the hidden reasons. Attending to all three will help the clients to feel understood and will facilitate the therapeutic process.

Themes, Types, and Priorities

Adler spoke of **types,** and discussed four possible ones. Mosak (1977) and Manaster and Corsini (1982) presented other possible types and central themes life-style convictions may cluster into. Manaster and Corsini (1982) also discussed the concept of priorities.

Mosak (1977) discussed certain **themes** which appear to be evident in certain diagnostic categories. For example, the Paranoid Personality Disorders generally are expected to have the themes of controlling, wanting to be right, being a victim, and being oppositional in their life-styles. Similarly, people diagnosed as having Hypochondriacal Disorder tend to have the themes of being a victim and craving excitement. Life-styles also seem to cluster into **priorities,** and Manaster and Corsini (1982) discussed four of them: pleasing, comfort, control, and superiority. Understanding the themes in clients' lives, or their possible priorities (which they emphasize and in what order) all serve to facilitate understanding clients and intervention strategies which will be particularly relevant for the individuals seeking help.

Winning Cooperation, Encouragement, and Finding A Place Usefully

Adler emphasized winning the clients' **cooperation.** Ideally, therapy should be an experience in useful, interpersonal interaction, perhaps one of the first truly meaningful experiences of that kind clients have encountered. Adler believed that all forms of psychopathology were the result of discouragement, that clients had become discouraged in their ability to find their place usefully. By providing **encouragement,** a sense of being accepted, understood, and valued as they are (not as they felt they "should be"), Adler attempted to re-educate clients about their values and beliefs. The particular techniques Adlerians use vary from practitioner to practitioner, but the overall goal is the same: to increase social interest.

CASE EXAMPLE

While the previous chapters have explored the various diagnostic conditions in detail as listed in DSM-III-R and explained the dynamics of each condition according to the aforementioned principles, it might be beneficial to present a brief clinical example which emphasizes more of the Adlerian formulation.

Case of Karen

Karen came into therapy because of marital dissatisfaction. She complained of being irritable, depressed, sexually frustrated, and on the verge of asking for a divorce. She was 44 years old and had been married for over 20 years.

Her family constellation revealed the following: She was an oldest born who helped raise her younger siblings, most of whom she described as "nice, but klutzy." She "had to" pick up after them, help them, and in general, "look after" them. She characterized her father as the head of the household, the breadwinner, but her mother as "the real organizer," the one who "ran things." She described her parents' relationship as "cooperative but not very affectionate." Her earliest recollection was this:

Age 3. "I remember Mother putting me in my crib. She was all dressed up, waiting for Father to take her out."

This woman's life-style was discussed with her. She was used to being "in charge" in life, but when it came to men, she had to assume a somewhat subservient role and "wait" for them to "bring the goodies" to her. Her usual pattern was to be a loyal, hard-working wife and caregiver. Her life-style dynamics were the following:

Life-style Type: Victim (she worked and worked, but felt unappreciated)

Central Themes: Men bring the goodies home, but they'd be nowhere without women. I find my place through being hard-working, loyal, and underappreciated.

Personal Priorities (in descending order of importance): Pleasing, Comfort, Superiority, Control

Frequent Hidden Reasons (self-statements): "I feel used." "I have a right to be depressed, he doesn't appreciate me." "Why should I have to ask, he should just know what to do."

Frequent Immediate Goals: Attention, orderliness, affection

Karen agreed wholeheartedly with the assessment. She even reported this as her first in-therapy dream:

"I'm looking after John [an adult male relative], but he's not an adult, he's a child. He slips in the mud and as I go to help him, I hit my head on something hanging from above."

Many of the above mentioned themes and issues are in this dream. Karen keeps rehearsing her life-style issues in her sleep, reinforcing both her depression and her typical style of living.

The precipitating problem for her was this: Her last and youngest child left home for college. Her husband, a kind but very success-driven man, devoted more time than ever to his career. For the first time in her life, Karen had no one to care for, and through her depressive symptoms and irritable moods, she had managed to catch not only the attention of her husband once again, but one or two of her children as well. Karen found her place through being a mother, wife, and caregiver who "sacrificed" for others. When no one was left to "sacrifice" for, she lost her place, felt insecure (i.e., inferior), and compensated on the useless side of life by choosing symptoms which would get the attention of those around her and bring them back into her life. Then once again, she could "muster up strength" and somehow "pull" herself together long enough to take care of them until they thought she was doing well enough, at which time they would leave to go about their own business, and she would feel insecure again, and the cycle would repeat itself.

REFERENCES

Adler, A. (1956). *The Individual Psychology of Alfred Adler.* H. L. Ansbacher & R. R. Ansbacher (Eds.). New York: Basic Books.

Adler, A. (1964). *Superiority and social interest.* H. L. Ansbacher & R. R. Ansbacher (Eds.). Evanston, IL: Northwestern University Press.

Adler, A. (1978). *Co-operation between the sexes: Writings on women, love and marriage, sexuality and its disorders.* H. L. Ansbacher & R. R. Ansbacher (Eds.). New York: Doubleday.

Dreikurs, R. (1953). *Fundamentals of Adlerian psychology.* Chicago: Alfred Adler Institute.

Dreikurs, R. (1967). *Psychodynamics, psychotherapy, and counseling.* Chicago: Alfred Adler Institute.

Dreikurs, R. (1973). The private logic. In H. H. Mosak (Ed.), *Alfred Adler: His influence on psychology today* (pp. 19-32). Park Ridge, NJ: Noyes Press.

Manaster, G. J., & Corsini, R. J. (1982). *Individual Psychology.* Itasca, IL: F. E. Peacock.

Mosak, H. H. (1977). *On purpose.* Chicago: Alfred Adler Institute.

Mosak, H. H. (1989). Adlerian psychotherapy. In R. J. Corsini & D. Wedding (Eds.), *Current psychotherapies* (4th ed.) (pp. 65-116). Itasca, IL: F. E. Peacock.

Shulman, B. H. (1973). *Contributions to Individual Psychology.* Chicago: Alfred Adler Institute.

Shulman, B. H., & Mosak, H. H. (1988). *Manual for life style assessment.* Muncie, IN: Accelerated Development.

INDEX

INDEX

A

Abraham, K. 81, 91, 117
Abrams, J.C. 523, 529, 557
Abramson, L.Y. 476, 503
Academic, inhibition 291-2
Ackerman, P.T. 512, 514, 529, 558
Activity, degree of 600-1
Addictions 418-24
Adler, A. 2, 3, 4, 5, 6, 13, 16, 17,
    21, 23, 33, 35, 46, 54, 57, 58,
    59, 60, 66, 67, 73, 75, 77, 81,
    96, 97, 100, 118, 137, 139, 146,
    147, 150, 153, 154, 159, 177, 178,
    183, 185, 198, 201, 202, 204,
    231, 252, 258, 273, 276, 281,
    282, 301, 346, 365, 372, 373,
    374, 383, 418, 424, 455, 456,
    468, 476, 481, 482, 483, 484,
    486, 488, 499, 526, 535, 556, 599,
    610
    Affective Disorders 95-8
    Individual Psychology 93-8
    organ inferiority 93-5
Adler, Alexandria 328, 365
Adler, G. 354, 365
Adler, K. 39, 50, 54, 96, 97, 103,
    118, 138, 139, 140, 145, 146, 147,
    148, 149, 151, 153, 156, 157, 158,
    159, 160
Adlerian dynamics in Childhood-
    onset Major Depressive Disorder
    481-9
    anger 482
    appearance 486
    attitude to fail 485-6
    constitutional factors 481

early training 481
family dynamics 486-7
family therapy 488-9
fantasy 488
goals of misbehavior 487-8
lacking in cooperation 483-4
life-style themes 481-2
life tasks 483
obfuscation 484
overambition 485
pampering 482-3
self pity 488
treatment strategy 487
using others 484-5
Adlerian perspective, dynamics
    64-9
    organic mental disorders 58-60
Adlerian psychotherapy,
    purpose of 415
Adlerian thought, associated with
    substance dependence or abuse
    394-9
Agoraphobia 171, 173-5
    Adlerian interpretation 177-9
    criteria 174
    developmental antecedents
        174-5
    treatment 179-80
Agras, W.S. 570-1, 578, 591
Akhtar, S. 376, 383
Akiskal, H. S. 87, 91, 95, 109,
    118, 123, 129, 160, 470, 472, 479,
    499, 500
Alcohol Abuse 390
Alcohol Dependence 390
Alcoholism 418-20
Allen, R.P. 510, 530, 563
Alloy, L.B. 476, 507

B

DuPaul, G.J. 539, 562
Dupertius, C. 327, 366
Dykman, R.A. 512, 514, 529, 558
Dysfunctions, Psychosexual 440-3
Dysthymia 128-30
    criteria 128-9

E

Eagle, M. 372, 384
Ebert, M.H. 133, 160, 529, 557
Eckert, E.D. 572, 592
Edelstein, C. 572, 588, 592, 594
Egeland, J.A. 131, 161
Egendorf, A. 196, 200, 213, 232
Ego-gravity, pull of, *Figure* 188
Ego-syntonic 300
Electroconvulsive therapy (ECT) 263
Elkin, I. 152, 161
Elkind, G.S. 519, 563, 565
Ellenberger, H. 91, 119, 259, 273, 277
Ellickson, P.L. 387, 395, 404
Ellis, A. 468, 501, 581, 592
Emery, G. 169, 183
Emotions, disturbance of 290
Encouragement 397-8, 608
Endicott, J. 126, 128, 161, 465, 472, 507
Environment, social
    Adlerian thought 395-6
Environment, supportive 275
Epidemiologic Catchment Area (ECA) study 170
Erickson, M. 202
Erickson, R.C. 60, 78
Erikson, E. 219, 229
Etiology 444-6
Evaluation, clinical 12
Everly, G. 302, 313, 332, 337, 366, 375, 384
Examination, mental status 70
Exhibitionism 435
Exner, J.E. 71, 78

Exposure, imaginal 180
Extein, I. 135, 161

F

Factors, Psychological 242-4
    Adlerian approach 244
    affecting physical condition 235-58, 242-4
    DSM-III-R 243-4
Fakouri, M.E. 101, 119
Fallon, P. 586, 593
Family
    intervention treatment 71-2
    training 67
Family constellation 604
Family dynamics 412-3
Fawcett, J. 470, 501
Fear 169
Feinberg, M. 123, 160
Feinberg, T.L. 459, 470, 471, 477, 479, 480, 504
Feingold, I. 538, 559
Feldman, L. 320, 365, 379, 384
Ferguson, H.B. 529, 558, 562
Fetishism 435
Fiedorowicz, C. 466, 503
Fiester, S.J. 152, 161
Fine, S. 468, 471, 502, 504
Fingarette, H. 397, 403
Finney, J.W. 396, 403
Finucci, J.M. 529, 558
Fisher, D. 558
Fisk, J.L. 528, 563
Flashback 217-22
    cause or effect 214-5
    regression during 218
Flor-Henry 88
Focus
    cognitive 9
    psychodynamic 9
    systems 9
Ford, C. 253, 258
Ford, D.H. 415, 425
Formulation

H

Halbreich, U. 135, 163
Hales, R.E. ix, 161
Haley, G.M.T. 468, 471, 502, 504
Hallucinogen dependence and abuse 391
Halmi, K.A. 572, 592
Haloperiodol 69
Halperin, J.M. 523, 530, 559
Handicap 76
Hanlon, C. 474, 506
Harms, E. 79
Hartdagen, S. 520, 534, 560
Harvald, B. 131, 132, 160
Hastings, J.E. 529, 559
Hauge, M. 131, 132, 160
Hawel, M. 120
Hay, W.M. 404
Heather, N. 402, 403
Heaton, R.K. 523, 559
Hechtman, L. 530, 533, 534, 559, 565
Hejazi, M.S. 475, 500
Helzer, J.E. 477, 507
Hendrickson, L. 529, 560
Heninger, G.R. 172, 183, 470, 500
Henker, B. 514, 515, 519, 530, 537, 538, 539, 540, 559, 565, 566
Herjanic, B. 467, 476, 477, 502, 506
Herjanic, M. 467, 476, 502
Hershberg, S.G. 469, 470, 476, 502
Herzog, D.B. 570, 592
Heymen, S.A. 592
Hinkle, D.E. 489, 501
Hirsch, M. 477, 500
Hirschfeld, R.M.A. 124, 131, 136, 161
Hirshfeld, M. 91, 118
Hirshfeld, R. 86, 87, 118
Hobbs, G. 529, 560
Holism 396-7
Holmes, C.S. 534, 538, 556
Holt, K.G. 475, 500
Homosexuality 439-40
Hooker, B. 217, 219, 230, 232
Hooker, E. 185
Hoover, G. 40, 54

Hopkins, J. 530, 533, 559, 565
Hoppe, K. 87, 119
Horevitz, R. 270, 277
Hoy, E. 518, 529, 565
Hozman, P. 101, 119
Hsu, L.K.G. 575, 593
Hughes, M.C. 469, 502
Hunt, R.D. 525, 559
Hutt Adaptation to the Bender-Gestalt Test 71
Hutt, M. L. 71, 78
Hyatt, R. 577, 592
Hyman, S.E. 592
Hynd, G. 520, 534, 560, 564
Hyperactivity, autonomic 190
Hyperavoidance 189
Hypervigilance 190
Hypnosis 260
Hypnotic dependence and abuse 393
Hypochondriasis 236-7, Figure 245
    DSM-III-R 236-7
Hypotheses, schizophrenic 41-3

I

Ideals, extravagant 33, 46
Identification 202
Imber, S.D. 152, 161
Individual Psychology 4, 81-120, 372-4, 378-9
    Adler, A. 93-8
    biopsychosocial aspects 60
    DSM-III-R 9-11
    primer of 597-611
    viewpoint of Psychosexual Disorders 429-56, 432-43
Inferiority
    causes 65
    complexes 65
    feelings 65
    organ 66, 76, 535-6
    physiology and organ 473-6
Inhalant dependence and abuse 392
Interest, social 395-6, 413-4, 600
Interpretation, dream 221
Interpreter, brain 36
Introduction 1-18
Isele, F.W. 422, 426

Obesity 422-3
Obsessions 175
Offord, D.R. 539, 558
Opioid dependence and abuse 392
Order-for-disorder 215-6
Organ inferiority 36, 58, 93-5
    psychic level 59
    somatic level 59
    sympathic level 59
Ornsteen, M. 473, 500
Ornstein, R. 1, 60, 71, 76, 78, 505
Overambition, definition 467
Ozols, E.J. 527, 561

P

Padian, N. 123, 163
Pain, complaints of 238
Pampering 66
Pancner, K.L. 153, 162
Pancner, R. 7, 8, 18, 22, 121, 132, 136, 153, 162, 410, 426,
Pandina, R.J. 396, 404
Pappas, B.A. 529, 558
Paradoxical intention 154
Paraphillias 434-5
Parloff, M.B. 152, 161
Pasamanick, B. 510, 560
Paternite, C.E. 534, 560
Pathology, organic, characteristics 68
Pattison,E. M. 394, 395, 403, 404
Pauls, D.L. 131, 161, 470, 504
Pavlidis, G. 558
Paykel, E.S. 124, 162
Pearl, D. 564
Pedophilia 436-7
Peele, S. 399, 404
Pelham, W.E. 539, 562
Pendulum, The 88, 120
Pennington, B.F. 524, 562
Perfectionism, *Figure* 188
Perlman, T. 530, 533, 534, 559, 565
Perry, H. 120
Personality
    definition 299
    factors in Bipolar Disorders 99-106

multiple 270-72
style 299
types 9-10
Personality Disorder, Antisocial 321-6
    characteristics, *Figure* 325
    clinical presentation 322-3
    developmental and etiological features 323-4
    DSM-III-R description and criteria 321-2
    treatment 324-6
Personality Disorder, Avoidant
    characteristics, *Figure* 334
    clinical presentation 331-2
    developmental and etiological features 332-3
    DSM-III-R description and criteria features 330-1
    treatment 333-5
Personality Disorder, Borderline 352-9
    characteristics, *Figure* 357
    clinical presentation 353-4
    developmental and etiological features 355-6
    DSM-III-R description and criteria 352-3
    treatment 356-9
Personality Disorder, Dependent 305-11, *Figure* 308
    clinical presentation 306
    developmental and etiological features 307, *Figure* 308
    DSM-III-R criteria 305-6
    treatment considerations 309
Personality Disorder, Histrionic 311-6
    characteristics, *Figure* 314
    clinical presentation 312
    DSM-III-R description and criteria 311-2
    developmental and etiological features 313-5
    treatment considerations 315
Personality Disorder, Narcissistic 316-21, 369-85, 375-8
    characteristics, *Figure* 319
    clinical presentation 317-8
    developmental and etiological

Sadists 437-9
Sadock, B. 87, 89, 90, 118-9, 277, 460, 478, 481, 502
Sadock, B. 286, 297
Safer, D.J. 510, 530, 563
Salameh, W. 232
Sallas, R. 578, 593
Salzman, L. 179, 180, 184, 212, 223, 345, 366
Samuelson, M.A. 475, 503
Sandbek, T.J. 576, 593
Sandberg, S.T. 519, 530, 563
Sandoval, J. 530, 560
Sasone, D.M. 530, 560
Satterfield, J.H. 529, 563
Satz, P. 528, 563
Scher, J. 43, 55
Schildkraut, J. 87, 120
Schilgen, B. 136, 163
Schizophrenia 25-55
    catatonic subtype 28-9
    childhood characterizations 39
    definition 25-6
    difference from Bipolar Disorder 47
    difference from Delusional Disorder 47
    differenial diagnosis 46-7
    disorganized subtype 29
    DSM-III-R diagnostic features 26-7
    frequency 25
    paranoid features of 47
    paranoid subtype 29
    residual subtype 29
    subtypes 28-9
    treatment 50-1
    undifferentiated subtype 29
Schloredt, K. 468, 475, 505
Schmaling, K.B. 534, 560
Schmidt, W. 403
Schoeler, Y. 539, 562
Schonhaut, S. 528, 563
Schuele, J.A. 396, 404
Schwartz, R. 578, 586, 593
Scott, J.L. 384
Sebrechts, M.M. 539, 564
Sedative dependence and abuse 393
Seime, R.J. 577, 592
Self, creative 40

Self psychology 370-2
Self-blame 224
Self-esteem (SE) 186, 192, 194, 195, 202, 203, 206, 228-9, *Figures* 187, 208
Seligman, L. 296, 297, 578, 579, 593
Seligman, M. 142, 163, 408, 426, 476, 507
Sense of humor (SH) 186, 194, 195, 203, 206, 229, *Figures* 187, 208
Sense, common 605-6
Separation, discouraging events from basic worth 229-30
Serum antidepressant levels in depression 136
Shaffer, D. 519, 530, 563
Shapiro, R.W. 470, 479, 480, 503
Shapiro, S.K. 519, 564
Sharpeners 101
Shaywitz, B.A. 539, 564
Shaywitz, S.E. 539, 564
Shea, M.T. 152, 160
Shea, S. 302, 366, 377, 384
Sheldon, W. 327, 366
Shenker, R. 530, 533, 534, 559, 561
Sherman, R. 66, 79
Shield, J.A. 507
Shock violence, *Figure* 208-9
    main reactions to unlimited absurd violence, Figure 208-9
Shock effects 67
Sholomskas, D. 123, 163
Shulman's model
    psychotic process 32-3
Shulman, B. 16, 18, 22, 25, 32, 39, 40, 44, 47, 48, 50, 51, 52, 55, 65, 79, 82, 96, 98, 100, 101, 102, 104, 106, 107, 120, 140, 158, 159, 162, 163, 274, 277, 354, 366, 378, 385, 410, 426, 429, 432, 438, 439, 451, 599, 602, 604, 611
    work with Bipolar Disorder 98-106
Siegel, L.S. 539, 558
Siegel, M. 576, 593
Silberman, E. 277
Silberstein, L. 572, 594

Weil, A. 202, 203, 216, 233
Weingartner, H. 529, 562
Weinshel, M. 576, 593
Weiss, G. 518, 529, 530, 533, 534, 559, 561, 565
Weissman, M. 86, 87, 118, 123, 124, 162, 163, 170, 172, 176, 183, 471, 472, 475, 477, 478, 479, 505, 507
Weller, E.B. 474, 507, 508
Weller, R.A. 474, 507, 508
Welne, Z. 477, 506
Wender, P.H. 474, 508, 529. 530, 533, 565
Wener, A. 530, 533, 565
Werry, J.S. 518, 519, 529, 563, 565
Whalen, C.K. 514, 515, 519, 530, 537, 538, 539, 540, 559, 565, 566
Wheeler, A. 159
White, W.C., Jr. 580, 592
Wiener, A.L. 577, 592
Wieselberg, M. 519, 530, 563
Wilbur, C. 275, 277
Wilerman, L. 91, 120
Williams, J.B.W. 417, 418, 427
Williams, S. 471, 472, 476, 479, 500, 504, 520, 556, 561
Williams, T.A. 507
Wilmer, H. 199, 200, 233
Wilner, P. 473, 508
Wilson, I.C. 135, 162
Wing, E.H. 523, 529, 557
Winokur, G. 86, 89, 120
Winsberg, B.G. 538, 563
Wiseman, M.M. 477, 507
Withdrawal 291
Wolf, E. 375, 385
Wolman, B. 231
Wolpert, E. 120
Wolraich, M. 556
Wong, B. 564
Wood, D.R. 533, 565
Work, inhibition 291-2
World design 34
Worlfe, W.B. 258
Wurtman, J. 594
Wurtman, R. 594

Y

"yes-but" responses 5
Yaeger, J. 260, 277, 572, 587, 594
Yerevanian, B. 91, 118
Young, W. 474, 508
Yudofsky, S.C. 161

Z

Zahn, T.P. 529, 562
Zametkin, A. 519, 563
Zametkin, A.J. 529, 538, 566
Zax, M. 405, 427
Zis, A.P. 478, 508
Zoophilia 436-7

BIOGRAPHIES

BIOGRAPHIES

Heinz L. Ansbacher, Ph.D., Emeritus Professor of Psychology, University of Vermont, and past president of the North American Society of Adlerian Psychology, is an Honorary President of the International Association of Individual Psychology. He and his wife, Rowena, have edited three volumes of Alfred Adler's writings: *The Individual Psychology of Alfred Adler* (1956), *Superiority and Social Interest* (1964), and *Cooperation Between the Sexes* (1978). They also have edited 17 volumes of the *Journal of Individual Psychology* (1957-1973). Dr. Ansbacher has written numerous chapters and journal articles on various topics of Adlerian psychology; he is currently engaged in synthesizing some of these.

James W. Croake, Ph.D., is Professor of Psychiatry and Behavioral Sciences, School of Medicine, University of Washington in Seattle. He has written numerous articles and books in Adlerian psychology. His most recent texts are *Dreikursian Theory Part I and II* with Dick Fowler and *Toward an Adlerian Theory of Learning.* The former is the unpublished writings of Rudolf Dreikurs obtained from the Library of Congress.

Elizabeth Hooker, Ph.D., served as a primary therapist and Clinical Coordinator of an inpatient behavioral health unit specializing in anxiety disorders and trauma/PTSD for 16 months. For over 11 years she has studied various forms and the residual effects of abuse. On the practical side, working as a therapist in private practice, Dr. Hooker has specialized in treating victim behavior, and as a seminar/lecture presenter and trainer for mental health professionals, she has shared this knowledge with others. Dr. Hooker has written one book on the assessment and treatment of victim behavior and has just completed a second one which moves beyond identifying the abuse into the healing/change process.

Judith A. Lewis, Ph.D., is a professor in the College of Health Professions at Governors State University, where she currently teaches in a graduate program focused on alcoholism and drug abuse. She is a licensed psychologist in Illinois.

Dr. Lewis does extensive publishing, training, and consulting in the fields of substance abuse and counseling. Among her recent publications are *Substance Abuse Counseling* (Brooks/Cole), *Community Counseling* (Brooks/Cole), *Counseling Women Over the Life Span* (Love Publishing Company), *Mannagement of Human Services Program* (Brooks/Cole), and a number of articles, book chapters, and journal issues. She serves on the editorial board of *Family Dynamics of Addiction Quarterly* and is associate editor of *Topics in Family Psychology and Counseling* and *The Family Journal.*

Donald N. Lombardi, Ph.D., is a Professor of Psychology, Seton Hall University, and a licensed practicing psychologist in New Jersey. He was attracted to Individual Psychology after reading *The Individual Psychology of Alfred Adler.* Dr. Lombardi learned much about Adlerian psychology in his 15-year association with Willard and Marguerite Beecher. He has authored numerous articles and a book, *Search for Significance,* in 1975.

Michael P. Maniacci, Psy.D., is a clinical psychologist in private practice in Chicago, Illinois. A graduate of the State University of New York at Stony Brook and the Alfred Adler Institute of Chicago, he is the consulting psychologist to Lovellton Academy, an inpatient residential program for adolescents. Dr. Maniacci is also adjunct faculty at the Adler School of Professional Psychology and on the board of consultants to the Parent and Child Education Society (PACES) of Illinois.

Mark Mays, Ph.D., J.D., is a clinical psychologist in private practice in Spokane, Washington. He is a consulting editor of *Individual Psychology* and is a past president of the Washington State Psychological Association. Dr. Mays has lectured and taught extensively in the field of psychology. Also an attorney, he is on the adjunct faculty of Gonzaga School of Law.

Harold H. Mosak, Ph.D., is a clinical psychologist in private practice. He has taught at the Alfred Adler Institute of Chicago for 40 years and is currently Chairman of the Board. He is also a past president of the North American Society of Adlerian Psychology. Among his publications are *On Purpose; Alfred Adler: His Influence on Psychology Today; Manual for Life Style Assessment* (with B.H. Shulman); and *Ha Ha and Aha: The Role of Humor in Psychotherapy.*

Kathleen Myers, M.D., M.P.H., M.S., is an Assistant Professor of Psychiatry and Child Psychiatry at the University of Washington in Seattle, Washington. She is also the Director of Mental Health at King County Juvenile Detention Center and a staff psychiatrist at Children's Hospital and Medical Center. Dr. Myers has published research regarding developmental psychopathology and mood disorders. She and her husband, James Croake, Ph.D., together have written and taught about the application of Adlerian methods to child development, therapy, and parenting. They have contributed several articles to the *Journal of Individual Psychology.*

Walter (Buzz) O'Connell, Ph.D., Diplomate in Clinical Psychology (ABPP), retired from clinical practice and research at the Veterans' Administration Medical Centers after 33 years and from teaching in Texas universities after 27 years. Dr. Buzz is a Fellow of the American Psychological Association and the International Academy of Eclectic Psychotherapists. He is a past president of the American Society of Adlerian Psychology and a past recipient of the V.A. annual Professional Service Award for psychologists (1983). His last V.A. commendation read " . . . teacher, therapist, psychodramatist, researcher, author, theorist, and mystic; Buzz was, and is, a man for all seasons."

Ronald J. Pancner, M.D., is in the private practice of psychiatry in Fort Wayne, Indiana, and is the Medical Director of Charter Beacon Psychiatric Hospital. He is a core professor of the Alfred Adler Institute of Chicago and Fort Wayne and a clinical instructor at the Indiana University of Medicine (Fort Wayne Center for Medical Education) and the Fort Wayne Medical

Education Program. He and his wife have authored several articles in the *Journal of Individual Psychology*. He has given numerous presentations at professional conventions and institutes on psychiatry and Individual Psychology.

Dorothy E. Peven, M.S.W., is a professor at the Alfred Adler Institute, Chicago, and a Licensed Clinical Social Worker in private practice in the Chicago metropolitan area. She has served as a delegate and as Vice President of the North American Society of Adlerian Psychology, and is a consultant and lecturer to Alfred Adler Institutes in the United States, Canada, and the Netherlands. Ms. Peven's interests include bipolar disorder and the psychological problems of women vis-a-vis the feminist movement. Ms. Peven has contributed several encyclopedia articles on Adler and a chapter in *The Psychotherapist's Casebook* (1986) on Adlerian Psychotherapy.

Bernard H. Shulman, M.D., is a past president of the North American Society of Adlerian Psychology and of the International Association of Individual Psychology. He is a Life Fellow of the American Psychiatric Association and formerly was a Clinical Professor of Psychiatry at both Northwestern Medical School and Loyola Medical School. He has made many contributions to the literature of Adlerian psychology, including *Essays in Schizophrenia.*

ABOUT

THE AUTHORS

Len Sperry, M.D., Ph.D., is Professor of Psychiatry and Preventive Medicine at the Medical College of Wisconsin and Co-Director of its Center for Aging and Development. Board certified in both psychiatry and clinical psychology, he has published over 200 professional articles and books and is associate editor of *Individual Psychology* and *The International Journal of Individual Psychology and Comparative Studies.*

Jon Carlson, Psy.D., Ed.D., is a Professor of Psychology and Counseling at Governors State University, University Park, Illinois, and a psychologist in Lake Geneva, Wisconsin. Dr. Carlson is a Fellow of the American Psychological Association, a Diplomate in Family Psychology of the American Board of Professional Psychology, and holds a certificate in psychotherapy from the Alfred Adler Institute in Chicago. Dr. Carlson has authored 14 books, 70 professional articles, and is the editor of four journals: *Individual Psychology: The Journal of Adlerian Theory, Research, and Practice; The Family Psychologist; Topics in Family Psychology and Counseling;* and the *International Journal of Individual Psychology and Comparative Studies.*